Indiana University
Glory of Old IU

By

**Bob Hammel
and Kit Klingelhoffer**

Sports Publishing Inc.
www.SportsPublishingInc.com

Photos courtesy of Indiana University Photo Service, Indiana University Archives, Bloomington *Herald-Times*, Rich Clarkson and *Sports Illustrated*.

Editors: Bob Hammel and Kit Klingelhoffer
Book Design: Michelle R. Dressen
Dustjacket Design: Julie L. Denzer
Book Layout: Erin J. Sands

ISBN: 1-58261-068-1
Library of Congress Number: 99-64585

Printed in the United States.

www.SportsPublishingInc.com

Table of Contents

Acknowledgments

by Bob Hammel

The list of people who deserve at least a nod of acknowledgment for contributions to *Glory of Old IU* would be a hundred years long. It includes dozens of people who died unsuspecting of the use that their chronicling of events in their time would be called up for replay generations later.

I did so a bit shamelessly. My life has been as a chronicler. I have left the paths of the '60s, '70s, '80s and '90s strewn with items that someone some time in a role similar to this can feel quite free to pick up and put to use. That makes me a typical modern-day American: use now, pay later.

Most critical of all in the evolution of this ongoing story was the century's never-ending flood of interesting people— primarily athletes, some remarkable coaches, and a few others who fit neither category but contributed to the glory of Indiana University in particular, special ways. A quick definition of that last category: the most beloved Hoosier of them all, Herman B Wells.

So, to him and to them—all those mentioned in the book and the deserving ones omitted or overlooked—a great debt is acknowledged. More directly, university files and records preserved in the tenures of Bob Cook and Tom Miller as IU's pioneer "sports publicity directors" were invaluable, as were the results of the continuing efforts of their successor, Kit Klingelhoffer, after the job title was updated to "sports information director." Three men, for the most part, were the chief stewards of two-thirds of IU's athletic history, as covered in this book. Brad Cook at IU Archives was unfailingly coopera- tive and helpful in running down pictures and items and suggesting others. Calls to the Alumni Records office at the IU Alumni Office must have run into three digits, in search of verification or information, and every one was handled cheer- fully and helpfully. Collections of *Arbutus*, the IU yearbook, at the Alumni Office and at the Monroe County Public Library also were major sources of information, particularly from the century's first twenty years.

My newspaper—*The Herald-Telephone* when I started, *The Herald-Times* today, a variety of ancestral titles before either of those—was probably the biggest information source. It also richly contributed to the store of pictures used, chief photographers Larry Crewell and David Snodgress heading teams that followed IU throughout America.

Rich Clarkson, a special friend and colleague and a photographic artist who fully deserves the legendary status he holds among peers, was generous in contributing some of his work. When called on for widely varying reasons, so many others responded quickly and well—Becky Parke and Gregg Elkin, Gregg Greenwell, Ryan Frantz, Cynthia Dosick, Herman Hudson, Sarah Melton, Alex Simon and Kristin Miller . . . Debbie O'Leary and Jay Jameson . . . Art Berke, the IU alum- nus who (practically) runs *Sports Illustrated* . . . Chuck Crabb, Beth Feickert and Dave Martin . . . Rose McIlveen, Gene Hedrick and Stewart Moon . . . the ladies with the smiles and the available dimes in the Indiana Room at the library . . . and all the others forgotten here, but not forgotten.

My voice is the one here, but hear it in duplicate (I started to say "as a duet," but that just didn't sound right). Kit Klingelhoffer had all the organizational jobs I sloughed off. It is he who kept the pipe flowing, who found all those intrigu- ing "Lists" you will meet, who painstakingly put together the letterman directory and the alphabetized index, the extras that augment this book's history function.

It is a project that has been tedious, and fun, two words not ordinarily linked. A hundred years of anecdotes isn't ordinarily done. Along with Kit, I hope it works for you in the ever-stimulating way it did for me, through most of those hundred years.

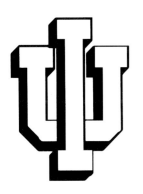

Acknowledgments

by Kit Klingelhoffer

My parents, Calvin and Jeanne Klingelhoffer, were graduated from Indiana University. For as many years back as I can remember, there was never a doubt as to where I would attend college. Mom and Dad saw to that—it would be IU, no questions asked.

I enrolled at Indiana in the fall of 1966, and beginning in the fall of 1968, thanks to former sports information director Tom Miller, as good a man as ever stepped on this earth, I've been associated with Indiana University athletics—32 years in a profession and at a school that I truly love.

When Mike Pearson, former sports information director at the University of Illinois and now Vice President with Sports Publishing Inc., first approached me about a book on the 100-year history of Indiana University athletics, I embraced the concept if, and only if, Bob Hammel and Tom Miller would agree to be involved in the project. They enthusiastically endorsed the idea.

If Bob Hammel is not the best writer in the country, I don't know who is. As Tom Miller, who was around many great journalists in his 37-year career at Indiana once told me, "I know writers who write good copy and I know writers who write a lot of copy, but I've never read anyone who writes as much good copy as Bob Hammel." Truer words were never spoken. As you read *Glory of Old IU*, you will certainly agree that Bob is an exceptional writer. And trust me on this, Bob's knowledge of Indiana University athletics and his tireless research, 100 years worth, is what has made *Glory of Old IU* possible. I also consider Bob Hammel a great friend. For that, I simply say, "Thank you."

Due to unforeseen health problems a year ago—fortunately which have now cleared up—Tom Miller was not able to contribute as much to this book as he would have liked. His long-standing love affair with IU began as a student and certainly didn't end with his retirement in December 1982 after his distinguished Hall-of-Fame tenure as IU's publicist. It was Tom and his first assistant, John Beatty, who were my mentors when I first began as a student assistant in the fall of '68. And then it was Tom who gave me, a young, wide-eyed, unexperienced 21-year old, the opportunity of a lifetime—to be his assistant in the sports information office. Tom may not have contributed to this book in the way he envisioned, but in many ways, what you read here is the direct result of Tom Miller's guidance, patience, understanding and loyalty. I know Bob Hammel would agree.

Glory of Old IU has been a two-year book-in-the-making. Challenging and time-consuming, yes, but what fun. There are many people to thank, far too many for me to mention here. For those I do not mention, I apologize.

First of all to Clarence Doninger, Indiana's Director of Athletics, who allowed me the available time and the resources to make *Glory of Old IU* possible. To everyone else in the athletic department who assisted, from the Varsity Club through a very special Media Relations staff, I say, thank you to one and all.

Erin Sands, Julie Denzer, and Mike Pearson with Sports Publishing are wonderful people. Mike was the guiding force behind this project and provided valuable assistance and sound advice, and Julie was most helpful in cover design. Erin, where would we have been without you? Through the many changes in copy and layout, you were never complaining and always helpful. Thanks.

I owe Indiana University, and it's athletic department, a great deal of gratitude.

For the past 32 years I have been privileged to be a part of something grand—whether it be an Anthony Thompson touchdown, a Steve Alford basket, a Mark Spitz championship or a myriad of achievements by teams and individuals—all those parts of *Glory of Old IU* left wonderful memories that will last a lifetime. It's been a great ride and to all of those athletes, coaches and administrators who have made it possible—words can never express the appreciation that comes with being a part of something so special.

My final thanks—to wife Rita for her encouragement and her support throughout this project and our life together; to daughters Kelly and Brooke, who bring me happiness and joy just by being who and what they are; and again, to Mom and Dad—I wouldn't have had this opportunity if it weren't for you.

Please now, take time to read and to enjoy *Glory of Old IU*. Here's hoping it brings as much pleasure to you as these experiences—both as IU sports information director and as co-author of *Glory of Old IU*—have brought to me.

Foreword
by Tom Miller

Two events of supreme importance to Indiana University's future came coincidentally and providentially just a few years apart at the turn of the century—IU's earlier-than-expected admission to the "Big Seven" Conference (1899) and young William Lowe Bryan's appointment to the school's presidency (1903).

IU joined the conference less than four years after its formation.

Purdue President James R. Smart called fellow presidents of Minnesota, Wisconsin, Illinois, Northwestern, Michigan and Chicago to meet with him February 8, 1896, in Chicago to discuss the problems threatening intercollegiate athletes. Out of this meeting came The Intercollegiate Conference of Faculty Representatives, popularly dubbed The Big Seven, progressing to Big Nine and finally to Big Ten, a name which stood for so much it was retained when Penn State's admission took the league past that number.

The presidents, in one bold stroke, solved almost all the problems threatening college athletics by placing total control and supervision under a faculty committee at each school, with conference control via a committee composed of each institution's faculty representative.

Armed with that power, the new conference curbed and eliminated such abuses as the tramp athlete, the unqualified student, the delinquent student, and professional aspects that already had begun creeping into college sports.

Over time, the conference's formation completely changed the fact—and future—of college athletics.

Indiana, uninvited in 1895, did not regard the omission as a slight. Neither its athletic standing nor its facilities were in the class of the original league membership. But Dr. Bryan, vice president before succeeding Joseph Swain as president, liked what the presidents had done in Chicago and he could foresee the many advantages cooperation in numerous areas would bring to conference members.

Dr. Bryan, an 1884 baseball letterman, urged caution but saw a need for a program of improvement in caliber of teams and facilities—to be ready when, and if, the call came.

Indiana had attempted a football program in 1884 but it had taken three years to get a team into a game. Coaches were unpaid volunteers. Finances were precarious and, on occasion, games had to be forfeited for non-appearances. After seven years teams had posted an overall 4-13-2 record, almost entirely against smaller institutions or clubs within the state.

Facility-wise, a move to Jordan Field for football, a site now a parking lot for the IU Union Building, was in the works. And a new gym, Assembly Hall, a frame building, famed as site of the first Indiana High School basketball tournament in 1911, was on paper.

For its day it was an ambitious undertaking. The University was just emerging from a trying period. A fire had destroyed most of it in 1883, so much so that it was moved from the old site, now named Seminary Square on the south side of downtown Bloomington, to a 20-acre tract on the east side of the city.

In the face of numerous bids from other cities, the university, bolstered by strong community support, picked up the pieces and started virtually anew in three buildings—Wylie, Owen and Maxwell Halls (later named Mitchell Hall). It was done on insurance money and a $50,000 gift voted by the Monroe County commissioners.

It had been a trying, penny-pinching time and enrollment dropped to 414 at one point. But the darkest days were behind and Vice President Bryan's goal of Big Seven stature was inching closer.

The first full-time football coach, Madison G. Gonterman, was enticed from Harvard. His teams produced 6-2 and 6-1-1 records, and Jimmy Horne, who succeeded him, posted winning records, 4-1-2 in 1898 and 6-2 in 1899. The latter included victories over Notre Dame, southern power Vanderbilt, and a first-in-history triumph over Purdue.

The 17-5 win over Purdue on Thanksgiving Day of 1899 was rewarded promptly by an invitation, as well as one to Iowa, to become members of the Big Seven.

The Hoosiers, once over the hump, never looked back. Jimmy Sheldon, who succeeded Horne, went 8-1-1 in 1905, including victories over Notre Dame and Ohio State and a tie with Purdue.

No mistake, the Hoosiers had arrived as respected and competitive members of the Big Nine.

In the century since that December day in 1899, Indiana teams have won 149 conference championships, hundreds of individual titles, 21 national collegiate team championships, 118 individual national titles. IU's five NCAA team championships in basketball rank third all-time; there were six consecutive NCAA swimming championships from 1968-1973; and men's soccer has dominated the collegiate scene for over the last two decades. But every sport has had its glorious moments, its share of great coaches and special athletes.

To the thousands of dedicated people—administrators, coaches, athletes and workers, and the thousands of students and alumni who have supported them so loyally and with great pride—we can say only:

Thank you. Well done.

Tom Miller
IU Sports Information Director
1953-1982

1899 1900

HOOSIER LIST

ADMITTED TO THE BIG TEN CONFERENCE

1896   University of Chicago
University of Illinois
University of Michigan
University of Minnesota
Northwestern University
Purdue University
University of Wisconsin

1899   Indiana University
State University of Iowa

1912   Ohio State University

1917   University of Michigan
(rejoined)

1949   Michigan State University

1990   Pennsylvania State
University

WITHDREW FROM CONFERENCE

1908   University of Michigan
withdrew, in protest against
"retroactive provisions" of cer-
tain Conference enactments.

1946   University of Chicago
withdrew, due to inability to
"provide reasonable equality
of competition."

INDIANA

LEGEND   *Martin Sampson*

WELCOME TO THE BIG TIME

When formed in 1896, the conference that was to be known most of its years as the Big Ten named itself the Intercollegiate Conference of Faculty Representatives.

That's why English professor Martin W. Sampson was Indiana University's representative in Chicago on Thanksgiving Day 1899 when the conference's seven charter members agreed to expand by admitting Indiana and Iowa.

Sampson telegraphed word back to Bloomington, and the one-paragraph announcement story ran on Page 4 of the *Bloomington World* December 1.

"Indiana and Iowa (have) been admitted to the Big Seven which is composed of Purdue, Chicago, Northwestern, Michigan, Wisconsin, Illinois and Minnesota . . . This speaks well for Indiana University, and the splendid football victory Thanksgiving Day doubtless helped to bring about the result."

The next week Sampson gave a report to the student body at chapel services. "(He) said we were admitted into the Big Nine because we were playing good, sportsmanlike games," *The World* reported. "The four most important rules of this organization are: None but bona fide students can (play). No professionals can play. No student can play on a team longer than four years. A (transfer) student must attend (his new school) at least one year before he can play."

Within a few years, the league had pioneered in even more restrictive legislation. In 1904, it was the first conference to require a student to complete a semester of academic work before gaining eligibility. In 1906, that was expanded to require one full year (*i.e.*, freshmen were ineligible) and permit just three years of competition (graduate students ineligible). It was the start of what became national adoption of those rules.

IU's 1899 football team had the first-ever win over Purdue; the 17-5 victory also gave IU the state championship.

2

IU ITEM

....

BREAKTHROUGH AGAINST PURDUE

James Horne had a 33-21-5 record as IU's football coach from 1898-1904.

B y far the biggest news in that December 1 newspaper was the splendid football victory cited by Professor Martin W. Sampson. Indiana's 17-5 Thanksgiving Day win at Purdue was the Hoosiers' first in the rivalry and IU's first claim to the state football championship.

The main headline on Page 1 read:

OUR VICTORY WAS GLORIOUS!

Indiana led 12-5 at halftime and let the Boilermakers inside the 40 just once afterward.

Notre Dame had beaten Indiana, 17-0, and tied Purdue, 10-10, but a pre-game *Bloomington World* story had noted: "In our game with Notre Dame, there were players who have since been contested and thrown out (on a charge of professionalism), Notre Dame herself admitting they were not eligible for a championship game."

One of those players was tackle Frank Hanley, "a man who took no small part in the (Indiana) game," the newspaper story said. Hanley had started for Notre Dame in 1896, missed two years, then come back in 1899 to reclaim his starting spot in the Irish line.

Indiana coach Jim Horne had no hesitation about counting Notre Dame out, although the Irish had finished 6-3-1, with losses to Chicago (which went 12-0) and Michigan (8-2).

"The defense of Indiana was good and would have kept Notre Dame from scoring," Horne said. "There is no doubt that Indiana has a clean title to the championship."

Snapshot In Time

'BIG RED' OUT OF THE RED

THE CROWD AT Purdue's Stuart Field totaled 2,630, at 50 cents apiece, the *Bloomington World's* game account said. That included fans from IU who went by train on $1 round-trip tickets.

Indiana's share of the game income was more than $700, and after expenses the Hoosiers cleared more than $600.

"The athletic association is now out of debt with a surplus on hand," the *World* said.

"This is the first balance in favor of the athletic association in its history."

The newspaper had a suggestion for how some of that profit could be spent.

"A good thing would be to make each member a present . . . a picture of the team," it said.

The crowd included about 200 people from Attica—just 22 miles from West Lafayette, but IU country for this day because the Hoosier captain, fourth-year player John Hubbard, was from there. Hubbard, the *Arbutus* said, "played at fullback and tackle for the '99 Hoosiers and was one of the most successful captains the team has ever had."

The school's enrollment topped 1,000 for the first time in 1900, about 90 percent of the student body from Indiana.

By then, all 92 Indiana counties were represented in the enrollment, and the total university budget was about $150,000.

Attica, 22 miles from West Lafayette, was IU country this day because of Hoosier captain John Hubbard.

IN THOSE DAYS . . .

'TOO MANY TRICK PLAYS'

A newspaper custom of the day was to interview game officials afterward, as well as coaches. Players were never interviewed.

The officials could be cryptic. Umpire Harry Hadden said, "After the Indiana-Purdue game, what chance Purdue had was thrown away by poor generalship in the first half. IU outplayed Purdue during the entire game and has improved 100 per cent in the last few weeks."

Referee Paul Brown said, "Purdue's Ed Robertson is truly a beautiful punter . . . he has few, if any, equals in the west. (Indiana quarterback John) Foster deserves great credit for the splendid way in which he handled the ball. Purdue should have kicked oftener in the first half."

It was just the second Purdue game for Indiana coach Jim Horne; he had to live with a 14-0 loss the first time.

This time, Horne said flatly, "The best team won, but it was evident that Purdue did not play her best game. Purdue tried too many trick plays."

1900 1901

INDIANA

HOOSIER LIST

IU BASKETBALL CAPTAINS

1901	Ernest Strange
1902	Phelps Darby
1903	Harry Ayres
1904	Leslie Maxwell
1905	Earl Taber
1906	None Listed
1907	Everett Sanders
1908	Ed Cook
1909	Arthur "Cotton" Berndt
1910	Dean Barnhart
1911	Homer Hipskind
1912	Merrill Davis
1913	H.J. Freeland
1914	Frank Whitaker
1915	Frank Whitaker
1916	Allan Maxwell
1917	Charles Buschmann
1918	Phillip Bowser
1919	Ardith Phillips
1920	Arlo Byrum
1921	Everett Dean
1922	Eugene Thomas
1923	Wilfred Bahr
1924	None Listed
1925	Paul Parker
1926	Palmer Sponsler
1927	Julius Krueger
1928	Robert Correll
1929	Dale Wells
1930	Branch McCracken
1931	None Listed
1932	None Listed
1933	Glendon Hodson
1934	Woodrow Weir
1935	Willard Kehrt, Robert Porter
1936	Lester Stout, Wendell Walker
1937	Kenneth Gunning, Vernon Huffman
1938	Joe Platt
1939	Ernie Andres
1940	Marvin Huffman
1941	None Listed
1942	Andy Zimmer
1943	Irvin Swanson
1944	Paul Shields
1945	Al Kralovansky
1946	Dick Whittenbraker
1947	Ralph Hamilton
1948	Ward Williams
1949	Don Ritter

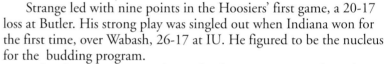

LEGEND — *Ernest Strange*

FIRST IU BASKETBALL CAPTAIN

A great, promising lifetime seemed ahead for Ernest Strange when he graduated from Anderson High School and enrolled at Indiana. His father, Joshua, described by the Marion *Tribune* as one of Grant County's wealthiest and most prominent farmers, was a populist candidate for governor in 1896. Ernest's brother, Leonard, was a dentist in Marion; their uncle, John Strange, was a Marion attorney.

As a sophomore, Ernest went out for the first basketball team IU ever had. He became its leading scorer and its captain—the first of those in a now-long list that includes virtually all the revered Hoosier basketball names.

Strange led with nine points in the Hoosiers' first game, a 20-17 loss at Butler. His strong play was singled out when Indiana won for the first time, over Wabash, 26-17 at IU. He figured to be the nucleus for the budding program.

A few days after he went home for the summer to work on the family farm near Arcana, nine miles east of Marion, a boiler operating a feed grinder exploded. Ernest, standing 12 feet away, was hit in the head by a piece of metal. He died within minutes, just 21.

Among the flowers at Ernest Strange's funeral was a handsome wreath from the students of Indiana University, the *Tribune* said in a story headlined, "Sad Ending of a Promising Career of a Bright Young Man."

Indiana's first basketball team, captained by Ernest Strange.

4

IUitem

PURDUE FIRST CONFERENCE VICTIM

John Foster captained the 1900 football team that beat both Notre Dame and Purdue.

John Foster, a senior who had been a turn-of-the-century Hoosier standout in track (he vaulted 10-6) as well as football, captained the first Indiana football team that played in what is now the Big Ten.

Zora Clevenger, the starting left halfback for the '00 Hoosiers as a freshman, was beginning an epic IU career that fall. John Foster was the reason, Clevenger said, "such a fine fellow that he is the one who influenced me to go to Indiana. He came to Muncie and talked with me. He was from northern Indiana (Kendallville), one of the finest fellows I ever knew."

Captain Foster, rookie Clevenger and the rest of coach Jim Horne's team lost to Northwestern, 12-0, in their first Big Ten game, and to Michigan by the same 12-0 score in their second. In between, they won 6-0 at Jordan Field over a little Indiana school just beginning to flex football muscles, Notre Dame.

But the Hoosiers still hadn't broken through with their first conference victory when they closed their season on Thanksgiving Day at Purdue. No. 1 came by a resounding 24-5 score and, with the Notre Dame game, justified another Indiana claim to the state championship.

NO GAME FOR LITTLE GUYS

FOOTBALL'S SCORING rules were different when the 31-year-old game entered the new century—touchdowns and field goals each worth five points, the field goals usually dropkicked.

That was a cosmetic difference compared to the way the game was played.

"There was no such thing as a forward pass," Zora Clevenger told author Allison Danzig for Danzig's book, *Oh, How They Played The Game*.

Teams had three downs to make five yards against a massed 10-man defense that didn't have to worry about a pass or a quarterback roll-out. "Since I am a small fellow, I wish I could have played under the present rules," Clevenger said.

Clevenger described the defense, "practically the same by all teams: seven men on the line, one man behind each tackle, generally just off his hip; another right behind the center, with just one man back from the line as a safetyman.

"Also at one time the field was longer. There was no end zone, that not being necessary because there was no forward passing."

The ball itself was different, "fatter, more rounded," Clevenger told Danzig. "At Indiana (in 1900) we had a fine punter, Roy Pike, who punted spirals of considerable distance with that big ball. For a while a rule permitted an onside kick from a punt.

"To be eligible to recover a punt, a player from the punting team had to be behind the punter when the ball was kicked, and the punt had to hit the ground. If trying for a recovery, the punter would aim low and away from the safetyman, and short."

And then there would be one wild chase.

IN THOSE DAYS . . .

WOMEN PLAYED GAME FIRST

Women were playing basketball at Indiana University before there was an official men's team. The women did not play teams from other schools, but there was official intraschool competition.

According to the yearbook, in the 1899-1900 academic year IU women played their first public game. "For several years before that," the *Arbutus* report said, "the gymnasium girls had given one game every spring for the women of the university, but men were not admitted. In 1899, it was decided to make this yearly game open to everybody."

In the spring 1901 game, the sophomores through seniors were on one team, wearing red, and the freshmen wore white. The Whites won, 9-4.

The game was in the spirit of the times, both nationally and on campus. During the year, IU President Joseph Swain and his wife, Frances, initiated a fund drive to build a Women's Building on campus. The Local Council of Women of Bloomington followed the Swains as the first donors.

INDIANA

LEGEND *Phelps Darby*

PLAYER-COACH

Phelps Darby, a law student and starting center on Indiana's first basketball team, returned in 1901-02 as the captain, a role that, with no designated coach, made him a virtual player-coach.

Darby, who also starred in football, was in charge of the 12-man varsity basketball squad. The rest of about 50 candidates for the team formed a class taught by athletic director and football coach Jim Horne (a young man himself: Bowdoin '97).

The class was necessary to widen the base of athletes familiar with the 10-year-old sport. Basketball's newness had other ramifications, too, the *Arbutus* noted. "The fact that the game has been so recently adopted as a college game, and there were so few experienced players in the university, prevented a general interest on the part of the student body."

The team did go 4-4 against collegiate opposition, all from within the state. Purdue games were disasters for the Hoosiers: 32-8 in Bloomington, 71-25 at Purdue. For more than 40 years, the Boilermakers' 71 was the highest score ever run up against Indiana, until George Mikan and DePaul beat the Hoosiers 81-43 December 18, 1943.

Darby and Alvah Rucker, another football player and returning starter, were the team's leading scorers.

A few years after graduation, Darby returned to join IU's law school faculty as a specialist in bankruptcy laws.

Darby practiced law in Evansville for 53 years, and he served in the Indiana legislature. He died in Evansville April 23, 1957.

View of the campus, looking east. From a photograph taken in 1895.

'GRAY-HAIRED' HELP

> **"Purdue charged that an old gray-haired man tripped the Purdue quarterback, who was pursuing Rucker . . ."**
>
> **—Arbutus**

It didn't take long for the Indiana-Purdue football rivalry to have some heated controversies. Indiana was humiliated in its first few games against the Boilermakers— 64-0, 60-0 and 68-0, before an outright forfeit that preceded a two-year lull in the series.

However, the Hoosiers turned the century with consecutive wins over Purdue, 17-5 in 1899 and 24-5 in 1900.

So, on October 26, Purdue was backed by a determined crowd of fans when the teams met at IU's Jordan Field. The game was 6-6 (five points awarded for a touchdown, one for an extra point) in the final minutes when Indiana end Alvah Rucker picked up a Purdue fumble and ran nearly the length of the field to give Indiana an 11-6 victory.

Let the *Arbutus* describe the scene that touched off:

"Purdue charged that an old gray-haired man tripped the Purdue quarterback, who was pursuing Rucker, but the officials decided, after carefully looking into the matter, that a touchdown was due Indiana.

"Then they began to pout and left the field before a goal could be kicked."

The 11-6 score stood, and the Hoosiers had a three-game winning streak over Purdue. That streak has been bettered by IU just one time in the century-old series, 1944-47, the last four years of the Bo McMillin era.

Snapshot In Time

A DOER AND A TALKER

ALVAH RUCKER'S moment of heroics against Purdue was nothing unusual for one of IU's earliest to obtain BMOC status: Big Man on Campus.

Rucker, from Evansville, spent his first two collegiate years at DePauw. His most noted athletic achievement there was playing on a doubles team that won the state intercollegiate tennis championship.

He arrived at Indiana in the school's first year of membership in the "Big Nine" conference and had key roles in the Hoosiers' first league football and basketball victories.

He continued to play tennis, lettering two years. As a senior, he was the only player given a tennis letter.

Rucker also distinguished himself as an orator. Debating was a major intercollegiate activity at IU as the new century opened. He won out in stiff campus competition to be IU's representative in the Central Oratorical League championship. Other schools in the league were Cornell, Ohio State, Illinois, West Virginia and Ohio Wesleyan.

Three-sport letterman Alvah Rucker.

IN THOSE DAYS . . .

ATHLETES ASSOCIATION

Phelps Darby's leadership was recognized off the playing fields and courts, too.

The new membership in the Western Conference (sometimes called the "Big Nine" then) led to some restructuring of the IU athletic program.

In the second year as a member, a decision was made to change control of athletics from a faculty committee to what was called "a more general body, in which faculty, students and alumni would be represented," the *Arbutus* said.

"To further this end the Athletes Association was organized and assumed complete control of all athletics, and it was stipulated that no man, unless a member of the association, could represent Indiana in any athletic event. Over 250 shares were immediately sold."

The association's first president was Darby, with J.P. Boyle, a baseball teammate of Darby, secretary.

IU'S FACULTY REPRESENTATIVES

1900-06	M.W. Sampson
1906-07	U.G. Weatherly
1907-08	E.O. Holland
1908-12	H.W. Johnston
1912-19	Charles W. Sembower
1919-41	William J. Moenkhaus
1941-42	Bernard C. Gavit
1942-43	Lee Norvelle
1943-51	William R. Breneman
1951-62	John F. Mee
1962-73	Edwin H. Cady
1973-78	Dan W. Miller
1978-85	Jack Wentworth
1985-93	Haydn Murray
1986-93	Marianne Mitchell
1994-99	William Perkins

INDIANA LEGEND

Bruce Lockridge

TRAGEDY TOOK A STAR

Bruce Lockridge, a faculty resolution said, was a young man "promising and brave . . . (with) frank and open disposition, hearty manner, earnestness, good sense, and strength of purpose."

An 1898 graduate of Roann High School in Wabash County, Lockridge served with an Indiana volunteer company in the Spanish-American War, then excelled as an athlete and student leader at IU. He was a starting end in football, captain and a sprinter-hurdler in track, and president of the school's Athletic Association.

As a senior, he paid some school expenses by doubling as track coach at Louisville Male High.

In Louisville with the IU track team for an evening indoor meet March 28, Lockridge called the Male team together for an afternoon instructional practice. He brought along his IU football and track coach, Jim Horne, to assist. Lockridge was working with the discus throwers when Horne, demonstrating the hammer throw for another group, lost direction with a whirling throw. About 150 feet away Lockridge heard warning cries, looked up, and was hit in the head by the 12-pound hammer.

He died two hours later, his skull crushed.

Horne was griefstricken. The track team and the IU community were stunned and sorrowed. President William Lowe Bryan, faculty representative Martin Sampson and Lockridge's fellow Phi Delt, Zora Clevenger, were among the speakers at a campus memorial service.

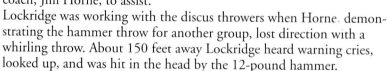

Bruce Lockridge, victim of a practice-field accident, was a young man "promising and brave . . . (with) frank and open disposition, hearty manner, earnestness, good sense, and strength of purpose."

—IU Faculty Resolution

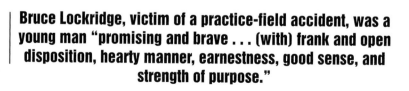

IUitem

SEMBOWER A SCHOLAR AND FAN

Charles Jacob Sembower, a distinguished professor of English and such a baseball enthusiast that the IU field is named for him, spoke out for the sport in a lecture carried in the *Arbutus.*

"It does not matter, you know, whether the baseball team is clever or not, the test which the Philistine makes is the test of the winning score," Sembower said.

"I think gentlemen can win a game if they know how, and they can be gentlemen if they know how to play. It is easy for gentlemen to quit on that excuse."

Sembower, who lettered in baseball all four of his undergraduate years at IU (1891-94), had other strong, sardonic views:

"The Harvard man is often an ass. I have met more asses from Harvard than from anywhere else, but whenever you find a good Harvard man, watch out for him. He is a wonder. I have met one or two . . ."

And, after relaying a report he had read about Kaiser Wilhelm of Germany:

"I do not know whether or not that is exactly true. I always mistrust the *Cincinnati Enquirer* a little . . ."

Indiana's baseball field is named after Charles Sembower.

Snapshot in Time

BRYAN: A BLOOMINGTON PRESIDENT

WHEN JOSEPH SWAIN resigned as Indiana University president to become president at Swarthmore College, he told IU trustees "the thing to do" was to give the job to vice president William Lowe Bryan.

It was done. At his inauguration January 21, 1903, Bryan said: "What the people need and demand is that their children shall have a chance, as good as any other children in the world, to make the most of themselves, to rise in any and every occupation . . . (and) open paths from every corner of the State, through the schools, to the highest and best things which man can achieve."

The new president, 42, had been born and raised two miles east of the campus, as William Julian Bryan, altering his name to insert wife Charlotte's maiden name after their marriage in 1899. Bryan was to serve as IU's president longer than anyone else: 35 years. It was a period of defining growth for the university, and for its athletic department. In *Indiana University: Midwestern Pioneer*, author Thomas D. Clark said that during the Bryan presidency, "Season after season an almost adolescent hope arose, that Indiana University would conquer its (Big Ten) rivals and Purdue University first of all. William Lowe Bryan was as ardent as any fan in this desire."

Bryan was the only I-man ever to serve as IU's president. He lettered in baseball in his senior year, 1884.

William Lowe Bryan is the only 'I' Man to serve as IU President.

IN THOSE DAYS . . .

A ROYAL IU FAMILY

Bruce Lockridge's family had a long-lasting relationship with IU.

His brother, Ross, was the first person contacted by the university after the accident occurred. Ross already had graduated from IU and begun a teaching career that ultimately brought him back to campus as a renowned history professor. His name became known to thousands of Indiana schoolchildren from throughout the state, because he made on-site lectures for schools at places important in Hoosier history.

His son, Ross Jr., grew up in Bloomington. At IU, he competed in track and cross country, lettering for the Hoosiers' 1932 Big Ten cross country champions. He went on to earn two IU degrees. After graduation, he wrote one of the most acclaimed novels of the early post-World War II years, *Raintree County*, later a major MGM movie that starred Elizabeth Taylor, Montgomery Clift, Eva Marie Saint and Lee Marvin.

Bruce Lockridge had spent his first two IU years teaching during the winter and attending the university in spring and summer. He was president of the sophomore class, and he was studying toward a career in medicine.

HOOSIER LIST

CLEVENGER AWARDS

The Z.G. Clevenger Award is presented to living I-Men who, as alumni, have made outstanding contributions to Indiana University through service to its athletic program. It is the highest honor bestowed upon a living I Man.

1963	Lloyd Balfour
	Everett Dean
	George Fisher
	Sherman Minton
	Ralph Tirey
1964	Frank Allen
	Edgar Davis
	Howard Mutz
1965	Charles Buschmann
	Roscoe Minton
	John Sutphin
1966	Branch McCracken
	Fred Seward
	William "Bill" Smith
1967	Noble Biddinger
	Paul Jasper
	Samuel Niness
1968	Daniel Bernoske
	James Strickland
	Paul Tobin
1969	Danny Danielson
	Merrill Davis
	Vern Huffman
1970	Bob Haak
	John Mellett
	Gerald Redding
1971	Tom Deckard
	Angelo Lazzara
	Bob Ravensberg
1972	Chuck Bennett
	Ted Kluszewski
	Pete Pihos
1973	Clum Bucher
	Charles Hornbostel
	Bob Skoronski
1974	George Belshaw
	Don Lash
	Edward VonTress
1975	Neal Baxter
	Campbell Kane
	Claude Rich
1976	Garnett Inman
	Ken Moeller
	Les Stout
1977	Brad Bomba
	Bob Menke
	Ed Schrader

LEGEND   *Zora Clevenger*

IU'S FIRST HALL OF FAMER

Zora Clevenger, little more than jockey-sized, was Indiana's first great Hall of Fame athlete.

Clevenger came to IU from Muncie and immediately starred in both football and baseball. He started at left halfback and shortstop all four of his college years.

Included were some heroic times.

The 1902 baseball Hoosiers closed their season at home against Minnesota. Clevenger came to bat down 10-8, two on, two out, last of the ninth. He homered, and the Hoosier fan section exploded. "It wasn't a big school then (about 1,000 students)," he said later, "but the students got together, took up a collection, and went uptown and bought me a gold watch. It's one of my most prized possessions."

As a 1903 football senior, 5-7, 143-pound team captain Clevenger kicked a field goal, ran a punt back for a touchdown and led his team to a shocking 17-0 win over Illinois. The crowd of 1,500 carried Clevenger and other Hoosiers off the field, then marched behind the band downtown for a celebration that lasted into the night.

Jordan Field was IU's football home as the new century opened.

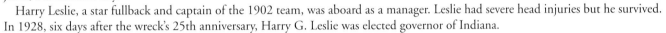

PURDUE TEAM'S TRAIN CRASH KILLED 16

Indiana and Purdue moved their football game to Indianapolis in 1903, and the event was an instant gala. Special trains were booked on game day at both Bloomington and Lafayette, each carrying the team and fans.

The 12-car Bloomington train packed 1,102 in so tightly that aisles were filled and some people stood. The Lafayette train carried nearly 1,000.

At 10 a.m., at a crossing near its Indianapolis arrival point, the Purdue train slammed into a freight. The front cars, carrying the players and coaches, splintered and crushed together. Sixteen died, and dozens more were injured.

The toll included 11 players and assistant coach Ed Robertson, Purdue's captain in both 1899 and 1900. Coach Oliver Cutts was injured, but not seriously.

Harry Leslie, a star fullback and captain of the 1902 team, was aboard as a manager. Leslie had severe head injuries but he survived. In 1928, six days after the wreck's 25th anniversary, Harry G. Leslie was elected governor of Indiana.

The tragedy nearly was doubled. Near Greencastle, the Indiana train's first car fell off the tracks and ran on crossties for more than 100 yards at high speed. Somehow, the car bounced back onto the tracks and continued without damage or alarm. President William Lowe Bryan and his wife, Charlotte, were aboard the train.

Reserved Seat	FOOTBALL
Section C	INDIANA vs. PURDUE
Row I	October 31st
Seat No. 6	Reserved Seat, $1.00

A ticket sold but never used for the game that was never played.

SHIDELER SILVER MEDALIST

THADDEUS "THAD" SHIDELER'S one year at Indiana gave him a role in not just IU record books but also in national and international track and field histories.

Shideler won a silver medal in the 110-meter hurdles at the 1904 Olympic Games in St. Louis, and weeks before that may have beaten a world record.

He won that Olympic medal competing in an IU, not a United States, uniform. The St. Louis Olympics, held coincident with the 1904 St. Louis World's Fair ("Meet me in St. Louie, Louie, meet me at the Fair"), were opened to almost all American athletes who could get there.

As a result, of the eight finalists in the high hurdles, seven were Americans. And the U.S. scored a 1-2-3-4 sweep.

Fred Schule, who had won the 1901 Big Ten long jump for Wisconsin, took the hurdles gold in 16.0 seconds, with Shideler second in 16.3.

Shideler said later that he enjoyed the Fair atmosphere too late into the night before the finals, possibly costing him a gold medal.

Shideler, who had graduated from Indianapolis Manual High School, did some hurdling for the Chicago Athletic Association. He was 82 when he died June 22, 1966.

IN THOSE DAYS . . .

WESTERN CHAMPIONS

Thad Shideler introduced himself to St. Louis in April by leading Indiana to its first major team track championship there.

Shideler's winning time of 15.0 bettered the world hurdles record as IU outscored Stanford, 32-27, for the Western Collegiate title.

Hoosier sprinter Hugh Martin had a brilliant meet. Martin won the 100 in a fast 10.2 (the world record was 9.7) and 200 in 21.8 (the world record was 21.2).

Vaulter Leroy Samse, previewing his own silver-medal performance in the Olympics, tied the world record (11-9) in winning.

The Hoosiers picked up enough seconds and thirds to head the 10-school field. Shideler was third in the low hurdles and high jump.

Shideler was clocked in 15.0 by two of the three timers. The third timer's watch didn't start, costing Shideler official verification. A 1987 book called *America's Best* gives it full credit.

The accepted world record going into the Olympics was 15.2, by 1900 gold medalist Alvin Kranzlein of Penn.

The 1970 edition of *Progressive World Record Lists* says the first hurdler to go 15.0 was Oregon State's Forrest Smithson in leading another 1-2-3-4 U.S. sweep at the 1908 London Olympics.

INDIANA

LEGEND   *George Thompson*

A BARRIER FALLS

George Thompson came down from Covington to become Indiana's first noted African-American athlete.

In an unenlightened era, being on a team helped. Once when a clerk questioned registering Thompson at a whites-only hotel, a teammate said, "He's from Hawaii." The clerk registered him and muttered, "Last year he was from Cuba."

Thompson lowered IU's 440-yard dash record to :51.4 when the Olympic record was :49.2. He won the event at a major Chicago indoor meet.

Thompson anchored Indiana's mile relay team to the Western championship by beating Illinois, before 7,000 people at St. Louis.

Fred Seward (the teammate who fibbed for him at Cincinnati), Bill Kercheval and George Zimmer were on that relay team with Thompson, who lost his senior outdoor season (1906) to illness.

His barrier-breaking didn't end with his track career, according to information dug up by Bloomington *Herald-Telephone* sports writer Lynn Houser for a 1998 story. Akron, Ohio, became Thompson's base, first as director of a new black YMCA, then as founder of the Association for Colored Community Work.

When he died of tuberculosis at 60 in 1944, an *Akron Beacon Journal* editorial noted:

"More than any other one individual, George W. Thompson is responsible for the understanding and mutual trust which prevails between the white and Negro populations of the city of Akron."

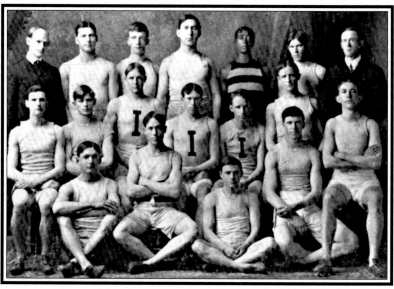

African-American George Thompson and the 1905 IU track team.

A TURN-AROUND AGAINST PURDUE

C het Harmeson of Anderson was one of IU's first basketball stars, but a teammate, Godfred Ritterskamp, beat him out for the distinction of being the first IU player to score 20 points in a game.

Ritterskamp did it the hard way with 10 field goals for an even 20 points in a 52-16 Hoosier victory over Indiana State.

The Ritterskamp record stood for just 38 days.

Purdue ripped Indiana at West Lafayette, 38-20, shutting Harmeson down with four points. It was all too typical for IU in the series up to then. Purdue had won all nine games, and the average score was 34-17.

When the rivals met for a second time at Bloomington, the Boilermakers' dominance ended resoundingly. One player shot all of a team's free throws under the rules then, and Harmeson hit 11 free throws and broke Ritterskamp's record with a 21-point contribution to a historic first victory over Purdue, 29-14.

It was the last season before basketball formally was added as a conference sport. The Hoosiers finished 5-12, ending the year with a 66-12 drubbing at Ohio State. The Buckeyes weren't in the conference yet, gaining membership in 1912.

The two Purdue games were the only ones the 1904-05 Hoosiers played against schools who at the time were league members.

Chet Harmeson was the star of IU's first basketball victory over Purdue.

Snapshot In Time

LOSS OF A WINNER

IU'S TRACK RECORDS were sharply upgraded after the 1904 season and summer, and the improvements continued in the spring of 1905.

Sprinter Hugh "Caddy" Martin's winning marks in the Western Intercollegiates at St. Louis gave him the IU records in both the 100 (10.0) and 220 (21.8), and Joe Barclay, who came back after graduation to help coach, had the marks in the two distance events, mile (4:41.6) and two-mile (10:48).

The only three-event recordholder was Bill Banks, a strong young athlete from Salem who played a year of football and then developed into Indiana's outstanding weight man of the early century.

In a dual meet with Purdue in the spring of 1905, Banks set an IU discus record with a throw of 114 feet. The same spring, he doubled in the State Intercollegiate meet, setting school records with 40-9 in the shot put and 147-5 in the hammer throw.

The track season carried into May. Classes wound up June 6. On June 26, nine days after going home to Salem from Bloomington, Bill Banks, off to so good a start toward the career as a physician and surgeon that was his dream, died of gastritis, possibly appendicitis, at 22.

Bill Banks set an IU discus record of 114 feet, and was the only three-event recordholder of his time.

IN THOSE DAYS . . .

REELING THEM IN

Recruiting when the century opened was a bit different from what it was as the century was closing.

In late August 1904, not long before fall classes were to begin in Bloomington, recruiting was still going on. Hard.

"During the last week," the September 4 *Indianapolis Star* reported, "Zora Clevenger, captain of last year's team and recruiting agent for the 1904 team, was in this city 'signing' material for the IU eleven.

"His efforts were quite successful and as a result some of the best brawn developed on the local high school teams will wear the red and white of old Indiana this fall."

The headliner of the group Clevenger landed was Shortridge captain Hezlep "Heze" Clark, who "will try for the position of halfback," the *Star* story said. "His line plunging and ability to back up the line make him pretty sure of a place.

"Floyd Payne, the 205-pound Shortridge guard, and George Steele, the husky guard and tackle (from Manual) . . . will report for the early football practice a week from today, as will Phillip Hill, the former Culver lineman."

Clark became a star; Steele and Hill each lettered three years and Payne two.

HOOSIER LIST

PROGRESSION OF IU'S BASKETBALL SCORING RECORDS
(Against collegiate opponents)

INDIVIDUAL

20	Godfred Ritterskamp vs. Indiana State, 1905
21	Chet Harmeson vs. Purdue, 1905
25	Dean Barnhart vs. DePauw, 1911
30	Ernie Andres vs. Illinois, 1938
31	Ralph Hamilton vs. Iowa, 1943
35	Don Schlundt vs. Purdue, 1952
41	Don Schlundt vs. Notre Dame, 1953
47	Don Schlundt vs. Ohio State, 1954
	Don Schlundt vs. Ohio State, 1955
56	Jimmy Rayl vs. Minnesota, 1962
	Jimmy Rayl vs. Michigan State, 1963

TEAM

54	vs. DePauw, 1903
64	vs. Rose Poly, 1915
71	vs. Connecticut, 1938
	vs. Iowa, 1943
84	vs. Ball State, 1946
93	vs. Earlham, 1947
94	vs. Northwestern, 1951
96	vs. Northwestern, 1951
105	vs. Butler, 1953
113	vs. Purdue, 1953
122	vs. Ohio State, 1959
	vs. Notre Dame, 1962

INDIANA LEGEND
Leroy Samse

MEDALIST AND WORLD RECORD-HOLDER

Leroy Samse won an Olympic medal before he won a conference championship.

But when his league title came, it was special, and not just because it was the first ever won by a Hoosier.

In 1906, a senior from Kokomo competing in his last conference championships, Samse soared 12-4 7/8, for not just first place but also the world record.

He followed up by winning the U.S. national championship, at a time when virtually all of the world's top vaulters were Americans.

Samse's emergence as king of the vault was a reward for his decision to stay in school. After he won a silver medal in the 1904 Olympics, the Bloomington *Evening World* reported, "He received offers from circus people to do trapeze work but turned them down (because) he did not wish to turn professional while still in school."

Samse probably could have handled the trapeze. He had arrived at IU more a gymnast than a track and field prospect. Tumbling and the horizontal bar were his specialties. He also was a fair high jumper, once holding the IU record at 5-6.

Competing in his last Conference championship meet, 1904 Olympic silver medalist Leroy Samse soared 12-4 7/8, for not just first place but also the world record.

IU item

SHELDON A STAGG MAN

Jimmy Sheldon led IU to an 8-1-1 record in 1905 and had a career record of 35-26-3.

Jimmy Sheldon's hiring as football coach represented Indiana's acceptance of the new necessities that went with membership in the proud Western Conference.

IU reached into the league's most distinguished program, Amos Alonzo Stagg's at Chicago, to hire its first trained football coach. Sheldon had started as a sophomore end on Stagg's unbeaten 1899 league champions. He was captain of the next two Maroon teams, and he had assisted Stagg for two years before Indiana hired him.

Sheldon made the move look brilliant, quickly. His third game put him against Stagg back at Chicago. The Maroons won, 16-5, but Charles Tighe's 45-yard TD dash, Indiana's first touchdown ever against Stagg, turned out to be the only points anyone scored against that 11-0 team.

It also was the only loss the Hoosiers were to have in an 8-1-1 season that stood as the school record for victories in a season until, 40 years later, the best of all IU teams went 9-0-1 and won the 1945 Big Ten championship for Bo McMillin.

Sheldon's first IU team outscored its opponents, 240 to 38.

He was instantly popular.

"Undersized and tow-headed but 'Oh my,'" the *Arbutus* said, calling him in a picture caption a coach "second only to his teacher, Stagg."

SAMSE IU'S FIRST MEDALIST

LEROY SAMSE'S COMBINATION of jumping and tumbling skills inspired Indiana track coach Jim Horne, who introduced him to the pole vault. Horne taught him the "shifting-hand" technique, the sport's newest thing.

By Samse's sophomore year, he was flying. He went 10-9 to set the IU record.

But many of the world's best vaulters were in the same league with him. Michigan's Charles Dvorak, an Olympic threat in 1900, won the first conference meet at 11-1 in 1901. In 1903, Samse's freshman year, Dvorak flew 11-9 at the conference meet, just under the world record.

A year later, Stanford's Norman Dole came into the conference meet (then open to non-members) as the world recordholder (12-1) and won at 11-6.

But Samse was coming on. A week after his loss to Dole, Samse went 11-9 and beat him in the Western Intercollegiate Championships at St. Louis—"no fluke," the *St. Louis Globe-Democrat* said. "Had the Hoosier been fresh, he would have cleared 12 feet."

Three months later, Dvorak won Olympic gold at 11-5. Samse took the silver, IU's first Olympic medal of any kind, with 11-3, well above the marks that had won the first two Olympics in 1896 and 1900.

Samse's medal was *barely* the first for Hoosiers. Both he and freshman high hurdler Thad Shideler won silvers on September 3, but the pole vault came earlier in the day.

IN THOSE DAYS . . .

A BASKETBALL FIRST

Basketball became an official conference sport with the 1905-06 season. Indiana's first league game was played January 20 at Champaign, and the Illini, despite 14 points by senior and captain Chet Harmeson, edged the Hoosiers, 27-24.

Three weeks later, Indiana lost another tight league game at Purdue, 27-25. The Hoosiers avenged that one in their final game of the year at Bloomington, 30-27, with Harmeson hitting 13 of 16 free throws and scoring 17 points.

Before that, they had evened things with Illinois, too. Harmeson and Godfred Ritterskamp scored 12 points each in a 37-8 rout of the Illini that went into history as IU's first conference basketball victory.

It stayed historic for a long while on another count. The 29-point winning margin wasn't topped by Indiana in a league game for 22 years.

A week after the first Illinois game, Harmeson had scored 28 points in a 48-21 basketball victory over the New Albany YMCA.

Though official school records could be set only against collegiate competition, Harmeson's 28 points stood untopped by a Hoosier for more than 32 years, until Ernie Andres set a Big Ten record with 30 points at Illinois March 4, 1938.

INDIANA LEGEND — *Lloyd Balfour*

FIRST BASEMAN AND BENEFACTOR

One athlete whose name assuredly will live forever at IU is Lloyd G. Balfour, not the greatest of Hoosier stars but one of the most generous.

After earning a law degree, Balfour chose to go on the road selling fraternity jewelry. Five years later, he started his own small company in Massachusetts and built it into the No. 1 manufacturer of fine jewelry in the world.

At IU, he funded the Balfour Awards, plaques given annually since 1929 to one person in each Hoosier varsity sport for outstanding performance and conduct.

He lettered two years in football (end) and baseball (first base). The spring of his final season, the *Arbutus* said: "Bally is gaining a reputation as a tall hitter who is playing first base in 'Frank Chance' fashion." Chance, of Tinker-to-Evers-to-Chance fame with the Chicago Cubs, exemplified in his era fielding style and grace.

Balfour said his biggest collegiate thrill came at Purdue in his last baseball game, when young coach Zora Clevenger surprised the Boilermakers by starting freshman pitcher Tate Siebenthal, who threw a two-hit shutout.

"They were fit to be tied," Balfour said 50 years later. "We escaped from Lafayette amid jeers and rocks by riding in a caboose back to Bloomington.

"That was a thrill I'll never forget."

It was IU's first conference baseball victory. Though Indiana first began playing baseball in the spring of 1866, barely a year after the end of the Civil War, IU was not counted in conference baseball standings until 1906.

> **"They were fit to be tied. We escaped from Lafayette amid jeers and rocks by riding in a caboose back to Bloomington. That was a thrill I'll never forget."**
>
> —Lloyd G. Balfour

'FUMBLING SEEMED INEVITABLE'

When football produced 18 deaths and 150 serious injuries in 1905, President Theodore Roosevelt ordered rulesmakers to reduce the game's brutality or risk losing their sport.

They opened the game with changes that Indiana, with several stars back from an 8-1-1 team, didn't welcome. In early practices, the *Arbutus* reported, "the double passes, the forward passes, the quick kicks all went amiss. Fumbling seemed inevitable. The game appeared changed from one of brawn to one of chance."

Jimmy Sheldon could teach that game, too. After losing at Chicago, 33-8, Indiana won at Notre Dame, 11-10, and went into the final game at Minnesota claiming the state championship.

The Gophers had beaten Chicago and lost only to Carlisle and Jim Thorpe. In the opening minutes, Indiana's Sam Heckaman took a recovered fumble 40 yards for the game's only touchdown. But Minnesota still won, 8-6, on a safety, a four-point field goal, and another safety, when star center Lloyd "Sag" Waugh snapped the ball over punter Frank Hare's head out of the end zone.

But the game Hoosiers operated with new respect. Senior Heze Clark was named All-Conference and he, Hare, Heckaman, Waugh and fullback George Steele all were named All-State.

Heze Clark was IU's first All-Conference halfback.

Snapshot In Time

WIT AND WISDOM OF ABE, JR.

INDIANAPOLIS NEWS CARTOONIST Kin Hubbard created a wise, Brown County-based character named Abe Martin, whose philosophies ran daily in an illustrated feature.

The 1907 *Arbutus* borrowed Kin's rustic character for a feature of its own under the title "Abe Martin Jr." Among the campus comments of Abe Jr., regarding times and topics of the academic year:

"By gum, Purdue knew when to quit, but W. J. Bryan never will."

"Ez Pash sez the list uv th' six best sellers dun't include that one under th' Pi Phi house."

And:

"Th' Law School has decided that stealin' bases from Northwestern is only petit larceny."

Translations:

Just ahead of what turned out to be two straight winless seasons for the Boilermakers, Purdue had broken off athletic relations with Indiana in a June 5, 1906, announcement that was headlined in the *Indiana Daily Student*:

PURDUE QUITS

The Bryan referred to was not IU president William Lowe Bryan but Democrat William Jennings Bryan, who lost in races for the presidency in 1896 and 1900 and was working toward the 1908 nomination that he won, before losing one more time in the presidential election.

As for the "seller" under the Pi Phi house ...

Albin Hayes

Larry Rosin

INDIANA

LEGEND *Johnny Johnson*

NO-HIT MAN

Morris "Johnny" Johnson picked up two degrees from IU and went on to a medical career.

His college days included five letters and two special memories.

In 1907, as a substitute end, he caught a touchdown pass at Chicago. It came in a 27-6 Hoosier loss to the league-champion Maroons, but it was just the third time a Hoosier ever had scored against Amos Alonzo Stagg's vaunted team.

The following spring, Johnson, a tall right-hander from Owensboro, pitched a no-hit, no-run game to beat Northwestern, 1-0. It was the first of just three one-man no-hitters that show up in IU's post-1900 baseball records.

Another Johnson, Harry, president of the sophomore class, in spring 1908 gave IU its second Big Ten track and field champion. Johnson won the long jump at 22 feet, 3 3/4 inches. It took almost another half-century for Indiana to produce a Big Ten champion in that event, but when it happened in 1956, it was with a budding Olympic gold medalist: Greg Bell.

Future doctor Johnny Johnson scored a touchdown against football powerhouse Chicago and the same academic year pitched IU's first recorded no-hitter to beat Northwestern.

WELL HOUSE ARRIVES

Generations before the Sample Gates went up on the western edge of the Indiana University campus, a banker-lawyer who served on the Board of Trustees dreamed of such an architectural welcoming at the end of Kirkwood Avenue.

Instead, his thinking produced another campus landmark.

Theodore Frelinghuysen Rose of Muncie wanted to make a gate of the porticos of the University Building that had been left behind when the campus moved from what is now the south edge of downtown Bloomington to the present site on the city's east side.

Symbolic but impractical, President William Lowe Bryan decided. Already access to the university was difficult. The narrow porticos would make it worse.

But Bryan applied the idea to a necessity of the times. Limited water access demanded a major well in the center of the campus. A physics professor, Arthur Lee Foley, worked out a well-house design that included the portals. On June 2, the new building was introduced as part of 1908 commencement, "the diamond stud on the shirt front of the University," a friend of Bryan's called it.

IU historian Thomas D. Clark called it "the central landmark of Indiana University folklore, tradition, and microbic exchange" for the custom that grew with the Well House: "the ardent midnight kissing which transformed plain innocent college lasses into full-fledged co-eds."

FRESHMEN RAISE HOPES

NOT MANY PEOPLE were around to see it, but on a Friday afternoon in mid-November 1907, some new Indiana athletic heroes emerged.

It was an off-week for the varsity football team, before the season-closer against Illinois.

Coach Jimmy Sheldon scheduled a game for the Hoosiers: against the freshmen, who under the rules couldn't play on the varsity and couldn't meet outside teams.

Sheldon, closing out his first year as Hoosier coach, knew what he was doing. The freshmen gave a dreary season a campus-electrifying highlight by beating the varsity, 11-9.

Quarterback Arthur "Cotton" Berndt previewed a popular, heroic career by scoring both touchdowns. Another future star, halfback Andy Gill, excelled, as did Homer Dutter, who was to be an All-Big Ten lineman in future years. The *Arbutus* hailed it as "the best freshman team that ever represented an Indiana college."

Three years later, that class was the nucleus Sheldon built around for the first outstanding football team at IU.

The experience didn't help his 1907 varsity, though. It came back a week later to lose to Illinois, 10-6.

IN THOSE DAYS . . .

A LEADER FROM START

Cotton Berndt didn't take long to be noticed on campus.

The rookie from Indianapolis Manual was the only freshman football player who shifted over to play basketball, too. Besides varsity play, the school had official inter-class play in many sports, capped by a championship tournament. The 1908 inter-class tournament was won by the freshmen.

Though young, Berndt had so good a grasp of how to play basketball that he helped the varsity even that freshman year when he couldn't play.

Football coach Jimmy Sheldon was the listed coach of the varsity basketball team that went 9-6 and won at Purdue, 26-21. A free throw after the buzzer cost the Hoosiers a 21-20 loss to Notre Dame.

The *Arbutus* review of the season said: "Much of the success was due to the coaching of Cotton Berndt."

1908 Ⓘ 1909

HOOSIER LIST

IU'S ALL-BIG TEN LINEMEN

1909	Homer Dutter, tackle
1910	Allen Messick, guard
1917	Russ Hathaway, center
1919	William McCaw, guard
1927	John Matthew, guard
1928	Clare Randolph, center
1931	Joe Zeller, guard
1933	Bob Jones, guard
1937	George Miller, center
	Bob Haak, tackle
1938	Bob Haak, tackle
1944	John Tavener, center
1946	Russ Deal, tackle
	John Cannady, center
1947	Howard Brown, guard
1964	Don Croftcheck, guard
1966	Tom Schuette, guard
1967	Gary Cassells, guard
1969	Don DeSalle, guard
1977	Charley Peal, tackle
1978	Mark Heidel, center
1987	Don Shrader, guard
1988	Don Shrader, guard
1989	Ian Beckles, guard
	Ron Vargo, center
1993	Hurvin McCormack, tackle
1996	Nathan Davis, end
1997	Adewale Ogunleye, end

INDIANA

LEGEND
Homer Dutter

FIRST ALL-LEAGUE LINEMAN

Homer Dutter from Orland in the state's northeastern corner moved into a starting job at right tackle as soon as he could: opening day of his sophomore season, 1908.

He never gave it up, playing three years for teams that went 13-8, including a historic 10-4 victory over Purdue closing out the 1908 season.

The game was the first between the schools since Purdue severed athletic relations with IU in 1906. The 1909 *Arbutus* called Indiana's victory "a mighty day" in IU football history because it not only got the two rivals back together but also showed Purdue "her real and proper sphere in State football circles, just below Indiana."

Dutter played on IU teams that beat Purdue three times. He was considered a major reason for the Hoosiers' success. In his junior year, he became the first Hoosier lineman ever to make All-Conference. As a senior, he was picked at fullback, the first IU player of any position to be a two-time All-Conference selection, and there wasn't another one for 28 years.

Dutter was more than a football player. A math major, he was president of the Senior Class of 1910, the Indiana Club, and the YMCA. He won a spot on the debating team for competitions against Illinois and Wabash.

Homer Dutter, IU's first All-Conference lineman (1909), repeated the honor as a fullback in 1910—Indiana's only two-time first-team All-Conference football player until 1938.

IUitem

FIRST BASKETBALL 'I'-MEN

Dean Barnhart tied an IU record with 21 points against DePauw in 1909 and set a new IU record with 25 against DePauw in 1911.

In its ninth year as an IU sport, basketball wasn't close to the popularity it was to attain on campus.

The sport's bottoming-out points at IU came a month apart, and so did a turnaround and newfound acclaim.

At Illinois January 9, the Hoosiers took an embarrassing 30-2 loss, the school's all-time low in points scored. Dean Barnhart, a sophomore from Rochester, scored just before halftime. That lone basket separated the Hoosiers from an even more humilating basketball shutout.

February 9, before taking the floor to play DePauw, the team split apart in what the *Arbutus* called "a rebellion." A six-man squad was left, and those six did all the playing the rest of the season, starting with an IU record-tying 21 points by Barnhart in a 31-20 victory over DePauw the night of the split.

Three weeks later, the five IU starters went all the way, Barnhart scored 13 points, and Indiana got even with Illinois, 23-13.

"As a well-earned reward," the *Arbutus* said, "the six members of the team were given the coveted 'I' . . . the first time it was ever done at Indiana."

Those first basketball monograms went to Barnhart, Arthur "Cotton" Berndt, George Trimble, Homer Hipskind, Frank "Sonny" Thompson and Arthur Rogers.

Snapshot In Time

KEEPING A COACH

WHEN JIMMY SHELDON went from Chicago to Indiana to coach football in 1905, he didn't plan a long tenure. He already had his law degree and had begun a practice.

Sheldon worked out a way to keep his law office going and spend autumns in Bloomington coaching football, trying to shrink the football gap between Indiana and his alma mater.

The 1908 meeting of the two was painful for Sheldon, who was expecting a tight battle after his captain and best player, Scott Paddock, returned an interception 50 yards for a touchdown and quick 6-0 lead. Before halftime, Paddock was thrown out for slugging and Chicago pulled away, 29-6.

The Hoosiers were 0-3 in the league and 1-4 overall when they prepared to close the season at Purdue. Before the game, Sheldon told his team that the time had come for him to become a full-time lawyer. The game would be his last as coach.

Paddock drop-kicked a 45-yard field goal, and Ashel "Heze" Cunningham returned an interception 60 yards to jump Indiana out front 10-0 in the game the Hoosiers won, 10-4.

Sheldon changed his mind. He came back in 1909, saw he had his best team coming up, and put off full-time lawyering plans until after 1910, at least.

"Heze" Cunningham

IN THOSE DAYS . . .

HEALING MED-SCHOOL BREACH

Indiana's 1908 football victory at Purdue capped the first year of resumption of athletic competition between the two schools, after bitterness over which university would get a medical school brought a break in 1905.

Indiana won the medical school fight, which was more contentious—and far more important to IU's future as a university—than any athletic battles between the two schools.

Still, Indiana's athletic program was losing ground financially without Purdue competitions to spark interest and contributions. Both schools saw the value of resuming the competition, and the restart began with two basketball games, Indiana winning at Purdue (26-21) and Purdue at Indiana (16-14).

Immediately after the 10-4 football victory in 1908, Thomas D. Clark said in *Indiana University, Midwestern Pioneer*, IU's Athletic Association received $1,750 from Hoosier fans, but still the association was about $1,000 in debt.

Sheldon's decision to return as coach put him in position to add a new role in charge of ticket sales. He arranged with Bloomington circus magnate Frank Gentry to get use of bleachers for Jordan Field in the circus off-season, and for the first time IU offered football season athletic passes, at $5 each.

It was a shocking figure to IU fans, who bought only about 100. Purdue sold 1,600.

HOOSIER LIST

IU TWO-SPORT CAPTAINS

- Ernie Andres, Basketball 1939, Baseball 1939
- Arthur "Cotton" Berndt, Basketball 1909, Baseball 1910, Football 1910
- Ray Briggs, Cross Country 1918, Track 1919
- Henry Brocksmith, Cross Country 1931, Track 1932
- Zora Clevenger, Football 1903, Baseball 1903
- Edgar Davis, Football 1913, Wrestling 1914, 1915
- Floyd Fleming, Football 1912, Baseball 1914
- Andy Gill, Football 1911, Baseball 1912
- Frank Hanny, Football 1922, Track 1923
- Charles Hornbostel, Cross Country 1933, Track 1934
- Bob Kennedy, Track 1991, Cross Country 1992
- Don Lash, Cross Country 1935, 1936, Track 1936, 1937
- Arthur Mogge, Cross Country 1917, Track 1918
- Jim Spivey, Cross Country 1982, Track 1981, 1982
- Wayne Tolliver, Cross Country 1940, Track 1941
- Mel Trutt, Cross Country 1938, Track 1939
- Frank Whitaker, Football 1915, Basketball 1914, 1915

INDIANA

LEGEND *Cotton Berndt*

ONLY THREE-SPORT CAPTAIN

Arthur "Cotton" Berndt, one of the most popular athletes in IU history, won eight varsity letters and captained four teams, the only Hoosier ever to be captain in three sports: twice in baseball, once each in football and basketball.

But, in the middle of all that, he lost a basketball season to bureaucracy.

Berndt, from Indianapolis Manual, was named all-state as a sophomore in 1908-09, when he was elected captain of that first IU basketball team to get varsity letters.

As a junior, though, he was benched in basketball by a new school rule that said no athlete could play more than two sports without special permission, which obviously didn't come. The Hoosiers missed him in a season that ended 5-8, and 3-7 in the Big Ten.

In the 1909 season, Berndt was part of a resounding 36-3 football victory over Purdue, which came after some back-and-forth wrangling.

Just before the Indiana-Purdue game, a Purdue official filed charges of professionalism against IU star Clarence Cartwright of New Harmony. He was right. Cartwright admitted playing summer baseball for pay for teams at Mount Vernon and Rockport. But, the resultant investigation brought admission from Purdue fullback R. S. Shade that he also had been paid for athletics and had been ineligible the whole season.

Popular Cotton Berndt won eight letters in his IU athletic career and became the only Hoosier to captain teams in three sports—football, basketball and baseball.

IUITEM

THE MAYOR WORE SWEATERS

> ## "He wore I-letter sweaters and one pair of blue serge pants."
>
> ### —Thomas Berndt

The football team that had junior Cotton Berndt as a star end finished 4-3, and that same academic year Berndt captained the baseball team that had its best Big Ten finish up to then: third, at 4-3.

Berndt came back as a senior to captain the football and baseball teams and return to the basketball team and lead the Hoosiers to an 11-5 year.

Berndt coached IU for two years each in basketball (1913-14 and '14-15) and baseball (1913 and '14). He adopted Bloomington as his new hometown and ultimately served as mayor.

When Berndt was inducted into the Indiana University Athletic Hall of Fame in 1997, his son, Thomas, said that during his father's days at IU, "he wore I-letter sweaters and one pair of blue serge pants. He kept a single quarter in his pocket all the time. He was afraid to spend it, because it was about all he had."

That report jibes with a teasing 1911 *Arbutus* description of senior and economics major Arthur Henry Berndt: "Cotton has bought less clothes than any man extant, the university athletic association having furnished him with enough sweaters and other wearing apparel to keep him well supplied throughout his entire career."

Snapshot In Time

TRACK DERAILED

INDIANA'S EARLY TASTE of national and international success in track and field didn't sustain the program for very long.

Just six years after Hoosiers Leroy Samse and Thad Shideler won silver medals at the 1904 St. Louis Olympics, IU didn't even have a track team.

The Hoosiers had fair success in the indoor season, thanks chiefly to two men: captain Ray "Cy" Bonsib and popular, competitive Harry Johnson, a senior from Sheridan who was captain the year before.

In a 1910 indoor dual meet at Northwestern, Johnson, the 1908 conference long jump champion, won the 50-yard high hurdles (7.0 seconds), 50-yard low hurdles (5.6), pole vault (9-0) and high jump (5-4) and came in second in the long jump for 23 personal points. Bonsib won the 440 and 880 for 10 more, but Northwestern won, 55 to 40.

When the season moved outdoors, dropoffs left the Hoosiers with just those two likely scorers. Then captain Bonsib withdrew, so Johnson did, too, switching to baseball. He didn't win a letter there, but he was part of a team. Outdoors, in the spring of 1910, Indiana had no track team at all.

Harry Johnson was conference long jump champion in 1908.

IN THOSE DAYS . . .

'LOVEY-DOVEY' BLUES

After starting the basketball season 5-3, including a 13-11 victory over Wisconsin in the teams' first meeting ever, the Hoosiers closed out with a five-game losing streak.

Four of the closing defeats were one-sided. The close loss was at Rose Poly, 23-21, to a team Indiana had beaten earlier, 37-21.

In explaining the turn-around to the *Indiana Daily Student* reporter, Hoosier coach John Georgen showed he hadn't lost his sense of humor.

Rose Poly plays its games on a dance floor, Georgen said, and the Rose players were more "socially inclined" than his.

Georgen seemed to be teasing. Baseball coach Ralph "Skel" Roach didn't when he said:

"There is too much 'lovey-dovey' business at IU for the good of the athletic teams . . . I attribute the lack of spirit to the presence of the girls in the University."

HOOSIER LIST

IU FOOTBALL SHUTOUTS (since the 1900s)

1900	IU 0, Illinois 0
IU 0, Alumni 0	1912
IU 18, Earlham 0	IU 20, DePauw 0
IU 62, Vincennes 0	1914
IU 6, Notre Dame 0	IU 27, Northwestern 0
IU 0, Illinois 0	1915
1901	IU 7, DePauw 0
IU 56, Rose Poly 0	IU 41, Miami (O.) 0
IU 76, Franklin 0	1916
IU 24, DePauw 0	IU 20, DePauw 0
1902	IU 0, Purdue 0
IU 34, Wabash 0	1917
IU 33, Vincennes 0	IU 50, Franklin 0
1903	IU 51, Wabash 0
IU 39, Earlham 0	IU 40, St. Louis 0
IU 17, Illinois 0	IU 35, DePauw 0
IU 70, DePauw 0	IU 37, Purdue 0
1904	1918
IU 12, Indiana Medics 0	IU 41, Fort Harrison 0
IU 8, Ohio State 0	IU 13, DePauw 0
IU 4, Wabash 0	1919
IU 27, Kent 0	IU 24, Kentucky 0
1905	1920
IU 5, Alumni 0	IU 47, Franklin 0
IU 31, Butler 0	IU 24, Mississippi 0
IU 29, Kentucky 0	1921
IU 39, Washington 0	IU 47, Franklin 0
IU 40, Wabash 0	IU 29, Kalamazoo 0
IU 11, Ohio State 0	IU 3, Purdue 0
1906	1922
IU 16, Alumni 0	IU 0, DePauw 0
IU 55, DePauw 0	1923
IU 12, Notre Dame 0	IU 32, Hanover 0
1907	IU 3, Purdue 0
IU 40, Alumni 0	1924
IU 0, Notre Dame 0	IU 65, Rose Poly 0
1908	IU 21, DePauw 0
IU 11, Alumni-Freshmen 0	1925
IU 16, DePauw 0	IU 31, Indiana Normal 0
1909	IU 0, Purdue 0
IU 30, St. Louis 0	1927
1910	IU 21, Kentucky 0
IU 12, DePauw 0	1928
IU 6, Chicago 0	IU 14, Wabash 0
IU 33, Millikin 0	IU 6, Michigan 0
IU 33, Butler 0	IU 6, Northwestern 0
IU 15, Purdue 0	1929
1911	IU 0, Ohio State 0
IU 42, Franklin 0	1930
IU 12, Washington (St.L) 0	IU 14, Miami (O.) 0
	(continued)

(continued)

INDIANA

LEGEND
1910 Football Team

NO ONE CROSSED ITS GOAL LINE

"Foxy Jimmy" Sheldon and his men of 1910 represented "the greatest football machine in the history of Indiana," the 1911 *Arbutus* trumpeted.

It's still the only IU football team whose goal line never was crossed.

This 6-1 team's loss was 3-0 to an Illinois team that went unbeaten, untied and unscored on in winning the conference championship. In the view of the *Arbutus*, the game—next-last of the season, played in the mud of a miserable November day at IU—and the conference championship got away because of "the unthinking mind of a rain god.

"No one denies, not even the most prejudiced, that had it not rained the night before the game, putting the field in a slop, the Crimson speed demons would have scored. Time and again the writhing and maddened whirlwinds, (Andy) Gill and (Paul) Davis, started on journeys to the Orange and Blue goal posts, only to lose their footing and fall."

The only other team to score on the 1910 Hoosiers was Wisconsin, beaten 12-3 at Madison.

Indiana came back from the Illinois loss to win 15-0 at Purdue. Cotton Berndt and Davis scored touchdowns and Gill kicked a field goal.

The 3-1 league record and third-place finish were conference high marks for IU. Indiana was 5-25-2 in previous conference games and never had won more than one in a season.

Three Hoosiers—end Berndt, tackle Homer Dutter and guard Allen "Feeb" Messick—were named All-Conference. That didn't happen again at Indiana for 27 years.

The *Arbutus* called Messick "our big, good-natured lineman, famous for his smile. But outside of that he plays like sin." And Dutter: "a tower of strength, both in offense and defense." And Berndt: "the famous starved cat player, the best captain and fiercest fighter in the west."

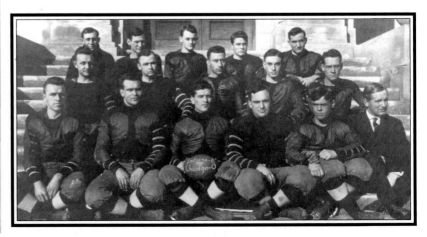

IU ITEM

"The greatest football coach in the west."

—1911 *Arbutus* on Indiana's football coach Jimmy Sheldon

CHICAGO FINALLY FALLS

The highlight of the six 1910 football victories came early at Chicago. Jimmy Sheldon went into the game 0-5 against Amos Alonzo Stagg.

The game was 0-0 at the half, Chicago losing an early touchdown to a holding call. The game still was scoreless entering the fourth quarter, but Indiana's Heze Cunningham moved the Hoosiers deep with a 25-yard pass to Cotton Berndt. Andy Gill fought his way free to score from the 15, and Indiana had a historic 6-0 victory, all the more meaningful to Hoosiers because, despite their relationship, Stagg had been less than cooperative to Sheldon in scheduling.

When Chicago did play Indiana, it was always on a take-it or leave-it date dictated by Stagg, at Chicago and early in the season. After a few of those games, Sheldon asked Stagg to move the Chicago-Indiana date later in the year, when Sheldon felt he could have his team better prepared to play. Stagg didn't budge; he offered the same early date. Sheldon, who deeply admired his coach, accepted it, and won anyway.

The 1911 *Arbutus* skipped over Stagg and called young Sheldon "the greatest football coach in the west."

Snapshot In Time

BODENHAFER IU'S FIRST CHAMPION

WRESTLING, THE SPORT of Billy Thom, Charley McDaniel, Dick Voliva, the Belshaw brothers and "Big Ed" Davis, began at Indiana University in a classroom.

Elmer Jones, an education professor, got his bachelor's degree at Monmouth College and his master's at Colorado before winning honors as a wrestler while getting his Ph. D. in 1908 at Columbia. Ross Netherton attended Columbia before lettering at IU in football in 1907 and '08, so he knew Jones' background. Netherton urged him to start the sport at IU.

Jones offered a class in wrestling in the 1908-09 academic year. One of the students was Walter Bodenhafer, a pre-law major from Kendallville. Bodenhafer showed such promise Jones continued to work with him and entered him in the 1911 Western Conference championships.

Bodenhafer won the middleweight title.

Letters weren't given cheaply then. Chester Teeter of Pennville lost in the lightweight finals at the same conference meet, but only Bodenhafer was awarded an "I", the first awarded at Indiana in wrestling.

Jones went from that start to build a team and a program. Wrestling had only four weights in 1912 and six after that, but Jones had at least one champion in every conference meet until he gave up coaching in 1914.

Walter Bodenhafer won IU's first conference wrestling title.

HOOSIER LIST

IU FOOTBALL SHUTOUTS
(continued)

1931	1945
IU 0, Iowa 0	IU 6, Illinois 0
IU 0, Illinois 0	IU 49, Minnesota 0
IU 6, Chicago 0	IU 19, Pittsburgh 0
1932	IU 26, Purdue 0
IU 12, Iowa 0	1946
IU 19, Mississippi State 0	IU 21, Minnesota 0
1933	1947
IU 7, Miami (O.) 0	IU 17, Nebraska 0
1934	IU 7, Ohio State 0
IU 27, Ohio University 0	1948
IU 0, Iowa 0	IU 7, Iowa 0
1935	1952
IU 14, Centre 0	IU 33, Temple 0
IU 24, Chicago 0	1958
IU 7, Purdue 0	IU 6, Minnesota 0
1936	IU 6, Michigan State 0
IU 38, Centre 0	1959
1937	IU 20, Illinois 0
IU 12, Centre 0	IU 0, Ohio State 0
IU 27, Cincinnati 0	1962
IU 10, Ohio State 0	IU 21, Kansas State 0
IU 3, Iowa 0	1969
1938	IU 16, Michigan State 0
IU 0, Nebraska 0	1976
1939	IU 7, Northwestern 0
IU 14, Wisconsin 0	1979
1940	IU 3, Wisconsin 0
IU 20, Michigan State 0	IU 30, Northwestern 0
IU 3, Purdue 0	1980
1941	IU 24, Wisconsin 0
IU 7, Purdue 0	1982
1942	IU 30, Northwestern 0
IU 53, Butler 0	1986
IU 12, Nebraska 0	IU 21, Louisville 0
IU 7, Minnesota 0	1990
IU 54, Kansas State 0	IU 42, Northwestern 0
IU 20, Purdue 0	1991
IU 51, Fort Knox 0	IU 31, Michigan State 0
1943	IU 24, Baylor 0
IU 52, Wabash 0	1992
IU 34, Wisconsin 0	IU 16, Miami (O.) 0
1944	1993
IU 72, Fort Knox 0	IU 12, Toledo 0
IU 20, Michigan 0	IU 24, Northwestern 0
IU 54, Nebraska 0	IU 10, Michigan State 0
IU 32, Iowa 0	
IU 47, Pittsburgh 0	

INDIANA

LEGEND   *Andy Gill*

'BIG WIDE SPACE IN HALL OF FAME'

The devilish wits of the 1912 *Arbutus* called Thomas Andrew Gill "a gentle-mannered and soft-tongued athletic major who has never comprehended why the college curriculum should interfere with the major sports."

It was a tease. Andy, an English major, was a leader from the time he arrived on campus from Linton and was elected captain of the freshman football team. A hard-charging back whose touchdown gave Indiana its first victory over Chicago (6-0 in 1910), a fiery, inspiring baseball shortstop, Gill lettered three years in each sport and captained both his senior year.

For him, that 1912 *Arbutus* said, "They have carved out a big wide space in the hall of fame, the biggest ever given to a name in athletics here."

In 1918, young Andy Gill was the football coach at Kentucky and he won his first game, 24-7, at Indiana.

Indiana got even the next year, 24-0, Gill's last as Kentucky coach, but he closed that 1919 season with a 13-0 victory over Kentucky's other big rival, Tennessee.

The win over Indiana was Kentucky's last in that series until 1974. And, after that final-game 1913 victory under Gill, Kentucky beat Tennessee just three times in the next 33 years.

Andy Gill's touchdown in 1910 gave Indiana its first football victory over the powerful Chicago program of legendary coach Amos Alonzo Stagg.

26

ARTHUR TROUT, A COACHING LEGEND

Arthur Trout in his IU playing days.

The 1911 Indiana football team included a future Hall of Famer, but nobody would have guessed how end Arthur Trout would get there.

Trout, from Bruceville, won three IU football letters. "He is not big but he is full up to the gills with the necessary ingredient called pepper," the *Arbutus* said. "He always has a sarcastic expression on his face, but in the fray he makes them think he has a family feud to settle."

Trout never played basketball at IU, but that became the sport of his lifetime. In 37 years as the basketball coach at Centralia, Illinois, High School, Trout's teams won 809 games and three state championships. His stars included Dwight "Dike" Eddleman, a Rose Bowl football player for Illinois, an NBA basketball player who once had 48 points in a game for Tri-Cities against Fort Wayne, and a 1948 Olympic high jumper. Trout was Eddleman's Centralia coach in all three sports, introducing football to a school that was thought too small for the sport before Trout's arrival.

But it was his long and brilliant career in basketball that earned him induction into the National High School Hall of Fame, as well as the Illinois version.

Snapshot In Time

A FIGHTER, SOMETIMES CAUGHT

MERRILL DAVIS, WHO was to have a career in medicine, captained the Indiana basketball team that was 5-3 when it went to Butler. The Hoosiers lost the game and more that night. Davis, hurt in the game, was out the rest of the year, and the Hoosier defense collapsed in a season that ended 6-11.

Davis was given a tongue-in-cheek appraisal in the *Arbutus*:

"Merrill Davis, captain of the team, fights hard all the time and sometimes the referee catches him at it. Then 'Davy' stamps on the sidelines."

Phil Graves, in the second of four seasons in which he lettered, carried a 10-point average for a team that averaged 19.5 points a game. The *Arbutus* called Graves "the cleanest player and the best point-getter on the team. Phil prefers dodging to bruising and consequently makes a few goals."

Davis received his M.D. from IU in 1914. He practiced in Marion and served on the IU Board of Trustees. Representing the trustees at dedication ceremonies for Memorial Stadium in 1960, he said: "On behalf of the Board of Trustees and for the athletes who have worn the Cream and Crimson, I glory in this day and occasion."

He died June 5, 1974.

Merrill Davis, as a doctor and trustee, helped dedicate Memorial Stadium in 1960.

IN THOSE DAYS . . .

STEEL OR PEWTER?

William Lowe Bryan, the man who served longest as Indiana University's president, was a gifted writer and speaker who included among his presidential duties, and pleasures, writing a regular column for the *Indiana Daily Student*. He counted himself among the Hoosiers' biggest fans, and he suffered when IU teams—and players, football players foremost—suffered, as they did frequently in his years.

So, Bryan (an 1884 baseball letterman) wrote, under the title "On Being Beaten:"

"One of the compensations for defeat, and every man must sometimes lose, is to find out for yourself whether you are made of steel or pewter.

"If you are one kind of man, defeat will crumple you up; you will whine or sulk or swear at somebody else; and you will quit. If you are another sort, you will discover in yourself, under the chagrin of defeat, one of the deepest joys of a man, the joy of finding that you possess an unbeaten heart.

"The great thing about Washington is not his victories in battles. He won few victories. The thing which lifts him into place with the few great world leaders is that through years of defeat upon defeat, he kept together a little army of men who were always ready for a fight. It was the unbeaten heart of Washington, more than anything else, which won American independence.

"A defeat can give you a chance to find out whether you are made of pewter or of steel."

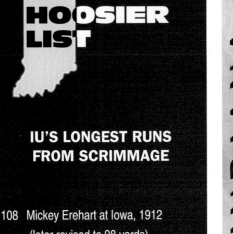

HOOSIER LIST

IU'S LONGEST RUNS FROM SCRIMMAGE

108 Mickey Erehart at Iowa, 1912
(later revised to 98 yards)

90 George Ross at Northwestern, 1929

89 Darrick Burnett vs. Miami (O.), 1977

85 Gene Gedman vs. Pittsburgh, 1951

85 Larry Marks at Northwestern, 1923

83 Bob Robertson vs. Notre Dame, 1953

82 Ric Enis vs. No. Carolina St., 1976

82 Rick Thompson vs. Baylor, 1968

82 Don Veller vs. Purdue, 1934

81 Alex Smith vs. Southern Miss., 1995

80 Vaughn Dunbar vs. Missouri, 1990

80 Johnnie Salters at Colorado, 1980

Darrick Burnett—89 yards vs. Miami in 1977.

INDIANA

LEGEND *Mickey Erehart*

RACE TO THE RECORD BOOK

Mickey Erehart's touchdown dash for Indiana at Iowa in 1912 might always be the longest scrimmage run a Big Ten player ever makes, whether official records say so or not.

Erehart, playing in just his fifth college game, almost had an early-game punt blocked by a hard-charging right end. Later, on fourth down at Indiana's 2, punter Erehart's heels were just inside the back of the end zone "when I got the ball, looked up, and there came that end again. So, being a sophomore and a fool, I decided to run.

"If the coach (Jim Sheldon) could have, I'm sure he'd have killed me right then and there.

"But I did get outside the end and suddenly I was in the open, so I kept running as hard as I could.

"I was all right for a while, but I had a broken nose and some kind of guard on it, so I could only breathe through my mouth. I kept running and wheezing and gasping and praying, and I guess something worked because nobody caught me.

"I was never so glad to see the end zone in my life."

It was called a 108-yard run. College scoring rules no longer include end zone yardage, so it was officially revised to 98, nearly a century later still the Big Ten record—tied by Minnesota's Darrell Thompson 75 years later (1987) but never beaten.

Unfortunately for Erehart and the Hoosiers, the long run was the only IU excitement in a 13-6 loss.

IU item

LINDLEY IU'S FRANGIPANI MAN

"Indiana, Our Indiana," the fight song that has celebrated Hoosier touchdowns and tournament championships over the years, came into being in the 1912 football season.

IU band director Russell P. Harker, lifted the melody from "The Viking March," written by the director of the band for the Barnum and Bailey Circus, Karl L. King. To King's music, Harker wrote:

Indiana, our Indiana,
Indiana, we're all for you.
We will fight for
The Cream and Crimson,
For the glory of Old IU.
Never daunted, we cannot falter,
In the battle, we're tried and true.
Oh Indiana, our Indiana,
Indiana, we're all for you!

Harker's band first performed it at the football Hoosiers' game with Northwestern in 1912—alas, a 21-6 Hoosier loss.

IU's Alma Mater was introduced in 1893, not at a football game but a state musical contest. Joseph T. Giles, organizer of the IU Glee Club, was invited to bring his group to the contest and he hurriedly wrote up the words that still are sung. The tune was borrowed from Cornell's "Far Above Cayuga Waters," the model for many university alma maters.

The IU song's key words, "Gloriana, frangipana, e'er to her be true," come from a cheer some enterprising IU students coined on the way to a football game in the 1890s. Making up the word gloriana to rhyme with Indiana wasn't too difficult, but frangipana was an inspiration.

The senior who came up with it, Ernest Hiram Lindley, was the son of a

druggist and he remembered selling perfume from the frangipani flower.

President William Lowe Bryan was the one whose research linked Lindley, perfume and frangipani.

Bryan admitted in a 1923 speech: "I have one qualm: I do not know how one is to make Indiana rhyme with Frangipani without mispronouncing one or the other."

Lindley later became chancellor at the University of Kansas. His son, Ernest K. Lindley, was a Rhodes Scholar at IU before becoming Washington bureau chief for *Newsweek* magazine and chairman of the U.S. State Department advisory board.

Lindley Hall at IU, the former Science Hall, is named for Ernest Hiram, the frangipana man.

Snapshot in Time

THE 'DEMON' BROTHERS

THE BIG AND FAST Erehart brothers from Huntington, Mickey and Archie, made an impact on the full IU athletic program.

Mickey came first at IU, but they already were recognized as stars before either reached campus. In the book *Before Rockne at Notre Dame*, author Chet Grant told of his own pre-Irish days, as a South Bend High School back who also covered the team for the *South Bend Tribune*. The town's only high school, South Bend High, was a football powerhouse. But Huntington came in and played the team to a 12-12 tie.

Grant's *Tribune* story was headlined "Demon of Visiting High School Is Star of Game," "the demon" unidentified further in the newspaper story because, Grant admitted, "I didn't know the name of the big back who scored both Huntington touchdowns." It was Mickey. Archie was there, too, one of "the demon Erehart brothers," Grant called them in his book.

Mickey won three IU letters in football, "captain and best player" on the 1914 team, the *Arbutus* said. He also lettered two years as a baseball outfielder and one year in track. Archie won three football letters and two in track, where his school-record 9.9 made him the first IU athlete to break 10 seconds in the 100-yard dash.

Both became doctors.

Archie Erehart

HOOSIER LIST

PAST I-MEN'S PRESIDENTS

1934-47	J. Leroy Sanders
1947-50	Clinton C. Prather
1950-52	James O. Birr
1952-53	Noble L. Biddinger
1953-54	James D. Strickland
1954-57	Paul G. Jasper
1957-62	Everett S. Dean
1962-65	W.T. "Bill" Smith
1965-71	R. Vernon Huffman
1971-76	Kenneth W. Moeller
1976-81	Merritt W. Smith
1981-84	Don R. Luft
1984-87	Norbert E. Herrmann
1987-90	Thomas McConnell
1990-93	Bruce R. Ellwanger
1993-96	Jerry W. Gates
1996-98	Patrick J. O'Connor
1999-	Dean Vonderheide

Pat O'Connor
Swimming 1971-74

INDIANA LEGEND — *Sherman Minton*

A POWER-HITTING JUSTICE

Sherman Minton was the first—and as the century closes still the only—IU graduate to sit on the U.S. Supreme Court.

Minton is also one of the few Americans to serve in Washington in all three governmental branches: legislative (U.S. Senator from Indiana, 1936-40); executive (administrative assistant to President Franklin Roosevelt), and judicial.

"Shay" Minton, from New Albany, also was an end and fullback on IU's 1912 and '13 football teams. He was even more noted as a baseball outfielder.

In the spring of 1913, a key to the Hoosiers' third-place conference finish was an early 6-5 victory at Ohio State. Minton scored the winning run on a two-out hit by Otto Englehart in the 10th inning. Minton opened the inning with a single and moved to second on a sacrifice.

Earlier that game came a home run that Minton in a 1956 interview called his greatest sports thrill.

The Buckeyes' diamond was encircled by a cinder track, he said. "The pitcher threw one where I had been swinging for three years (high and outside) . . . and away it went over the centerfielder's head.

"(He) chased the ball clear out of the playing field, and there it went down the cinder track, the centerfielder still chasing it. I walked in . . ."

Minton was appointed to the Supreme Court September 15, 1949, by his friend and one-time Senate colleague, Harry S. Truman, who called Minton his "top notch appointment after the Chief Justice (Fred Vinson)." He resigned from the Court for health reasons seven years later. He died at 74 in 1965. The Interstate 64 bridge linking Indiana and Kentucky at Louisville is named for him.

IU item

I-MEN FORMED

I n the fall of 1913, before Indiana was to meet Illinois in a football game at Indianapolis, a group of former Hoosier letterwinners met at the Claypool Hotel and formed an organization that continues today: the I-Men's Association.

The purpose was to tie all Hoosier athletes together in support of the program. When the group marked its first anniversary in 1914, more than 300 former letterwinners were on the Jordan Field sidelines supporting the Hoosiers in a game with Washington and Jefferson.

The first I-Men's officers all played in the 1800s: president Carl Endicott (football, 1893-1896), vice president C.J. Sembower (baseball, 1891-94), and secretary George Cook (football, 1895).

Later, the group opened its membership ever so judiciously to include some honorary members. The first was Jacob Gimbel, the Vincennes store owner who underwrote the Gimbel awards. Another was Paul McNutt, the baseball player who became governor and twice was on the cover of *Time* magazine. In 1944, the honor went to a World War II Medal of Honor recipient, Jerry Kisters of Bloomington.

Three IU presidents are among the honorary members: Herman B Wells, 1962, Elvis J. Stahr, jr., 1964, and John W. Ryan, 1973.

Paul McNutt played baseball at IU and became governor of Indiana.

MINTON ON FAST TRACK

"SHAY" MINTON MIGHT have won more than four IU letters if he hadn't been on so fast an academic track.

After two undergraduate years, students could go straight into the three-year law school. Minton did and finished law school in just two years, graduating first in his law class with all A's except for a few B-pluses and B's.

He also waited tables at his Phi Delta Theta fraternity house to cut costs. He was elected president of the Indiana Union.

A two-year member of the varsity debating team, Minton won the 1914 William Jennings Bryan prize in oratorical competition administered by IU's history and political science departments. The prize included some cash, the annual interest on a $250 contribution Bryan made to the university.

The subject of Minton's prize-winning speech, previewing his career was: "The Relation of the Executive to the Legislative Department."

Justice Minton

HOOSIER LIST

IU BIG TEN WRESTLING CHAMPIONS

1911 Walter Bodenhafer, middleweight
1912 Ed Davis, heavyweight
1913 Ed Davis, heavyweight
1914 Ralph Williams, 125; Floyd Demmon, 158;
Ed Davis, heavyweight
1923 Omar Held, 175
1924 Ralph Wilson, 175
1928 C.O. Swain, 145
1931 Delmas Aldridge, 118
1932 Eddie Belshaw, 135; Dale Goings, 145;
George Belshaw, 155; Bob Jones, Hwt.
1933 Pat Devine, 135; Dale Goings, 145; Glen Brown,
155; Olden Gillum, 165; Bob Jones, Hwt.
1934 Pat Devine, 135; Frank Krahulik, 155;
Olden Gillum, 165; Richard Voliva, 175
1936 Clifford Myers, 118; Willard Duffy, 126
1937 Clifford Myers, 118
1938 Willard Duffy, 126; Charley McDaniel, Hwt.
1939 Angelo Lazzara, 155; Chauncey McDaniel, 165;
Chris Traicoff, 175
1940 Jim Sefton, 121; Ben Wilson, 136;
Chauncey McDaniel, 165
1941 Ben Wilson, 136; Angelo Lazzara, 155
1943 Bob Bruner, 128; Chet Robbins, 136;
Jim Wilkinson, 155; Harry Traster, 175
1945 Joe Roman, 155
1946 Mike Rolak, 121; Elias George, 145
1947 Chet Robbins, 136
1949 Andy Puchany, 145
1952 Bob Carlin, 115; Jim Ellis, 147
1953 Charles Pankow, 147
1962 John Maroni, 177
1964 Dick Isel, 177
1968 Tim McCall, 123
1969 Jim Lentz, 145
1971 Bill Willetts, 142
1975 Sam Komar, 134
1977 Sam Komar, 142
1989 Brian Dolph, 150
1990 Brian Dolph, 150; Jim Pearson, 158
1997 Roger Chandler, 142

INDIANA LEGEND 'Big Ed' Davis

THREE-TIME CHAMPION

They called Edgar Clarence Davis "Big Ed." They still should. His role in Indiana's athletic history is gigantic.

Davis, from Salem, played three years of football for the Hoosiers. As a senior, he captained the 1913 team, but a second-game injury at Chicago ended his season.

The injury did not end his IU career. Davis moved from football into wrestling, where he made his biggest Hoosier impact. Heavyweight Davis became the first wrestler to win three straight conference championships, captained the Hoosier team his last two years, and led the 1914 team to the school's first Western Conference championship. Six men made up a wrestling team then, and all six Hoosiers contributed to the 15 points that beat Wisconsin's 13 and won the title.

Besides Davis, Indiana's Ralph Williams (125) and Floyd Demmon (158) won championships.

Davis picked up an additional letter as a weightman in track, then entered medical school and stayed with the IU wrestling program as coach for two seasons. He picked up his M.D. in 1919 and, blending in three years of professional football, went on to a distinguished career as a physician in Muncie.

In 1964 he was brought back to campus to receive one of the earliest Z.G. Clevenger awards.

He remains the only Hoosier wrestler ever to win three conference championships.

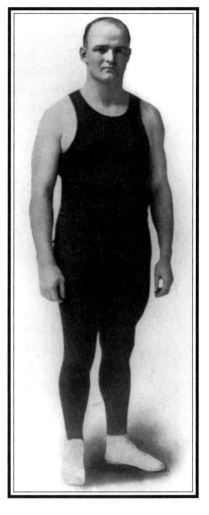

BIG TEN MEDAL
Matthew Winters

A CHAMPION RETURNS

Dick Porter was one of the first stars of an Indiana high school basketball tournament to move on to IU and excel. Porter's Lebanon High School team was the runnerup to Crawfordsville in the first state tournament ever played, in 1911, at IU. Porter had four points in that game, a 24-17 loss.

As a senior, he led Lebanon back to Bloomington, and to a resounding state championship, 51-11 over Franklin in the final game in 1912. Porter's 26 points in that game stood as the championship-game record for 34 years. The 40-point final-game margin never has been topped.

As a Hoosier, his low point may have come his junior year, 1914-15, when an Illinois team that was to finish the season unbeaten came in to Bloomington and won, 20-4, without allowing an IU basket. Porter had three of the free throws that averted a shutout that night.

Just 18 days later on the same court, Porter had 13 points, teammate Allan Maxwell 20 and the Hoosiers routed Rose Poly, 64-15.

The 64 remained IU's team scoring record for 24 years.

Porter was an honor student at IU, picking up his M.D. in 1919 and returning to Lebanon as a doctor.

Snapshot In Time

JIM THORPE, HOOSIER

Clarence Childs

Jim Thorpe

CLARENCE CHILDS OF Yale and Jim Thorpe of Carlisle Institute were teammates on the 1912 U.S. Olympic track team at Stockholm, and that's why Thorpe wound up as a part of Indiana's athletic history.

Childs won the bronze medal in the hammer throw at Stockholm, and Thorpe was the dominant athlete of those 1912 Games. He won both the decathlon and pentathlon, gold medals he had to give back a year later when it was learned he had earned $25 a week playing semi-pro baseball in the summers of 1909 and '10. Seventy years later the ban was lifted and his gold medals were given to his descendants; Thorpe had died 30 years before.

From 1913 through 1919, Thorpe played in baseball's major leagues, with undistinguished marks.

Childs, who had been coached in football by Walter Camp at Yale, was named Indiana's football coach in 1914. He talked Thorpe into joining him as backfield coach for both 1914 and '15, building the coaching around Thorpe's baseball career.

Thorpe, voted in 1950 America's Athlete of the Half-Century, had been an all-time All-America football star under Pop Warner at Carlisle.

He scored all the points when his 1911 team beat Harvard, 18-15. In 1912, he ran 92 yards for a touchdown against Army and a linebacker named Dwight Eisenhower. The play was called back because of a penalty. Next play, Thorpe went 97 yards to score. Carlisle won, 27-6.

All-America teams were Ivy League-dominated then, but Thorpe was a first-team pick in both 1911 and 1912.

Thorpe's fame was unique. "Men came from distances to see Jim's exhibitions of punting between halves," the 1915 *Arbutus* said. "At Northwestern after the game had been won, a little boy came running up to (equipment manager) Jake Van Buskirk, who was carrying the football that had just been won. The chap touched the ball reverently and then exclaimed exultantly, 'Jim Thorpe touched the ball, and so did I.'"

HOOSIER LIST

IU GIMBEL AWARD WINNERS

1916	Claude Ewing	1960	Ted Smith
1917	Russell Hathaway	1961	Bob Reinhart
1918	Wilbur Dalzell	1962	Charles Hall
1919	Arthur Mogge	1963	Tom Bolyard
1920	Spencer Pope	1964	Lary Schulhof
1921	Edward Mumby	1965	Fred Schmidt
1922	Elmer Lucas	1966	John Durkott
1923	Eugene Thomas	1967	Bob Russell
1924	Theodore Koontz	1968	Bob Russell
1925	Earl Moomaw	1969	Jerry Grecco
1926	Robert Rose	1970	Jim Henry
1927	Walter Fisher	1971	E.G. White
1928	Victor Salmi	1972	Mark Spitz
1929	William Moss	1973	John Ritter
1930	Wilbert Catterton	1974	Bill Armstrong Jr.
1931	Bernard Miller	1975	Steve Green
1932	George Belshaw	1976	Tom Abernethy
1933	Clifford Watson	1977	Kent Benson
1934	Charles Hornbostel	1978	Peter Murao
1935	Willard Kehrt	1979	Joe Norman
1936	Daniel Caldemeyer	1980	Angelo Marino
1937	Don Lash	1981	Glen Grunwald
1938	Robert Kenderdine	1982	Rob Bollinger
1939	Paul Graham	1983	Gregg Thompson
1940	James Logan	1984	Bobby Hicks
1941	Bob Menke	1985	Joe Fitzgerald
1942	Andy Zimmer	1986	John Stollmeyer
1943	Guy Wellman	1987	Steve Alford
1944	Kermit Wahl	1988	Jeff Stout
1945	Leon Kaminski	1989	Charles Wright
1948	Ward Williams	1990	Brian Dolph
1949	Don Ritter	1991	Shaun Micheel
1950	James Roberson	1992	Mike Anhaeuser
1951	Edwin Reisig	1993	Mike Clark,
1952	Larry Meyer		Glenn Terry
1953	Jim Schooley	1994	Jody Roudebush
1954	Lowell Zellers	1995	Brian
1955	Tom Dailey		Maisonneuve
1956	Bob Skoronski	1996	Sam Gasowski
1957	Bill Woolsey	1997	Micah Nori
1958	Don Brodie	1998	Andrew Held
1959	Tom McDonald	1999	Mike Collier

INDIANA

LEGEND *Frank Allen*

ATHLETE AND A.D.

Frank Allen came to Bloomington from Summitville, but not directly out of high school. Allen played three years of high school football as a halfback, then worked the next four years and spent some autumn time playing end on an amateur team.

He was 23 when he played as a sophomore tackle on the 1914 Indiana team. He moved back to end under coach Clarence Childs as a junior, then graduated the next spring with a degree in geology.

Allen went on to a rich career in education. He coached basketball and football at New Castle, then moved to Muncie and built the Bearcats into a football power. In South Bend, he advanced to superintendent of schools and drew credit for the number of bright young coaches brought into the public school system there.

Allen's contacts with his alma mater remained strong. From 1940 to 1954, he served on IU's Board of Trustees. That board picked him to move to Bloomington in 1955 as Athletic Director, a role he had during the planning and construction of Memorial Stadium and other facilities. He resigned as athletic director in 1961; in 1989, he was elected to the university's Athletic Hall of Fame.

1915-16 was the last full season of use for the original Assembly Hall, IU's first basketball home.

BIG TEN MEDAL
George Shively

GIMBEL AWARD
Claude Ewing

GIMBEL A PRIZE

Jake Gimbel

Claude Ewing

Jake Gimbel, described as "a merchant and psychological student" from Vincennes, funded an annual prize to go to a junior or senior athlete "for the building of mental attitude in athletics."

The prize, the *Arbutus* said, is "a very earnest effort on the part of a man who is deeply interested in Indiana to improve her athletics."

The first Gimbel Prize, given in December 1915, went to Claude Ewing, a Clinton senior who lettered two years in football and also competed in track and gymnastics.

The year before, the Western Conference began an annual award on each campus, intended to recognize outstanding performance by a senior in both athletics and academics. Matthew Winters, who went on to become a doctor, was IU's first winner. Winters lettered in football on the same teams with Ewing in 1914 and '15, and won a letter as well with the 1912 baseball team.

In 1917, Gimbel, whose name was to be known nationally after he opened a store in New York and began a legendary commercial war with Macy's, underwrote a similar mental attitude award for the Indiana high school basketball tournament. It continued as the Gimbel Prize for 27 years. Since 1945, it has been the Arthur L. Trester Award, renamed to honor the first IHSAA commissioner.

Snapshot In Time

SOME EXCUSE

WHEN COTTON BERNDT resigned as basketball and baseball coach, the baseball job went to Illinois graduate and seven-year major league pitcher Fred Beebe.

Indianapolis alumni set up a welcoming luncheon for Beebe, an *Indianapolis Star* story said. "But it was quite like a good mess of ham and eggs, without the ham. Beebe didn't come."

Too late to cancel the luncheon, Beebe wired from Colorado that he wouldn't make it. When he finally arrived in Bloomington, he explained why:

"Just before our train reached Marshall Pass, Colorado, it ran into a cut of 30 feet of snow. We stuck and laid there 24 hours. There was no dining car and the passengers soon began to get hungry. I left the train and, wading through snow above my waist, finally reached the cabin of a miner and found something to eat.

"I helped the miner's wife prepare a dinner for 40 passengers, all of whom reached the cabin after fighting through the drifts. The woman had a goodly supply of fresh sausage on hand, and I helped mix a breadpan of pancakes, which soon disappeared." How happy the miner's wife was to see Beebe and his party leave was not recorded.

Beebe coached the Hoosiers for just one season. His 1916 team finished third in the conference with a 4-3 record. He was the first of three straight one-season baseball coaches at IU.

Beebe had a good excuse for leaving. After being out of the major leagues for four seasons, he went from the spring in Bloomington to a pitching job with the Cleveland Indians. After a 5-3 season, he was released. He had seven major league seasons, mostly with the Cardinals. His career record was 63-84, but his lifetime earned run average was 2.86.

IN THOSE DAYS . . .

NO PRESIDENT, BUT A MEMORY

Washington & Lee came out of Lexington, Virginia, to fill a spot on the Indiana football schedule.

It was the first time Indiana had met a football team from Virginia, and Indiana Senator John Worth Kern went to the White House to invite the time's most noted son of Virginia, President Woodrow Wilson, to make the trip by train to see the game. Wilson was renowned as a distinguished law professor and the first lay president of Princeton, but he also had coached a strong football team at Wesleyan while he was teaching there. And his vice president, Thomas R. Marshall, was from Indiana.

Still, the invitation was not accepted.

The little school turned out to be something of a ringer for Indiana. The Generals' only loss was 40-21 to a Cornell team that was acclaimed as national champion, Cornell's 9-0 record including a 34-7 rout of Michigan.

It was Washington & Lee, though, that got the early shock in Bloomington. Freal McIntosh caught the opening kickoff at the goal line and ran it back for the only Hoosier score in a 7-7 tie.

That 100-yard run stood unmatched in IU history for 83 years, till freshman Derin Graham returned the second-half kickoff 100 yards in a 24-20 loss to Wisconsin in 1998.

1916 1917

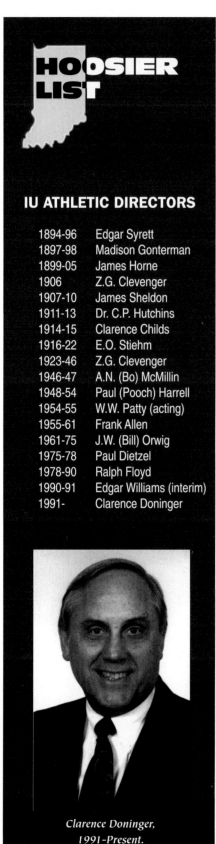

IU ATHLETIC DIRECTORS

1894-96	Edgar Syrett
1897-98	Madison Gonterman
1899-05	James Horne
1906	Z.G. Clevenger
1907-10	James Sheldon
1911-13	Dr. C.P. Hutchins
1914-15	Clarence Childs
1916-22	E.O. Stiehm
1923-46	Z.G. Clevenger
1946-47	A.N. (Bo) McMillin
1948-54	Paul (Pooch) Harrell
1954-55	W.W. Patty (acting)
1955-61	Frank Allen
1961-75	J.W. (Bill) Orwig
1975-78	Paul Dietzel
1978-90	Ralph Floyd
1990-91	Edgar Williams (interim)
1991-	Clarence Doninger

Clarence Doninger, 1991-Present.

LEGEND *'Jumbo' Stiehm*

A BADGER GREAT TAKES OVER

Ewald Ortivin Stiehm was called "Jumbo" because he was a giant of his day, about 6-3, 180 pounds.

His was a sinewy, athletic frame. At Johnson Creek, Wisconsin, Stiehm was a high school basketball and football star. He was Wisconsin's first All-Big Ten football player in 1906, the sophomore center on an unbeaten conference champion. In 1907, a key to Wisconsin's 11-8 win over Indiana was Stiehm's touchdown on a recovered blocked punt. His four Badger basketball teams went 43-11, sharing the 1908 championship with Chicago. He added track, tennis and water polo to his sports, winning nine letters.

At the end of his fifth year as football and basketball coach at Nebraska, Indiana hired him in the spring of 1916 to be its football coach and athletic director. His Nebraska football teams had gone 35-2-3 (both losses to Minnesota) and won five straight Missouri Valley Conference championships.

The Bloomington Chamber of Commerce set up a banquet to welcome Stiehm, who noted the hospitality with a message that he sent ahead:

"I appreciate the courtesy of your invitation, but I regret to inform you I am not a public speaker.

"However, I am willing to sit down and do my share of eating."

BIG TEN MEDAL
DeWitt Mullett

GIMBEL AWARD
Russell Hathaway

36

IU item

RECORD LOW SCORE FOR DEDICATION

A day of festive excitement preceded the Indiana-Iowa basketball game in Bloomington January 19, 1917.

The university celebrated its 97th birthday with a Founder's Day observance led by President William Lowe Bryan. Classes were called off to encourage student participation.

And that night, the Hoosiers and Hawkeyes played the first game in IU's glistening new $250,000 Fieldhouse.

Construction took just about a year on the 240 x 328-foot Tudor Gothic structure. The gymnasium floor, 190 x 90, was the central part of the second floor.

It was part of a major upgrading of the Indiana athletic program, which started when C. P. Hutchins came to IU from Wisconsin in 1911 and took on impetus in 1916 with the hiring of E.O. "Jumbo" Stiehm as football coach and IU athletic director.

Stiehm had coached basketball as well as football in highly successful years at Nebraska. At Indiana he turned basketball over to Guy Lowman, who had played at Iowa State and coached against Stiehm at Kansas State.

Lowman had his team ready that first night in the new gym. The Hoosiers won, 12-7. The score is a part of IU history for more than its timing. It's the lowest-scoring basketball game ever involving IU, and the Hoosiers' 12 is the lowest score ever to win an Indiana game, by either Indiana or an opponent.

Snapshot In Time

1-0 — IN 17 INNINGS

EARLY IN THE 1917 baseball season, Indiana whipped Ohio State, 7-2, behind captain and pitching ace "Big Ed" Ridley. It was to be the only league game the champion Buckeyes lost.

So, Indiana went into the last weekend of the season hoping to use a two-game set with Purdue as a springboard into second place.

The Boilermakers spoiled that with a 2-1 victory over Ridley in the opener.

The next day, Ken Kunkel was the Indiana pitcher through the first nine innings of a scoreless tie. On came captain Ridley, to keep the game 0-0 through three more innings, then four . . . five . . . six . . . seven . . . eight.

In the bottom of the 17th, Indiana's Roy "Curly" Rayl doubled to drive in the only run of what may be the longest 1-0 game in Big Ten history.

It made the difference between a winning and losing season for the Hoosiers in conference play. Their 5-4 record was good for third. Charlie Buschmann, captain of the basketball team that year and a football player as well, won the last of his eight varsity letters as a third-year player on the baseball team.

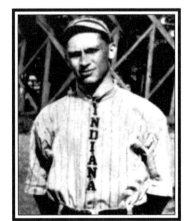

"Big Ed" Ridley

1917  1918

HOOSIER LIST

IU'S HIGHEST SCORING FOOTBALL TEAMS

33.0 (1988)

32.1 (1917)

29.2 (1944)

27.9 (1945)

27.4 (1990)

26.9 (1994)

26.3 (1989)

26.2 (1979)

25.6 (1942)

25.4 (1991)

25.2 (1969)

25.0 (1968)

LEGEND — *Russ Hathaway*

LEADER OF A POWERHOUSE

Center Russell Hathaway of Linton was the captain and a first-team All-Big Ten pick for a 5-2 team that made people notice what second-year coach E. O. "Jumbo" Stiehm was doing at Indiana.

It was a remarkable record for a team cut drastically by the man-power demands of World War I. Just 12 players reported for the first practice. Only 14 made an October trip to Minnesota.

But for more than 70 years, this team stood as IU's highest-scoring football team ever.

The Hoosiers drubbed four non-conference opponents 176-0 and added a fifth shutout victory over Purdue (37-0, the Hoosiers' most one-sided win in the series' first 97 years).

They lost to the Big Ten's two best teams, 33-9 at Minnesota and 26-3 at Ohio State.

Indiana's 32.1 scoring average stood as the school record until the 8-4 Liberty Bowl-champion Hoosiers of 1988 averaged 33.0.

Hathaway, IU's 1917 Gimbel Award winner, entered military service as a Navy ensign. After World War I, he began a seven-year career in the new National Football League.

In 1967, at age 83, he went back to the campus to be honored as a 50-year I-Man, on Homecoming of the greatest Hoosier football season of the last half-century.

Wrestler Wilbur Dalzell was the first IU athlete to win both the Big Ten Medal and the Gimbel Award.

BIG TEN MEDAL
Wilbur Dalzell

GIMBEL AWARD
Wilbur Dalzell

38

AT LAST: THE BIG TEN

T he Western Conference in 1917 became, for the first time, a 10-member league. Immediately, to the press and public, it took on the unofficial title that has stuck with it ever since: "the Big Ten."

After reaching nine members with admittance of Indiana and Iowa in 1899, the conference slipped back to eight in 1908 when Michigan withdrew, angered by new eligibility restrictions that the conference had enacted upon the recommendation of Michigan president J.B. Angell.

Ohio State was added in 1912, bringing the league back to nine members. On June 9, 1917, Michigan was invited to return, and the invitation was accepted, effective with the start of fall competition that year.

Michigan played just one league football game in 1917, losing at Northwestern, 21-12. The next year, though, the Wolverines claimed a title share by beating Chicago and Ohio State in the war-abbreviated season.

The popular, public name of the conference has been the "Big Ten" almost from then on. From 1944 to 1949, between Chicago's decision to drop out of the league and Michigan State's acceptance as a replacement, the league did operate as the "Big Nine." When its membership went the opposite direction, however—in 1990 when the 10-team league added Penn State—the numbers reality was ignored and the conference formally announced it would keep the name Big Ten.

A NEAR-STRIKE, AND A ROUT

THE 1917 PURDUE game almost wasn't played, and war demands had nothing to do with that.

On Monday of game week, Purdue demanded that Indiana declare two starters ineligible—tackle Howard Ewart for playing a pro game with Hammond, and fullback Lynn Howard for playing a baseball game at Creighton and not sitting out a year after transferring.

"Unfortunately," Russ Hathaway said in an interview 50 years later, "they were right."

Hoosier players felt Purdue timed its protest for game week for maximum effect. Manpower-short even with Ewart and Howard, the reduced Indiana squad voted not to play the game. The Hoosiers didn't practice Monday, Tuesday, Wednesday or Thursday.

Thursday, Hathaway received a telegram from president William Lowe Bryan: "It would reflect on the honor of Indiana University not to play Purdue. Fight it out on Jordan Field." The players voted to play.

"Jumbo" Stiehm took it from there. After his pregame talk, Hathaway said, "Half of us were so emotional we were crying. We tore up those Boilermakers."

Hathaway was particularly roused. His Linton teammate and friend, Bill Berns, was Purdue's captain.

After the Hoosiers' 37-0 victory, relations between the two schools were so strained they didn't meet again in football until 1920. The series has been unbroken since.

President William Lowe Bryan
"Fight it out."

IN THOSE DAYS . . .

'THE LORD BLESS PURDUE'

Don Herold, an IU graduate who went on to acclaim as a national writer and humorist, celebrated Indiana's one-sided football victory by thanking Purdue "for getting us good and sore."

Under the heading "The Lord Bless Purdue" in the *Bloomington World*, Herold wrote:

"Indiana found out Saturday what she can do when she gets mad. Some of Purdue's methods of the first of last week made us sorer than we have ever been before. It was the first time we have been gloriously sore. There was every reason in the world why Purdue should have licked the tar out of Indiana Saturday, but she didn't. We tore some new stuff loose out of ourselves.

"The Indiana football team started something Saturday that ought to last Indiana 150 years."

The *Lafayette Courier* reported: "Several players on the Boilermaker squad have bruised places that will attest to the slugging of the Indiana players. The officials did not see it, of course."

And in the *Lafayette Journal*: "The traditional fighting spirit of the Boilermakers against their time-worn rivals waned and they seemed dumfounded . . . It was not the same team that at least fought against the other teams played this season. Indiana fought with a dogged determination that would not be curbed, that is the primary reason of the Purdue downfall."

HOOSIER LIST

WHEN IU PLAYERS OUTSCORED OPPONENTS

20 Godfred Ritterskamp vs. Indiana State, 1905 (52-16)
21 Chet Harmeson vs. Purdue, 1905 (29-14)
16 Leslie Maxwell & 14 Chet Harmeson vs. Butler, 1906 (42-11)
16 Chet Harmeson vs. Wabash AC, 1906 (20-13)
28 Chet Harmeson vs. New Albany YMCA, 1906 (46-21)
15 Chet Harmeson vs. Indiana State, 1906 (27-12)
12 Chet Harmeson & 12 Godfred Ritterskamp vs. Illinois, 1906 (37-8)
12 Charles Cook & 10 Hugh Martin vs. Butler, 1907 (42-7)
15 Harlan McCoy vs. Indiana State, 1908 (37-13)
11 Harlan McCoy, 8 Clifford Woody & 6 Arthur Rogers vs. DePauw, 1908 (25-4)
13 Clifford Woody vs. Northwestern, 1908 (36-10)
20 Clifford Woody vs. Rose Poly, 1908 (30-11)
12 Arthur Rogers vs. Indiana State, 1908 (28-10)
21 Dean Barnhart vs. DePauw, 1909 (31-20)
18 Dean Barnhart vs. Butler, 1911 (41-16)
25 Dean Barnhart vs. DePauw, 1911 (45-20)
16 Dean Barnhart vs. Chicago, 1911 (22-14)
21 Dean Barnhart, 12 Phil Graves & 8 Homer Hipskind vs. Rose Poly, 1911 (45-6)
10 Dean Barnhart & 8 Glen Munkelt vs. Indiana State, 1913 (24-6)
20 Allan Maxwell vs. Rose Poly, 1915 (64-15)
13 Charles Buschmann, 10 Allan Maxwell & 6 Charles Prather vs. DePauw, 1916 (37-5)
12 Bob Rogers vs. Indiana Dental College, 1917 (40-10)
10 Charles Buschmann vs. Rose Poly, 1917 (35-9)
19 Herman Schuler, 12 Bill Zeller & 10 Herschel Bowser vs. Central Normal, 1917 (61-9)
24 Bill Zeller vs. Manchester, 1918 (45-18)
15 Bill Zeller, 8 Dick Easton & 8 Ardith Phillips vs. Rose Poly, 1918 (43-7)
15 Everett Dean vs. Notre Dame, 1919 (29-11)
16 Everett Dean vs. North America Gymnastics Union, 1920 (32-10)
10 Everett Dean, 8 Herman Schuler, 8 Harry Donovan & 6 Mark Wakefield vs. Hanover, 1920 (46-5)
18 Everett Dean vs. Valparaiso, 1920 (24-15)
12 Everett Dean vs. Ohio State, 1920 (22-11)
14 Everett Dean vs. Northwestern, 1920 (32-11)
12 Bobby Marxson vs. Northwestern, 1921 (31-10)
21 Everett Dean vs. Ohio State, 1921 (33-11)
15 Wilfred Bahr vs. Indiana Dental College, 1923 (28-12)
23 Harlan Logan & 18 Mike Nyikos vs. Rose Poly, 1924 (51-15)
16 Harlan Logan vs. Northwestern, 1924 (30-13)
15 Julius Krueger, 13 Harlan Logan & 8 Palmer Sponsler vs. Cincinnati, 1925 (51-7)
12 Harlan Logan vs. Chicago, 1925 (40-11)
24 Branch McCracken vs. Chicago, 1928 (32-13)
16 Maurice Starr vs. Coe, 1928 (35-14)
31 John Ritter vs. Notre Dame, 1972 (94-29)

LEGEND *Everett Dean*

INDIANA

FIRST BASKETBALL ALL-AMERICAN

On January 2 at Vincennes, Indiana introduced its first great basketball player.

Sophomore Everett Dean of Salem started and scored four points in a 47-16 rout of the Vincennes YMCA.

That was his start in basketball, but not as an IU athlete. Though he never lettered in football, Dean, who had played on Salem High School's first football team, caught a pass for Indiana's only touchdown in a 24-7 season-opening loss to Kentucky.

In basketball, Dean's biggest point total as a sophomore was 17 in a 37-31 victory at Ohio State, eight days after his 13-point performance wasn't quite enough in a 22-21 home-court loss to the Buckeyes. Dean scored in double figures five other times and averaged 8.4 in conference play.

On March 3 in the handsome new IU Fieldhouse, Dean personally outscored Notre Dame with 15 points in a 29-11 victory. That wasn't unheard of in the sport's early days. More than 40 times between 1905 and 1928, one Indiana player scored more points than an opposing team.

Dean did it most frequently of all Hoosiers: seven times.

BIG TEN MEDAL
Bill Zeller

GIMBEL AWARD
Arthur Mogge

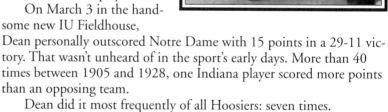

··

THREE I-MEN KILLED IN WAR

Claude Whitney   Harry Gray

The 1923 *Arbutus* listed 52 Indiana University students who were killed in World War I. Three were letter-winning athletes.

Joe Barclay was one of the Hoosiers' first track stars. A distance runner, he lettered three years before graduating in 1905. He captained the team as a senior and left with school records in the mile (4:41.6) and two-mile (10:48). Active in campus organizations inside and outside athletics, Barclay stayed on to coach track and cross country while working toward the law degree that he picked up in 1908.

Claude Whitney came from Muncie to play on the 1909-10 and 1910-11 Hoosier basketball teams. Whitney went on to earn two IU degrees before wartime came. An outstanding student, Whitney was a member of IU's charter class of inductees into the national arts and sciences honorary, Phi Beta Kappa, in 1911.

Harry Gray of Pennville won football letters in 1915 and 1916, and he was one of the thousands who interrupted their college years to enter the military. Gray was a halfback who hadn't played football before trying out as a Hoosier.

Joe Barclay (above) set IU records as a runner and later coached at IU.

Snapshot In Time

BIG TEN TAKES A BREAK

IU'S CONCERNS ABOUT how to mix war preparedness with athletics were shared throughout the troubled nation, and they grew as the war lengthened.

In fall of 1918, the Big Ten voted to suspend athletic operations "as a controlling body."

On October 3, control of college football was assumed by the War Department, which invoked immediate limits on practice time and travel. The new rules also granted freshmen varsity eligibility, for the duration of the war.

Indiana was forced to cancel scheduled games with Wisconsin, Minnesota and Iowa as the conference closed down. An abbreviated league schedule was worked out among some of the schools, and Illinois (4-0 in conference play), Michigan (2-0) and Purdue (1-0) each claimed parts of the championship.

Indiana was the only school totally left out in the redrawn schedule. Coach Jumbo Stiehm patched together a four-game schedule that included two college teams (Kentucky, which defeated the Hoosiers, 24-7, and DePauw, which lost in Bloomington, 13-0, after beating Purdue earlier, 9-7).

The Hoosiers' other games were with military teams. Indiana lost 7-3 at Camp Taylor and routed Fort Harrison, 41-0.

The short football season was barely over when world peace came. Formal treaties were signed at 11 a.m. on 11-11, November 11. The date became a national holiday, first as Armistice Day, later Veterans Day in honor of U.S. servicemen from all wars.

IN THOSE DAYS . . .

CO-EDS GET A CHANCE

A formal intercollegiate women's athletic program wasn't to come for another half-century, but one effect of the wartime manpower shortage was to give women new opportunities in athletics.

Wilma Lloyd

"Co-ed activities came to life and were more visible in Indiana's athletic activities," Thomas D. Clark wrote in *Indiana University, Midwestern Pioneer*. "The girls played baseball and basketball, swam, and performed on the track. In April the co-ed baseball team defeated Chicago."

President William Lowe Bryan had challenged male students to become "Soldiers of the Soil." To answer an anticipated food shortage related to taking young men off farms to go to war, Bryan offered academic credit to properly registered students who put in required time in gardening or farming—males or females.

"With the (athletic) accomplishments tucked away in the record books, the girls turned to war work," Clark wrote. "The leading female athlete, Wilma Lloyd, joined Bryan's 'land army.'"

HOOSIER LIST

HOOSIERS IN FOOTBALL HALL OF FAME

A.N. (Bo) McMillin
IU coach 1934-47
inducted 1951
deceased

Pete Pihos
played 1942-43, 1945-46
inducted 1966
lives in Winston-Salem, NC

Zora G. Clevenger
played 1900-03
inducted 1968
deceased

George Taliaferro
played 1945, 1947-48
inducted 1981
lives in Bloomington, IN

John Tavener
played 1941-44
inducted 1990
deceased

INDIANA

LEGEND *Roscoe 'Cow' Minton*

A BUDDY OF BO

Roscoe "Cow" Minton followed brother Sherman to Indiana and had an even better IU athletic career than did Sherman, the future Supreme Court justice.

The two boys from near New Albany spent some early years in Fort Worth, Texas, where they met and played ball with young Alvin "Bo" McMillin. The three worked together later on the summertime Chautauqua lecture and revival circuit.

The Mintons tried to get McMillin to go to IU, but Bo followed his high school coach and some other Fort Worth friends to Centre College in Danville, Kentucky.

On a rainy October day in 1919, Centre for the first time played Indiana. "Cow" Minton and Bo McMillin met at midfield as captains, so stirred by the moment they wept.

Charles Mathys kicked a field goal for a 3-0 lead the Minton-led Hoosier defense fiercely protected until—with three minutes left, Indiana fans gathering excitedly on the sidelines for a victory march—McMillin passed the Colonels deep, and Texan Red Roberts scored to put Centre ahead, 6-3.

Indiana tried to rally, but McMillin intercepted a pass and scored to complete a 12-3 Centre victory that "went down in Indiana's football history as The Heartbreaker," the 1920 *Arbutus* said.

BIG TEN MEDAL
Willard Rauschenback

GIMBEL AWARD
Spencer Pope

IUitem

'THREE-FINGER' WAS HERE

Mordecai "Three-Finger" Brown, whose Hall of Fame pitching career ended in 1916, came over from his Terre Haute home to be pitching coach for the 1920 Hoosiers.

Brown, who won 20 games six straight years and was the pitching leader of the last two Cubs teams to win World Series championships (1907 and '08), didn't find any major league arms in Bloomington. But, the Hoosiers did end their season merrily by sweeping Purdue, 6-5 at IU (on junior Everett Dean's bases-loaded hit in the 10th) and 8-4 at Purdue.

Then, behind Brown's ace, Ken Kunkel, the Hoosiers defeated Notre Dame, 4-1, and claimed the state championship.

Brown, born at Nyesville in Parke County, went 23-8 and led the Three-I League in victories when he began his professional career with Terre Haute in 1901.

He made his major league debut with a 9-13 season for the 1903 Cardinals. After that season, he was traded to the Cubs, and he was the team's pitching ace through an eight-year tenure that included four National League pennants. Brown led the National League with a 1.04 earned run average in 1906. His 2.06 career ERA is baseball's third-best all-time.

Brown managed Indianapolis in 1919. After his spring with IU, he managed Terre Haute's Three-I League team. He was elected to baseball's Hall of Fame in 1949, a year after his death at age 71.

Mordecai Brown—as a Cub.

'COW' SCORED ON PURDUE

BO MCMILLIN WAS a hero in victory for Centre College in his first football appearance at IU, but McMillin had much greater days ahead, even before his return to Bloomington as IU's most successful football coach.

In 1920, he was a first-team All-American and in '21 he scored the touchdown in Centre's 6-0 victory at Harvard, usually considered college football's all-time top upset.

Roscoe "Cow" Minton, IU's captain in the 1919 IU-Centre game, had an outstanding career of his own. World War I had interrupted his college years. He entered military service after starring in the Hoosiers' 37-0 rout of Purdue in 1917, and he returned to campus in time to be there in 1920 when the bitter rivals got together again. He scored Indiana's touchdown in a 10-7 victory. He also had scored the Hoosiers' first touchdown that year.

Minton lettered as a senior in baseball and came back the next year as an assistant baseball coach, moving up to head coach in 1923 and '24.

Both "Cow" and brother "Shay" were among the first 11 recipients of the Zora Clevenger Award, for service to the university by an I-Man.

Their greatest service of all, though, may have been their boyhood friendship that eventually linked Bo McMillin with Bloomington.

Roscoe Minton scored IU's touchdown in a 10-7 victory over Purdue in 1920.

IN THOSE DAYS . . .

BILL MCCAW: THREE-YEAR STAR

Bill McCaw came out of Chicago high school competition to give Indiana three strong years of football line play.

McCaw won a starting spot as soon as he could, as a sophomore on the 1919 Indiana team that won three of seven games.

McCaw won first-team All-Big Ten honors that year, and he had at least some all-conference mention each of the next two seasons. "For three years," the 1922 *Arbutus* said, "he has been a mighty defensive bastion . . . one of the most powerful and resourceful linemen who ever fought on Jordan Field."

He was the first IU player to make All-Big Ten in his first year of eligibility, according to conference records. It was another 22 years before the next one to do it: halfback Billy Hillenbrand in 1941. The only others through the end of the century were Bob Hoernschemeyer (1943) and George Taliaferro (1945) as freshmen and Harry Gonso (1967) as a sophomore. All but McCaw were backs.

McCaw, an outstanding student who won IU's Big Ten Medal as a senior, played one season of professional football, with the Racine Legion in 1923.

HOOSIER LIST

IU'S BIG TEN TENNIS CHAMPIONS

Singles

1921	Frederick Bastian, #1
1951	Eli Glazer, #3
1952	Eli Glazer, #2; Duane Gomer, #3; John Hironimus, #4; Bob Martin, #5; Tom Lynch, #6
1953	John Hironimus, #2; Duane Gomer, #3; Bob Martin, #4
1954	Bob Martin, #3; Bob Barker, #4; Carl Dentice, #6
1955	Carl Dentice, #5; George Fryman, #6
1956	Elam Huddleston, #5; Ken Dillman, #6
1957	Bob Gray, #6
1963	Alan Graham, #4; Charlie Fichter, #6
1964	Alan Graham, #4; Jim Binkley, #5; Charlie Fichter #6
1965	Rod McNerney, #2
1966	Mike Baer, #3
1970	Tom Dunker, #5
1971	Geoff Hodsdon, #2
1972	Doug Sullivan, #2
1973	Joe Kendall, #3
1977	Bill Rennie, #1
1979	Tom Rogers, #4

Doubles

1952	John Hironimus & Tom Lynch, #2
1953	John Hironimus & Ed Harrison, #3
1954	John Hironimus & Bob Martin, #1
1956	Carl Dentice & Elam Huddleston, #2; George Fryman & Ken Dillman, #3
1963	Gary Baxter & Jim Binkley, #3
1964	Alan Graham & Charlie Kane, #2; Jim Binkley & Charlie Fichter, #1
1965	Dave Power & Rod McNerney, #1
1970	Geoff Hodsdon & Darrel Snively, #2
1971	Mark Bishop & Geoff Hodsdon, #1
1972	Tom Dunker & Joe Kendall, #2

INDIANA

LEGEND   *Babe Pierce*

FUTURE TARZAN A HOOSIER STAR

Senior James "Babe" Pierce, the 1921 *Arbutus* said, was "a wonder at roving center," a key reason why Indiana went 3-1 in the Big Ten and 5-2 overall.

Pierce, from Freedom in Owen County, was a giant for the era: 6-feet-4, 220 pounds. After graduation from IU in 1921, he coached high school football in Arizona and tried amateur acting. The two interests took him to Glendale, California, where one of his high school football stars was a young man who later played at Southern Cal as Marion Morrison before becoming an American hero as the actor John Wayne.

At a party in 1926, Pierce's blind date was his future wife, Joan Burroughs. Joan's father was Edgar Rice Burroughs, author of the Tarzan novels. Burroughs, who said Pierce "came nearer approaching my visualization of Tarzan than any man I'd ever seen," talked him into seeking, and getting, the lead role in the 1927 silent movie, "Tarzan and the Golden Lion."

Pierce, never Tarzan again, did appear in other movies. He and wife Joan were Tarzan and Jane for seven years in a nationwide radio serial.

Pierce later worked with the Burroughs family's Tarzana operations. John Wayne never forgot him. Frequently, after Wayne became one of Hollywood's biggest stars, he insisted on bit parts in his films for Babe Pierce, ex-Hoosier, ex-coach.

In 1999, the small town of Freedom put up highway signs noting it was the hometown of Babe Pierce.

BIG TEN MEDAL
Everett Dean

GIMBEL AWARD
Edward "Ted" Mumby

IU item

BASTIAN NATIONAL CHAMPION

Fritz Bastian is IU's only national champion in men's tennis.

Frederick "Fritz" Bastian of Indianapolis gave Indiana's men's tennis program its first exposure to glory, and its only national tennis championship.

Bastian, Big Ten singles runnerup as a junior, started a championship run in his senior year by beating his brother, Dick, for the state college title. Dick played for Butler, and he combined with Fritz to put on a long, competitive match that Fritz won in straight sets, 6-3, 6-3, 6-4, his second straight victory in the tournament.

Bastian's late-May victory in Big Ten singles gave Indiana its first conference team championship in tennis.

In June, the left-handed Bastian represented IU in the National Intercollegiate Championships at Merion Cricket Club in Haverford, Pennsylvania. There, in a five-day meet involving 68 players from 21 colleges, Bastian won the championship. In the finals, he defeated Carl Fischer of Penn State, again in straight sets.

The tennis championship went with the 1921 wrestling title to mark the first time Indiana had won two conference championships in the same academic year. Bastian and fellow senior Bruce DeMarcus were the only tennis players given letters in the championship season.

Fritz Bastian beat his brother for the State championship, gave IU its first Big Ten title, and won out in a 68-man field in the National Intercollegiate Championships.

Snapshot In Time

MUMBY 'BIGGEST LITTLE MAN'

WHEN INDIANA UPSET Eastern power Syracuse 12-6 closing out the 1919 season, a Hoosier hero was a 165-pound junior lineman, guard Ted Mumby.

Syracuse had a two-time consensus All-American opposite him, Joe Alexander, who was impressed. Alexander called Mumby "the biggest little man in the country."

Mumby, the smallest lineman to make All-State, came back as a senior to star on an outstanding team.

And football wasn't his main sport. He lettered three times in wrestling, and he was team captain as a junior.

The team he captained defeated Iowa, 32-6, and Iowa State, 27-12. He was a competitive leader. He won his match against Purdue, and when the Hoosiers faced a forfeit at heavyweight because of an injury, he stepped way up in weight and won that match, too, in a 37-0 victory.

As a senior, he won a Western Conference championship and led his team to its second league wrestling title, before a happy crowd in Bloomington. Albert Stanley (115) and Orville Ratcliff (125) contributed second-place finishes to the Hoosiers' 16-15 edge over runnerup Iowa.

Mumby, who upon graduation entered missionary work in India, won IU's 1921 Gimbel Award.

Ted Mumby

IN THOSE DAYS . . .

GIPP'S LAST TD

The 1920 Indiana team's biggest role in football history was not its 10-7 victory over Purdue in their first game since Indiana's near-strike in 1917.

The Hoosiers, grudgingly, gave up all-time All-America George Gipp's last touchdown and extracted from him his last great effort.

A week before playing Purdue, Indiana lost 13-10 at Indianapolis to a Notre Dame team en route to a second straight perfect season. Its leaders were Gipp and coach Knute Rockne.

Against Indiana, the Irish fell behind 10-0, on Elliott Risley's 36-yard field goal and Russ Williams' 22-yard touchdown pass to Frank "Duke" Hanny. IU took that lead into the fourth quarter.

Gipp, who had left the game with a shoulder injury, returned to score a touchdown, then set up the game-winner in Notre Dame's narrowest escape of the year.

Just 31 days later, Gipp was dead.

The injury kept him out of an easy windup victory at Northwestern, till Rockne answered late-game fan pleas by letting him play, almost strictly as a passer. He threw well: 5-for-6, 157 yards, two touchdowns.

Gipp stayed in Chicago to demonstrate punting for a former teammate's high school team. There, he contracted strep throat and, at 25, died of pneumonia.

HOOSIER LIST

ATHLETIC FACILITIES

Baseball

1867-1898	IU Athletic Park
1899-1950	Jordan Field
1951-present	Sembower Field

Basketball

1901-1917	Original Assembly Hall
1917-1928	Men's Gymnasium
1928-1959	Old IU Fieldhouse (7th street)
1960-1971	New IU Fieldhouse (17th street)
1972-present	Assembly Hall

Football

1897-1923	Jordan Field
1924	Indiana Field
1925-1959	Memorial (10th Street) Stadium
1960-present	Memorial Stadium

Golf

1957-present	IU Championship Golf Course

Swimming

1916-1960	Men's Gymnasium
1961-1995	Royer Pool
1996-present	Counsilman Billingsley Aquatics Center

Soccer

1981-present	Bill Armstrong Stadium

Track

1966-present	E.C. (Billy) Hayes Track

INDIANA

LEGEND

Johnny Kyle

ONLY DROP-KICK BEAT PURDUE

Hard interior running characterized Johnny Kyle's three years as Indiana's fullback, but he did lots more than that on the day that made him a figure in Hoosier football lore.

Kyle's last game came in rain and mud at home against Purdue. The Boilermakers slogged their way to 13 first downs, to Indiana's 2, but neither team could score. Purdue missed three field goals and late in the game was driving again when Kyle recovered a fumble at the Indiana 15.

His own team couldn't advance the ball, so Kyle punted to Purdue's 18, and when the ball squirted loose from the hapless Boilermaker who tried to return the kick, it was hustling punter Kyle who recovered the fumble at the Purdue 17.

On third down from Purdue's 10, Kyle fielded a poor center snap and, with Boilermakers charging in, drop-kicked a 30-yard field goal that made the Hoosiers 3-0 winners.

Kyle was "the king and captain of them all," the *Arbutus* said, "one of the greatest football players who ever played at Indiana, or anywhere else . . . the best line plunger of the season in the Middle West."

That game-winning field goal was the first drop-kick Kyle had ever tried.

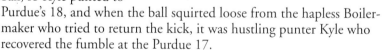

BIG TEN MEDAL
Bill McCaw

GIMBEL AWARD
Elmer Lucas

BASEBALL AMBASSADORS TO JAPAN

Indiana skipped usual Big Ten baseball play in 1922 to spend most of its spring in Japan. The trip was a major event. Governor Warren T. McCray on a March trip to Bloomington talked to the IU team. The day before departure, President William Lowe Bryan met the players in his office, reminded them they were representing not just IU but also America, and predicted they would find their trip as educational as "a half-year in college."

On the morning of March 28, classes were dismissed, and students marched behind the band to the Monon Railroad depot for an 11 a.m. sendoff.

The traveling group—12 players (from an original tryout group of 60); head coach George Levis and his wife; Dean of Students Clarence E. Edmondson and his wife, and assistant coach Roscoe Minton—went by train to Seattle and sailed from there April 1. Even choice of the ship drew attention. Waseda University of Tokyo was paying Indiana's travel expenses and assigned the Indiana travelers to a Japanese ship because its cost was $200 below any American liner. Senator Harry S. New intervened, got an American company to lower its bid, and New triumphantly, jingoistically announced that the Hoosiers would travel under an American flag, not Japanese.

After 12 days at sea, the team landed in Japan. The Hoosiers went 2-7-1 against college teams (and one semi-professional club, the Osaka Stars).

They completed their two-month, 14,000-mile tour by returning to Bloomington May 27. Ten miles out of town, they ran into their only travel delay: three hours, because of a freight train wreck at Unionville.

The team practiced a week and played seven June games that included a 1-2 record against Purdue, the only Big Ten games the '22 baseball Hoosiers played.

ARBUTARIANS? WAMPUS CATS?

HARVARD WAS COLLEGE football's king when Indiana coach Jumbo Stiehm coaxed an invitation to play at legendary Soldiers' Stadium in Cambridge.

The game was treated in Bloomington as Indiana's biggest football event ever. Stiehm and 25 Hoosier players, after a hometown sendoff on Tuesday of game week, arrived in Boston Thursday morning. Practices Thursday and Friday tuned up the Hoosiers, who had a cluster of backing from a hardy group of fans who made the trip out by car or train.

Saturday, October 8, was a day of New England sleet, then rain in torrents. Harvard, 3-0 and unscored on as a follow-up to two straight unbeaten, national-championship seasons, sent the Hoosiers home soaked and drubbed, 19-0.

Considering the alternatives, Scrappin' Hoosiers seemed good enough.

The Crimson, the Eastern Crimson, got its legend-making 6-0 comeuppance from Centre three weeks later.

The other Crimson, the Indiana Cream and Crimson, that very fall had a slight change in nickname. The football team solicited suggestions for a new team name, something sounding more menacing than Hoosiers.

Suggestions came, among them Wampus Cats (which Cambridge City High School already was using), Arbutarians, Bloodhounds, Red Clovers, Unlicked Cubs and Fighting Foxes.

The team called off the hunt and happily settled for Scrappin' Hoosiers.

IN THOSE DAYS . . .

MILLION-DOLLAR EFFORT

Indiana University faced up to three major needs in the spring of 1922 and met them with one all-out push: The Million-Dollar Memorial Drive.

In June 1921, the IU Alumni Council announced plans for the campaign to fund a Student Union building ($500,000), athletic stadium ($250,000) and women's dormitories ($250,000).

The buildings were to go up as memorials to all from IU who fought in wars, and the money was to come from private donations, not taxes.

Launching day for the drive was March 7, 1922. Governor Warren T. McCray spoke to more than 4,000 people in the school gymnasium, and President William Lowe Bryan followed him. At 11:50 p.m. the next day, the victory signal rang out, the first notes of the alma mater, "Gloriana, Frangipana," announcing via the chimes in the Student Building tower that the $400,000 goal in campus pledges had been topped.

Students spilled out into the night. President Bryan, a Monroe County native and 1884 IU graduate, spoke to a semicircle of gathered students, estimated in the thousands. Bryan said:

"The greatest emotion I ever had in my life was when I first crossed the campus of Indiana University as a student years ago. Today I again crossed the campus and shed tears of rejoicing. I thank God I was born to work with these boys and girls at Indiana."

HOOSIER LIST

THREE-SPORT LETTERMEN

Edmund Elfers, Track 1899, 1900, 01, 02; Football 1900, 01; Basketball 1901, 02

George Teter, Football 1899; Track 1901, 05; Basketball 1905

Phelps Darby, Football 1900, 01; Basketball 1901, 02, Capt. 02; Baseball 1901, 02

Alvah Rucker, Football 1900, 01, 02; Tennis 1900, 01, 02; Basketball, 1901, 02

Willis Coval, Football 1901, 02, 03, 04, Capt. 04; Basketball 1902, 03; Track 1902, 03

Clyde Dreisbach, Football 1902; Basketball 1902, 03; Track 1903

Leslie Maxwell, Basketball 1903, 04, 05; Football 1904; Track 1904

Hal Driver, Baseball, 1904, 08, 09; Football 1907; Track 1907

Arthur (Cotton) Berndt, Football 1908, 09, 10, Capt. 10; Basketball 1909, 11, Capt. 09, Baseball 1909, 10, 11, Capt. 10

Andy Gill, Football 1909, 10, 11, Capt. 11; Baseball 1910, 11, 12, Capt. 1912; Track 1911, 12

Floyd Fleming, Football 1910, 11, 12, Capt. 12; Basketball 1912; Baseball 1914, Capt. 14

Edgar Davis, Football 1911, 12, 13, Capt. 13; Wrestling 1912, 13, 14, Capt.13 &14; Track 1914

Mark (Mickey) Erehart, Football 1912, 13, 14; Baseball 1912, 13; Track 1913

Ward Gilbert, Basketball 1913, 14; Track 1914, Baseball 1916, 22

Russell Wallace, Cross Country 1913; Football 1914; Track 1914, 15, 16

Frank Whitaker, Football 1913, 14, 15; Basketball 1914, 15, 16; Baseball 1915, 16

Charles Buschmann, Football 1915, 16; Basketball 1915, 16, 17, Capt. 17; Baseball 1915, 16, 17

Phares Hiatt, Football 1916, 17, 19; Baseball 1918; Track 1919

Kermit Maynard, Football 1919, 20, 21; Basketball 1920, Baseball 1920

Eugene Thomas, Football 1920, 21, 22; Basketball 1921, 22, 23; Baseball 1922, 23; Track 1922, 23

Joseph Sloate, Football 1922, 23, 24; Basketball 1922; Baseball 1922, 23

George Fisher, Football 1923, 24, 25; Wrestling 1924, 25; Track 1924, 25

Harlan Logan, Basketball 1924, 25; Tennis 1924; Track 1925

Walter Fisher, Football 1925, 26; Wrestling 1925, 26, 27; Track 1926, 27

Ambrose Rascher, Football 1929, 30, 31; Baseball 1930, 31; Wrestling 1931, 32

William Dickey, Football 1930, 31, 32; Basketball 1931, 33; Baseball 1931, 32, 33

Otto Kuss, Football, 1931, 33; Wrestling 1932, 34; Track 1932

Vernon Huffman, Football 1933, 35, 36; Basketball 1934, 36, 37, Co-Capt. 37; Baseball 1934

Kenneth Gunning, Basketball 1935, 36, 37, Co-Capt. '37; Baseball 1935; Track 1936, 37

Del Russell, Football 1944, 47, 48; Basketball 1945; Baseball 1949

Don Luft, Football 1949, 50, 51; Basketball 1951; Baseball 1951, 52

INDIANA

✦ LEGEND

Ernie Pyle

MANAGED TO MAKE AN IMPACT

Indiana University in 1922 formally recognized a role always important but hitherto undistinguished.

Each varsity sport was authorized to name a senior manager and two junior managers. The senior, in charge of equipment and publicity, was seen as a link between the students and Athletic Department. He would travel with the team to each road game, and for the first time receive a full varsity "I."

The first senior football manager under that system, the 1923 *Arbutus* said, "was Ernest T. Pyle, senior."

It's the Ernie Pyle, of Dana, Indiana, whose name now is on the IU School of Journalism's building and in every journalism hall of fame.

Pyle, a noted traveling reporter-columnist for Scripps-Howard newspapers in the 1930s, achieved unique renown for his writings during World War II. A colleague said Pyle "went into war as a newspaper correspondent among newspaper correspondents. He came back a figure as great as the greatest, as Eisenhower or MacArthur or Nimitz."

On April 18, 1945, after covering the D-Day invasion, winning a 1944 Pulitzer Prize, returning to the U.S. for a November respite that included acceptance of an honorary degree from IU, and resuming his war coverage with American troops island-hopping their way toward anticipated invasion of Japan, Pyle was killed by a sniper's bullet on the island of Ie Shima.

Charles Kuralt, who was to do for CBS-TV what the pre-war Pyle did for newspapers, said, "Ernie Pyle showed everybody else the way. He was a hell of a reporter."

BIG TEN MEDAL
Omar Held

GIMBEL AWARD
Eugene Thomas

GENE THOMAS: 10-LETTER MAN

Eugene Thomas is IU's only four-sport letterman.

Eugene "Gene" Thomas missed out on the baseball trip to Japan his junior year to stay home and compete in track but he didn't miss much else athletically in a career that made him unique in Hoosier history.

Thomas, an economics major from Fortville, is IU's only four-sport letterman, the only Hoosier to win 10 letters in all.

Thomas won three letters each in football (as a starting halfback) and basketball (guard), captaining the basketball team as a junior. He added two letters each in track (long jump) and baseball (outfield) his junior and senior seasons, the only times an IU athlete lettered in four sports in one year.

He was able to achieve the first four-letter year because after his track season had ended and his 1922 baseball teammates were back from Japan, Thomas joined them and played enough games to letter in that sport, too.

Thomas capped his senior season by winning IU's 1923 Gimbel Award.

He went into coaching and had immediate success. His 1926 Marion team won the school's first state basketball championship. He moved to Michigan and coached teams that won two more state high school basketball championships there.

> **Four-sport letterman Gene Thomas coached State basketball champions in Indiana and Michigan.**

'TRAMP' PYLE SAW THE WORLD

Sports' greatest allure for Ernie Pyle was travel, author James Tobin said in *Ernie Pyle's War.*

Pyle wrote an aunt one baseball spring: "I wish I was a good ballplayer so I could get to make some of those trips. They went all through the south on their training trip, and went to Ohio and got to go through the state penitentiary."

In 1922, he and three other students went by ship to Tokyo with the IU baseball team. The team got off as scheduled but Japanese authorities made Pyle and his friends stay aboard because they weren't on the official travel list, a bonus for Pyle because the ship went to China and the Philippines before returning to America.

Even after riding out a Pacific typhoon, the excited Pyle told his parents from Shanghai: "I never felt better in my life."

Along on the trip accompanying the baseball team were Dean of Students Clarence Edmondson and his wife, who became lifelong friends of student Pyle. Mrs. Edmondson filed dispatches from abroad with the *Bloomington Evening World* and in one reported, "Our four 'tramps' (students working their way over) seem to be getting along fine."

Back in Bloomington, Dean Edmondson spoke to the Rotary Club about his observations in Japan and introduced Pyle, who was editor of the *Indiana Daily Student.* Pyle told the Rotarians that on the return voyage the four students had formed a friendship with a Filipino stowaway, Jean Eberhart, whom they hid in a clothes closet every day at inspection time and brought safely to Bloomington. Pyle introduced Eberhart to the Rotarians, and a newspaper account said the young man "received a reception worthy of a foreign ruler."

IN THOSE DAYS . . .

DEATH OF STIEHM ROCKS IU

The fear that Indiana University fans had been living with for a year was realized August 18, 1923.

"Jumbo" died.

Ewald O. Stiehm, just 37, lost an 11-month battle with stomach cancer. After six seasons as IU's football coach and athletic director, Stiehm had to pull out of football on the eve of the 1922 season to undergo tests. At the Mayo Clinic in Rochester, Minnesota, he learned his illness would be fatal.

Stiehm, who went 3-0-1 against Purdue, had a national reputation for success when pointing his team for a game. His 1919 Hoosiers were 2-6 before the 12-6 season-closing win over Eastern power Syracuse. From then on, a wide Stiehm grin was called "his Syracusin' smile."

Stiehm's parents, his wife and their two daughters were aboard the train that left Bloomington 52 minutes after midnight to take his body back to his hometown, Johnson Creek, Wisconsin, for burial.

A turnout of Bloomington friends was at the depot. One remembered, according to the *Bloomington Evening World*, that seven years earlier "the big, athletic coach stepped from a similar late-hour train to view for the first time the city where he was to make his home."

HOOSIER LIST

HOOSIER BASKETBALL COACHES

1901	J.H. Horne
1902	Phelps Darby
1903-04	Willis Coval
1905-06	Zora G. Clevenger
1907	James Sheldon
1908	Ed Cook
1909	Robert Harris
1910	John Georgen
1911	Oscar Rackle
1912	James Kase
1913	Arthur Powell
1914-15	Arthur "Cotton" Berndt
1916	Allan Willisford
1917	G.S. Lowman
1918-19	Dana Evans
1920	Ewald "Jumbo" Stiehm
1921-22	George Levis
1923-24	Leslie Mann
1925-38	Everett Dean
1939-43	Branch McCracken
1944-46	Harry Good (interim)
1947-65	Branch McCracken
1966-71	Lou Watson
1970	Jerry Oliver (acting)
1972-present	Bob Knight

INDIANA LEGEND — *Les Mann*

IU COACH A WORLD SERIES HERO

Leslie Mann, a 30-year-old Nebraskan schooled in coaching at an academy at basketball's birthplace, the Springfield, Massachusetts, YMCA, brought a fast-paced game to IU as the Hoosiers' new basketball coach in the 1923-24 season.

Indiana had scored in the 50s just once in 19 years before beating Rose Poly 51-15 in Mann's second game and Drake 53-30 in his third. Mann's Hoosiers came within a 26-25 March 1 loss at Chicago of the school's first share of a Big Ten basketball championship.

Les Mann had coached at Rice before coming to IU, but he was far better known as a big league outfielder.

He was a second-year player and starter for the 1914 "Miracle Braves," who came from last place on the Fourth of July to win the pennant, then swept Connie Mack's vaunted Philadelphia A's in the World Series. Mann's two-out ninth-inning hit beat Hall of Famer Eddie Plank, 1-0, in Game 2. He scored the 12th-inning run that won Game 3.

In 1918, Mann was a Cub and back in the World Series. The Red Sox won in six games, but Mann's two-out, eighth-inning RBI hit in Game 4 ended pitcher Babe Ruth's World Series-record string of 29 scoreless innings.

Mann averaged .282 in playing 16 seasons, through 1928. He coached IU just two seasons.

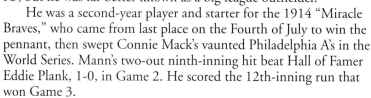

BIG TEN MEDAL
John Nay

GIMBEL AWARD
Ted Koontz

'MR. CLEV' RETURNS TO LEAD

Zora Clevenger as athletic director.

Zora Clevenger served Indiana University in about every way possible, which is why his name is on the most prestigious award given by the school to its athletic alumni.

After his IU playing career, Clevenger coached football at Nebraska Wesleyan, Tennessee (his 1914 Vols went 10-0), Kansas State and Missouri.

His performances as a player and as a coach won him 1968 induction into the College Football Hall of Fame.

But his most significant role at Indiana began in 1923 when he was named athletic director.

Quiet, beloved little "Mr. Clev" lifted the whole IU program into the major leagues. He brought in Billy Hayes to coach track and cross country, then Everett Dean for basketball and baseball, and Billy Thom for wrestling. He completed what he called his "Four Aces" by adding football coach Bo McMillin in 1934. Each took his sport (or sports) to heights IU never had approached. When Dean left Indiana in 1938, Clevenger brought in young Branch McCracken, and the basketball climb continued.

Clevenger retired in 1947, his IU program already owning national championships in track, wrestling, cross country and basketball, plus 32 Big Ten championships. He died, at 88, on November 24, 1970.

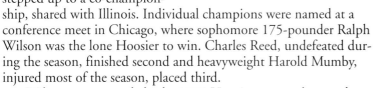

THE CHAMP BUILDS A CHAMPION

JACK REYNOLDS **WAS** the world welterweight wrestling champion averaging about a match a week, calendar-round, when he coached the Indiana wrestling team in the early 1920s.

The Big Ten championship was decided by dual meets from 1922 through '25. Reynolds' first Hoosier team had a shot at the 1923 title but lost a battle of unbeatens to Ohio State in the final match of the season, before a roaring Bloomington crowd.

In '24, the Hoosiers stepped up to a co-championship, shared with Illinois. Individual champions were named at a conference meet in Chicago, where sophomore 175-pounder Ralph Wilson was the lone Hoosier to win. Charles Reed, undefeated during the season, finished second and heavyweight Harold Mumby, injured most of the season, placed third.

Wilson went on to help the 1925 Hoosiers to another co-championship and to captain the 1926 team. Then he picked up an undergraduate degree and graduated from the IU School of Medicine.

Ralph Wilson won Big Ten titles in 1925 and 1926.

IN THOSE DAYS . . .

ELMER WILKENS MAN OF HISTORY

The successful Memorial Stadium fund drive meant that IU would move out of Jordan Field, its football home since 1896.

The 1923 Purdue game was designated as the last game at Jordan, and President William Lowe Bryan led in a campaign to make it a time of celebration.

Bryan released a statement citing the field's place in IU history. "For 30 years, the Cream and Crimson have fought on that field. We have seen great victories there. We have seen the greatest universities of the West go down to defeat there. We have seen the hitherto champion of the East fall before our Hoosier men. Again and again we have seen Purdue come to us in the sure expectation of victory and go from us in the sorrow of defeat."

He called on former players and other alumni to return and for "the men of 1923 . . . to win the last game on Jordan Field."

A gala crowd came, and the Hoosiers, who had lost that season at Jordan Field to DePauw and Wabash, delivered. Substitute quarterback Elmer Wilkens of Fort Wayne, one of just two seniors on first-year coach "Navy Bill" Ingram's team, drop-kicked a 44-yard field goal to give Indiana a 3-0 victory over Purdue.

The kick stood as IU's longest field goal for 41 years, until Tom Nowatzke set a Big Ten record with a 50-yard place kick against Ohio State in 1964.

HOOSIER LIST

BILLY HAYES' CHAMPIONS AND OLYMPIANS

Olympians

1932 - Ivan Fuqua, gold, 1600-relay; Charles Hornbostel, 6th, 800 meters

1936 - Charles Hornbostel, 5th, 800 meters; Don Lash, 8th, 10,000 meters; 14th, 5,000 meters; Tommy Deckard, 5,000 meters.

NCAA Champions

1932 - Charles Hornbostel, 800; Bryce Beecher, pole vault

1933 - Charles Hornbostel, 880

1934 - Charles Hornbostel, 880

1936 - Don Lash, 5,000 meters

1940 - Campbell Kane, 880; Archie Harris, discus

1941 - Campbell Kane, 880; Fred Wilt, cross country; Fred Wilt, two mile; Archie Harris, discus

Big Ten Champions

1926 - Walter Caine, 880 outdoor

1927 - Mile Relay, outdoor

1928 - Wilmer Rinehart, javelin outdoor

1929 - Wilmer Rinehart, javelin outdoor

1930 - Rodney Leas, cross country, two mile indoor, Mile Relay indoor; Henry Brocksmith, two mile outdoor

1931 - Henry Brocksmith, cross country; Rodney Leas, mile outdoor

1932 - Bryce Beecher, pole vault indoor; Henry Brocksmith, mile and two mile indoor and outdoor; Charles Hornbostel, 880 indoor and outdoor; Noble Biddinger, hammer outdoor

1933 - Charles Hornbostel, 880 indoor, 880 and mile outdoor; Ivan Fuqua, 440 indoor, 220 and 440 outdoor; Cliff Watson, two mile indoor and outdoor; Noble Biddinger, hammer outdoor; Wes Busbee, discus outdoor; Mile Relay indoor

1934 - Steve Divich, pole vault indoor and outdoor; Charles Hornbostel, 880 and mile indoor and outdoor; Ivan Fuqua, 400 indoor, 220 and 440 outdoor; Dan Caldemeyer, high jump outdoor; Wes Busbee, discus outdoor, Mile Relay outdoor

1935 - Don Lash, two mile indoor, mile and two mile outdoor

1936 - Don Caldemeyer, hurdles indoor; Don Lash, mile and two mile outdoor

1937 - Don Lash, two mile indoor, mile and two mile outdoor; Robert Collier, 220 outdoor

1938 - Mel Trutt, cross country

1939 - Roger Poorman, javelin outdoor; Roy Cochran, low hurdles outdoor

1940 - Wayne Tolliver, cross country; Archie Harris, shot put indoor, shot put and discus outdoor; Campbell Kane, 880 and mile indoor, mile outdoor; Roy Cochran, 440 indoor

1941 - Fred Wilt, cross country; Bob Burnett, long jump indoor; Campbell Kane, 880 and mile indoor and outdoor; Roy Cochran, 440 indoor and outdoor; Fred Wilt, two mile indoor; Archie Harris, shot put and discus outdoor; Wayne Tolliver, two mile outdoor

1942 - Earl Mitchell, cross country, two mile, indoor and outdoor; Campbell Kane, 880 and mile, indoor,

1943 - Lou Saban, shot put, indoor; Mile Relay, indoor;

LEGEND — *Billy Hayes*

INDIANA

A BUILDER OF CHAMPIONS

Earle C. "Billy" Hayes, though still in his 20s, already had a reputation as a builder of champions and Olympians when IU athletic director Zora Clevenger reached down to Mississippi State to bring Hayes back to his Hoosier homeland.

Hayes, hired by Clevenger as IU's head track coach and a football assistant to Bill Ingram, grew up near Madison, Indiana. At Albion College in Michigan, he captained

the football team, won eight athletic letters, and was president of his Class of 1910.

In 1912, he went to Mississippi State as head basketball and track coach and manager of the bookstore. He was head football coach there for four years before Clevenger hired him.

Quickly, he built Indiana into a national track and cross country power, even during the three years (1931-33) when he added duties as head football coach and brought in his 1928 Olympic 1,500-meter runner from Mississippi State, Sid Robinson, to help with the distance runners. Hayes and Robinson stayed together as a remarkable team, Robinson achieving esteem as an eminent researchist in physiology in addition to his role as a Hayes aide.

Hayes' runners, jumpers and throwers won an Olympic gold medal and 11 NCAA titles, and he coached 23 different athletes who won Big Ten championships.

He was a charter member of the IU Athletics Hall of Fame and an assistant coach on the 1936 Olympic team.

BIG TEN MEDAL
Harlan Logan

GIMBEL AWARD
Earl Moomaw

HOME-GROWN HOOSIER STARS

New coach Everett Dean's first basketball team made a run at the Big Ten championship with a school and league rarity: its top three scorers were from the same high school.

They didn't have far to go, either. Harlan Logan, Palmer Sponsler and Julius Krueger were from Bloomington.

Logan, the No. 2 scorer in the Big Ten, led the Hoosiers back into contention after they opened the league season with losses at Ohio State and Illinois. The Hoosiers won seven games in a row, including a 39-36 win over Purdue (featuring Logan's career-high 19 points), and a second-half comeback from 10 points down that beat Illinois, 30-24. Purdue ended the streak, 38-29, and Ohio State (11-1) won the championship.

Logan, a junior, was a first-team All-Big Ten pick. He would have been an All-America possibility as a senior, but he spent his senior year instead as a Rhodes Scholar at Oxford. He went on to be editor of *Look* magazine and speaker of the New Hampshire House of Representatives.

Logan scored 154 points for the full season. Sophomore Krueger had four double-figure games in scoring 137 points, and Sponsler, an outstanding ballhandler and defensive player, had 85.

After his time at Oxford, Logan returned to Bloomington, and in 1930 became the school's first official tennis coach. He had lettered in tennis as a sophomore and in track as a junior.

Harlan Logan, the Big Ten's No. 2 scorer in 1925, was a Rhodes Scholar who became IU's first tennis coach.

Snapshot In Time

FIRST BASEBALL TITLE

JUST AS HE had done in his playing days, Everett Dean went right from basketball to baseball, and there he delivered the school's first Big Ten championship.

Two early losses dropped the Hoosiers in the standings, but they surged from there. A 3-1 victory over Chicago kept their league hopes alive. Closing against Purdue, they fell behind 3-0 before a bases-loaded triple by Walter Hall started them toward an 8-6 victory that meant a 9-2 league finish.

Then they waited. Ohio State took an 8-2 record into two games against Michigan. The Wolverines won both, and Indiana was the champion.

Shortstop Dorsey Kight led the league in hitting. Football players Sam Niness (captain and centerfielder) and Dick Woodward (No. 1 pitcher) played key roles.

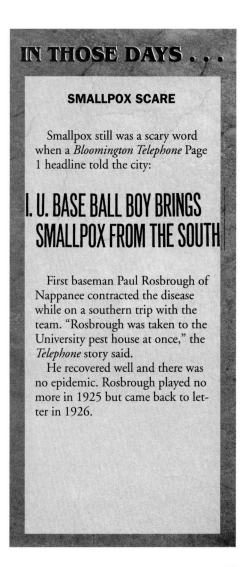

Football star Sam Niness was the centerfielder and captain of IU's first Big Ten baseball championship.

IN THOSE DAYS . . .

SMALLPOX SCARE

Smallpox still was a scary word when a *Bloomington Telephone* Page 1 headline told the city:

I. U. BASE BALL BOY BRINGS SMALLPOX FROM THE SOUTH

First baseman Paul Rosbrough of Nappanee contracted the disease while on a southern trip with the team. "Rosbrough was taken to the University pest house at once," the *Telephone* story said.

He recovered well and there was no epidemic. Rosbrough played no more in 1925 but came back to letter in 1926.

1925 1926

HOOSIER LIST

OLD OAKEN BUCKET SCORES

1925	Indiana 0, Purdue 0
1926	Purdue 24, Indiana 14
1927	Purdue 21, Indiana 6
1928	Purdue 14, Indiana 0
1929	Purdue 32, Indiana 0
1930	Indiana 7, Purdue 6
1931	Purdue 19, Indiana 0
1932	Purdue 25, Indiana 7
1933	Purdue 19, Indiana 3
1934	Indiana 17, Purdue 6
1935	Indiana 7, Purdue 0
1936	Indiana 20, Purdue 20
1937	Purdue 13, Indiana 7
1938	Purdue 13, Indiana 6
1939	Purdue 7, Indiana 6
1940	Indiana 3, Purdue 0
1941	Indiana 7, Purdue 0
1942	Indiana 20, Purdue 0
1943	Purdue 7, Indiana 0
1944	Indiana 14, Purdue 6
1945	Indiana 26, Purdue 0
1946	Indiana 34, Purdue 20
1947	Indiana 16, Purdue 14
1948	Purdue 39, Indiana 0
1949	Purdue 14, Indiana 6
1950	Purdue 13, Indiana 0
1951	Purdue 21, Indiana 13
1952	Purdue 21, Indiana 16
1953	Purdue 30, Indiana 0
1954	Purdue 13, Indiana 7
1955	Purdue 6, Indiana 4
1956	Purdue 39, Indiana 20
1957	Purdue 35, Indiana 13
1958	Indiana 15, Purdue 15
1959	Purdue 10, Indiana 7
1960	Purdue 35, Indiana 6
1961	Purdue 34, Indiana 12
1962	Indiana 12, Purdue 7
1963	Purdue 21, Indiana 15

INDIANA

LEGEND
Art Beckner

A GRANGE ON THE FLOOR

Art Beckner led Muncie to the state high school championship game in 1923, then entered IU in the second semester of the 1923-24 season. Thus, he didn't become eligible as a sophomore until January 1925, just in time to spark that team's seven-game winning streak.

But that Hoosier team had lost its first two league games without Beckner and couldn't make up for it.

The 1925-26 season, with Beckner there all the way, Indiana won its first share of a Big Ten basketball championship. And Beckner's 9.0 league average made him IU's first Big Ten scoring champion.

The Hoosiers had to come from down in the pack to get their title share. Heartbreaking mid-February losses at Purdue (31-29) and at home to Illinois (21-20) sank them to 4-4 in the Big Ten.

But, they didn't lose again to finish 8-4 and tie Purdue, Michigan and Iowa for the championship.

The last week of the season, the Hoosiers avenged the home-court loss to Illinois by winning at Champaign, 28-25, with Beckner scoring 12 points. They clinched their title share by avenging another loss—35-20 over visiting Wisconsin, Beckner again leading the way with 13 points.

"Beckner on the basketball floor is like (Red) Grange on the football field," Illinois coach Craig Ruby said.

Junior Julius Krueger, the Hoosiers' No. 2 scorer, made All-Big Ten.

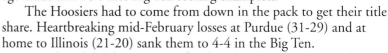

BIG TEN MEDAL
Dan Bernoske

GIMBEL AWARD
Robert Rose

FIRST BUCKET GAME

The Old Oaken Bucket became a part of the Indiana-Purdue football series with the 1925 game, but at that point, not a big part.

The week of the game, a three-paragraph story in the *Bloomington Telephone* said alumni of the two schools were contributing the trophy as an annual prize that would be the game-winner's to keep until beaten. A gold link would go on the bucket for each game, a block I for Indiana victories, a block P for Purdue's, the emblem carrying the game score.

The first game was a tie, 0-0, which put an I-P fittingly at the top of the chain.

Chicago alumni of the two schools came up with the trophy idea. Dr. Clarence Jones of IU and Russell Gray of Purdue, mindful of the nostalgic tune from an 1802 Samuel Woodworth poem, recommended an old oaken bucket from a well somewhere in Indiana would be most fitting. Wiley J. Huddle of IU and Fritz Ernst of Purdue came up with the bucket, from the Bruner farm in deep southeastern Indiana, between the Jefferson County communities of Kent and Hanover. Legend says Morgan's Raiders drank from it on a sortie into Indiana.

Although the IU-Purdue rivalry dates back to 1891, the Old Oaken Bucket wasn't the prized trophy until 1925.

IU'S NEW STADIUM

THE 1925 BUCKET game was dedication day for IU's 22,000-capacity, $250,000 stadium.

The stadium was one part of a $1-million fund drive among IU students, faculty and alumni, memorializing the school's war dead, from all wars. Memorial Stadium and Memorial Hall, a new women's dormitory, were dedicated on the pre-Thanksgiving weekend. The third building funded by the drive, the Indiana Memorial Union, was finished later.

The stadium was supposed to be done in 1924, the year Purdue opened Ross-Ade Stadium, but Memorial Stadium's concrete walls began to crumble during construction. The structure was torn down and work began anew.

Captain Larry Marks of Wabash scored the first touchdown in the stadium, in the second quarter of a 31-0 season-opening victory over Indiana State.

Marks almost was the hero of the first Bucket game, too. In the final minutes of the scoreless game, Marks, a track sprinter, broke free on a daring run from punt formation at the Indiana 10. He made it to the end zone untouched, but an official ruled his foot touched the sideline around the 50-yard line. The game ended a few minutes later.

HOOSIER LIST

OLD OAKEN BUCKET SCORES
(continued)

1964	Purdue 28, Indiana 22
1965	Purdue 26, Indiana 21
1966	Purdue 51, Indiana 6
1967	Indiana 19, Purdue 14
1968	Purdue 38, Indiana 35
1969	Purdue 44, Indiana 21
1970	Purdue 40, Indiana 0
1971	Indiana 38, Purdue 31
1972	Purdue 42, Indiana 7
1973	Purdue 28, Indiana 23
1974	Purdue 38, Indiana 17
1975	Purdue 9, Indiana 7
1976	Indiana 20, Purdue 14
1977	Indiana 21, Purdue 10
1978	Purdue 20, Indiana 7
1979	Purdue 37, Indiana 21
1980	Purdue 24, Indiana 23
1981	Indiana 20, Purdue 17
1982	Indiana 13, Purdue 7
1983	Purdue 31, Indiana 30
1984	Purdue 31, Indiana 24
1985	Purdue 34, Indiana 21
1986	Purdue 17, Indiana 15
1987	Indiana 35, Purdue 14
1988	Indiana 52, Purdue 7
1989	Purdue 15, Indiana 14
1990	Indiana 28, Purdue 14
1991	Indiana 24, Purdue 22
1992	Purdue 13, Indiana 10
1993	Indiana 24, Purdue 17
1994	Indiana 33, Purdue 29
1995	Purdue 51, Indiana 14
1996	Indiana 33, Purdue 16
1997	Purdue 56, Indiana 7
1998	Purdue 52, Indiana 7

INDIANA

LEGEND   *Clare Randolph*

A LION IN THE LINE

In 1969, the 50th anniversary of the National Football League, each franchise was asked to pick an all-time team. In Detroit, sports columnist Joe Falls deferred to a colleague who had seen every Lions team.

Ed Hayes' all-time Lions team included expectables Bobby Layne, Doak Walker, Leon Hart, Joe Schmidt and Alex Karras, and, at center, Clare Randolph (Indiana 1926-28).

Randolph, from Elkhart, was a three-year IU starter. For a 3-5 team his sophomore year, he went the full 60 minutes six times and 59 in another.

It was the start of three big seasons for Randolph, a first-team All-Big Ten pick his senior year with some All-America mention. His fumble recovery that year was a key to Indiana's 10-7 comeback victory over an Oklahoma team led by Tom Churchill, who was to finish fifth in the 1928 Olympic decathlon.

Also in 1969 college football celebrated its centennial. In a poll of former IU captains, Most Valuable Players and All-Big Ten or All-America selections, Clare Randolph was voted to a third-team spot, 41 years after his last Hoosier play. One voter, whose first Hoosier game came 10 years after Randolph's last, gave him his vote as IU's all-time best player, at any position.

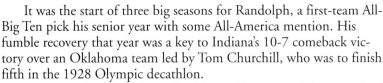

BIG TEN MEDAL

Charles Benzel

GIMBEL AWARD

Walt Fisher

IU item

BILL EASTON, A HAYES DISCIPLE

Bill Easton was born in Stinesville, a tiny Monroe County limestone quarry town named for his great-grandfather. He grew up in Sandborn, then earned a degree in 1927 from IU where he lettered as a senior in cross country and track, under Billy Hayes, but before Hayes really got the Hoosier programs rolling.

That time under Hayes led Easton to a career that put him in the United States Track and Field Hall of Fame.

Easton coached at Ellettsville, Lowell, Hobart and Hammond high schools before getting the track coaching job at Drake.

His Drake teams won three straight NCAA cross country championships (1944 through '46). He moved on to Kansas, and NCAA championships in outdoor track (1959 and '60) and cross country (1953). His athletes, among them four-time Olympic gold-medalist discus thrower Al Oerter, miler Wes Santee, sprinter Charlie Tidwell, and Billy Mills, America's only Olympic 10,000-meter gold medalist (1964), won 20 NCAA individual track or cross country titles.

His key? "I ran cross country under Billy Hayes, the greatest track coach who ever lived," he told a 1975 interviewer. "He knew more about boys and the schedules they should maintain, and some of us simply carried it over when we left Indiana."

Bill Easton

Snapshot In Time

AS PREDICTIONS GO. . .

CHICAGO'S HARLAN "Pat" Page may have been the best all-round athlete in the Big Ten's opening years, a star end on championship football teams in 1907 and '08, a starting guard on three straight league basketball champions, and pitcher for yet another conference champion in the 1909 baseball season.

Upon graduation, he had major-league offers but he passed them up to start a coaching career in baseball with the Maroons. By 1920, he had added basketball, and he won the Big Ten title.

He went to Butler as head basketball and baseball coach, then moved on to Indiana as football coach in 1926.

Considering his own rich background in the sport, it probably was a bit jarring when he attacked something sacred in Indiana: high school basketball.

In a late-December *Bloomington Evening World* interview, Page said:

"Just when the weather is good for outdoor exercise, many high schools hold basketball games inside, and instead of it being beneficial, it is detrimental to high school boys who need more fresh air and outdoor activity."

> **"Basketball inside is detrimental to high school boys who need more fresh air and outside activity."**
>
> **—Pat Page**

The interviewer added: "Basketball, according to Page, has reached its zenith in Indiana, and it is time that other sports are developed more, especially outdoor sports."

IN THOSE DAYS . . .

AIR APPARENT

Pat Page went to great lengths, and heights, to try to find the football answers at Indiana.

Before his team's first game, in late-September 1926, Page went up in a small airplane piloted by a student aviator to ride low over Memorial Stadium and learn some things.

When the low-flying plane would take a sudden dip, that to Page meant obstructions and air currents had formed an air pocket. Page noted the places, for future use with punts and long passes.

It was privileged information, of course. Page had no intention of passing his secrets along to anyone but his players.

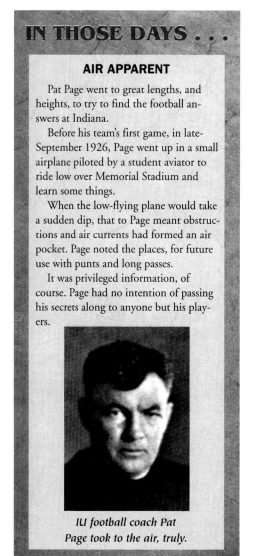

IU football coach Pat Page took to the air, truly.

IU HEAD COACHES IN MORE THAN ONE SPORT

Coach	Sport (Years Coached)
James Horne	Baseball (1899-1900) Basketball (1901) Football (1898-1904)
Zora G. Clevenger	Baseball (1905-06) Basketball (1905)
James Sheldon	Basketball (1906-07) Football (1905-13)
James Kase	Basketball (1912) Wrestling (1917-21)
A.H. (Cotton) Berndt	Baseball (1913-15) Basketball (1914-15)
Ewald Stiehm	Basketball (1920-21) Football (1916-21)
Clarence Childs	Football (1914-15) Track (1915-16)
Guy Rathbun	Baseball (1918) Swimming (1919-20) Track (1920) Wrestling (1922)
Dana Evans	Basketball (1918-19) Cross Country & Track (1918-19)
George Levis	Baseball (1921-22) Basketball (1922-23)
Lester Null	Cross Country & Track (1922) Swimming (1922)
Everett Dean	Baseball (1925-38) Basketball (1925-38)
E.C. (Billy) Hayes	Football (1931-33) Cross Country & Track (1925-43)

INDIANA LEGEND — *Billy Thom*

TOOK IU TO WRESTLING HEIGHTS

Born in Illinois, Billy Thom grew up in Nebraska, started in college in Missouri and finished up in Iowa, where he was an outstanding football player.

He was a high school football coach at Wabash, Indiana, when he got the call to be head wrestling coach and an assistant in football and track at Indiana.

Big things happened fast for Thom and IU wrestling. In 1927, his first coaching year, the Big Ten meet was at IU and Hoosier captain Charles Swain won the 145-pound title, the first of 32 Big Ten titles IU wrestlers were to win in Thom's 18 coaching seasons.

In 1931 at Chicago, with 118-pounder Delmas Aldridge of Kokomo their only champion, the Hoosiers won the Big Ten championship, their first of eight under Thom.

And in 1932 in Bloomington, with the home crowd roaring for every Indiana move, the Hoosiers won the school's first NCAA championship in any sport, and senior Eddie Belshaw of Gary was the first winner of the meet's Outstanding Wrestler Award.

In 1936, still a young man himself, Thom coached the United States team in the Olympic Games at Berlin.

He died at 73 in December 1973, nine years before the IU Athletics Hall of Fame began. He was a charter inductee.

BIG TEN MEDAL
Art Beckner

GIMBEL AWARD
Vic Salmi

58

IU**item**

Branch McCracken also won three letters in football.

ARRIVAL OF BRANCH MCCRACKEN

Branch McCracken, described by coach Everett Dean as "a big, husky fellow, about 6-4, (with) the weight to handle himself under the basket—and he could shoot, too," came to Indiana straight off a farm near Monrovia, about 20 miles from the IU campus.

Few athletes ever had the impact on a college program that Emmett Branch McCracken had at Indiana.

One other did: Dean, who came from Salem nine years ahead of McCracken, became IU's first basketball All-American and coached the school's first Big Ten basketball and baseball champions.

McCracken had no pre-college football background but, like Dean, scored a touchdown before he ever scored a basket. In 1927, when Indiana blemished Minnesota's unbeaten season with a 14-14 tie, sophomore end McCracken ran a recovered fumble 20 yards into the end zone.

He made a bigger splash in basketball.

After averaging 12.7 a game in leading the Hoosiers to three straight pre-conference victories, McCracken exploded for 24 points in a 32-13 league-opening rout of Chicago. It set an IU record for Big Ten play, topping a record (21) set seven years earlier by Dean against Ohio State.

McCracken's 24 remained IU's Big Ten high for 10 years.

STREAKING TO A TITLE

INDIANA STOOD 3-2 in Big Ten basketball after early road losses to league powers Michigan (42-41) and Purdue (28-25). At that point, closing out the first semester, the Hoosiers lost their most noted player. Art Beckner, who was the Big Ten scoring leader in 1926 when he starred on IU's first conference basketball champion, had just that first semester of eligibility left before graduating, with grades that won him IU's 1928 Big Ten medal.

Sophomore Jim Strickland, who had 15 points in IU's eight games up to then, stepped into Beckner's spot and amazing things happened.

Strickland, from little Owensburg, scored 19 in his first start, a 48-29 romp over Kentucky, then 16 when IU avenged the Purdue loss, 40-37. Including a 48-29 rout of Kentucky, IU's winning streak was seven with two games left. Strickland scored 17 points and McCracken 16 as the Hoosiers squeezed by Michigan, 36-34, despite seven points each by two-sport All-American Bennie Oosterbaan and guard Bill Orwig, IU's future athletic director.

That sent the streaking Hoosiers to Illinois with a chance for their second title in three years. They got it. Strickland and Dale Wells scored overtime baskets and IU won, 27-23, to finish 10-2 and tie Purdue for the title.

Wells and Bob Correll were named All-Big Ten. "Wells was a marvelous player," coach Everett Dean told Ray Marquette in *Indiana University Basketball*. "He was so good that you didn't notice what or how much he was contributing until the game was over. He was a fine scorer and an excellent defensive player."

Dale Wells was All-Big Ten for IU's 1928 Big Ten co-champions.

IN THOSE DAYS . . .

LET'S PLAY TWO

Football coach Pat Page, his 1926 call for a de-emphasis of Indiana high school basketball ignored, came out with another idea involving his own sport:

Football doubleheaders.

Indiana opened the 1928 season by beating Wabash, 14-0. Then Hoosier reserves came out and won 39-0 over Indiana State. The second game wasn't counted as a varsity game.

Six Saturdays that year, the Hoosiers played two games, though the opener was the only time both were on the same bill. More common was a match-up of the varsities at one school while the reserves were playing at the other.

Indiana did that twice, when the varsity played at Illinois and at home against Northwestern. Page passed players back and forth between the two teams. George Ross scored three touchdown in the reserves' victory over Indiana State and started for the varsity the next week against Oklahoma.

Page's doubleheader idea got a different interpretation in Ann Arbor. From 1929 through '31, mighty Michigan opened its season with doubleheaders, and counted all the games. The Wolverines went 6-0 against Albion and Mount Union ('29), Denison and Eastern Michigan ('30), and Central State and Michigan Normal ('31), outscoring the lot of them 156-6.

1928 · 1929

HOOSIER LIST

IU'S BIG TEN MVPs IN FOOTBALL

1928	Chuck Bennett, HB
1936	Vern Huffman, QB
1937	Corby Davis, FB
1979	Tim Clifford, QB
1988	Anthony Thompson, TB
1989	Anthony Thompson, TB

Tim Clifford, the 1979 Big Ten Most Valuable Player.

INDIANA

LEGEND — *Chuck Bennett*

IU'S FIRST BIG TEN MVP

Linton's Chuck Bennett scored two touchdowns in his first college game, a 31-7 victory over DePauw opening the 1926 season. He was to score seven of that 3-5 team's eleven touchdowns.

Bennett had some All-Big Ten mention his junior year, which included consecutive 60-minute performances against powers Chicago, Minnesota and Harvard.

As a senior, offensive captain Bennett's 29-yard scoring run in a 13-7 loss at Illinois was the only touchdown that unbeaten championship team allowed, and he had the Hoosiers at the Illini 2 when the game ended. Bennett played 60 minutes in Indiana's first football victory over Michigan, 6-0 at Ann Arbor, and 60 more in the mud against Northwestern, when his 72-yard second-quarter breakaway won his last home game, 6-0.

At Purdue, he battered away: 35 carries, 149 net yards, including gains of 28, 23, 14 and 12 yards. But Purdue won, 14-0.

The next week, Bennett and center Clare Randolph were named first-team All-Big Ten.

Then Bennett, from the league's ninth-place team, was named the fifth winner of the silver football as the Big Ten's Most Valuable Player.

Picked for the East-West Game, Bennett scored two touchdowns in the East's 20-0 victory, earning himself another Outstanding Player award.

BIG TEN MEDAL
Wilmer Rinehart

GIMBEL AWARD
Bill Moss

BALFOUR AWARDS
Football - Chuck Bennett
Basketball - Branch McCracken
Baseball - Paul "Pooch" Harrell
Track - Harold Fields
Wrestling - Auree Scott

Harold Fields

Paul "Pooch" Harrell

THE MAN FROM RUSSIAVILLE

Claude Rich served IU in some capacity—officially or unofficially—for almost 70 years.

C laude Rich put Russiaville—*roosh*-uh-vill, not *rush*-uh—on the Indiana map, four decades before the Palm Sunday tornadoes in 1965 almost blew it off. Russiaville was his high school, but not his hometown. That was New London, in Russiaville's northern suburbs.

And the Claude Rich who left there in late-summer 1925 to begin his college education was "the greenest kid ever," he said a lifetime later.

Rich got his degree as a history major. He also got an "I" as the senior manager in football in 1928, and he was one of 10 students named by President William Lowe Bryan to the Board of Aeons, a liaison group between students and the Chancellor.

The green kid from New London had found a home in Bloomington. He was IU's assistant alumni secretary for 15 years, alumni secretary for 21, and director of university relations until his retirement in 1976. In 1988 when a letter informed him he had been elected to the IU Athletics Hall of Fame for his long service in administration, he called himself "the most surprised person in the state of Indiana. I sent a letter right back: 'I may question the wisdom of the committee, but I accept immediately before they change their mind.'"

Rich died in 1999.

FIELDHOUSE OF DREAMS

ON JANUARY 5, 1928, Indiana University trustees announced plans to build a $300,000 basketball fieldhouse. Eleven months later, on December 13, they dedicated it.

Its 10,000 seats made it a showpiece of the time. An IU-record crowd of 8,000, including Big Ten commissioner John Griffith and Governor-elect Harry Leslie, watched the Hoosiers win that dedication game from eastern power Pennsylvania, 34-26. Also there was Frank Dailey, an IU letterman in football (1891 and '92) and baseball (1889, '90 and '92, captain in '89 and '90). He was the Democrat whom Republican and 1902 Purdue football captain Leslie beat in the governor election five weeks earlier.

Guard Dale Wells scored on the opening tipoff play, and Indiana led 30-15 before Penn scored 11 straight points.

It wasn't the building's first game. Goals were installed December 7, and the next night Washington of St. Louis was the Hoosiers' first Fieldhouse opponent. The Bears pulled a shocker, never trailing in a 31-30 victory tightened by Wells' basket at the gun.

IU's first point in the arena was a free throw by Branch McCracken, who was to come back as a coach and build four Big Ten and two NCAA championship teams there.

It was to become one of the greatest home courts in college basketball, but it took the Hoosiers a while to make it seem advantageous. They lost nine of their first 16 games there, including a 5-4 record in the debut season.

IN THOSE DAYS . . .

BALFOUR AWARDS BEGIN

The Balfour Awards, one a year in each major sport, underwritten by jewelry magnate and IU letterman Lloyd Balfour, began at Indiana in 1928-29.

The first winners were a Hall of Fame lot: Chuck Bennett in football, Branch Mc-Cracken in basketball, Paul "Pooch" Harrell in baseball, Harold Fields in cross country and Auree Scott in wrestling.

Harrell, later IU's baseball coach (1938-47) and athletic director (1948-54), still is in IU's record books in football and baseball. Just before a late-game injury knocked him out of his last three college games, Harrell launched an 86-yard punt against Ohio State. The punt stood alone at IU till matched 64 years later by Jim DiGuilio against Wisconsin.

In baseball, Harrell remains IU's only .400 career hitter. His three-season average was .404.

Fields, from Indianapolis, captained the Indiana cross country team that won its first Big Ten championship. Fields finished third, Rodney Leas eighth and Ed Clapham ninth at Madison, Wisconsin, in leading Billy Hayes' team to what proved to be the starting point for the great Hayes era in IU, Big Ten and national cross country and track and field. Clarence Banks, James Abromson and Paul Shafer also ran on the championship team.

HOOSIER LIST

HOOSIERS IN BASKETBALL HALL OF FAME

Branch McCracken (inducted 1960)

All-American at IU in 1930. Finished career as Big Ten's all-time leading scorer. Coached Hoosiers to NCAA championships in 1940 and 1953.

Everett Dean (inducted 1966)

All-American at IU in 1921. Coached at IU for 14 seasons winning three Big Ten titles. Later coached Stanford to 1942 NCAA championship.

Bob Knight (inducted 1991)

IU coach since 1972 who has led Hoosiers to national championships in 1976, 1981 and 1987 and 11 Big Ten titles. Also coached NIT, CCA, Pan American Games and Olympic Games champions.

Walt Bellamy (inducted 1993)

Two-time All-American at IU who led Hoosiers in scoring and rebounding all three seasons. U.S. Olympic team member in 1960, NBA Rookie of the Year in 1962. Played 14 NBA seasons.

Branch McCracken coached IU to NCAA titles in 1940 and 1953.

INDIANA

LEGEND *Branch McCracken*

REVOLUTIONALIZED POST PLAY

Branch McCracken, coach of IU's first two NCAA basketball champions (1940 and 1953), had an All-American playing career that was good enough to rank him with the best players he ever coached, and with the best of any era who ever played basketball for IU.

There's proof: he's in the Basketball Hall of Fame, the first man ever voted there for his performance as an IU player.

His IU coach and predecessor, Everett Dean, called McCracken "rough and tough." McCracken never missed a game. Once, when slowed by injuries, he planted himself near the foul line, back to the basket, from there passing off to players cutting by him or keeping the ball and rolling to the basket himself. "Once we saw what he could do, we let him go," Dean said. "He was one of the first college centers who played the pivot the way it's played today."

He scored 32.3 percent of the points his three Hoosier teams scored. He led the Big Ten with a 12.3 average his senior year and graduated as the league's career scoring recordholder. A consensus All-American in 1930, in 1960 he was elected to the Hall of Fame.

McCracken, who coached IU from 1938-39 through 1964-65, died in 1969.

BIG TEN MEDAL
Ed Clapham

GIMBEL AWARD
Wilbert Catterton

BALFOUR AWARDS
Football - Paul Balay
Basketball - Branch McCracken
Baseball - Claron "Lefty" Veller
Track - Jim Hatfield
Wrestling - Jacob Unger

IU item

SHAVING IT CLOSE

George Ross scored two touchdowns in a 19-14 win over Northwestern.

A week before 1929 national champion Notre Dame was to open its season at IU's Memorial Stadium, Indiana was embarrassed there by Ohio University, 18-0. At a campus pep rally the following Monday, coach Pat Page angrily attacked the student body's lack of "spirit and loyalty."

After the Hoosiers lost 14-0 to Notre Dame, 13-7 at Chicago and 21-6 at home to Colgate, some male students vowed not to shave again till Indiana won a game.

Page ridiculed them. "Get over that high school stuff and get serious-minded," Page said.

The pledge stood, through a 0-0 tie at Ohio State, a 19-7 loss at Minnesota, and a week off. In the next-last game, at Northwestern on Homecoming against a team that had beaten Illinois, Wisconsin, Ohio State and Chicago, the Hoosiers trailed 14-6 in the fourth quarter. Then halfback George Ross scored on a 13-yard run, and, seconds later, on a stunning 83-yard breakaway for a 19-14 victory.

Twenty-five days after taking their pledge, the "No-Shavers" led 2,000 students and a Bloomington fire truck to the Monon Railroad station for the winning team's early Sunday morning arrival back in Bloomington.

The victory came just in time to avoid a hairy winter for the zealous pledge-takers. The next week at IU, Purdue won 32-0.

Snapshot In Time

A CARNEGIE SNUB

THE CARNEGIE FOUNDATION for the Advancement of Teaching made national headlines in late October 1929 by accusing more than 100 major universities of subsidizing athletes, through a slush fund, scholarships or loans.

The charge came after a survey of 130 schools, only 28 found taint-free.

The report wasn't in the headlines long. The Wall Street stock market crash began a day later, triggering the Great Depression.

Still, the charge was noticed in Bloomington, where football coach Pat Page seemed irritated that Indiana wasn't among the 130 schools surveyed.

"Of course we could be put on either the lily-white or coal-black list," Page said. "We have tried to uphold the Big Ten ideals which have elevated the standard and now set the pace for the entire country.

"Our past record with athletic material at hand probably speaks for our alumni. I do not believe that they have been over-ambitious."

Humorist Will Rogers saw in the following weekend's games the public's answer to the Carnegie report. "A half-million people paid to see seven games where the athletes were paid," Rogers said, "and less than half that many went to 50 games where the athletes were pure."

HOT TIME IN THE OLD TOWN

Purdue's only home loss in going 30-3-1 in football from 1929 through '32 came in a 7-6 shocker that put Indiana's first block I on the Old Oaken Bucket. The 1930 Hoosiers didn't score a Big Ten point till Gene Opasik's last-quarter touchdown pass to future Phi Beta Kappa Ray Dauer, and Eddie Hughes' kick.

Bloomington's celebration was immediate and wild. Bonfires blazed on all four corners of the Courthouse square. With firemen fretting, president William Lowe Bryan calmed things with an announcement: no classes Monday.

A few days later, *The Indianapolis Star* ran a bitter, open letter from coach Pat Page to IU fans. "It's tough to have a gang of cutthroats in your midst," said Page, who didn't spare his own players: "We haven't a single man over 200 pounds, (and) our 190-pound men are dubs."

In January, Page "resigned," revealed as a firing when he sued the university. Claiming his contract had a year remaining, he sought $15,000, though his contracted salaries his first three years were $3,000, $6,500 and $7,000. Page testified additional pay from alumni, unbeknownst to athletic director Zora Clevenger, made his real salaries those years $10,000, $11,000 and $12,000. Page lost the suit.

Bucket game hero Ray Dauer was a Phi Beta Kappa student.

Snapshot In Time

BUCKET DELAYED IN TRANSIT

WINNING THE OLD Oaken Bucket and truly possessing it were two different things for the Hoosiers.

The 7-6 IU victory in 1930 was so unexpected nobody brought the Bucket to Ross-Ade Stadium. Arrangements were made to send it to Bloomington by bus the next day. Purdue students, angered by an IU group's theft of the clapper from its Victory Bell, intercepted the Bucket and hid it away.

Two weeks later, the Bucket showed up at a Lafayette newspaper and December 10, eighteen days after the game, Purdue officials made the delivery to Bloomington.

Architect's drawing, Union Building

HOOSIER LIST

IU'S NATIONAL CHAMPIONSHIPS

1932   Wrestling
      Coach Billy Thom
1932   Men's Outdoor Track
      Coach Billy Hayes
1938   Men's Cross Country
      Coach Billy Hayes
1940   Men's Basketball
      Coach Branch McCracken
1940   Men's Cross Country
      Coach Billy Hayes
1942   Men's Cross Country
      Coach Billy Hayes
1953   Men's Basketball
      Coach Branch McCracken
1968   Men's Swimming
      Coach Doc Counsilman
1969   Men's Swimming
      Coach Doc Counsilman
1970   Men's Swimming
      Coach Doc Counsilman
1971   Men's Swimming
      Coach Doc Counsilman
1972   Men's Swimming
      Coach Doc Counsilman
1973   Men's Swimming
      Coach Doc Counsilman
1976   Men's Basketball
      Coach Bob Knight
1981   Men's Basketball
      Coach Bob Knight
1982   Women's Tennis (AIAW)
      Coach Lin Loring
1982   Men's Soccer
      Coach Jerry Yeagley
1983   Men's Soccer
      Coach Jerry Yeagley
1987   Men's Basketball
      Coach Bob Knight
1988   Men's Soccer
      Coach Jerry Yeagley
1998   Men's Soccer
      Coach Jerry Yeagley

INDIANA

LEGEND
Joe Zeller

A ROCKNE FAVORITE

Because its soon-to-be-legendary stadium was being built, Notre Dame's 1929 national champions played just one game in the state of Indiana: a 14-0 victory at IU in the Irish season opener.

An Indiana sophomore playing his second college game impressed Notre Dame coach Knute Rockne. "I wish to goodness I had one lineman like that fellow Zeller," Rockne said.

Joe Zeller, from East Chicago, lived up to Rockne's praise. He went on to one of the most honored careers any Hoosier lineman ever had. Twice he was his football team's Most Valuable Player, on some All-Big Ten teams as a junior, on all of them as a senior. He also was a basketball starter, and a good one.

Other Hoosiers played, even starred in both sports, but only Joe Zeller won Balfour Awards in football and basketball the same academic year: 1931-32, when he also was senior class president.

Zeller closed his college football career by playing all 60 minutes in the last four games, then 60 minutes again in the Thanksgiving Day charity tournament. "A whale of a battler," football coach E. C. "Billy" Hayes called him.

Zeller played in the NFL with the Bears and the Packers.

BIG TEN MEDAL
Henry Brocksmith

GIMBEL AWARD
George Belshaw

BALFOUR AWARDS
Football - Joe Zeller
Basketball - Joe Zeller
Baseball - Clifton Wright
Track - Bryce Beecher
Wrestling - Eddie Belshaw

NCAA CHAMPIONS
Team
Wrestling (Billy Thom)
Track (Billy Hayes)

Individual
Wrestling - Eddie Belshaw, 135
Track - Charles Hornbostel,
800 meters, 1:52.7
Bryce Beecher, pole vault, 13-10

IU item

BEECHER: A PRESSURE CHAMPION

Pole vaulter Bryce Beecher shows up just twice on IU's list of Big Ten and NCAA champions, but his titles were epochal.

In the Big Ten indoor championships at Chicago, with all other events over, and all eyes on the vault, Beecher cleared 13 feet, 8 inches to deliver IU's first league track title. A Beecher tie wouldn't have done it; the champion Hoosiers scored 27 5/6 points, to runnerup Michigan's 27.

Coach Billy Hayes called Beecher's clutch performance "the climax to a great meet." Beecher had finished seventh in the high jump, starting at 7 p.m. His meet-winning vault came at 11, "a full evening's work," Hayes noted.

Outdoors, Beecher lost in the Big Ten to Ohio State vaulter John Wonsowitz's 13-3. At the NCAA meet, Wonsowitz and five others cleared 13-6, but Beecher soared 13-10 and both he and his team were national champions.

At the Olympic Trials, where 13-10 put UCLA's George Jefferson on the team and later won him a bronze medal, Beecher made just 13-4 and missed the Games.

The senior from Linton won IU's Balfour Award in track and field, an award even more prestigious than usual because of the depth of great performers.

Pole vaulter Bryce Beecher won Big Ten and NCAA titles.

Bryce Beecher's pole vault victories brought IU Big Ten and NCAA team championships.

Snapshot In Time

KUSS ON BOTH NCAA TITLE TEAMS

TALL, STRONG, WAVY-HAIRED Otto Kuss of Pine City, Minnesota, has a unique role in IU's athletic history: He lettered on two NCAA championship teams, in one year.

Before lettering on the 1932 wrestling and track teams that won IU's first two NCAA titles, sophomore Kuss won a football letter. He couldn't get into the wrestling lineup because of sophomore Bob Jones, national AAU heavyweight champion as a freshman. The 1932 NCAA championships served as an Olympic qualifier so weights were adjusted to Olympic limits. That let coach Billy Thom use both Jones (at 191 pounds, after shedding 10 pounds) and the 220-pound Kuss (heavyweight).

Kuss had been in just one match in the entire season up to then, and lost it. He also lost his only two NCAA matches, but honorably. He was beaten in overtime by eventual champion Jack Riley of Northwestern. His second loss was to runnerup Pete Mehringer, the Big Six champion for Kansas. Meet officials did advance Kuss, 0-3 for the year, to the Olympic Trials.

After missing out there, he lettered as a weightman for Billy Hayes' championship track team.

From IU, Kuss went on to a long career as a professional wrestler, competing in 38 states and New Zealand.

Otto Kuss remains IU's only athlete to letter on NCAA-championship teams in two sports.

IN THOSE DAYS . . .

ANOTHER BASEBALL CROWN

Indiana's unprecedented glut of championships in the 1931-32 academic year was filled out by Everett Dean's baseball team, which won the school's second Big Ten baseball championship by winning at Purdue on the last day of the season.

The Hoosiers opened their season by going 7-0 through non-conference play. Indiana won two of three games from Ohio State and split two with Purdue for the losses that made them 5-2 going to the final game. Purdue (6-3) would have tied Illinois (7-3) for the championship, if the Boilermakers had beaten Indiana.

Early in the year, pitcher Ralph Gatti broke an arm, straining a thin pitching staff. At Purdue, Dean pulled a surprise. Gatti, back from his injury, started, and he pitched well. Indiana won 8-3 to clinch what remains the school's most recent outright Big Ten baseball championship.

The captain of the team, hard-hitting outfielder Merrill May of Laconia, signed with the Yankees and, as "Pinky" May, played five years in the major leagues with the Phillies. May's son, Milt, a catcher, followed him to the majors and played 15 years.

LEGEND   *Henry Brocksmith*

INDIANA

THE DOCTOR COULD RUN

In all its history, Indiana University has had few people who took a combination of academic and athletic excellence to the levels that middle-distance runner Henry Brocksmith did.

Brocksmith, from Freelandville in Knox County northeast of Vincennes, was an honor student. He won IU's Big Ten Medal in his senior year, 1932, and earned his M.D. degree from IU in 1936.

He was the first Hoosier runner to win six Big Ten championships, for teams that won three league cross country titles and one, the school's first, in indoor track. With two second-place finishes, the strong 5-10, 160-pound Brocksmith was the highest-scoring contributor to the only NCAA team championship in IU's strong track and field history.

Brocksmith won the Big Ten indoor two-mile title as a sophomore in 1930, when the Hoosiers made their first real run at a Big Ten track team championship—third, four points behind champion Wisconsin. He won the league's cross country race in 1931, in the midst of the three straight team titles.

In spring 1932, an Olympic year, he put his name among the top middle-distance runners in the nation. In the Big Ten indoor meet that Indiana won by five-sixths of a point, Brocksmith took more than nine seconds off the meet mile record by winning in 4:12.5, only 2.1 seconds slower than Paavo Nurmi's world outdoor record. An hour later, he cut eight seconds off the league's two-mile record with 9:18.4.

Outdoors, he beat Kansas great Glenn Cunningham and broke a 20-year-old U.S. intercollegiate record by four seconds in winning the two-mile at the Drake Relays, then anchored IU to victory in the four-mile relay. The Hoosiers couldn't repeat their Big Ten title outdoors, but Brocksmith repeated his indoor double, in the mile and two-mile.

Two weeks later in Chicago, at the NCAA outdoor championships that served as a qualifying meet for the U.S. Olympic Trials, Brocksmith ran his fastest mile, only to lose by about five yards to Cunningham's American-record 4:11.1.

Again Brocksmith came back in the two-mile, where he lost by a scant yard to a fresh runner, Charles Shugert of Miami (Ohio). "No runner of (his) ability ever experienced two such bitter disappointments in one afternoon," Wilfrid Smith wrote in the *Chicago Tribune*.

All disappointment disappeared when Indiana piled up 56 points and edged league rival Ohio State (49 1/2) for the national championship.

At the Olympic Trials, Brocksmith set the pace into the final lap but finished fifth in the 1,500 meters, two spots too low to get him to the Olympics.

He still had a semester of eligibility left and used it to finish second and help IU to one more Big Ten cross country title. Then he entered medical school, where the honors continued. He was elected president of the medical honorary, Phi Beta Pi.

IU WINS FOOTBALL 'TOURNEY'

BIG TEN FOOTBALL teams raised $154,000 for the Great Depression's Midwest jobless by adding a weekend to their 1931 schedule.

The league's top six teams met in normal games. The four others played a one-day, four-team Thanksgiving Day tournament at Chicago's Stagg Field.

Indiana was at the Illinois 3 when their 30-minute game ended 0-0, IU awarded the victory for an 8-4 edge in first downs. Chicago scored on a punt return to beat Iowa, 7-0. In the finals, Stan Saluski's 37-yard TD run gave Indiana a 6-0 win and the championship of the only Big Ten football tournament ever played.

Ohio State, Wisconsin and Northwestern teams, their own games two days later, were in the crowd of 8,000 that raised $13,000 for the jobless.

IN THOSE DAYS . . .

SWIMMING SEASON SHORTENED

Baseball games called off because of rain are nothing unusual, but what happened to the 1931 IU swimming team was. Its whole season was called off because of a lack of rain.

An extended Southern Indiana drought caused so dire a water shortage that the city of Bloomington and the university agreed to take some emergency steps. Among them was ruling out swimming, the IU varsity included.

No varsity letters were given, but Elmer Delo, Dudley Jordan, Jack Shaffer, Richard Stanbro and Lawrence Welch were awarded numerals.

When IU resumed swimming competition in 1932, Stanbro was the only one of the '31 numeral recipients to come back and win a letter.

IUitem

BELSHAW BROTHERS: KEYS TO AN ERA

Eddie (left) and George (right) Belshaw were all-everything—champions, Gimbel and Balfour Award winners.

The Belshaw brothers, Eddie and George, epitomized the athletes Billy Thom built his Indiana University wrestling program around— tough, smart, courageous, and very nearly unbeatable.

Their early years were in Montana, where in 1918 a flu outbreak caused them to miss a full year of school. When they were back in classes, Eddie, 14 months younger, moved into the same seventh-grade class with George, and the two stayed together the rest of the way.

The family moved to Lowell, Indiana, where they were undersized, submarining football linemen, but there was no wrestling team. Their start in that sport came at the Gary YMCA, which in 1928 took its team by train to Bloomington to compete against Thom's IU team. Thom recruited the two brothers, virtual novices in the sport, after the meet, and when they were sophomores he had them ready to deliver three years of victories at two weights: 135 for Eddie, 155 for George.

> **"When they handed me the first-place medal and the (Outstanding Wrestler) cup, it was a dream come true."**

They were seniors and leaders when Indiana won its first NCAA championship, in competition at IU's Men's Gym in March 1932. Eddie in that meet became Indiana's first NCAA wrestling champion. He also was the first winner of a new award that became the most prestigious in the college sport: Outstanding Wrestler at the NCAA championships. Eddie was overcome by the honor. "When they handed me the first-place medal and the cup, it was a dream come true," he said.

George went into that meet unbeaten for the year, the Big Ten champion. He lost in the first round to Michigan's Carl Dougovito, an outstanding wrestler who went on to win the NCAA championship. George probably shouldn't have wrestled at all that day. Two days before, flu hit him hard. Literally, he came out of a sickbed to compete and fought his way into overtime before Dougovito finally won.

Eddie's junior year, he was unbeaten, but he didn't win any championships. In his Big Ten semifinal match, he broke three ribs, but he continued to battle through the pain and won the match with a pin. Then, he was withdrawn.

Eddie was captain of the IU team in 1931. George was co-captain in 1932. Eddie won IU's Balfour Award in wrestling in 1932, then as now given to an athlete in each sport for bringing honor and distinction to the school. George won the school's Gimbel Award that year, then as now given annually to one senior athlete for academic and athletic achievement.

The 1932 NCAA meet was a qualifier for the U.S. Olympic Trials. College and Olympic wrestling had seven weights then; all seven IU entrants in the NCAA meet were sent on to the Trials at Ann Arbor. There, Eddie made it to the finals, George to the semifinals, before they were eliminated.

Wrestling ended there for George, who after a few years in coaching entered IU's medical school and had a distinguished career in obstetrics/gynecology. In his 90s, he lived in retirement in a Montana canyon home, hiking about four miles daily.

Eddie's degree and academic honors didn't get him a job in those Depression depths. A year after graduation, married to a young teacher, he tried to supplement family income as a professional wrestler. A severe mat burn infected, and he became gravely ill. On the way back to health, he got another chance to wrestle. Too soon. The infection returned and, in 1933, Eddie Belshaw died.

Indiana's first two NCAA championship teams were the 1932 trackmen of Billy Hayes and the 1932 wrestlers of Billy Thom. Both Hayes and Thom served the United States as Olympic coaches in 1936.

HOOSIER LIST

IU'S OLYMPIC MEDALISTS IN TRACK AND FIELD

Year	Name	Event	Medal
1904	Leroy Samse	Pole Vault	Silver
1904	Thad Shideler	110-Hurdles	Silver
1932	Ivan Fuqua	1600-Relay	Gold
1948	Roy Cochran	400-Hurdles	Gold
		1600-Relay	Gold
1952	Milt Campbell	Decathlon	Silver
1956	Milt Campbell	Decathlon	Gold
	Greg Bell	Long Jump	Gold
1960	Willie May	110-Hurdles	Silver
1984	Sunder Nix	1600-Relay	Gold
	Timi Peters (Nigeria)	1600-Relay	Bronze

Hurdler Willie May won a silver medal in the 1960 Olympics in Rome.

INDIANA

LEGEND *Ivan Fuqua*

IU'S FIRST OLYMPIC GOLD MEDALIST

As a sophomore in 1932, Ivan Fuqua helped IU to its first Big Ten indoor track championship but won no Big Ten titles himself. It was a rather mild introduction to college eligibility for a man who came into IU with a national reputation and left with a greater one.

When the Hoosiers won the 1932 outdoor NCAA title, Fuqua ran second to Canadian Alex Wilson of Notre Dame in the 400 meters. He won the 400 at a midwest Olympic qualifying meet, then finished fifth in a tight pack at the U.S. Olympic Trials.

Fifth put Fuqua on the Olympic team in the 4x400-meter relay. At Los Angeles, he ran the leadoff leg for an American team that won by 20 yards and set a world record that stood for 20 years.

It was IU's first Olympic gold medal, in any sport.

Back at IU, he won the rare 220-440 double at two straight Big Ten outdoor meets, anchoring Indiana to mile relay victories each time. He also won two Big Ten 440 titles indoors.

Fuqua went on to coach track at Connecticut and at Brown. He was inducted into the IU Athletics Hall of Fame in 1988.

BIG TEN MEDAL
Noble Biddinger

GIMBEL AWARD
Cliff Watson

BALFOUR AWARDS

Football - John Keckich
Basketball - Woody Weir
Baseball - Howard Koenig
Track - Charles Hornbostel/
Ivan Fuqua
Wrestling - Pat Devine

NCAA CHAMPIONS
Individual
Wrestling - Pat Devine, 135
Track - Charles Hornbostel, 880, 1:50.9

NO NCAA REPEAT, BUT ALL-OUT TRY

Indiana didn't repeat its two 1932 NCAA team championships, but the defending wrestling and track champs tried valiantly.

The track Hoosiers won eight Big Ten outdoor events, two each by Olympians Ivan Fuqua and Charles Hornbostel, but finished second to Michigan. In the NCAA meet, Hornbostel won the 880 and Fuqua was second in the 440 as Indiana finished third, behind LSU and Southern Cal.

Billy Thom's wrestlers left the NCAA meet at Lehigh thinking they had won again, with 22 points to 20 for Iowa State and 19 for Oklahoma A&M. Subsequent records list Iowa State and Oklahoma A&M as co-winners of the "unofficial" team title. Each had three champions to Indiana's one (Pat Devine, at 135 pounds). Indiana's team points included second-place finishes by Dick Voliva (175) and Bob Jones (heavyweight).

The '33 Hoosier wrestlers won five (of the seven) individual championships in retaining their Big Ten title. That's the highest total ever for Indiana, and it wasn't topped by anyone in the league meet till 1969 (when there were nine weight divisions).

Devine, Dale Goings (145), Glen Brown (155), Olden Gillum (165) and heavyweight Jones won IU's '33 titles. Devine's NCAA championship capped an unbeaten season for him.

> **Billy Thom's wrestlers left the NCAA meet at Lehigh thinking they had won again.**

Pat Devine won Big Ten titles in 1933 and 1934 and the 1933 NCAA championship at 135 pounds.

Snapshot In Time

'KIDNAPPED' BY A GOVERNOR

IVAN FUQUA'S WELCOME back to Indiana after the Olympics included a 100-car escort, a parade and a rousing public reception in his hometown, Brazil.

Fuqua had made Brazil proud many times before.

As a high school freshman, he led off a mile relay team that won the state meet in a record 3:29.6. As a junior, he won the 220-yard hurdles, 440 and long jump and anchored the winning mile relay team at the state, then won the 220 hurdles (24.7) and the 440 (49.4) at the National Interscholastic Meet in Chicago. His senior year, he won the 100 and 440 at the state, then at Chicago won the 220 (21.6) and anchored a record-setting mile relay team in leading Brazil to a second-place team finish. At the 1930 Kokomo Relays, he set a national high school record of 9.7 in the 100.

Fuqua always joked that he was more kidnapped than recruited to IU. Another IU student from Brazil told Fuqua that's where he was going to go, packed him into his car, and drove him to Bloomington for enrollment. The driver, George Craig, had won freshman wrestling numerals at IU. He went on to be the state's governor.

George Craig, future state governor, drove Ivan Fuqua to IU.

IN THOSE DAYS . . .

AWARDS SWEPT BY TRACKMEN

Track's dominance over even basketball and football at Indiana in the '30s was suggested by the university's annual awards in the 1932-33 athletic year.

For the first time (and still the only time), the school's Big Ten Medal and Gimbel Award both went to track and field athletes. Senior class president Noble Biddinger, two-time Big Ten hammer throw champion and Drake Relays recordholder in the event, won the school's Big Ten Medal, and distanceman Cliff Watson was the Gimbel Award winner. The Balfour Award in track then was split between two other richly deserving athletes: Olympians Charles Hornbostel and Ivan Fuqua.

For both Hornbostel and Fuqua, the Olympics and the Balfour, not to mention lifetimes of great achievement, almost didn't happen.

One of the three cars carrying IU's track team to the 1932 Drake Relays overturned twice in an accident near Sullivan, within 30 miles of home for Fuqua.

In the car were the team's legendary coach, Billy Hayes, and six athletes, among them Fuqua, Hornbostel, Don Harpold and Abe Streicher, who had been expected to take a shot at the Drake Relays mile relay record. Cuts and bruises scratched the four relayers from that meet, but all were competing again a week later.

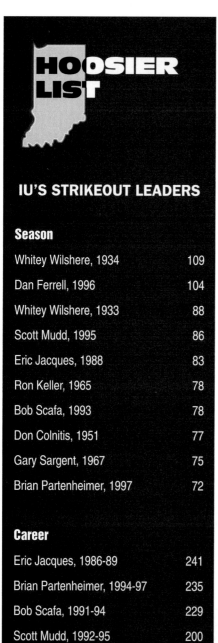

HOOSIER LIST

IU'S STRIKEOUT LEADERS

Season

Whitey Wilshere, 1934	109
Dan Ferrell, 1996	104
Whitey Wilshere, 1933	88
Scott Mudd, 1995	86
Eric Jacques, 1988	83
Ron Keller, 1965	78
Bob Scafa, 1993	78
Don Colnitis, 1951	77
Gary Sargent, 1967	75
Brian Partenheimer, 1997	72

Career

Eric Jacques, 1986-89	241
Brian Partenheimer, 1994-97	235
Bob Scafa, 1991-94	229
Scott Mudd, 1992-95	200
Larry Rosin, 1975-78	199
Gary Sargent, 1966-68	198
Whitey Wilshere, 1933-34	197
Dan Ferrell, 1994-96	194
Kyle Boyd, 1995-98	187
Ron Keller, 1963-65	185
John Barnefield, 1974-77	182

INDIANA

LEGEND *Charles Hornbostel*

A WORLD-RECORD DOUBLE

Charles Hornbostel accomplished several things unmatched in IU track history, and one unmatched anywhere.

Hornbostel never lost a collegiate race in his specialty, the half-mile run. Three straight years, Hornbostel won Big Ten 880 titles indoors and out, then added the NCAA championship, IU's first and still only three-time NCAA track champion.

He won three Big Ten mile titles, too. He doubled in the 880 and mile, then combined with Ivan Fuqua, Don Harpold and Chuck Bicking to win the mile relay at both the '33 and '34 Big Ten outdoor meets.

Hornbostel, the first Hoosier to run in two Olympics, reached the 800-meter finals both times, finishing sixth (1932) and fifth (1936). A 1934 IU graduate, he had come back to international track in '36 after earning an MBA at Harvard.

Eleven days after his 1936 Olympic race, Hornbostel and three other American Olympians set a world record in the two-mile relay. The same day, August 15, 1936, at London, in essentially his farewell to track, Hornbostel and three different U.S. Olympians set a world four-mile relay record. No other man ever has held both of those marks simultaneously, let alone set them in one day.

BIG TEN MEDAL
Ray Dauer

GIMBEL AWARD
Charles Hornbostel

BALFOUR AWARDS
Football - Bob Jones
Basketball - Woody Weir
Baseball - Whitey Wilshere
Track - Charles Hornbostel/
Ivan Fuqua
Wrestling - Dick Voliva

NCAA CHAMPIONS
Individual
Wrestling - Dick Voliva, 175
Track - Charles Hornbostel, 880, 1:51.9

IU item

IU'S BEST PITCHER?

Whitey Wilshere posted a 17-2 record and struck out 197 batters in 159 innings in his IU career.

Vernon "Whitey" Wilshere won just 10 major league games, but he may be the best pitcher IU ever had.

Wilshere, from upstate New York, lost just two games in his two varsity years, both to Michigan.

Opening the May Big Ten homestretch in 1934, Wilshere struck out 16 and, with a two-run triple by Vern Huffman, won 5-2 over Purdue. As a relief pitcher at Chicago, he struck out the side in the seventh and eighth; he and Indiana won 3-2 with a run in the ninth. With more than 3,000 people jamming the Hoosier field, Wilshere struck out 10 as Indiana beat Michigan.

The Hoosiers went to Ann Arbor sharing the league lead but lost, 4-2. A closing split on Memorial Day at Ohio State left Indiana 6-3 and second in the Big Ten, two games behind champion Illinois.

Though he pitched only two seasons, Wilshere's 17 career victories was the IU record for 42 years; his 197 career strikeouts, for 34 years. His 1.12 career earned average still is IU's all-time best. His junior-year marks sparkled: 9-1, 1.10 ERA, 109 strikeouts in 84 innings, 10.9 per game.

In 1996, he was the first baseball-only letterman inducted into IU's Athletics Hall of Fame.

He remains the only IU baseball player to step straight from campus to the major leagues.

Snapshot In Time

A DEATH, AND A RAID

COACH EVERETT DEAN planned a grand windup to his baseball team's season, taking it east for games at Rutgers and Temple. The Hoosiers won both games, by 6-4 scores, finishing 21-5.

But it wasn't a happy trip.

Three days before the Hoosiers left, their captain and star second baseman, Kenny Dugan, was killed in an Indianapolis auto crash. His baseball teammates were pallbearers.

A day after Dugan's accident, outfielder Bill Cox left the club and signed with the Tigers.

At Temple, with A's owner-manager Connie Mack watching, Whitey Wilshere struck out 15 in outdueling Temple star Eddie Cramer, who was 8-0 going into the game.

Wilshere had a year of eligibility left, but he didn't return with the team. Mack signed him and started him against Detroit, the American League champion that year. Wilshere led into the fifth inning but a five-run rally beat him. He pitched in eight more games that year, but the loss to the Tigers was his only decision.

Whitey Wilshere won at Temple and never made it back to IU.

The next year, he went 9-9 for a last-place team. Early in the 1936 season, he hurt his arm and never pitched again.

A member of Blue Key honorary, he returned to IU and earned his bachelor's and master's degrees. Then he went back to New York to teach and coach.

IN THOSE DAYS . . .

BOB JONES ON FIRST ALL-STARS

Baseball's All-Star Game was the 1933 brainchild of *Chicago Tribune* columnist Arch Ward, whose newspaper tabulated the nationwide fans' voting that picked the teams.

That same year the *Tribune* began a football All-Star Game: a summer matchup of the previous fall's best collegians and the pro champion. Fans' votes picked the college players.

In 1934, the No. 3 vote-getter, and the first Hoosier to play in the game, was All-Big Ten guard Bob Jones, a three-year starter in football and a standout heavyweight wrestler as well. Heavyweight Jones won two Big Ten championships and one AAU. His Big Ten title as a sophomore came over Northwestern's Jack Riley, the only loss for Riley in two straight NCAA-championship years. Jones contributed a third-place NCAA finish to the Hoosiers' 1932 team championship.

In the All-Star Game, Jones started across from 1931 IU teammate Joe Zeller of the champion Chicago Bears. Their battle was as even as the final score: 0-0. Those Bears went on to be 13-0 when the New York Giants beat them 13-6 in the 1934 NFL championship game.

Jones played a year for Green Bay, then became one of Indiana's high school football coaching legends at South Bend Central.

HOOSIER LIST

LONGEST-TENURED IU COACHES

33 James (Doc) Counsilman, swimming, 1958-90

33 Bob Fitch, golf, 1957-89

30 Hobie Billingsley, diving, 1960-89

29 Sam Bell, cross country & track, 1969-98

28 Bob Knight, basketball, 1972-99*

27 Charles McDaniel, wrestling, 1946-72

26 Jerry Yeagley, soccer, 1973-98*

25 Ernie Andres, baseball, 1949-73

24 Branch McCracken, basketball, 1939-43, 1947-65

22 Lin Loring, women's tennis, 1978-99*

19 E.C. (Billy) Hayes, cross country & track, 1925-43

19 Sam Carmichael, women's golf, 1981-99*

18 W.H. (Billy) Thom, wrestling, 1928-45

17 Gordon Fisher, cross country & track, 1945-61

16 Bob Morgan, baseball, 1984-99*

15 Bill Landin, men's tennis, 1958-72

* Still active

INDIANA

LEGEND *Charley McDaniel*

AN OLYMPIAN AND A TACKLE

Charley McDaniel was a college wrestling rookie when unbeaten Indiana and unbeaten Illinois stood 10 to 10 going into the last match of the last meet of the 1935 regular season. Home boy "Charley Mac" beat the Illini's undefeated co-captain, Andy Dahl, in overtime, and the campus had a new hero.

McDaniel went on to make history time and time again as Indiana's only two-time NCAA champion, an Olympian, and a three-year football starter as well.

McDaniel won a state high school wrestling championship and led Bloomington High to the state's first team championship as a senior in 1933.

For winning the 1935 NCAA heavyweight title, McDaniel became the first sophomore to win one of IU's Balfour Awards. He went to Berlin in 1936 as an alternate on the U.S. Olympic team. As a senior in 1938, he won Big Ten and NCAA titles, and the school's Big Ten Medal for academic and athletic proficiency.

McDaniel coached high school football and wrestling. When Billy Thom retired in 1944, McDaniel succeeded him in wrestling and joined Bo McMillin's football staff as an assistant. McDaniel coached IU wrestling teams through 1972. He was a charter member of IU's Athletics Hall of Fame, and, in 1966, he was inducted into the National Wrestling Hall of Fame.

BIG TEN MEDAL - Don Veller   **GIMBEL AWARD -** Willard Kehrt

BALFOUR AWARDS

Football - Don Veller; Basketball - Willard Kehrt; Baseball - Willis "Babe" Hosler; Track - Don Lash; Wrestling - Charley McDaniel

NCAA CHAMPION

Wrestling - Charley McDaniel (heavyweight)

IU ITEM

....

'GRAVEYARD' DOESN'T SCARE

> ## "It has thrilled the kids of Indiana to know that Bo is going to coach here."
>
> —Sherman Minton on new IU football coach Bo McMillin

When Ohio University coach Don Peden turned down the open Indiana football coaching job, Hoosiers were pessimistic about the sport's IU future. Walter Bradfute, writing in the *Bloomington Telephone*, called the school "the graveyard of football coaches" and warned dourly: "Another poor football season and (athletic director Zora) Clevenger's head will be demanded on a platter."

The Hoosier mood changed instantly when the new man turned out to be one of the sport's golden names: Bo McMillin, creator of legends with his play in leading Centre over Harvard and a man who already had achieved a turn-around at another football "coaching graveyard," Kansas State.

Clevenger, in announcing the hiring, called McMillin "one of the greatest quarterbacks the country has had (and) one of the outstanding coaches of the country."

At McMillin's campus introduction, a boyhood friend, former Hoosier football and baseball star Sherman Minton, eight months away from being elected a U.S. Senator, said: "His ambition as a boy was to be a great player. He was. His ambition is to be a great coach. He is. It has thrilled the kids of Indiana to know that Bo is going to coach here."

VELLER BUCKET HERO

A FOOTBALL COINCIDENCE brought Don Peden, the coach reported to have rejected the IU job, and Ohio University to Bloomington for Bo McMillin's Hoosier debut.

Indiana won, 27-0.

Then the Hoosiers scored just one touchdown in the next five games, salvaging ties with Iowa (0-0) and Temple (6-6, against a strong Pop Warner-coached team that stayed unbeaten till a 20-14 loss to Tulane in the first Sugar Bowl).

Even after outlasting Maryland in their seventh game, 17-14, the Hoosiers were given little chance at Purdue, against a team 3-0 in the Big Ten, closing in on at least a co-championship.

Indiana jumped ahead on Wendel Walker's touchdown pass to Ettore Antonini. In the second quarter, 156-pound Don Veller, once a Purdue freshman who left because he felt the coaches ignored him, bolted 82 yards on an end sweep to score. The Veller run still is the longest scrimmage run ever in an Old Oaken Bucket game and among the 10 longest in IU history. It keyed a 17-6 victory that launched McMillin's mastery of the Old Oaken Bucket series. Veller, an outstanding student, won IU's Big Ten Medal, Balfour and Most Valuable Player awards and played in the East-West Game.

Don Veller's 82-yard run beat Purdue in 1934. He later coached football and golf at Florida State.

IN THOSE DAYS . . .

VELLER ON BO: 'JUST BRILLIANT'

At his IU Athletics Hall of Fame induction in 1986, Don Veller gave an inherited senior player's perspective of the Bo McMillin he played for.

"He had a tremendous ego," Veller said. "He really felt he was a great coach.

"And he was.

"Bo was just brilliant. If he had a fault as a coach, it was that he wasn't good about delegating. But he had one of the greatest minds ever.

"We had so many plays . . . The Purdue game, he let me call the plays, I was supposed to be smart. But I had a hard time remembering them all.

"He was such a great communicator, able to fire you up so high. His teams were always good for an upset or two over teams they shouldn't have beaten."

Veller, son of a Bicknell coal miner, was the first football coach at Florida State, after the hitherto all-girls school admitted males in the 1940s. He coached the Seminoles from 1948 through '52. "When I was coaching, I used Bo's stuff," Veller said.

After football, he coached Florida State's golf team for 30 years, retiring in 1982.

INDIANA LEGEND

Don Lash

AMERICA'S BEST

Don Lash, it is said, developed leg speed by running down rabbits on his family's farm. In any chase that lasted a mile or two, a bunny was overmatched.

Golden-haired, effortless Don Lash, running indoors and out, on paved ovals and cross-country courses, became America's answer to Paavo Nurmi and track's Flying Finns. Young and inexperienced internationally, he didn't run well in the 1936 Olympics. Billy Hayes, his Hoosier coach and an assistant coach for that U.S. team, said two years later:

"I believe Don Lash can better the world records in both the mile and the two-mile . . . Lash should reach his peak in 1940 (and) make up for his showing in the Berlin Olympics by beating the Finns in the Japan Olympics."

There was no 1940 Olympics. By the time world peace allowed resumption of the Games at London in 1948, Lash was running down criminals as a career FBI agent. He went on to serve in the state legislature and as an IU trustee.

For the running career he did have, despite the predictions he didn't get a chance to justify, Don Lash was one of the 25 charter electees to IU's Athletics Hall of Fame. He also is in the U.S. Track and Field Hall of Fame. Lash died in 1994.

BIG TEN MEDAL - Reed Kelso   **GIMBEL AWARD -** Dan Caldemeyer

BALFOUR AWARDS

Football - Reed Kelso; Basketball - Vern Huffman; Baseball - Willis "Babe" Hosler; Track - Don Lash; Wrestling - Willard Duffy

NCAA CHAMPION

Track - Don Lash, 5,000 meters, 14:58.5

OLYMPIC MEDALIST

Wrestling - Dick Voliva, 174, silver

IUitem

VOLIVA A CHAMPION AND A MEDALIST

Dick Voliva is the only IU wrestler to win a medal in Olympic competition. He won silver in 1936.

Former Hoosier wrestler Harold Mumby had his own great program going at Bloomington High School when Billy Thom got Indiana's on its way. Bloomington High under Mumby won six of the first 11 state high school team championships. It was a natural step for the best of those athletes to move right into Thom's program across town.

Dick Voliva brought honors to both programs.

Voliva won two state championships under Mumby. He lettered as a sophomore on Thom's 1932 NCAA champions, and he was the national runnerup at 175 pounds for the third-place Hoosiers in 1933. He lettered in football the fall of his senior year, then as a wrestling co-captain won the 1934 Big Ten 175-pound title and completed a 12-0 season by winning the NCAA championship for a team that was runnerup to Oklahoma State.

Voliva stayed in training under Thom while working toward a master's degree. He won a spot on the U.S. Olympic team, and at Berlin he won a silver medal, the only Olympic medal ever for an IU wrestler.

Voliva coached for 10 years at Montclair State College in New Jersey, then for 32 years at Rutgers. He was elected to the National Wrestling Hall of Fame and inducted into IU's Athletics Hall of Fame in 1987.

Snapshot In Time

VOLIVA THRILLED U.S. COACH THOM

BILLY THOM WAS not yet 36 when he coached the United States wrestling team at the 1936 Olympics.

Thom's U.S. squad included three of his IU wrestlers: Dick Voliva, the only one of the three to compete at Berlin, and alternates Charley McDaniel and Willard Duffy.

Both Voliva and McDaniel were from Harold Mumby's Bloomington High program, and Duffy had won four state high school titles for Muncie Central.

The Great Depression's grip was tight in 1936. The U.S. Olympic Committee indicated it might not have the funds to send wrestlers to Berlin. Thom attacked that problem personally.

Even while coaching, he had wrestled professionally. He won the world middleweight championship in 1928 and held it through 1937 before retiring unbeaten. He headlined two benefit exhibition matches in Bloomington, risking his title in one. The matches raised $360, and the three Hoosier wrestlers went to the Olympics.

There, Thom watched Voliva win all but one of his matches and receive a silver medal. Thom expressed his feelings:

"A boy I had seen grow up in Bloomington, had coached to a Big Ten championship, an NCAA championship, a National AAU championship, and then the Olympic team . . . if I were to pick one incident as my greatest thrill, that would be it."

IN THOSE DAYS . . .

BIG YEAR FOR 'ACES'

Athletic director Zora Clevenger's "Four Aces" delivered big things for him in 1935-36.

Everett Dean's basketball team set school records by going 18-2 overall and 11-1 in sharing the Big Ten championship.

Olympic coach Billy Thom's IU wrestlers, with league champions Clifford "Two-Bits" Myers (118 pounds) and Willard Duffy (126), won their fourth Big Ten title.

Bo McMillin's 4-3-1 team beat Chicago 24-0 (stopping first Heisman Trophy winner Jay Berwanger) and Purdue 7-0 (on Wendel Walker's third-quarter touchdown pass to Vern Huffman). All-Big Ten center (and Big Ten Medal winner) Reed Kelso captained IU's first winning football team in 15 years.

Olympic distance coach Billy Hayes' team won IU's first Big Ten outdoor track championship, with Don Lash doubling in the mile (4:10, a meet record) and two-mile.

Lash's year also included his:
• First world record (8:58.4 in a two-mile race at Princeton);
• Second of six straight National AAU cross country victories (leading Tommy Deckard and Jim Smith in a 1-2-3 IU finish);
• One-year slam never duplicated: NCAA, AAU and Olympic Trials 5,000-meter victories.

Lash also won the Trials 10,000, his Berlin finishes eighth (10,000) and fourteenth (5,000).

INDIANA

IU TRACK AND FIELD WORLD RECORDHOLDERS

Two Miles
Don Lash, 8:58.4, June 19, 1936, at Princeton, New Jersey.

4X400 Meter Relay
Ivan Fuqua, 3:08.2, August 17, 1932, at Los Angeles, California with Edgar Ablowich, Karl Warner, Bill Carr (USA National Team).

4X800 Meter Relay
Charles Hornbostel, 7:35.8, August 15, 1936 at London, England with Robert Young, Henry Williamson, John Woodruff (USA National Team).

4XMile Relay
Charles Hornbostel, 17:17.2, August 15, 1932 at London, England with Gene Venzke, Archie San Romani, Glenn Cunningham (USA National Team).

Mel Trutt, Jim Smith, Tom Deckard, Don Lash, 17:16.2, April 24, 1937 at Philadelphia, Pennsylvania.

120-Yard Hurdles
Thad Shideler, :15.0., June 11, 1904, at St. Louis, Missouri

Milt Campbell, :13.4, May 31, 1957, at Compton, California

440-Yard Hurdles
Roy Cochran, :52.2, April 25, 1942, at Des Moines, Iowa.

Discus
Archie Harris, 174-9, June 20, 1941, at Palo Alto, California.

Pole Vault
Leroy Samse, 12-4 7/8, May, 1906, at Chicago, Illinois.

LEGEND — *Vern Huffman*

BASKETBALL, FOOTBALL ALL-AMERICA

Vernon "Vern" Huffman led basketball-rich New Castle to (so far) its only state high school championship—in 1932, over Winamac and another future Hoosier, Lester Stout, in the final game.

At Indiana, Bo McMillin talked Huffman into trying football, too. He became the only athlete in IU history to be named to major All-America teams in both sports.

After a knee injury took him out of the 1934-35 athletic year, Huffman was a consensus All-American in basketball in '36 for the 18-2 team that was Everett Dean's best at IU.

His senior football season, a team captained by IU Athletics Hall of Famer Chris Dal Sasso won at Michigan, 14-3, and lost only at Ohio State (7-0) and Nebraska (13-9). At Purdue, in a game tied 0-0 at halftime, Huffman and Purdue's Cecil Isbell each threw three touchdown passes and the teams tied, 20-20, and 3-1-1 in the Big Ten, and 5-2-1 overall.

Huffman, the Big Ten's Most Valuable Player and IU's Big Ten Medal winner, earned a law degree before a career that included the NFL (two years with Detroit), the FBI and eventually a return to Bloomington to enter private business. He was a charter selection for the IU Athletics Hall of Fame.

Huffman died on March 18, 1995.

BIG TEN MEDAL
Vern Huffman

GIMBEL AWARD
Don Lash

BALFOUR AWARDS
Football - Vern Huffman
Basketball - Ken Gunning
Baseball - Russ Grieger
Track - Don Lash/Bob Collier
Wrestling - Clifford "Two-Bits" Myers

IU item

LASH, DAVIS 1-2 AS BIG TEN'S BEST

Don Lash

An IU student poll named Don Lash the school's 1936-37 Athlete of the Year, over two other outstanding candidates: runnerup Corby Davis and basketball-football All-American Vern Huffman.

An Associated Press poll of coaches and sportswriters named Lash 1937's Big Ten Athlete of the Year, with Davis second, basketball's John Townsend of Michigan third, and Purdue quarterback Cecil Isbell fourth. Fifth was future baseball Hall of Famer Lou Boudreau, a bigger star in basketball than baseball during his career at Illinois.

Lash was AP's fifth Big Ten Athlete of the Year. Purdue football-track star Duane Purvis was the first, in 1933. Chicago's Jay Berwanger won in both 1934 and 1935, and Olympic hero Jesse Owens of Ohio State won in 1936.

Lash's 1937 track season included combining with Tommy Deckard, Jim Smith and Mel Trutt to set a world record in the four-mile relay at the Penn Relays. The record they broke was the one fellow Hoosier Charles Hornbostel helped to set in 1936.

A year later, as a graduate running toward the 1940 Olympics chance that never came, Don Lash of Indiana won the Sullivan Award as the nation's No. 1 amateur athlete, the first of IU's four Twentieth Century Sullivan winners.

BERT LAWS: VOICE OF AN ERA

ONE MAN DID his job for both the unbeaten 1945 Indiana football team and the 1967 Hoosier Rose Bowlers; for both Indiana's 1940 NCAA basketball champions and IU's unbeaten 1976 national championship team.

Public address system announcer Bert Laws was the man. From November 1936 through the next 200-plus home football games, and for more than 500 basketball games, his rich, smooth voice was as much a part of IU home games as "Indiana, Our Indiana."

Bert Laws lettered on the Washington Hatchets' first Final Four basketball team in 1925. At IU, he was vice president of his sophomore class and earned a degree in education. He won freshman numerals in basketball and lettered in track.

Laws got his P.A. job because he spurned a career in teaching to work as an electrician at IU. He got the announcing job because he knew better than anyone else how IU's first public address system worked; he installed it at old Memorial Stadium. Athletic director Zora Clevenger gave him the job, starting with football and continuing with basketball when the system was moved indoors to the old IU Fieldhouse.

Laws retired after the IU-Ohio State basketball game March 5, 1977.

For more than 40 years, Bert Laws was the PA voice of IU athletics.

IN THOSE DAYS . . .

DECKARD AT HOME WITH STARS

Tommy Deckard first impressed IU coach Billy Hayes when, still at Bloomington High, he regularly worked out and ran with Hayes' world-class Hoosier runners.

Deckard's record 4:26.3 in winning the 1934 state high school mile stood for nine years. At IU, he ran on world-record relay teams, on Big Ten championship teams, and in the 1936 Olympics.

Hayes knew he was never likely to beat Don Lash in standard distance events and suggested Deckard aim at the 1940 Olympics in the steeplechase.

Deckard quickly excelled. He won the 1937 Penn Relays in 9:21.0, that meet's record for 24 years. In 1939, in a two-mile steeplechase race, he set an American record that stood until 1957.

World War II killed his Olympic dream. He served as a lieutenant commander in the navy. "I and a whole bunch of good athletes from IU, like Campbell Kane and Roy Cochran, not only missed an Olympics but had to serve in war and get shot at," Deckard said later, after a coaching career that took him to Drake University as coach and director of the Drake Relays.

Deckard died at 66 in 1982. He was inducted into IU's Athletics Hall of Fame in 1992.

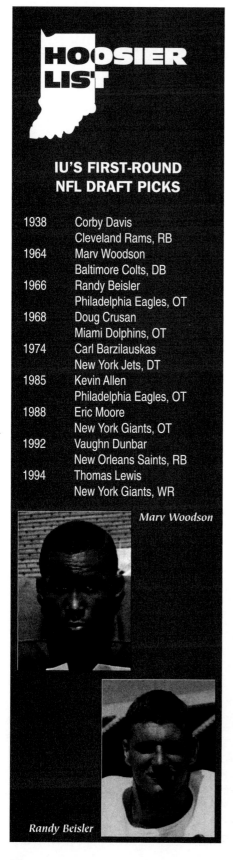

HOOSIER LIST

IU'S FIRST-ROUND NFL DRAFT PICKS

1938	Corby Davis Cleveland Rams, RB
1964	Marv Woodson Baltimore Colts, DB
1966	Randy Beisler Philadelphia Eagles, OT
1968	Doug Crusan Miami Dolphins, OT
1974	Carl Barzilauskas New York Jets, DT
1985	Kevin Allen Philadelphia Eagles, OT
1988	Eric Moore New York Giants, OT
1992	Vaughn Dunbar New Orleans Saints, RB
1994	Thomas Lewis New York Giants, WR

Marv Woodson

Randy Beisler

INDIANA LEGEND
Corby Davis

NO. 1 WITH NFL

No one ever questioned Richard Corbett Davis's toughness, but in a rawhide sport he was cursed with sensitive skin. He missed what would have been his senior season, 1936, because of boils.

When Corby Davis finally had that senior football season, it was historic.

"The greatest fullback in America," coach Bo McMillin called him. "He makes the hard plays look easy. And when the going gets tough, he gets better."

Davis, from Lowell, Indiana, was All-Big Ten and on many All-Americas. He played in the East-West Game, the College All-Star game. He was the Big Ten's Most Valuable Player.

And, in the third National Football League draft, the Cleveland Rams made Corby Davis of Indiana the No. 1 player taken. No other Hoosier ever has been the NFL's first pick.

World War II cut his pro career short, and so did that congenitally sensitive skin. A man who stormed ashore at Normandy came back from the war with feet permanently damaged by combat frostbite. He stayed in football as an official and once worked the Rose Bowl. He died on a hunting and fishing trip in 1969.

In 1991, he was inducted into IU's Athletics Hall of Fame.

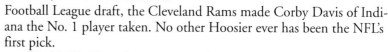

BIG TEN MEDAL - Charley McDaniel

GIMBEL AWARD - "Jick" Kenderdine

BALFOUR AWARDS
Football - Corby Davis; Basketball - Ernie Andres; Baseball - Bill Smith; Track - Mel Trutt; Wrestling - Charley McDaniel/Willard Duffy

NCAA CHAMPION
INDIVIDUAL:
Wrestling - Charley McDaniel (heavyweight)

HEAVYWEIGHTS AT TACKLE

The '37 Hoosiers had more than Corby Davis. Passer Frankie Filchock went on to an NFL career. The tackles were the NCAA's two best heavyweight wrestlers: Charley McDaniel and Bob Haak (two-time All-Big Ten in football and another future pro). Center George Miller made All-Big Ten; captain "Jick" Kenderdine was a pass-catching hero of the 1936 Purdue game.

Coach Bo McMillin, with that nucleus, sought two IU football "firsts:" three straight winning seasons and first-division Big Ten finishes.

The Hoosiers played well but lost 6-0 at Minnesota, which won the league at 6-0 and finished No. 5 in the land. Indiana lost 7-0 at No. 9 Nebraska, despite dominating play (14-1 in first downs, 263-113 in yardage) after a first-play 65-yard breakaway.

The next week, McMillin's unsinkable team won 10-0 at No. 13 Ohio State, which went 5-0 against other league teams.

Ohio State was one of four 60-minute games for Davis, who also starred as IU edged Illinois (13-6) and Iowa (3-0) to carry championship hopes into the final weekend.

Spoiler Purdue scored with two minutes left and beat McMillin for the first time, 13-7. Still, Indiana did achieve those two targeted "firsts," finishing 5-3 and third in the Big Ten.

Snapshot In Time

ANDRES FIRST TO SCORE 30

IU'S GREAT basketball link-up with Everett Dean didn't formally end till June, but his last basketball victory was 45-35 at Illinois, in a season-ending game that became historic on its own.

The Hoosiers' best player, junior guard Ernie Andres, approached game time with a heavy cold and stomach pain.

Andres, who also starred for Dean in baseball and later played in baseball's American League and the National Basketball League, played at Illinois though obviously ill.

He delivered the first 30-point performance in IU and Big Ten history, topping the league record of 29 that was shared by four. Andres sank 13 of 34 shots and four of five free throws.

Ernie Andres' 30 points against Illinois was not only an IU record but a Big Ten record as well.

Andres reached 28 points with five minutes left and asked Dean to pull him as soon as he set the record. With a minute to go, he scored on a rebound of his own miss. He was taken out immediately.

On June 8, after key hits by Andres won two big games and Dean's last IU team shared the Big Ten baseball title with Iowa, Stanford hired Dean to coach basketball and baseball.

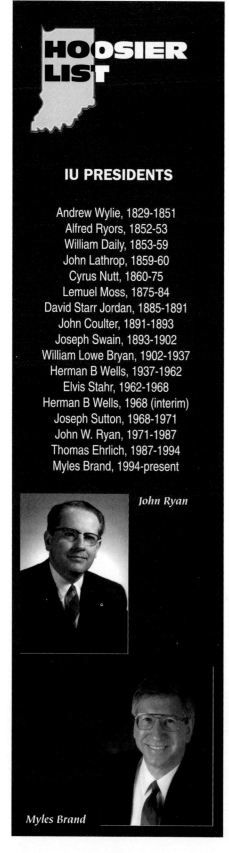
LEGEND *Herman B Wells*

HISTORIC CHOICE, AT AGE 35

Indiana University's biggest hiring of the century was no big surprise. IU trustees needed just 17 minutes at a March 22 meeting to vote in Herman B Wells as the school's new president.

His official inauguration came in the fall.

Wells was 35 when picked, the youngest president in IU history and youngest at the time at any state university in the United States.

Wells, from Jamestown in Boone County, already was experienced in the IU presidency. An IU graduate named dean of the School of Business three years earlier, he had been appointed acting president July 1, 1937, after the retirement of William Lowe Bryan.

"His observed experience, practiced wisdom, admirable temperament and high ideals give conspicuous assurance of enduring achievement," the trustees' prescient announcement statement said.

"I love to teach, love the administration of research work more than anything else in the world," Wells said. "I'm going to miss that.

"I love to talk to students."

> **Prescient trustees saw signs "of enduring achievement."**

BIG TEN MEDAL - Chris Traicoff   **GIMBEL AWARD** - Paul Graham

BALFOUR AWARDS

Football - Bob Haak; Basketball - Ernie Andres; Baseball - Tom Gwin; Track - Roy Cochran; Wrestling - Chris Traicoff

NCAA CHAMPIONS
TEAM: Cross Country (Billy Hayes)
INDIVIDUAL: Wrestling - Chris Traicoff (175)

SULLIVAN AWARD
Don Lash

IU item

FIRST NCAA CROSS COUNTRY CHAMPS

The first NCAA cross country title was won by IU's Hoosiers, (l to r) Mel Trutt, Paul Bente, Vernon Broertjes, Edgar Hedges, Harry Robins, Roger Poorman and Robert Barter.

After years of Big Ten and National AAU cross country dominance, Indiana finally got to run for an NCAA championship in the sport, and, on a nippy November day at East Lansing, Michigan, the Hoosiers won the first NCAA meet.

Captain Mel Trutt finished fourth and Ed Hedges eighth to lead the Hoosiers, whose edge over runnerup Notre Dame was 51-61.

The NCAA meet came just three days after Trutt won the Big Ten championship and led the Hoosiers to their sixth straight team title—an 11-year dominance, actually, because there was no Big Ten meet from 1933 through '37. Indiana had 30 points to 45 for runnerup Wisconsin. Harry Robins finished sixth and Hedges eighth in that meet at Purdue.

Bob Barter, Paul Bente, Vern Broertjes and Roger Poorman were the other lettermen with Trutt, Hedges and Robins on the national-championship team. Hedges, Barter, Bente and Broertjes were all sophomores, running in major meets for the first time.

Trutt had run the leadoff half-mile leg when Indiana set a world distance medley record in the spring of 1938. As a sophomore, Trutt also ran the leadoff leg when he, Jim Smith, Tommy Deckard and Don Lash set a world record in the four-mile relay by winning at the Penn Relays in 17:16.2. That stood as a world record for six years.

Snapshot In Time

TRAICOFF A BELSHAW DELIVERY

George Belshaw's route from IU wrestling great to eminent physician included a stop as basketball coach at Calumet High. He had a basketball guard there who "had a crouch I thought looked perfect for wrestling."

He was right. He sent Chris Traicoff to IU, and Billy Thom, the man who had developed George and Eddie Belshaw, did the same for Chris Traicoff, who had one of the greatest senior seasons of all the Thom-era Hoosier stars.

Traicoff finished the year unbeaten, won at his weight and captained the team that won the Big Ten championship, then went on to win the NCAA 175-pound championship. He also received IU's Big Ten Medal and its Balfour Award in wrestling.

Then he went back to Calumet and coached, basketball. Chris and cousin Carl combined to have Calumet High's basketball in the coaching hands of a Traicoff for 50 years before Carl's retirement in 1998.

Chris Traicoff's undefeated 1939 season included Big Ten and NCAA championships.

IN THOSE DAYS . . .

BO WINS WITH ALL-STARS

Bo McMillin's four-year success story at Indiana made such an impact in college football that fans elected him head coach of the 1938 College All-Stars.

With him in the game at Chicago's Soldier Field were Big Ten MVP Corby Davis and end Jim Birr, plus quarterback Frankie Filchock, who was hurt and unable to play. Davis scored the first All-Star touchdown by a Hoosier, ramming over from a yard out in the 28-16 victory over Sammy Baugh and the NFL-champion Washington Redskins.

McMillin could have used the three players in the months to come. The Hoosiers' upward climb in the Big Ten and in national respect temporarily stopped. After a 1-6-1 season ended in defeat at Purdue, McMillin said at the football banquet:

"I haven't had much experience with losing teams, and I may be wrong but I don't expect to have much experience with losing teams in the future. I want real men first and then good football players, but it doesn't hurt a man to be a winner."

At that banquet, he gave letters to an uncharacteristically high 33 players, including 22 sophomores, "to see if boys play harder wearing an I."

1939 1940

LEGEND '40 NCAA Champions

HALL OF FAMERS ABOUND ON TITLE TEAM

Tournament basketball already was part of the culture in Indiana, the state was playing its 30th high school basketball tournament in March of 1940, when the National Collegiate Athletic Association put on its first tournament.

On the night of March 31, in Kansas City's Municipal Auditorium, Jayhawk Country, Indiana ran away from Kansas, 60-42, to win that first officially backed NCAA national tournament.

Legends? That championship 1940 IU team may be the most honored basketball group in state history.

Ten players from that team are in the Indiana Basketball Hall of Fame at New Castle, Paul "Curly" Armstrong and Herm Schaefer of Fort Wayne Central, Bill and Bob Menke of Huntingburg, Bob Dro of Berne, Marv Huffman of New Castle, Jay McCreary of Frankfort, Chet Francis of Avon, Jim Gridley of Vevay and Andy Zimmer of Goodland, plus coach Branch McCracken, the man from Monrovia who also is in the Basketball Hall of Fame at Springfield, Massachusetts.

McCracken, Dro and Huffman are in IU's Athletics Hall of Fame.

They didn't get there on size. The Menke brothers were 6-3, Huffman 6-2, Francis 6-1, Schaefer and Gridley 6-0, Dro and Armstrong 5-11, and McCreary 5-10—with starters averaging 6-0, maybe the shortest of all NCAA champions.

> **With starters averaging 6-0, IU's '40 team may be the shortest of all NCAA champions.**

HOOSIER LIST

IU'S RANKING IN THE NCAA BASKETBALL TOURNAMENT

Championships

UCLA	11
Kentucky	7
Indiana	5
North Carolina	3
Cincinnati	2
Duke	2
Kansas	2
Louisville	2
No. Carolina St.	2
Oklahoma State	2
San Francisco	2

Tournament Wins

Kentucky	86
UCLA	79
North Carolina	76
Duke	65
Kansas	59
Indiana	52
Louisville	48
Michigan	41
Arkansas	39
Villanova	37
Syracuse	37
Georgetown	36
Ohio State	35
Cincinnati	34
Utah	32
UNLV	30

Final Four Appearances

UCLA	15
North Carolina	13
Kentucky	12
Duke	12
Kansas	10
Ohio State	9
Indiana	7
Arkansas	6
Cincinnati	6
Michigan	6

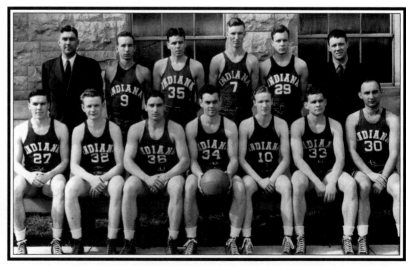

Front row (l to r): Jim Gridley, Herm Schaefer, Bob Dro, Marv Huffman, Jay McCreary, Paul (Curly) Armstrong and Ralph Dorsey. Second row: Head Coach Branch McCracken, Chet Francis, Bill Menke, Andy Zimmer, Bob Menke and assistant coach Ralph Graham.

FIRST SWEEP OVER PURDUE KEY

The 1940 tournament wasn't college basketball's first national meet, nor by history's reckoning is it counted as the NCAA's first. But it was.

In 1938, Madison Square Garden and promoter Ned Irish conducted the first National Invitation Tournament. It figured to be a crowning moment for the powerful program legendary coach Clair Bee had built at New York's own Long Island University. But, Temple came down from Philadelphia and defeated LIU in the first NIT final.

A few weeks after that, in the spring of 1938, the National Association of Basketball Coaches asked and received NCAA approval to set up its own tournament the next season. Oregon defeated Ohio State at Evanston, Illinois, for the championship of the NABC's 1939 tourney, which had a net loss of $2,531, more than the coaches' organization could afford. By the next year, the NCAA had agreed to take over the tournament, and it counted the 1939 tourney as its first.

The new rival didn't diminish the stature of the NIT, its New York base giving it a big edge over the NCAA tournament in national publicity. Colorado defeated Duquesne in the 1940 NIT finals at Madison Square Garden. Then both NIT finalists were included in the eight-team field picked for the NCAA meet by committees in each of eight geographical sections.

Butler coach Tony Hinkle's Midwest selection committee included coaches George Keogan of Notre Dame and Bill Chandler of Marquette. News accounts said their unanimous pick was Big Ten runnerup Indiana (17-3) over champion Purdue (16-4), apparently because Indiana, for the first time in series history, had swept both games from Purdue.

Acceptance of the invitation wasn't automatic. Years later, zoology professor Bill Breneman remembered the into-the-night Athletics Committee meeting that finally brought approval of IU's entry into the tournament.

Breneman, who later was IU's faculty representative to the Big Ten, also had a different memory of the invitation's source.

"Dr. William Moenkhaus was the chairman of the committee," Breneman said. "He called us together in the Faculty Lounge, (athletic director Zora) Clevenger, Bill Thornberry, Ross Bartley, Lee Norvelle, Joe Franklin, Willard Patty, Branch McCracken (and Breneman). He told us Purdue had called him and offered to waive its right to the NCAA. We were assured that the president, the athletic director and Piggy (Lambert, the Purdue coach) felt we should go, because we had beaten them twice. That was the way it was explained to us.

"We debated a long time, several hours, actually. Even Branch had reservations. He thought the team that won the championship should go.

"Finally we agreed we would take it and express our appreciation to Purdue. It really was an act of great sportsmanship on their part."

STARTED WITH SPRINGFIELD

THE NCAA'S FOUR EASTERN selections met for a two-night tournament at Butler Fieldhouse in Indianapolis. Indiana overwhelmed Springfield College the first night, 48-24, then came back against a Duquesne team that had lost just twice—38-36 to IU at Pittsburgh in December, and in the NIT finals to a Colorado team the Dukes had beaten earlier.

Indiana jumped out to a 25-13 halftime lead and, with center Bill Menke scoring 10 points and Bob Dro playing all 40 minutes, handled Duquesne more easily than in the teams' first meeting, 39-30.

The four western teams had met in Kansas City. Southern Cal, with a mostly Indiana team led by All-American Ralph Vaughn, a teammate of IU's Jay McCreary on Frankfort's 1936 state champions, dumped NIT champion Colorado. But, a step away from a colorful, Hoosier-dominated final game, USC lost to Kansas.

BIG TEN MEDAL	BALFOUR AWARDS	NCAA CHAMPIONS
Bob Hokey	Football - Jim Logan	TEAM
	Basketball - Marvin Huffman	Basketball (Branch McCracken)
GIMBEL AWARD	Baseball - Dale Gentil	
Jim Logan	Track - Archie Harris/	INDIVIDUAL
	Campbell Kane	Wrestling - Bob Antonacci (121)
	Wrestling - Chauncey McDaniel	Track - Campbell Kane, 880 (1:51.5)
		Archie Harris, discus (162-4 1/2)

85

'40 TEAM ALL-HOOSIER, ALMOST

Marvin Huffman was the first Outstanding Player award recipient at the NCAA finals.,

B ranch McCracken built IU's first national collegiate basketball championship team with Indiana players who had played on strong high school programs and enjoyed success in the tournament biggest to all Hoosiers of the era.

The only two who started every 1939-40 game were Bob Dro, who as a sophomore had led little Berne to the 16-team 1935 State tournament, and center Bill Menke, who played with brother Bob in the Huntingburg program.

Captain Marv Huffman, who had watched brother Vern lead New Castle to its only state title in 1932 before a two-sport All-America career at IU, was the team's only prominent senior. McCracken didn't start Huffman in two early Big Ten games. Otherwise, he started with Dro and Menke in every game.

With them, McCracken mixed and matched from a nucleus that included Paul "Curly" Armstrong and Herm Schaefer from Fort Wayne Central's 1936 runnerup team and Jay McCreary, captain of the Frankfort team that won the '36 tournament.

Others—Bob Menke, Andy Zimmer, Jim Gridley and Ralph Dorsey (the only non-Hoosier, from Horse Cave, Kentucky)—played in almost every game and logged some important minutes.

For the most part, though, McCracken went with some combination from his six "starters," never starting the same five-man group more than three straight games.

The Hoosiers, who started 17-1 in McCracken's first coaching season before losing their last two games at Purdue and Michigan to finish second in the Big Ten, opened the 1939-40 season with nine straight victories. At Minnesota, they trailed 29-16 at halftime, then blitzed the Gophers 20-1 to lead 36-30. With a minute and a half left, Indiana led 44-40, but the Gophers caught up, got the ball back, and won on Willie Warhol's buzzer shot from a step past center-court.

Indiana also lost 40-36 at Northwestern and by a mystifying 44-26 score at Ohio State, when the Fort Wayne Central pair, Armstrong and Schaefer, combined to hit one of 20 shots and the team shot .156 (12-for-77).

Four nights later, against a Purdue team closing in on the league championship, the Hoosiers won 45-39. That and an earlier 46-39 home-court victory represented IU's first sweep in a series Purdue led 51-11. The losses to Indiana, the only ones in league play for champion Purdue, were IU's key to the NCAA tournament.

Even in the tournament, McCracken continued his lineup shuffle. Armstrong, the Hoosiers' leading scorer and only representative on the coaches' first-team All-Big Ten, came off the bench in the first two tournament games. And when Armstrong did start again in the championship game, McCreary came off the bench to score 12 points, his season high.

In tournament play alone, Schaefer led the Hoosiers (with 31 points, to 24 for Huffman and 23 for Armstrong).

Half of Huffman's came in the championship game, though he fouled out with 14 minutes left. By then, the Hoosiers had firm command, and Huffman's play won him an honor given for the first time: Outstanding Player at the NCAA finals. His 12 points in his last college game was his highest total in more than 50 games, stretching to January of his sophomore year.

Hoosiers celebrate the championship.

Branch McCracken receives the game ball from Kansas Coach Phog Allen.

Snapshot In Time

ANTONACCI NCAA CHAMPION

BILLY THOM HAD NCAA championship hopes for his 1940 team, till key pieces started to fall away.

Defending Big Ten 155-pound champion Angelo Lazzara, who had strong grades across the board, ran into problems with a math course and was declared ineligible. His backup, Homer Faucett, was hit by a truck and never competed again for the Hoosiers.

Despite similar problems at other positions, Indiana edged Michigan 24-23 for its seventh Big Ten championship under Thom. The winning point came in the meet's last match, when co-captain Joe Roman salvaged third at 145 pounds.

At the NCAA meet, Thom dropped some of his key men one weight. One was Bob Antonacci, who had begun the season with a torn knee ligament. He lost in the Big Ten semifinals at 128 pounds.

In the NCAA meet at Illinois, 121-pounder Bob Antonacci of Hammond won, the last NCAA wrestling title a Hoosier was to win for 50 years.

His fellow NCAA semifinalists didn't fare as well. Roman (at 136 pounds, down from 145), Chauncey McDaniel (165) and Garnett "Tuffy" Inman (175) all lost in the championship match. Oklahoma A&M won at two weights and defended its NCAA championship 24-14 over runnerup Indiana.

Inman later became mayor of New Albany.

Bob Antonacci didn't win the Big Ten championship but came back to be NCAA champion.

IN THOSE DAYS . . .

EXCEPT FOR THE FOOTBALL GAME . . .

The *Bloomington Telephone* drily informed its November 13, 1939, readers:

"Thirty-six scrappin' Hoosiers unpacked their pajamas last night after returning from a three-day round trip to New York City, where they visited the Empire State Building, Central Park, Broadway, saw 'Hellzapoppin' and played a football game.

"Except for the football game, a very enjoyable time was had by all." Fordham (6-2) won 13-0 at the Polo Grounds.

For Indiana (2-4-2), the year's highlight game was a 32-29 loss at Iowa, a shootout between IU's Hal Hursh (the Big Ten's passing champion) and Iowa's Nile Kinnick (the 1939 Heisman Trophy winner).

Hursh hit 16 of 29 passes for 258 yards, in a season when teams averaged 5-for-14 for 66 yards. Kinnick passed for three touchdowns and ran 55 yards to Indiana's 3 to set up another.

Hal Hursh's 258-yard game wasn't quite good enough at Iowa.

IU's Hal Hursh had the numbers edge in pitchers' duel, but Heisman Trophy winner Nile Kinnick's team won.

Indiana lost despite scoring more points than in its nine previous games (21 in the whole 1938 season, seven in an opening tie with Nebraska). The Hoosiers scored just 34 points the rest of '39.

Hursh also was an outstanding baseball pitcher. Kinnick was one of the most beloved athletes in Iowa history; the Hawkeyes play in Nile Kinnick Stadium. Tragically, both of the game's heroes died in World War II.

1940  1941

HOOSIER LIST

McCRACKEN'S 25-GAME WIN STREAK IN OLD IU FIELDHOUSE

1939

Indiana 52, Ball State 28
Indiana 49, Miami (O.) 23
Indiana 47, Wabash 23
Indiana 71, Connecticut 38
Indiana 43, Wisconsin 19
Indiana 39, Purdue 36
Indiana 46, Ohio State 34
Indiana 44, Northwestern 37
Indiana 45, Iowa 40
Indiana 49, Minnesota 37

1940

Indiana 37, Wabash 24
Indiana 58, Xavier 24
Indiana 51, Pittsburgh 35
Indiana 38, Illinois 36
Indiana 45, Iowa 30
Indiana 46, Purdue 39
Indiana 57, Michigan 30
Indiana 38, Chicago 34
Indiana 52, Ohio State 31

1941

Indiana 44, Georgia 31
Indiana 53, Marshall 22
Indiana 52, Northwestern 32
Indiana 45, Ohio State 25
Indiana 50, Iowa 40
Indiana 44, Minnesota 34

INDIANA

LEGEND *Archie Harris*

SCHOOLBOY STAR BLOSSOMS AS A HOOSIER

As an Ocean City, New Jersey, High School junior, Archie Harris missed the discus finals at the 1936 Olympic Trials by just one place.

Harris, also an outstanding football player, later blazed the New Jersey-to-IU trail that in 15 years another great track and football star, Milt Campbell, followed.

Football end Harris lettered three years and started two. His senior year he led the Big Ten in pass receiving yards and excelled on defense. Against Michigan State, Harris caught a touchdown pass and blocked a punt for another TD in a 20-0 victory. His defense helped Indiana beat Purdue, 3-0, on a field goal by Gene White. Coaches named him second team All-Big Ten.

Harris as a junior in 1940 became IU's first Big Ten shot put champion. Outdoors, he doubled in the discus and won the NCAA discus title.

In 1941, Harris repeated his Big Ten shot put-discus double, then in the NCAA meet achieved a long-held goal: his winning mark, 174 feet, nine inches, broke the six-year-old world discus record by seven inches.

Another discus victory days later made him the only Hoosier, still, to win a field event at the NCAA and U.S. national championships in one year.

BIG TEN MEDAL - Harold Zimmer   **GIMBEL AWARD -** Bob Menke

BALFOUR AWARDS

Football - Dwight Gahm; Basketball - Bill Menke; Baseball - Don Dunker; Track - Archie Harris/Campbell Kane; Wrestling - Ben Wilson

NCAA CHAMPIONS

TEAM: Cross Country (Billy Hayes)

INDIVIDUAL: Track - Campbell Kane, 880 (1:51.2); Fred Wilt, 2-mile (9:14.4); Archie Harris, discus, (174-9) (world record)

BEAT JACKIE, BUT NOT BADGERS

Indiana's reigning NCAA basketball champions kept every key player but Marvin Huffman and entered the 1940-41 season with national popularity.

Look magazine ran a picture feature on the Hoosiers, titling the story "Point-a-Minute Men" because of Indiana's record 43.3 conference scoring average in 1940.

On a holiday trip west, the Hoosiers won 60-59 from former coach Everett Dean's Stanford team, then beat California and UCLA (51-26, despite a team-high nine points by future baseball barrier-breaker Jackie Robinson). Southern Cal ended the Hoosiers' four-game, eight-day California swing with a 41-39 victory, but two nights later the Hoosiers were in New Orleans for a 48-45 Sugar Bowl victory over Kentucky.

The Hoosiers lost at Purdue, 40-36, but seemed headed for the Big Ten championship and an NCAA tournament return till Wisconsin came into Bloomington and upset them, 38-30. It was the first home loss of the three-year McCracken era, snapping a 25-game streak.

It was no fluke. Coach Bud Foster's Wisconsin team, 11-1 in the league to Indiana's 10-2, won the NCAA championship. It was just the third NCAA tournament, and already the Big Ten had supplied two champions (Indiana and Wisconsin) and a runnerup (Ohio State, beaten by Oregon in the finals of the first tournament in 1939).

FIRST 'TRACK TRIPLE'

EVEN FOR ULTRA-SUCCESSFUL Billy Hayes, Indiana's achievements in the Hayes-coached sports in the 1940-41 competitive year were exceptional.

The Hoosiers scored the school's first "Track Triple," sweeping Big Ten team titles in cross country, indoor track and outdoor track for the only time in the Hayes era. It was another 32 years before Indiana achieved the "Triple" again.

The 1940 cross country team, behind Big Ten champion Wayne Tolliver, middle-distance great Campbell Kane and newcomer Fred Wilt, also won IU's second NCAA championship.

And the outdoor track team, on a day when Archie Harris set a world record in winning the discus, Kane won the 880 and Wilt won the two-mile, had its second-best NCAA finish ever. In competition at Stanford, IU scored 50 points to finish as runnerup to Southern Cal (81).

Wilt, from Pendleton, had begun his college career as a basketball player at Indiana Central College (now the University of Indianapolis). He transferred to IU, with hopes of running track for Billy Hayes. He became eligible in the spring of 1940 and won the Big Ten indoor two-mile title that year.

In 1941, he was unbeaten in 12 track races until teammate Tolliver beat him in the Big Ten two-mile race outdoors. Wilt came back from that loss to win the NCAA two-mile. That fall he became IU's first NCAA cross country champion.

The '40 championship team included Kay Hilkert, Vernon Broertjes, Edgar Hedges, Campbell Kane, Wayne Tollliver, Murlyn Wilson and Delmar Persinger.

IN THOSE DAYS . . .

WHITE BUCKET HERO

Bo McMillin's football frustrations at Indiana were building when he took a 2-5 team to Purdue for the season finale.

McMillin was to be known as a Purdue killer in his 14 Hoosier years, but Indiana had lost to the Boilermakers three times in a row, after a 20-20 tie in 1936, when Old Oaken Bucket time rolled around again in 1940.

Ross-Ade Stadium was soaked. Neither team could advance the football on a rain-drenched, muddy day. First downs wound up just 6-5, in Indiana's favor.

The score was 0-0 in the last minute of play when Indiana's Cobb Lewis intercepted a pass at the Indiana 35 and ran it to Purdue's 40. With three end runs, Harold "Red" Zeller moved the ball to the Boilermakers' 19. From there, with 14 seconds left, Gene White kicked a 36-yard field goal and Indiana had the Bucket back.

Starting with that victory, McMillin's teams won the Bucket battle seven times in eight years.

Game hero White was named the Hoosiers' captain for 1941; Zeller won the Big Ten Medal, and center Dwight Gahm, who snapped the ball for the winning kick, won the football Balfour Award.

HOOSIER LIST

McCRACKEN AGAINST PURDUE

1939	Indiana 39, Purdue 36 (H)
	Purdue 45, Indiana 34 (A)
1940	Indiana 46, Purdue 39 (H)
	Indiana 51, Purdue 45 (A)
1941	Purdue 40, Indiana 36 (A)
	Indiana 47, Purdue 29 (H)
1942	Indiana 40, Purdue 39 (H)
1943	Indiana 53, Purdue 35 (H)
	Purdue 41, Indiana 38 (A)
1947	Indiana 62, Purdue 46 (A)
	Indiana 54, Purdue 38 (A)
1948	Purdue 58, Indiana 49 (A)
	Purdue 51, Indiana 49 (H)
1949	Indiana 56, Purdue 42 (H)
	Indiana 56, Purdue 50 (A)
1950	Indiana 49, Purdue 39 (A)
	Indiana 60, Purdue 50 (A)
1951	Indiana 77, Purdue 56 (A)
	Indiana 68, Purdue 53 (H)
1952	Indiana 81, Purdue 77 (A)
	Indiana 93, Purdue 70 (H)
1953	Indiana 88, Purdue 75 (A)
	Indiana 113, Purdue 78 (H)
1954	Indiana 73, Purdue 67 (H)
	Indiana 86, Purdue 50 (A)
1955	Indiana 75, Purdue 62 (H)
	Purdue 92, Indiana 67 (A)
1956	Purdue 73, Indiana 71 (H)
1957	Purdue 70, Indiana 64 (A)
1958	Purdue 68, Indiana 66 (A)
	Indiana 109, Purdue 95 (H)
1959	Indiana 77, Purdue 69 (H)
	Purdue 94, Indiana 89 (A)
1960	Purdue 79, Indiana 76 (H)
1961	Purdue 64, Indiana 55 (A)
1962	Purdue 105, Indiana 93 (A)
	Indiana 88, Purdue 71 (H)
1963	Indiana 85, Purdue 71 (H)
	Indiana 74, Purdue 73 (A)
1964	Purdue 87, Indiana 84 (A)
	Indiana 92, Purdue 79 (H)
1965	Purdue 82, Indiana 70 (A)
	Indiana 90, Purdue 79 (H)

Won 28, Lost 15

INDIANA

LEGEND *Campbell Kane*

A HARRIER HOOSIER

Campbell Kane of Valparaiso High, big for his era at 6-3, went to IU hoping to play basketball. Hoosier coach Branch McCracken "wanted all his guys to go out for cross country, to get in shape," Kane said.

That's how track coach Billy Hayes discovered one of the school's all-time great runners.

Kane, fourth in the 440 at the state high school meet, surprised himself when in his cross country training he began beating some IU marks of such world-class distance stars as Don Lash and Tommy Deckard.

Lash and Deckard, though out of IU by then, still were training with Hayes for the 1940 Olympics. "I was good friends with all those guys," Kane said. "I heard about some of the trips those fellows made in track—New York, Boston, Philadelphia."

Goodbye, basketball.

"I just stuck to track."

As a sophomore, Kane won the 1940 Big Ten indoor and outdoor mile titles, then dropped to the 880 and won the NCAA championship.

The next year, Kane swept almost everything. He ran on IU's 1940 Big Ten and NCAA cross country championship team; doubled in the 880 and mile indoors and out as Indiana won both team titles, then won another NCAA 880.

Injuries took Kane out of cross country and the NCAA track meet his senior season, but he repeated his Big Ten indoor-outdoor "double-double" in the 880 and mile.

BIG TEN MEDAL - Hugh McAdams **GIMBEL AWARD -** Andy Zimmer

BALFOUR AWARDS

Football - Jim Trimble; Basketball - Andy Zimmer; Baseball - Johnny Logan; Track - Campbell Kane; Wrestling - None

NCAA CHAMPION

INDIVIDUAL: Cross Country - Fred Wilt, 20:32.1

IU item

BIG NIGHT FOR LITTLE IRV

The Indiana-Purdue basketball rivalry heated up considerably when Branch McCracken, with players brought to campus by Everett Dean, began beating Piggy Lambert and Purdue with unprecedented regularity.

IU's first home-and-home sweep of the Boilermakers in 1939-40 led to the Hoosiers' first NCAA championship. The teams split the next year, Purdue's 40-36 February victory costing Indiana a title share.

The 1941-42 schedule matched Indiana and Purdue just once, in January at IU. Purdue went into the game unbeaten in league play; IU, straight from a 64-44 flogging at Minnesota two nights before.

The littlest Hoosier, 5-9 junior Irv Swanson of LaPorte, capped what was to stand as his highest career scoring night (14 points) with a free throw that edged Indiana ahead 38-37. Purdue's Frosty Sprowl sank a long shot that seemed to swing the Boilermakers on top, but an official ruled he traveled just before launching the basket. Indiana held on to win, 40-39.

Leaving the court afterward, umpire Earl Townsend "was swarmed in" by Purdue players, the *Bloomington Telephone* game story said, "and, according to observers, Purdue's captain and guard, Don Blanken, swung a hard right off Mr. Townsend's handsome chin.

" . . . Indiana fans had no kind words for (the officials), either."

Irv Swanson scored a career-high 14 points in a 40-39 win over Purdue.

Snapshot In Time

KANE STARDOM 'ALL BILLY HAYES'

THE SPECTACULARLY SUCCESSFUL track career of "retired" basketball player Campbell Kane "was all Billy Hayes," Kane said.

"He was the one who pulled everything out of me.

"He'd say: 'Kane is a lazy runner. If you run a mile in 4:20, Kane will run 4:19. If you run 4:10, Kane will run 4:09.' He was right. I didn't want to run any faster than I had to. In practice if I was running a quarter-mile, he'd start somebody 50 yards ahead of me. He knew if we started together, I'd wait till the last 50 yards to run."

Kane went from track straight into World War II, serving as a Navy pilot. When he came out, his collegiate track eligibility gone, he considered but dismissed thoughts of re-entering training with an eye on the 1948 Olympics.

He completed work for his degree in education, then, married to the daughter of a Valparaiso contractor, studied architecture. He passed state exams in both Illinois and Indiana and became a registered architect on the way to a long, successful career that included his selection for IU's Clevenger Award (1975).

Kane was inducted into the IU Athletics Hall of Fame in 1985.

Campbell Kane at his IU Hall-of-Fame induction.

IN THOSE DAYS . . .

AN OLYMPIC SHOCK

Cancellation of the 1940 Olympics because of the war already raging in Europe was a major disappointment to Billy Hayes and to the stars he had pointed toward the Games.

Hayes' teams won the 1938 NCAA cross country championship, tied for that title in 1940, and won three events in finishing second at the 1941 NCAA track meet, all with athletes who would have been primed for the U.S. Olympic Trials.

But the 1940 Olympics, originally assigned to Helsinki but switched because of European war conditions to Tokyo, finally were scratched altogether because of war clouds there, too.

"We didn't hear of the cancellation till just a few months before," said two-time NCAA 880-yard champion Campbell Kane. "It was a big disappointment to all our guys."

That was a long, distinguished list that included 1936 Olympians Don Lash and Tommy Deckard, who had worked four years to be ready for supreme efforts; Fred Wilt, 1941 NCAA two-mile (and 1941 NCAA cross country) champion; Archie Harris, two-time NCAA discus champion (and world recordholder); Roy Cochran, 1939 AAU intermediate hurdles champion, and Kane.

Wilt and Cochran were able to come back after the war, Wilt reaching the Olympics in both 1948 and 1952 and Cochran winning two gold medals at London in 1948.

For the others, 1940 was the last Olympic chance.

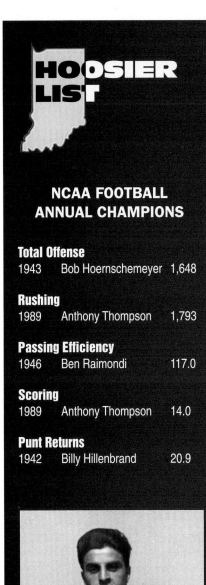

HOOSIER LIST

NCAA FOOTBALL ANNUAL CHAMPIONS

Total Offense
1943   Bob Hoernschemeyer   1,648

Rushing
1989   Anthony Thompson   1,793

Passing Efficiency
1946   Ben Raimondi   117.0

Scoring
1989   Anthony Thompson   14.0

Punt Returns
1942   Billy Hillenbrand   20.9

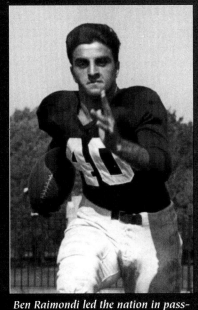

Ben Raimondi led the nation in passing efficiency in 1946.

INDIANA

⊕ LEGEND   *Billy Hillenbrand*

FIRST ALL-AMERICA BACK

Billy Hillenbrand came out of Evansville Memorial High School with rare acclaim and pulled his first surprise by spurning Notre Dame to go to Indiana and Bo McMillin.

After Hillenbrand's first college game, Grady Bennett said in the *Bloomington Telephone*: "Much has been written about him, but after seeing him in action, you can take it from us. He is the works."

After IU's 21-13 victory over '41 Rose Bowler Nebraska, the *Omaha World-Herald* said: "Hillenbrand has been acclaimed as the sophomore back of the year. These reasons encompass about everything a back is supposed to do. He accomplished them."

He led the nation in punt returns. United Press named him first-team All-Big Ten and left off the year's Heisman Trophy winner, Bruce Smith of Minnesota.

Hillenbrand was the first Indiana player to receive significant voting support in the Heisman Trophy race. He placed fifth in 1942 voting, when Frankie Sinkwich of Georgia won. Hillenbrand came in second to Sinkwich in Midwest voting. As a junior, he became IU's first consensus All-America back. When that 7-3 season ended, he enlisted in the Army. He completed degree work at IU by correspondence school, then moved straight into the pros after the war. He played one year with the Chicago Rockets, then two with the Baltimore Colts. Each year, he led his team in scoring.

Then he left football for a business career, back in his native Evansville. He was a 1983 inductee into IU's Athletics Hall of Fame.

Hillenbrand died July 17, 1994.

BIG TEN MEDAL - Fred Huff   **GIMBEL AWARD -** Guy Wellman

BALFOUR AWARDS

None Given

NCAA CHAMPIONS

TEAM:
Cross Country, co-champion/Penn State (Billy Hayes)

IU item

IU, HAMILTON LEAD SCORING BREAKTHROUGH

Ralph Hamilton set an IU record with 31 points at Iowa.

The 1942-43 season introduced the Big Ten to high scoring.

Junior Ralph Hamilton of Fort Wayne set an IU record with 31 points in a 71-55 victory at Iowa, the first time a team scored 70 points in a Big Ten game. The next two digit barriers fell before the season was over: Illinois beat Northwestern 86-44, then closed its season with a 92-25 rout of Chicago, the Maroon's 40th straight loss.

League coaches put four Illinois "Whiz Kids" on their All-Big Ten team, dominance unmatched until Indiana's 1975 team. The fifth all-league player was future NFL Hall of Famer Otto Graham of Northwestern. Hamilton and IU sophomore Ward Williams of Colfax were second-team picks by the coaches. United Press named a team of three Illini, Graham and Williams.

The Illini leader was a future basketball Hall of Famer, guard Andy Phillip, who broke other league barriers by averaging 21.3 and scoring 40 points in the Chicago game.

War broke up the "Whiz Kids" even before 1943 NCAA tournament play. As sophomores in '42, they had been eliminated in the Mideast Regional by Kentucky, 42-38.

Earlier in '42 at Bloomington, a defense led by Ed Denton held Phillip without a field goal and IU won, 41-36, the only time the teams met in those two historic Illini seasons.

Snapshot In Time

'43 HOOSIERS MIGHT HAVE BEEN IU'S BEST

OTHER TEAMS HAD better records—far better in 1945, Indiana's only unbeaten football season, and in 1967, IU's only Rose Bowl trip.

But the 1942 Hoosiers may have been the most talented team Indiana ever put on a football field, raising a legitimate question about how good the '43 team would have been without World War II.

None of that mattered when the nation's biggest and strongest were being gathered together for the collective effort that won the war. But, back from that 7-3 '42 team, in addition to All-American Billy Hillenbrand should have been IU Hall of Famers Howard Brown, Russ Deal, Pete Pihos, Lou Saban and John Tavener, plus freshmen John Cannady, Bob Hoernschemeyer and Bob Ravensberg and many other players assembled by Bo McMillin.

"I've always felt the '43 team would have been the best ever," Hillenbrand said in 1969. "We had all but one or two players back from our first 33 in that '42 team, and we were picking up a tremendous freshman class."

In a special vote of IU captains, MVPs and All-Americans that football centennial year, 1969, both Hillenbrand and Pihos voted the '42 team IU's best ever. And Pihos had played on the unbeaten '45 team.

IN THOSE DAYS . . .

WHIZZED RIGHT BY

Indiana's 1942-43 basketball team won its first 16 games, a school-record winning streak at the time, and at one point was ranked No. 2 in the nation.

But the Hoosiers had second-billing all season to the legendary team playing at Illinois at the time, a group called "The Whiz Kids."

The Illini blitzed the Big Ten to finish 12-0 and win their second straight league title. Wartime travel restrictions caused a change of normal scheduling and played a role. Both Indiana and Purdue were left without a 1943 shot at Illinois. Bud Foster, who had taken Wisconsin to the 1941 NCAA championship, fumed: "The Big Ten has handed Illinois the title with this new schedule." Foster, scoffing at the travel-restrictions justification, pointed out that Purdue was the closest team in the league to Illinois, and Indiana wasn't much farther away.

Ironically, Foster's Badgers gave Illinois all the help it needed by ending Indiana's streak 57-53 at Madison, two nights after Indiana (under wartime scheduling that minimized travel with frequent two-game visits) had won there, 51-44. The Hoosiers' only other loss was in their final game, 41-38 at Purdue, a defeat that came after Illinois had finished unbeaten to eliminate Indiana. IU had beaten Purdue 53-35 at Bloomington.

HOOSIER LIST

HOERNSCHEMEYER IN THE IU RECORD BOOK

Touchdown Passes—Game
6 Bob Hoernschemeyer vs. Nebraska, 1943
5 Jay Rodgers vs. Ball State, 1997
5 Tim Clifford vs. Colorado, 1980

Touchdown Passes—Season
14 Steve Bradley, 1983
13 Dave Schnell, 1987
13 Tim Clifford, 1979
13 Tim Clifford, 1980
13 Bob Hoernschemeyer, 1943

Touchdown Passes—Career
35 Steve Bradley, 1983-85
32 Harry Gonso, 1967-69
31 Tim Clifford, 1977-80
27 Dave Schnell, 1986-89
23 Trent Green, 1989-92
20 Bob Hoernschemeyer, 1943-44

Passing Yards—Game
408 Jay Rodgers vs. Ball State, 1997
390 Babe Laufenberg vs. Iowa, 1982
385 Antwaan Randle El vs. W. Michigan, 1998
379 John Paci vs. Penn State, 1993
345 Bob Hoernschemeyer vs. Nebraska, 1943
345 Tim Clifford vs. Colorado, 1980

Completion Percentage—Game
.786 Tim Clifford vs. Colorado, 1980
.777 Bob Hoernschemeyer vs. Nebraska, 1943
.722 Babe Laufenberg vs. Iowa, 1982

Total Offense—Game
467 Antwaan Randle El vs. W. Michigan, 1998
458 Bob Hoernschemeyer vs. Nebraska, 1943

Punt Return Yards—Season
635 Bob Hoernschemeyer, 1943
561 Billy Hillenbrand, 1941

Punt Return Yards—Career
1042 Billy Hillenbrand, 1941-42
817 Bob Hoernschemeyer, 1943-44

INDIANA

LEGEND *Bob Hoernschemeyer*

'HUNCHY' HAS BIG DAY

When World War II denied All-American Billy Hillenbrand his senior season at tailback, freshman Bob "Hunchy" Hoernschemeyer got his chance.

On October 9, 1943, Hoernschemeyer, 16 days past his 18th birthday, led Indiana over Nebraska, 54-13, with what *Chicago Tribune* sportswriter Arch Ward called "one of the most brilliant individual performances ever seen in Lincoln."

Hoernschemeyer ran for 113 yards and hit 14 of 18 passes for 345 yards and six touchdowns. Six TD passes is still the NCAA record for a freshman. The 458 yards was the NCAA freshman total-offense record until 1996 and the IU record until another freshman, Antwaan Randle El, totaled 467 yards in 1998 against Western Michigan.

Hoernschemeyer, a third-team All-American, led the nation in total offense. Only one other freshman has done that.

The 5-5 Hoosiers began in 1943, Hoernschemeyer recalled, with "only two players who had played any college ball, Pete Pihos and John Tavener." Pihos, Tavener and Hoernschemeyer are in IU's Hall of Fame.

Hoernschemeyer was the Big Ten passing leader when Indiana went 7-3 in '44 and, for the first time in school history, won four league games. In 1945, he helped No. 2 Navy to a 9-0 start but injuries cost him four games, including the year-ending 32-13 loss to No. 1 Army.

Hoernschemeyer went on to an outstanding professional career, starring on Detroit Lions teams that won NFL championships in 1952 and '53 and lost in the title game in 1954.

BIG TEN MEDAL
None Given

GIMBEL AWARD
Kermit Wahl

BALFOUR AWARDS
None Given

NCAA CHAMPIONS
None

IU LOSES ITS ROCKNE

In December 1943, Billy Hayes, a native Hoosier who came back to his home state to build the nation's model track and field program at Indiana, caught a heavy cold. The cold advanced to influenza. Late in the second week of his illness, pneumonia set in and Hayes was placed under oxygen at Bloomington Hospital. His condition grew so grave fifteen IU football players reported to the hospital to give blood.

But they couldn't save him; 59-year-old E.C. "Billy" Hayes died at 4 in the morning on Wednesday, December 13, and the campus was stunned.

President Herman B Wells called him "truly irreplaceable . . . one of the most beloved men on campus . . . his like will not soon again be seen."

At the funeral, athletic director Zora Clevenger called Hayes "the foremost coach in his field in the country." Faculty representative W. R. Breneman said, "In a school which has pointed with pride to its many educators, the sorrowful fact has dawned upon many that our finest teacher has closed his rollbook."

A memorial fund was started in his name. One of the first contributors enclosed a note that said:

"Notre Dame had its Rockne and Indiana had its Hayes."

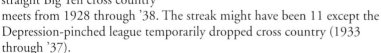

BILLY AND SID

DISTANCE RUNNING BECAME the Hoosier specialty under Billy Hayes and aide Sid Robinson, whom Hayes had developed at Mississippi State into a 1928 U.S. Olympic 1,500-meter runner. Robinson already had started toward achieving his own world-recognized eminence as a physiologist when in 1930 Hayes brought him to IU to help coach.

Sid Robinson and Don Lash at the U.S. Track Hall of Fame dinner in 1973.

Their program won six straight Big Ten cross country meets from 1928 through '38. The streak might have been 11 except the Depression-pinched league temporarily dropped cross country (1933 through '37).

With no NCAA meet either, Indiana focused on National AAU cross country team competition and dominated it. In 1936 Indiana won with a perfect score, 15, on a 1-2-3-4-5 finish.

The first NCAA cross country meet (1938) was won by Indiana, which won again in 1940 and tied for the title in 1942. The NCAA meet's team championship award was The Billy Hayes Trophy until a 1970s policy change took all names off NCAA trophies.

The distancemen helped Hayes win five Big Ten track championships and the 1932 NCAA outdoor title. Five IU athletes made the '32 and '36 Olympic teams. The number might have doubled if war hadn't canceled the 1940 Olympics, when the Hayes program was at its height.

HOOSIER LIST

HOOSIER MAJOR LEAGUERS

Ernie Andres, Boston AL (1946)

Ralph Brickner, Boston AL (1952)

John Corriden, Jr., Brooklyn (1946)

Sammy Esposito, Chicago AL (1952-63); Kansas City (1963)

Barry Jones, Pittsburgh (1986-88), Chicago AL (1988-90), Montreal (1991-92), Philadelphia (1992), New York NL (1992) Chicago AL (1993)

Ron Keller, Minnesota (1966-68)

Ted Kluszewski, Cincinnati (1945-57), Pittsburgh (1958-59), Chicago AL (1959-60), Los Angeles AL (1961)

Mike Kosman, Cincinnati (1944)

Merrill (Pinky) May, Philadelphia NL (1939-43)

Bruce Miller, San Francisco (1973-76)

Mike Modak, Cincinnati (1945)

Mickey Morandini, Philadelphia (1990-97), Chicago NL (1998-99)

Kevin Orie, Chicago NL (1997-98), Florida (1998-99)

Chris Peters, Pittsburgh (1996-99)

Kermit Wahl, Cincinnati (1944-45, 1947); Philadelphia AL (1950-51), St. Louis AL (1951)

John Wehner, Pittsburgh (1991-96), Florida (1997-98), Pittsburgh (1999)

Guy Wellman, Cincinnati (1947)

Whitey Wilshere, Philadelphia AL (1934-36)

INDIANA

LEGEND *John Tavener*

ALL-AMERICA ON WAY TO HALL

John Tavener was one of three freshman fullbacks who reported to Bo McMillin in 1940. Lou Saban and Howard Brown were the others. None stayed at fullback. All are in IU's Athletics Hall of Fame.

Tavener became a center and stands at century's end as IU's only interior lineman to make consensus All-America (1944). In 1990, he was inducted into the College Football Hall of Fame. There he joined his one-time teammate and Beta house roommate, 1966 inductee Pete Pihos, and their IU coach: 1951 inductee McMillin.

The 6-foot, 220-pound Tavener's position switch came his freshman year. "They told me later Bo always had wanted a center who could pull like a guard and lead plays and trap," Tavener said.

A head injury that freshman year caused Tavener's rejection when he tried to enter the Marines. He wound up playing four years, starting all but his first two college games. IU's first two-year captain, he led teams that beat Michigan (20-0, 1944), Ohio State (20-14, 1943) and Purdue (7-0, 20-0 and 14-6, 1941, '42 and '44).

He felt IU's 7-0 loss to unbeaten Purdue in 1943 best showed McMillin's coaching skills.

"Purdue had a great team, a lot of great players (military transfers)," Tavener said. IU, virtually all-freshman except for Tavener and Pihos, "didn't have a chance in the world," Tavener said. "In one week, Bo rigged up a 4-4 defense, a four-man line with four linebackers, worked it up himself. It all went just beautifully.

"He was way ahead of his time."

In 1991, Tavener was inducted into the IU Athletics Hall of Fame.

BIG TEN MEDAL
None

GIMBEL AWARD
Leon Kaminski

NCAA CHAMPIONS
None

BALFOUR AWARDS
None Given

IU item

'TERRIFIC COACH' THOM RETIRES

> "He was such a terrific wrestling coach that there was a time we couldn't get meets, he won so many championships other teams wouldn't meet him."
>
> —IU Athletic Director Zora Clevenger

The end of the 1945 wrestling season brought an end as well to the Billy Thom era at Indiana. Days after the season ended, Thom resigned to enter private business. Thom's 1943 team won his eighth and last Big Ten championship. Bob Bruner (128), Chet Robbins (136), Jim Wilkinson (155) and Harry Traster (175) won individual titles as IU outscored Michigan, 28-22, at Northwestern.

Thom's Indiana years also included 32 individual Big Ten titles, plus the 1932 NCAA team championship, and eight NCAA individual titles.

At the height of Thom's Hoosier era his teams won 34 straight matches.

"We were a terror in the conference," said athletic director Zora Clevenger, the man who hired him.

"He was such a terrific wrestling coach that there was a time we couldn't get meets—he won so many championships other teams wouldn't meet him."

Thom's successor was one of his greatest wrestlers, Charley McDaniel, the Bloomington native who was the only Thom wrestler to win two NCAA titles. "Charley Mac" also was an Olympian and a football starter at tackle. He went on to coach IU wrestling for 27 years and assist in football. He was the scout who watched and previewed every IU opponent in the 1967 Rose Bowl season.

Snapshot In Time

REDS, IU FORM A FRIENDSHIP

THE CINCINNATI REDS' management grew to love the team's War Duration spring training base in Bloomington, weather difference and all.

The Reds, welcomed with a community banquet March 18, 1943, played outdoors at Jordan Field, near the Student Union. When necessary, they moved across the street to Seventh Street Fieldhouse, which was spacious, with the basketball floor and bleachers out.

Cincinnati sportswriter Tom Swope, writing in *The Sporting News*, said in 1943, "The first week the Reds trained inside, 4.91 inches of rain fell outside." Manager Bill McKechnie called it "the first weatherproof camp" he had ever run and said, "I'm all for it."

After the first year there, McKechnie told IU athletic director Zora Clevenger, "If this war and baseball both continue for another year, you already have our invitation to invite us back."

IU's baseball team was working, too, and the watching Reds signed the Hoosiers' 1944 captain and Gimbel Award winner, infielder Kermit Wahl, as soon as that season ended. Wahl played his first big league game a month later.

Kermit Wahl played five seasons in the majors with Cincinnati, Philadelphia and St. Louis.

IN THOSE DAYS . . .

PYLE DEATH 'SADDENS' NATION

World War II was just four months from being over when, in early-spring 1945, America was jolted by two deaths.

On April 12, 12-year President Franklin D. Roosevelt died. On April 18, his successor, Harry S. Truman, had to announce:

"The nation is quickly saddened again by the death of Ernie Pyle. No man in this war has as well told the story of the American fighting man, as American fighting men wanted it told."

Pyle, killed by a Japanese sniper's bullet on the island of Ie Shima, was "an illustrious son" of Indiana, IU President Herman B Wells said, "a homespun Hoosier, a discerning reporter, an unexcelled interpreter of the minds and hearts of men in peace and war, and advocate for the rights of soldiers in the ranks."

Just five months earlier, Wells conferred an honorary Doctor of Humane Letters degree on the most renowned journalist ever to attend the university. Pyle left school in 1923, hours short of a degree. Now, the IU School of Journalism's building carries his name.

In January 1945, IU had lost another favorite son. Bill Menke, a prototypical student-athlete as the center on IU's 1940 NCAA basketball champions, never was seen again after the three-year Navy pilot left on a training mission to Puerto Rico.

1945 1946

HOOSIER LIST

THE '45 HOOSIERS

Head Coach
A.N. (Bo) McMillin

Assistant Coaches
John Kovach
Paul (Pooch) Harrell
Gordon Fisher
Charles McDaniel
Carl Anderson
C.A. (Tim) Temerario

Starting Lineup (Purdue game)
Bob Ravensberg, end
Ted Kluszewski, end
John Goldsberry, tackle
Russ Deal, tackle
Howard Brown, guard
Joe Sowinski, guard
John Cannady, center
Ben Raimondi, quarterback
George Taliaferro, halfback
Mel Groomes, halfback
Pete Pihos, fullback

Reserves (Lettermen)
Charles Armstrong
William Armstrong
Frank Ciolli
Dick Deranek
Bob Harbison
Allan Horn
John Kokos
Nick Lysohir
Bob Meyer
Lou Mihajlovich
Bob Miller
Tom Schwartz
Nick Sebek
Leroy Stovall

Scores
Indiana 13, Michigan 7
Indiana 7, Northwestern 7
Indiana 6, Illinois 0
Indiana 54, Nebraska 14
Indiana 52, Iowa 20
Indiana 7, Tulsa 2
Indiana 46, Cornell (Ia.) 6
Indiana 49, Minnesota 0
Indiana 19, Pittsburgh 0
Indiana 26, Purdue 0

INDIANA

LEGEND   *Ted Kluszewski*

AN IU TWO-SPORT STAR, A REDS ALL-TIMER

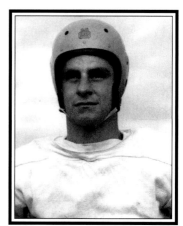

Wartime restrictions that forced the Cincinnati Reds to do their 1943-45 spring training in Bloomington gave them an unexpected bonus: one of their greatest stars.

In 1945, when IU baseball players shared facilities with them, the Reds first saw Ted Kluszewski, recruited to IU as a football end. That '45 baseball season Kluszewski, a centerfielder whose only diamond experience before college was sandlot softball back home in Argo, Illinois, hit .443, an IU record that stood for 50 years. It was a hard .443, football teammate Bob Ravensberg testified: "Ted would hit the ball and it would just sort of scream."

The impressed Reds let Kluszewski play out the championship 1945 football season, then signed him with a $15,000 bonus.

He became one of the Reds' greatest and most popular players, a four-time All-Star first baseman who hit .300 seven times. From 1953 through '55, he hit 40, 49 and 47 home runs and struck out just 34, 35 and 40 times. Kluszewski, batting coach during the "Big Red Machine" days of the 1970s, is in the Reds' Hall of Fame. In 1998 the Reds retired his jersey No. 18.

He played 15 major-league seasons. At 35 in his only World Series (with the White Sox in 1959), he set a six-game Series record with 10 RBI.

His IU teammates in that 9-0-1 1945 football season never doubted he could have been an NFL star—"the greatest tight end in the world," NFL veteran George Taliaferro said. "He was an excellent athlete, a lot more agile than his muscularity made him appear. And with those hands, he caught almost anything thrown to him."

He caught 10 passes for 112 yards and three touchdowns. Each touchdown was big: IU's first of the season, in the 13-7 victory at Michigan; the Hoosiers' next-last of the year, virtually clinching a 26-0 victory over Purdue, and a third-game Ben Raimondi bullet that came in the fourth quarter and beat Illinois, 6-0.

Kluszewski also ran the ball once on an end-around, pulled up four times on the end-around play and passed, punted once (for 52 yards), kicked an extra point, kicked off regularly (to the opponents' 5, on average), and returned one kickoff.

On defense, Kluszewski's backup, freshman basketball-football star Tom Schwartz, said, "When blockers came out around that end, they'd hit him and just bounce off, and he'd grab the runner.

"He had such great hands. In my opinion he would have been one of the best ends in the NFL."

98

TALIAFERRO GOT IT STARTED

Indiana's only undefeated football season began in a place where historically visiting teams' hopes of unbeaten seasons have died: Michigan Stadium.

The '44 Hoosiers had won there, 20-0. That doubled the difficulty for the '45 Indiana team that nevertheless opened its season with a 13-7 victory. Indiana's '44 victory "was termed one of the season's upsets," W.W. Edgar wrote in the *Detroit Free Press*. "No such claim can be made this time. Bo McMillin's men outplayed the Wolverines from the start, and only a mistake (a short punt, to the Indiana 49) prevented them from blanking the Maize and Blue."

It was a Michigan team that finished No. 6 in the land and 7-3, winning the rest of its Big Ten games and losing only to No. 1 Army and No. 2 Navy.

The game introduced Indiana tailback George Taliaferro, just 18, a freshman from Gary Roosevelt. Taliaferro ran for a net 96 yards in 20 carries, losing a 100-yard game on the last play of the game when he took a seven-yard loss running out the clock. He also hit all three passes he tried and handled the Hoosiers' punting. Maurice Shevlin of the *Chicago Tribune* called Taliaferro "a brilliant freshman;" George Barton in the *Detroit Morning Tribune* called him "185 pounds of dynamite. His brilliant running, pass catching and pass throwing played a vitally important role."

Taliaferro's running led a first-quarter drive that set up Ben Raimondi's 12-yard touchdown pass to Ted Kluszewski. In the second quarter, Mel Groomes caught Raimondi's 46-yard touchdown pass and Indiana led 13-0.

Michigan pulled close with a third-quarter touchdown and in the final minutes drove inside the Indiana 10. "They got down to our 8 in a hurry," Indiana coach Bo McMillin said. After reaching the 4, "On the third play, they didn't gain an inch," McMillin said. "On the fourth, maybe a yard."

In an *Indianapolis News* column headlined "On The Verge of Greatness," Bill Fox noted what Indiana had achieved in its back-to-back Ann Arbor visits. "Notre Dame has had some fine football teams, but Notre Dame cannot point to such triumphs over Michigan as Indiana has gained in the last two years."

George Taliaferro burst on the scene with 96 rushing yards in his first game, a 13-7 IU win at Michigan.

HISTORIC ROUT AT MINNESOTA

IF THERE WAS a moment in the 1945 season when the rest of the college football world shed its last doubts about Indiana, it was November 10 at Minnesota.

Minnesota was the Big Ten football dynasty of the era. On a bitter-cold day, a wall of scraped-off snow surrounding the field, Indiana opened a 35-0 halftime lead, hiked it to 49-0 ten minutes into the second half and played the game out with substitutes to win by that shocking 49-0 score.

In 11 years, just four teams had scored in the 20s against legendary coach Bernie Bierman's teams, which in that time had won seven Big Ten championships and five national titles.

"The disparity between these teams was so great it defies description," Wilfrid Smith wrote in the *Chicago Tribune*. "The Hoosiers just can't be as strong as they appeared."

NO AWARDS GIVEN

INDIANA

WAR HEROES RETURN TO LEAD A CHAMPION

The Indiana team that beat Michigan became a whole lot tougher, in every sense, when Pete Pihos and Howard Brown, each destined to be named to a spot on IU's 11-man All-Time Football Team, came back from the war in time to join the Hoosiers for their second game

Pihos won a battlefield promotion to Lieutenant with General George Patton's 35th Infantry Division in bloody fighting in Europe during World War II. Brown won three Purple Hearts in the same war theater.

> **"We knew we had a pretty good ball club. With Howard Brown and Pete Pihos, there wasn't any doubt."**
>
> **—George Taliaferro**

No Hoosier, ever, exuded more toughness and leadership than the two buddies from earlier IU days who—still in the Army, on 60-day leave, the war over—came back together to play for Bo McMillin in 1945.

They re-entered school on Tuesday of Northwestern week and reported that day for practice. After practicing three days, they played almost all the way when Indiana fought from behind to salvage a 7-7 tie at Northwestern.

Indiana trailed 7-0 in the fourth quarter when the Hoosiers drove to the Northwestern 6. The call was a flat pass to fullback Pihos, who caught the ball at the Northwestern 5 and determinedly carried Wildcats with him into the end zone. "I didn't know exactly what to do," Pihos said. "All I knew was I was going to get in the end zone, somehow. We had to score."

Off the bench came another last-minute team addition, kicker Charley Armstrong, a three-year bomber pilot with a Distinguished Flying Cross among his decorations. His kick tied the game.

Pihos was one of the greatest ends in the history of college and professional football, a Hall of Famer in both, but he was a fill-in fullback in '45. With Ted Kluszewski and Bob Ravensberg, end was a strength of the team McMillin had set up in Pihos's absence. So Pihos plugged a hole at fullback and played linebacker, too, an ultimate team player, a star wherever used.

Howard Brown

Brown played in the middle of the line on both offense and defense, so well that, at season's end on a team of stars, lineman Howard Brown was named IU's Most Valuable Player.

Neither started the Northwestern game, the only non-start in Pihos's college career. Northwestern's 7-0 lead came on a blocked punt in the game's opening minutes, and McMillin immediately put the two in. He never took them out.

"Howard and I were dead tired," Pihos remembered, years later. The travel agenda called for the team to stay overnight in Chicago after the game before returning home. The two Army buddies wearily went out together. "I don't drink," Pihos said, "but that night, Howard and I had a few beers."

The tie turned out to be the only blotch on the Hoosiers' 9-0-1 record, but that day in Evanston was the one when Indiana became a champion, freshman star George Taliaferro felt.

"It showed Indiana and showed the world it wasn't what we had, it was what we were going to get," Taliaferro said. "We knew we had a pretty good ball club. With Howard Brown and Pete Pihos back fulltime, there wasn't any doubt about it."

Pete Pihos

CENTER-BY-NECESSITY AN ALL-TIME STAR

John Cannady set an IU record with six interceptions in 1946.

John Cannady had no thought of replacing graduated All-American John Tavener at center when pre-season practice began in 1945. Bob Meyer had that job. After lettering at blocking back as a freshman, Cannady was hoping to win the fullback job.

"And play linebacker," Cannady said. "I always played linebacker."

On opening day at Michigan, Meyer broke a leg. Cannady had missed the game with a knee he hurt in workouts before practice began. On Monday after the Michigan game, Cannady said, "Bo threw me a football and said, 'You're the center.' I had played everything else. I figured I might as well play that."

That Saturday he played center and linebacker at Northwestern, in a 7-7 tie.

"It rained," he said. "I had never snapped the ball in the rain. The morning of the game at our hotel, Bo took me upstairs with the backs. He put six footballs in the bathtub. A coach would hand one to me, I'd snap it to the quarterback, and they ran plays right there in the room. For about 45 minutes."

Halfback George Taliaferro was one of those backs. "Everybody was Bubba to John," Taliaferro said. "He'd say, 'You gotta stay with ol' John, Bubba. This is something I never did before.' And he played center like he'd been doing it his whole life."

Cannady started at center the rest of the way, for two years.

On defense, Cannady was side-by-side with Pete Pihos, whose first game back from service also was the 7-7 tie at Northwestern. "We were the two best linebackers in the nation," Cannady said later. "You couldn't run against us."

Or pass. As a junior, linebacker Cannady set an IU record with six interceptions.

After making All-Big Ten in 1946, Cannady, with a year of eligibility left, signed with the New York Giants. When the pros went to two-platoon football in 1950, Cannady was the linebacker in a 6-1 defense. That year, the new Cleveland Browns won the NFL championship. Their only losses all year were in regular-season play to the Giants, who also finished 10-2. In a divisional playoff, the Browns and Otto Graham beat New York, 8-3, and went on from there to the championship.

> "Everybody was Bubba to John. He'd say, 'You gotta stay with ol' John, Bubba. This is something I never did before.' And he played center like he'd been doing it his whole life."
>
> —Halfback George Taliaferro

ARMY-IU: THE CLASSIC THAT DIDN'T HAPPEN

BIG TEN RULES at the time prohibited post-season play for its football teams, but there was a strong movement for a bowl matchup of Big Ten champion Indiana with national champion Army, "for war relief, at Soldier Field (in Chicago), with 125,000 people," Pete Pihos recalled.

It was the unbeaten, unchallenged Army team that always is listed among college football's greatest. It had 1945 Heisman Trophy winner Felix "Doc" Blanchard at fullback and '46 Heisman winner Glenn Davis at halfback, "Mr. Inside" and "Mr. Outside" in legendry. It whipped Notre Dame 48-0 and unbeaten Navy 32-13.

Indiana Senator Homer Capehart said, "If there is one team in the United States today which can beat the squad from West Point, that team is Indiana." Indiana Congressman Gerald Landis said an Army-Indiana game "would be the biggest athletic event of our time."

It didn't happen. The only available comparison was through Michigan, which lost to Indiana 13-7 and to Army 28-7. The Indiana game was at Ann Arbor, the week before the return of Pete Pihos and Howard Brown and the move of John Cannady to center solidified a team that grew stronger as the year went on. The Army-Michigan game was at the Cadets' second home, Yankee Stadium.

ARMY-IU? DIDN'T SCARE BO

Bo McMillin is in the College Football Hall of Fame for his legendary feats as a Centre College player. Only Amos Alonzo Stagg and Bobby Dodd are in the Hall in dual roles, as a player and as a coach. McMillin is among a handful who deserve that kind of consideration.

There was no doubt about his coaching qualifications in 1945. He swept national coaching honors, Coach of the Year by vote of his peers in the American Football Coaches Association, football's Man of the Year by vote of the Football Writers Association of America.

McMillin did his most impressive winning at two of college football's historically poor programs, Kansas State and Indiana. Until Bill Snyder built a strong program at Kansas State closing out the century, McMillin was the only coach at either school to have a winning record over a number of years.

When McMillin received his Coach of the Year Award, he made it clear he felt he had a team that could challenge even Doc Blanchard, Glenn Davis and the mighty Army club.

"I haven't seen Blanchard," McMillin said at the Coach of the Year dinner, "but until I do, I'll settle for Pete Pihos any time. He is a great football player in any position.

"I've heard a lot about DeWitt Coulter, Army's wonderful left tackle. I never saw Coulter play, but until I have, I'll take John Goldsberry, our 230-pound left tackle and the fastest man on our line.

"Maybe you've never heard of Ted Kluszewski and Bob Ravensberg, our ends. They were the best ends Fritz Crisler of Michigan saw all season, by his own quotes.

"And don't forget John Cannady, our 210-pound center."

He mentioned guards Howard Brown and Joe Sowinski and the team captain, tackle Russ "Mutt" Deal, another who was fighting in Europe in the spring.

"Our line was probably the best in the Big Ten in 10 years, the real secret of our unbeaten season and Big Ten championship," McMillin said. "That line allowed only one touchdown all season, and that was by Michigan in the first game, before Brown, Cannady and Pihos were in the lineup. Even that score was around end. It was a hell of a line . . .

"It's too bad Army had a full schedule. We'd have loved to meet them."

Surrounding coach Bo McMillin, Hoosiers celebrate 26-0 win over Purdue to cap undefeated season.

1945 Football Team—Front Row (l to r): Bob Walther, Pat Kane, Joe Gingery, Joe Postulka, Frank Bossart, Nick Sebek, Nick Lysohir, Bill Bradley, Francis Oleksak, Russell Moore, George Erath, Allan Horn, George Gallant. Second Row: Al Lesniak, Leroy Stovall, George Giljum, Bob Harbison, Charles Armstrong, Frank Ciolli, Lou Mihajlovich, Bob Meyer, Jack Adams, Bob Miller, Ted Kluszewski, Tom Sfura. Third Row: Simon Rainge, Jerry Morrical, Dick Deranek, Larry Napolitan, Don Jones, Ben Raimondi, George Taliaferro, Bob Ravensberg, Mel Groomes, Bill Stratton, John Kokos, Charles Weiss, C.R. Bauer, Joe Novosel. Fourth Row: Bob Joseph, Al Peterson, John Gorkis, Joe Sowinski, John Roper, Howard Wright, John Cannady, George Guetzloff, Art Lehman, Don Smith, Russ Deal, Chester Sanders, John Goldsberry, Tom Schwartz.

RAVENSBERG ALL-AMERICAN

JUNIOR END BOB
Ravensberg, a two-time state high school pole vault champion for Bellevue in his native Kentucky, was the 1945 Hoosiers' only consensus All-America selection. He joined Billy Hillenbrand (1942) and John Tavener (1944) as IU's only consensus All-America players up to that time.

Sophomore end Ted Kluszewski, freshman halfback George Taliaferro and junior fullback Pete Pihos were first-team All-Big Ten picks from the championship team.

Quarterback Ben Raimondi led Big Ten passers and, in an efficiency grading system adopted by the NCAA 34 years later, came out with a strong 145.1 rating for the full season. He threw 83 passes and 12 went for touchdowns, with just three interceptions.

Ravensberg, Kluszewski, Taliaferro and Pihos are all in the IU Athletics Hall of Fame.

The only consensus All-American on the '45 team was end Bob Ravensberg.

103

1946 1947

LEGEND — Lou Watson

'RIVER RAT' A FOUR-YEAR STAR

Lou Watson, tall, raw-boned and tough, provided all the qualities Branch McCracken was looking for when "The Big Sheriff" returned from three years of military duty to rebuild his basketball program.

Watson, a self-styled "River Rat" from Jeffersonville, served in the Navy after high school. McCracken recruited him to IU, and the two stayed together for most of the next 20 years.

Almost from the start, Watson gave McCracken a floor leader, and, at 6-5, one of the game's first big guards. As a freshman, he played little in seven games leading up to Big Ten play, then came off the bench to score 10 points in a 62-39 win at Ohio State. He was a starter from there on. By season's end, on that Big Ten-runnerup team, only All-American Ralph Hamilton topped rookie Watson's 8.9 league scoring average.

The rest of his career, Watson was the team leader—Most Valuable Player his last two years, captain and All-Big Ten as a senior.

He graduated with IU's career scoring record, 757 points, topping Hamilton's 646.

Watson joined McCracken's coaching staff, left for three years (1953-55) to coach at Huntington High School, then returned and was the automatic pick as head coach when McCracken retired after the 1964-65 season. His six-year tenure included a Big Ten co-championship in 1966-67.

BIG TEN MEDAL
Ralph Hamilton

GIMBEL AWARD
None Given

BALFOUR AWARDS
None Given

IUitem

A MARINE BETWEEN TWO TITLES

Earl Mitchell won Big Ten cross country titles in both 1942 and 1946.

F oremost among the trackmen whose varsity careers bridged World War II duty was Earl Mitchell, who put four years and wartime Marine duty between two Big Ten cross country championships.

Mitchell, two-time state high school mile champion at Anderson, ran a year at Butler before transferring to Billy Hayes' IU program.

Quickly, he showed he was another prize Hayes pupil. He won the '42 Big Ten two-mile indoors and ran second behind teammate Campbell Kane in the mile. Then, on boards at Cleveland, he beat the great Gil Dodds with a 4:10.7 mile.

Outdoors in '42, he took a four-second bite off Don Lash's Indiana Intercollegiates two-mile record and won the event in the annual Big Ten-Pacific Coast dual.

That fall, he won his first Big Ten cross country title in leading the Hoosiers to the team championship (IU's Charlie Labotka second, Paul Kendall seventh and Tom Judge eighth). A week later, Mitchell ran second and Labotka 10th as IU tied Penn State for the NCAA championship, Hayes' last team title.

Mitchell entered service, then returned to win the '46 Big Ten cross country championship and lead his team to a co-championship.

Had there been a 1944 Olympics, Mitchell's chances of making the team would have been good. By the resumption of the Games in 1948, he was no longer nationally competitive.

ROSE BOWL PACT A YEAR TOO LATE

IRONIES ABOUNDED IN 1946 for Bo McMillin, Pete Pihos, Howard Brown, John Cannady, Ben Raimondi, Russ Deal and all others from the unbeaten 1945 IU football team, which was denied post-season play by a Big Ten rule.

The very next year, the conference struck a deal with the Rose Bowl that carried through the rest of the century. The first team to represent the Big Ten in Pasadena was Illinois, which lost in league play only to Indiana, 14-7 at IU.

The '46 Hoosiers lost early to Cincinnati, Michigan and Iowa. They won their last four games (including a 34-20 victory over Purdue) to finish third in the Big Ten and 20th nationally, the last time in 21 years Indiana ended a season nationally ranked.

Raimondi, center Cannady and tackle Deal were first-team All-Big Ten. Pihos, hurt much of the year, was on the second team, but he was IU's MVP, "the greatest player this country has produced in the last 25 years," McMillin said.

In July, McMillin for the second time coached the College All-Stars to victory over the NFL champions, this time 16-0 over Bob Waterfield and the Rams before 97,380 at Chicago's Soldier Field.

McMillin's All-Stars included former Hoosiers Billy Hillenbrand, Bob Hoernschemeyer, John Tavener, Gene White, Chuck Jacoby and Ed Bell, plus Elroy Hirsch of Wisconsin and Otto Graham of Northwestern.

IN THOSE DAYS . . .

'A HONEY' FROM COLFAX

Ward Williams

Ward Williams was on his way to being one of Indiana's all-time best basketball players when World War II interrupted his college years.

As a rookie, sophomore Williams averaged 10.7 points a game in league play and made one All-Big Ten team.

Michigan coach Bennie Oosterbaan said, "I've never seen a sophomore in this league with the poise that Williams demonstrates under fire."

Oosterbaan asked Indiana coach Branch McCracken where he had found Williams. McCracken told Oosterbaan he was traveling in northern Indiana when he heard about a team and a player worth seeing "at a Hoosier crossroad known as Colfax. I just slipped in the back door of the Colfax gym on a Friday night and you saw tonight what I saw then. "He's a honey, isn't he?"

After that season, Williams spent three years in military service. He rejoined IU and McCracken in the fall of 1946 for his last two college seasons.

As a senior in the 1947-48 season, he was the Hoosiers' captain and MVP.

HOOSIER LIST

BIG TEN MEDALS
(continued)

1958	Gregory Bell
1959	Ronald Walden
1960	Donald Noone
1961	Gary Long
1962	William Elyea
1963	Chester Jastremski
1964	James Binkley
1965	Douglas Spicer
1966	Wayne Witmer
1967	Kenneth Sitzberger
1968	Eugene Denisar
1969	Richard Fuhs
1970	William Wolfe
1971	Mark Stevens
1972	Chuck Thomson
1973	Gary Hall
1974	Dan Hayes
1975	Orlando Fernandez
1976	Bruce Dickson
1977	James Montgomery
1978	Richard Hofstetter
1979	David Abrams
1980	Marc Schlatter
1981	Kevin Speer
1982	Bob Stephenson
1983	Tony Nelson
1984	George Gianakopoulos
1985	Uwe Blab
1986	Terry Brahm
1987	Steve Alford
1988	Sven Salumaa
1989	Simon Katner
1990	Scott Holman
1991	Scott Boatman
1992	Mark Hagen
1993	Dave Held
1994	Vito Maurici
1995	Erik Barrett
1996	John Hammerstein
1997	Tom Lukawski
1998	Rob Iglinski
1999	Bryan Holcomb

INDIANA

LEGEND   *Roy Cochran*

DECADE LATE, TWO GOLDS

Roy Cochran was five years old when his brother Commodore won a gold medal in the 4x400-meter relay at the 1924 Paris Olympics.

Commodore, known as Com, or Racehorse, had won two NCAA 440-yard dash titles for coach Billy Hayes at Mississippi State. When Roy came along, Hayes was at Indiana. Recruitment was automatic.

Roy was an immediate Hoosier star. As a sophomore in 1939, he won the Drake Relays 440-yard intermediate hurdles and the Big Ten 220-yard low hurdles, then introduced himself nationally by winning the AAU 400-meter intermediate hurdles. With a year to go to the 1940 Olympics, he was ranked best in the world in the intermediates.

A few months after that, war cancelled the 1940 Olympics.

At IU, Cochran kept adding laurels. He won the 440 at the Big Ten indoor meet as a junior. As a senior, he won the Big Ten 440 indoors and out and the team won both meets.

Cochran was serving at Great Lakes Naval Training Center when, back at Drake on April 25, 1942, he won his second 440-yard intermediate hurdles title and set a world record: 52.2 seconds.

Then he went to war.

In June 1948, at 29, he returned to track, specializing in the 400-meter intermediate hurdles. Nine years after his first National AAU title, he added his second. In the Olympic Trials at Evanston, Illinois, he beat the young stars of the NCAA meet and had his Olympic chance.

And at London, he blew away the field, winning his gold medal. A week later, he ran the third leg as America won the 4x400-meter relay—a second gold for Roy, a second for the Cochran family in that one event.

BIG TEN MEDAL - LeRoy Deal

GIMBEL AWARD - Ward Williams

BALFOUR AWARDS

Football - Howard Brown; Basketball - Ward Williams; Baseball - Bill Stearman; Track - Chuck Peters; Wrestling - Chet Robbins

OLYMPIC MEDALIST

Track - Roy Cochran, 400 hurdles, gold (51.1), 4x400 relay, gold (3:10.4)

IU ITEM

BO, SENIORS GO OUT WINNING

O n the afternoon of November 22, Rex Grossman kicked a 30-yard field goal early in the fourth quarter to give underdog Indiana a 16-0 lead over Purdue. The Boilermakers scored two late touchdowns to make the game close, 16-14. Hoosier coach Bo McMillin, boosting his Old Oaken Bucket record to 9-4-1, was unrattled by the Purdue rally. As was his custom, he played out the final minutes with his seniors on the field, starters and non-starters.

"There are other Indiana-Purdue games coming," McMillin said. "Our seniors have meant too much to Indiana football for the coaches to have denied their request to play."

There were other Indiana-Purdue games to come, but not for McMillin. The most successful IU football coach in history was hearing some grumbles at the end of the 5-3-1 season, despite four straight Bucket victories and a 7-1 record against Purdue in the '40s, despite the unbeaten season, Big Ten championship and No. 4 national ranking just two years earlier.

McMillin had moved up to the dual role of football coach and athletic director after Zora Clevenger's retirement the year before. Three months after the 16-14 victory over Purdue, McMillin, 63-48-11 in 14 IU seasons, resigned both jobs and signed a $30,000 contract as coach of the Detroit Lions.

Rex Grossman helped beat Purdue in 1947. Sons Dan and Dobby also played football at IU.

Snapshot In Time

A BARRIER FALLS IN BLOOMINGTON

BIG TEN BAS-KETBALL history was made in the Bryan Hall office of Indiana University president Herman B Wells in late-spring 1947.

Shelbyville and "Mr. Basketball" Bill Garrett were the state's heroes of the hour after they had whipped unbeaten Terre Haute Garfield and its 6-9 junior star, Clyde Lovellette, in the state championship game.

Coach Branch McCracken and Bill Garrett.

Wells, when he was inducted into IU's Athletics Hall of Fame, told of being approached by Shelbyville alumni on Garrett's behalf. "I was astonished to learn that we didn't recruit black basketball players," Wells said.

"I called Branch (McCracken) in and asked him if he'd like to have Bill Garrett next fall. He said, 'Of course I'd like to, but there is a gentleman's agreement in the Big Ten that we won't recruit black players. My fellow coaches may make it hard for me.'

"I told him, 'I happen to be chairman (of the Big Ten presidents' organization) this year. If any of the other coaches says so much as one word to you, you tell me and I'll take it to his president, and that will be the last word you will hear about it, I'm sure.'"

Wells, McCracken and IU made Bill Garrett the first African-American basketball player in Big Ten history, to the great benefit of all.

IN THOSE DAYS . . .

FOR OPENERS: THREE COACHES-TO-BE

December 12, 1919, junior Everett Dean scored 16 points as Indiana opened its basketball season with a 32-10 victory over the North American Gymnastics Union.

Dean's performance set a record for an IU player in a season opener.

It stood as that for 10 years, until December 7, 1929, when Branch McCracken opened his All-America senior season with 19 points in a 26-24 loss at DePauw.

McCracken's record stood for 18 years, until December 6, 1947, when sophomore Lou Watson scored 22 points when that team opened with a 59-43 victory over DePauw.

Dean was McCracken's coach.

McCracken was Watson's coach.

Watson succeeded McCracken as coach, the three opening-game recordholders combining to hold the IU basketball coaching position for 44 seasons, from 1924-25 through 1970-71 (interrupted by McCracken's service duty from 1944-46).

Watson's opening-game record fell December 4, 1955, when Wally Choice scored 29 points in a 77-66 win over Valparaiso.

IU's opening game scoring record, as the century ends, is 35, by Jimmy Rayl in a 90-59 victory over Virginia on December 1, 1962.

HOOSIER LIST

IU'S BIG TEN CHAMPIONSHIPS

Indiana has won 149 Big Ten men's and women's championships, third all-time behind Michigan and Illinois among conference schools. (*co-championship)

23 Men's Swimming (1961, 1962, 1963, 1964, 1965, 1966, 1967, 1968, 1969, 1970, 1971, 1972, 1973,1974, 1975, 1976, 1977, 1978, 1979, 1980, 1983, 1984,1985)

19 Men's Basketball (1926*, 1928*, 1936*, 1953, 1954, 1957*, 1958, 1967*, 1973, 1974*, 1975, 1976, 1980, 1981, 1983, 1987*, 1989, 1991*, 1993)

15 Men's Indoor Track (1932, 1933, 1941, 1957, 1973, 1974, 1975, 1979, 1980,1983, 1984, 1985, 1990, 1991, 1992)

13 Men's Cross Country (1928, 1929, 1930, 1931, 1932, 1938, 1940, 1942, 1946*, 1967, 1972, 1973, 1980*)

13 Women's Tennis (1982, 1983, 1984, 1987, 1988, 1989, 1990, 1991, 1992, 1993, 1994, 1995, 1998)

12 Men's Outdoor Track (1936, 1941, 1950, 1957, 1970, 1971, 1973, 1974,1979, 1985, 1990, 1991)

12 Wrestling (1914, 1921, 1924*, 1925*, 1931, 1932*, 1933, 1934, 1936, 1939, 1940, 1943)

8 Men's Golf (1962, 1968, 1970, 1973, 1974, 1975, 1991, 1998)

7 Women's Golf (1986, 1987, 1990, 1992, 1995, 1996, 1998)

7 Men's Soccer (1991, 1992, 1994, 1995*, 1996, 1997, 1998)

5 Men's Tennis (1921*, 1952, 1953, 1954, 1964)

4 Baseball (1925, 1932, 1938*, 1949*)

3 Softball (1983, 1986, 1994)

2 Football (1945, 1967*)

2 Women's Cross Country (1989, 1990)

2 Women's Indoor Track (1988, 1991)

1 Women's Basketball (1983*)

1 Women's Soccer (1997)

INDIANA

LEGEND *George Taliaferro*

'DEVASTATING,' AND HISTORIC

George Taliaferro's debut game may have been the best any IU football freshman ever had, importance of the performance and the game factored in. It started him on a career that established him as not just one of Indiana's but college football's all-time best.

Taliaferro didn't score in IU's 13-7 opening victory at Michigan, but in the first quarter when Indiana drove 56 yards to jump ahead, Taliaferro ran for 14, passed for 14, ran for 13, then slashed into the Michigan end zone, only to lose the touchdown to a holding call. Indiana got the touchdown anyway, on Ben Raimondi's pass to Ted Kluszewski, but Taliaferro's role as a gifted running back was established. Bill Fox in *The Indianapolis News* called Taliaferro "devastating. Inside the tackles and around the end, this sturdy lad ran beautifully."

Four weeks later at Iowa, Taliaferro scored on runs of 62 and 73 yards as Indiana opened a 52-0 lead and won, 52-20. In the *Des Moines Sunday Register*, Bert McGrane described the 73-yard run: "Mr. Taliaferro busted through left guard and simply flew into the Iowa secondary, then through it like a startled deer."

Taliaferro started the shocking 49-0 rout at Minnesota by returning the opening kickoff 94 yards, to Minnesota's 4. On the next play, he lost the ball on a fumble. An interception stopped the Hoosiers the next time they got inside Minnesota's 10. Very little stopped them afterward. Taliaferro scored the first three touchdowns, one on an 82-yard interception return, then sat out the second half.

Taliaferro ended his freshman season as the only Big Ten back who averaged more than 100 yards a game running and passing. Just 18 through that season, he entered the army before his sophomore year came. He returned to play in 1947 and '48, making at least one All-America team each of his three IU seasons and All-Big Ten twice. He gave up his last year of eligibility to turn pro, with the Los Angeles Dons of the All-American Conference, after the Chicago Bears made him the first black athlete ever drafted in the NFL.

He was the AAC's Rookie of the Year in 1949. In a seven-year career that wound up in the NFL with the Baltimore Colts, Taliaferro was a three-time Pro Bowl selection.

In 1972, he returned to IU as a special assistant to President John Ryan. In 1981, he was inducted into the College Football Hall of Fame and in 1992, into IU's Athletics Hall of Fame.

BIG TEN MEDAL
Joe Lawecki

GIMBEL AWARD
Don Ritter

BALFOUR AWARDS

Football - John McDonnell; Basketball - Lou Watson; Baseball - Don Ritter; Track - Chuck Peters; Wrestling - Andy Puchany

COURTING A BASEBALL TITLE

A major leaguer himself in both baseball and basketball, new IU baseball coach Ernie Andres won right away with a team built around basketball players.

Second baseman Gene Ring (.349) and first baseman Don "Tex" Ritter (.387) hit third and fourth. Bill Tosheff (6-1) led the pitchers. Lou Watson (.325) was a backup outfielder. All were basketball players, good ones. Watson set IU's career scoring record; Tosheff set a Big Ten record by hitting his last 28 straight free throws and went on to an NBA career; Ritter led IU in scoring as a junior; Ring was a fiery, effective guard.

Ring, Ritter and Bill Stearman, a future Indiana high school basketball coaching great at Columbus, had big hits when the Hoosiers won 8-5 at Purdue to move within a game of an outright Big Ten championship. The next day, IU lost 7-1 at Purdue, which blew a chance for its first championship since 1909 by losing a season-ending doubleheader at Ohio State. Purdue's coup de grace was a two-homer, six-RBI day by Buckeye first baseman Fred Taylor, who after playing pro baseball had a Hall of Fame career as Ohio State's basketball coach.

Indiana, Iowa and Michigan (8-4) shared the championship, Purdue finishing 7-5 and Ohio State 6-6. Indiana, in its first NCAA tournament, lost 8-3 at Western Michigan.

Ritter, from Aurora, won the Big Ten batting title at .439 with a league-record 25 hits. He was named first-team All-America.

Andres had the longest tenure of any IU baseball coach, 25 years, and his teams won 388 games. The title share was his only one, and, as the century closed, IU's most recent regular season crown.

Indiana's 1949 Big Ten champions were led by first-year coach Ernie Andres.

Snapshot In Time

THE MAN CALLED 'POOCH'

In the late 1920s, Paul "Pooch" Harrell enjoyed a good football career at IU and left behind some baseball batting records that still weren't challenged when the century ended.

After signing with the Cincinnati Reds and playing pro baseball for a season, he returned to IU to coach. But Harrell's most lasting contributions to the university came as an administrator.

"Pooch" was IU's head baseball coach from 1939 through '47, and he assisted Bo McMillin in football. In 1948, when coach-athletic director McMillin left to go to the Detroit Lions, Harrell became athletic director.

He stayed in that role until 1954, when health problems led to his reassignment to coordinate IU's athletic facilities expansion. The direct results were the new Memorial Stadium, opened in 1960, and Assembly Hall, dedicated in 1971.

"There was a big boom all around the conference after the war," Harrell said. "When everybody else was building bigger and better facilities, we were building steel bleachers on an outdated football stadium."

First plans for the present complex seven blocks north of what was then the campus edge were developed in 1949. President Herman B Wells gave final approval in 1953.

Harrell died in 1973. He was elected to IU's Athletics Hall of Fame in 1983.

Paul "Pooch" Harrell

IN THOSE DAYS . . .

GARRETT WINNER IN DEBUT

Twelve months after Jackie Robinson ended major league baseball's color barrier, Bill Garrett quietly brought one down in Bloomington.

On December 4, 1948, at IU Fieldhouse, the 6-foot-2 sophomore from Shelbyville started the season opener against DePauw and contributed eight points to the Hoosiers' 61-48 victory.

In the same building five weeks later, on January 8, 1949, before a full house of 10,013, Garrett became the first African-American to play in a Big Ten basketball game. Illinois won the game, 44-42, as Garrett scored just two points, but the Hoosiers went on to a 14-8 season, 6-6 in the Big Ten.

HOOSIER LIST

IU'S BIG TEN SPRINT DOUBLES IN TRACK

Indoor

1975 Mike McFarland, 60 and 300 yards
1986 Albert Robinson, 55 meters and 300 yards

Outdoor

1948 Chuck Peters, 100 and 220 yards
1949 Chuck Peters, 100 and 220 yards
1950 Chuck Peters, 100 and 220 yards
1969 Larry Highbaugh, 100 and 220 yards
1984 Albert Robinson, 100 and 200 meters
1985 Albert Robinson, 100 and 200 meters

Mike McFarland doubled in the sprints at the 1975 indoor meet.

INDIANA LEGEND — *Chuck Peters*

THE ONLY 'TRIPLE-DOUBLE'

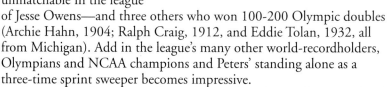

Chuck Peters as an 85-pound high school freshman wrestled at 125 pounds and went 0-15. Then he tried cross country running.

It wasn't the usual path to success for a track sprinter who did something no other Big Ten sprinter has matched.

Peters, from Blue Island, Illinois, won both sprints at three straight Big Ten outdoor meets.

That doesn't sound unmatchable in the league of Jesse Owens—and three others who won 100-200 Olympic doubles (Archie Hahn, 1904; Ralph Craig, 1912, and Eddie Tolan, 1932, all from Michigan). Add in the league's many other world-recordholders, Olympians and NCAA champions and Peters' standing alone as a three-time sprint sweeper becomes impressive.

Peters won the 220 and finished second in the 100 for Blue Island at the 1945 Illinois state high school meet. He seemed headed to Illinois but a chance trip to a 1946 Indiana football game brought introduction to IU track coach Gordon Fisher and a revision of college plans. In his first Big Ten outdoor meet as a freshman in 1947, Peters placed in the two sprints.

The next three years, he swept them.

Since then, half a dozen sprinters have doubled at two straight Big Ten meets, or two out of three—including Indiana's Albert Robinson in 1984 and 1985. But the Chuck Peters "Triple-Double" of 1948, '49 and '50 stands alone.

Peters went on to coach for more than 30 years while heading the Science Department at Evanston, Illinois, High. He married Jean Robinson, daughter of Sid and Aline Robinson. Both Peters and Sid Robinson (an eminent physiologist who coached cross country at IU) are in Indiana's Athletics Hall of Fame, and Aline Robinson's name is on awards given annually in each IU women's sport.

BIG TEN MEDAL - Walt Bartkiewicz   **GIMBEL AWARD** - James Roberson
BALFOUR AWARDS -
Football-Walt Bartkiewicz; Basketball-Lou Watson; Baseball-Willard Litz; Track-Chuck Peters; Wrestling-Bob Brabender; Swimming-Larry Meyer; Gymnastics-Norm Schulte; Golf-Bob Cleveland; Tennis-Tom Hay

IUitem

CROWD FAVORITE STUTEVILLE KILLED

Jerry Stuteville had a team-high 12.3 scoring average in the Big Ten.

Seven games into his junior season, Jerry Stuteville had scored just four points. Then he came off the bench to rally Indiana from behind to a 50-47 victory over Notre Dame in the Hoosier Classic at Butler Fieldhouse in late December.

From there on, the fiery 6-3 forward from Attica was a crowd favorite and a starter. As a senior, his pell-mell play earned him a school-record 95 free-throw points, and his 12.3 Big Ten scoring average tied Bill Garrett for the team lead.

The last weekend of the season, he scored 18 points in a 59-53 loss to Iowa and 20 as Illinois fell, 80-66. He was invited to play with an Indiana All-Star team in an exhibition game against the NBA Indianapolis Olympians, and he scored nine points. The Olympians and Sheboygan Redskins offered him contracts for the next season, and he had three high school coaching offers.

He was to pick up his degree in education at commencement exercises June 12. Early on the morning of May 30, he and two friends were headed for Indianapolis and the 500-Mile Race when the car Stuteville was driving sideswiped a truck on a narrow bridge seven miles southwest of Indianapolis. The car slammed against the bridge and Stuteville, 22, died instantly of a broken neck.

> **Two pro contracts, three coaching offers for popular Jerry Stuteville.**

Snapshot In Time

SEVENTH TO FIRST

INIDANA FINISHED SEVENTH in the nine-team Big Ten indoor track and field championships in 1950.

Never—before or since—has a team that finished lower than fifth indoors come back to win the outdoor championship that same year. The 1950 Hoosiers did, because outdoors they got two events, rather than one, from:

• Chuck Peters, who won the 100 and 220 (the only indoor sprint was the 60);

• Weightmen Clifton "Doc" Anderson (the Big Ten pass receiving leader) and Jim Roberson, who went 1-2 in the shot put with an additional second-place from Roberson in the discus (the discus is unthinkable indoors).

The '50 outdoor Hoosiers had one other big advantage: basketball star Bill Garrett was available.

Garrett, a state-meet hurdler at Shelbyville High, ran courageously in the Big Ten meet with a gashed heel and finished second in the 440, for four points.

Peters and Garrett also were factors when the meet came down to the mile relay. Kevin Grindlay and Phil Snyder kept Indiana alive on the opening legs. Peters, summoned back from the showers to run for the first time in the relay, delivered a strong third leg. Garrett's 49.5 anchor leg brought Indiana in fourth, just ahead of Minnesota—the champion if those positions had been reversed.

Indiana scored 37 points, Minnesota and Illinois 36. It was IU's first track championship in nine years and the first of three Big Ten crowns for 15-year coach Gordon Fisher.

IN THOSE DAYS . . .

BASKETBALL TV OKAYED

The Big Ten, operating with nine members after the University of Chicago's pullout in 1946, reached full membership again by admitting Michigan State for the start of competition in the 1950-51 season.

Meanwhile, the league's administrative bodies searched for answers to a brand new problem:

Television.

At its spring meeting in 1950, the Big Ten's faculty representatives banned live telecasts of football games played at member schools. "Deferred" television was permitted.

In July, the league approved a one-year experiment allowing theater television of 1950 games.

It was another season before the league formally allowed its members "to cooperate with the NCAA in the conduct of any controlled experiments" with any live football telecasts "which the NCAA might consider to be worthwhile for experimental purposes."

The faculty representatives "further voted that conference institutions (in 1951) could make available for general simultaneous television broadcast any other intercollegiate contest under their control."

Translation: basketball, too, could be televised.

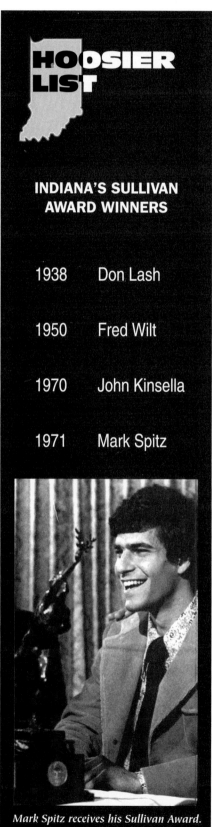

HOOSIER LIST

INDIANA'S SULLIVAN AWARD WINNERS

1938   Don Lash

1950   Fred Wilt

1970   John Kinsella

1971   Mark Spitz

Mark Spitz receives his Sullivan Award.

INDIANA

✦ LEGEND   *Bill Garrett*

LAST OF THE GREAT 6-2 CENTERS

Bill Garrett was—in Indiana University, Big Ten and even national intercollegiate athletics—a first and a last:

• The first African-American basketball player in the Big Ten;

• The last 6-foot-2 center to win All-America honors.

The Sporting News named Garrett to its All-America first team after Garrett led Indiana to a 19-3 record, best among Big Ten teams although Illinois (12-1 in league play) edged the Hoosiers (11-2) for the Big Ten championship and NCAA tournament bid.

Indiana finished seventh in the final Associated Press poll, behind two teams it had defeated. Kansas State, No. 4 in the poll and runnerup to Kentucky in the NCAA tournament, lost to Indiana 58-52 in the dedication game for its new Ahearn Fieldhouse. Illinois, which lost to Kentucky in the NCAA semifinals, split with the Hoosiers—a 71-65 Illini win at Champaign February 19 deciding the league race.

Indiana also had lost 64-62 at Peoria (to a Bradley team that had the stars back from its team that had been runnerup in both the NCAA and NIT the year before), and 61-54 at Minnesota—the one slip that separated Illinois and Indiana in the final standings.

Garrett led his team in scoring each of his three seasons and graduated with IU's career scoring record, 792 points. "Mr. Basketball" on Shelbyville's 1947 state champions, Garrett coached Indianapolis Attucks to the 1959 championship, the second man to play on a state champion and coach one. Heart problems forced him out of coaching and led to his death in 1974, in his mid-40s.

In 1984, he was inducted into IU's Athletics Hall of Fame. Shelbyville's handsome gymnasium carries his name.

BIG TEN MEDAL - Jack Phillips   **GIMBEL AWARD -** Ed Reisig

BALFOUR AWARDS
Football - Ernie Kovatch; Basketball - Bill Garrett; Baseball - Gene Ring; Track - Cliff Anderson; Wrestling - Harry Arthur; Swimming - Larry Meyer; Gymnastics - George Cross; Golf - Charles Schultz, Jr.; Tennis - Jim Shannon

SULLIVAN AWARD - Fred Wilt

IU item

WILT WINS SULLIVAN AWARD

F red Wilt was nearly 30 when he won the 1950 James Sullivan Award as America's top amateur athlete.

Even more meaningful to two-time Olympian Wilt was that he was the last great runner representing Billy Hayes in championship international competition.

"With the exception of my mother, Coach Hayes influenced my life more than any other individual," Wilt said. Hayes, he said, "inspired unbelievable confidence."

Hayes, who died in 1943, got Wilt as a transfer from Indiana Central and a convert to track from basketball. Wilt won NCAA two-mile and cross country championships for Hayes in 1941, then entered the navy. After the war, he began a 30-year career with the FBI, and continued to run.

He made the 1948 and '52 Olympic teams, won three straight U.S. 5,000-meter titles (1949-51) and one in the 10,000 and, in the summer of 1950, set American records at 3,000 and 5,000 meters. He set an American mile record indoors (4:05.5) and won four straight U.S. 3,000-meter championships indoors, and three national cross country titles.

After retirement from the FBI, Wilt coached women's track and field at Purdue for 11 years. He wrote 20 books on track and field physiology, and he was named to the IU Athletics, USA Track and Field, and New York Athletic Club halls of fame. He died at 73 in 1994.

Fred Wilt was the second of four Hoosiers to win the Sullivan Award, symbolic of America's top amateur athlete.

Snapshot In Time

THE DAY NOTRE DAME FELL AT IU

NOTRE DAME OPENED the 1950 football season ranked No. 1, carrying the longest unbeaten streak in school history—39 when, in the second game of the season, Purdue shocked the Irish, 28-14.

Two weeks later, Notre Dame was 2-1 and No. 10 in the land when it came to IU's Memorial Stadium.

Indiana jumped ahead 6-0 in the first six minutes on Lou D'Achille's touchdown pass to Don Luft. The Hoosiers led 13-0 at halftime.

Sophomore Bobby Robertson's 83-yard touchdown run on the first play of the second half set up a 20-7 Hoosier victory.

In the jubilant locker room, third-year coach Clyde Smith counseled his players, "Go to your classes on Monday. Act as if nothing has happened."

There were few classes Monday. The Page 1 headline on the Monday afternoon Bloomington *Herald-Telephone* read "IU In 'Unequaled' Victory Celebration," with a picture that showed "thousands of joyous IU students" packing the Courthouse Square Sunday night, more than 30 hours after the game.

Smith's advice was good, but wasted. Indiana came out of the game 2-1-1, popping into the polls at 16th, but lost the next week to Illinois, 20-0, and beat only Marquette the rest of the way in a 3-5-1, eighth-place season.

IN THOSE DAYS . . .

LITTLE 500 LAUNCHED

After five hours of competition, Bob Moore crossed the finish line to a standing ovation as South Hall won IU's first Little 500 bicycle race.

Glen Wilson, John Skomp and captain Russ Keller completed the first championship team on a sun-blessed day before 7,000 at old Memorial Stadium.

South Hall averaged 18.99 mph and won by more than four minutes—about five laps—over runnerup Sigma Alpha Epsilon. South Hall was in the pits for more than three minutes getting a bent pedal straightened after a 150th-lap accident.

The same day at Indianapolis, Duke Nalon averaged a record 136.498 in putting the popular Novi on the Indy pole. He did it while Tony Hulman Jr. and Speedway president Wilbur Shaw were in Bloomington. They rode with IU President Herman B Wells in the pace car, and Indy starter Seth Klein sent the pack off with a green flag. The renowned Voice of the 500, Sid Collins, joined with IU's Bert Laws as the track announcers for the first "Little Five."

The race grossed $10,000 for student scholarships. It was the idea of IU Foundation executive director Howard S. "Howdy" Wilcox, who predicted a "humdinger" of a second edition in 1952. "The way the fans turned out this year was proof enough for me that the race holds their interest."

HOOSIER LIST

MEDAL COUNT OF IU ATHLETES AT SUMMER OLYMPIC GAMES

Year Site	Gold	Silver	Bronze	Total
1904 St. Louis	0	2	0	2
1908 London	0	0	0	0
1912 Stockholm	0	0	0	0
1920 Antwerp	0	0	0	0
1924 Paris	0	0	0	0
1928 Amsterdam	0	0	0	0
1932 Los Angeles	1	0	0	1
1936 Berlin	0	1	0	1
1948 London	2	0	0	2
1952 Helsinki	1	1	0	2
1956 Melbourne	2	1	1	4
1960 Rome	4	2	1	7
1964 Tokyo	7	1	4	12
1968 Mexico City	7	5	5	17
1972 Munich	11	3	1	15
1976 Montreal	5	0	2	7
1980 Moscow	1	0	2	3
1984 Los Angeles	2	0	2	4
1988 Seoul	1	0	0	1
1992 Barcelona	1	0	0	1
1996 Atlanta	0	0	1	1
	45	**16**	**19**	**80**

INDIANA

LEGEND *Gene Gedman*

'POWER RUNNER WITH SPEED'

Throughout his Indiana years Eugene William Gedman was known as both Gene and Pat. But he was known, early.

In his fourth college game, sophomore Gedman returned a punt 65 yards to set up Indiana's first touchdown in its 20-7 victory over Notre Dame. In a 13-6 victory over Pittsburgh, junior Gedman— from Duquesne, just outside Pittsburgh—broke an 85-yard touchdown run. His 187 yards that day set an IU record that stood for 24 years.

He ended that season with an IU-record 731 rushing yards, 240 more as a receiver, 280 more as a kick returner, and eight of the team's 18 touchdowns.

He was the Hoosiers' MVP that year and his senior season, when he made All-Big Ten. His 1,562 rushing yards stood as IU's record for 17 years. IU assistant coach Howard Brown called him "a power runner with speed, and a great clutch player."

Gedman and linebacker Joe Schmidt headed one of the Detroit Lions' greatest rookie groups. They joined an NFL championship team and helped it repeat in 1953.

After two years of military duty, Gedman led the '56 Lions in rushing. In 1957, his touchdown got the Lions past San Francisco in the Western Conference championship game, and he scored again when Detroit beat Cleveland for the NFL championship.

He had another strong season in '58, but a knee injury in the next-last game ended his career. In 1974, just 42, Gedman died of a heart attack.

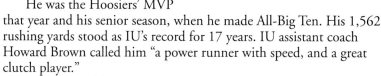

BIG TEN MEDAL - Bob Masters   **GIMBEL AWARD -** Larry Meyer

BALFOUR AWARDS

Football - Gene Gedman; Basketball - Bob Leonard; Baseball - Sammy Esposito; Track - Jim Anderson/Bill Taylor; Wrestling - Bob Carlin; Swimming - Nevin Phillips; Gymnastics - Bill Lee; Golf - Jack Leer; Tennis - Bob Burnham

OLYMPIC MEDALISTS

Swimming: Bill Woolsey, 800-meter freestyle relay, gold;
Track: Milt Campbell, decathlon, silver (6,795).

IU item

ESPOSITO: FROM IU TO WORLD SERIES

Sammy Esposito played seven years in the major leagues.

Sammy Esposito, All-City in football, basketball and baseball at Chicago Fenger, won freshman numerals in all three sports at IU.

As a sophomore, he skipped football and was a star member of one of IU's greatest basketball classes. His roommate, team MVP Bob Leonard, was the only sophomore who outscored him. By year's end Esposito, Leonard, sophomore Dick Farley, freshman center Don Schlundt and senior Bobby Masters were the starters on a 16-6 team that laid the groundwork for championships ahead.

In baseball, IU finished last in the Big Ten at 1-13, but Esposito hit .333, led the league in stolen bases and played shortstop as maybe no other Hoosier ever played it.

His hometown White Sox ended his IU days by signing him after the 1952 season. Four years later, Esposito arrived in the majors with bad timing. Another 1956 White Sox rookie was shortstop Luis Aparicio— Rookie of the Year, then a perennial All-Star on his way to the Hall of Fame. Esposito spent seven years as a backup, playing in more than 500 games—two in the White Sox' only World Series (1959) in the century's last 81 years.

After his player years, Esposito became baseball coach at North Carolina State. He also was a basketball assistant when the Wolfpack won the 1974 NCAA championship.

BELOVED BO DIES

SUCH WAS THE affection of Indiana football fans toward Bo McMillin that with his move to pro football in 1948, they adopted a Sunday team: Bo's Detroit Lions.

McMillin took over a team that had gone 4-19 in the two previous years. Trades and drafts brought in ex-Hoosiers Howard Brown and Bobby Hoernschemeyer, plus Bobby Layne, Doak Walker, Leon Hart and others who were to make the Lions champions.

Bo's third year, after a 6-6 season and a reported player revolt led by the free-living Layne, McMillin was fired. He wasn't out of a job long. From many offers, he chose the Philadelphia Eagles, where his players would include the best of all his IU stars, Pete Pihos, by then All-NFL headed for the Hall of Fame.

McMillin coached Philadelphia for just two games, both wins, before stomach cancer forced him out. Six agonizing months later, on March 31, 1952, back home in Bloomington, he died. McMillin—All-America player, star of the Centre-Harvard game considered college football's grandest upset, coach of Indiana's only unbeaten team—was 57.

"All who knew Bo loved him," IU President Herman B Wells said. "As a leader of young men he was unexcelled." A *New York Times* obituary called him "one of football's immortals."

He was buried at Rose Hill Cemetery in Bloomington. His pall-bearers were Pihos, 1945 MVP Brown, 1945 captain Russ "Mutt" Deal, 1945 All-American Bob Ravensberg, football-basketball All-American Vern Huffman and a star from Bo's pre-IU years at Kansas State, Eldon Auker, a 10-year major league pitcher.

IN THOSE DAYS . . .

SMITH ERA ENDS

Clyde Smith played for Bo McMillin at Geneva College and coached Frankie Filchock in two undefeated high school seasons at Redstone High in Republic, Pennsylvania. In 1934 McMillin brought Filchock to IU to play and Smith to help coach.

When McMillin left after the 1947 season, IU promoted Smith.

His tenure was a highlight film: great moments that glistened in a bleak period. His 1948 team opened with Big Ten victories over Wisconsin and Iowa, then didn't win again. A 39-0 drubbing at Purdue ended the four-year Old Oaken Bucket winning streak McMillin had left behind.

Smith's '49 Hoosiers beat only Pittsburgh. In 1950, Indiana defeated Notre Dame 20-7, then went 1-4.

In '51 at Columbus, Indiana beat Ohio State, 32-10. It was the first Big Ten loss for new Buckeye coach Woody Hayes, who legends say vowed Indiana would never beat him again. Ohio State didn't lose to IU during the rest of Hayes' 28-year tenure.

The '51 Hoosiers didn't beat anybody after Ohio State, and Smith—8-27-1 overall, 4-19 in the Big Ten, 0-4 against Purdue—resigned. He started anew at Arizona State. Three decades later the Sun Devils were a major national power, and the start of their rise traced to the arrival of Clyde Smith.

1952  1953

HOOSIER LIST

IU'S HIGH-POINT BASKETBALL GAMES

122 at Ohio State, 1959
122 vs. Notre Dame, 1962*
118 vs. Iowa, 1990
117 vs. Tennessee Tech, 1994
116 vs. Iowa, 1988
115 vs. Iowa State, 1990
114 vs. Wisconsin, 1976
113 vs. Purdue, 1953
113 vs. Michigan State, 1963
113 vs. Northern Illinois, 1971
113 vs. Tennessee Tech, 1975
112 vs. Michigan State, 1965
112 at Illinois, 1975
112 vs. Michigan, 1991
111 vs. Butler, 1971
110 vs. Detroit, 1964
110 vs. Ohio State, 1965
110 vs. South Dakota, 1977
110 vs. Grambling, 1983@
110 vs. Iowa, 1995
109 vs. Purdue, 1958
109 vs. Loyola (Chi.), 1965
109 vs. Illinois, 1991
108 vs. George Washington, 1999$
108 vs. Notre Dame, 1964*
108 vs. Wisconsin, 1964
107 vs. North Carolina, 1965
107 vs. Notre Dame, 1965*
107 vs. Illinois, 1974
107 at Michigan State, 1975
107 vs. Auburn, 1987@
107 vs. Austin Peay, 1993
106 at Notre Dame, 1971
106 vs. Columbia, 1976+
106 vs. Purdue, 1992
106 vs. UCLA, 1992#
106 vs. San Francisco, 1999
105 vs. Butler, 1953
105 vs. Minnesota, 1962
105 vs. Arkansas-Little Rock, 1989
105 at Northwestern, 1991
105 vs. St. John's, 1993
105 vs. Penn State, 1993

* at Fort Wayne, Indiana
@ at Indianapolis, Indiana
+ at New York, New York
# at Albuquerque, New Mexico
$ at Orlando, Florida

INDIANA LEGEND

The 1953 Champions

NO. 1 OF IU'S NO. 1'S

Indiana's first 52 basketball teams won one NCAA championship but never an outright Big Ten title and never were ranked No. 1 in the nation.

The 1952-53 Hoosiers achieved all those things.

Coach Branch McCracken entered the 23-3 season knowing he had three experienced stars in juniors Bob Leonard and Dick Farley and sophomore center Don Schlundt. McCracken added junior Charley Kraak and sophomore Burke Scott and went virtually the entire way with that as his lineup.

Last-second shots beat the Hoosiers twice in their first three games (71-70 at Notre Dame, 82-80 at Kansas State).

The Hoosiers didn't lose again for almost three months. By then, they had won 17 straight games, and—after a title-clinching 91-79 victory over defending champion Illinois February 28 at Champaign—moved to the top of both national polls.

Their streak ended with another last-second shot at Minnesota, but the Hoosiers still were No. 1 when they opened NCAA tournament play at Chicago by beating DePaul, 82-80, then Notre Dame, 79-66, as Schlundt, on his 21st birthday, set IU and Chicago Stadium records with 41 points.

In the Final Four at Kansas City, Schlundt had 29 points and Leonard 24 as Indiana got past Louisiana State and its All-American, Bob Pettit, 80-67. The championship-game matchup and site were the same as 1940. Again, Kansas and coach Forrest "Phog" Allen lost, this time just 69-68. Rebounding leader Kraak scored a career-high 17 points, Schlundt 30 and Leonard 12, including the game-winning free throw at 0:27.

Front row (left to right): Bobby Leonard, Charley Kraak, Don Schlundt, Dick Farley, Burke Scott. Second row: Manager Ron Fifer, Dick White, Jim Deakyne, Coach Branch Mc-Cracken, Paul Poff, Phil Byers, Assistant Coach Ernie Andres. Third row: Ron Taylor, Jim Schooley, Goethe Chambers, Jack Wright.

BIG TEN MEDAL - George Branam   **GIMBEL AWARD** - Jim Schooley

BALFOUR AWARDS

Football - Gene Gedman; Basketball - Jim Schooley; Baseball - Paul Underwood; Track - Dave Martin; Wrestling - Charles Pankow; Swimming - Frank Pisacreta; Gymnastics - Herb Vogel; Golf - Jack Leer; Tennis - Eli Glazer

NCAA CHAMPION

TEAM: Basketball (Branch McCracken)

IU TRIES AN IRISHMAN

Bernie Crimmins, a three-sport star at Louisville St. Xavier High School, made some All-America teams as a guard on an unbeaten team at Notre Dame in 1940. He came back from World War II to play a year at Green Bay, then gave up professional football to go back to Notre Dame. He coached the quarterbacks—Johnny Lujack, George Ratterman, Frank Tripucka, Bob Williams, Ralph Guglielmi—for Frank Leahy on four unbeaten Irish clubs.

At 32, Crimmins brought Irish optimism and enthusiasm to Bloomington in 1952 as Indiana's head coach.

Certainly he was tough enough. As a PT-boat commander in the South Pacific, he won the Silver Star, a Presidential Citation and three battle stars.

But, try as he and his teams did, Crimmins couldn't deliver traditional Fighting Irish results.

In Crimmins' first IU first game, a red-haired freshman came off the Ohio State bench to score three touchdowns—Howard "Hopalong" Cassady starting his own Hall of Fame career at the expense of Crimmins and Indiana, 33-13.

The score's numbers were prophetic. Five years later, they almost represented Crimmins' Indiana record: 13-32, and just 6-24 in the Big Ten. The Crimmins Era at IU ended with a 39-20 loss at Purdue in 1956, his fifth straight Old Oaken Bucket loss and Indiana's ninth straight.

Bernie Crimmins served as IU football coach from 1952 to 1956.

Snapshot In Time

SCHOOLEY: A RING AND A KEY

SENIOR JIM SCHOOLEY'S late-game tip-in on opening night of the 1952-53 season against Valparaiso ignited a fan explosion worthy of a game-winning play. It came in the closing seconds of a 95-56 Hoosier victory, and every celebrating fan knew it was Schooley's first IU basket.

At Auburn High School, he had led his team to the state tournament's Final Four and made the Indiana All-Star team. But at IU, Schooley recalled later, "I was a mediocre basketball player. My size was almost my only asset."

That wasn't true. He also had a passion for the game that made him a crowd favorite, and he was far from mediocre off the court. He's the only Hoosier basketball player who graduated with an NCAA championship ring and a Phi Beta Kappa key.

At California-Berkeley he earned a master's degree, then a doctorate in nuclear studies. In 30 years as a scientist at the National Bureau of Standards, he became America's ranking authority on thermometry.

Schooley is the only athlete to win both IU's Gimbel Award and the high school mental attitude award that Jake Gimbel set up and the IHSAA perpetuated in the name of former Commissioner Arthur L. Trester. "For me, both in high school and college," he said, "basketball was a dream come true."

Jim Schooley won the IHSAA's Trester Award and IU's Gimbel Award—both given for mental attitude.

IN THOSE DAYS . . .

SCHLUNDT REVISES STANDARDS

Don Schlundt in his sophomore year took scoring to levels never before approached at Indiana.

In his 40th college game—February 23 of his sophomore season, in IU Fieldhouse against Purdue—Schlundt's first basket made him IU's all-time leading career scorer. Bill Garrett, an All-American himself, had set IU's record with 792 in his three seasons, just before the 6-foot-9 Schlundt's arrival from little Washington-Clay High School, on South Bend's outskirts.

Schlundt started the Purdue game with 791 points and finished it with 822, contributing 31 points to IU's Big Ten-record 113-78 victory.

It was the first time Indiana scored 100 points in a conference game. IU's first 100-point game had come three weeks earlier, 105-70 over Butler. Reserve guard Jack Wright's two free throws with 2:14 to play put IU at 100 the first time. Wright also scored the last basket just ahead of the buzzer against Purdue.

Coach Branch McCracken substituted liberally in each game. IU's halftime lead was 60-39 over Butler, 61-35 over Purdue. Schlundt played just 24 minutes in scoring 33 against Butler, 26 minutes in getting his 31 against Purdue.

Schlundt won his first of three Big Ten scoring championships with 459 points in the 18-game league schedule (25.5 average). His 661-point season total made him IU's first 1,000-point scorer—1,037, with two full seasons to go.

1953 1954

HOOSIER LIST

IU'S ALL-BIG TEN BASEBALL PLAYERS*

Don Ritter, OF, 1949
Willard Litz, 2B, 1950
Gene Ring, SS, 1951
Paul Underwood, RF, 1953
Bobby Robertson, RF, 1954
Bob Lawrence, IB, 1958
James Howe, RF, 1959
Paul Michaels, P, 1960
Eddie LaDuke, 2B, 1961, 62
Jack Campbell, IB, 1966
Jim Lee, RF, 1967
Bruce Miller, SS, 1969
Mike Baughman, LF, 1969
Barry Burnett, IB, 1973
Randy Miller, 2B, 1974
Dale Thake, SS, 1974
Ken St. Pierre, C, 1974
Dave Wilson, OF, 1975
Terry Jones, OF, 1976
Mark Laesch, OF, 1976
Scott Weiner, DH, 1976, 78
Bob Johnson, 2B, 1978; 3B, 1979
Larry Blackwell, DH, 1979
Bob Waite, OF, 1981
Dan Winters, C, 1984
Bill Mueller, DH, 1985
Mickey Morandini, 3B-SS, 1986, 87, 88
Bill Jordan, DH, 1989
Phil Dauphin, OF, 1990
Mike Smith, SS, 1991, 92
Kevin Orie, DH, 1992
Marty Wolfe, OF, 1992
Bob Scafa, P, 1993
Matt Braughler, C, 1996
Dan Ferrell, P, 1996
Kevin Zaleski, P, 1996
Doug DeVore, OF, 1999

*Official Big Ten records start with the 1949 season

INDIANA LEGEND — *Bobby Leonard*

BEST IN LAND, POUND-FOR-POUND

Jim Enright, a Chicago sportswriter and referee, in one role or the other saw college basketball's best. In the 1952-53 season Enright wrote:

"This fellow Leonard is to basketball what Robin Roberts is to baseball, Ben Hogan to golf and Eddie Arcaro to horse racing. Pound-for-pound, dribble-for-dribble, pass-for-pass and shot-for-shot, Bob is without question the game's greatest individual player in my book."

Leonard's point total rarely matched teammate Don Schlundt's. But he did follow Schlundt as just the second 1,000-point scorer at IU.

His long, high, two-handed set shots were as deflating for road crowds as they were exhilarating for home.

And he was brash. When IU won 91-79 at Illinois to clinch the 1953 league championship, Leonard missed his first two shots. The crowd jeered, "Shoot! Shoot!" He did and sank seven shots before halftime, ending with ten, and 23 points.

"I see a lot of All-American picks, but they forget Leonard," Hoosier coach Branch McCracken said after that game.

"He belongs . . ."

Leonard's seven-year NBA career ended as player-coach with the Chicago Zephyrs and—after a franchise move—the Baltimore Bullets. In mid-season 1969-70, he took over the Indiana Pacers. He stayed for 10 more seasons, winning three ABA championships and coaching the team in its first four NBA seasons.

Both Leonard and Schlundt were among the 25 charter members of IU's Athletics Hall of Fame. A star under Howard Sharpe at Terre Haute Gerstmeyer before going to IU, Leonard also is in the Indiana Basketball Hall of Fame.

BIG TEN MEDAL - Duane Gomer   **GIMBEL AWARD** - Lowell Zellers

BALFOUR AWARDS -
Football - Jerry Ellis; Basketball - Charley Kraak; Baseball - Bobby Robertson; Track - Lowell Zellers; Wrestling - Dick Anthony; Swimming - Dick Knight; Gymnastics - Ron Johnson; Golf - Elliott Phillips; Tennis - Duane Gomer

IU item

ROBERTSON TWO-SPORT CHAMPION

A Big Ten batting champion in baseball, Bobby Robertson also held IU's punting record in football for 16 years.

Bobby Robertson's biggest day as an Indiana football player came as a sophomore against the team from his home town, Notre Dame, which got him pretty good coverage back home.

"The prancing feet of Bobby Robertson shook Memorial Stadium like thunder," Paul Neville wrote in Robertson's hometown newspaper, the *South Bend Tribune*, after Indiana's 20-7 victory in 1950.

That day Robertson set an IU record with 185 rushing yards, and he caught passes for another 20.

He went on to a 1,220-yard career, just the fourth back in IU history to top 1,000 yards.

He's in the Big Ten record book, though, for two achievements that didn't involve carrying the football.

Twice—in 1949 as a freshman and in 1951—he led the Big Ten in punting. His career average, 38.0, stood as IU's record for 16 seasons.

And, in 1954, after missing the 1952-53 athletic season for military duty, he played his only season of baseball at IU and led the Big Ten with a .438 average. That gave him the honor that had never come to him in his standout football career: first-team All-Big Ten selection.

LEWIS TAKES IU TENNIS TO TOP

WHEN DALE LEWIS took over as Indiana's tennis coach in 1949, the Hoosiers hadn't won a Big Ten dual match in 12 years. In the 1948 Big Ten tournament, Indiana didn't score a point; in the '46 conference meet, Indiana didn't win a set.

In his fourth year, Lewis and Indiana won the Big Ten title. Junior Eli Glazer, sophomores Duane Gomer and Tom Lynch, and freshmen John Hironimus and Bob Martin gave IU a sweep of singles titles from 2 through 6. Hironimus and Lynch added the No. 3 doubles title as Indiana opened a 70-56 margin over Michigan State for the 1952 Big Ten title.

Dale Lewis coached Indiana to Big Ten tennis titles in 1952-53-54, the '54 team going 19-0.

The next year, Hironimus, Gomer and Martin won at 2 through 4, and the Hironimus-Ed Harrison doubles combination won at No. 3 for a 64 to 56 margin over runnerup Michigan State.

In 1954, the Hoosiers swept through their season 19-0 and opened a record winning margin (52 to 36) over second-place Michigan. Martin won his third straight Big Ten title at No. 3 and combined with Hironimus to win the No. 1 doubles title, the third doubles championship for Hironimus. Sophomore Carl Dentice completed an undefeated season by winning the title at No. 6.

IN THOSE DAYS . . .

'IT'S INDIANA' FOR CAMPBELL

In an era when recruiting made no headlines and few high school athletes were known outside their state, Milt Campbell was an exception.

The summer before his senior year at Plainfield, New Jersey, High School, Campbell was the decathlon silver medalist at the 1952 Olympics. The 6-foot-3, 205-pound Campbell returned to Plainfield High and scored 23 touchdowns, then made high school All-America in swimming, then won both the high hurdles and high jump at a national high school meet—and in the summer of '53 won his first national decathlon title.

So, it was a national news story when a top Associated Press sports writer, Will Grimsley, talked to Campbell in March and wrote: "It's Indiana."

Days later, speculation rose that he had changed his mind and picked Penn State.

On Saturday, August 22, the Bloomington *Herald-Telephone* pulled out its biggest headline type and announced at the top of its front page:

'GREATEST' ATHLETE IU BOUND

Campbell had announced that morning in Plainfield he would leave the next day to enroll at Indiana. Three other Plainfield-area Hoosier athletes helped recruit him— Archie Harris, Clifton "Doc" Anderson and Jim Roberson.

HOOSIER LIST

IU'S GYMNASTICS CHAMPIONS

NCAA

1955	Dick Albershardt, trampoline

Big Ten

1952	Dick Albershardt, trampoline
1956	Dick Albershardt, trampoline
1957	Dick Albershardt, trampoline
1959	Ron Walden, tumbling
1971	Benny Fernandez, rings
1972	Benny Fernandez, rings
1973	Benny Fernandez, rings
1974	Benny Fernandez, rings
1975	Landy Fernandez, rings
1977	Pete Murao, floor exercise
1978	Pete Murao, floor exercise

All-Americans

1971	Benny Fernandez, rings
1972	Benny Fernandez, rings
1973	Benny Fernandez, rings
1974	Benny Fernandez, rings
1978	Pete Murao, floor exercise

INDIANA LEGEND — *Don Schlundt*

47-POINT EXIT, 2,132-POINT CAREER

Don Schlundt spent his first three college basketball years surrounded by some of the best players Indiana ever had, on some of the best teams the Big Ten ever saw.

Schlundt's senior season introduced him to losing.

He still had high-quality teammates, but they were younger and greener and opponents were more inclined to swarm around Schlundt —in a way they couldn't do with Bobby Leonard sniping from outside and Dick Farley scoring from close range.

After starring on the first two IU teams to win clear-cut Big Ten championships, Schlundt as a senior captained a team that lost seven of eight games at one stretch, five of six in another in falling into the league's second division.

With a farewell crowd cheering him on in the season finale against Ohio State, Schlundt matched his career high with 47 points and set Big Ten records by hitting 25 of 30 free throws in an 84-66 victory.

The big game assured a record third straight Big Ten scoring championship for Schlundt, whose career closed with 2,132 points and 10 Big Ten scoring records. IU sports information director Tom Miller noted the extra season given Schlundt under temporary Korean War eligibility rules and said in a news release: "Schlundt seems likely to go down in history as the Big Ten's all-time greatest scorer."

BIG TEN MEDAL - Mike Cusick **GIMBEL AWARD -** Tom Dailey

BALFOUR AWARDS
Football-Florian Helinski; Basketball-Don Schlundt; Baseball-Charles Mead/Art Herring; Track-Jim Lambert/Mike Cusick; Wrestling-Dick Anthony; Swimming-Bill Woolsey; Gymnastics-Dick Albershardt; Golf-Jim Balch; Tennis-Carl Dentice/John Hironimus

NCAA CHAMPIONS
Gymnastics-Dick Albershardt, trampoline; Track-Milt Campbell, 120 hurdles (:13.9)

IU item

ALBERSHARDT SCORES A FIRST

Dick Albershardt won trampoline competition at the 1952 Big Ten gymnastics championship. He missed the next two seasons, on military duty.

He returned to school in the fall of 1954 and showed his readiness in a clinic, where he defeated the reigning NCAA champion (Jim Norman of Iowa) and the expected Big Ten favorite (Jeff Austin of Illinois). Before regular competition began, however, he injured a knee and missed all regular-season events and the Big Ten meet.

So, the 1955 NCAA championship meet at Los Angeles was his first competition in almost three years.

He was ready. Though he had resumed practice just two weeks earlier, he scored 284 of a possible 300 points, and his 12-point winning margin over runnerup Austin set an NCAA record for the event.

In both 1956 and '57, he won Big Ten trampoline titles.

When IU dropped men's gymnastics after the 1982 season, it solidified Albershardt's role in Hoosier history as the school's only NCAA gymnastics champion. In 1994, he was inducted into the IU Athletics Hall of Fame.

Dick Albershardt is IU's only NCAA gymnastics champion. He won on trampoline in 1955.

> In his first competition in almost three years, Dick Albershardt won the 1955 NCAA trampoline championship.

Snapshot In Time

HELINSKI HERO AT MICHIGAN

IN ITS FIRST 100 years of Big Ten football, Indiana has won at Michigan just seven times. One of those seven—the last time Indiana won at Ann Arbor over a nationally ranked Wolverine team—came under unpromising conditions October 30, 1954.

Going into the game, third-year coach Bernie Crimmins was 0-12 at IU in road games. Michigan was ranked No. 11 in the country, among its stars future college and pro Hall of Famer Ron Kramer. Indiana was 1-4, its only win over outmanned College of Pacific at Memorial Stadium.

And the Hoosiers' 5-10, 170-pound senior quarterback, Florian Helinski, was fighting a sore shoulder that had kept him out of one game.

Helinski was the game's star. He played 59 minutes, scored one touchdown, passed for another, and on defense set an IU record with three interceptions. He extended to 106 his own NCAA record of consecutive passes without an interception.

He also was one of the nation's top punters. Recruited out of Hurley, Wisconsin, Helinski stepped in as a freshman in a blizzard-like game at Wisconsin—35 mph winds, heavy, swirling snow—and kept the Hoosiers alive with his punting: 14 times (still the IU one-game record) for a 37.1 average. The Badgers won, 6-0.

Florian Helinski led IU in passing ('53-'54), scoring ('54) and punting ('52, '53, '54). His 14 punts against Wisconsin in '54 is still an IU record.

HOOSIER LIST

IU'S OLYMPIC GOLD MEDALISTS

1932	Ivan Fuqua, track, 1600-relay
1948	Roy Cochran, track, 400-hurdles
	Roy Cochran, track, 1600-relay
1952	Bill Woolsey, swimming, 800-fr
1956	Greg Bell, track, long jump
	Milt Campbell, track, decathlon
1960	Walt Bellamy, basketball
	Mike Troy, swimming, 200-butterfly
	Mike Troy, swimming, 800-freestyle
	Frank McKinney, swimming, 400-mr
1964	Ken Sitzberger, diving, springboard
	Fred Schmidt, swimming, 400-mr
	Bob Windle, swimming, 1500-freestyle
	Kevin Berry, swimming, 200—butterfly
	Lesley Bush, diving, platform
	Kathleen Ellis, swimming, 400-fr
	Kathleen Ellis, swimming, 400-mr
1968	Charlie Hickcox, swimming, 200-im
	Charlie Hickcox, swimming, 400-im
	Charlie Hickcox, swimming, 400-mr
	Don McKenzie, swimming, 100-breaststroke
	Don McKenzie, swimming, 400-mr
	Mark Spitz, swimming, 400-fr
	Mark Spitz, swimming, 800-fr
1972	Mark Spitz, swimming, 100-freestyle
	Mark Spitz, swimming, 200-freestyle
	Mark Spitz, swimming, 100-butterfly
	Mark Spitz, swimming, 200-butterfly
	Mark Spitz, swimming, 400-mr
	Mark Spitz, swimming, 400-fr
	Mark Spitz, swimming, 800-fr
	Mike Stamm, swimming, 400-mr
	John Murphy, swimming, 400-fr
	Fred Tyler, swimming, 800-fr
	John Kinsella, swimming, 800-fr
1976	Jim Montgomery, swimming, 100-freestyle
	Jim Montgomery, swimming, 400-mr
	Jim Montgomery, swimming, 800-fr
	Quinn Buckner, basketball
	Scott May, basketball
1980	Mark Kerry, swimming, 400-mr
1984	Steve Alford, basketball
	Sunder Nix, track, 1600-relay
1988	Mickey Morandini, baseball
1992	Mark Lenzi, diving, 3-meter

Coaches of gold-medal teams

1984	Bob Knight, basketball
1996	Tara Van Derveer, basketball

fr - freestyle relay; mr - medley relay

LEGEND   *Milt Campbell*

INDIANA

WORLD'S GREATEST ATHLETE

Milt Campbell excited Indiana imaginations as a football player, and he played well enough to have an NFL career.

But track was his Hall of Fame sport. Campbell is one of just 23 athletes, worldwide, who have won the decathlon at the Olympic Games and with it unofficial recognition as the world's greatest athlete.

Campbell competed in just five decathlons in his life. His first put him in the 1952 Helsinki Olympics, where his second decathlon won him—at 18—a silver medal. His hometown, Plainfield, New Jersey, had raised the funds to send him to Tulare, California, for the 1952 Olympic Trials, and the town honored him further by hosting the 1953 U.S. decathlon championship. That was Campbell's third decathlon, and his first victory.

He didn't try another till placing second to Rafer Johnson in the 1956 U.S. Olympic Trials at Crawfordsville, Indiana. In the Olympics at Melbourne, Campbell defeated Johnson to win a gold medal in his fifth and last decathlon.

He had thought he would make the U.S. team in the 110-meter hurdles. He won both the NCAA and AAU national championships in the event in 1955 as an IU sophomore, and he was to tie the world record (13.4) in 1957. But in the 1956 U.S. Trials, he finished fourth. "I was stunned," he said later. "But then God seemed to reach into my heart and tell me He didn't want me to compete in the hurdles, but in the decathlon."

Campbell was a charter member of the IU Athletics Hall of Fame, and in 1989 he was inducted into the National Track and Field Hall of Fame.

BIG TEN MEDAL - Sam Reed   **GIMBEL AWARD -** Bob Skoronski

BALFOUR AWARDS

Football-Tom Hall; Basketball-Wally Choice; Baseball-Art Herring; Track-Greg Bell/Don Ward; Wrestling-Dick Anthony/ Jim Ellis; Swimming-Bill Woolsey; Gymnastics-Dick Albershardt; Golf-Bob Dyar; Tennis-Elam Huddleston/Ken Dillman

NCAA CHAMPIONS

Swimming - Bill Woolsey, 220 freestyle (2:04.7), 440 freestyle (4:31.1);
Track - Greg Bell, long jump, 25-9

IU item

WOOLSEY FIRST NCAA SWIM KING

Olympian Bill Woolsey was IU's first NCAA swim champion.

The moment Hawaiian Bill Woolsey enrolled as a freshman, he was the best swimmer Indiana University had ever had.

Woolsey won a gold medal on the U.S. 800-meter freestyle relay team at Helsinki in 1952. He enrolled at IU the next fall, and as a junior in 1956 he won the 220-yard and 440-yard freestyles—the first of the 62 NCAA events Indiana swimmers were to win in the century.

Woolsey repeated in the two events the next year.

Indiana also got 1956 NCAA points from Woolsey's fellow Hawaiians Dick "Sonny" Tanabe, second in the 200-yard individual medley, and Ron Honda, fourth in the 200-yard butterfly. IU's sixth-place finish was its all-time high, though just a hint of the dynasty to come.

Woolsey had tripled in the 220, 440 and 1,650 freestyles in the '56 Big Ten championships. There, Tanabe was second in both the 220 freestyle and 200 medley, and Honda placed fourth in the 200-yard butterfly as the Hoosiers tied Iowa for third.

Tanabe joined Woolsey on the 1956 U.S. Olympic team, as an alternate on the 800-meter freestyle relay team at Melbourne. Woolsey won a silver medal with that relay team.

Snapshot In Time

A LEADER OF THE PACK

BOB SKORONSKI'S NAME is forever linked with football glory and success. Skoronski for seven years was the offensive captain of the Green Bay Packers—Vince Lombardi's Packers, including the first two Super Bowl champions.

Success took a while in coming to Skoronski, whose three IU teams went 8-19. Skoronski, a tackle on both offense and defense, was IU's 1954 captain, 1955 MVP (he recovered eight fumbles), and 1956 Gimbel Award winner.

Skoronski, Green Bay's fifth-round draft pick, played in the College All-Star game before going to the Packers' camp. Dispirited, the second day in Green Bay's camp he left, to enter law school at IU. Packers coach Lisle Blackbourn talked him into returning.

After a 4-8 rookie season, Skoronski entered military service for two years and returned to find Lombardi had arrived, one of football's legendary eras a-dawning.

In the '60s, the Green Bay teams Skoronski captained won five NFL championships and the two Super Bowls. Lombardi left after the 1967 season; Skoronski played one more season and retired in 1968. He developed a successful private business in Wisconsin. He was a charter member of the IU Athletics Hall of Fame.

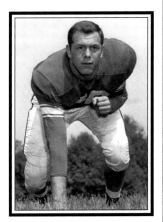

Bob Skoronski captained five NFL championship teams and two Super Bowl winners for the Green Bay Packers.

IN THOSE DAYS . . .

THE 6-4 BUCKET LOSS

Purdue's eighth straight Old Oaken Bucket victory came by the oddest score of the entire series: 6 to 4.

Indiana led 2-0 on a third-quarter safety till Purdue scored a fourth-quarter touchdown but missed the extra-point kick. Down 6-2, the iron-man Hoosiers summoned one last victory push.

On fourth-and-1 at the Purdue 2, IU fullback and captain John Bartkiewicz — an ex-Marine who went from high school to Korean front lines, the last of four Chicago brothers and honor students who played at Indiana — plunged into the line. Officials spotted the ball four inches short of first-and-goal at the 1.

Purdue intentionally took a second safety, creating the 6-4 score, then kicked the ball away, and time ran out.

Indiana used just 19 players. Ten played at least 50 minutes, five all 60 — linemen Bob Skoronski, Ron Rauchmiller, Tom Hall and Brad Bomba and quarterback Gene "Chick" Cichowski.

Purdue finished 5-3-1. Indiana's 3-6 record included 20-13 losses to champion Ohio State and runnerup Michigan State. "We had our chances in every game," coach Bernie Crimmins said. "I couldn't be much prouder. In the last minute of the season these men were working their hearts out. This was a season of inches."

123

HOOSIER LIST

IU'S ACADEMIC ALL-AMERICANS

Baseball
Dave Wilson, 1975

Men's Basketball
Dick Van Arsdale, 1964, 1965
Tom Van Arsdale, 1965
John Ritter, 1973
Steve Green, 1974, 1975
Kent Benson, 1976, 1977
Wayne Radford, 1978
Randy Wittman, 1982, 1983
Uwe Blab, 1985

Football
Brad Bomba, 1956
Harry Gonso, 1967
Glenn Scolnik, 1972
Kevin Speer, 1980
John Hammerstein, 1994

Softball
Pam Lee, 1985
Karleen Moore, 1986, 1987

Volleyball
Joy Jordan, 1990

Women's Basketball
Ann Mooney, 1989

⬡ LEGEND *Greg Bell*

LATE, BUT GREAT

Greg Bell was well into his 20s before he realized he had exceptional long-jump talent. For Terre Haute Garfield, he finished second in the state high school meet. After high school, he worked for a Chicago packing company, drove a semi-trailer, went into the Army for two years that included some long jumping, then came out of the Army and worked night shift in a Terre Haute factory for $1.59 an hour.

All the while, his body was maturing. In a state AAU meet, he jumped 24 feet for the first time. That fall Bell, almost 24 years old, entered IU.

And his life turned golden.

As a freshman, he jumped 26 feet for the first time and won the National AAU championship. In his first year of collegiate eligibility, sophomore Bell won Big Ten titles indoors and outdoors, the NCAA, the U.S. Olympic Trials (tied) and—at Melbourne, Australia, just turned 26—the Olympic gold medal.

He didn't leave himself much room for improvement but he won four more Big Ten titles, a second NCAA, and—nearly 30, a full-time dentistry student by then—came within an inch and a half of making the 1960 U.S. Olympic team.

Twice in his career, he came within that same bitsy margin, an inch and a half, of taking the world long jump record away from Jesse Owens. Owens went 26-8 1/4 in winning the 1935 Big Ten title; Bell jumped 26-7 twice, in winning the 1957 NCAA championship (a meet record at the time) and in beating Soviet star Igor Ter-Ovanesyan in the high-pressure U.S.-Soviet Union dual meet in 1958. He added second-place finishes in both sprints to his long jump title in helping the 1957 Hoosiers to the Big Ten outdoor title.

Bell spent a long career as a dentist. A charter member of IU's Athletics Hall of Fame, he was inducted into the U.S. Track and Field Hall of Fame in 1988.

BIG TEN MEDAL - Dick Neal   **GIMBEL AWARD -** Bill Woolsey

BALFOUR AWARDS
Football-Brad Bomba; Basketball-Charley Hodson; Baseball-Carl Kirkpatrick; Track-Greg Bell/Clarence Lane; Wrestling-Joe Shook; Swimming-Bill Woolsey; Gymnastics-Ron David; Golf-Jack Rouhier; Tennis - Gerry Parchute/Bob Gray

NCAA CHAMPIONS
Swimming - Bill Woolsey, 220 freestyle (2:02.1), 440 freestyle (4:38.2);
Track - Greg Bell, long jump, 26-7

OLYMPIC MEDALISTS
Track-Greg Bell, long jump, gold (25-8); Milt Campbell, decathlon, gold (7,657);
Swimming- Bill Woolsey, 800-meter freestyle relay, silver (8:31.5); Frank McKinney, 100 backstroke, bronze (1:04.5)

Dick Neal set a Big Ten record with a .512 field goal percentage.

TWO SURPRISES, ONE TITLE

First-semester grades cost Indiana two basketball players at the start of 1956 Big Ten play and two more as the 1957 league season began.

A door opened to senior Dick Neal, from little Reelsville High in Putnam County. Neal had scored just 43 points in 51 career games when Branch McCracken started him in the Big Ten opener against Michigan.

Neal's 22 points, vital in the Hoosiers' 73-68 victory, started a remarkable Big Ten season for him and IU. Neal averaged 15.6 points, 10th-best in the conference, and shot .512 to set a Big Ten record. Led by league MVP and scoring champion Archie Dees, Indiana tied Michigan State for the league championship. Neal made second-team All-Big Ten, and in May he won IU's Big Ten medal, for academic and athletic excellence.

Clarence Doninger had played on strong Evansville Central teams and on the IU freshman team. Cut as a sophomore, Doninger excelled as a student, in campus politics (student body president) and as a Little 500 bicyclist (his Sigma Nu team won in '57). With the basketball roster down to 10, senior Doninger was asked if he would help as a practice player. He played little in games but "proved a real asset" for scrimmaging, Bloomington *Herald-Telephone* columnist George Bolinger wrote. "Doninger will go down in IU cage history alongside such inspirational players as Jim Schooley."

Thirty-four years later, successful lawyer Doninger became IU's 18th athletic director.

A DOCTOR ALL THE WAY

BRAD BOMBA WENT to Indiana to be a doctor, and a chance to play in the National Football League didn't dissuade him. Bomba stuck with his studies and went on to a long practice in Bloomington, including more than 25 years as an IU team doctor.

Bomba saw son Matt win four IU football letters and take charge of the weight program under coach Cam Cameron.

But it was his own outstanding Hoosier football career that made Brad Bomba a 1994 inductee into IU's Athletics Hall of Fame.

Bomba was Indiana's first Academic All-America, after three outstanding seasons at end. He led Big Ten pass catchers in 1956, and he was a first-team All-Conference pick—he and Wisconsin's Pat Levenhagen the first to make Academic All-Big Ten three times. He won IU's Balfour Award and Most Valuable Player Award, and he played in the East-West Game, Senior Bowl, and—back home in Chicago where he had starred at Mount Carmel High—the College All-Star Game.

Bomba's 154-yard day at Northwestern as a sophomore was IU's one-game receiving record for 12 years. Two years later he caught nine passes against Northwestern, and that was IU's receptions record for 10 years.

Brad Bomba—football end—was IU's first Academic All-American.

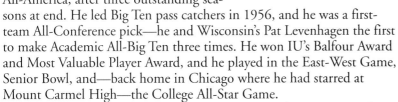

HAYES: A NO-HITTER, A LOSS

In the second game of Albin Hayes' IU varsity career, he sat in the dugout and watched two teammates pitch a no-hit game. Woody Ratterman worked the first five innings, giving up a run on an error, and Harold Summers faced 12 batters in four innings in a 9-1 no-hit victory over Indiana Central.

Just 11 days later, it happened again. Once more, Hayes was a spectator as Bill Dooley pitched the first four innings and Summers finished a 21-0 seven-inning no-hit victory over Bakalar Air Force Base. Summers, who faced the minimum 21 batters in his seven relief innings, combined with Dooley for 14 strikeouts against Bakalar.

Hayes was part of the Hoosiers' starting rotation throughout his career. He started his senior season with two straight shutout victories.

Then, on May 4, 1957, he achieved what he had only watched before. He pitched a no-hit game against Ohio State.

And he lost.

In the third inning, Hayes walked the bases loaded and a run scored on a fly ball. In the sixth, a walk, stolen base and overthrow, and another sacrifice fly delivered the run that decided a 2-1 Ohio State victory

It's the only losing no-hitter in IU history.

HOOSIER LIST

IU BIG TEN BASKETBALL MVP'S

1953
Don Schlundt

1957
Archie Dees

1958
Archie Dees

1973
Steve Downing

1975
Scott May

1976
Scott May

1977
Kent Benson

1980
Mike Woodson

1981
Ray Tolbert

1983
Randy Wittman

1987
Steve Alford

1993
Calbert Cheaney

1996
Brian Evans

INDIANA

✦ LEGEND   *Archie Dees*

BIG TEN'S FIRST TWO-TIME MVP

Archie Dees grew up just across the Indiana-Illinois line in Mount Carmel, watching IU's 1953 national champions play on TV and even attending a few games—a big Hoosier fan.

He also grew up to 6-8 and was one of the top national recruits when he decided to wear that Indiana uniform himself.

He knew the pressure he was inheriting, as the successor to record scorer Don Schlundt. He was the worthiest of successors. After averaging 17.4 on a 13-9 team as a sophomore, he led the Big Ten in scoring twice in a row in leading Indiana to championships—a share of the title with Michigan State in 1957 and an outright championship in '58.

He finished more than 100 points ahead of runnerup Frank Howard, a future baseball great, when he averaged 25 points a game as a junior. His senior year, he boosted that to 25.5—with four straight 30-point games and a 28.8 average in the five-game closing rush that pulled out a league championship for the Hoosiers.

His performance made him the first player in league history to win the Most Valuable Player silver basketball trophy twice.

Dees had a four-year NBA career before building a business in Bloomington. He was inducted into the IU Athletics Hall of Fame in 1983.

BIG TEN MEDAL - Greg Bell   **GIMBEL AWARD -** Don Brodie

BALFOUR AWARDS

Football-Del Gales; Basketball-Archie Dees; Baseball-Bob Lawrence; Track-Greg Bell/Hal Caffey; Wrestling-Nick Petronka; Swimming-Ron Honda; Gymnastics-Jeryl Wright; Golf-Ron Terrell; Tennis-Gerry Parchute/Bob Gray

IU item

FIRST BIG TEN TRIPLE CROWN

Bob Lawrence was the Big Ten's first Triple Crown winner. He later coached at IU.

Bob Lawrence introduced himself to Big Ten baseball in the spring of 1958 and left after just a few months—a few pretty good months that made an impact on the league's records.

In his one varsity season, Lawrence became the first Triple Crown winner in 20 years of official Big Ten record-keeping. In 15 league games, Lawrence hit .472, with five home runs and 14 runs batted in, sharing the RBI lead.

Lawrence, 2-for-2 in a season-ending 6-1 victory over Purdue, topped teammate Don Foreman (.424) for the batting title. He was the Hoosiers' first All-Big Ten selection in four years. The league's top pitchers that year all made the major leagues—Ron Perranoski and Dick Radatz of Michigan State and Ron Nischwitz of Ohio State.

Lawrence signed a bonus contract with the Boston Red Sox. He had a 30-home run, 127-RBI season with Waterloo in 1961, reaching Triple-A before going back to IU to complete his degree work.

He joined his college coach, Ernie Andres, as an assistant in 1965 and in 1974 succeeded Andres as Hoosier coach. His best of seven IU seasons was a third-place finish in 1976, including a 6-0 closing rush.

Lawrence was from Beaver Dam, Pennsylvania, where in addition to baseball, he starred in football—five years ahead of the town's most famous football player, Joe Namath.

Snapshot in Time

DICKENS' START STORMY

Interim coach
Bob Hicks

ON SATURDAY, JANUARY 19, 1957, Indiana brought North Carolina football coach Jim Tatum—National Coach of the Year in 1953 when he took Maryland to the national championship—to campus to offer him the IU coaching job.

After a long afternoon session with IU officials, Tatum left town and said, "I'm sorry, I can't leave North Carolina."

Within minutes, the job was offered by telephone to Phil Dickens, a former Tennessee tailback whose 1956 Wyoming team had gone 10-0. Dickens, 42, accepted and left immediately for Indiana, bringing his Wyoming staff with him.

Their Big Ten reception wasn't rosy.

On July 19th, six months to the day after Dickens' hiring, Big Ten Commissioner Kenneth "Tug" Wilson notified IU that he was suspending Dickens for the 1957 season for what he termed "a consistent pattern" of excessive offers to prospects. In *The Big Ten*, a 1967 book he co-authored, Wilson called it "probably the first time a football coach had been forced to sit out the whole season before he had fielded a team."

Assistant coach Bob Hicks, who came to IU from Wyoming with Dickens, was interim head coach in a 1-8 season, the victory 14-7 over Villanova.

HOOSIER LIST

THE DOC DYNASTY

From July 11, 1959, to August 27, 1977, there was never a day when at least one of the 12 major individual swimming world records didn't have a Hoosier connection.

Year-by-year, the number of world records held by IU swimmers, before, during or after their Hoosier competitive seasons:

Year	Records
1959	2
1960	2
1961	6
1962	8
1963	6
1964	5
1965	1
1966	1
1967	5
1968	5
1969	6
1970	9
1971	6
1972	7
1973	5
1974	5
1975	3
1976	3
1977	1

INDIANA

LEGEND — *Frank McKinney*

FIRST COUNSILMAN CHAMPION

Frank McKinney Sr. was a national Democratic chairman (Harry S. Truman a frequent houseguest); owner of the Pittsburgh Pirates; president of one of Indianapolis' biggest banks, and an IU trustee. Through son Frank Jr., McKinney also developed an interest in swimming and played a role in the coinciding arrivals at IU of freshman Frank and designate-coach Jim "Doc" Counsilman in 1957-58.

Young Frank was the cornerstone for construction of Counsilman's swimming dynasty at IU. He won two Pan American Games gold medals and an Olympic bronze while still in high school, and as an IU freshman, he won two of his 14 National AAU championships. His Indianapolis and IU teammate, Alan Somers, said, "There never has been a prettier backstroker. When he swam, there was no splash."

Sophomore McKinney won both backstrokes at the 1959 Big Ten and NCAA meets. McKinney went on to win four more Big Ten titles.

McKinney returned to the Olympics in 1960 and won a gold medal in the medley relay as well as a silver in the 100-meter backstroke.

After getting bachelor's and master's degrees from IU's School of Business, McKinney became a business and civic leader in Indianapolis and a four-year IU trustee.

September 11, 1992, McKinney and three other prominent Indianapolis businessmen died in an airplane crash. His will included one of the major gifts that funded construction of IU's Counsilman-Billingsley Aquatic Center.

BIG TEN MEDAL - Ron Walden   **GIMBEL AWARD -** Tom McDonald

BALFOUR AWARDS
Football-Mike Rabold; Basketball-Frank Radovich; Baseball-John Anderson; Track-Willie May/Ron Long; Wrestling-Bill Bane/Fred Redeker; Swimming-Dick Kennedy; Gymnastics-Jerome Jacquin; Golf-Darl Kriete; Tennis-Dean Dixon

NCAA CHAMPIONS
Swimming - Frank McKinney, 100 backstroke (56.1), 200 backstroke (2:01.4)

IUitem

RABOLD: AN IU, BEARS STAR

All-American Mike Rabold was a member of the 1963 NFL champion Chicago Bears.

Chicagoan Mike Rabold had some football dreams when he arrived at Indiana in fall 1955.

Lineman Rabold, named IU's outstanding freshman, was a three-year varsity starter, playing almost every minute. After 3-6 and 1-8 seasons, captain Rabold led IU to successive November victories over Minnesota (6-0), Michigan State (6-0) and Michigan (8-6).

IU was 5-3, its first winning season in 11 years assured, going to Purdue (6-1-1) in 1958. The teams tied 15-15, and the Hoosiers—after 10 straight losses to Purdue—carried coach Phil Dickens off the field. "We talked all week about making him Coach of the Year," Rabold said. They came close; national coaches voted Dickens third.

Rabold made All-Big Ten and third-team All-America. He played back home in Chicago as a College All-Star, and after four NFL seasons, he was dealt to his dream team, the Bears, in time to play guard on their 1963 NFL champions. He started every game with the Bears from 1964 till his retirement at the end of the 1967 season.

Rabold returned to Bloomington as a partner in a beer distributorship. He was 33 when, returning from an Indianapolis business meeting, he lost control of his car on a rain-slicked curve. He died of neck and head injuries.

In 1969, Rabold was named to a first-team spot on an all-time IU team, selected by fans' vote.

Snapshot in Time

SILVER FOR MAY AFTER IU TITLES

WILLIE MAY'S HEAD was an Olympic champion, but his body finished second.

Before all that, the football recruit from Blue Island, Illinois, went into Hoosier history as one of the Big Ten's all-time great hurdlers.

May gave the 1957 Hoosiers a boost toward their Big Ten title sweep by edging Ohio State Olympic gold-medalist Glenn Davis to win the 70-yard hurdles indoors, then winning both the highs and lows outdoors.

That started a three-year reign in the outdoor high hurdles for May, a seven-time Big Ten champion. He won his second Big Ten low-hurdles championship in 1959 in :22.9; only Jesse Owens, with a world-record :22.6 in 1935, ever ran it faster in the conference meet.

May ran second to native Hoosier Lee Calhoun (Gary) in the 1960 U.S. Olympic Trials. In the hurdles finals at Melbourne, the two hit the finish line virtually together, the 6-3 May's head thrust forward out front in the photofinish but 6-1 Calhoun's torso—the determining factor—just ahead of May's to make Calhoun the first two-time hurdles champion in Olympic history.

May, also a silver medalist at the 1963 Pan-American Games, went on to a long and successful career as track coach at Evanston, Illinois, High.

IN THOSE DAYS . . .

COUNSILMAN ERA BEGINS

Indiana University's most dominant coaching era began quietly in fall 1957 when James "Doc" Counsilman arrived in Bloomington. Bob Royer, IU's swimming coach since 1932 except for a World War II interruption, was terminally ill with cancer. Counsilman, already nationally recognized, came in as Royer's titled assistant during the 1957-58 season, and he became head coach when Royer died.

The summer of 1958, Counsilman coached the Indianapolis Athletic Club to its first of seven National AAU outdoor championships. The team included stars who were the nucleus of Counsilman's first great IU team: backstroker Frank McKinney, butterflyer Mike Troy, freestyler Alan Somers and medleyist Bill Barton, all high school stars.

Counsilman brought in former Ohio State teammate Hobie Billingsley as the first collegiate diving coach. Counsilman recalled standing with Billingsley on the top level of brand new Royer Pool in 1960 and noting that the wall included 24 niches "tailor-made for large team pictures. I jokingly (more or less) told Hobie we'd fill them all with championship team pictures. We didn't quite make it." The two had 23 Big Ten championship teams, six of them NCAA champions, and each coach attained international stature as the world's best in his field.

1959 1960

HOOSIER LIST

IU'S LEADING REBOUNDERS

Game

33	Walt Bellamy vs. Michigan, 1961	
28	Walt Bellamy vs. Wisconsin, 1961	
26	Dick Neal vs. Wisconsin, 1957	
26	Dick Van Arsdale vs. Missouri, 1964	
26	Steve Downing vs. Ball State, 1972	

Season

428	Walt Bellamy, 1961
377	Steve Downing, 1972
352	George McGinnis, 1971
345	Archie Dees, 1958
335	Walt Bellamy, 1959
325	Walt Bellamy, 1960

Season Average

17.8	Walt Bellamy, 1961
15.2	Walt Bellamy, 1959
15.1	Steve Downing, 1972
14.7	George McGinnis, 1971
14.4	Archie Dees, 1957
14.4	Archie Dees, 1958
13.5	Walt Bellamy, 1960

Career

1091	Alan Henderson, 1992-95
1088	Walt Bellamy, 1959-61
1031	Kent Benson, 1974-77
914	Archie Dees, 1956-58
889	Steve Downing, 1971-73

INDIANA

LEGEND *Walt Bellamy*

OLYMPIAN, ROOKIE OF YEAR, HALL OF FAMER

His curse was to play without a championship, as a collegian or a pro. But by many standards, including election to the Basketball Hall of Fame, the best player in IU history may have been the man they called "Big Bell"— Walter Bellamy.

Bellamy came out of New Bern, North Carolina. He filled out the best decade of basketball centers any Big Ten school ever put together: barrier-breaker Bill Garrett at the start of the decade, Don Schlundt for four record years, then Archie Dees for three, leading up to Bellamy.

Each of the four made a major All-America team. Bellamy gave IU representation on perhaps the greatest amateur team ever, the gold-medal U.S. Olympic team that also included Oscar Robertson, Jerry West, Jerry Lucas, Bob Boozer and Terry Dischinger.

Bellamy averaged 17.4 points and 15.2 rebounds as an IU sophomore. His junior year, the averages were 22.4 and 13.5 on one of Branch McCracken's best clubs: 20-4, winner of 11 in a row and No. 7 in the nation closing out the year.

As a senior, Bellamy averaged 17.8 rebounds (still IU's record) and 21.8 points on a 15-9 team that was No. 4 in early polls before falling out. His final college game, he set IU and Big Ten records that still stand with 33 rebounds (and 28 points) in an 82-67 win over Michigan. IU's three-time MVP, he made All-Big Ten twice and second-team All-America his senior season.

Bellamy became the first Hoosier taken No. 1 in the NBA draft and the first Hoosier named Rookie of the Year. Not Robertson, not West, not Elgin Baylor or Michael Jordan—only Wilt Chamberlain— topped his rookie numbers: 31.6 scoring average, 19.0 rebounds.

BIG TEN MEDAL - Don Noone **GIMBEL AWARD -** Ted Smith

BALFOUR AWARDS

Football, Elvin Caldwell; Basketball, Frank Radovich; Baseball, John Anderson; Track, Joe Carroll; Wrestling, George Ihnat; Swimming, Gerry Miki/John Parks; Gymnastics, Jerome Jacquin; Golf, John Sommer; Tennis, John Fitzpatrick.

NCAA CHAMPIONS

Swimming, Mike Troy, 100 butterfly (53.1), 200 butterfly (1:57.8); 400 medley relay, Frank McKinney, Gerry Miki, Mike Troy, Pete Sintz, 3:40.8.

OLYMPIC MEDALISTS

Basketball - Walt Bellamy, gold. Swimming - Mike Troy, 200 butterfly, gold (2:12.8); 800 freestyle relay, gold (8:10.2); Frank McKinney, 100 backstroke, silver (1:02.1); 400 medley relay, gold (4:05.1); Track, Willie May, 110 hurdles, silver (13.8).

IU item

NCAA HAMMER DROPS

I U's darkest athletic hours of the century began with a thunderbolt April 27, 1960, headlined in that day's Bloomington *Herald-Telephone*:

"IU SOCKED WITH FOUR-YEAR NCAA POST-SEASON PENALTY"

Three months later, the Big Ten added to the penalty by putting IU's football program on a one-year probation that included prohibition from participating in distribution of the league's TV revenue, about an $85,000 "fine."

The NCAA move covered all sports, although Big Ten Commissioner Kenneth "Tug" Wilson—who joined IU officials in an appeal of the decision—said only football was involved in the charges against IU. The NCAA's infractions committee stuck with its penalty, particularly upset because of the six NCAA violations it charged against IU, five came in 1958 when the football program already was on probation.

The Big Ten penalty lasted just one year, but from April 27, 1960, through April 27, 1964, no IU athletic team could participate in post-season NCAA championship competition. "It meant that Indiana, which had the best swimming team in the country, would be denied a crack at the NCAA championship . . . (and) banned any chance for their basketball team to compete in the NCAA championship," Wilson said in his 1967 book, *The Big Ten*. The swimming team was allowed to compete in the 1964 NCAA meet, a month before the original penalty expired.

> ## "It meant that Indiana, which had the best swimming team in the country, would be denied a crack at the NCAA championship . . ."
>
> **—Big Ten Commissioner Kenneth "Tug" Wilson**

SOPHOMORE SWEEP FOR MIKE TROY

FEW ATHLETES IN history have had the debut year—or career—that swimmer Mike Troy did at Indiana.

Only Doc Counsilman knew how really good Troy was until the summer of 1959 when he won the U.S. National 200-meter butterfly championship with a world-record performance.

Then, in 1960, his first year of collegiate eligibility, butterflyer Troy:

• Twice broke the American record in the 200-yard butterfly in regular-season competition, the first man to take the record under two minutes;

• Won both the 100 and 200 butterflies in the Big Ten meet;

• Won both in the NCAA championships, taking the 200 record on down to 1:57.4;

• Won both in the AAU indoor championships; and

• Won the 200-meter title, only butterfly event contested, and reset his world record in the AAU outdoor championships;

• Won the butterfly, again in world-record time, in the Rome Olympics, where he also picked up a gold as a member of the 800-meter freestyle relay team.

Six times in his career Troy broke the 200-meter butterfly record. A charter member of the IU Athletics Hall of Fame, Troy also is in the International Swimming Hall of Fame.

Mike Troy—Big Ten, NCAA, AAU & Olympic Champion, world record-holder.

IN THOSE DAYS . . .

ARRIVAL DAY FOR IU SWIMMING

If there was a defining moment for Doc Counsilman's fledgling swimming program at Indiana, it was Saturday, February 20, 1960, at Ann Arbor—"a wintry afternoon," Counsilman once recalled.

"As we walked in, I looked up to see a young man dangling half-in and half-out of a window. The building was literally stormed by the student body."

The overflow crowd of 4,000 saw IU open the meet stunningly. Frank McKinney, Mike Troy, captain Gerry Miki and Pete Sintz took 4.3 seconds off the listed American record in the 400-yard medley relay.

Troy set another American record in winning the butterfly. McKinney led a 1-2 Indiana finish in the backstroke. The Hoosiers had things clinched going into the concluding 400-yard freestyle relay but won it anyway for a 58-47 score—reigning NCAA champion Michigan's first dual-meet loss in four years.

Michigan regrouped to win the Big Ten and edge Indiana 73-69 for second in the NCAA meet behind Southern Cal (87).

But this meet in Ann Arbor that *Sports Illustrated* covered started an annual no-stops-pulled battle whenever the two teams met in Bloomington or Ann Arbor. "Oh," Counsilman said, "the dual meets were monumental."

131

HOOSIER LIST

BIG TEN CHAMPIONSHIPS DURING BILL ORWIG'S TENURE

1961	Men's Swimming
1962	Men's Golf
	Men's Swimming
1963	Men's Swimming
1964	Men's Swimming
	Men's Tennis
1965	Men's Swimming
1966	Men's Swimming
1967	Men's Basketball
	Men's Swimming
1968	Men's Cross Country
	Football
	Men's Golf
	Men's Swimming
1969	Men's Swimming
1970	Men's Golf
	Men's Swimming
	Men's Outdoor Track
1971	Men's Swimming
	Men's Outdoor Track
1972	Men's Swimming
1973	Men's Basketball
	Men's Cross Country
	Men's Golf
	Men's Swimming
	Men's Indoor Track
	Men's Outdoor Track
1974	Men's Basketball
	Men's Cross Country
	Men's Golf
	Men's Swimming
	Men's Indoor Track
	Men's Outdoor Track
1975	Men's Basketball
	Men's Golf
	Men's Swimming
	Men's Indoor Track

INDIANA

⊛ LEGEND   *Earl Faison*

'TREE' REACHED FULL BLOOM IN AFL

Earl Faison jumped from prospect to star with one play in Indiana's 6-0 victory over Michigan State in 1958, his sophomore year.

The six points came when defensive end Faison blocked a field-goal try, picked up the ball and ran a Big Ten-record 92 yards to score. "It seemed like I'd never reach the end zone," the 6-5, 240-pound Faison said. "But it wasn't the run that made me the tiredest. It was surviving all those people jumping on me in the end zone. I don't know where they came from."

That was the game when Faison picked up a nickname. On the way to the shutout, an impressed Spartan mentioned Faison to a teammate and said, "Did you see the legs on that guy?" The response: "Those aren't legs, they're roots. That guy's a tree." Faison was "Tree" after that.

Faison was IU's MVP his senior season, when he also made All-Big Ten and third-team All-America.

Faison, from Newport News, Virginia, roomed as a freshman with another big rookie from the South, 6-11, 250-pound basketball center Walt Bellamy. "We shared our intimate secrets, our uncertainties, our fears," Faison said.

Four years later, Faison was Rookie of the Year in the American Football League and Bellamy was Rookie of the Year in the National Basketball Association.

For Faison, that was the first of four first-team All-AFL seasons on Chargers' teams that reached the AFL championship game four times and won in 1963—three years before the first Super Bowl game. He was elected to the Chargers' Hall of Fame and the Virginia Hall of Fame before his induction in 1990 into the IU Athletics Hall of Fame. "I appreciated them all," Faison said in Bloomington, "but this one means the most."

BIG TEN MEDAL - Gary Long   **GIMBEL AWARD -** Bob Reinhart

BALFOUR AWARDS

Football, Earl Faison; Basketball, Walt Bellamy; Baseball, Paul Deem/Max Bailey; Track, Reggie Flood/Reggie Laconi; Wrestling, Dick Zboray; Swimming, Frank McKinney; Gymnastics, Tom Lancaster; Golf, Dave Pelz; Tennis, Gil Lortz/Don Thorne.

IU item

START OF A BIG TEN DYNASTY

"We're going to break some more records. In a few years we'll look back and wonder how we could have been so slow."

—IU swim coach
Doc Counsilman

From 1931 through 1960, Michigan or Ohio State won the Big Ten swimming championship 29 times.

That ended in 1961, and it was another 20 years before any team but Indiana won the meet.

The transfer of power came in the Columbus, Ohio, pool where both Doc Counsilman and diving coach Hobie Billingsley helped Ohio State to some Big Ten and NCAA championships.

Indiana's 205.5 to 201.8 victory over Michigan included 4.5 surprise last-night points from Keith Craddock and John Lovestedt of Billingsley's brand new diving program. That avoided a repeat of 1960, when IU's swimmers outscored Michigan's but diving points made the Wolverines champions.

Counsilman squeezed points every way he could. Olympian Mike Troy doubled the final day and contributed thirds in both the 400-yard freestyle and 100-yard butterfly. Double-winner Frank McKinney "was great, just great," Counsilman said. "Here's a kid who has done it all—a record-breaker, Olympic team member . . . and all he thought about was the team effort."

Indiana led in the meet's record onslaught, but Counsilman was prescient. "We're going to break some more records," he said. "In a few years we'll look back and wonder how we could have been so slow."

ORWIG TAKES OVER

ON FEBRUARY 13, 1961, ten months into its four-year NCAA probation, Indiana named Bill Orwig athletic director.

Orwig, who had starred in football and basketball at Michigan, was in his ninth years as athletic director at Nebraska when Indiana hired him, effective Aug. 1.

Orwig sent a clear message in his first Bloomington speech—to the Bloomington Varsity Club March 11.

"No strong athletic program has been built on fraud," he said. "We'll never have a part of that as long as I am the director at Indiana University.

"I know there have been mistakes made here, but I think they've been honest ones. These are mistakes to be corrected."

Orwig was IU's director for 14 years, in which Hoosier teams won 37 Big Ten championships in seven sports. His hirings included Bob Knight in basketball, Sam Bell in track and John Pont in football. In his era, soccer became a varsity sport and Jerry Yeagley was the Hoosier coach from the start. And, swimming, under two coaches he inherited, Doc Counsilman and Hobie Billingsley, reached its peak with six straight national championships.

At 86, Bill Orwig died July 30, 1994. He had been inducted into IU's Athletics Hall of Fame in 1987.

Under Bill Orwig's leadership, Indiana won 37 Big Ten championships.

IN THOSE DAYS . . .

NEW STADIUM DEDICATED

Indiana moved into its gleaming new football home in 1960 and played that season as a non-team.

Big Ten Commissioner Kenneth "Tug" Wilson, in penalizing the football program for illegal recruiting, declared Indiana's Big Ten games would not count in conference standings.

Indiana went 0-7 in league play. Without IU's penalty, Minnesota (a 42-0 winner over Indiana) would have won the Big Ten title outright at 6-1 instead of sharing it at 5-1 with Iowa, which didn't play IU that fall.

Fourth-year coach Phil Dickens had some fun with his plight at a Chicago luncheon attended by Wilson. "I've had a great career at Indiana," Dickens said. "One year I wasn't allowed to coach and this season the results don't count."

October 8, Indiana lost its first game in the stadium 20-6 to Oregon State and 1962 Heisman Trophy winner Terry Baker. Wingback Nate Ramsey scored the historic IU touchdown.

Dedication came October 22. Homecoming queen Judy Curtis of Monon broke across a goalpost a bottle filled with Jordan River water.

Then Michigan State routed the Hoosiers, 35-0.

IU's first victory of the season (and only 1960 win) was 34-8 over Marquette.

HOOSIER LIST

HOOSIERS IN INTERNATIONAL SWIMMING HALL OF FAME

United States

Hobie Billingsley, coach/diver, 1983

Lesley Bush, diver, 1986

James 'Doc' Counsilman, coach, 1976

Kathleen Ellis, swimmer, 1991

Gary Hall, swimmer, 1981

Charles Hickcox, swimmer, 1976

Chet Jastremski, swimmer, 1977

John Kinsella, swimmer, 1986

Don McKenzie, swimmer, 1986

Frank McKinney, swimmer, 1975

Jim Montgomery, swimmer, 1986

Cynthia Potter, diver, 1994

Ken Sitzberger, diver, 1994

Mark Spitz, swimmer, 1977

Ted Stickles, swimmer, 1975

Tom Stock, swimmer, 1989

Mike Troy, swimmer, 1971

Australia

Kevin Berry, swimmer, 1980

Bobby Windle, swimmer, 1990

LEGEND — *Chet Jastremski*

'BEST SWIMMER IN THE WORLD'

Chet Jastremski may be the greatest Indiana University swimmer who never won an NCAA championship or an Olympic gold medal. Nine world records make a good starting point for that argument.

The three NCAA meets IU missed because of probation were Jastremski's three varsity seasons (1961, '62 and '63). In '62, his winning breaststroke times in the Big Ten meet were 1:01.7 at 100 yards and 2:13.7 at 200; the winning NCAA times were 1:01.7 (by Michigan's Richard Nelson, whom he had beaten in the Big Ten) and 2:16.8. The differences were greater in '63: Jastremski 1:00.9 and 2:13.2 in the Big Ten, NCAA winners 1:02.2 and 2:17.0.

Before any of those performances, Arlie Schardt in the January 29, 1962, *Sports Illustrated* called Jastremski "beyond argument the best swimmer in the world. Last summer (he) broke world records in his specialty not once but again and again, and in doing so changed the basic conception of the stroke itself."

Jastremski's nine world breaststroke records included six at 100 meters in the seven-week 1961 stretch Schardt mentioned.

He was luckless in the Olympics. As a 15-year-old Toledo high schooler, Jastremski had the second-best 200-meter breaststroke qualifying time in the 1956 Olympic Trials but was disqualified because an official said he kicked one leg six inches deeper than the other coming out of a turn. At the 1960 Trials, he placed second in the 200-meter breaststroke but U.S. officials misunderstood Olympic rules and left him at home. In '64, he finally made the team with a world-record 200-meter performance in the U.S. Trials and won a bronze medal. He almost made the U.S. team in 1972—at 31 and already a doctor, he reached the Olympic Trials finals before losing out.

He did win a gold medal at the 1963 Pan-American Games and 13 U.S. championships indoors and outdoors.

As a doctor, Jastremski went into family practice in Bloomington, serving for a time as IU's women's swimming coach. He was elected to the International Swimming Hall of Fame in 1997 and to IU's Athletics Hall of Fame in 1983.

BIG TEN MEDAL - Bill Elyea   **GIMBEL AWARD -** Charley Hall

BALFOUR AWARDS

Football, Byron Broome; Basketball, Jerry Bass; Baseball, Eddie LaDuke; Track, Jim Clinton; Wrestling, John Maroni; Swimming, Mike Troy; Gymnastics, John Burkel/A.J.Canning; Golf, Forrest Jones; Tennis, Charles Jenness.

IU item

STAHR SUCCEEDS WELLS

Secretary of the Army Elvis J. Stahr, jr., who left the presidency of the University of West Virginia to take office with the new John F. Kennedy administration in January 1961, was announced on Founders Day, May 2, as the choice to succeed popular Herman B Wells as IU's president.

Wells had asked the Board of Trustees to allow him to leave the job July 1, 1962, after 25 years. Stahr's appointment took effect on that day.

Wells called Stahr "a recognized scholar, a skilled academic administrator and an experienced public servant."

President Kennedy, in a letter accepting Stahr's resignation, saluted him for "a job well done and a service truly performed for the government and the people of our country."

Just as Wells liked his middle initial B run without a period, Stahr liked the junior in his name run jr., uncapitalized. "Call it an eccentricity if you like," he said.

At his first press conference, athletics did come up. The 46-year-old Kentucky native said he loved basketball and would be "delighted" to see IU win in football.

January 2, 1968, Stahr became the only IU president of the century to ride in the Rose Bowl parade representing a competing team.

Elvis J. Stahr, jr.

Snapshot In Time

RECORD RUNAWAY, YEAR OF NAMES

ON THE DAY after New Year's 1962, Indiana's basketball team celebrated, at Notre Dame's expense.

Playing their annual game at the Fort Wayne Coliseum, the Hoosiers roared to a 122-95 victory. The total matched the school record set in a 122-92 victory at Ohio State in 1959, and it still stands.

Fort Wayne native Tom Bolyard had an off-night with eight points, but Jimmy Rayl (28), Charley Hall (22) and Jerry Bass (21) filled in well.

Notre Dame's nine players in the game included junior Ed Malloy, who didn't score. In 1987, the Rev. Edward A. Malloy, C.S.C., became the school's president.

It was a year of "name" opponents for the Hoosiers, who:
• Won at North Carolina, 76-70, despite 22 points by Larry Brown and 11 by Donnie Walsh, later coach and general manager of the Indiana Pacers;
• Split with Michigan State, with Pete Gent, who was to write a best-seller, *North Dallas 40*, scoring 13 and 22 points;
• Split with Illinois, with future pro sports owner Jerry Colangelo scoring 17 and 15 points;
• Lost its only game with defending national champion Ohio State, which got eight points from future IU coach Bob Knight, who had sat in the stands with fellow freshmen Jerry Lucas and John Havlicek and watched the 122-point record set three years earlier.

1962  1963

HOOSIER LIST

IU'S 40-POINT SCORERS

56   Jimmy Rayl vs. Minnesota, 1962*

56   Jimmy Rayl vs. Michigan State, 1963

48   Mike Woodson vs. Illinois, 1979

47   Don Schlundt vs. Ohio State, 1954

47   Don Schlundt vs. Ohio State, 1955

47   Steve Downing vs. Kentucky, 1972**

45   George McGinnis vs. Northern Illinois, 1971

44   Jimmy Rayl vs. Wisconsin, 1962

44   Jimmy Rayl vs. Michigan State, 1963

42   Walt Bellamy vs. Illinois, 1960

42   Dick VanArsdale vs. Notre Dame, 1964

42   Steve Alford vs. Michigan State, 1987

41   Don Schlundt vs. Notre Dame, 1953

41   Don Schlundt vs. SMU, 1955

41   Jimmy Rayl vs. DePaul, 1962

41   George McGinnis vs. San Jose State, 1971

41   Steve Downing vs. Illinois, 1973

41   Scott May vs. Wisconsin, 1976

41   Alan Henderson vs. Michigan State, 1994

40   Ted Kitchel vs. Illinois, 1981

*Overtime

**Double overtime

INDIANA

LEGEND   *Jimmy Rayl*

56 POINTS, TWICE

Jimmy Rayl

Jimmy Rayl shot the basketball like no other Hoosier before or since.

Shot it often. Shot it high. Shot it well.

Already an Indiana high school legend by the time he left Kokomo, Rayl had a disappointing sophomore season at IU—just 79 points for the full season, zero in the last five games. By contrast, Tom Bolyard, who had come out of Fort Wayne South with high school credentials similar to Rayl's, had an outstanding sophomore year, just missing IU's first-season varsity record with 371 points.

The magic came back for Rayl his junior year. He scored 34 in the second game of the year against New Mexico State, then headed into semester exams with his first collegiate 40-point game, 41 in a 98-89 victory at DePaul.

In the first game after exams, Rayl exploded. He had 25 points the first half against Minnesota (IU trailed 53-48). He was at 48 after leading a comeback from 11 points down with 10 minutes left to force overtime. Then, his 20-foot shot with two seconds left in overtime won the game, 105-104, and lifted him to a Big Ten-record 56.

A year later, Dave Downey of Illinois scored 53 in a 103-100 loss at IU, and a record claim went up—he had done it in the regulation 40 minutes. In a 72-71 win over Iowa two nights later, Rayl went to the opposite extreme. He hit just one of seven shots and scored two points, ending his 43-game string of double-figure performances.

His bounce-back was spectacular: another 56-point game as IU routed Michigan State, 113-94. He put up 48 shots and hit 23. All of those numbers—23 field goals, 48 shots, 56-points—are still IU records.

Seventeen games in their three shared years, Rayl and Bolyard each scored 20 or more points. That's an IU record. So is their combined 48.4 average as juniors (29.8 for Rayl, 18.6 for Bolyard).

Both were All-Big Ten as seniors. Both are in the Indiana Basketball Hall of Fame and IU's Athletics Hall of Fame.

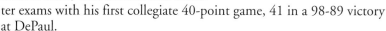

BIG TEN MEDAL - Chet Jastremski   **GIMBEL AWARD** - Tom Bolyard

BALFOUR AWARDS

Football-Woody Moore; Basketball-Jimmy Rayl; Baseball-Dave Granger; Track-Ted Jackson; Wrestling-Bill Gavin; Swimming-Chet Jastremski; Gymnastics-Jim Woodward; Golf-Art White; Tennis-Gary Baxter

IU item

WOODSON BRINGS BUCKET BACK

Through 14 Old Oaken Bucket games ending 14 football seasons, the best thing Indiana had to celebrate was a 15-15 tie in 1958.

Maybe the slowest touchdown in Bucket history ended the ignominy for IU.

Purdue led 7-6 late in the second quarter with first down at the Indiana 14. Quarterback Ron DiGravio's pass skipped off a receiver to IU's Marv Woodson at the 8.

Woodson headed up the east sideline, and DiGravio angled in to cut him off at Indiana's 25. Play seemed in slow motion as Woodson faked, cut, stopped, cut back, stopped, faked—DiGravio, looking over one shoulder, then another, giving ground slowly, waiting for help.

The help that came was for Woodson. Guard Don Croftcheck's block flattened DiGravio and Woodson completed the 92-yard touchdown run 1:12 before halftime.

The 12-7 score stood up. Purdue receiver Ray Schultz was tackled at the IU 7 on the last play of the game.

Woodson, from Hattiesburg, Mississippi, was the Hoosiers' best offensive player, gaining 101 yards in a 10-7 loss to Ohio State and a team-high 540 for the season. He went on to a strong six-year pro career, mostly as a defensive back with Pittsburgh.

Captain Nate Ramsey proudly displays the Old Oaken Bucket after the 12-7 win over Purdue in '62.

Snapshot in Time

AUSTRALIAN GOLD MEDALISTS PICK IU, DOC

DOC COUNSILMAN'S IU swimming program became global in the summer of 1963 when Australian butterfly star Kevin Berry signed with the Hoosiers.

Berry at 15 was a 1960 Olympic finalist in the 200-yard butterfly. He finished sixth and sat on the pool deck to watch the ceremony that honored gold medalist Mike Troy. "I wrote to Mike in Bloomington after I got home," Berry said, "and he sent me a postcard. I carried it around for a couple of years.

"Why Indiana for me? It was that postcard, and Troy giving me a T-shirt that had 'Indiana Swimming' on it, and Doc writing to (Australian Olympic coach Don) Talbot, and Tom Dinsley (a Canadian diver at IU) coming down to the Commonwealth Games in 1962 with a message to recruit me."

Berry attended the fall semester at IU in 1963, then went home to prepare for Tokyo. The 1964 Olympic 200-meter butterfly gold-medal ceremony was for him.

When he returned to IU, Australian teammate Bob Windle, the 1964 Olympic 1,500-meter freestyle winner and a one-time world recordholder at 200 meters, joined him. Both won Big Ten championships for IU, and Windle anchored an 800-yard freestyle relay team that won in the 1967 NCAA meet.

Kevin Berry won a gold medal for Australia in the 200-butterfly in '64.

HOOSIER LIST

GOLD MEDALISTS IN SWIMMING AND DIVING

1952 *Bill Woolsey:* 800-Freestyle Relay, Gold
1956 *Bill Woolsey:* 800-Freestyle Relay, Silver
Frank McKinney: 100-Backstroke, Bronze
1960 *Mike Troy:* 200 Butterfly, Gold; 800-Freestyle Relay, Gold; *Frank McKinney:* 400-Medley Relay, Gold; 100-Backstroke, Silver
1964 *Ken Sitzberger:* Springboard diving, Gold
Fred Schmidt: 400-Medley Relay, Gold; 200-Butterfly, Bronze; *Chet Jastremski:* 200-Breaststroke, Bronze
Bob Windle (Aus): 1500 Freestyle, Gold; 400-Freestyle Relay, Bronze; *Kevin Berry (Aus):* 200-Butterfly, Gold; 400-Medley Relay, Bronze; *Lesley Bush:* Platform Diving, Gold; *Kathleen Ellis:* 400-Freestyle Relay, Gold; 400-Medley Relay, Gold; 100-Butterfly, Bronze; 100-Freestyle, Bronze; *Terri Stickles:* 400 Freestyle, Bronze
1968 *Charlie Hickcox:* 200-Ind. Medley, Gold; 400 Ind.Medley, Gold; 400 Medley Relay, Gold; 100-Backstroke, Silver; *Don McKenzie:* 100-Breaststroke, Gold; 400-Medley Relay, Gold; *Mark Spitz:* 400-Freestyle Relay, Gold; 800 Freestyle Relay, Gold; 100-Butterfly, Silver; 100-Freestyle, Bronze; *Gary Hall:* 400-Ind. Medley, Silver; *John Kinsella:* 1500-Freestyle, Silver; *Jack Horsley:* 200 Backstroke, Bronze; *Jim Henry:* Springboard Diving, Bronze; *Win Young:* Platform Diving, Bronze; *Bob Windle (Aus):* 800-Freestyle Relay, Silver; 400-Freesyle Relay, Bronze
1972 *Mark Spitz:* 100-Freestyle, Gold; 200-Freestyle, Gold; 100-Butterfly, Gold; 200-Butterfly, Gold; 400-Medley Relay, Gold; 400-Freestyle Relay, Gold; 800-Freestyle Relay, Gold; *Mike Stamm:* 400-Medley Relay, Gold; 100-Backstroke, Silver; 200-Backstroke, Silver; *Gary Hall:* 200-Butterfly, Silver; *John Murphy:* 400 Freestyle Relay, Gold; 100-Backstroke, Bronze; *Fred Tyler:* 800-Freestyle Relay, Gold; *John Kinsella:* 800 Freestyle Relay, Gold
1976 *Jim Montgomery:* 100-Freestyle, Gold; 400-Medley Relay, Gold; 800-Freestyle Relay, Gold; 200-Freestyle, Bronze; *Gary Hall:* 100-Butterfly, Bronze; *Cynthia Potter:* Springboard Diving, Bronze
1980 *Mark Kerry (Aus):* 400-Medley Relay, Gold; 200-Backstroke, Bronze; *Djan Madruga (Brazil):* 800-Freestyle Relay, Bronze
1984 *Mark Kerry (Aus):* 400-Medley Relay, Bronze
1988 *Sergio Lopez (Spain):* 200-Breaststroke, Bronze
1992 *Mark Lenzi:* Springboard Diving, Gold
1996 *Mark Lenzi:* Springboard Diving, Bronze

⬖ INDIANA LEGEND *Lesley Bush*

A MIRACLE FROM 10 METERS UP

Hobie Billingsley calls it the greatest upset in the history of diving, "a miracle."

It began in the spring of 1964 and resulted in a gold medal that 17-year-old diving unknown Lesley Bush won in 10-meter platform competition at the Tokyo Olympics.

Bush trained under Billingsley the summer of 1964, after he watched her finish 11th at the national indoor championships in April and told her: "There's an outside, outside, outside chance you could make the Olympic team."

At the U.S. Trials, she just missed on the springboard, finishing fourth, but she came back to make the team in her first "high-dive" competition.

At Tokyo, East German Ingrid Kramer already had won the springboard gold, her second straight Olympic sweep all but conceded.

But, Bush nailed her opening dive for 9s from the judges and took a lead she stubbornly kept all the way. With 7s on the meet's last dive, she beat Kramer by 1.35 points.

Billingsley said Bush's father back home got a post-midnight call. "A wire-service reporter said, 'Congratulations, your daughter just won the Olympic gold medal.' He said, 'That's a fine trick to play on someone in the middle of the night,' and hung up. They had to call him back.

"*Nobody* could believe it."

At IU, Bush earned a degree in biology and won five national championships on one- and three-meter springboards and in platform. She won another platform gold medal at the 1967 Pan-American Games and made it back to the Olympics in 1968 but didn't medal. In 1987, she was the first woman inducted into IU's Athletics Hall of Fame.

BIG TEN MEDAL - Jim Binkley   **GIMBEL AWARD -** Lary Schulhof

BALFOUR AWARDS
Football, Tom Nowatzke; Basketball, Dick Van Arsdale/Tom Van Arsdale; Baseball, Don Dilly; Track, Cornelius Miller; Wrestling, Dick Isel; Swimming, Ted Stickles; Gymnastics, Bob Lilly; Golf, Byron Comstock; Tennis, Alan Graham.

NCAA CHAMPIONS
Swimming: Fred Schmidt, 200 butterfly (1:53.5); Diving: Rick Gilbert, 1-meter springboard.

OLYMPIC MEDALISTS
Swimming - Kathy Ellis, 400 freestyle relay, gold (4:03.8), 400 medley relay, gold (4:33.9), 100 freestyle, bronze (1:00.8), 100 butterfly, bronze (1:06.0); Kevin Berry (Australia), 200 butterfly, gold (2:06.6); 400 medley relay, bronze (4:02.3); Bob Windle (Australia), 1,500 freestyle, gold (17:01.7), 400 freestyle relay, bronze (3:39.1); Fred Schmidt, 200 butterfly, bronze (2:09.3), 400 medley relay, gold (3:58.4); Chet Jastremski, 200 breaststroke, bronze (2:29.6); Terri Stickles, 400 freestyle, bronze (4:47.2); Diving - Ken Sitzberger, springboard, gold; Lesley Bush, women's platform, gold.

NOWATZKE: A STEP-IN ALL-AMERICAN

Tom Nowatzke scored 21 points against Oregon in 1964, an IU record for 14 years.

A third-game knee injury to pre-season All-American Marv Woodson gave Indiana's 1963 football team an early body blow. Junior fullback Tom Nowatzke stepped up.

Woodson's darts and slants became Nowatzke power blasts. Nowatzke (6-3, 228 pounds) more resembled Dick Butkus (6-3, 234) than he did Jim Grabowski (6-2, 211) or other 1960s power backs.

Like center Butkus, Nowatzke also was a linebacker. He played 51 minutes a game in 1963, all 60 in the Hoosiers' 21-15 loss to Purdue.

Nowatzke's 124 rushing yards against Purdue gave him an IU-record 756 for the season. He was IU's first Big Ten rushing champion since league record-keeping began in 1939, and the first Hoosier ever named to the American Football Coaches' 11-man All-America team (which started in 1945).

Drafted No. 1 by both the Detroit Lions and New York Jets, he played four years for Detroit, then four for Baltimore. In Super Bowl V, he scored the tying touchdown in Baltimore's 16-13 victory over Dallas—the only Super Bowl touchdown by an IU player.

Nowatzke also kicked. Straight-on, not soccer-style, he launched the first 50-yard field goal in Big Ten history against Ohio State in 1964, breaking Elmer Wilkens' 41-year-old IU record.

In 1995, Nowatzke entered the IU Athletics Hall of Fame.

Snapshot In Time

ASSASSINATION DELAYS IU-PURDUE

FOR THE FIRST time since 1948, Indiana owned the Old Oaken Bucket going into a Purdue game. The 1963 game was at IU, and Purdue's senior quarterback, Big Ten passing and total offense leader Ron DiGravio, had a sore shoulder, his availability uncertain.

About 24 hours before kickoff, news of President John F. Kennedy's assassination stunned the world. Indiana-Purdue was one of many games postponed that black Friday.

The teams played one Saturday later. Circumstances had changed. IU coach Phil Dickens had entered Mayo Clinic in Rochester, Minnesota, on Monday for long-scheduled tests. Assistant coach Bob Hicks took charge.

DiGravio showed up sharp. He hit 10 of 14 passes for 187 yards, including a 55-yard first-quarter touchdown strike to Randy Minniear. Indiana matched that touchdown, then fell behind 14-7 by halftime.

A late-game Indiana drive died on downs at Purdue's 5. A Purdue fumble gave the ball back. IU quarterback Rich Badar ran the ball in from the 9, then, with 2:37 left, passed to Trent Walters for the two-point conversion that put Indiana up 15-14.

The lead lasted 26 seconds. Gordon Teter ran the kickoff back to Indiana's 25, and DiGravio passed to Minniear for the touchdown that won for Purdue, 21-15.

IN THOSE DAYS . . .

DOC-COACHED OLYMPIANS SHINE

Doc Counsilman from 1961 through 1963 had probably the strongest college team in America but couldn't prove it because of NCAA probation.

Doc's peers knew what he had built and by vote strongly recommended him for the job that he did get: head men's swimming coach in the 1964 Olympics.

It was a golden choice. Where the American men had won four of the eight available swimming golds in 1960 and just one of seven in 1956, Counsilman's 1964 team won seven of the ten events.

Counsilman did even better than that.

Two of the three men's golds that got away were won by his Australian recruits, butterflyer Kevin Berry and freestyler Bobby Windle.

And, Kathy Ellis, the first woman swimmer named to IU's Athletics Hall of Fame, won golds as a member of two U.S. women's relay teams and bronze medals in two individual events. In 1998, she was the first woman swimmer inducted in IU's Athletics Hall of Fame.

The Hoosier success at Tokyo also carried over to diving, where freshman Ken Sitzberger previewed his NCAA success by winning the men's springboard gold. Another Hobie Billingsley pupil, Lesley Bush, was the women's platform diving gold medalist.

HOOSIER LIST

IU'S TOP NBA SCORERS

	Points	Seasons
Walt Bellamy	20,941	14
Isiah Thomas	18,822	13
George McGinnis	17,009*	11
Dick Van Arsdale	15,079	12
Tom Van Arsdale	14,232	12
Mike Woodson	10,981	11
Jon McGlocklin	9,169	11
Kent Benson	6,168	11
Quinn Buckner	5,929	10
Calbert Cheaney	5,499#	6
Bobby Wilkerson	5,424	7
Bobby Leonard	4,204	7
Randy Wittman	4,034	9
Scott May	3,690	6
Johnny Logan	3,196	5
Butch Carter	3,137	5
Alan Henderson	2,162#	4
Herm Schaefer	1,903	7
Bill Tosheff	1,859	3
Tom Abernethy	1,779	5
Archie Dees	1,548	4
Dean Garrett	1,410#	3
Dick Farley	1,378	3
Steve Green	1,179*	4
Jimmy Rayl	1,125*	2
Curly Armstrong	1,040	8

* Includes ABA points
\# Active through 1998-99

INDIANA

LEGEND — Tom and Dick Van Arsdale

IDENTICAL, AND INCOMPARABLE

America has never seen twin athletes more alike in appearance, achievement and exceptional performance than IU's Van Arsdales, Tom and Dick.

They came to Indiana after enchanting the state with their play for state basketball runnerup Indianapolis Manual. They were the first co-winners of the state's Trester Award, the first co-Mr. Basketballs for the Indiana All-Star series. Each scored 26 points in the first game against Kentucky's All-Stars, 14 in the second.

At IU Tom finished with 1,252 points, Dick 1,240 (with five college games to go, each had 1,150 points). Tom had 723 career rebounds, Dick 719.

In 72 college games, Dick's scoring high was 42 points against Notre Dame as a junior. Tom's IU high was 34 points, in the same game—their 76 probably the NCAA record for brothers *and* twins.

At IU, each scored 30 points just one other time, in their junior year. Each scored 20 or more points 27 times—14 times in the same game.

As juniors and seniors, they were IU's co-MVPs.

Both won gold medals with the U.S. team in the World University Games. Both were second-round draft picks, and both made the five-man NBA All-Rookie team. Their NBA careers peaked in the same four seasons, 1968-69 through 1971-72, during which Tom averaged 21.1 points a game, Dick 21.0.

Each played 12 NBA seasons and they retired after the 1976-77 season, when for the first time as pros they were teammates (with the Phoenix Suns).

They were inducted into the IU Athletics Hall of Fame in 1985 and the Indiana Basketball Hall of Fame in 1986.

Tom Van Arsdale

Dick Van Arsdale

BIG TEN MEDAL - Doug Spicer   **GIMBEL AWARD -** Fred Schmidt

BALFOUR AWARDS
Football-Tom Nowatzke; Basketball-Jon McGlocklin; Baseball-Tom Erickson; Track-Terry Shy; Wrestling-Dick Conway; Swimming-Rick Gilbert; Gymnastics-Jim Everroad; Golf-Paul Williams; Tennis-Rod McNerney

NCAA CHAMPIONS
Swimming-Fred Schmidt, 100 butterfly (51.0), 200 butterfly (1:54.4); Tom Tretheway, 200 breaststroke (2:10.4); 400 medley relay, Pete Hammer, Tom Tretheway, Fred Schmidt, Bob Williamson (3:30.7). Diving: Ken Sitzberger, 1-meter springboard, 3-meter springboard.

IU item

SCHMIDT LED RECORDHOLDERS

Olympian Fred Schmidt was one of IU's many world record-holders during the '60s.

O f the cluster of world record-setters who missed NCAA swimming meets because of IU's probation, only butterflyer Fred Schmidt stayed on top long enough to win a championship when eligibility returned to IU.

Schmidt was Indiana's only swimming winner in the '64 NCAA meet when the Hoosiers, in their first year back, lost the team title to Southern California, 96-91. Schmidt's NCAA victory was in the 200-yard butterfly, on his way to a bronze medal in the 200-meter butterfly at the Tokyo Olympics. He also won a gold at Tokyo as the 'flyer on the U.S. medley relay team.

Schmidt, from Northbrook, Illinois, had set a world record in winning the National AAU outdoor championship before entering IU as a freshman. In his Hoosier career, he won three Big Ten championships and three more National AAU titles.

At one point during the probation, Schmidt (100 butterfly), Tom Stock (100 and 200 backstroke), Chet Jastremski (100 and 200 breaststroke) and Ted Stickles (400 individual medley) all held world records. Jastremski's three varsity years passed during those NCAA-ineligible years. Stickles and Stock, who had combined to win 12 National AAU championships and set 10 world records, managed just a fourth (Stickles, 400 individual medley) and a fifth (Stock, 200 backstroke) in their only NCAA chance.

Schmidt's swimming skills came into use after graduation. As a U.S. Navy Seal, his duties included being on the recovery team for Apollo 12.

DISAPPOINTMENT AT END OF ERA

ALL-AMERICAN CAZZIE RUSSELL led No. 1-ranked Michigan into sold-out IU Fieldhouse on February 15, 1965 and the No. 9 Hoosiers were ready.

Both teams were 15-2, but Indiana's losses had come in Big Ten play, so the game was a Hoosier "must." IU led 81-74 with 1:05 left but a late one-and-one miss let Michigan catch up. A 92-88 Indiana lead with 30 seconds left in overtime got away after a two-shot free-throw miss. In overtime, a late one-and-one misfired, and Michigan won, 96-95 —over the team that still ranks best ever at IU in free throw percentage (.768) but missed 15 that night.

The deflated Hoosiers lost two of the next three games to sink in the league standings. After a 110-90 rout of Ohio State March 1, word leaked out that Branch McCracken had given president Elvis J. Stahr, jr., a letter of retirement that afternoon. A day later, the job was given to McCracken's assistant and one-time captain, Lou Watson.

McCracken planned to coach the rest of the season. Sick with flu, he led the Hoosiers to a 90-79 victory over Purdue in his final home game, but he stayed in Bloomington while his last team closed out 19-5 by winning under Watson at Wisconsin, 92-73.

McCracken's 24 Hoosier seasons produced two NCAA championships and four Big Ten titles. His IU teams won 364 games and lost 174. In 49 other years, Indiana teams won 379 games and lost 296. His 28-15 record against Purdue included a 13-game winning streak from 1949 through 1955.

IN THOSE DAYS . . .

FROM ONE STREAK TO ANOTHER

The same weekend Michigan's top-ranked basketball team spoiled the season for Indiana, Michigan's swimmers delivered their own disappointment to an Indiana team unused to losing.

In the same Matt Mann Pool where a dual-meet victory in 1961 had signaled Indiana's arrival as a power, Michigan ended a 47-meet winning streak for Indiana, 70-53.

It was a match typical of the era for the two, Olympians abounding. Indiana's Fred Schmidt edged Michigan's Carl Robie in the 200-yard butterfly; six months earlier both had stood on the medal stand at Tokyo. Robie won the 200-yard individual medley from IU's Chuck Richards, who three years later was an American Olympian in the modern pentathlon. Olympic gold medalist diver Ken Sitzberger won his specialty for IU, but Michigan won both relays and breezed.

Three weeks later, it was Indiana's turn. The Hoosiers set two American records and opened a 447-409 victory over runnerup Michigan for their fifth straight Big Ten championship.

As the years passed, the 1965 dual meet at Ann Arbor took on its own historical significance. Not until January 20, 1979 — 140 dual meets and nearly 14 years later — did Indiana lose one again.

HOOSIER LIST

LOU SABAN
THROUGH THE YEARS

Head Coach, Case Institute	1950-52
Asst. Coach, Washington	1953
Asst. Coach, Northwestern	1954
Head Coach, Northwestern	1955
Sold Insurance	1956
Head Coach, Western Illinois	1957-59
Head Coach, Boston Patriots (AFL)	1960-61
Head Coach, Buffalo Bills (AFL)	1962-65
Head Coach, Maryland	1966
Head Coach, Denver Broncos (NFL)	1967-71
Head Coach, Buffalo Bills (NFL)	1972-76
Head Coach, Miami (Fla.)	1977-78
Head Coach, Army	1979
Manager, Tampa Downs	1980
President, New York Yankees	1981
Head Coach, Central Florida	1982-84
Scout, New York Yankees	1985-86
Asst. Coach, Martin County, Florida H.S.	1986

INDIANA

⊕ LEGEND   *John Pont*

FROM YALE, VIA WOODY AND ARA

After a 2-8 season that made Indiana 11-34 in the '60s, John Pont was brought in from Yale to replace Phil Dickens.

Pont, 37, was an Ohioan (Canton) who played at Miami of Ohio for Woody Hayes and Ara Parseghian. Pont's 42 football jersey was the first number Miami ever retired.

As a coach, he was 55-27-3 in five years at Miami and two at Yale.

The Hoosiers beat Kansas State 19-7 in Pont's IU opener. They were 1-4 going against Washington State (4-1). In the final seconds, they led 7-0 but lost Glenn Holubar's game-clinching interception to an off-side penalty. Washington State passed for a touchdown as time ran out and for a two-point conversion with 0:00 on the board to win, 8-7.

Indiana led No. 1 Michigan State 13-10 in the fourth quarter but lost 27-13. The Hoosiers, 2-7 when they met No. 10 Purdue (6-2-1), trailed 20-0 early but scrambled back on two touchdown catches by team MVP Bill Malinchak. On the last play of the third quarter, IU's Mike Krivoshia drove 11 yards to Purdue's 12, but he lost the gain and the first down to a rare unnecessary roughness call—against the ball-carrier.

Purdue won, 26-21.

No Hoosiers made first- or second-team All-Big Ten. Four IU seniors were drafted and signed quickly, defensive tackle Randy Beisler of Gary the third player taken in the NFL draft—by Philadelphia, as an offensive lineman. Beisler played 10 NFL seasons.

BIG TEN MEDAL - Wayne Witmer   **GIMBEL AWARD -** John Durkott

BALFOUR AWARDS
Football-Bill Malinchak; Basketball-Max Walker; Baseball-Jack Campbell; Track-Randy Weddle; Wrestling-Bob Campbell; Swimming-Pete Hammer; Gymnastics-Mike Rose; Golf-Jim Jewell; Tennis-Dave Power

NCAA CHAMPIONS
Swimming - Bill Utley, 200 individual medley (1:58.55); Ken Webb, 400 individual medley (4:19.01); Diving - Ken Sitzberger, 1-meter springboard.

IU item

LOU SABAN: IU STAR, COACHING NOMAD

1942 IU football MVP Lou Saban coached the Buffalo Bills to American Football League championships in both 1964 and 1965.

In 1942, one of Indiana's best and most talented football teams picked Lou Saban as its MVP—Billy Hillenbrand, Pete Pihos, Howard Brown and John Tavener among the eligibles. Just a junior then, Saban entered the Army and after World War II captained and played linebacker for Paul Brown's first four Cleveland Browns teams.

Then this Chicago-raised son of a Yugoslavian immigrant, this man Luka Shabon till he Americanized his name, began an amazing, nomadic coaching career that took him to all levels of the game he loved.

Paul Brown's players were such heroes in the Cleveland area that Saban started out in the field as head coach at Case Institute. In three years there, his teams went 10-14-1. Then Case dropped football. Saban took a job as an assistant coach at Washington in 1953, moved to the Northwestern staff in 1954, and in 1955 he replaced Bob Voigts as head coach at Northwestern.

He went 0-8-1. He was fired. He sold insurance for a year. Then he coached at Western Illinois for three good years (20-5-1).

A new professional league was formed, the American Football League an instant rival to the old, established National. The AFL's Boston franchise chose as its first coach Lou Saban—and fired him five games into his second season. The next year, Buffalo picked him up.

Bingo.

After two 7-6-1 seasons, Saban's 1964 Bills (Cookie Gilchrist, Jack Kemp) went 12-2 and beat San Diego for the AFL championship. They repeated in '65— the last two years before the NFL and AFL got together for the first Super Bowl. Both championship seasons Saban was AFL Coach of the Year.

Then he moved again. Maryland, college football's national champion a decade before, charmed him with its promise. After one 4-6 season, he went back to the AFL for five years with Denver (Floyd Little), then four more at Buffalo that included O.J. Simpson's historic 2,003-yard season in 1973.

After 15 years of AFL paychecks came collegiate stops at Cincinnati (athletic director, for 19 days), Miami, Florida (football coach for two years, 9-13) and Army (one year, 2-8-1). George Steinbrenner, who had coached receivers on Saban's Northwestern staff, hired him to run his Tampa Downs race track, then named him president of the Yankees (combined, two years). Then he was Central Florida's first varsity coach (three years, 6-12). He went back with Steinbrenner as a scout (two years). Then a coach on his Central Florida staff asked him to come to Martin County High in Stuart, Florida, as defensive coordinator.

Luka Shabon touched all the bases, and as Lou Saban was one of the 25 charter members of IU's Athletics Hall of Fame.

Snapshot In Time

WALKER EMERGES AS WATSON DEBUTS

THE SEVEN SENIORS who left with retired basketball coach Branch McCracken were the top seven scorers on IU's 1964-65 team.

Maxie Walker of Milwaukee showed new coach Lou Watson he had just been waiting for a chance. A 6-1 guard, Walker had scored 13 points his junior year. He topped that with 16 when Indiana beat St. Joseph's of Indiana, 76-62, in Watson's debut. Walker went on to a bigger year than even Dick Neal (1956-57) and Sam Gee (1957-58) had in their senior-year breakthroughs under McCracken.

Walker averaged 14.0 as Indiana went 4-5 in pre-conference play. In the Big Ten, the left-hander stepped it up—24 points in a loss to Michigan, 27 in a win over Illinois. He scored 17 but severely injured an ankle in a rout of Ohio State. He sat out an 83-82 home-court loss to Northwestern, and Indiana won just one game the rest of the way to share last place in the league with Purdue at 4-10—8-16 overall in Watson's tough first year. Walker, the man who scored 13 points the whole season before, finished with a league average of 18.5 a game.

Max Walker averaged 18.5 points in Big Ten play in 1966.

1966 1967

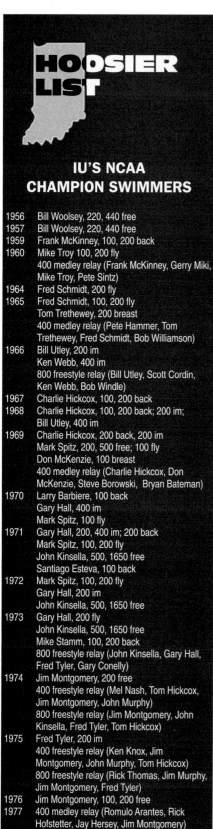

IU'S NCAA CHAMPION SWIMMERS

1956	Bill Woolsey, 220, 440 free
1957	Bill Woolsey, 220, 440 free
1959	Frank McKinney, 100, 200 back
1960	Mike Troy 100, 200 fly
	400 medley relay (Frank McKinney, Gerry Miki, Mike Troy, Pete Sintz)
1964	Fred Schmidt, 200 fly
1965	Fred Schmidt, 100, 200 fly
	Tom Trethewey, 200 breast
	400 medley relay (Pete Hammer, Tom Trethewey, Fred Schmidt, Bob Williamson)
1966	Bill Utley, 200 im
	Ken Webb, 400 im
	800 freestyle relay (Bill Utley, Scott Cordin, Ken Webb, Bob Windle)
1967	Charlie Hickcox, 100, 200 back
1968	Charlie Hickcox, 100, 200 back; 200 im; Bill Utley, 400 im
1969	Charlie Hickcox, 200 back, 200 im
	Mark Spitz, 200, 500 free; 100 fly
	Don McKenzie, 100 breast
	400 medley relay (Charlie Hickcox, Don McKenzie, Steve Borowski, Bryan Bateman)
1970	Larry Barbiere, 100 back
	Gary Hall, 400 im
	Mark Spitz, 100 fly
1971	Gary Hall, 200, 400 im; 200 back
	Mark Spitz, 100, 200 fly
	John Kinsella, 500, 1650 free
	Santiago Esteva, 100 back
1972	Mark Spitz, 100, 200 fly
	Gary Hall, 200 im
	John Kinsella, 500, 1650 free
1973	Gary Hall, 200 fly
	John Kinsella, 500, 1650 free
	Mike Stamm, 100, 200 back
	800 freestyle relay (John Kinsella, Gary Hall, Fred Tyler, Gary Conelly)
1974	Jim Montgomery, 200 free
	400 freestyle relay (Mel Nash, Tom Hickcox, Jim Montgomery, John Murphy)
	800 freestyle relay (Jim Montgomery, John Kinsella, Fred Tyler, Tom Hickcox)
1975	Fred Tyler, 200 im
	400 freestyle relay (Ken Knox, Jim Montgomery, John Murphy, Tom Hickcox)
	800 freestyle relay (Rick Thomas, Jim Murphy, Jim Montgomery, Fred Tyler)
1976	Jim Montgomery, 100, 200 free
1977	400 medley relay (Romulo Arantes, Rick Hofstetter, Jay Hersey, Jim Montgomery)

LEGEND *Charlie Hickcox*

'CHARLIE WAS RESPONSIBLE'

Unlike some IU swimming greats who came before and after him, Charlie Hickcox arrived on campus with no world records, no national championships.

It took him a while, but when he got to the top, he took IU with him.

The Hickcox breakthrough came in his sophomore year at the 1967 NCAA championships. Michigan State backstroker Gary Dilley, silver medalist in the 1964 Olympics, was unbeaten as a college backstroker until the NCAA meet his senior year—in his home pool at MSU. Hickcox beat him in both backstroke events.

A year later, on opening night of the 1968 NCAA championships at Dartmouth, Hickcox won the 200-yard individual medley. From there on he was a towel-waving, emotional leader of the first IU swimming team that got over a historical hump and won the NCAA championship.

Hickcox added both backstroke titles in that meet, swept the backstrokes and the 200 medley again in the National AAU meet, and went on that summer to win Olympic gold medals in the 200- and 400-meter individual medleys and medley relay. He was World Swimmer of the Year.

As a senior, he captained the IU team that won the 1969 NCAA meet by a record margin in IU's Royer Pool. And then he retired, with 23 national or international championships in a three-year period. A graduate from Salmon P. Chase College of Law, Hickcox was a charter inductee in IU's Athletics Hall of Fame.

In 1990, when Doc Counsilman retired and thought back over all the grand moments in an unparalleled coaching career, winning that first NCAA championship at Dartmouth "may have been the highest point," he said. "Charlie was responsible for that one."

BIG TEN MEDAL - Ken Sitzberger   **GIMBEL AWARD** - Bob Russell

BALFOUR AWARDS
Football-Tom Schuette; Basketball-Vernon Payne; Baseball-Jim Lee; Track-Rich Dilling; Wrestling-Tim McCall; Swimming-Bill Utley; Gymnastics-Joel Sutlin; Golf-Jim Cheney; Tennis-Jim Nolan

NCAA CHAMPIONS
Swimming - Charlie Hickcox, 100 backstroke (53.17), 200 backstroke (1:55.30); Diving - Ken Sitzberger, 1-meter springboard, 3-meter springboard.

THE LAST-TO-FIRST SEASON

I n Branch McCracken's 24-year basketball coaching era, Indiana never finished last. In successor Lou Watson's first year, it happened. Hoosier hopes weren't soaring when much the same club—minus MVP Max Walker but adding a bona fide center in 6-9 sophomore Bill DeHeer—opened a new season.

DeHeer started and scored only two points in his college debut, but five Hoosiers scored in double figures in an 84-71 victory over DePauw. Just 6,472 saw that game, barely over 5,100 the next two home games.

But a trend began in that opener. Watson saw it early and talked of it at the 18-8 season's end—"unselfish team spirit. Everyone put the team ahead of himself, working together and getting the ball to the open man."

Ten times this Hoosier team put five men in double figures, six in a 93-81 victory over Wisconsin that gave the Hoosiers a six-game winning streak and a share of the Big Ten lead at 5-1.

The streak ended in an 86-77 loss at Michigan State that was doubly costly: Erv Inniger, a 6-3 senior guard whose first chance as a starter had produced backcourt leadership and consistent double-figure scoring, cracked a bone in his hand and went out for the year.

Senior Bill Russell—from Columbus, not San Francisco—stepped in and led the club with 20 points in his first start, an 81-79 squeaker at Northwestern. Inniger had averaged 15.7 the first seven Big Ten games; Russell averaged 15.1 the last seven.

Junior Butch Joyner (team MVP, All-Big Ten with a 20.3 league average) and sophomore Vernon Payne (second team All-Big Ten, 15.7 a game) were the Hoosiers' stars. DeHeer and Jack Johnson helped an IU team that had finished last in Big Ten rebounding the year before outrebound its league opponents.

The last night of the season, with IU Fieldhouse packed (9,554) for the first time all year, the Hoosiers beat Purdue, 95-82, to tie Michigan State for the championship and advance to the NCAA tournament for the first time in nine years. Virginia Tech cut them down, but they had made Big Ten history with their last-to-first surge.

AFTER GOLD, SITZBERGER IMPROVED

As an IU freshman, Ken Sitzberger won the springboard gold medal at the 1964 Olympics.

His victory was unusual. American Frank Gorman outscored him on each of nine dives but missed badly on the other and Sitzberger edged him out for the gold.

Hobie Billingsley went back a long way with his memories that day. Sitzberger grew up in Downers Grove, Illinois, and Billingsley remembered sitting at a Chicago pool on a summer day—several times, several summers. "Every summer, this little kid would come up and say, 'Hi, Mr. Billingsley. I'm Kenny Sitzberger, do you remember me? Would you please watch my dives?'

"Then one day when he was still in high school he just wiped out all our divers in the nationals. I said, 'Hi, Mr. Sitzberger, I'm Hobie Billingsley. Do you remember me?' "

After his Olympic championship, Sitzberger got better and better, for three seasons—five NCAA championships, four Big Ten, three National AAU.

After graduation, Sitzberger had a 16-year career as ABC's commentator at diving telecasts. He was contracted to do that role at the 1984 Olympics in Los Angeles. On New Year's Day 1984, at 38, Sitzberger died in his sleep. He and his IU-alumna wife, Jeanne—Jeanne Collier when she won a U.S. springboard championship in 1983 and a silver medal at the same Tokyo Games where Sitzberger won a gold—had four children.

Ken Sitzberger was a three-time NCAA champion and 1964 Olympic gold medalist.

IN THOSE DAYS . . .

ORWIG "SICK OF LOSING"

Indiana's surprise drive to the Rose Bowl may have started ten months before the 1967 season, when athletic director Bill Orwig declined to join in the traditional platitudes at the annual football banquet.

The Michigan man who had endured successive football seasons of 2-7, 3-6, 3-6, 2-7, 2-8 and 1-8-1 after taking over as IU's director in February 1961 looked straight at the Hoosier underclassmen and said:

"I'm sick of losing . . . I'm sick of the attitude of some of our players have on the field. I'm sick of seeing some of our players do things off the field that they know the coaches don't expect them to do.

"Boys, if you don't want to play football next year, please don't come out. Winning isn't easy. If you want to win next year, you'd better start preparing yourself Monday. It takes work."

• Indiana's freshmen gave the John Pont program a boost by winning 13-8 at Ohio State. Harry Gonso ran 22 yards for a touchdown and threw six yards to Jade Butcher for the other . Gonso also ran 34 yards for a touchdown and passed ten yards to Butcher for another when the rookies lost a week later at home to Michigan State, 25-13.

HOOSIER LIST

INDIANA

IU'S ROSE BOWL LINEUP

Offense

SE	Eric Stolberg
LT	Rick Spickard
LG	Gary Cassells
C	Harold Mauro
RG	Bob Russell
RT	Al Schmidt
TE	Al Gage
QB	Harry Gonso
TB	John Isenbarger
FL	Jade Butcher
FB	Terry Cole
K	Dave Kornowa

Defense

LE	Tom Bilunas
LT	Doug Crusan
RT	Harold Dunn
RE	Cal Snowden
OLB	Brown Marks
LB	Jim Sniadecki
LB	Ken Kaczmarek
OLB	Kevin Duffy
CB	Dave Kornowa
CB	Nate Cunningham
S	Mike Baughman
P	John Isenbarger

Coaches

John Pont
Bob Baker
Howard Brown
Herb Fairfield
Jay Fry
Bob Hicks
Charley McDaniel
Nick Mourouzis
Ernie Plank
Jake Van Schoyck

LEGEND
Doug Crusan

THE CAPTAIN MADE A SACRIFICE

John Pont never asked more of a captain than he did of 1967 senior Doug Crusan. The NFL had Crusan ranked among the best offensive tackles in the nation. Pont asked him to shed 30 pounds and move to defense.

Tackle Crusan, from Monessen, Pennsylvania, was the last piece that made Pont's new four-linemen, four-linebackers defense a quiet key to the Hoosiers' great season.

Illinois trailed 13-7 and had the ball at the IU 15 with four minutes left. Brown Marks' tackle and Jim Sniadecki's fumble recovery stopped that threat, and linebacker Ken Kaczmarek's last-minute TD interception return made the victory look much easier than it was, 20-7.

Wisconsin was at the Indiana 10 when a game-ending pass misfired and IU won, 14-9.

No. 3-ranked Purdue was at IU's 4 with six minutes left when linebacker Ken Kaczmarek jolted the ball loose from Purdue's Perry Williams and safety Mike Baughman recovered at the IU 1, preserving a 19-14 victory.

Offensive guard Gary Cassells was the only Hoosier who made a major All-America team, but Crusan and Kaczmarek got some All-America mention and those two plus Sniadecki and end Cal Snowden were on the first or second All-Conference defensive team.

Miami made Crusan its No. 1 draft pick, as an offensive lineman. Crusan was a starting guard and Terry Cole—a hero of the Purdue game with up-the-middle bursts of 63 and 42 yards—was a running back for the only unbeaten team ever to win the Super Bowl: the 17-0 Miami Dolphins of 1972.

BIG TEN MEDAL - Gene Denisar   **GIMBEL AWARD -** Bob Russell

BALFOUR AWARDS

Football-Harry Gonso; Basketball-Vernon Payne/Butch Joyner; Baseball-Gary Sargent; Track-Dick Swift; Wrestling-Tom Blankenship; Swimming-Charlie Hickcox; Gymnastics-David Keller; Golf-Jim Cheney; Tennis-Dave Brown

NCAA CHAMPIONS

TEAM: Swimming - (Doc Counsilman); INDIVIDUAL: Charlie Hickcox, 100 backstroke (52.18), 200 backstroke (1:54.66), 200 individual medley (1:52.56); Bill Utley, 400 individual medley (4:10.85). Diving - Jim Henry, 1-meter springboard.

PONT JOINS BO AS COACH OF THE YEAR

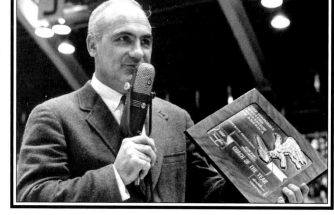

In his early days at Indiana, John Pont told prospects to come to Indiana *because* it hadn't won, to be part of something new. A skeptic asked: "How can you sell something that negative?" Pont's answer: "They sell life insurance every day."

The policy paid off in 1967 for Indiana's so-very-long-suffering football fans.

Never has a team, through force of will, skill or luck, won out in more games that went into the final minutes as 50-50 propositions, winnable and losable.

The Hoosiers' formula was solid, conservative, dependable defense that kept every game tight and an offense that could be ineffective most of the day but unstoppable at crisis time.

The offense came from behind or broke ties late in victories over Kentucky (12-10), Kansas (18-15), Iowa (21-17), Michigan (27-20) and Michigan State (14-13); the defense held on to beat Illinois (20-7), Wisconsin (14-9) and Purdue (19-14).

The point averages of the two units were a statistical gem: offense 19 a game, defense 14. The Purdue game score.

Seven games into the season, Pont said: "I wish there was a book out on this so I could read the next chapter." He lived it instead. For his frights and delights, and for his steady hand through all of both, Pont joined Bo McMillin (1945) as IU's only winners of the national Coach of the Year award.

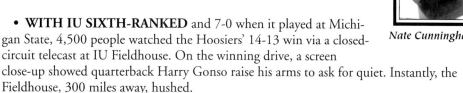

NUGGETS FROM A GOLDEN SEASON

Nate Cunningham

Cal Snowden

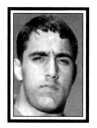
Gary Cassells

• **WITH IU SIXTH-RANKED** and 7-0 when it played at Michigan State, 4,500 people watched the Hoosiers' 14-13 win via a closed-circuit telecast at IU Fieldhouse. On the winning drive, a screen close-up showed quarterback Harry Gonso raise his arms to ask for quiet. Instantly, the Fieldhouse, 300 miles away, hushed.

• At 8-0, going to Minnesota, the Hoosiers were fifth in both wire-service polls,—with one No. 1 vote in each. Not even the 1945 team got one of those.

• Guard Bob Russell, taking pre-medicine courses, in spring 1967 won IU's Gimbel Award, given only to seniors. Russell postponed medical school a year and came back for a fifth year—a decision that made future doctor Robert Russell a Rose Bowl starter and IU's only two-time Gimbel Award winner.

Mike Baughman

• Terry Cole's 63-yard touchdown run against Purdue was the longest of his IU career. Before that, it was his 42-yard gain on the same trap play earlier in the game.

• Linebacker standouts Ken Kaczmarek and Jim Sniadecki were teammates at South Bend St. Joseph.

• The IU pass defense allowed only three touchdown passes, none over junior halfback Nate Cunningham.

Ken Kaczmarek

Jim Sniadecki

• Sophomore safety Mike Baughman, whose fourth-quarter fumble recovery at the 1 against Purdue may be IU's all-time biggest, made All-Big Ten as a baseball outfielder.

Bob Russell

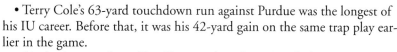
Terry Cole

In the faculty section, by game 4, there were signs of an imminent miracle.

INDIANA

GONSO, ISENBARGER, BUTCHER LED WAY TO PASADENA

Their stamp was on every game. Indiana's Rose Bowl season, in consensus Hoosier memory, is Harry, John and Jade, the three irrepressible sophomores who dominated the spotlight that bathed Bloomington in autumn 1967.

Not till September did Harry Gonso, of Findlay, Ohio, beat out John Isenbarger of Muncie Central for starting quarterback. Isenbarger moved to tailback and, all along, Jade Butcher of Bloomington was the team's No. 1 receiver.

Opening day, Kentucky led at halftime 10-0, but Gonso ran and passed for 236 yards and two touchdowns (to Butcher and Al Gage) to win, 12-10.

He did the same thing, 100-yard days passing and rushing, in a 21-17 victory over Iowa. That day he scrambled for a first down on a fake field goal (fourth-and-12, Iowa 22), then passed to Butcher at 0:53 for the touchdown that won.

Butcher, the hometown boy, caught touchdown passes in his first six college games, nine of them all told, as the Hoosiers won all six games and burst into the national polls.

By then, Isenbarger was their most famous player. Early against Iowa, he ran by design as the punter on fourth-and-9 at the IU 17, and made it. Later, he saw the same keys, ran by inspiration, and came up short, setting up the Iowa touchdown that forced the Gonso heroics.

The next week at Michigan, Isenbarger's passes and runs jumped IU out front, 20-0. Michigan caught up after a foiled run by erstwhile punter Isenbarger (at the IU 16). On his first 100-yard day (101), the determined Isenbarger slashed and powered the Hoosiers to the game-winning score with 1:10 left in a 27-20 win.

The 5-0 Hoosiers breezed the next week, 42-7, at Arizona, where Isenbarger's mother sent him a fabled pre-game telegram that said: "Dear John: Please punt." From there came the "Punt, John, Punt" title of Dan Jenkins' *Sports Illustrated* feature on the fall's biggest surprise team.

In rain at Michigan State, IU had little offense till taking the ball at its 31 with 6:33 left. Again, Isenbarger was a racehorse sniffing victory down the stretch. He ran for 13, 14 and 12 yards, caught a Gonso pass for 15 and, with 2:50 left, took a Gonso option pitch to score from the 4 for a 14-13 win.

After Minnesota stopped the Hoosiers, 33-7, all championship and Rose Bowl hopes rode on the Old Oaken Bucket game. With 6:27 left and IU leading 19-14, sophomore Mike Baughman recovered Perry Williams' fumble at the IU 1. On second down, Gonso ran across the end zone before unloading an incomplete pass. On fourth down from the 4, Isenbarger's best punt of the year sailed out of the end zone 63 official yards, backed the Boilers to their 40, and IU held on to win.

Each of the three closed his college career owning virtually every IU record at his position. All three are in IU's Athletics Hall of Fame. And, in 1969, their senior season, Hoosier fans, as part of college football's centennial observance, voted all three to spots on the 11-man all-time IU team.

The Cinderella Year

Indiana 12, Kentucky 10
Indiana 18, Kansas 15
Indiana 20, Illinois 7
Indiana 21, Iowa 17
Indiana 27, Michigan 20
Indiana 42, Arizona 7
Indiana 14, Wisconsin 9
Indiana 14, Mich. St. 13
Minnesota 33, Indiana 7
Indiana 19, Purdue 14
Southern Cal 14, Indiana 3

Harry Gonso

John Isenbarger

Jade Butcher

INDIANA

HICKCOX, DIVERS LEAD THE WAY

For three years, Doc Counsilman had the best team in college swimming but couldn't compete for the NCAA championship. For the next three years, he came so close that he had to think of the recruits NCAA ineligibility had cost him—when one more good swimmer might have won each championship.

Finally, on a brisk March weekend in Hanover, New Hampshire, Counsilman's Indiana swimming program reached the top. Junior Charlie Hickcox, establishing himself as America's best swimmer, and Hobie Billingsley's diving corps led by sophomore Jim Henry left the field far behind as Indiana won its first NCAA championship.

IU scored 346 points to 253 for distant runnerup Yale. A decade-long crusade had found its Holy Grail.

The Hoosiers' opening was rough. In afternoon qualifying, the medley relay team counted on for first place and 32 points was disqualified for an illegal takeoff—an enormous first-day jolt to a team that had lost each of those three previous NCAA meets by fewer than 30 points. Leadoff man Hickcox was outraged. Counsilman took him aside for a few words. They were, Hickcox said later with a grin: "Shut up and swim."

In the second event of the evening finals, Hickcox swam. In the 200-yard individual medley, he finished almost two seconds under the listed American record and four seconds ahead of teammate Bill Utley in a 1-2 finish that gave IU 29 quick points.

In the next event, sprinter Bryan Bateman figured to score a point or two. In the qualifying round, he tied for sixth and the last spot in the finals. He won the swim-off to get in the finals, then surged at the finish to get second place, and 13 unexpected points.

The Hoosiers' knockout punch came next. Henry won the one-meter title, followed by teammates Win Young (fourth), Jon Hahnfeldt (fifth), Luis Nino de Rivera (sixth) and Nick Carlton (eighth)—51 total points, a meet record for one event, swimming or diving.

In the next two nights, Hickcox set two more meet records in winning the backstrokes; Utley won the 400-yard individual medley, and the diving corps delivered 45 more points on the three-meter board. Indiana scored at least five points in every event but the disqualified medley relay, a display of depth that surprised even Counsilman.

Only four teams in the field, including Indiana, topped the Hoosier divers' 96 points. Only 10 full teams beat the 51 points IU got from the one-meter dive alone.

First Row (left to right): Manager Terry Weisman, Win Young, Jim Henry, Dave Perkowski, Bill Utley, Luis Nino de Rivera, Nick Carlton, Jon Hahnfeldt, Manager Jeff Bankston. Second Row: Coach 'Doc' Counsilman, Dave Bayless, Fred Southward, Charlie Hickcox, Bryan Bateman, Dave Usrey, Don McKenzie, Tito Perez, Diving Coach Hobie Billingsley. Third Row: Manager Mark Wallace, Bob Windle, Bill Burrell, Ron Jacks, Steve Ware, Steve Borowski, Manager Corby Sanders, Assistant Coach Jack Pettinger.

IN THOSE DAYS . . .

FROM NO. 3 TO NOWHERE

Indiana's basketball team kept the football-generated enthusiasm going on campus well into December.

Butch Joyner and Vern Payne, the stars of the surprise co-championship team the year before, returned as seniors and Joe Cooke and Ken Johnson headed a sophomore class of promise, so Indiana expectations soared.

The Hoosiers boosted them with a 6-0 start that included a 101-97 overtime victory at North Carolina State and a 96-91 win over Notre Dame at Fort Wayne. Indiana was No. 3 in the national polls, behind powers UCLA and Houston.

The football team was at Pasadena when the basketball team went to Dallas for a tournament. Western Kentucky ended the winning streak, 110-91, and SMU denied the Hoosiers consolation, even. The ship never got righted again, Joyner battling an ankle injury most of the season. Their 10-4 Big Ten co-championship record of the year before reversed to 4-10 and started a three-year stretch of last-place finishes.

HOOSIER LIST

IU'S ALL-TIME FOOTBALL TEAM
(as voted by fans in 1969)

1st Team

E Pete Pihos '46
E Jade Butcher '69
L Howard Brown '47
L Bob Skoronski '55
L Mike Rabold '58
L Doug Crusan '67
L Don Croftcheck '64
B John Isenbarger '69
B Harry Gonso '69
B George Taliaferro '48
B Billy Hillenbrand '42

2nd Team

E Earl Faison '60
E Bill Malinchak '65
L John Cannady '46
L John Tavener '44
L Gary Cassells '67
L Russ Deal '46
L Ken Kaczmarek '67
B Tom Nowatzke '64
B Vern Huffman '46
B Bob Hoernschemeyer '44
B Corby Davis '37

3rd Team

E Ted Kluszewski '45
E Brad Bomba '56
L Jim Sniadecki '68
L Bob Russell '67
L Bob Haak '38
L John Goldsberry '48
L Gene White '41
B Terry Cole '67
B Gene Gedman '52
B Marv Woodson '63
B Chuck Bennett '28

INDIANA

⊗ LEGEND   *Jim Henry*

'GREATEST ONE-METER DIVER EVER'

In Jim Henry's first diving competition, as a Dallas 9-year-old, "I was so green I couldn't even give them my dives," he said. "Like, I had never called it an 'inward.' It was a 'cutaway' to me. All that jargon—I didn't know what they were talking about. I didn't win."

As an IU freshman, he practiced with the king of collegiate diving, Ken Sitzberger. "I was always watching him," Henry said. "You can pick up a lot of things that way."

When Sitzberger's NCAA reign ended, Henry's began: five collegiate championships, 13 more National AAU titles. Coach Hobie Billingsley called him "probably the greatest one-meter diver ever."

In 1970, *Swimming World* magazine ranked him No. 1 among the world's springboard divers. "A wonderful honor," Henry called it. But it wasn't the Olympic gold medal he sought.

At the 1968 Games in Mexico City, Henry entered the final round of springboard competition leading the field. "I had been doing pretty well—two points was a pretty good lead," he said. "I blew two dives (in the finals)—the first and the last. In practice I had been doing them very well. It ticked me off." He took home a bronze, then began his three-year collegiate sweep. His career ended when he missed out in the 1972 Olympic trials.

A dentist, in 1984 Henry was inducted into IU's Athletics Hall of Fame.

BIG TEN MEDAL - Rich Fuhs   **GIMBEL AWARD** - Jerry Grecco

BALFOUR AWARDS
Football-Harry Gonso; Basketball-Ken Johnson; Baseball-Bruce Miller; Track-Mark Gibbens; Wrestling-Jim Lentz; Swimming-Charlie Hickcox; Gymnastics-Paul Graf; Golf-Walt Cisco; Tennis-Mike Meis

NCAA CHAMPIONS
TEAM: Swimming (Doc Counsilman); INDIVIDUAL: Swimming, Mark Spitz, 200 freestyle (1:39.53), 500 freestyle (4:33.48), 100 butterfly (49.69); Charlie Hickcox, 200 backstroke (1:53.67), 200 individual medley (1:54.43); Don McKenzie, 100 breaststroke (58.36), 400 medley relay, Charlie Hickcox, Don McKenzie, Steve Borowski, Bryan Bateman (3:25.89). Diving: Jim Henry, 1-meter springboard, 3-meter springboard.

OLYMPIC MEDALISTS
Swimming: Charlie Hickcox, 200 individual medley, gold (2:12.0), 400 individual medley, gold (4:48.4), 100 backstroke, silver (1:00.2), 400 medley relay, gold (3:54.9); Don McKenzie, 100 breaststroke, gold (1:07.7), 400 medley relay, gold (3:54.9); Mark Spitz, 100 freestyle, bronze (53.0), 100 butterfly, silver (56.4), 400 freestyle relay, gold (3:31.7), 800 freestyle relay, gold (7:52.3); Gary Hall, 400 individual medley, silver (4:48.7); John Kinsella, 1,500 freestyle, silver (16:57.3); Jack Horsley, 200 backstroke, bronze (2:10.9); Bobby Windle (Australia), 400 freestyle relay, bronze (3:34.7), 800 freestyle relay, silver (7:53.77). Diving: Jim Henry, springboard, bronze; Win Young, platform, bronze.

FOR DOC AND HOBIE: THE PERFECT MEET

For three days and nights, Doc Counsilman and Hobie Billingsley watched their efforts and their dreams align, with a basketball-style crowd at Royer Pool to celebrate it all—at the 1969 NCAA swimming and diving championships.

Indiana won nine of the eighteen events, scored in all of them, and blew the field away with 427 points and a 121-point margin over runnerup Southern Cal—each of those numbers NCAA meet records, by lots.

It was the first year of the modern freshman-eligibility rule. The timing was perfect for IU. Freshman Mark Spitz won an event every night. Senior Charlie Hickcox won two events and got the revenge he hoped for when, on opening night, the Hoosiers won the event they had lost to disqualification at the 1968 NCAA meet: the medley relay.

Indiana divers were denied their 96-point harvest of the year before by a rule that for the first time restricted the number of entries a team could have: 18, swimmers and divers. Billingsley got three diving spots. Opening night, Jim Henry, Win Young and Jon Hahnfeldt finished 1-2-3 in one-meter competition. Down to two for three-meter diving because Hahnfeldt cut a heel in practice, Henry—with a ninth-dive perfect-10 score—and Young again went 1-2.

That was 70 points out of a maximum 70. Hoosier breaststrokers beat even that with 81 points, including a 1-2-4 finish from Olympic champion Don McKenzie, Dave Perkowski and freshman Jim Counsilman Jr. in the 200-yard event (with teammate Peder Dahlberg ninth).

Counsilman Sr. called it "the greatest college swimming team in history, because of Spitz and Hickcox. No team ever had two swimmers like that, because there never were two swimmers like them."

Snapshot In Time

'OWENS SLAM' FOR HIGHBAUGH

JIM LAVERY, WHO once anchored three winning relay teams to give coach Tommy Deckard and Drake their greatest Drake Relays memories, announced before the 1969 outdoor season that he would be leaving to take an administrative role at Ohio University.

At Lavery's last Big Ten meet, sophomore Larry Highbaugh gave the seven-year coach a spectacular sendoff and showed successor Sam Bell what he would be inheriting.

Highbaugh became the first Big Ten athlete to pull off a "Jesse Owens Slam"—victories in the two sprints (100 and 220), the long jump and the sprint relay, just as Owens had done at the 1936 Olympics. Owens had won those three individual events, plus the no longer contested 220-yard low hurdles, at both the 1935 and '36 Big Ten meets, when there was no sprint relay.

Highbaugh, who had played football at IU in 1968 and lettered on a state-championship basketball team at Indianapolis Washington in 1965, won the long jump at 24-7 1/2 on the first day of competition. The second day, he anchored IU's 4x100-meter relay team in a meet-record 40.1 victory; 70 minutes later won the 100 in 9.6 seconds, and 30 minutes after that won the 220 in 21.0.

His performance helped the Hoosiers to their best finish of the Lavery years, second with 64 points to champion Wisconsin's 80.

Larry Highbaugh had one of the great meets in the history of the Big Ten—winning the long jump, 100 and 220 yard dashes, and anchoring the 4X100 relay team that won.

IN THOSE DAYS . . .

A RE-MARK-ABLE YEAR

• Seventeen past, present or would-be Indiana swimmers and divers combined to win five gold medals, five silver and five bronze at the 1968 Olympic Games. Just seven nations won more golds, and—in not just swimming but all competitions at the Games—only nine nations topped those 15 IU medals.

• One of the future Hoosiers winning medals at Mexico City was California teenager Mark Spitz, who delayed selecting a college till the late-October Olympic swimming competition ended. That led to a wintertime visit to IU. "He came out during a snowstorm," Coach Doc Counsilman recalled. "I took him to see Mrs. Robinson (Aline, IU's registrar) at her home. He got out of the car, slipped and fell on his butt. I thought: That's the end of that. But when left to go home, he said, 'I want you to send out the scholarship.' I almost died."

•Canadian Wayne McDonald, seventh in the 1969 Big Ten tournament when teammate Don Padgett was medalist, tied for second in the NCAA championships, IU's highest finish ever there. McDonald made All-America and came back the next year to lead IU to a Big Ten championship and become the only repeat All-American in IU golf history.

INDIANA

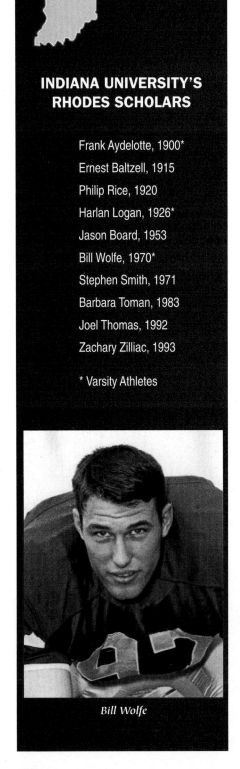

HOOSIER LIST

INDIANA UNIVERSITY'S RHODES SCHOLARS

Frank Aydelotte, 1900*

Ernest Baltzell, 1915

Philip Rice, 1920

Harlan Logan, 1926*

Jason Board, 1953

Bill Wolfe, 1970*

Stephen Smith, 1971

Barbara Toman, 1983

Joel Thomas, 1992

Zachary Zilliac, 1993

* Varsity Athletes

Bill Wolfe

LEGEND *Sam Bell*

GLORY RETURNS TO INDIANA TRACK

Sam Bell blew into Bloomington on a spring night—to be introduced as Indiana's new track coach, to meet his team, to meet the press. Bell had coached an NCAA cross country championship team at Oregon State. He was leaving California, where he had built a team good enough to win the NCAA track title.

"Do you think," someone asked, "you can build a national contender at Indiana?"

"I wouldn't have taken the job if I hadn't," he said.

He elaborated. "We won't go after anything but blue-chippers," he said. "There are enough of those around you don't have to."

Billy Hayes remains the only Indiana coach who has won NCAA track or cross country championships. Bell did bring back the aura of the Hayes era, though, with 25 Big Ten team championships over a 29-year tenure that ended with his retirement in 1998, at 70. He was to become the most prominent college coach in American track and field development, and a coach in the Olympics (Montreal 1976). He coached eight of his athletes to Olympic Games berths—one of those going three times, another two.

As a final act, he led a drive that turned Billy Hayes Track into one of the nation's showpieces and brought the 1997 NCAA meet to Bloomington.

Even at the end, people still asked him: "Why *would* a track coach leave California to go to Indiana?"

"Those people," Sam Bell said, a twinkle of humor in the eyes where the glint of determination flashed that first night in Bloomington 29 years before, "didn't live in Berkeley in the '60s."

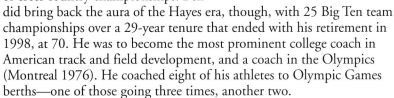

BIG TEN MEDAL - Bill Wolfe   **GIMBEL AWARD -** Jim Henry

BALFOUR AWARDS
Football-John Isenbarger; Basketball-Ken Johnson; Baseball-Kent DeFord/Larry Trzaskowski; Track-Terry Musika; Wrestling-Everette Barnard; Swimming-Gary Hall; Gymnastics-Al Gatti; Golf-Wayne McDonald; Tennis-Chuck Parsons/Darrel Snively

NCAA CHAMPIONS
TEAM: Swimming (Doc Counsilman); INDIVIDUAL: Swimming-Larry Barbiere, 100 backstroke (51.91); Mark Spitz, 100 butterfly, (48.62); Gary Hall, 400 individual medley (4:07.32); Diving: Jim Henry, 1-meter springboard, 3-meter springboard.

SULLIVAN AWARD - John Kinsella

BOYCOTT WILTS ROSY DREAM

It was a crisis that came up suddenly and ended quickly, with a universally devastating outcome that nobody involved seemed to want.

Indiana's 1969 football team opened November with a 16-0 victory at Michigan State that made a return to Pasadena a realistic hope. The Hoosiers were 3-1 in Big Ten play, a Rose Bowl return seeming likely if they could close by beating Iowa and Northwestern as expected, and Purdue in what would have been an upset.

On Tuesday, the team's 14 African-American players— who said later they felt grievances they had voiced about racial issues hadn't been handled satisfactorily—skipped practice. John Pont met with his coaches most of Wednesday, then on request of the 14 players met with them. Pont said he told the players they could return to practice with no penalty, "under the policies set by the coaches." Starters John Andrews (tight end) and Bob Jones (defensive tackle) and reserves Steve Porter (defensive halfback) and Tim Roberson (defensive tackle) practiced. Seniors Mike Adams (a starting outside linebacker), Charlie Murphy, Benny Norman, Clarence Price and Greg Thaxton, juniors Larry Highbaugh (a starting defensive halfback whose punt runback scored the only touchdown at Michigan State), Don Silas and Bobby Pernell, and sophomores Greg Harvey and Gordon May did not practice, and they were dismissed from the team.

The five non-seniors were invited back for spring practice. Harvey lettered with the team in 1970 and '71, May in '71. For most of the others, football was over—Highbaugh a notable exception. He had a long, outstanding career as a defensive back and kick-return specialist on Grey Cup championship teams at Edmonton in the Canadian Football League.

Pont's football program took a major hit. Indiana was 19-9 up to that week in games played after the Rose Bowl sophomores had become varsity-eligible. The reduced team lost all three closing games, 20 of the 22 that followed the boycott. It was another 19 years before Indiana won as many as 19 football games in a three-year period.

Snapshot In Time

AT 18, KINSELLA WINS SULLIVAN AWARD

OF THE FOUR IU athletes who have won the James E. Sullivan Award as America's best amateur athlete, 1970 winner John Kinsella was the youngest. Indeed, of the nearly 60 men who have won the award since its inception in 1930, only 1948 Sullivan winner and Olympic decathlon gold medalist Bob Mathias was younger than Kinsella—and he by just a few months, each of them 18 when honored.

Kinsella and teammate John Murphy came out of Hinsdale, Illinois—Kinsella a distance swimmer, Murphy a sprinter, each tight end-sized at 6-4 and 200-plus pounds. In late-summer 1970, days before he began his freshman year at IU, Kinsella outswam 1968 Olympic gold medalist Mike Burton in an epic 1,500-meter race at the National AAU championships. Kinsella's 15:57.1 made him the first to break 16 minutes in the event. Three days earlier, he had claimed his first world record, in the 400-meter freestyle.

At IU, Kinsella doubled in the 500 and 1,650 freestyles for three straight NCAA team champions. Both he (4x200) and Murphy (4x100) won relays gold medals in the 1972 Olympics.

In 1988, Kinsella entered IU's Athletics Hall of Fame.

John Kinsella won the Sullivan Award as a freshman.

IN THOSE DAYS . . .

BILL WOLFE: RHODES SCHOLAR

As a sophomore, Bill Wolfe started at defensive tackle most of IU's charmed Rose Bowl season.

Wolfe also was a 3.66 student in IU's School of Business, the 1970 winner of IU's Herman B Wells Senior Recognition Award, and a Rhodes Scholar in 1970-71. After his year at Oxford and fulfilling his military obligation, Wolfe completed graduate work in business and his dissertation at Stanford. His business career included two years in Saudi Arabia.

His home in Naperville, Illinois, includes a few 1967 mementos. More prominent is an oar won in crew competition at Oxford.

As he drove back to IU in 1997 for the Rose Bowl team's 30th-anniversary reunion, Wolfe mused. "I remembered those 'old men' who used to come back as 50-Year I-Men— now I was closer to them than to the players. And I thought of my youngest child, Christine—if she goes to IU, when she's a senior, I'll *be* one of those 50-Year I-Men.

"That 1967 season, the coaches and players truly were in synch, from start to finish. I've always thought, as I voted then, the team's true MVP was Doug Crusan. He could have been an All-American on offense but he switched to defense and led that team."

HOOSIER LIST

IU'S 1ST ROUND NBA/ABA DRAFT PICKS

1958	Archie Dees, Cincinnati
1961	Walt Bellamy, Chicago
1971	George McGinnis, Indiana (ABA)
1973	Steve Downing, Boston
1975	Steve Green, Utah (ABA)
1976	Scott May, Chicago
1976	Quinn Buckner, Milwaukee
1976	Bobby Wilkerson, Seattle
1977	Kent Benson, Milwaukee
1980	Mike Woodson, New York
1981	Isiah Thomas, Detroit
1981	Ray Tolbert, New Jersey
1983	Randy Wittman, Washington
1985	Uwe Blab, Dallas
1993	Calbert Cheaney, Washington
1993	Greg Graham, Charlotte
1995	Alan Henderson, Atlanta
1996	Brian Evans, Orlando

INDIANA

LEGEND *George McGinnis*

IU'S GREATEST ONE-YEAR CAREER

George McGinnis played one year at IU, the greatest one-season career in Hoosier basketball history.

In that 17-7 season, the 6-8, 235-pound forward:

• Led the Big Ten in both scoring (29.9) and rebounding (14.9), one of just five players to do that in 41 years of conference record-keeping;

• Set IU's record with the 29.9 average for the full season;

• Scored 20 or more points in 21 of his 24 college games, including an IU-record 14 times in a row;

• Scored over 30 points 12 times, an IU one-season record;

• Scored 41 points against San Jose State and 45 in the highest-scoring Hoosier game ever, a 113-112 victory over Northern Illinois.

McGinnis and teammate Steve Downing led Indianapolis Washington to the 1969 state championship, one of just five unbeaten champions in tournament history.

In his last game as a high schooler, McGinnis rewrote all series records with 53 points and 31 rebounds against the Kentucky All-Stars at Louisville's Freedom Hall.

A back injury hampered Downing during their one season of college basketball together. However, February 23 in an 88-79 victory over Big Ten leader Michigan, McGinnis had 33 points and 15 rebounds. Downing's totals in his first big college game were 28 points, 17 rebounds and 10 blocked shots—IU's only recorded "Triple Double."

BIG TEN MEDAL - Mark Stevens   **GIMBEL AWARD -** E.G. White

BALFOUR AWARDS
Football-Chris Morris; Basketball-John Ritter; Baseball-Frank Grundler; Track-Mike Goodrich; Wrestling-Bill Willetts; Swimming-Mark Spitz; Gymnastics-Chuck Earle; Golf-Don Padgett; Tennis-Geoff Hodsdon

NCAA CHAMPIONS
TEAM: Swimming (Doc Counsilman). INDIVIDUAL: Swimming, Gary Hall, 200 backstroke (1:50.60), 200 individual medley (1:52.20), 400 individual medley (3:58.25); Mark Spitz, 100 butterfly (48.82), 200 butterfly (1:50.11); John Kinsella, 500 freestyle (4:27.39), 1,650 freestyle (15:26.51); Santiago Esteva, 100 backstroke (51.72).

SULLIVAN AWARD - Mark Spitz

Mark Spitz' victory in the 200-meter butterfly started his seven-gold, seven-world record performance in the 1972 Olympics.

PHOTO BY RICH CLARKSON

To the cheers of a home crowd, triumphant Bob Kennedy closed his college career with a record victory in the 1992 NCAA cross country championships.

PHOTO BY DAVID SNODGRESS

■■■■■■■■■■■■■■ **ANTHONY THOMPSON'S TOUCHDOWNS** ■■■■■■■■■■■■■■

1986

Opponent, site, score	TD	Yds.	Score	Time-Qtr
Ohio State, h, L 22-24	1	1	14-24	2:12-4
Michigan, h, L 14-38	2	3	0-38	13:24-4
	3	3	7-38	2:15-4
Michigan St., a, W 17-14	4	3	0-0	2:49-1
Purdue, a, L 15-17	5	2	0-10	6:01-3

BOWL GAMES*

Opponent, bowl, score	Yds.	Score	Time-Qtr
Tennessee, Peach '87, L 22-27	12	10-21	8:44-3
South Carolina, Liberty '88, W 34-10	7	0-0	9:23-1
South Carolina	8	27-10	8:31-4

*Do not count for NCAA records

1987

Opponent, site, score	TD	Yds.	Score	Time-Qtr
Rice, h, W 35-13	6	4	7-7	11:27-2
	7	2	28-10	3:41-3
Northwestern, h, W 35-18	8	52	0-0	9:35-1
	9	2	28-12	8:28-4
Ohio State, a, W 31-10	10	3	0-0	6:57-1
Iowa, a, L 21-29	11	1	7-20	3:20-3
Illinois, h, W 34-22	12	1	3-16	9:51-3
	13	3	27-22	2:29-4
Purdue, h, W 35-14	14	5	7-0	4:00-1
	15	1	14-0	12:58-2
	16	3	21-14	6:43-4

Anthony Thompson's NCAA-record 60th touchdown.

PHOTO BY LARRY CREWELL

THOMPSON'S TOUCHDOWNS CONTINUED

1988

Opponent, site, score	TD	Yds.	Score	Time-Qtr
Rice, a, W 41-14	17	23	3-0	14:54-2
	18	3	10-0	7:25-2
	19	32	24-0	9:10-3
Kentucky, h, W 36-15	20	5	0-0	13:48-2
	21	1	30-15	0:00-4
Missouri, a, T 28-28	22	5	7-7	7:40-3
	23	4	21-21	8:35-4
Northwestern, a, W 48-17	24	11	0-0	11:52-1
	25	1	7-7	2:26-1
	26	1	14-7	12:52-2
Ohio State, h, W 41-7	27	1	0-0	6:16-1
	28	6	7-0	0:27-1
	29	12	14-0	9:47-2
	30	4	21-0	1:49-2
Minnesota, h, W 33-13	31	4	9-0	14:20-2
	32	1	19-7	7:35-3
	33	10	26-7	11:28-4
Iowa, h, W 45-34	34	1	7-3	1:18-1
	35	4	28-3	1:33-2
	36	1	35-26	13:01-4
Illinois, a, L 20-21	37	1	0-0	8:04-1
Purdue, a, W 52-7	38	1	0-0	6:45-1
	39	7	7-7	10:43-2
	40	4	31-7	8:34-3

1989

Opponent, site, score	TD	Yds.	Score	Time-Qtr
Kentucky, a, L 14-17	41	10*	0-7	1:28-1
	42	1	7-7	9:49-2
Missouri, h, W 24-7	43	12	0-7	1:12-2
	44	3	7-7	5:57-3
	45	35	17-7	3:52-4
Toledo, h, W 32-12	46	1	9-0	5:46-1
	47	3	16-0	8:10-2
Northwestern, h, W 43-11	48	10	0-0	11:00-1
	49	1	14-3	3:10-2
	50	11	22-3	14:48-3
	51	1	29-11	6:44-3
	52	1	36-11	14:11-4
Ohio State, a, L 31-35	53	9	0-7	11:04-2
	54	2	14-35	4:17-3
	55	6	21-35	3:29-4
Minnesota, h, W 28-18	56	5	0-0	5:29-1
	57	1	7-7	5:15-2
	58	16	21-18	0:29-4
Michigan, a, L 10-38	59	1	3-31	12:40-4
Michigan St., h, L 20-52	60	1**	7-17	6:33-2
Wisconsin, a, W 45-17	61	3	0-0	11:21-1
	62	7	10-0	13:55-2
	63	1	24-17	6:00-3
	64	19	31-17	8:21-4
Illinois, a, L 28-41	65	20	14-35	8:05-3

* Pass from Dave Schnell   ** Set NCAA record

Keep
him
happy.

Support **IU** sports!

 INDIANA UNIVERSITY FOUNDATION

Part of the IU Tradition since 1936

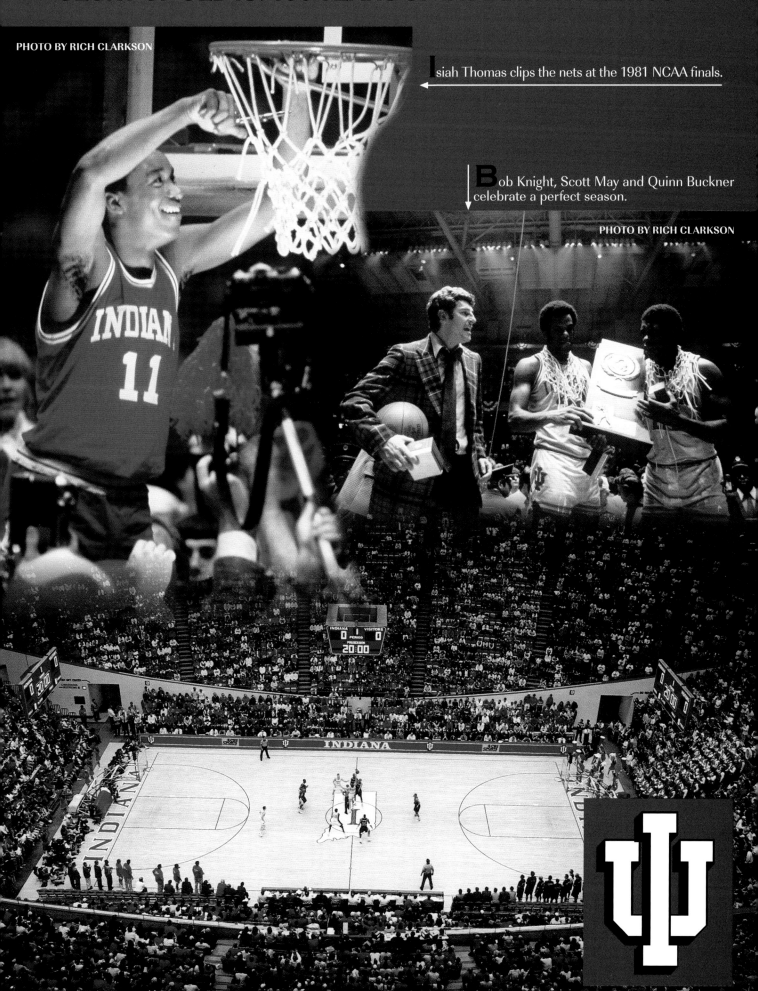

Isiah Thomas clips the nets at the 1981 NCAA finals.

Bob Knight, Scott May and Quinn Buckner celebrate a perfect season.

You can help write the next chapter of IU Golden Moments

Nearly all of the Golden Moments chronicled in this special edition book were made possible, in part, by the generous contributions of IU sports fans like you. The Indiana University Department of Intercollegiate Athletics does not receive funds from the university or state to support IU's 23 varsity teams and over 600 student-athletes. This means the next generation of IU achievers is depending on your support to help them realize their Golden Moments . . . on the field, in the classroom, and beyond.

Your tax-deductible donation to the IU Varsity Club entitles you to:

- Ten free issues of the Varsity Club newsletter, *Hoosier Scene*
- Invitations to special Varsity Club events, including golf outings and pre-game gatherings
- Priority points good for season ticket and parking upgrades
- IU Dept. of Intercollegiate Athletics press releases e-mailed to you at the same time as the media

But best of all, you'll know that 100 percent of your donation will help deserving athletes make the most of their IU experience.

Your Golden Moment is just a click away . . . make your donation to the IU Varsity Club online when you visit www.athletics.indiana.edu/varsityclub/ and click "Pledge Form."

There are hundreds more IU Golden Moments just waiting to happen . . . we hope you'll want to be a part of them.

If you have any additional questions about your contribution, or the IU Varsity Club, please call us at: (812) 855-0866.

Thank you!

9 WORLD RECORDHOLDERS—GREATEST TEAM?

The argument was raised in late-summer 1970 that Indiana might have on-campus the greatest team in history. In any sport.

Freshman John Kinsella checked in fresh from setting world records at 400 and 1,500 meters in the National AAU outdoor meet, at a time when international swimming certified world records in just 12 individual events. For 20 days from late August to early September, enrolled IU swimmers held nine of those.

It was the peak of the 19-year period in which at least one world record always was held by a present, past or future Hoosier.

The 1970-71 team's world recordholders were Mark Spitz (100 and 200 freestyle, 100 and 200 butterfly), Mike Stamm (200-meter backstroke), Gary Hall (200 and 400 individual medley), and Kinsella.

At the same time, IU's Jim Henry was world-ranked No. 1 in springboard diving.

Going by recorded times, a dual meet matching on-campus Hoosiers against all the rest of the world, including all other Americans, would have gone down to the last relay for a nip-and-tuck decision.

That was the basis for a Bloomington *Herald-Telephone* story built into a feature by *Sports Illustrated* contending that no team—not the Yankees or the Celtics, no Super Bowl or Stanley Cup champion—was ever as superior in its field as the Doc Counsilman-Hobie Billingsley program in 1970-71.

> **Of men's swimming's twelve world records, on-campus Hoosiers in late-summer 1970 held nine.**

Snapshot in Time

'THIRD TWIN' McGLOCKLIN
AN NBA CHAMPION

DURING THEIR IU years together, Jon McGlocklin sometimes was called "The Third Twin." It was a high compliment, linking him in size (6-5, 205), skill and competitiveness with the two teammates he had throughout his IU years, Tom and Dick Van Arsdale.

McGlocklin grew up just 17 miles from the Vans, in Johnson County—McGlocklin at Franklin, the Twins at Greenwood (though they played at Indianapolis Manual). An excellent outside shooter, McGlocklin played little as a sophomore at IU but the next two years fit in wherever he could help, much of the time at center.

Jon McGlocklin played on an NBA championship team in 1971 and was an NBA All-Star in 1969.

Those two years, Tom averaged 19.8 points a game, Dick 19.7 and "Third Twin" McGlocklin 18.5. Seven times all three scored in the 20s; another 21 times, McGlocklin and one of the Twins did.

In 1971, McGlocklin achieved something even the Twins never did: an NBA championship. At guard alongside Oscar Robertson for champion Milwaukee, McGlocklin averaged 15.8 points and led all NBA guards by shooting .535. He scored more than 9,000 points in his 11 pro seasons, averaging 19.4 in 1968-69 when he was an All-Star —with Dick, just ahead of the two years when both Van Arsdales were All-Stars.

IN THOSE DAYS . . .

WATSON RESIGNS;
KNIGHT BROUGHT IN

With the scars of the 1969 football walkout still fresh, Indiana faced another team split and near walk-out late in the 1970-71 basketball season.

This time, the division crossed racial lines. Sixth-year coach Lou Watson, whose development of the team and handling of star sophomore George McGinnis were questioned by several players on the 13-man team, resigned during the tense final week of the 17-7 season.

The search for a replacement took on a clear priority: a disciplinarian who could win—in a critical year: the Hoosiers' first in spacious Assembly Hall.

March 27, athletic director Bill Orwig, faculty representative Ed Cady and a search committee came back from the NCAA Final Four in Houston with their man: Bob Knight, at 30 already the winner of 102 games (in six Vietnam-era seasons at Army), a player for respected Fred Taylor during Taylor's peak seasons at Ohio State.

McGinnis, who was not among the objecting players, turned pro. He helped his hometown Indiana Pacers to two straight championships and in four ABA seasons averaged 25 points a game (his high 58, still the team record). McGinnis joined the Philadelphia 76ers and immediately made first-team All-NBA. His 17,000-point pro career ended in 1982 with the Pacers, who made his No. 30 one of three they have retired.

HOOSIER LIST

MARK SPITZ' 1972 OLYMPICS

INDIVIDUAL EVENTS

Monday, Aug. 28
200 butterfly, 2:00.70
Record broken was set 6-3-76
New record lasted 1,375 days*

Tuesday, Aug. 29
200 freestyle, 1:52.78
Record broken was set 8-23-74
New record lasted 724 days*

Thursday, Aug. 31
100 butterfly, :54.27
Record broken was set 8-27-77
New record lasted 1,822 days*

Sunday, Sept. 3
100 freestyle, :51.22
Record broken was set 6-21-75
New record lasted 1,021 days*

*Average for other men's events, set at Munich or standing: 565 days

RELAYS

Monday, Aug. 28
4X100 freestyle, 3:26.42
(John Murphy on team)

Thursday, Aug. 31
4X200 freestyle, 7:23.22
(John Kinsella, Fred Tyler on team)

Monday, Sept. 4
4X100 medley, 3:42.22
(Mike Stamm on team)

INDIANA LEGEND — *Mark Spitz*

'GREATEST ATHLETE EVER'—DOC

Two years before the Munich Olympics, a fan letter addressed "Mark Spitz, USA" reached him in Bloomington. After Munich, Bob Hope said Spitz's achievements "made Superman seem like Truman Capote." *Los Angeles Times* columnist Jim Murray called Spitz "the nearest thing to a dolphin this country has ever produced" and said he "may be the most handsome specimen ever to achieve championship status in world athletics. In a film with Omar Sharif, he'd get the girl."

Doc Counsilman called it "valid to consider him the greatest athlete who ever lived. I don't think his seven gold medals in the Olympics will ever be matched."

That's Mark Spitz, who called choosing Indiana and Counsilman in January 1969 "the biggest decision of my life (and) the best."

Spitz knew better than anyone how he felt after going to the Mexico City Olympics in 1968 a spotlighted high school athlete talking of winning six golds—and leaving there without a single individual victory. "I went through an identity crisis," he said. "The things that happened (at IU) enabled me to stay in swimming and keep going four years after Mexico City. I don't think Doc received enough recognition for that."

Eight NCAA-meet victories by Spitz that helped IU to four team championships left Counsilman feeling amply repaid.

BIG TEN MEDAL - Chuck Thomson   **GIMBEL AWARD -** Mark Spitz

BALFOUR AWARDS
Football-Mike Heizman/Larry Morwick; Basketball-John Ritter/Steve Downing; Baseball-Ken St. Pierre; Track-Steve Kelley; Wrestling-Bill Willetts; Swimming-Mark Spitz; Gymnastics-Benny Fernandez; Golf-Gar Hamilton; Tennis-Mark Bishop

NCAA CHAMPIONS
TEAM: Swimming (Doc Counsilman). INDIVIDUAL: Swimming, Mark Spitz, 100 butterfly (47.99), 200 butterfly (1:46.90); Gary Hall, 200 individual medley (1:51.51), 400 individual medley (3:58.72); John Kinsella, 500 freestyle (4:24.50), 1,650 freestyle (15:33.58).

OLYMPIC MEDALISTS
Swimming: Mark Spitz, 100 freestyle, gold (51.22), 200 freestyle, gold (1:52.78), 100 butterfly, gold (54.27), 200 butterfly, gold (2:00.70), 400 freestyle relay, gold (3:26.42), 800 freestyle relay, gold (7:35.78), 400 medley relay, gold (3:48.2)—all seven times world records; Mike Stamm, 100 backstroke, silver (57.70), 200 backstroke, silver (2:04.09), 400 medley relay, gold; John Murphy, 100 backstroke, bronze (58.35), 400 freestyle relay, gold; Gary Hall, 200 butterfly, silver (2:02.86); Fred Tyler, 800 freestyle relay, gold; John Kinsella, 800 freestyle relay, gold.

FOOT INJURY STOPS CYNTHIA

Cynthia Potter won a record 28 national diving championships.

On her last practice dive two days before competition began at Munich, Cynthia Potter experienced an Olympian's nightmare. The top of her right foot banged against the diving board—no fracture, just a deep bruise likely to cause major problems for only a few days. Those were gigantic days.

Before the injury, Cynthia—tiniest of all IU sports champions at 5-1 and 98 pounds—seemed sure to win the springboard gold medal and maybe the 10-meter platform gold. A 15-time national champion, she had been the dominant woman diver at the U.S. Trials.

On her 22nd birthday, injury and all, she tried. Olympic rules denied her most pain-killers. She grittily took a few warm-up dives (her first since the injury) and then competed, hobbling on each advance to the board. She qualified 10th and finished seventh. Micki King, whom she had beaten in the Trials, won the gold easily.

At 17, Cynthia had surprised herself by coming within two points of a 1968 Olympic berth. At 25, her national-championship total at 22, she tried again and finally won that elusive first Olympic medal—third on the springboard at Montreal.

She retired as one of America's all-time diving greats, her final national championship total 28, still the women's diving record.

She entered the International Swimming Hall of Fame in 1987 and IU's Athletics Hall of Fame in 1989.

Snapshot in Time

DOWNING, RITTER CHRISTEN HALL

AN 84-77 VICTORY over Ball State December 1, 1971, officially launched the Assembly Hall Era, and the IU era of basketball coach Bob Knight.

Frank Wilson's free throw went into history as the building's first point. Ball State guard Steve Tucker's only basket of the game was The Hall's first field goal. John Ritter scored IU's first basket. Steve Downing had 26 rebounds, still the building's record, and 33 points.

The Hoosiers were 3-0 when they went to Louisville for a historic matchup: Knight, in his first IU year, against Adolph Rupp, in his last at Kentucky. Hobbling on a sore knee, Downing played all 50 minutes and had 47 points and 25 rebounds in IU's double-overtime 90-89 victory.

Assembly Hall's dedication game was Saturday, December 18, against Notre Dame and its first-year coach, Digger Phelps. An IU-record crowd of 14,992 saw the Irish lead 5-4. Then IU spurted to a 16-5 lead on the way to a 94-29 outcome, although Indiana had just nine available players and used Downing (four points) for less than 10 minutes. Ritter's 31 points led Indiana and made him the only Hoosier since 1928 to outscore a basketball opponent.

John Ritter's 31 points outscored Notre Dame in Assembly Hall's dedication game.

IN THOSE DAYS . . .

SPITZ JOINS OWENS AT TOP

An international poll in 1980 rated Jesse Owens No. 1 among all-time American athletes, and Mark Spitz No. 2—ahead of Muhammad Ali and Joe Louis, of Jim Thorpe and Babe Ruth.

The "Spitz Olympics" did that. At the Olympic Games in Munich in 1972, Spitz swam in seven events, won seven gold medals, and set seven world records.

Three golds and records came in relays. On his own in individual events at Munich, Spitz set four world records in seven days. Four weeks earlier, he set five world records in four days at the U.S. Trials in Chicago—nine world-record swims for him in 32 days.

No, world-record swims do not happen every time a good swimmer gets in the water. Of America's greatest male swimmers, only Don Schollander (13), John Hencken (12) and Gary Hall (10)—not Spitz successors John Naber (4) or Mike Biondi (5)—had more than nine world-record performances in a whole career.

In 1983, the U.S. Olympic Hall of Fame was inaugurated with 25 charter selections. One-two in the voting were Jesse Owens and Mark Spitz.

The only other Hoosier in the U.S. Olympic Hall of Fame is Walter Bellamy, taken in with the 1960 basketball team.

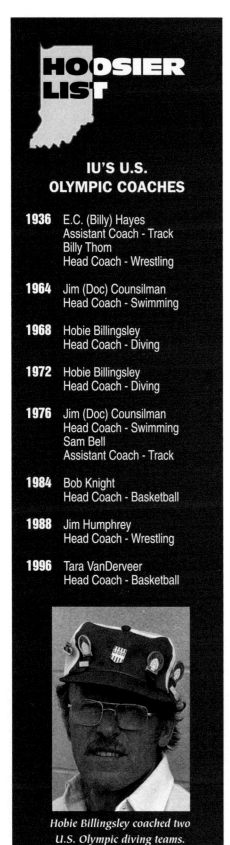

HOOSIER LIST

IU'S U.S. OLYMPIC COACHES

1936 E.C. (Billy) Hayes
Assistant Coach - Track
Billy Thom
Head Coach - Wrestling

1964 Jim (Doc) Counsilman
Head Coach - Swimming

1968 Hobie Billingsley
Head Coach - Diving

1972 Hobie Billingsley
Head Coach - Diving

1976 Jim (Doc) Counsilman
Head Coach - Swimming
Sam Bell
Assistant Coach - Track

1984 Bob Knight
Head Coach - Basketball

1988 Jim Humphrey
Head Coach - Wrestling

1996 Tara VanDerveer
Head Coach - Basketball

Hobie Billingsley coached two U.S. Olympic diving teams.

INDIANA

⟨✦⟩ LEGEND — *Steve Downing*

IU RIDES DOWNING TO VICTORIES

Steve Downing emerged from longtime pal George McGinnis's huge shadow when Bob Knight built his first Indiana team around the 6-8 junior center.

In the second game of the season, Knight's plans teetered when Downing injured a knee. A week later, he surmounted the injury to play what Knight has called the greatest game ever for one of his Hoosiers: in a 90-89 double-overtime victory over Kentucky, 47 points, 25 rebounds—and fifty minutes played. He was never taken out.

The knee injury that year eventually did slow Downing, who averaged 21.8 in pre-Big Ten games and 14.7 in the conference. The next year, he averaged 24 points in the Hoosiers' last eight Big Ten games, including 41 against Illinois. He had 20 points in a season-ending 77-72 victory over Purdue—on Knight's first "Senior Day," starting a tradition. When Northwestern upset Minnesota later that day, the Big Ten-champion Hoosiers were NCAA tournament-bound.

Downing scored 29 points as No. 6 Indiana dumped No. 5 Marquette, 75-69, then 23 in a 72-65 victory over Kentucky that sent the Hoosiers to the Final Four. There, against No. 1 UCLA, Downing faced Player of the Year Bill Walton. After nearly 10 minutes, IU led 18-13. Downing's third foul came early in a 29-4 UCLA barrage wrapped around halftime, opening a 46-24 lead. It was 54-34 with 13:14 left, before a shocking 17-0 Indiana run that John Wooden called "the best comeback anybody has ever made against us."

Walton, out with four fouls, returned when the meltdown reached 54-47. At 54-51, Walton wheeled to drive, Downing cut him off, and whistles signaled a foul—a Downing block, not a Walton charge that would have ended the All-American's day. Downing's fifth foul came seconds later and UCLA won, 70-59. Downing outscored Walton, 26-14.

Downing was All-Final Four, the Big Ten MVP, and the Boston Celtics' No. 1 draft pick. He won an NBA championship ring with the Celtics in 1974.

BIG TEN MEDAL - Gary Hall   **GIMBEL AWARD -** John Ritter

BALFOUR AWARDS
Football-Dan Grossman; Basketball-Steve Downing; Baseball-Barry Burnett; Track-Bob Someson; Wrestling-Bill Willetts; Swimming-Gary Conelly; Gymnastics-Benny Fernandez; Golf-Kevin Proctor; Tennis-Doug Sullivan.

NCAA CHAMPIONS
Team: Swimming (Doc Counsilman); Individual: John Kinsella, 500 freestyle (4:26.32), 1,650 freestyle (15:29.09); Mike Stamm, 100 backstroke (50.91), 200 backstroke (1:50.56); Gary Hall, 200 butterfly (1:48.48); 800 freestyle relay, John Kinsella, Gary Hall, Fred Tyler, Gary Conelly (6:36.39)

GARY HALL: A SPECIAL SCHOLAR-ATHLETE

Gary Hall may be the greatest all-round swimmer in IU's remarkable history. He's surely the greatest scholar-athlete ever at IU, giving equal weight to both sides of the hyphen.

Hall set world records in four different swimming events. Among all swimmers in the world ever, only three-year IU teammate, Mark Spitz, topped that (five).

And only Hall of all IU's swimming greats made three Olympic teams—once as a high schooler, once as a Hoosier, once as a medical student. He medaled each time.

Twice, Hall was named World Swimmer of the Year—in 1970 and '71, during the remarkable run of six such honors for Hoosiers present and future (Charlie Hickcox won the award in 1968, Spitz in 1967, '69 and '72).

America's 1976 Olympic swimming team elected Hall captain at Montreal. There, U.S. team captains (IU's Quinn Buckner in basketball included) picked him to carry the flag in the Games' Opening Ceremonies.

Hall and Spitz were the first collegiate swimmers to win at least one event a year on teams that won four straight NCAA championships. Spitz scored 218 career NCAA points, Hall 214 1/2—the first 200-point men in meet history.

Hall's career highlight came in the 1971 NCAA meet. Sophomore Hall swam in five events and—including two relay legs—each time swam his distance faster than anyone ever. "That ranks next to Mark's Olympics (as) the two greatest meets any swimmer ever has had," Doc Counsilman said.

Hall, a charter member of IU's Athletics Hall of Fame and a 1981 inductee into swimming's, has had a distinguished career as an eye surgeon. In 1998, the NCAA gave him and diver Cynthia Potter its Silver Anniversary Award—two of six scholar-athletes from all sports cited for their achievements in athletics and afterward in their life's work.

Three-time Olympian Gary Hall carried the U.S. flag in opening ceremonies in the 1976 Olympics.

Snapshot In Time

BURNETT EDGED OUT WINFIELD

BARRY BURNETT FOLLOWED the Dick Farley trail from Winslow High to Indiana. Like 1950s star Farley, Burnett did carry a high scoring average in basketball as a Winslow Eskimo (18.5 his senior year), but basketball wasn't Burnett's college game.

He hit .616 his senior baseball season at Winslow, and he was all set to go to Kentucky Wesleyan on a basketball-baseball grant until IU baseball coach Ernie Andres saw him hit in summertime American Legion ball and recruited him.

Burnett was a starter as a sophomore at IU. His junior year, he became the school's first Big Ten batting champion in 11 years, with the highest average (.471) the league had seen in nine years.

He struck out just three times in the Big Ten season, the last time against the pitcher-outfielder who was runnerup to him in the batting race. Burnett went 1-for-3 that day. If that Minnesota pitcher-outfielder had blanked him that game, he—future major league star Dave Winfield—would have been the league batting champion at .453.

Instead, Burnett finished the season on an 11-for-14 tear and stole the title away from one of the league's all-time great athletes.

Barry Burnett won the Big Ten batting title with a .471 average.

IN THOSE DAYS . . .

IU WOMEN, TARA START WELL

Women's varsity basketball began at IU with a 70-40 victory over Valparaiso in fall 1971.

Indiana won its first 15 games before losing to Northern Illinois in the opening round of a regional tournament, 42-35. That team finished 17-2.

The next year, the Hoosiers went 15-1 to qualify for the 16-team National Women's Collegiate Tournament. Debbie Oing had 18 points and Debbie Milbern 15 as Indiana opened with a 46-43 victory over Lehman. In a 55-51 win over East Stroudsburg, sophomore Tara VanDerveer was the leader with 16 points. Queens, down 36-32 after three quarters, beat IU in the semifinals, 52-40.

Oing, IU's first All-America player (1975), was the first women's basketball player named to the IU Athletics Hall of Fame. VanDerveer joined her in 1995.

VanDerveer coached Stanford to NCAA championships in 1990 and '92. She took a year away from the college game in 1995-96 to coach the U.S. women's Olympic team to the gold medal at Atlanta.

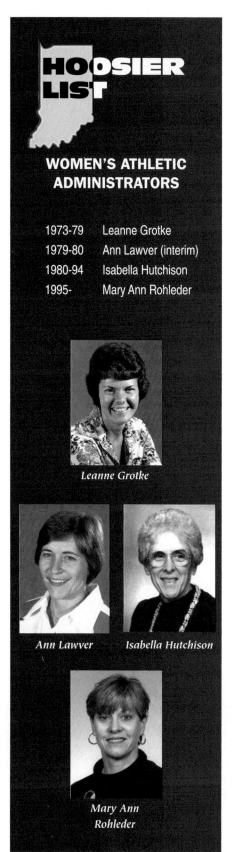

HOOSIER LIST

WOMEN'S ATHLETIC ADMINISTRATORS

1973-79 Leanne Grotke
1979-80 Ann Lawver (interim)
1980-94 Isabella Hutchison
1995- Mary Ann Rohleder

Leanne Grotke

Ann Lawver   *Isabella Hutchison*

Mary Ann Rohleder

LEGEND *Jim Montgomery*

'HE COULD INTIMIDATE'

Jim Montgomery looked good on the Olympic medal stand—he won three golds and broke a special swimming barrier at Montreal in 1976. And he looked good powering through a pool—"he'll get up high and plane water like a speedboat," Tennessee coach Ray Bussard said.

Doc Counsilman's favorite memory of Montgomery, though, was on the starting blocks

"*He* could intimidate," Counsilman said. "He was 6-6, 212, and he'd tell the swimmer beside him, 'I'm gonna beat the hell out of you.'

"Jim was probably the greatest competitor I ever had."

And, he added with a smile, "the meanest."

Montgomery went on at IU to win three NCAA sprints and—one of college swimming's all-time great relays swimmers—helped five Hoosier relay teams to victories.

World recordholder in the 100-meter freestyle going into the 1976 Olympics, he bettered his record in the preliminaries. Then, in the race that carried with it the unofficial title of "World's Fastest Swimmer," he became the first ever to go under 50 seconds. His finals time was 49.99, "the best swim of the meet," his IU and Olympic coach, Counsilman, called it.

"Fifty seconds," Counsilman said, "was the last barrier. It's like breaking a minute, which happened 50 years ago. It has taken that long to get down (from 60 seconds to 50), and there's no way anyone's ever going to break 40.

"This is actually more important than the gold medal, although Jim doesn't realize it now and won't until he's about 20 years older."

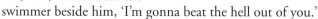

BIG TEN MEDAL - Dan Hayes   **GIMBEL AWARD** - Bill Armstrong, Jr.

BALFOUR AWARDS
Football-Carl Barzilauskas; Basketball-Steve Green; Baseball-Dale Thake; Track-Pat Mandera; Wrestling-Marty Hutsell; Swimming-John Kinsella; Gymnastics-Benny Fernandez; Golf-Cole Mahan; Tennis-Doug Sullivan

NCAA CHAMPIONS
Swimming: Jim Montgomery, 200 freestyle (1:39.19); 400 freestyle relay, Mel Nash, Tom Hickcox, Jim Montgomery, John Murphy (3:00.36); 800 freestyle relay, Jim Montgomery, John Kinsella, Fred Tyler, Tom Hickcox (6:40.32).

FAST START FOR SOCCER

Soccer began at Indiana University as a club sport, coached first by Joe Guennell and then, in 1963, by a young Pennsylvanian just two years away from playing on an NCAA champion at little West Chester State, Jerry Yeagley.

Yeagley's program earned promotion to varsity status in 1973. Friday night, September 14, a new IU era began at Notre Dame. Ibrahima Fall, a junior from Senegal, scored the first IU varsity goal. Freshman Steve Burks, the Hoosiers' first big scorer, scored twice in the 5-1 victory that opened a 12-2 introductory season.

The sixth of those victories, 10-0 over Indiana State, featured six goals by Burks, still the IU one-game record.

Win No. 9, by a 6-0 score at Ohio State, started an unbeaten streak against Big Ten opponents that was to stretch through 18 seasons and 68 games before a 1-0 loss to Wisconsin in 1991.

In the club-sport days, the teams of Guennell and Yeagley had several players named All-America—Tom Morrell (1952), Gus Omary (1954), John Hicks (1955 and '56), Joe Singer (1955), Elon Rothmuller (1956), Umit Kesim (1966), Karl Schmidt (1967) and Bob Nelson (1972).

Burks in 1976 became the first first-team All-America of the varsity era. He had 20 goals that first season, then 22 in each of the next two—the IU record until All-American Robert Meschbach's 27-goal season in 1980. Burks' 77 career goals was IU's record until four-time All-American and two-time Hermann Trophy winner Ken Snow scored 84 (1987-90). Burks' 77 still is No. 2 on the IU career list.

Steve Burks was IU's first first-team All-American in soccer.

Snapshot In Time

HOOSIER HORROR AT LONG BEACH

IN THE AFTERNOON preliminaries on opening day of the NCAA swimming meet at Long Beach, California, officials ruled breaststroker Brock Ladewig began his leg too soon and Indiana's medley relay team was disqualified. A potential 32 points, almost certainly 26 or 24, became zero.

It was the start of a three-day horror show for the Hoosiers. Up and down the lineup, expected points kept slipping away. Even John Kinsella, seeking to be the first Hoosier to double at the NCAA meet four straight years, finished sixth in both his specialties (500 and 1,650). And every key ruling by meet officials seemed to go against the growingly frustrated Hoosiers.

The nadir came in the next-last event, when the pro-Southern Cal crowd was allowed raucous heckling that cracked IU diver Gary James' composure—heckling that was as foreign in championship diving as on a PGA tour green. The effect was to sink a probable contender for a championship to a 10th-place finish, to drop IU from a possible 16 points (for first) to the 3 James got for 10th.

Indiana won the closing freestyle relay for 32 points but second-place Southern Cal scored 26 and won the meet, 339 to 338.

Leo Zainea of the *Chicago Tribune* noted that when "brawny freshman Jim Montgomery climbed the victory stand (after the relay), he wept unashamedly. They were not tears of joy." Indiana's six-year reign as national champion was over.

IN THOSE DAYS . . .

CORSO, BENNY AND TRIPLE

• Lee Corso, who felt fun and football co-mingled comfortably, was brought in as the replacement for John Pont, who—five years after his Rose Bowl season—resigned under some trustee pressure and became Northwestern's coach. Corso had coached Louisville to a 9-1 season and No. 16 national ranking in 1972. He also had ridden an elephant, among other stunts aimed at drawing attention to his Louisville program. Before his IU debut against Illinois at Memorial Stadium, he promised an unforgettable pre-game warmup, packing the stands an hour before game time. No IU player stepped on the field until, just before kickoff, a red double-decker English-style bus nosed through the gates of the stadium and Corso's first Hoosier team came running down a hill onto the field. The charged-up Hoosiers scored a quick touchdown, but Illinois won, 28-14, the start of IU's 2-9 season, 0-8 in the Big Ten.

• Benny Fernandez, on rings, became IU's first four-time Big Ten gymnastics champion—and last. Citing high insurance costs, Indiana dropped men's gymnastics after the 1982 season. Fernandez was a four-time All-American.

• Indiana in 1971-72 and 1972-73 became the first Big Ten track program ever to win the league's "Track Triple" two years in a row. The Hoosiers' championships in cross country and indoor and outdoor track went with titles in basketball, golf and swimming each year for an all-time IU high of six Big Ten championships in a season.

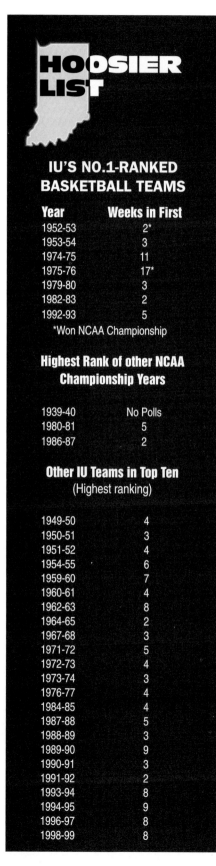

HOOSIER LIST

IU'S NO.1-RANKED BASKETBALL TEAMS

Year	Weeks in First
1952-53	2*
1953-54	3
1974-75	11
1975-76	17*
1979-80	3
1982-83	2
1992-93	5

*Won NCAA Championship

Highest Rank of other NCAA Championship Years

1939-40	No Polls
1980-81	5
1986-87	2

Other IU Teams in Top Ten
(Highest ranking)

1949-50	4
1950-51	3
1951-52	4
1954-55	6
1959-60	7
1960-61	4
1962-63	8
1964-65	2
1967-68	3
1971-72	5
1972-73	4
1973-74	3
1976-77	4
1984-85	4
1987-88	5
1988-89	3
1989-90	9
1990-91	3
1991-92	2
1993-94	8
1994-95	9
1996-97	8
1998-99	8

INDIANA LEGEND — *Steve Heidenreich*

IU'S ROGER BANNISTER

Early in Steve Heidenreich's Indiana career, Sam Bell described him with extraordinary words: "Terrific leg speed, one of the real premier runners—in the Dave Wottle and Steve Prefontaine class." Implied was a prediction of upcoming greatness. "I'm really hesitant to think about it," Heidenreich said. "Something like that—you just don't know till it happens."

Both were right.

The 5-10, 134-pound high school mile champion from Watertown, South Dakota, was IU's Roger Bannister, the school's first four-minute miler— Heidenreich's breakthrough 3:59.6 in a 1975 dual meet at Western Kentucky.

"Heidi" won the Big Ten outdoor mile championship in 1975 and ran for IU teams that won six Big Ten cross country and track championships. July 23, 1975, he outran Wilson Waigwa of Kenya to win the mile in an IU-record 3:58.4 at an international dual meet. He won a silver medal in the 1975 World University Games and ran second in a dual meet with the Soviet Union.

Late on the night of March 16, 1976—101 days before 1,500-meter preliminaries at the U.S. Olympic Trials—Heidenreich's life changed. Aiming at a straight-A semester as well as the Olympics and facing a next-day exam, Heidenreich delayed an all-nighter cram session and left his apartment to run. On a dark road, running on the left side, Heidenreich was hit from behind by a car that left the scene. He was critically hurt, his skull split open.

Miraculously, he survived—even more, he conquered the brain damage that wiped out much of what he had learned, relearned everything he needed and graduated with a degree in business in 1977.

He even returned to the track, not in championship form but competitive. CBS told his story in a national telecast. St. Louis sports writer Dave Dorr told it in the 1979 book, *Running Back*.

BIG TEN MEDAL - Orlando "Landy" Fernandez **GIMBEL AWARD -** Steve Green

BALFOUR AWARDS
Football, John Babcock; Basketball, John Laskowski; Baseball, Tim McGonagle; Track, Steve Cobb; Wrestling, Sam Komar; Swimming, John Murphy; Gymnastics, Jack Malmedahl; Golf, Bob Ackerman; Tennis, Doug Sullivan.

NCAA CHAMPIONS
Swimming: Fred Tyler, 200 individual medley, 1:50.62; 400 freestyle relay, Ken Knox, Jim Montgomery, John Murphy, Tom Hickcox (2:58.42); 800 freestyle relay, Rick Thomas, John Murphy, Jim Montgomery, Fred Tyler (6:36.29). Outdoor Track-Craig Caudill, 440 intermediate hurdles, 50.44.

GREEN AND 'LAZ' FOUNDATION BLOCKS

Steve Green   *John Laskowski*

Steve Green, Bob Knight's first IU recruit, and John Laskowski were senior leaders on the team Knight calls the best he has coached.

The 1974-75 Hoosiers became the first team to sweep through an 18-game Big Ten schedule unbeaten, and they did it by a record average winning margin of 22.8 points a game. They were IU's first team to complete regular-season play unbeaten, but in their 26th game—an 83-82 victory at Purdue that clinched the Big Ten championship—they lost consensus All-America forward Scott May to a broken left arm. May returned to play a few minutes in late-season games, but the No. 1-ranked Hoosiers' tournament hopes died with a 92-90 Mideast Regional championship-game loss to Kentucky.

So dominant were the Hoosiers that May, Green, center Kent Benson and guard Quinn Buckner all made the coaches' five-man All-Big Ten team. The other starter, guard Bobby Wilkerson, made the third team.

Deadly shooting was three-year starter Green's trademark. He hit 17 of 24 shots in scoring 37 points against Michigan his junior year. When May broke his arm, senior Green stepped up to average 26 points a game the last month. Included was a 13-for-15, 29-point game-saver that May-day afternoon at Purdue.

Laskowski was IU's "Super Sub." He came off the bench to score in the 20s six times—in double figures 40 times. Laskowski replaced May as a starter and scored a career-high 28 points the first time out at Illinois.

The Chicago Bulls took Green and Laskowski two spots apart in Round 2. Laskowski played two seasons with Chicago, averaging 9.2 as a rookie. Green, the fifth player taken in the ABA draft, signed with Utah instead of the Bulls, then joined the Indiana Pacers for their first three NBA seasons. He completed dental school and went into practice. Laskowski stayed close to IU basketball as an announcer for Hoosier network telecasts.

BURGER DAY AT THE HALL

AFTER INDIANA REACHED 13-0 by opening the Big Ten season with a road sweep over Michigan State and Michigan, college basketball's No. 1 ranking settled on the Hoosiers. Only the 1952-53 NCAA champions and the 1953-54 Big Ten champions, of all previous IU teams, had ever been there.

The Hoosiers' first game in the new role was a 102-49 home blowout of Lute Olson's first Iowa team.

It wasn't a matter of running up the score; 15 Hoosiers scored.

But, his first visit to Assembly Hall still left Olson flabbergasted. When a last-second Iowa shot was in the air, the crowd of 17,256 screamed as if the game were riding, then exploded in joy when the shot missed.

Hoosier bloodlust wasn't responsible, Olson learned later. A McDonald's promotion in Bloomington offered ticketholders a free hamburger and fries for any home game when IU held the opponent under 50. The final buzzer sent the 17,256 out into the late afternoon.

At the closest McDonald's, less than a mile from Assembly Hall, "We wrapped hamburgers for four solid hours," a manager said. The two Bloomington McDonald's outlets reported they gave away 6,000 hamburgers and 10,000 orders of fries.

A promotions disaster? *Time, Sports Illlustrated* and *People* magazines all ran stories, and the young Bloomington-raised employee who thought up the offer, David Campaigne, got a company promotion.

IN THOSE DAYS . . .

CAUDILL, COURTNEY AND CO.

• Senior hurdler Craig Caudill won the 440-yard intermediate hurdles at Provo, Utah, to become IU's first NCAA track and field champion in 18 years.

• In Indiana's second of three straight Big Ten men's golf championships, Hoosiers Gary Biddinger and Bob Ackerman were co-medalists—just the second time in league history teammates had done that. Ackerman was 14th and Biddinger 20th as IU shared eighth place in the NCAA tournament Biddinger and Ackerman were All-Americans.

• In a 1-10 season, sophomore Courtney Snyder revised the Hoosier football record book. Snyder's 1,254 rushing yards took the IU record away from John Isenbarger (1,217) and stood as the Indiana mark for 14 years. He was named to the writers' All-Big Ten team alongside Heisman Trophy winner Archie Griffin of Ohio State.

• The 1974-75 athletic year was the last time around for Bill Orwig, who retired after his 14th year as IU's athletic director. Orwig's assistant, Bob Dro, was the interim director until former LSU and Army football coach Paul Dietzel was hired as Orwig's replacement.

• A 14-2 record in its second varsity season earned Indiana's soccer team its first NCAA tournament invitation. Southern Illinois-Edwardsville ended it quickly for the visiting Hoosiers, 2-0. But, it was a major milestone for Jerry Yeagley's program.

1975 1976

HOOSIER LIST

THE PERFECT SEASON

Pre-Conference

Indiana 84, UCLA 64
Indiana 83, Florida State 59
Indiana 63, Notre Dame 60
Indiana 77, Kentucky 68 (OT)
Indiana 93, Georgia 56
Indiana 101, Virginia Tech 74
Indiana 106, Columbia 63
Indiana 97, Manhattan 61
Indiana 76, St. John's 69

Big Ten

Indiana 66, Ohio State 64
Indiana 78, Northwestern 61
Indiana 80, Michigan 74
Indiana 69, Michigan State 57
Indiana 83, Illinois 55
Indiana 71, Purdue 67
Indiana 85, Minnesota 76
Indiana 88, Iowa 73
Indiana 114, Wisconsin 61
Indiana 72, Michigan 67 (OT)
Indiana 85, Michigan State 70
Indiana 58, Illinois 48
Indiana 74, Purdue 71
Indiana 76, Minnesota 64
Indiana 101, Iowa 81
Indiana 96, Wisconsin 67
Indiana 76, Northwestern 63
Indiana 96, Ohio State 67

NCAA Tournament

Indiana 90, St. John's 70
Indiana 74, Alabama 69
Indiana 65, Marquette 56
Indiana 65, UCLA 51
Indiana 86, Michigan 68

INDIANA LEGEND

The 1976 Basketball Team

THE LAST PERFECT TEAM

Indiana's 1975-76 team showed quite quickly it wasn't brooding over the disappointing finish to its 1974-75 highride.

Starters Scott May, Quinn Buckner, Bobby Wilkerson and Kent Benson were back. Fifth-year coach Bob Knight moved senior Tom Abernethy into Steve Green's starting spot. The Hoosiers were No. 1 in pre-season, and in quick order, they:

• Crushed by a 94-78 score a Soviet Union National team that included the two stars of the Soviets' gold-medal victory in 1972, Aleksandr Belov and Sergei Belov. From 40-40, Indiana roared away to 79-49 before a sellout crowd of 17,377 at new Market Square Arena in Indianapolis. May signaled his return with 34 points, and 13-for-15 shooting in the preseason exhibition game.

• Ruined John Wooden-successor Gene Bartow's debut as UCLA coach with an 84-64 season-opening victory in one of the first made-for-TV games: in St. Louis, the starting time nearly 11 p.m. for maximum national airing. This time May had 33 points against the team

Bobby Wilkerson, Tom Abernethy, Scott May, Jim Crews and Quinn Buckner were the seniors on the undefeated 1976 national champions. The assembled trophies and plaques were from accomplishments in 1973, 1974 and 1975—before the perfect season.

that won the '75 national championship that Indiana, until May's injury, seemed to have in its sights.

• Went back to Market Square Arena and stunned Florida State, 83-59, with 24 points from May and 22 from Benson. The Seminoles' coach, Hugh Durham, said before the game: "They beat Russia to prove they're the best in the world. And they beat UCLA to prove they're the best in the United States. Now I'd like to see them prove they're human and have a bad game." At halftime, Indiana led 47-20. "I'm glad this isn't like baseball," Durham said. "I'd hate to play these guys in a three-game homestand."

The Hoosiers—as the century closes still college basketball's last unbeaten champions—weren't so overpowering every night out, but their resolve got them through even on off-nights. Rebound baskets by Benson got them into their only two overtimes—a 77-68 December victory over Kentucky at Louisville and a 72-67 escape from Michigan in February at Assembly Hall. Michigan led 60-56 and had the basketball, but a turnover and a missed free throw in the last 33 seconds let Indiana catch up in the second of three games between the teams that were to meet in the first NCAA championship game involving teams from the same conference.

First Row (left to right): Bobby Wilkerson, Jim Crews, Scott May, Quinn Buckner, Tom Abernethy, Kent Benson. Second Row: Student Manager Tim Walker, Rich Valavicius, Mark Haymore, Scott Eells, Wayne Radford, Bob Bender, Student Manager Chuck Swenson. Third Row: Head Coach Bob Knight, Assistant Coach Harold Andreas, Jim Roberson, Jim Wisman, Assistant Coach Bob Donewald, Assistant Coach Bob Weltlich.

BIG TEN MEDAL

Bruce Dickson

GIMBEL AWARD

Tom Abernethy

BALFOUR AWARDS

Football-Donnie Thomas; Basketball-Quinn Buckner/Scott May; Baseball-Scott Weiner/Tom Abernethy; Track-Steve Heidenreich; Wrestling-Sam Komar; Swimming-Jim Montgomery; Gymnastics-Greg Sangalis; Golf-Rob Jackson; Tennis-Rick Fink

NCAA CHAMPIONS

TEAM: Basketball (Bob Knight); INDIVIDUAL: Swimming - Jim Montgomery, 100 freestyle (44.39), 200 freestyle (1:36.53). Diving - Brian Bungum, 3-meter springboard.

OLYMPIC MEDALISTS

Basketball, gold, Quinn Buckner (captain), Scott May; Swimming, Jim Montgomery, 100 freestyle, gold, (49.99), 400 medley relay, gold (3:42.22), 800 freestyle relay, gold, (7:32.22), 200 freestyle, bronze, (1:50.58); Gary Hall (captain, U.S. flag bearer, opening ceremonies), 100 butterfly, bronze (54.65); Diving - Cynthia Potter, springboard, bronze.

LEGEND

40-0 YEAR, AND TWO SPECIAL CHAMPIONSHIPS

Scott May and Quinn Buckner enjoyed an all-conquering senior year in 1975-76.

The two close friends led Indiana to a 32-0 basketball season capped by an 86-68 victory over Michigan for the NCAA championship. Four months later, they were starters and leaders on the U.S. Olympic team that went 8-0 at Montreal and won the gold medal. Theirs was a 40-0 year, and it included the two biggest championships in amateur basketball.

May was college basketball's 1976 Player of the Year as a followup to his All-America junior season that ended in the supreme disappointment of his broken arm and Indiana's broken dreams.

Led by Quinn Buckner-Bobby Wilkerson backcourt, IU's defense to coach Bob Knight was "offense without the ball."

Buckner was the driving, demanding captain of a veteran team that had only one goal left after achieving everything but a national championship in going 31-1 the year before.

May was the '76 team's leading scorer, its most dependable clutch scorer, and an outstanding defensive player and rebounder, too.

Buckner teamed with Bobby Wilkerson to form perhaps the strongest defensive backcourt in college basketball history—"offense without the ball," coach Bob Knight called the defense Buckner and Wilkerson led.

May, a football and basketball star at Sandusky, Ohio, High, made the NBA All-Rookie team after averaging 14.2 for the Chicago Bulls. Injuries reduced him to seven NBA seasons, but he doubled his career by playing in Europe.

Scott May—Player of the Year

Buckner, whose father, Bill, played on IU's 1945 Big Ten football champions, was the most noted high school football-basketball doubler in the nation his last two years at Dolton, Illinois, Thornridge. He was a two-year starter at defensive back for IU, likely the only major college freshman to start the season opener in both football and basketball since freshmen became eligible in 1972.

Buckner played 10 NBA seasons, and in 1984, with the Boston Celtics, he joined Jerry Lucas as the only players ever to be on championship teams in high school, college, the Olympics and the NBA. After the Olympics allowed pros to play, Magic Johnson joined them in 1992.

Buckner was a captain and longtime leader of strong teams with the Milwaukee Bucks, before going to the Celtics. He played with the Indiana Pacers to close out his career. He interupted a television career for a brief tenure as coach of the Dallas Mavericks, then returned to television.

In 1986, May and Buckner were inducted into IU's Athletics Hall of Fame.

Quinn Buckner—Always a captain

In 1975-76, May and Buckner led teams that went 40-0 and won amateur basketball's two biggest championships.

TOUGH TOURNEY TRAIL

I n the 1976 NCAA tournament, Indiana whipped the toughest route ever dealt to a No. 1-ranked team—a route that included a regional matchup of No. 1 and No. 2 (Marquette) and convinced the NCAA Tournament Committee to begin seeding the tournament.

Indiana's tourney route, concluding what remains college basketball's last perfect season:

• No. 18 St. John's, 90-70—Scott May scored 33 points in victory over a 23-6 team that had been unbeaten when Indiana beat the Redmen, 76-69, in the championship game of the Holiday Festival before a college-record Madison Square Garden crowd of 19,964 in December;

• No. 7 Alabama, 74-69—The Tide, who had eliminated No. 4 North Carolina to get to IU, led 69-68 when May hit a jump shot with 2:02 left. May's numbers: 25 points, 16 rebounds against the 23-5 team Bob Knight called the best any of his teams ever played.

• No. 2 Marquette, 65-56—Marquette coach Al McGuire threw a box-and-one defense at Scott May, who scored 15 points but sat out 13 minutes with foul problems. Knight got 40-minute performances from Kent Benson, Quinn Buckner and Tom Abernethy against the 27-2 team that won the NCAA championship the next year.

• No. 5 UCLA, 65-51—The Bruins finished the season 28-4, 27-2 between their Indiana losses. Bobby Wilkerson, the 6-7 guard who jumped at center on opening tipoffs, had 19 rebounds. Abernethy, assigned to 6-11 All-American Richard Washington after Benson drew two quick fouls, outscored Washington, 14-10, after the switch.

• No. 9 Michigan, 86-68—The Wolverines went 25-4 against everyone else, but 0-3 against Indiana. Michigan led at half-time, 35-29, after Indiana lost Wilkerson early (concussion). May had 26 points, Buckner 16 and Outstanding Player Award winner Benson 25, with strong off-the-bench play from Jim Crews and Jim Wisman, filling in for Wilkerson.

Snapshot In Time

BIG TIME FOR IU AT MONTREAL

INDIANA'S STAMP ON the 1976 Montreal Olympic Games was more prominent than even in "The Spitz Olympics" in 1972 at Munich.

Almost every day a Hoosier was in the headlines coming out of Montreal, starting with the Opening Ceremonies when graduated IU swimming great Gary Hall was picked by team captains to carry the U.S. flag in the Parade of Nations.

IU's Quinn Buckner was the captain and Scott May a consistent scoring leader of the U.S. team that brought the Olympic men's basketball gold medal back after a controversial four-year stay in the Soviet Union.

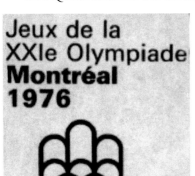

The swimming star of the Games again was a Hoosier—Jim Montgomery, who won three gold medals and shattered the 50-second barrier in the 100-meter freestyle, winning in 49.99.

Hall won a bronze in the 100-meter butterfly, and IU diver Cynthia Potter—a 28-time national champion—won a bronze in springboard competition.

IU's Doc Counsilman was the head coach of the most successful U.S. Olympic swimming team ever: 12 gold medals, 10 silvers, in just 13 events.

Hoosier track coach Sam Bell was an assistant coach on the U.S. team, coaching the men's distance runners.

HOOSIER LIST

BIG TEN'S FRESHMAN 1,000-YARD RUSHERS

1976	Mike Harkrader, Indiana	1,003
1983	D.J. Dozier, Penn State	1,002*
1986	Darrell Thompson, Minnesota	1,240
1990	Robert Smith, Ohio State	1,064
1994	Alex Smith, Indiana	1,475
1996	Ron Dayne, Wisconsin	1,863
1996	Sedrick Irvin, Michigan State	1,086

* Not in Big Ten at the time.

Alex Smith

INDIANA

LEGEND   *Kent Benson*

THE BIG RED'S BIG RED

Red-headed Kent Benson, "Mr. Basketball" in 1973 at New Castle, felt a shiver when—as a spectator at the state championship game at Assembly Hall—he stood and joined in a roaring tribute when the triumphal IU team, back from the NCAA Regional, walked across the court to its locker room. Benson's announcement for IU came soon afterward.

At IU, he was an immediate starter, but not a big scorer. Not until his 15th college game did he hit his first free throw. Three weeks later he had a 20-point, 15-rebound game against Michigan, and he was on his way. He averaged 15 points a game the rest of the way, and when Indiana—Big Ten co-champion but deprived of an NCAA tournament chance by a playoff loss to Michigan—won the Collegiate Commissioners Association's shortlived tournament, freshman Benson was the MVP.

Sophomore Benson made some big contributions to the 31-1, No. 1-ranked 1974-75 Hoosiers. His biggest came in the one loss. Benson had 33 points and 23 rebounds, fouling out three Kentucky centers in the 92-90 regional loss.

"Big Red" of the Big Red was All-Big Ten that year, a consensus All-American the next two years. At the Final Four in Philadelphia in 1976, Benson, with 25 final-game points, won the Outstanding Player Award.

A year later, he was the first player taken in the NBA draft. It was at the end of a long season for IU—16-11 on the court, the last four games played without Benson, who had back surgery after an injury at Purdue. Freshman Mike Woodson, with 104 points in those last four games, wound up the team's leading scorer. Benson was named the Big Ten MVP.

Benson played eleven NBA seasons and returned to Bloomington for a business career. In 1989, he was inducted into the IU Athletics Hall of Fame and in 1999 into the Indiana Basketball Hall of Fame.

BIG TEN MEDAL - Jim Montgomery **GIMBEL AWARD** - Kent Benson

BALFOUR AWARDS

Football, Steve Sanders; Basketball, Kent Benson; Baseball, Carl Imburgia; Track, Bill Foley; Wrestling, Sam Komar; Swimming, Jim Montgomery/Kenny McLaughlin; Gymnastics, Greg Sangalis; Golf, Rob Jackson; Tennis, Mike McLoughlin.

NCAA CHAMPIONS

Swimming, 400 medley relay, Romulo Arantes, Rick Hofstetter, Jay Hersey, Jim Montgomery, 3:17.14. Diving: Brian Bungum, 3-meter springboard.

IU item

GUTTY HARKRADER FIT THE HOLES

Freshman Mike Harkrader started 1976 No. 4 at tailback and ended with 1,003 rushing yards.

P re-season All-America nominee Courtney Snyder broke a leg in the ninth minute of the opener against Minnesota. Backups Darrick Burnett and Tony Suggs were gone because of injuries, too, after a second-game loss to Nebraska.

All Lee Corso had left was 5-7, 174-pound freshman Mike Harkrader.

At Washington, in the year between two Huskies Rose Bowl appearances, against a team led by Warren Moon, Indiana won, 20-13. Harkrader gained 76 yards and led the Hoosiers on the game-winning fourth-quarter scoring drive, prompting from defensive tackle Russ Compton a classic post-game appraisal:

"I think we've had the holes there all the time. We just had to find someone small enough to fit 'em."

A week later in his first Big Ten start, Harkrader gained 179 yards and Indiana beat Northwestern, 7-0. A week later, his 18-yard fourth-quarter touchdown run beat Iowa, 14-7, and his 191 yards set a Big Ten freshman record.

Indiana (4-6) went to Purdue with a four-game Old Oaken Bucket game losing streak. Early in the game, Harkrader cracked a bone in one leg. He kept playing. Just before halftime, with the Purdue band massed on the sidelines, he was thrown into a tuba. Broke his other leg. Even he had to quit then.

But he already had 79 yards, which gave him 1,003 as the fourth freshman in NCAA history to top 1,000 yards. He also had Indiana on its way to winning the Bucket back—20-14, on a touchdown by *his* backup, Burnett.

Snapshot In Time

ST. LOUIS ROUT PINPOINTED IU

THE JERRY YEAGLEY soccer program won no-doubt acceptance as a national collegiate soccer power on a sunny Sunday afternoon, October 14, 1976, at Memorial Stadium.

St. Louis came in No. 6-ranked, winner of 10 national championships in the previous 17 years. A crowd estimated at 6,000 turned out.

No. 12 Indiana took the Billikens apart, 5-1. "This was our greatest victory," Yeagley said that day.

A freshman corps headed by Angelo DiBernardo settled in alongside a veteran group that included senior Steve Burks, the link between the fast-developing IU program and its roots. Burks, who scored two goals in Indiana's first varsity game, was to close his senior season with 77—and first-team All-America honors, the first for a Hoosier in the varsity soccer era.

Burks scored a goal in a 5-0 rout of Cleveland State, avenging a late-season 1975 loss that probably cost Indiana an NCAA tournament invitation.

Indiana went into the '76 tournament 15-0-1 and No. 2-ranked nationally.

First Akron fell (2-1, Indiana's first NCAA tournament victory ever), then Southern Illinois-Edwardsville (1-0), then Hartwick (2-1), and the Hoosiers were in the NCAA championship game against reigning national champion San Francisco.

The Dons won, 1-0.

But Indiana had introduced itself, on the way to becoming college soccer's dominant team of the 20th century's last 25 years.

IN THOSE DAYS . . .

58 NCAA CHAMPIONS, 16 YEARS

• At Cleveland State in his last NCAA swimming championships, Olympian Jim Montgomery's record-shattering 42.51-second anchor leg—almost a full second under the American record for the open 100-yard freestyle (43.49)—squeezed Indiana in a touch ahead of Southern Cal in the medley relay. Backstroker Romulo Arantes, breaststroker Rick Hofstetter and butterflyer Jay Hersey were the other Hoosiers in a victory that proved historic. It was the last of Doc Counsilman's 58 NCAA individual or relay champions—at least one a year for 16 straight meets in which IU participated.

• Indiana had one other champion in the Cleveland State meet—diver Brian Bungum, who joined Hall of Famer Jim Henry as the only Hoosiers ever to win two straight NCAA championships on the three-meter springboard.

• In a meet that had been taken over by 1972 Olympic gold medalist Dan Gable's Iowa program, 142-pounder Sam Komar gave IU a breakthrough. His Big Ten championship, IU's first in six years, lifted the fifth-year program of another Olympic gold medalist, Doug Blubaugh, to a sixth-place finish in the nation's strongest wrestling conference— the Hoosiers' highest Big Ten finish of the '70s.

HOOSIER LIST

BIG TEN CHAMPIONSHIPS DURING RALPH FLOYD'S TENURE

1979	Men's Indoor Track
	Men's Swimming
	Men's Outdoor Track
1980	Men's Basketball
	Men's Indoor Track
	Men's Swimming
	Women's Tennis
1981	Men's Cross Country
	Men's Basketball
	Women's Tennis
1982	Women's Tennis
1983	Men's Basketball
	Men's Indoor Track
	Men's Swimming
	Softball
	Women's Basketball
	Women's Tennis
1984	Men's Indoor Track
	Men's Swimming
	Women's Tennis
1985	Men's Indoor Track
	Men's Swimming
	Men's Outdoor Track
1986	Softball
	Women's Golf
1987	Men's Basketball
	Women's Golf
	Women's Tennis
1988	Women's Indoor Track
	Women's Tennis
1989	Men's Basketball
	Women's Tennis
1990	Men's Indoor Track
	Men's Outdoor Track
	Women's Cross Country
	Women's Golf
	Women's Tennis

LEGEND *Angelo DiBernardo*

IU'S FIRST HERMANN WINNER

In an era when Brazilian star Pele was restyling international soccer, Angelo DiBernardo came out of Argentina to lend the same Latin American flair and inventiveness to Indiana soccer.

DiBernardo graduated in just three years, but he used those three seasons to help lift the Hoosiers' national stature.

The day when Indiana stunned St. Louis, 5-1, freshman DiBernardo reached full bloom. He scored all five goals, "the greatest individual performance I have ever seen," coach Jerry Yeagley called it.

In the NCAA semifinals, DiBernardo's two second-half goals got Indiana by Hartwick, 2-1, and into the NCAA championship game for the first time.

As a sophomore, DiBernardo had three three-goal hat tricks and scored the goal in a 1-0 victory over St. Louis. He was named first-team All-America.

In his final season, he became IU's first winner of the Hermann Award, as college soccer player of the year.

In an early sweep over strong opponents that vaulted Indiana to No. 1 in the rankings, DiBernardo's tie-breaking goal won at San Francisco, 2-1.

Those teams met again in the 1978 championship game at Tampa, and—as it had done in 1976—San Francisco denied the Hoosiers a national title, 2-0.

DiBernardo played as a professional for eight years, six with the New York Cosmos. He was on U.S. Olympic teams in 1980 and '84, and in 1991, he was the first soccer player inducted into IU's Athletics Hall of Fame.

BIG TEN MEDAL - Rick Hofstetter   **GIMBEL AWARD -** Peter Murao

BALFOUR AWARDS

Football, Keith Calvin; Basketball, Wayne Radford; Baseball, Bob Johnson; Track, John Dudeck; Wrestling, Sam Komar; Swimming, Rick Hofstetter; Gymnastics, Peter Murao; Golf, Bill Parker; Tennis, Bill Rennie.

IU item

FLOYD LED IU INTO NEW ERA

Big and burly Ralph Floyd played in the line on two bowl teams at William & Mary, then spent two decades in coaching that included some administrative roles. In March 1976, Floyd joined a former associate, Indiana athletic director Paul Dietzel—just in time to be in on the Hoosiers' NCAA basketball championship.

When Dietzel left Indiana in 1978 to be athletic director at LSU, chief assistant Floyd succeeded him.

Floyd supervised the fast development of the IU women's athletic program in the early 1980s. In a nine-year period from 1983 through 1991, IU's women's program graded out best in the Big Ten eight times. For five straight years, from 1987 through '91, IU's combined men's and women's program was the Big Ten's all-sports leader.

Floyd headed IU's hosting role for Bob Knight's U.S. Olympic basketball team in the summer of 1984, including three team appearances that packed Assembly Hall's 17,000-plus seats and a game that launched the new Hoosier Dome in Indianapolis with an all-time record U.S. basketball crowd, 67,596. He was co-commissioner for basketball when Indianapolis was host to the 1987 Pan-American Games.

He also handled negotiations that led to five bowl appearances for IU football teams from 1979 through 1990. In his 12 years, IU teams won 37 Big Ten championships and five national championships, including the 1981 and '87 NCAA basketball titles.

Floyd died December 15, 1990. The man primarily responsible for IU's beginning its Athletics Hall of Fame, Floyd was inducted into it posthumously in 1997.

Ralph Floyd directed Hoosier teams to 37 Big Ten and five NCAA championships and IU football teams went to five bowl games during his tenure.

Snapshot In Time

LORING IMMEDIATE SUCCESS

IN FOUR YEARS as women's tennis coach at his alma mater, California-Santa Barbara, Lin Loring made a national factor out of a hitherto losing program.

His four-year record there made him the choice when Indiana's job came open after the 1977 season.

Loring's first recruiting class brought in Kelly Ferguson, Bev Ramser and Tina McCall, who became All-Americans and, he said, "the backbone of the team in the early years."

Official Big Ten women's competition didn't begin until Loring's fifth season, and by then Loring had a four-year unbeaten streak going against Big Ten teams. Indiana won the first four Big Ten women's tennis championships, lost two in a row, then won nine straight—a streak ended in 1986 by a semifinal loss to Wisconsin, coached by Ferguson.

In 1982, Indiana finished 39-3, ranked sixth in the nation. And that spring, IU's Heather Crowe won the AIAW national women's singles championship and the Hoosiers won the AIAW National team title.

Since the Big Ten instituted a Player of the Year Award in 1984, Loring's Hoosiers have won the award six times, including 1992 when teammates Stephanie Reece and Deb Edelman were co-winners. Reece, Edelman, Kelly Mulvihill and Jody Yin were sole winners of the award. Mulvihill also was a co-winner once.

Lin Loring built a tennis powerhouse at IU quickly.

IN THOSE DAYS . . .

AMID CHILL, RADFORD HEATED UP

Wayne Radford

A 2 1/2-month-old national coal strike caused such an energy shortage in Indiana in February that schools went without heat and night-time sports events were banned.

That's why Indiana and Wisconsin met before just 11,403 in chilly Assembly Hall at 4 o'clock on a Thursday afternoon.

The teams played cold. Jim Wisman scored on Indiana's first possession. Then, for almost seven minutes, the score stayed 2-0. Indiana scored the last six points to win, 58-52.

Wayne Radford scored 13 points for Indiana, the only time in his last nine college games he didn't score at least 20. Prior to that streak, Radford had scored in the 20s just six times in 103 college games.

Indiana heated up with Radford, winning the first eight of those games to share second in the Big Ten and make the NCAA tournament field. Radford's run made him second-team All-Big Ten, IU's MVP, and a first-team Academic All-American. Drafted in the second round, he played an NBA season in his hometown with the Pacers.

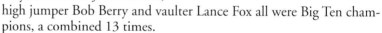
HOOSIER LIST

NCAA CHAMPION DIVERS

1964	Rick Gilbert,	1-meter
1965	Ken Sitzberger,	1 and 3-meter
1966	Ken Sitzberger,	1-meter
1967	Ken Sitzberger,	1 and 3-meter
1968	Jim Henry,	1-meter
1969	Jim Henry,	1 and 3-meter
1970	Jim Henry,	1 and 3-meter
1976	Brian Bungum,	3-meter
1977	Brian Bungum,	3-meter
1981	Rob Bollinger,	3-meter
1982	Rob Bollinger,	1-meter
1989	Mark Lenzi,	1-meter
1990	Mark Lenzi,	1-meter
1996	Kimiko Hirai,	1-meter

Rob Bollinger

INDIANA LEGEND — *Robert Cannon*

AN OLYMPIAN WHO WALKED ON

At Eastmoor High School in Columbus, Ohio, wideout Robert Cannon played a little football with Archie Griffin's brothers and did okay in track: 23-5 as a long jumper, 45 feet in the triple jump. Okay, but not enough to win a scholarship.

He became the most productive of the many walk-ons Sam Bell was to use and develop in a run of Big Ten championships around the turn of the decade.

Cannon headed a remarkable class. Sprinter Tim Graf, quartermilers Timi Peters and Tommy Hughes, long jumpers Wayne Pate and James Ewald, high jumper Bob Berry and vaulter Lance Fox all were Big Ten champions, a combined 13 times.

That didn't count Cannon, who won six championships and scored 115 points for teams that won three Big Ten titles and finished second four other times. Then, eight years after his last jump at IU, he made the 1988 U.S. Olympic team.

Cannon shot up to 52-9 in the triple jump as a freshman. The 45-foot high school jumper told coach Sam Bell drily, "I figured if I added seven feet every year, I might get to be pretty good."

It was a jumper's joke, but he did add more than five more feet before he was done to rank him with America's all-time bests.

In both 1978 and '79, he doubled at the Big Ten outdoor meet in the long jump and triple jump and led IU to an indoor-outdoor title sweep in '79. Then, in competition at Detroit, he gave IU its first NCAA indoor championship by winning the triple jump.

He topped 56 feet for the first time by winning the 1982 U.S. Olympic Festival at the new Indianapolis track with 56-4 1/2. He didn't top 57 feet until he was back at the same site for the 1988 U.S. Olympic Trials when he had the four best jumps of his life, topping out at 57-10 1/2 to make the U.S. team for Seoul.

BIG TEN MEDAL - Dave Abrams   **GIMBEL AWARD -** Joe Norman

BALFOUR AWARDS

Football, Joe Norman; Basketball, Scott Eells; Baseball, Dave Zuerner; Track, Mark Shroyer; Wrestling, Butch Marino; Swimming, Paul Sigfusson; Gymnastics, Tim Connelly; Golf, John Mealia; Tennis, Mike Dickinson.

NCAA CHAMPIONS

Indoor Track, Robert Cannon, triple jump, 54-8 1/2.

IU item

AFTER NIT TITLE, PAN-AM GOLD

Butch Carter's jump shot beat Purdue in the NIT finals.

When Indiana went to Illinois to close the 1978-79 basketball season, the Hoosiers' 17-12 record was out of consideration for the 40-team NCAA tournament field and questionable for the 24-team National Invitation Tournament. Mike Woodson had a career day at Champaign, outscoring Illinois for much of the game and finishing a 78-59 victory with 48 points, the Knight era record. From the NIT, that got Indiana the tournament's last invitation, a true "18-12 overture."

Woodson's scoring led the Hoosiers through to New York and the finals against Purdue, the Big Ten tri-champion that had been left out of the NCAA field. With five seconds left, Butch Carter scored from the top of the key and Indiana won, 53-52. Carter and Indiana center Ray Tolbert were named the tournament's co-MVPs.

The championship put Bob Knight (at 38) and IU among the coaches and schools that had won both the NCAA and NIT.

A few months later, Knight led a U.S. team that included Woodson (as its captain and leading scorer), Tolbert and incoming freshman Isiah Thomas to a gold medal in the Pan-American Games at San Juan, Puerto Rico. There wasn't much joy in the occasion. Knight spent much of his last week in Puerto Rico in courtrooms after a practice-floor time dispute led to controversial assault charges.

Snapshot In Time

SWIM STREAK ENDS; NORMAN EXITS HITTING

• **FRESHMAN DIVER ROB BOLLINGER**, who had been in kindergarten when Indiana last lost a swimming dual, gamely whipped two veteran SMU All-Americans in the next-last event to keep his team alive, but the Mustangs' 400-yard freestyle relay victory won the meet, 60-53, at Dallas. Snapped was Indiana's 14-year, 140-meet winning streak. Bollinger, a gymnastics whiz in his boyhood years, went on to win NCAA diving titles as a junior and senior.

• **JOE NORMAN**, too small at 6-1 and 205 to be a Big Ten inside linebacker, grew more and more reckless with his body as his season moved along. After a 24-0 lead at Minnesota sank into a 31-30 loss, Norman—diving over center, smashing into holes—had 23 tackles against Purdue after a career-high 26 against Ohio State. Still Purdue won the Old Oaken Bucket for the first time in three years, 20-7, and Ohio State's 21-18 scrape-through at IU turned out to be the last victory for Woody Hayes, whose first Big Ten loss had come from IU 27 years before. Norman, a Buckeye himself (Middlebury), made All-Big Ten and, a second-round draft pick, had an injury-shortened but good National Football League career with Seattle.

Linebacker Joe Norman was IU's Most Valuable Player in both 1977 and 1978.

IN THOSE DAYS . . .

BREAKING AWAY CHARMED WORLD

Hollywood came to Bloomington in late-summer 1978 to film a movie called *Bambino*.

Sometime after director Peter Yates and his dozen actors, three dozen technical assistants and four big trucks left seven weeks later, the name became *Breaking Away* and America had one of its greatest low-budget film hits.

Writer Steve Tesich rode on a winning Little 500 team as an IU student in 1962. He wove the story line around the bicycle race. Real-life people showed up in the film—president John Ryan, IU Foundation president Bill Armstrong, and hundreds of IU and Bloomington people made actors-for-a-day as extras. Bloomington scenes were the film's backdrops; actors dropped in at Memorial Stadium and were filmed sprawled on the grass at the stadium's south end, watching an IU football practice. The climactic race was run at old Memorial Stadium, where the real Little 500 had been run five months before.

Breaking Away's premiere was in Bloomington April 21, 1979. It became a worldwide hit, and 11 months later, it was one of five movies nominated for the Best Picture Oscar.

It didn't win, but Tesich won the Oscar for Best Screen Play.

HOOSIER LIST

IU IN BOWL GAMES

1967 Rose Bowl
Pasadena, California
Southern Cal 14, Indiana 3

1979 Holiday Bowl
San Diego, California
Indiana 38, Brigham Young 37

1986 All American Bowl
Birmingham, Alabama
Florida State 27, Indiana 13

1987 Peach Bowl
Atlanta, Georgia
Tennessee 27, Indiana 22

1988 Liberty Bowl
Memphis, Tennessee
Indiana 34, South Carolina 10

1990 Peach Bowl
Atlanta, Georgia
Auburn 27, Indiana 23

1991 Copper Bowl
Tucson, Arizona
Indiana 24, Baylor 0

1993 Independence Bowl
Shreveport, Louisiana
Virginia Tech 45, Indiana 20

INDIANA

LEGEND *Mike Woodson*

AN MVP, IN SIX GAMES

After Mike Woodson's performance as captain of the USA's Pan-American Games gold medal team in July, Bob Knight felt Woodson was the best player in the country, headed for a spectacular senior season.

And Woodson *was* the star as Indiana jumped to No. 1 in the polls with a rare 78-50 blowout of the Soviet National team and four straight collegiate victories. Then in one devastating week, the Hoosiers lost Randy Wittman for the season (broken foot) and Woodson to back surgery—out seven weeks.

The Hoosiers, barely alive in the Big Ten at 7-5, got Woodson back on Valentine's Day at Iowa. He hit his first three jump shots, scored 18 points, and began a 6-0 finishing streak in which his 20.5 average sparked Indiana to the Big Ten title.

Indiana and Ohio State went into their last-day game tied, winner take all. The Sunday national-TV game may have been Assembly Hall's best game ever. Of the 14 players used, nine had NBA careers. Butch Carter's free throws with seven seconds left tied the game. In overtime, Woodson and freshman Isiah Thomas (21 points each) pulled the Hoosiers through, 76-73.

Woodson, the man who played just six league games, was named the Big Ten's MVP.

The NCAA Final Four was in Woodson's hometown, Indianapolis, and the championship game was on his birthday. Perfect script.

But Woodson's adrenaline tank was dry. Indiana lost to Purdue in the tournament's second round.

Woodson went on to an 11-year, 10,981-point NBA career. And in 1984, when Isiah Thomas was the NBA All-Star Game's MVP, he was asked if that was his biggest basketball thrill. No, Thomas said, "My biggest thrill was my freshman year at Indiana when Mike Woodson came back from back surgery and hit his first three jump shots at Iowa."

BIG TEN MEDAL - Marc Schlatter   **GIMBEL AWARD -** Angelo "Butch" Marino

BALFOUR AWARDS
Football, Tim Clifford; Basketball, Mike Woodson; Baseball, Jim Caplis; Track, Mark Shroyer; Wrestling, Butch Marino; Swimming, Marc Schlatter; Gymnastics, Tim Connelly; Golf, Robbie Dew; Tennis, Randy Druz; Soccer, Mike Freitag.

NCAA CHAMPIONS
Swimming, Mark Kerry (Australia), 400 medley relay, gold (3:45.70), 200 backstroke, bronze (2:03.14); Djan Madruga (Brazil), 800 freestyle relay, bronze (7:29.30).

IUitem

AT 58, DOC SWIMS THE CHANNEL

(photo courtesy of Terrence Spencer, *Sports Illustrated*)

Doc Counsilman embarking on his historic swim.

Fall classes for 1979-80 already had begun when 58-year-old James "Doc" Counsilman conquered the English Channel, the oldest person ever to swim it. Counsilman entered the water at 6:13 a.m. Thursday, September 14, and 13 hours and four minutes later, he stepped out 26 miles away at Saint-Pol, France. He was the 214th swimmer to make it, the oldest by more than three years. Wife Marge accompanied him, riding in a small boat, sick all the way. "I saw Marge turn red, then green," Counsilman said. "When she got to purple, I thought, I'd better hurry up."

Back in Bloomington, people gathered around radios to listen to live coverage by the public FM radio station, WFIU. "The thing that amazes me is how much interest this caused," Counsilman said later.

He arrived home to a Bloomington celebration September 26. Hundreds, including IU President John Ryan, IU Foundation president Bill Armstrong, athletic director Ralph Floyd and many of Counsilman's present and past swimmers, greeted his late-afternoon arrival at Monroe County Airport. After an airport greeting, he rode back to campus in a police-led cavalcade.

On October 26, he was riding again, in an open convertible as the grand marshal for IU's Homecoming parade.

"I found out a lot about myself, and a lot about coaching," he said. "I didn't realize how hard you can swim—a guy my age swimming 12,000 meters a day.

"It made me realize how important goals are."

AFTER FIRST IU BOWL WIN, CLIFFORD BIG TEN MVP

INDIANA, BEHIND AT Iowa 26-3, spoiled Hayden Fry's Hawkeye coaching debut, 30-26—on Tim Clifford's 66-yard touchdown pass to Lonnie Johnson with 58 seconds left.

Indiana won 3-0 October 6 at Wisconsin over a team that lost four turnovers and missed three field goals and might have been the first team to be shut out without ever punting. Indiana won on Steve Straub's first-quarter field goal and a 23-play, 92-yard, 12-minute fourth-quarter drive launched by coach Lee Corso's daring call: a Clifford sneak on fourth-and-one at the *Indiana* 11.

At Michigan October 27, Clifford's pass to Dave Harangody at 0:55 pulled IU within 21-20. That time, with Clifford injured on the TD play, Corso didn't gamble, kicking to tie 21-21. Michigan, helped by time saved with a hotly disputed out-of-bounds toss that averted a midfield tackle, won at the gun on pass-catcher Anthony Carter's 45-yard breakaway.

The first Big Ten team invited to the Holiday Bowl, Indiana (7-4) met 10th-ranked Brigham Young (10-0). A fourth-quarter BYU punt bumped a Cougar player's leg. BYU players watched Indiana's Tim Wilbur slip in, snatch up the undowned football and dash to a 62-yard touchdown return for a wild 38-37 Indiana victory.

Days later Clifford became the first Hoosier in 42 years named the Big Ten's football MVP.

Tim Wilbur's 62-yard punt return gave IU its first-ever bowl win.

IN THOSE DAYS . . .

BELL BATTLES THROUGH

In spring 1980, 52-year-old IU coach Sam Bell had a practice-field heart attack. He barely survived. But he kept coaching. "Quit?" he said. "It never crossed my mind."

From his hospital bed, he coached that team via telephone to a victory over rival Wisconsin. "He sounded like himself, but it was kinda weird coming out of a speaker," said triple jumper Robert Cannon, who remembered hearing: "I'm not going to be there, but everyone knows what we want to do."

Cannon won two events and high jumper Bob Berry went 7-2 to win.

In '91 Bell had triple-bypass surgery the week of the two-day Big Ten outdoor championships.

He was directing both the men's and women's programs then and neither team had a good first day. They gathered in a hotel room to hear, in telephoned words relayed by women's assistant coach Roseann Wilson: "This was a horrible first day. Some of you have to get your heads out of your ... "

What men's captain Bob Kennedy called "the best final day we've ever had" vaulted IU to a 47-point win, Bell's last of 22 Big Ten men's championships. And the women surged to third.

HOOSIER LIST

'81 HOOSIERS AMONG BEST

Only nine NCAA basketball champions won each tournament game by at least 10 points:

	Games	Avg.	Low	High
Oregon, 1939	3	15.3	13	18
Kentucky, 1949	3	17.3	10	29
San Francisco, 1956	3	14.0	11	18
Ohio State, 1960	4	19.5	17	22
UCLA, 1967	4	21.2	13	49
UCLA, 1970	5	18.0	11	23
UCLA, 1973	4	15.3	11	17
Michigan State, 1979	5	20.8	11	34
Indiana, 1981	5	22.6	13	35

The 1981 Hoosiers rank second among NCAA basketball champions with the biggest average winning margins:

	Games	Avg.	Low	High
Loyola, 1963	5	23.0	2	69
Indiana, 1981	5	22.6	13	35
Kentucky, 1997	6	21.5	7	38
UCLA, 1967	4	21.3	13	49
UCLA, 1968	4	21.3	9	32
Michigan State, 1969	5	20.8	11	34
Ohio State, 1960	4	19.5	17	22
Oklahoma A&M, 1945	3	18.7	4	27
UNLV, 1990	6	18.7	2	30

INDIANA

✦ LEGEND *Isiah Thomas*

A LITTLE LEADER IN NO. 11

Photo by Rich Clarkson

Isiah Thomas was a third-grader playing on a sixth-grade team when a coach first gave him uniform 11. It's only coincidence that the Bible verse, "a little child shall lead them," is in the Book of Isaiah, Chapter 11.

No. 11 and a cherubic smile stayed with Thomas all the way through a Hall of Fame career.

The summer before he entered IU, Thomas played on Bob Knight's gold-medal Pan-American Games team at San Juan. Thomas scored 21 points in the tense championship game to lead a U.S. breakaway to a 113-94 victory over rabidly supported Puerto Rico. "Isiah played his butt off," U.S. captain Mike Woodson said.

Thomas started every college game he played, on two IU teams that won outright Big Ten championships. He was a 1980 U.S. Olympic starter (on a team kept home from Moscow by a U.S. boycott), and a consensus All-American in 1981.

When the '81 Hoosiers opened their championship drive by beating Maryland, 99-64, Thomas had 19 points, 14 assists and zero turnovers—a "time capsule" game, St. Joseph's coach Jim Lynam called it.

In the 63-50 championship-game victory over North Carolina, two steals and baskets by Thomas in the first two minutes of the second half "were the turning point," Carolina coach Dean Smith said. Thomas, who led both teams with 23 points, received the Outstanding Player Award.

Four weeks later, he announced he was turning pro. The No. 2 draftee, an instant NBA success, Rookie of the Year, and a starting All-Star from his first year on, in 1987 he completed the work and was awarded the IU degree he had promised his mother he would get. Isiah was involved in the playoffs with Detroit on graduation day. Mary Thomas accepted her son's diploma.

In 1993, he was inducted into IU's Athletics Hall of Fame, and in 1996, his No. 11 was retired by the team he had led to two NBA championships, the Pistons.

LEGEND

INDIANA

1981 NCAA Champions

FINAL PLAYED UNDER A CLOUD

Big Ten champion Indiana's 63-50 victory over ACC Tournament champion North Carolina is an NCAA final less remembered than are its circumstances.

Earlier that day in Washington, President Ronald Reagan was shot in the chest by attempted assassin John Hinckley. Bulletins updated by the minute stressed that the President's life was in no real danger, and NCAA tournament administrators decided to go ahead with the game.

At the halftime buzzer, Randy Wittman's baseline shot gave Indiana its first lead, 27-26. Twice in the first 90 seconds of the second half, Isiah Thomas converted steals into layups. Six minutes later, Indiana's lead was 45-34 on the way to history.

No previous NCAA champion ever had lost as often as 26-9 Indiana.

In their first trip back to Dayton since their 1975 regional nightmare, the Hoosiers blistered 18th-ranked Maryland, 99-64, to open their tournament drive. In the regional at Assembly Hall, Alabama Birmingham (87-72) and St. Joseph's (78-46) fell—in the semifinals at Philadelphia, LSU (67-49).

The losingest champions were the ninth—and, as the century turns, the last—to win all their tournament games by double-figure margins. Their 22.6-point average winning margin in the tournament is history's second-best, behind 1963 winner Loyola's 23.0 average.

Sophomore Isiah Thomas, who scored 23 points in the championship game and turned pro days after the tournament, won the Outstanding Player Award. Landon Turner and reserve Jim Thomas made the All-Final Four team. Wittman, who had 16 final-game points, finished sixth in the voting.

First Row (left to right): Student Manager Steve Skoronski, Eric Kirchner, Ray Tolbert, Glen Grunwald, Steve Risley, Phil Isenbarger. Second Row: Assistant Coach Gerry Gimelstob, Assistant Coach Jene Davis, Chuck Franz, Randy Wittman, Isiah Thomas, Ted Kitchel, Assistant Coach Jim Crews, Trainer Bob Young. Third Row: Dr. Brad Bomba, Head Coach Bob Knight, Landon Turner, Mike LaFave, Steve Bouchie, Tony Brown, Jim Thomas, Steve Downing.

BIG TEN MEDAL
Kevin Speer

GIMBEL AWARD
Glen Grunwald

BALFOUR AWARDS
Football, Tim Clifford; Basketball, Ray Tolbert; Baseball, Bob Waite; Track, Robert Cannon; Wrestling, Mark Galyan; Swimming, Mac Teskey; Cross Country, Jim Spivey; Gymnastics, Bob Hill; Golf, Eric Kaufmanis; Tennis, Bill Funk; Soccer, Robert Meschbach.

NCAA CHAMPIONS
Team: Basketball (Bob Knight); Individual: Diving, Rob Bollinger, 3-meter springboard; Outdoor Track: Dave Volz, pole vault (17-8 1/4).

TOLBERT, TURNER AND TRAUMA

The thought of 6-9 Ray Tolbert and 6-10 Landon Turner playing together tantalized Indiana fans with its potential from the time freshman Turner joined sophomore Tolbert in fall 1978.

Their combined work on Purdue star Joe Barry Carroll was a key to Indiana's National Invitation Tournament championship in '79. But Turner in particular had ups and downs into his junior season. At Iowa, late in a 78-65 Hawkeye victory, coach Bob Knight assigned Turner to guard 6-5 Kevin Boyle, with results that surprised even Knight.

Indiana didn't lose again, in large part because both Turner and Tolbert could blanket forwards on defense and leave post defense to 6-8 sophomore shooter Ted Kitchel.

Senior Tolbert, an Assembly Hall favorite for his leaps and dunks, was named the Big Ten's Most Valuable Player, and he was a first-round NBA draft pick.

> **"He never once . . . complained about not getting to play. He just kept working. He became as good a player as there was in college basketball."**
>
> **—Bob Knight**

Turner closed his junior season a player on the rise, his future limitless. He was All-Final Four after scoring 20 points against LSU and outscoring future NBA star James Worthy 12-7 in the championship game.

Four months later, he and a date were headed for a July outing at Kings Island amusement park when an accident left him paralyzed from the chest down.

Knight led a statewide drive, with help springing from small Hoosier towns and big ones, to take financial pressures off Turner and his family. Turner took it from there, graduating from IU in 1984 and going on to a successful career as a counselor and motivational speaker.

Turner's supporters weren't limited to Indiana. U.S. Basketball Writers named him to an honorary position on their 1982 All-America team and in 1989 gave him their Most Courageous Athlete award. In the 10th round of the 1982 NBA draft, general manager Red Auerbach announced:

"The Boston Celtics take Landon Turner of Indiana."

Landon Turner, All-Final Four, came back from tragedy triumphantly, graduating in 1984.

Snapshot In Time

TALE OF SWIM STRINGS:
ONE LIVES, ONE DIES

THE MEDLEY RELAY was added to the Olympic swimming program in 1960 at Rome, and the first gold-medal team was led off by IU backstroker Frank McKinney.

After that, in every Olympics, the United States won the event and at least one Hoosier brought home a gold medal from it, and somewhere during the span at least one Hoosier swam each of the four strokes that make up the medley.

IU's U.S. medley relay gold medalists after McKinney were butterflyer Fred Schmidt in 1964; backstroker Charlie Hickcox and breaststroker Don McKenzie, 1968; backstroker Mike Stamm and butterflyer Mark Spitz, 1972, and freestyler Jim Montgomery, 1976.

America's streak ended when the U.S. boycotted the 1980 Moscow Games, but IU's didn't. Backstroker Mark Kerry led off Australia's gold-medal team.

Another notable Hoosier swimming streak did end in 1980-81. By a 30-point margin, Iowa ended Indiana's streak of Big Ten championships at 20. The Hawkeyes won again in 1982, but the Doc Counsilman-Hobie Billingsley program regrouped to add three more championships from 1983 through '85—23 in all for IU, all under Counsilman and Billingsley.

IN THOSE DAYS . . .

THREE DIMENSIONS OF SHARPNESS

• Baseball pitcher Tim Clifford and track hurdler Nate Lundy hooked up well in football—particularly well in a 49-7 victory at Colorado. At halftime, Indiana led 35-0, and wideout Lundy already had caught touchdown passes of 75, 74 and 43 yards. He finished his day with five catches for a Big Ten-record 256 yards. And Clifford—11-for-14 for 345 yards and five touchdowns—still is in the NCAA record book for the highest efficiency grade for one game: 403.4.

• Kevin Speer started at center for much of his last two seasons at Indiana, on teams that went 14-9, including a Holiday Bowl victory. Speer, valedictorian of his class at Evansville Harrison, is one of IU's five football players who made Academic All-America. Speer graduated from Johns Hopkins University's School of Medicine—and did his residency in orthopedics. He is on the faculty at Duke University School of Medicine, in orthopedics.

• Sophomore Ted Kitchel's 9.2 scoring average was the lowest among the starters on IU's 1981 national champions, but Kitchel had the team's biggest day. In a 78-60 home victory over Illinois, he was 11-for-13 on field goals and a Big Ten-record 18-for-18 on free throws, Indiana's all-time most efficient 40-point game.

Nate Lundy (left) caught 5 passes for 256 yards against Colorado, the yardage total a Big Ten record at the time.

Ted Kitchel (center) hit a Big Ten record 18-18 free throws in scoring 40 points against Illinois.

Kevin Speer (right)— Academic All-America.

1981 [U] 1982

HOOSIER LIST

INDIANA'S MALE ATHLETE-OF-THE-YEAR

1982 *Jim Spivey, track and cross country

1983 Randy Wittman, basketball

1984 *Sunder Nix, track

1985 Paul DiBernardo, soccer

1986 Steve Alford, basketball

1987 *Steve Alford, basketball

1988 Mickey Morandini, baseball

1989 Anthony Thompson, football

1990 *Anthony Thompson, football

1991 Bob Kennedy, track and

cross country

1992 Mike Smith, baseball

1993 Calbert Cheaney, basketball

1994 Mark Buse, track

1995 Brian Maisonneuve, soccer

Todd Yeagley, soccer

1996 Brian Evans, basketball

1997 Roger Chandler, wrestling

1998 Randy Leen, golf

1999 Mike Collier, diving

Lazo Alavanja, soccer

* Also named Big Ten Athlete of Year

INDIANA

LEGEND *Jim Spivey*

FIRST BIG TEN ATHLETE-OF-THE-YEAR

Jim Spivey, the fastest miler ever to wear an Indiana uniform, was the first Hoosier runner ever to compete in three Olympics.

He had done neither of those things in late-spring 1982 when he won the Big Ten's first Athlete of the Year Award. Spivey, winner of 14 Big Ten championships and two NCAA, edged Michigan halfback-sprinter Butch Woolfolk.

Spivey ran on five IU teams that won Big Ten championships. He doubled in the 1,500 and 5,000 meters outdoors twice, the mile and two-mile indoors three times.

For all the great IU middle distance runners over the years, Spivey in 1982 became the first Hoosier to win an NCAA 1,500-meter or mile title outdoors, a year after winning IU's first NCAA indoor mile title.

He graduated owning every IU record from 800 meters through 5,000 outdoors and from 880 through two miles indoors. He held all-time Big Ten records in the mile indoors (3:57.04) and the 1,500 outdoors (3:37.24).

Spivey went on to win four U.S. championships outdoors at 1,500 meters. At Oslo in 1986, a 3:49.80 mile made him the third American to break 3:50. In 1984, an Olympian for the first time, Spivey ran fifth in the 1,500 meters in 3:36.07, still the best finals time ever for an American.

Spivey missed the 1988 Olympics, running fourth in the 1,500 at the U.S. Trials in Indianapolis. In '92, he won the Trials at New Orleans and finished seventh at Barcelona. In '96, he switched to 5,000 meters and—at 36—made the U.S. team again. Elimination in the semifinals ended his running career. He became track and cross country coach at the University of Chicago.

In 1993, he was inducted into IU's Athletics Hall of Fame.

BIG TEN MEDAL - Bob Stephenson & Karen Marinsek   **GIMBEL AWARD -** Rob Bollinger

ATHLETE OF THE YEAR - Jim Spivey (also, Big Ten)

BALFOUR AWARDS
Football, Steve Mitchell; Basketball, Jim Thomas; Baseball, Larry Blackwell; Track, Jim Spivey; Wrestling, Kevin Weber; Swimming, Tom Cole; Cross Country, Robbie Pierce; Gymnastics, Tom Gould; Golf, Denny Dennis; Tennis, Mike Dickinson; Soccer, Armando Betancourt.

NCAA CHAMPIONS
Team, Soccer (Jerry Yeagley); Individual: Diving, Rob Bollinger, 1-meter springboard; Outdoor Track, Jim Spivey, 1,500 (3:45.42).

AIAW CHAMPIONS
TEAM: Tennis (Lin Loring); INDIVIDUAL: Tennis - Singles, Heather Crowe.

IU ITEM

BETANCOURT WINS HERMANN

Armando Betancourt fell short of his goal of leading Indiana to its first NCAA soccer championship, but the Honduran star's productive play lifted the Jerry Yeagley program ever closer.

Betancourt still has IU's record for post-season goals after scoring six times in the Hoosiers' four-game drive to the 1980 finals. In his 20-3 farewell season in '81, he scored in almost every game—27 goals in all, tying the IU record Robert Meschbach set the year before.

When Bill Armstrong Stadium opened September 13, 1981, Betancourt scored the winning goal in the 17th minute of overtime as Indiana defeated its two-time championship-game conqueror, San Francisco, 2-1. Betancourt's goal came on an assist from Pat McGauley, who had scored the new Stadium's first goal.

Indiana closed the season 11-0 at Armstrong. All three losses came on the road, the last 1-0 at Philadelphia Textile in the second round of the NCAA tournament.

Betancourt, a first-team All-American for the second time, became IU's second Hermann Trophy winner. A 1980 Olympian, he also played for Honduras in the World Cup in 1982. In 1990, *Soccer America* magazine named him college soccer's Player of the Decade. In 1992, he entered IU's Athletics Hall of Fame.

Armando Betancourt became the second Hoosier to win soccer's Hermann Trophy.

Snapshot In Time

CROWE, IU NATIONAL CHAMPIONS

SOMETHING CLOSE TO a form letter introduced Indiana and tennis coach Lin Loring to Heather Crowe of Topsfield, Mass.

She visited, signed and stepped right in at No. 1 for Loring. She was a senior in 1982, when women's athletic programs achieved recognition in the Big Ten and NCAA. That spring IU won the first Big Ten title but Loring passed on the first NCAA championship for one last shot at the AIAW title.

Indiana and California, sixth and eighth in the final college rankings, were the AIAW's top seeds. They met in the finals, and straight-sets singles victories by Crowe, Tracy Hoffman (at No. 2), Bev Ramser (4), Diane McCormick (5) and Anne Hutchens (6) clinched IU's first national women's team championship.

The next week, No. 4 seed Crowe and top seed Vicki Nelson of Rollins met in the singles finals. Serving in the first set at 5-5, down love-40, Crowe's aggressive serve-and-volley game pulled out the game and set. "The best I've ever played" made her a straight-sets national champion.

In 1994 she became the first woman from the varsity sports era to be inducted into the IU Athletics Hall of Fame.

Heather Crowe led IU to the 1992 AIAW title and went on to capture the national singles championship.

IN THOSE DAYS . . .

A TEAM OF FIRSTS

• Tennis was the only championship Indiana won in the first year of Big Ten women's competition. The Hoosiers' best other finishes were third in indoor track and swimming and fourth in basketball, softball and field hockey.

• Partly with income from the hit movie *Breaking Away*, Indiana's $4-million new soccer and Little 500 home—Bill Armstrong Stadium—went up. After going 11-0 in their first season there, the Hoosiers lost for the first time in their 1982 opener, 2-1 in overtime to Alabama A&M. In 1988, Indiana won its third national championship there, 1-0 over Howard.

• The nation came to the Little 500 for the first time when CBS moved in a full crew to telecast the 1982 event. A 17-minute taped segment ran on the network's "Sports Saturday" hours after a *Breaking Away*-style finish—a record 28,632 standing and roaring as Phi Delta Theta anchorman Jim Mahaffey came off Turn 4 in second place but edged a wheel in front of Delta Chi anchor Chip Gutowsky in the fastest race ever. Gutowsky had been on Delta Chi teams that had won the previous three years, including the 1981 race that was the first event at Armstrong Stadium—before construction was completed.

HOOSIER LIST

IU IN NCAA SOCCER FINAL FOUR

1976	Indiana 2, Hartwick 1
	San Francisco 1, Indiana 0
1978	Indiana 2, Philadelphia-Textile 0
	San Francisco 2, Indiana 0
1980	Indiana 5, Hartwick 0
	San Francisco 4, Indiana 3
1982	Indiana 1, SIU-Edwardsville 0
	Indiana 2, Duke 1 (8OT)**
1983	Indiana 3, Virginia 1
	Indiana 3, Columbia 0 (OT)**
1984	Indiana 2, Hartwick 1
	Clemson 2, Indiana 1
1988	Indiana 1, Portland 0
	Indiana 1, Howard 0**
1989	Santa Clara 4, Indiana 2
1991	Santa Clara 2, Indiana 0
1994	Indiana 4, UCLA 1
	Virginia 1, Indiana 0
1997	UCLA 1, Indiana 0 (2 OT)
1998	Indiana 4, Santa Clara 0
	Indiana 3, Stanford 1**

**National Champions

Tony Nelson & Trish Eiting

Gregg Thompson

Randy Wittman & Denise Jackson

Football, Babe Laufenberg; Basketball, Randy Wittman; Baseball, Tony Nelson; Track, Sunder Nix; Wrestling, Dave DeLong; Swimming, Rojer Madruga; Cross Country, Jim Spivey; Golf, Tim Koressel; Tennis, Pablo Salas; Soccer, Gregg Thompson.

TEAM: Soccer (Jerry Yeagley); INDIVIDUAL: Indoor Track, Sunder Nix, 600 (1:10.01), Jim Spivey, mile (3:59.95). Outdoor Track: Kerry Zimmerman, decathlon (7,810).

INDIANA

LEGEND   *Kings of Soccer*

THOMPSON 8TH-OVERTIME HERO

Gregg Thompson

Four games into the 1982 soccer season, Indiana had tied a school record for losses in a season—three. The Hoosiers also had lost their No. 1 returning scorer, Pat McGauley—for the year, broken leg.

And still this was the year, this was the team, when the Hoosiers finally won their first national championship.

It came very late on a Saturday night in Fort Lauderdale, Fla.

In the sudden-death eighth overtime—the longest game in NCAA championship history, 44 seconds shy of being two hours old—Indiana All-American Gregg Thompson was tripped on a breakaway run. That gave Indiana a direct free kick, and Thompson, the man the Hoosiers called "Thumper," elected to take it himself.

He curled it into the lower left corner of the net, and Indiana was a 2-1 winner over previously unbeaten Duke.

Thompson—a Minnesotan who had passed up Big Ten football opportunities to play soccer at Indiana—had scored Indiana's first goal just 15 minutes into the marathon. Duke's Sean McCoy tied it with just 8:30 left, and the overtimes began. Three times Thompson had to leave the game with leg cramps, but he kept returning.

Strong defense shut down the two high-powered offenses. Indiana goalie Chris Peterson had to make just five saves all night, Duke goalie Pat Johnston six.

The championship came in the 10th year of varsity play for Indiana, the 20th year as Hoosier coach for Jerry Yeagley, who played on a national champion at West Chester in 1961. "I feel great happiness and relief," Yeagley said after the victory.

Losses in the 1976, '78 and '80 championship games "weighed heavily upon me," he said. "I feel like a 500-pound monkey is off my back."

Front Row (left to right): Manager John Gotschal, Manuel Gorrity, Mark Laxgang, Steve M Pat McGauley, Chris Oswald, Chris Peterson, Gregg Thompson, Greg Kennedy, Dan King, I Meyer. Back Row: Assistant Coach Don Rawson, Assistant Coach George Perry, John Stollm Henry Riggs-Miller, Chris Cotton, Silvio Iung, Craig Layman, Christian Fauser, Tom Ferl Dave Boncek, Mike McCartney, Mike Hylla, Paul DiBernardo, Assistant Coach Joe Kelley, I Coach Jerry Yeagley.

WITTMAN, KITCHEL AND A BANNER YEAR

R andy Wittman and Ted Kitchel didn't plan to be five-year roommates when they arrived on campus in fall 1978. Back problems forced Kitchel to red-shirt that first year, and a cracked foot took Wittman out of the 1979-80 season. They were starters together on the '81 national champions. Kitchel emerged as one of the Big Ten's best scorers his junior season. Wittman, always a picture shooter, waited till his senior year to take on a scoring load.

Kitchel and Wittman topped an all-senior lineup that was 10-0 and No. 1 in the country when it began Big Ten play with a 70-67 loss at Ohio State. The Hoosiers took command of the league race, but on a two-game weekend trip to Michigan, Kitchel sank an early 3-point shot and crumpled, the back problem back, his season over. The stunned Hoosiers lost to both Michigan and Michigan State and sank into a tie for the lead with three games left.

All were at home. All were against teams in the title chase. Coach Bob Knight asked for rousing backing from the Assembly Hall fans. It came, and the Hoosiers earned it. With Wittman taking charge, Indiana shot a combined .629 in routing Purdue, 64-41; Illinois, 67-55, and Ohio State, 81-60, to win the championship by two games.

Kitchel was back to attend Senior Night, when Knight made an announcement: The two rows of banners above the court that had up to then recognized only national achievements would get one for that 1983 Big Ten title, for that homestretch fan support. "That's for every one of you," Knight told the 17,343 at the final game.

Wittman, who shot .543 for the season and averaged 18.9, was IU's third Big Ten MVP in four years and sixth of the 12 Knight years. Both he and Kitchel were inducted into IU's Athletics Hall of Fame.

In July 1999, after a nine-year NBA career and seven years as an NBA assistant coach, Wittman was named head coach of the Cleveland Cavaliers.

WYCHE REPLACES CORSO

LEE CORSO, A QUIP-A-MINUTE man throughout his 10 years as IU's football coach, always called Indiana vs. Purdue "a JS game"— for Job Saver, to whichever coach won.

In 1982, he was fired, 24 days after a 13-7 victory at Purdue closed out a 5-6 season and 41-68-2 record in what was then the second-longest tenure in IU football history.

It was a bottoming-out point for the unsinkable Corso. Within three years, he was re-established in a new career that brought him success: as an analyst, controversial and colorful, for ESPN's college football coverage.

His Indiana replacement was another quick-quipping coach. Sam Wyche was the quarterback coach and heir-apparent to coach Bill Walsh with the San Francisco 49ers, the 1982 Super Bowl champions. In January, Wyche left the NFL to join an old friend, IU athletic director Ralph Floyd.

A flurry of Walsh retirement stories surfaced just before Wyche's appointment, and Wyche was the name forwarded as the likely replacement had Walsh left (he stayed for six more seasons).

"I didn't jump ship," Wyche said when he accepted the Indiana job. "Bill has encouraged me to take a college job.

"I don't intend to go anywhere else. I'm coming here to be a college coach, period."

A year later, after a 3-8 season and leading a sales campaign that started a "Twelfth-Man Club" of $10,000 contributors to upgrade IU's football facilities, Wyche got the NFL coaching chance that had been his career aim. The Cincinnati Bengals hired him, and Wyche's farewell gift to IU was his own $10,000 check for membership as an Indiana "Twelfth-Man."

IN THOSE DAYS . . .

DECATHLON AND MARATHON MAN

• There was no NCAA decathlon in the mid-'50s when IU's Milt Campbell was the Olympic gold medalist. So, when hitherto long jump star Kerry Zimmerman scored 7,810 points and won the 1983 event in searing heat at Houston, he achieved an Indiana first. No other Hoosier

Randy Wittman

has come close in an event which has had just three Big Ten winners in 30 years of competition.

• Randy Wittman graduated as the No. 5 scorer in IU basketball history but since has been pushed out of the Top 10. He may stay No. 1 forever in minutes played: 4,699—95 ahead of the next-closest Hoosier, Steve Alford. Wittman played four full seasons plus 147 minutes in five games before cracking a foot as a sophomore. As a freshman, he ran the offense—always a player Bob Knight prized for his care with the basketball. Wittman's scoring role increased as a senior, when he was a Basketball Writers All-American, but his career turnover average was under 2.0 per 40 minutes. He frequently played 40 minutes—45 times, easily a Knight era record.

HOOSIER LIST

INDIANA'S FEMALE ATHLETE-OF-THE-YEAR

1983	Denise Jackson, basketball
1984	Carla Battaglia, track
1985	Karleen Moore, softball
1986	Amy Unterbrink, softball
1987	Karna Abram, basketball
1988	Kim Betz, track and cross country
1989	Michelle Dekkers, track and cross country
1990	Michelle Dekkers, track and cross country
1991	Stephanie Reece, tennis
1992	Kristen Kane, diving
1993	Deb Edelman, tennis
1994	Kristen Kane, diving
1995	Michelle Venturella, softball
1996	Erika Wicoff, golf
	Kimiko Hirai, diving
1997	Hilary Bruening, track
1998	Erin Carney, golf
1999	Erin Carney, golf

INDIANA

LEGEND — *Sunder Nix*

A GOLD FOR BIG TEN'S BEST

In the Illinois state track meet his senior year, Chicago high school star Sunder Nix ran second in his future specialty, the 440—and in the 100 and the 220 as well, all in one day.

Once he arrived at IU and specialized, Nix quickly became one of America's best. As a sophomore in 1982, running in the U.S. Olympic Festival at the new IU Track in Indianapolis, Nix won the 400 meters in 44.68 seconds—the best mark in the world that year. At a school with a long and rich track and field history, it's still the best 400 ever —by nearly a full second.

Nix won the U.S. championship at 400 meters in 1983, and he brought home a bronze medal from the World Championships. He won the Big Ten indoor 440 all four of his college years, and two 400s outdoors—plus one NCAA indoor 600 title.

In 1984, he ran fifth in the 400 at the Olympic Games, .04 of a second away from a medal. Three days later he ran leadoff on the gold-medal U.S. 4x400 relay team.

That year, gold medalist Sunder Nix won the Jesse Owens Award as the Big Ten's male Athlete of the Year. He was inducted into IU's Athletics Hall of Fame in 1996.

Nix went on after graduation to a career in law enforcement—his goal, service with the Federal Bureau of Investigation.

BIG TEN MEDAL - George Gianakopoulos & Lynne Beck

GIMBEL AWARD - Bob Hicks

ATHLETES OF THE YEAR - Sunder Nix (also Big Ten) & Carla Battaglia

BALFOUR AWARDS

Football, Jim Sakanich; Basketball, Dan Dakich; Baseball, Dan Winters; Track, Sunder Nix; Wrestling, Jeff Bentley; Swimming, Paul Lenihan; Cross Country, Terry Brahm; Golf, Andy Shuman; Tennis, Joey Christoff; Soccer, Chris Peterson.

OLYMPIC MEDALISTS

Basketball, Steve Alford, gold (Coach Bob Knight); Track, Sunder Nix, 4x400 relay, gold (2:57.91), Rotimi Peters (Nigeria), 4x400 relay, bronze (2:59.32). Swimming, Mark Kerry (Australia), 400 medley relay, bronze (3:55.69).

IU item

KNIGHT'S OLYMPIANS WIN GOLD

Olympic Coach Bob Knight is carried off the floor by his players after winning Olympic gold.

Bob Knight was paid one of his profession's highest honors when he was named coach of the 1984 U.S. Olympic basketball team.

He shared the glory with IU and Bloomington, making Assembly Hall the base for a team headed by Michael Jordan.

Picked as coach in May 1982, Knight spent the next two years planning and preparing. He brought 73 of America's best amateur players to Bloomington for Trials Week April 17-22. The last two nights, the 32 remaining candidates played in doubleheaders that packed Assembly Hall. Twenty of them were brought back May 10. In June, 14 finalists gathered for the final drive.

The 12-man team never did lose, not in the Olympics nor in nine exhibition games played across the country—the highlight July 9 when 67,596, a record U.S. crowd for basketball, christened Hoosier Dome in Indianapolis by watching Larry Bird, Isiah Thomas and other pro stars lose 97-82 to the Olympians.

July 29, Olympic competition began with a 97-49 victory over China. On Friday night, Aug. 10, a 96-65 victory over Spain made the Americans gold medalists.

Jordan played just 28 minutes in the gold-medal game and led both teams with 20 points. "Every one of us discovered we could be pushed to a limit we didn't even know we had," Jordan said.

IU's representative on the team, freshman Steve Alford, worked up to a starting point on the team by mid-Olympics and hit five of six shots for 10 final-game points.

"I didn't think players in this era could ever come together in as many ways and play as hard as these kids did," Knight said.

Snapshot In Time

THE NIGHT JORDAN FELL

INDIANA IN THE Bob Knight era was not in position to pull many upsets, but the one the Hoosiers achieved March 22 at Atlanta was an all-timer.

No. 1-ranked North Carolina fell, 72-68, in Michael Jordan's last collegiate game.

This was the team Virginia coach Terry Holland had called "the finest college basketball team ever"—Player of the Year Jordan, All-American Sam Perkins, and future longtime pros Brad Daugherty and Kenny Smith all starters. Indiana started freshmen Steve Alford and Marty Simmons, sophomore Mike Giomi, and 7-foot West German center Uwe Blab and 6-5 Dan Dakich, both juniors.

Dakich's sixth start of the year paired him with Jordan. "Give up the 17-foot shot, not the lob or the back-cut," Knight told him. "Just don't let him dunk on you. That will embarrass you and me both." Dakich learned his assignment the afternoon of the game. "I went back to my room and threw up," he said.

Jordan scored 13 points and fouled out. Blab scored 16. Alford's 27 points offset Perkins' 26. Indiana shot .649 and led by 12 with 5:30 left before missed one-and-ones let Carolina get within two points. It wasn't the perfect game, but it was classic.

Dan Dakich, now head coach at Bowling Green, helped hold Michael Jordan to 13 points.

IN THOSE DAYS . . .

SOCCER CHAMPS REPEAT

Pat McGauley

After so long and frustrating a wait before getting there, Indiana's soccer team served notice in 1983 it was in no hurry to surrender its national championship.

The Hoosiers lost their opening game in overtime at Penn State, 2-1, but never lost again—tied four times, but never beaten.

And on December 10, back at Fort Lauderdale, for the second year in a row matched against an unbeaten and untied team in the national championship game, Jerry Yeagley's Hoosiers went into overtime before beating Columbia, 1-0.

The goal came from an appropriate hero. Pat McGauley had figured to be a senior leader of the 1982 national champions, but a broken leg took him out of the season and made him a sideline spectator in the eight-overtime victory over Duke.

McGauley hadn't scored a goal in two months when he took a pass from Rodrigo Castro and scored the overtime goal.

Rugged John Stollmeyer, a sophomore his teammates called "The Hub," and goalie Chris Peterson led the defense in the final-game shutout.

1984 [IU] 1985

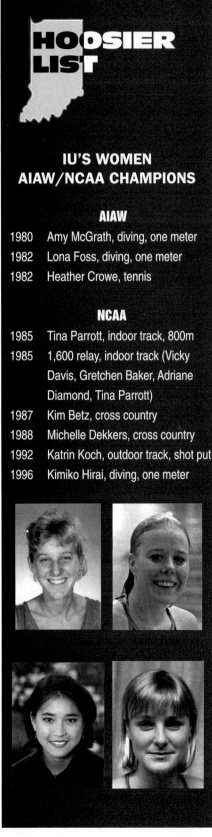

HOOSIER LIST

IU'S WOMEN AIAW/NCAA CHAMPIONS

AIAW

1980 Amy McGrath, diving, one meter
1982 Lona Foss, diving, one meter
1982 Heather Crowe, tennis

NCAA

1985 Tina Parrott, indoor track, 800m
1985 1,600 relay, indoor track (Vicky Davis, Gretchen Baker, Adriane Diamond, Tina Parrott)
1987 Kim Betz, cross country
1988 Michelle Dekkers, cross country
1992 Katrin Koch, outdoor track, shot put
1996 Kimiko Hirai, diving, one meter

INDIANA LEGEND — *Tina Parrott*

TWO TRACK FIRSTS BACK HOME

As an Indianapolis Tech senior, tiny Tina Parrott won a state 400-meter championship after being just barely edged in the 100-meter finals and before anchoring Tech's 4x400-meter relay team to third.

Three years later back in her hometown at the NCAA Indoor championships in the Hoosier Dome, 5-3, 102-pound Tina won IU's first NCAA women's track title by taking the 800-meter run.

The same day she combined with Vicky Davis, Adriane Diamond and Gretchen Baker to win the mile relay—the only relay championship ever for an IU track team: men's or women's, indoors or outdoors.

At the 1986 Big Ten outdoor championships, Parrott had the greatest performance ever by a Hoosier in the women's meet. She doubled in the 800 and 1,500 and ran on the winning 4x400 relay team.

In her career, she won two other Big Ten individual titles indoors and ran on four other Big Ten-champion relay teams.

Back in Indianapolis one more time, she closed her collegiate career with an outstanding performance in the NCAA outdoor championships. She ran the fastest 800 in Big Ten history and bettered the NCAA meet record with 2:01.02 but lost out to 2:00.85 by Karen Bakewell of Miami, Ohio.

A day later, she combined with Davis, Diamond and Karen Lewis to finish sixth in the 4x400 relay in 3:34.00. Both NCAA times still are IU records.

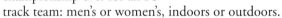
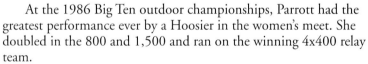

BIG TEN MEDAL - Uwe Blab & Kelly Greenlee   **GIMBEL AWARD -** Joe Fitzgerald

ATHLETES OF THE YEAR - Paul DiBernardo & Karleen Moore

BALFOUR AWARDS

Football, Dave Zyzda; Basketball, None given; Baseball, Bill Mueller; Track, Albert Robinson; Wrestling, Ken Johnson; Swimming, Tony Anderson; Cross Country, Terry Brahm; Golf, Richard Rousseau; Tennis, Frank Guengerich; Soccer, Paul DiBernardo.

NCAA CHAMPIONS

Indoor Track, Tina Parrott, 800, 2:08.69; Vicky Davis, Gretchen Baker, Adriane Diamond, Tina Parrott, 4x400 relay, 3:40.40.

AFTER 'THE CHAIR', A CHEERY FINISH

A Big Ten basketball season that started with a record-setting 87-62 blowout of Michigan at Crisler Arena was unraveling for Olympics veterans Bob Knight and Steve Alford when Purdue came to Assembly Hall February 23.

The Hoosiers, after losing three home games, had slipped to 6-7 in the league, and Alford was in the one shooting slump of his IU career—5-for-23 in two home games just ahead of Purdue.

Early in the game Knight, assessed a technical foul, tossed his chair onto the court.

The incident, which brought him expulsion and a one-game Big Ten suspension, had a life of its own. Thereafter, Knight was The Coach Who Threw a Chair and the toss was played and replayed on TV hundreds of times.

Alford struggled on, 3-for-12 in Purdue's 72-63 victory, 6-for-22 in two more homecourt losses that followed.

In a season-ending 73-71 buzzer-shot loss to turn-around champion Michigan, Alford's touch returned: 11-for-16 shooting, 22 points, and senior Uwe Blab scored 23.

The two led IU, denied an NCAA tournament bid for the only time in the '80s or '90s, to four NIT victories before a 65-62 championship-game loss at New York to UCLA. Future Indiana Pacer Reggie Miller, a UCLA sophomore who was named the tournament MVP, scored 18 points in his first of many memorable performances in Madison Square Garden.

Alford had 16 points in that championship game, 108 and a 21.6 average in the tournament.

0-11 IN CENTENNIAL YEAR

INDIANA AND 48-YEAR-OLD football coach Bill Mallory were ready for each other in December 1983, after one-year Hoosier coach Sam Wyche took the Cincinnati Bengals job.

Mallory, who played at Miami of Ohio under Ara Parseghian and captained the first team John Pont coached, had come back to coach his alma mater to success that was unprecedented even there. He took Colorado to the Bluebonnet Bowl, then the Orange Bowl, but a conflict with the CU program's biggest donors got him dismissed. He regrouped with a league champion and bowl winner at Northern Illinois, and he was athletic director Ralph Floyd's quick choice to succeed Wyche—IU's third football coach in three years.

His first year was IU's 100th in football. Indiana has had lesser teams, never one less lucky. The Hoosiers jumped ahead 14-0 in their opener at Duke but lost, 31-24. They went ahead 14-0 at Purdue but lost, 31-24. In between, they lost by scores of 40-37, 14-6, 33-24, 13-6, 20-16 and 24-20, but every week they lost to finish as IU's only 0-11 team ever.

In the bowl-rich decade that followed, Mallory always credited the unrewarded '84 team with laying the groundwork.

Bill Mallory took Indiana to six bowl games after an 0-11 beginning, winning the Liberty Bowl in 1988 and the Copper Bowl in 1991.

IN THOSE DAYS . . .

IU'S INTERNATIONAL TEAM

• At 7-foot-2, Uwe Blab—*oo*-vay *blop*—was IU's biggest IU basketball player ever, and greenest. A West German, he had barely begun in the game before playing as an exchange student at Effingham, Ill. Landon Turner's summertime accident shortcut Blab's chance to learn before jumping into a major role with IU. But he was All-Big Ten as a senior, averaging 17.6 in the league with highs of 33 and 31. He graduated No. 10 on IU's all-time point list with 1,357. A first-round NBA draft pick (Dallas), he played four NBA seasons and for West Germany in the 1984 Olympics. Blab was the first IU basketball player since Jim Schooley (1953) elected to Phi Beta Kappa.

• Coach Bob Knight took 12 underclassmen on a summertime trip around the world—with games in Canada, Japan, China, Yugoslavia and Finland. The Hoosiers won their last 10 games to finish 12-6, but their memories were greater of seeing The Great Wall of China, the Ming Tombs, Hiroshima, Hong Kong and lots more.

• His older brother, Angelo, and Armando Betancourt were IU's first Hermann Award winners in soccer, but Paul DiBernardo scored a first of his own. The veteran of IU's 1982 and '83 NCAA championships was the first soccer player named IU's Male Athlete of the Year.

HOOSIER LIST

BIG TEN MEDAL WINNERS — WOMEN

1982	Karen Marinsek
1983	Trish Eiting
1984	Lynne Beck
1985	Kelly Greenlee
1986	Lynn Dennison
1987	Karleen Moore
1988	Karen Dunham
1989	Ann Mooney
1990	Julie Goedde
1991	Joy Jordan
1992	Katrin Koch
1993	Courtney Cox
1994	Anne Eastman
1995	Michelle Venturella
1996	Gina Ugo
1997	Mary Vajgrt
1998	Jennifer Gray
1999	Melissa Rooney

INDIANA LEGEND *Terry Brahm*

AN OLYMPIAN FROM THE HILLS

Heritage Hills High School graduates about 175 kids a year. It will remember its athletic Class of 1981 for a while. Chris Sigler played football and baseball at IU and played in the Canadian Football League. Bruce King played football at Purdue and made the NFL. Then there was a skinny kid who tried tight end for a while and switched to track.

Terry Brahm took the Class of '81 all the way to the Olympic Games.

Brahm was from St. Meinrad, where the population is 500 and the tourist attraction is a monastery. "There isn't really what you would call a social whirl there," he said. "I started running for entertainment. That shows how boring it was."

He ran fourth in the 1981 State meet 1,600 as a senior. Three years later, at a meet in Burnaby, British Columbia, the day before the Olympics opened at Los Angeles, Brahm ran a mile in 3:54.56—still the IU record and a Big Ten record for 12 years.

Brahm won five Big Ten titles, and in 1986 at Indianapolis, he ran the last 200 meters in 25 seconds to win the NCAA 5,000-meter championship. "That's definitely the fastest I've ever finished a race," Brahm said. "Heck, I think my record for a 200 is 24." That's without running three miles first.

Two years later on the same track, Brahm eased in second in the 5,000 at the U.S. Olympic Trials to win his way to Seoul, which is several miles east of St. Meinrad.

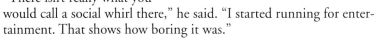

BIG TEN MEDAL - Terry Brahm & Lynn Dennison

GIMBEL AWARD - John Stollmeyer

ATHLETES OF THE YEAR - Steve Alford (also Big Ten) & Amy Unterbrink

BALFOUR AWARDS
Football, Bobby Howard; Basketball, Winston Morgan; Baseball, Alex Smith; Track, Terry Brahm; Wrestling, Bill Paxton; Swimming, Cliff Looschen; Cross Country, Marty Bassett; Golf, John Kernohan; Tennis, Sven Salumaa; Soccer, John Stollmeyer.

NCAA CHAMPION
Outdoor Track: Terry Brahm, 5,000, 13:56.64

IU item

John Stollmeyer was a three-time All-American and played on U.S. Olympic and World Cup teams.

NO ONE LOAFED AROUND STOLLMEYER

To Jerry Yeagley it was no coincidence that John Stollmeyer and Indiana played in national championship games his first three seasons.

"Probably more than any other player we've had, John played in a way that brought everybody to their highest standards," Yeagley said. "He was a great player himself. He led by example. He was a powerful player—he had one of the hardest kicks we've ever had.

"But he also forced his personality onto his teams. No one cheated on effort when John was out there."

Ranked the top high school player in the nation coming out in his senior year, the Virginia native starred on IU's first two NCAA champions (1982 and '83). In '84, Indiana was back in the championship game, trying to be the first team to win three straight years, but a 2-1 overtime loss to Clemson averted that.

He made second- or third-team All-America three times. He played on the 1988 U.S. Olympic team and on the 1990 U.S. World Cup team. In 1990, when *Soccer America* magazine named an All-Decade college team, John Stollmeyer—never a first-team All-American—was on it.

Emerging from college prior to the real arrival of professional soccer in the U.S., Stollmeyer played indoor soccer before beginning a career in investments.

BRINK OF A CHAMPIONSHIP

A basketball season that laid the groundwork for a national championship took on a controversial fame of its own.

Washington Post sports writer John Feinstein took a year away from regular duties to follow the Hoosiers and write what became a national best-selling book, *Season on the Brink*—a book Hoosier coach Bob Knight angrily contended that, by focusing on him, took a sharply different approach from what he had agreed to in opening his program's doors.

The season included its own historic controversy. Indiana had to play its fourth game at Kentucky without junior guard Steve Alford, whose picture on a charity calendar bruised an NCAA rule and caused a one-game suspension. Kentucky won the game, 63-58.

The Hoosiers were 8-2 when they opened Big Ten play with two close losses at home to Michigan and Michigan State. A 13-2 stretch let them finish in second place in the conference, just a game back of champion Michigan, but a first-round NCAA tournament loss to Cleveland State ended the 21-8 season in disappointment.

A year-long Hoosier key was 6-7 junior Daryl Thomas's play at center, a by-product of the Round-the-World trip. Thomas, a part-time player his first two years, averaged 14.5 points a game and made third-team All-Big Ten.

Alford, averaging 22.5 as a consensus All-American, was the first basketball player to be named the Big Ten's Jesse Owens Award winner as male Athlete of the Year.

1986 1987

HOOSIER LIST

IU'S BIG TEN COACHES OF THE YEAR

Baseball
Bob Morgan 1993

Football
Bill Mallory 1886, 1987

Men's Basketball
Bob Knight 1973, 1975, 1976, 1980, 1981, 1989

Men's Diving
Hobie Billingsley 1988, 1989
Jeff Huber 1997, 1998, 1999

Men's Golf
Sam Carmichael 1991, 1998

Men's Soccer
Jerry Yeagley 1993, 1994, 1996, 1997, 1998

Men's Swimming
Kris Kirchner 1991

Men's Tennis
Ken Hydinger 1992

Men's Track
Sam Bell 1990, 1991, 1992

Softball
Diane Stephenson 1994

Women's Cross Country
Carol Stevenson 1987
Sam Bell 1989
Roseann Wilson 1990

Women's Diving
Jeff Huber 1991, 1997

Women's Golf
Sam Carmichael 1985, 1986, 1987, 1988, 1995, 1996, 1998

Women's Tennis
Lin Loring 1988, 1992, 1995

Wrestling
Joe McFarland 1990

INDIANA LEGEND
'87 NCAA Champions

IN THE CLUTCH, THE BEST

Indiana might have twice as many national championship flags as the five that hang above the Assembly Hall playing court, if injuries had been avoided in 1975, 1980, 1982 and 1993—maybe 1983, too. Or if just a little better luck had come in 1941, 1954, 1973 and 1992.

But one banner that is up there marks a year when the Hoosiers probably didn't have national-championship material but went out and won anyway.

No NCAA champion in the last 40 years went so long with so little impact on the NBA as did the 1987 Hoosiers.

And none ever cut it any closer on the way to the championship.

A key for the '87 Hoosiers was winning a No. 1 seeding that let them open their tournament drive with first- and second-round games at the Hoosier Dome in Indianapolis. They needed last-day help from Michigan, in beating Purdue, for their own closing victory over Ohio State to blossom into a Big Ten co-championship. With it came the No. 1 seeding for them at 24-4.

Bob Knight receives congratulations from NCAA basketball tournament chairman Dick Schulz.

190

One more loss anywhere along the season probably would have rerouted the Hoosiers, whose Indiana Classic title included a 73-72 scrape past unheralded North Carolina Wilmington. In Big Ten play, where one more slip definitely would have changed things, the Hoosiers won at Michigan, 85-84; at Northwestern, 77-75; at Wisconsin in triple overtime, 86-85, and at home over Minnesota, 72-70, all but Northwestern on virtual last-second shots.

They won solidly over Fairfield, Auburn and Duke in NCAA play but needed Ricky Calloway's rebound lay-in to beat LSU, 77-76, and get to the Final Four.

There, the Hoosiers' finest hour was a 97-93 shock dropped on No. 1-ranked Nevada-Las Vegas—a shock that the Hoosiers dared to run with the Runnin' Rebels and whipped them on a day when UNLV guard Freddie Banks hit ten 3-point shots, still the Final Four record.

Indiana was not so sharp two nights later. Syracuse, with three future long-time pros in Derrick Coleman, Rony Seikaly and Sherman Douglas, led 73-70 in the last minute but lost to two Keith Smart baskets, the last one a tournament legend, at 0:05.

"The greatness in this team," coach Bob Knight said, "may be a greatness no other team here has had, to the degree that this one did—almost a total resolve not to recognize or be a part of defeat. This team played the last five minutes of critical games as well as I've ever seen a team play."

*Keith Smart's winning field goal—
IU 74, Syracuse 73*

Senior co-captains Todd Meier, Daryl Thomas and Steve Alford proudly display the NCAA championship trophy won in New Orleans.

BIG TEN MEDAL
Steve Alford
& Karleen Moore

GIMBEL AWARD
Steve Alford

ATHLETES OF THE YEAR
Steve Alford & Karna Abram

BALFOUR AWARDS

Football, Alex Green; Basketball, Steve Alford/Todd Meier/Daryl Thomas; Baseball, Mickey Morandini; Track, Charles Marsala; Wrestling, Scott Duncan; Swimming, Juan Carlos Vallejo; Cross Country, Scott Williams; Golf, Remi Bouchard; Tennis, Sven Salumaa; Soccer, Tim Hylla.

NCAA CHAMPIONS
Team: Basketball (Bob Knight).

LEGEND   *Steve Alford*

LEADER OF A TIGHT PACK

Steve Alford's always-in-place hair had nothing to do with how he played the game, but typified it perfectly. Alford's game was not flash and flair but efficiency: work, work, work for an open jump shot, and hit it. No one in the history of the college game ever did those things better, or more often.

Alford was Indiana's "Mr. Basketball" for his dad and coach, Sam, at New Castle. He averaged 37 points a game as a senior, and he never dipped under 20 in a game in his last two seasons.

At Indiana, Bob Knight built a four-year offense around Alford, whose contributions to it included an untiring determination to make his team-mates' maze of screens pay off for them and him with a basket.

Disciplined shooting, efficient and proficient, got him to the Olympic Games his freshman year and later made him a two-year consensus All-American.

He took fourteen shots and hit nine, attempted ten free throws and hit nine the night his freshman year when Indiana beat No. 1 North Carolina and Michael Jordan, 72-68.

His shooting got him into the Olympic team's starting lineup, and led that star-filled team. "Steve Alford," Knight said the night the gold medal was won, "carried his weight."

In his last IU season, Alford settled into a more rounded role. He, Daryl Thomas and Todd Meier were the team's senior leaders, taking especially under their wing junior college newcomers Dean Garrett and Keith Smart.

Alford had averaged 22.5 as a junior on a good 21-8 team that had just two other primary scorers. He averaged 22.0, and Thomas averaged 15.7, Ricky Calloway 12.6, Garrett 11.4 and Smart 11.2 his senior year when Indiana won the national championship.

Alford's high was 42 points in an 84-80 squeaker past Michigan State. In the first year of college basketball's 3-point shot, Alford took 202 of his team's 256 3-point attempts. As a result, the Hoosiers' .508 percentage for that first season not only led the nation but also remains the one-year NCAA record.

Alford's seven 3-point baskets against Syracuse still shares the championship-game record.

After a brief NBA career, Alford went into coaching. In spring 1999, at the age of 34, he was named Iowa's head coach.

Front Row (left to right): Todd Jadlow, Keith Smart, Todd Meier, Steve Alford, Daryl Thomas, Dean Garrett, Kreigh Smith, Joe Hillman. Second Row: Tony Freeman, Dave Minor, Jeff Oliphant, Brian Sloan, Steve Eyl, Magnus Pelkowski, Rick Calloway. Third Row: Trainer Tim Garl, Assistant Coach Ron Felling, Assistant Coach Joby Wright, Head Coach Bob Knight, Assistant Coach Kohn Smith, Assistant Coach Royce Waltman, Dr. Brad Bomba. Fourth Row: Graduate Assistant Julio Salazar, Manager Mike McGlothlin, Manager Bill Himebrook, Graduate Assistant Murry Bartow, Graduate Assistant Dan Dakich.

FRESHMAN STAR IN BREAKTHROUGH

A bright new era in Indiana football dawned in October 1986 when freshman Anthony Thompson led a downfield drive and scored the touchdown that pulled Indiana within 24-22 of Ohio State—as close as the Hoosiers were to get that day but as close as they had been to the Buckeyes in 27 years.

Two weeks later, Indiana was down 38-0 against Michigan when coach Bill Mallory turned the fourth quarter over to Thompson and red-shirt freshman quarterback Dave Schnell. They drove to two touchdowns, "mop-up" touchdowns, but Mallory was convinced. The next week, he gave both rookies their first start, and an Indiana turn-around had come.

Thompson blasted through Wisconsin for 207 yards and Indiana won, 21-7. He followed with four more 100-yard games, the last against Bobby Bowden, Deion Sanders and Florida State in a 27-13 Seminoles victory at the All-American Bowl in Birmingham, Alabama—the first Mallory Era bowl game, the third in IU history, a swift and dramatic change from the 0-11 season just two years before.

For the rise, Mallory won his first of two straight Big Ten Coach of the Year Awards. And he had his offense in place for the three years to come.

TWO TRUE *HOOSIERS*

AT 32, IU GRADUATE Angelo Pizzo was in Philadelphia cheering Indiana to the 1981 NCAA championship. He went away inspired "to do this script" he'd been thinking about.

The result was the 1986 movie *Hoosiers,* which blended some Bob Knight coaching basics with the charming improbability of little Milan's 1954 drive to the state high school basketball championship and became a movie classic.

Gene Hackman played the coach who—unlike Milan's Marvin Wood in real life—had some discipline problems to whip and some notoriety to live down in taking Hickory to its championship.

Angelo Pizzo stuck with the Hoosiers at Oscar time.

Both critics and the ticket-buying public loved *Hoosiers.* Pizzo's first movie script was nominated for a 1986 Oscar, and the film— directed by Pizzo's college friend and fellow IU alumnus, David Anspaugh —also was up for best picture.

The Oscars presentation was on the same night as the national championship game—March 30. Pizzo (from Bloomington) and Anspaugh (Decatur) skipped the Oscars and watched the game at a party at Anspaugh's house.

"We had three or four televisions (bringing in both events)," Pizzo said. "Once the game started, I didn't pay *any* attention to the Academy Awards. You go back to your roots in times of stress."

As the century closed, *Hoosiers* generally was ranked among the five best sports-theme movies ever.

HOOSIER LIST

WOMEN'S BASKETBALL CAREER SCORING LEADERS

Denise Jackson, 1981-84	1,917
Karna Abram, 1984-87	1,910
Cindy Bumgarner, 1985-88	1,836
Rachelle Bostic, 1981-84	1,827
Shirley Bryant, 1992-95	1,503
Lisa Furlin, 1993-96	1,451
Quacy Barnes, 1995-98	1,428
Sue Hodges, 1978-81	1,265
Zan Jefferies, 1988-91	1,173
Linda Cunningham, 1983-86	1,169
Dawn Douglas, 1990-93	1,128
Dani Thrush, 1996-99	1,017
Kristi Green, 1996-99	1,006
Kris McGrade, 1991-94	1,005
Tisha Hill, 1989-92	934
Kim Land, 1981-84	888
Cindy Kerns, 1996-99	839
Diann Nestel, 1976-79	818
Pam Owens, 1988-91	798
Ann Mooney, 1986-89	797
Deb McClurg, 1981-84	758
Joan Ryann, 1978-80	757

INDIANA LEGEND — *Albert Robinson*

OLYMPIAN PERFORMANCE AND DISMAY

At 6-2 and 187 pounds, Albert Robinson stood out as a giant in most sprint groups.

And that's what he became, the fastest sprinter of the modern Big Ten era.

Robinson doubled impressively in the 100 and 200 at the 1982 Illinois high school meet and achieved the same double as Athlete of the Meet for IU at the 1984 and '85 Big Ten championships. Nationally ranked throughout his college years, he won no national titles. At the 1984 Olympic trials, he ran seventh in the 200 and was eliminated in the 100 semifinals.

Two years out of college, he had almost been forgotten as a top national sprinter when he made an explosive return at the 1988 Olympic Trials at Indianapolis.

A tailwind kept the 100-meter finals from going down, officially, as the fastest 100 ever, but—when the American record was 9.93—Carl Lewis flashed home in 9.78 seconds, just ahead of Dennis Mitchell (9.86), Calvin Smith (9.87) and Robinson (9.88).

Only the top three go to the Olympics.

Four days later Robinson was in the 200 finals. There, Joe DeLoach (19.96) edged Lewis (20.01) for first place. Judges, after long study, broke a virtual third-place tie at 20.05 in favor of Roy Martin over Robinson—who went into history as the first American sprinter to finish fourth in both Olympic Trials finals.

Robinson did get the thrill of running in the Olympics—but the experience did not include a medal. He ran in the second leg in the opening round of qualifying in the 4x100 relay. The final American exchange of that qualifying race was bobbled; the U.S. team was disqualified.

BIG TEN MEDAL - Sven Salumaa & Karen Dunham   **GIMBEL AWARD -** Jeff Stout

ATHLETES OF THE YEAR - Mickey Morandini and Kim Betz

BALFOUR AWARDS
Football, Tim Jorden; Basketball, Steve Eyl; Baseball, Mickey Morandini; Track, Charles Marsala; Wrestling, Brian Dolph; Swimming/Diving, Mark Lenzi; Cross Country, Bob Kennedy; Golf, J.D. Meyer; Tennis, Eoin Collins; Soccer, Bruce Killough.

NCAA CHAMPION
Cross Country, Kim Betz (16:10.85).

OLYMPIC MEDALISTS
Baseball, Mickey Morandini, gold; Swimming, Sergio Lopez (Spain), 200 breaststroke, bronze (2:15.21).

IU item

GOLD, WORLD SERIES FOR MORANDINI

Mickey Morandini was a high-scoring basketball guard at Leechburg, Pennsylvania, but baseball was his game. At Indiana, he was an immediate starter—in center field. Then at third base. Finally at shortstop.

He's the only Hoosier baseball player ever to make All-Big Ten three times. He had a chance to turn pro after his junior year, but the offer wasn't good enough to dissuade him from a dream: playing in the 1988 Olympics. So he stayed on and made second-team All-America, graduating as—still—IU's career recordholder in runs, doubles, triples, total bases and steals.

And he made that 1988 Olympic team, the only American baseball team so far to win a gold medal. Robin Ventura and Tino Martinez were teammates of his on that team, which did what the '84 team with Mark McGwire, Barry Larkin and Will Clark couldn't.

Philadelphia's fifth-round draft pick, Morandini made his major league debut at second base in 1990, his second professional season. A Phillies starter in 1992, he played with the Phils in the 1993 World Series (1-for-5, in three games). In 1995, he played in the All-Star Game—the first Hoosier to do it since Ted Kluszewski almost 40 years before.

Traded to the Cubs, Morandini hit a career high .296 and led the league in fielding as Chicago reached the 1998 National League playoffs.

Current Chicago Cub Mickey Morandini is the only IU baseball player named All-Big Ten three years.

'BLACKEST' DAY, BUT NOT FOR IU

ON OCTOBER 10, 1987, a gray and damp day in Columbus, Ohio, Ohio State was 3-0-1, No. 9 in the land, when unranked Indiana won 31-10 before 90,032, still the largest crowd ever to see an IU football victory.

In 1951, Sandusky High School junior Bill Mallory had sat high in Ohio Stadium and watched Indiana beat the Buckeyes, 32-10—young Woody Hayes' first Big Ten defeat. Legend says Hayes vowed Indiana would never beat him again. Indiana didn't. His last coaching victory in 1978 was 21-18 at IU. Hayes died in 1987, months before Mallory's Hoosiers ended that 36-year, 30-0-1 hex with their thorough victory.

Hayes' successor, Earle Bruce, had been a Hayes assistant with Mallory. Stunned, Bruce said, "You just saw an Ohio State team that, in the second half, got the devil kicked out of it . . . This has got to be the darkest day for Ohio State football."

Two weeks later, Michigan came into Memorial Stadium with 15 straight victories over Indiana. Dave Schnell's 3-yard TD run on an option keeper gave Indiana a 14-10 lead that—through wind and rain—the Hoosiers preserved to the end.

In 15 days, Indiana achieved what no other IU football team ever did, beating both Ohio State and Michigan in the same year.

The Hoosiers went to Michigan State for their next-last game with a chance to win a Rose Bowl trip. An appendectomy had taken Schnell out a week earlier. Michigan State won the game, 27-3, and won the Rose Bowl as well. Indiana (8-3) went to the Peach Bowl, led Tennessee in the last minute but lost, 27-22. Mallory, for the second year in a row, was the Big Ten Coach of the Year.

IN THOSE DAYS . . .

BREAKTHROUGH, AND A CONTINUATION

• Kim Betz, a surprising second in the Big Ten cross country championships at IU, compounded the surprise by winning the NCAA championship three weeks later at Charlottesville, Virginia. She won by almost five seconds, surging back after leading early and then falling behind. "I just got mad at myself," the sophomore from Turpin High School in Cincinnati said.

• The IU-Doc Counsilman string of Olympic medals, which started in 1952, ran through a 10th Olympics when breaststroker Sergio Lopez of Spain won a bronze in the 200-meter event at Seoul. IU's run of gold medals reached nine straight Olympics with Mickey Morandini's gold in baseball.

• IU fans formed much of the crowd at the 1988 Olympic track and field trials in Indianapolis, and their cheers were rewarded with extraordinary performances that put Albert Robinson (sprint relay), Terry Brahm (5,000), Robert Cannon (triple jump) and IU assistant coach Randy Heisler (discus) on the U.S. team. A Hoosier dilemma came in the 1,500, however, when IU's Mark Deady closed with a rush that overtook another Hoosier favorite, Jim Spivey, for the third and last spot in the 1,500. Extra irony: Deady, as an IU student, rented an apartment from "landlord" Spivey.

195

HOOSIER LIST

IU SOCCER HONORS

Hermann Award

1978	Angelo DiBernardo
1981	Armando Betancourt
1988	Ken Snow
1990	Ken Snow
1994	Brian Maisonneuve

All-Americans

(First-team selections)

1976	Steve Burks
1977	Angelo DiBernardo
	George Perry
	David Shelton
1978	Angelo DiBernardo
	Charlie Fajkus
1979	Armando Betancourt
	Mike Freitag
1980	Robert Meschbach
1981	Armando Betancourt
1987	Ken Snow
1988	Ken Snow
1989	Ken Snow
	Chad Deering
1990	Ken Snow
1994	Brian Maisonneuve
	Todd Yeagley
1997	Dema Kovalenko
1998	Lazo Alavanja
	Dema Kovalenko

INDIANA

LEGEND
Pete Stoyanovich

IU'S BEST EVER IN CONCURRENT SPORTS

Pete Stoyanovich is the only Indiana football kicker to earn letters as a soccer player, too.

It's a difficult double because the seasons are concurrent. For three years, Stoyanovich spent a lot of weekends playing soccer on Friday night and/or Sunday afternoon and splicing football duties in between.

He concentrated on football as a senior in 1988, planning—if that didn't lead to an NFL contract—to play his fourth soccer season in '89.

The decision had good and bad results for him. He had his best Hoosier season, hitting 17 of 24 field goal tries, including two of 53 yards, the IU record at the time. He also ran his IU and Big Ten extra-point record to 107-for-107. His 96 points in 1988 still is IU's record for a kicker.

He was All-Big Ten and second-team All-America. And, as he had hoped, he became one of the rare kickers taken in the draft—in the eighth round, by Miami.

Ten years later, Stoyanovich had passed 1,000 career points, leading the NFL with 124 in 1992. His 80.66 career field-goal percentage was the league record. His 58-yard field goal against Kansas City in 1991 is the NFL's post-season record.

So what was bad about his 1988 move?

He was far more noted as a soccer player than football player at Dearborn, Mich., Crestwood High—a two-time All-American, playing on the U.S. Junior National team at 17. He starred as well on three IU teams, scoring 23 career goals.

But the year he didn't play, 1988, was the season when the Hoosiers won their third NCAA championship.

BIG TEN MEDAL - Simon Katner & Ann Mooney

GIMBEL AWARD - Charles Wright

ATHLETES OF THE YEAR - Anthony Thompson and Michelle Dekkers

BALFOUR AWARDS

Football, Brad Money; Basketball, Joe Hillman; Baseball, Phil Dauphin; Track, Alan Turner; Wrestling, Chuck Poulson; Swimming, Jeff Oristaglio; Cross Country, Bob Kennedy; Golf, Dan Olsen; Tennis, Eoin Collins; Soccer, Han Roest.

NCAA CHAMPIONS

Team: Soccer (Jerry Yeagley); Individual: Cross Country, Bob Kennedy (29:20), Michelle Dekkers (30:15). Diving, Mark Lenzi, 1-meter springboard.

Michelle Dekkers was NCAA cross country champion in 1988.

HOOSIER RUNNERS SWEEP

Bob Kennedy and Michelle Dekkers in 1988 at Iowa State made Indiana the first —and still the only—school to win both the men's and women's individual NCAA cross country championships.

They had achieved the same double at the Big Ten championships, the first of what was to grow into 20 Big Ten titles for 18-year-old freshman Kennedy.

Two-thirds of the way through the men's NCAA race, Kennedy was about 10 yards back of the front-running pack, thinking, "I'm up here in the top five and that's pretty good." Then he heard coach Sam Bell scream: "*Get back in contact!*"

"I got moving," Kennedy said.

The six-mile race boiled down to a sprint. In the last 50 yards, Kennedy raced by Clemson's Yehezkel Halifa and won.

Dekkers, a South African who by choice ran barefooted in the 28-degree chill, won the women's race by 25 yards—the four-second winning margin, making it her closest race of an unbeaten season.

Dekkers was IU's second winner of the women's race—second straight, with 1987 champion Kim Betz sidelined in 1988 by a leg injury.

Kennedy also was IU's second men's winner, 47 years after Fred Wilt won the first. Kennedy's father, Bob, ran on IU's 1967 Big Ten cross country champions.

CHAMPIONS AT HOME

KEN SNOW, whose 28-goal freshman season in 1987 broke IU's soccer scoring record, had an even bigger year as a sophomore.

Snow dipped to 22 goals but swept every available honor and became IU's first Hermann Award winner to play on a national champion, too.

Ken Snow won the Hermann Award in IU's NCAA championship season.

The 1988 championship came to the Hoosiers in their own Bill Armstrong Stadium, for more than 5,000 fans to see.

Indiana entered the NCAA tournament 15-3-3. The Hoosiers' 3-1 victories at Armstrong over Boston University and Seton Hall put them in the Final Four—as its host. On Saturday, December 3, goalie Juergen Sommer made Simon Katner's goal stand up for a 1-0 semifinal victory over Portland.

The next day, crisp and sunny, Sean Shapert's penalty kick put Indiana ahead of Howard. Sommer was forced out with a broken nose with more than 28 minutes left, and Matt Olson came on to complete the 1-0 victory behind an IU defense that allowed just 13 goals in 25 games. IU's 19th NCAA team championship was just the second that was won in Bloomington. The other was the school's first: in wrestling in 1932.

IN THOSE DAYS . . .

PARADE OF CHAMPIONS

• In Bob Knight's first 568 games as a college coach, only one opponent scored 100 points. It happened three times in 10 days early in the 1988-89 season, in one-sided losses to Syracuse, North Carolina and Louisville. Knight went to a "three-guard" lineup— 6-2 senior Joe Hillman with sophomores Jay Edwards and Lyndon Jones, starters on three straight state high school champions at Marion. Indiana won 21 of its next 23 games to clinch the championship in the strongest recent Big Ten season. Conference runnerup Illinois lost in the Final Four to third-place Michigan, on the Wolverines' way to their only NCAA basketball championship.

• Junior Anthony Thompson took IU's one-season touchdown record from 13 up to 26 in making consensus All-America and earning the Big Ten's Most Valuable Player trophy. Thompson's last two touchdowns came in a 34-10 Liberty Bowl victory over South Carolina, when game MVP Dave Schnell passed for 378 yards.

• When 30-year IU diving coach Hobie Billingsley retired after the 1989 season, he went out on top. His last protege, junior Mark Lenzi, won the NCAA one-meter championship—the 16th NCAA champion for Billingsley, winner on both boards himself for Ohio State in 1945.

HOOSIER LIST

HOOSIERS IN HEISMAN VOTING

Billy Hillenbrand
Year: 1942
Finished: 5th

Pete Pihos
Year: 1945
Finished: 8th

Anthony Thompson
Year: 1988
Finished: 9th
Year: 1989
Finished: 2nd

Vaughn Dunbar
Year: 1991
Finished: 6th

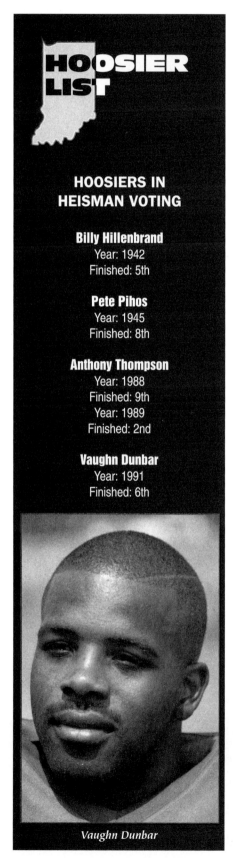

Vaughn Dunbar

INDIANA

LEGEND *Anthony Thompson*

TD RECORD FOR HEISMAN RUNNERUP

Anthony Thompson was strong and indestructible, a football yardage machine. But more than anything and anyone else, Thompson could score. And did.

When the man they called A.T. arrived from Terre Haute, IU's career record for touchdowns was 30.

When he scored his 60th touchdown with three games left in his career, he topped a national record that had stood for a while, shared at 59 by two greats of the game: Glenn Davis (Army 1943-46) and Tony Dorsett (Pittsburgh 1973-76).

He put the record at 65, where it stood until 1998. He still has the Big Ten record—68 in Big Ten books, counting three bowl touchdowns the NCAA records do not recognize.

Thompson ran for 5,299 yards (he's still seventh on college football's all-time list, second on the Big Ten's). As a senior, he led the nation in both rushing (1,793 yards) and scoring (25 touchdowns, 154 points).

At Wisconsin, Thompson carried 52 times for an NCAA-record 377 yards and four touchdowns in a 45-17 pullaway. In 44 college games he topped 100 yards 28 times—scored touchdowns in 31, twelve games in a row once. In three starts against Ohio State, he gained 493 yards and scored eight touchdowns. In going 2-0 against Wisconsin, he gained 584 yards. That's an NCAA record.

He's the only Hoosier to make consensus All-America twice. He was just the third two-time MVP in Big Ten history.

As a senior, Thompson was named Player of the Year by the American Football Coaches, the Walter Camp Foundation and the Maxwell Club. But he was runnerup to Houston's Andre Ware in the fourth-closest Heisman Trophy race ever.

BIG TEN MEDAL - Scott Holman & Julie Goedde   **GIMBEL AWARD -** Brian Dolph

ATHLETES OF THE YEAR - Anthony Thompson (also Big Ten) & Michelle Dekkers

BALFOUR AWARDS

Football, Anthony Thompson; Basketball, Jeff Oliphant; Baseball, Phil Dauphin; Track, Bob Kennedy; Wrestling, Brian Dolph; Swimming, Mark Lenzi; Cross Country, Bob Kennedy; Golf, Shaun Micheel; Tennis, Gunnar Salumaa; Soccer, Sean Shapert.

ALINE ROBINSON AWARDS

Basketball, Zandrea Jefferies; Volleyball, Joy Jordan; Track, Jennifer Goldy; Cross Country, Michelle Dekkers; Tennis, Gretchen Doninger; Golf, Debbie Lee; Swimming-Diving, Caroline Teskey; Softball, Marjorie Ledgerwood.

NCAA CHAMPIONS

Diving: Mark Lenzi, 1-meter springboard. Outdoor Track: Bob Kennedy, 1,500, 3:40.42.

IU item

SWIMMERS TELL DOC GOODBYE

A year after Hobie Billingsley—his partner in championships—retired, Doc Counsilman coached Indiana in his last dual swimming meet.

The handsome Counsilman Aquatic Center already was taking shape, but Doc's farewell came in Royer Pool, the functional facility that had opened with the Counsilman era—a pool where he almost never lost, but, more pertinent to his style and approach, the laboratory in which he tested and photographed and experimented as well as coached in advancing his sport far forward from where he had found it.

Inside walls that carried pictures and faces that brought back memories of unparalleled achievement and success, Counsilman's last team sent him off with a 71-33 victory over his alma mater, Ohio State.

First, captain Geof Clippert read the inscription on a plaque the team was giving its coach: "Dr. James Counsilman, The World's Greatest Swimming Coach, Father of Swimming."

"Grandfather," Counsilman corrected.

Royer Pool was nearly full for the first time in a generation. Some swimmers made it back for the day; others checked in by telephone.

"At midnight last night Mark (Spitz) called," Counsilman said. "Talked to me for an hour and a half. Charlie (Hickcox) called from Phoenix. There were lots of calls . . ."

Those calls came from once-young men who were on 34 teams that won 23 Big Ten championships and six NCAA championships, and who, as individual pupils of a master teacher, won considerably more than 100 Olympic, Pan-American Games, NCAA or national championships.

Legends Doc Counsilman and Hobie Billingsley.

NCAA BREAKTHROUGH FOR DOLPH

WRESTLING REARED ITS head at Indiana in 1991 as in the great old days, with Brian Dolph leading the way.

Dolph won his second straight Big Ten championship at 150 pounds. That made him just the third Hoosier since World War II to win two Big Ten titles and the first in 49 years to win the same weight title two years in a row (Ben Wilson, 134, 1940-41, the last).

Then as a senior, Dolph gave IU its first national champion in 50 years. He had been All-America twice before, for finishing eighth in the 1988 NCAA meet and third in 1989.

Jim Pearson also won a Big Ten championship at 158 pounds, the first time in 37 years IU had two conference winners. And, the Hoosiers' second-place Big Ten finish represented IU's high since 1946. Second-year Hoosier coach Joe McFarland, a former NCAA champion himself at Michigan, was the league's Coach of the Year.

Two-time Big Ten champion Brian Dolph became IU's first NCAA wrestling champion in 50 years; he holds the IU record with 127 career wins.

IN THOSE DAYS . . .

KNIGHT JOINS IN TRIBUTE TO ISIAH

Isiah Thomas ranked with professional basketball's best from the day he left IU with an 1981 NCAA championship ring. But it took a while for Detroit to build a title contender around its little captain.

In 1989, the Pistons won the franchise's first NBA championship. And in 1990, when they repeated, Thomas became the first IU player ever named MVP of the championship series.

That put him with Kareem Abdul-Jabbar, Bill Walton, Magic Johnson and James Worthy—just five who have won the Most Valuable or Outstanding Player award for championship teams at both the Final Four and the NBA finals.

On February 17, 1996, when the Pistons retired Thomas' No. 11 and named the street in front of the Auburn Hills Palace Isiah Thomas Drive, club president Bill Davidson's "speech" was 16 words: "In 1981, we drafted Isiah Thomas. I had a dream, and Isiah fulfilled it. Thank you."

Bob Knight, speaking immediately afterward, countered with a quip: "Mr. Davidson, you had a dream in 1981. Dammit, you took *my* dream away from me . . ."

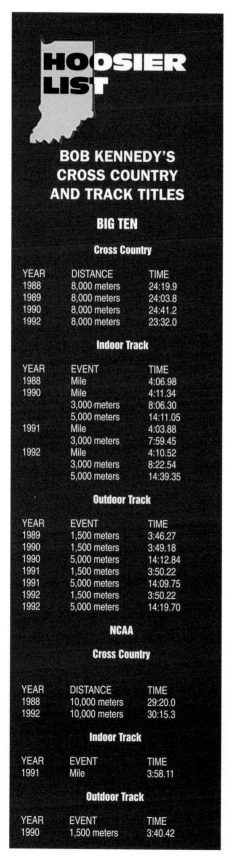

HOOSIER LIST

BOB KENNEDY'S CROSS COUNTRY AND TRACK TITLES

BIG TEN

Cross Country

YEAR	DISTANCE	TIME
1988	8,000 meters	24:19.9
1989	8,000 meters	24:03.8
1990	8,000 meters	24:41.2
1992	8,000 meters	23:32.0

Indoor Track

YEAR	EVENT	TIME
1988	Mile	4:06.98
1990	Mile	4:11.34
	3,000 meters	8:06.30
	5,000 meters	14:11.05
1991	Mile	4:03.88
	3,000 meters	7:59.45
1992	Mile	4:10.52
	3,000 meters	8:22.54
	5,000 meters	14:39.35

Outdoor Track

YEAR	EVENT	TIME
1989	1,500 meters	3:46.27
1990	1,500 meters	3:49.18
1990	5,000 meters	14:12.84
1991	1,500 meters	3:50.22
1991	5,000 meters	14:09.75
1992	1,500 meters	3:50.22
1992	5,000 meters	14:19.70

NCAA

Cross Country

YEAR	DISTANCE	TIME
1988	10,000 meters	29:20.0
1992	10,000 meters	30:15.3

Indoor Track

YEAR	EVENT	TIME
1991	Mile	3:58.11

Outdoor Track

YEAR	EVENT	TIME
1990	1,500 meters	3:40.42

LEGEND *Bob Kennedy*

AMERICA'S BEST—BIG TEN'S, TOO

INDIANA

Though he grew up in Columbus, Ohio, Bob Kennedy was born in Bloomington to a dad who had run on a Big Ten cross country championship team at IU and a mom who was fighting cancer, her pregnancy a terrifying balance between protecting her baby and battling kidney cancer with radiation.

Years later, when Barbara Kennedy saw the wonders being accomplished by the child who had come through all that, she smiled and said, "Maybe more (mothers) should try it."

She was joking, of course, the prerogative of proud mothers. Young Bob is Bob and Barbara Kennedy's only child.

His calling card at Indiana as an 18-year-old freshman was an NCAA cross country championship, and so was his exit line—in November 1992 at IU Golf Course by a 40.8-second victory gap that is the meet's widest on record.

Kennedy also won NCAA track championships indoors (mile, 1991) and outdoors (1,500 meters, 1990).

He went on after college to be not just America's best distance runner but also a vista-changer who trained with the world-dominant Kenyans to raise his and U.S. standards. Kennedy ran in the 1992 and 1996 Olympics and set American records at 3,000 and 5,000 meters.

Where collegian Kennedy likely will be toughest to overtake in the record books is in Big Ten championships. He won 20 of them: four in cross country, nine in indoor track, seven in outdoor track.

None was at a distance shorter than 1,500 meters. Added together they required more than 40 miles—every inch in determined, thought-out pursuit of a Big Ten championship that was achieved.

That's seven Everests. That's Bob Kennedy of Indiana.

BIG TEN MEDAL - Scott Boatman & Joy Jordan   **GIMBEL AWARD -** Shaun Micheel

ATHLETES OF THE YEAR - Bob Kennedy & Stephanie Reece

ALINE ROBINSON AWARDS
Basketball, Tisha Hill; Volleyball, Diane Hoereth; Track, Mary Beth Driscoll/Dawn Gelon; Cross Country, Amy Legacki; Tennis, Gretchen Doninger; Golf, Courtney Cox; Swimming-Diving, Caroline Teskey; Softball, Heather Darrow.

BALFOUR AWARDS
Football, Mike Dumas; Basketball, Eric Anderson; Baseball, Mike Smith; Track, Alan Turner; Wrestling, Adam Caldwell; Swimming, Richard Granneman; Cross Country, Bob Kennedy; Golf, Shaun Micheel; Tennis, David McCallum; Soccer, Ken Snow.

NCAA CHAMPIONS
Indoor Track, Bob Kennedy, mile, 3:58.11; Alan Turner, long jump, 26-5 1/2_.

IUitem

MICHEEL LEADS IU TO RECORD

A s a junior in 1990 Indiana golfer Shaun Micheel made All-Big Ten but placed 20th in the Big Ten championships when his team finished ninth.

He came back as a senior with one of the greatest years in IU golf history.

Micheel became the second Hoosier to win the Big Ten's Les Bolstad Award for low stroke average for the year (72.1). Then he put together the best tournament any IU player ever had, anywhere, and led his team to a record victory.

At Purdue, Micheel's final-day 67 gave him 276 and a four-shot victory. His team won by 11 strokes over Ohio State—with 1,138, still the lowest score in tournament history.

No Big Ten golf team ever had moved from ninth to first in a year. No Hoosier ever had shot 276 in a tournament, the previous IU four-round record 283 by Kelly Roberts in the 1974 Northern Invitational at IU. Micheel was IU's first Big Ten medalist in seven years (Mike Ingram, 1984), and just the sixth ever.

IU's first golf All-American in 16 years led the Hoosiers' first Big Ten championship team in 16 years. Bill Miller (290), Kyle Wieneke (291), Freshman-of-the-Year Jody Roudebush (292) and Joe Tomaselli (293) also contributed for Coach-of-the-Year Sam Carmichael.

Micheel turned professional after college and won two tournaments on the PGA's Nike tour.

Shaun Micheel was Big Ten medalist and an All-American.

Snapshot In Time

KNIGHT ENTERS BASKETBALL HALL

IN MAY 1991, in the town that was basketball's birthplace, Indiana's Bob Knight became one of the youngest coaches ever enshrined in the Basketball Hall of Fame.

Knight was 50 when he was elected to join some of his career heroes in the Hall at Springfield, Massachusetts—his Ohio State coach, Fred Taylor, plus Pete Newell, Clair Bee and Henry Iba, each among his advisers and confidantes all along the way.

"Some of the best minds this game has ever known have been close to me," he said at Springfield. "And now they can feel, despite all the trials and tribulations I gave them, that I listened after all."

He went in with three NCAA championships, plus Olympic and Pan-American Games championships. Already by then he had every Big Ten coaching record, and by decade's end he had passed 700 career victories and been recognized as an offensive and defensive innovator. His impact on IU also included credit for raising more than $5 million for the IU Library Fund, by former university president Thomas Ehrlich's figuring.

Nate Archibald
Dave Cowens
Larry Fleisher
Harry Gallatin
Bob Knight
Larry O'Brien
Boris Stankovic

1991

Bob Knight was a 1991 inductee into the Basketball Hall of Fame.

IN THOSE DAYS . . .

CHAMPIONS A-PLENTY

• Ken Snow closed his college soccer career with IU's goal records for a season (28, as a freshman in 1988) and career (84). He was the IU program's first four-time All-American and first two-time winner of the college game's top honors: the Hermann Award and the Missouri Athletic Club's Player of the Year Award.

Alan Turner

• Michelle Dekkers, the only IU woman to win a Big Ten cross country championship, won her third in a row with the 1990 race at Minneapolis and led Indiana to its second straight team title. Mary Beth Driscoll, Kathy Gobbitt and Amy Legacki ran with Dekkers on both Big Ten championship teams.

• Olympic gold medalist Greg Bell's IU long jump record—26-7, set in winning the 1957 NCAA championship—lasted 34 years, and it fell to another international champion. Alan Turner jumped 26-10 to win the World University Games gold medal at Sheffield, England. Turner also had set IU's indoor record under championship demands with 26-5 1/2 in winning the 1991 NCAA indoor meet at Indianapolis. Bob Kennedy won the mile (3:58.11) in the same meet.

IU'S CAREER
BATTING LEADERS

Paul "Pooch" Harrell, 1927-29	.404
Alex Smith, 1982-86	.393
Mickey Morandini, 1985-88	.392
Bob Waite, 1981-82	.387
Don Foreman, 1958-60	.381
John Wehner, 1986-88	.374
Mike Smith, 1989-92	.369
Geoff Flynn, 1987-89	.366
Bob Johnson, 1978-79	.363
Kevin Orie, 1991-93	.358
Ken Smith, 1957-60	.357

IU'S SEASON
BATTING LEADERS

Mike Smith, 1992	.490
Ted Kluszewski, 1945	.443
Bob Waite, 1981	.437
John Wehner, 1988	.436
Alex Smith, 1985	.434
Jeff Howard, 1988	.432
Mike Smith, 1991	.431
Barry Burnett, 1973	.427
Dan Winters, 1984	.426
Mike Crotty, 1995	.423

LEGEND   *Mark Lenzi*

SUCCESSOR TO INSPIRATION

Mark Lenzi was one of Virginia's top high school wrestlers when in the summer of 1984 he sat mesmerized and watched American Greg Louganis dominate the field in the Olympic Games.

Lenzi the Wrestler took his muscular 5-foot-5, 145-pound body to the closest pool and began a new sport.

Lenzi was a fast learner. Within two years he caught the eye of former IU diver Paul Lenihan, who relayed what he had seen to Hobie Billingsley, who made a call from Bloomington and—sight unseen—offered Lenzi a scholarship.

He barely missed making the field for the 1988 U.S. Olympic diving trials. By '92, he had won two NCAA championships, three national championships and two World Cups and—Louganis and all—recorded history's first 100-point dive.

At Barcelona in 1992, he stepped onto the medal stand where Louganis had stood in 1984 and '88. He won IU's last gold medal of the 20th century by 17 points over Chinese diver Liangde Tan, who missed a 1988 Olympic upset of Louganis by one agonizing point.

Lenzi dropped out of diving for a while between Olympics, then talked Billingsley—at 69—into one last run together. Lenzi ran his national championship total to eight and beat a Louganis record with 762 points in an 11-dive program. But he also ran into injury problems.

He made the Olympic team in the Trials at Indianapolis. He placed third in Atlanta in 1996 and smiled. "I shouldn't even be here," he said. "A couple of months ago (because of a torn rotator cuff) I couldn't lift my arms up, and here I am with a bronze medal at the Olympic Games."

BIG TEN MEDAL - Mark Hagen & Katrin Koch   **GIMBEL AWARD -** Mike Anhaeuser

ATHLETES OF THE YEAR - Mike Smith & Kristen Kane

ALINE ROBINSON AWARDS
Basketball, Tisha Hill/Amy Cherubini; Volleyball, Jill Kerkhoff; Track, Amy Legacki; Cross Country, Amy Legacki; Tennis, Stephanie Reece; Golf, Amy McDonald; Swimming-Diving, Christine Osterhues; Softball, Ann Tuttle.

BALFOUR AWARDS
Football, Mark Hagen; Basketball, Calbert Cheaney; Baseball, Mike Smith; Track, Glenn Terry; Wrestling, Jeff Lyons; Swimming, Dave Burgess; Cross Country, Derek Kelleher; Golf, Derek Clouse; Tennis, David Held; Soccer, Mike Anhaeuser.

NCAA CHAMPIONS Outdoor Track, Katrin Koch, shot put, 57-6 1/4.

OLYMPIC MEDALISTS Diving, Mark Lenzi, springboard, gold.

FALL AND WINTER FINAL FOURS

Only in 1991-92 did both the Indiana soccer and basketball teams reach the NCAA Final Four in the same academic year. The soccer Hoosiers won the championship in the first year of Big Ten competition—ironically, after having their 68-match unbeaten streak against Big Ten teams snapped in midyear at Wisconsin. Indiana avenged that loss 2-0 in the Big Ten tournament's championship game, then repeated over the Badgers 2-0 opening their NCAA tournament bid.

Mike Clark, Blake Rodgers, Mike Anhaeuser, Matt Coyer and Steve Keller scored on tie-breaker penalty kicks to get Indiana past SMU and into the Final Four at Tampa. There, Santa Clara ended IU's 19-3-2 season, 2-0.

The mostly junior Hoosier basketball team reached as high as second in the rankings after winning two games from early-'90s rival Ohio State. A shooting chill the last two Sundays of the season cost the Hoosiers defeats at Michigan and Purdue, giving Ohio State the league championship.

But Indiana's touch returned in tournament play. The Hoosiers blazed past Eastern Illinois, LSU (despite 36 points and 12-for-12 free-throw shooting by Shaquille O'Neal in his last college game) and Florida State to get a return shot at UCLA, which had ruined the IU opener in a special Hall of Fame game commemorating basketball's 100th anniversary. Calbert Cheaney scored 23 points, Damon Bailey 22 and Indiana shot 58 percent in dominating the rematch, 106-79.

At Minneapolis, the Hoosiers led No. 1-ranked, defending champion Duke 39-27 before an accumulation of fouls swung control to the Blue Devils. Duke won, 81-78, despite Todd Leary's last-minute 3-point blitz—three in 25 seconds—and went on to the only repeat championship in the final quarter-century.

The Hoosiers' 27-7 season also included an 82-77 victory over St. John's in another centennial game— before a full house at Madison Square Garden on Dec. 21, the 100th anniversary of James Naismith's introduction of the new game.

BOWL SHUTOUT,
AND LOTS OF OFFENSE

INDIANA COMPLEMENTED ALL-AMERICAN 1,805-yard rusher Vaughn Dunbar with Trent Green, a pro-prospect 2,627-yard passer, and may have deserved to finish better than its 7-4-1 record in 1991.

The Hoosiers augmented all that offense with a defense that delivered the first bowl shutout by a Big Ten team in 44 years. Competitive losses at Notre Dame, Ohio State and Michigan damaged the season record.

Dunbar, whose yardage beat one Anthony Thompson record, had 161 yards at Notre Dame, 116 at Michigan and 125 at Ohio State—plus a career-high 265 in a 27-27 tie at Missouri, and 153 as Indiana edged Purdue, 24-22.

Mark Hagen was defensive MVP in the Copper Bowl win over Baylor.

Dunbar ran for 205 yards at Wisconsin in a game for history. The previous week, Heisman Trophy winner Desmond Howard caught three touchdown passes in Michigan's 24-16 victory over the Hoosiers—one of them after a controversial defensive holding call. IU coach Bill Mallory's critical remarks two days later got him suspended for a game—though the official he criticized was penalized even more harshly.

Minus Mallory, the Hoosiers fell behind 20-0 but rode Dunbar and Green to a 28-20 victory under assistant coaches Joe Novak and George Belu.

Green passed and ran for 2,829 yards and 25 touchdowns in directing the 5,032-yard offense to 39 touchdowns and 305 points. Linebacker Mark Hagen was the defensive MVP and leader in IU's 24-0 Copper Bowl victory over Baylor.

Dunbar, IU's fifth consensus All-American, was a first-round NFL draft pick whose career was shortened by a knee injury. Green emerged as the Washington Redskins' starter in 1997 and in 1999 his hometown team, St. Louis, signed him to the biggest contract ever for an IU football player.

Trent Green set IU season records for passing and total offense.

LEGEND *Dave Volz*

COMEBACK OF A 'WHAT-IF' KID

There always will be a "What if?" element to the story of pole vaulter Dave Volz. Still, in the summer of 1992, Volz wrote a surprise and happy ending to it all.

Volz grew up in Bloomington with the build, speed and agility of a halfback, but the adventure of the pole vault captured his focus early. All those physical gifts were invaluable assets, and a fearless recklessness didn't hurt, either.

As a 16-year-old high school sophomore under coach Marshall Goss, he cleared 15-8. He won state championships the next two years, reaching 16-9 as a junior and joining the elite over 17 feet as a senior.

IU's first freshman to win an NCAA track and field championship, he reached 18-3 1/2 that year. At the 1982 Big Ten meet, he started a foot after all other vaulters had been eliminated. Then they lined the runway to cheer him on to a league-record 18-1.

That summer, he set the American record with 18-9 1/2 in an international meet at Durham, N.C. Seven weeks later at Nice, France, he moved the record on up to 18-10 1/4, two inches from the world record.

Three days after the Nice jump—at 20 years old, "the best vaulter in the world," *Track and Field News* called him in a cover article—Volz hurt an ankle in practice for a meet at Zurich. Severely. He never fully recovered.

That was August 17, 1982. As a junior in March 1983, he visibly limped running to an 18-0 1/2 vault in the NCAA indoor meet—the guttiest effort IU coach Sam Bell ever remembered seeing. A month later in Boston, Volz underwent ankle reconstruction surgery.

His days as a collegiate star were over, but he kept working to get back the speed that had been a key to his superiority. At the 1984 Olympic Trials, he remembered, "I could barely walk—I cleared one height." He made 19 feet for the first time at the 1986 Millrose Games— just the fourth American to reach that level—an inch-and-a-half beyond where he was four years before.

Then in 1987 he broke his other leg and considered his career over.

And in 1992, he vaulted in the Olympic Games at Barcelona.

A comeback he began at Bell's urging, after four years without a vault, got him to the U.S. Trials at New Orleans. There he cleared 19-0 1/4 and made the team.

At Barcelona, in wind that baffled world recordholder Sergei Bubka into early elimination, Volz used his wiles to come within one more clearance of a medal. As it was he finished fifth in a brilliant field.

What if he had never been hurt?

There's a good chance history's first 20-foot vaulter would have been a Hoosier.

Instead, the happiest 1992 Olympian was.

"I always felt the only thing I missed out on in my vaulting career was a legitimate chance at making the Olympic team," Hoosier Dave Volz said.

NATIONAL TRIPLE CROWN FOR MIKE SMITH

S hortstop Mike Smith put together quite a junior season, his .476 Big Ten batting average putting him first among the eight Hoosiers (now nine) who have won the league title.

Smith took off from there as a senior, making college baseball history.

Smith in 1992 was the first player to score a national Triple Crown. He led all college baseball with 27 home runs, 95 runs batted in (1.73 per game) and a .490 batting average. His slugging average was 1.000—202 total bases in 202 times at bat. That also led the nation.

Smith also had a Big Ten Triple Crown (.472, with a league-record 14 home runs and 36 RBI).

The American Baseball Coaches Association named him second-team All-America, and Big Ten coaches divided Player of the Year honors between him and Iowa pitcher Brett Backlund—the only time the 18-year-old award has gone to a Hoosier.

Smith is the only two-time Big Ten batting champion from IU, and only he and Wisconsin's Rick Reichardt (1963-64) have won back-to-back titles in 61 years of Big Ten record-keeping.

Smith, from Piqua, Ohio, signed as a fourth-round draft pick with the Texas Rangers. He reached as high as Triple-A but never played in the major leagues.

Mike Smith led all of college baseball with a .490 batting average, 27 homers and 95 runs batted in.

Snapshot In Time

A CONSOLATION CHAMPIONSHIP

KATRIN KOCH WON IU's Big Ten medal for academic excellence as a fine arts major. Tall and graceful, she loved the flowing beauty of the discus throw. The native German dreamed of being the American collegiate discus champion.

It was within her grasp, on finals day at the NCAA meet in Austin, Tex. "And then I tied up and got third," she said. She cried in frustration and anger that night—"I was *very* upset." She got up the next morning thinking, "I lost to 179 (feet). I've gone 180 the last four meets and I lost to 179."

All that was left was an event she hated: the shot put. Admittedly "mad—it was like my makeover," she heaved the shot two feet farther than she ever had before and became IU's first woman to win an NCAA outdoor track and field championship.

She already had five Big Ten shot put and discus championships and Big Ten records in the shot put indoors and out and the discus. She still has those records, impressive for young athletes to hear about in meeting her in her post-competitive role: strength and conditioning coach of IU athletics.

Katrin Koch, NCAA shot put champion and a 5-time Big Ten champion.

IN THOSE DAYS . . .

HOOSIER POTPOURRI

• Jim Spivey and Bob Kennedy, the best of Sam Bell's wave of outstanding middle-distance runners at IU, made it to Barcelona as Olympic teammates—Spivey in the 1,500 meters for the second time, Kennedy in the 5,000 for the first. Both made the Olympic finals, Spivey finishing eighth and Kennedy 12th.

• It hadn't happened often at IU—Zora Clevenger first, then Paul "Pooch" Harrell and Frank Allen. In 1991, lawyer Clarence Doninger became the fourth IU letterman to become the university's athletic director. Doninger succeeded Ed Williams, the interim director after the death of Ralph Floyd in December 1990.

• Sophomore Kristen Kane was named Big Ten women's Diver of the Year after winning three-meter and platform league championships. Kane, who went on to be a four-time All-American, repeated the three-meter title and Diver of the Year Award as a senior in 1994. She won a U.S. Outdoor championship in 1992 and dived for the U.S. in the Pan-American Games in 1995, finishing sixth.

• John Tavener, 47 years after making his last snap as a center and linebacker for Indiana, was inducted into the College Football Hall of Fame. Tavener in 1944 was IU's second consensus All-American.

HOOSIER LIST

MEN'S BASKETBALL CAREER SCORING LEADERS

Calbert Cheaney, 1990-93	2613
Steve Alford, 1984-87	2438
Don Schlundt, 1952-55	2192
Mike Woodson, 1977-80	2061
Alan Henderson, 1992-95	1979
Damon Bailey, 1991-94	1741
Kent Benson, 1974-77	1740
Eric Anderson, 1989-92	1715
Brian Evans, 1993-96	1701
Scott May, 1974-76	1593
Greg Graham, 1990-93	1590
Randy Wittman, 1979-83	1549
Archie Dees, 1956-58	1546
A.J. Guyton, 1997-99*	1481
Walt Bellamy, 1959-61	1441
Ray Tolbert, 1978-81	1427
Jimmy Rayl, 1961-63	1401
Uwe Blab, 1982-85	1357
Ted Kitchel, 1979-83	1336
Andrae Patterson, 1995-98	1316
Tom Bolyard, 1961-63	1299
Joby Wright, 1969-72	1272
Steve Green, 1973-75	1265
Tom VanArsdale, 1963-65	1252
Dick VanArsdale, 1963-65	1240
Steve Downing, 1971-73	1220
Quinn Buckner, 1973-76	1195

* Still Active

INDIANA LEGEND — *Calbert Cheaney*

PLAYER OF THE YEAR ON TEAM OF THE YEAR

Calbert Cheaney, Bob Knight's first left-handed player, is the only IU freshman to start the season opener and score 20 points.

Cheaney, 6-6 and smooth, went from there to be the Hoosiers' leader for the full four years. The last three of those years Indiana spent all but two of 53 poll weeks in the Top 10—38 of them in the Top 5. The Hoosiers were 87-16 those years, 105-27 for the four Cheaney seasons.

As a senior, he was the best player on the best team in the country. The Hoosiers were No. 1-ranked and 12-0 toward the first 18-0 Big Ten season in 17 years when in a practice February 19, sophomore Alan Henderson, the team's leading rebounder, hurt a knee.

Knight reshaped his offense around the team's shooting depth—Greg Graham, Damon Bailey, Pat Graham and freshman Brian Evans, exceptional 3-point shooters along with Cheaney. But it was Cheaney's team.

An overtime loss at Ohio State left the Hoosiers 17-1 as Big Ten champions. March 4 against Northwestern at Assembly Hall, Cheaney sank a jump shot that made him the all-time top Big Ten scorer. He was to take that record on up to 2,613, and he's still No. 1.

He scored 29 points as No. 1-ranked, No. 1 seed Indiana routed Wright State at the Indianapolis Hoosier Dome to open tournament play; 23 in a 73-70 escape from Xavier; 32 as the star of a splendidly played Midwest Regional opener at St. Louis, an 82-69 victory over Louisville.

Henderson, the knee encased, tried to help against tall Kansas but couldn't. Kansas won, 83-77. No. 4-ranked North Carolina beat Big Ten runnerup Michigan for the national championship.

Every post-season honor came to Cheaney: national Player of the Year, unanimous All-American, Big Ten MVP. Taken No. 6 in the NBA draft, he signed a six-year contract with Washington and in 1999 joined Boston.

BIG TEN MEDAL - Dave Held & Courtney Cox   **GIMBEL AWARD -** Mike Clark & Glenn Terry

ATHLETES OF THE YEAR - Calbert Cheaney & Deb Edelman

ALINE ROBINSON AWARDS
Basketball, Dawn Douglas; Volleyball, Jill Kerkhoff; Track, Nancy Goldman; Cross Country, Nancy Goldman; Tennis, Deb Edelman; Golf, Courtney Cox; Swimming-Diving, Christine Osterhues; Softball, Ann Tuttle.

BALFOUR AWARDS
Football, Scott Bonnell; Basketball, Calbert Cheaney; Baseball, Dave Snedden; Track, Gregg Hart; Wrestling, Andy Trevino; Swimming, Chuck Jennings; Cross Country, Bob Kennedy; Golf, Jody Roudebush; Tennis, Nigel Russell; Soccer, Matt Coyer.

NCAA CHAMPIONS
Indoor Track, Glenn Terry, 55 hurdles, 7.13; Outdoor Track, Glenn Terry, 110 hurdles, 13.43; Mark Buse, pole vault, 18-4 1/2.

IU item

TERRY, BUSE SCORE NCAA DOUBLE

Mark Buse won the NCAA pole vault.

Hurdler Glenn Terry and vaulter Mark Buse gave Indiana its first pair of NCAA outdoor track and field champions in 52 years.

Their victories and a third-place finish by Gregg Hart in the discus lifted Indiana to a tie for seventh in team standings—another high point unmatched since the 1941 Hoosiers, with victories by Campbell Kane (880), Fred Wilt (2-mile) and Archie Harris (discus), finished second to champion Southern Cal.

Terry joined Olympic decathlon champion Milt Campbell as IU's only NCAA outdoor hurdles champions (Campbell won the highs in 1955). Terry, a senior from Cincinnati, became the first Hoosier in any event to win NCAA titles both indoors and outdoors in the same year.

He won the NCAA outdoor hurdles in 13.43 seconds, just off his Big Ten-record 13.42 in winning the Penn Relays. He closed his career with the four fastest hurdles times in IU and Big Ten history.

Buse, whose uncle Don was a pro basketball star with the Pacers, won the vault with the best jump of his life—18-4 1/2. A two-time state champion from Southridge, Buse had cleared 18 feet for the first time in pulling out a third-place finish at the 1992 NCAA meet.

Glenn Terry was NCAA hurdles champion.

EDELMAN'S CAREER FULL OF WINS

DEB EDELMAN WAS associated with very little losing in her years as a three-time All-American tennis player for IU.

Lin Loring's team won four straight Big Ten championships with Edelman and was pressed only once. In the 1991 tournament finals, the Hoosiers edged Wisconsin (coached by one of Loring's program building blocks, Kelly Ferguson), 5-4. Only Edelman (at No. 2) and Gretchen Doninger (No. 6) won singles matches, but a straight-set 3-0 doubles sweep pulled out the title before a disappointed crowd at Madison.

The next two years, Indiana blew through the tournament in minimum time, winning each of its three matches as soon as the first five singles scores were in. Edelman was both Player of the Year and Freshman of the Year in the Big Ten in 1990. She was Co-Player of the Year with teammate Stephanie Reece in 1992.

Edelman closed out her Hoosier years by reaching the 1993 NCAA doubles quarterfinals with partner Rachel Epstein.

That year, Edelman was IU's woman Athlete of the Year, just the second tennis player to win the award. Teammate Reece (in 1991) was the first. Reece and Edelman also are the IU program's only three-time All-Americans.

Deborah Edelman, four-time All-Big Ten, two-time Big Ten Player-of-the-Year, and a three-time All-American.

IN THOSE DAYS . . .

SUDDEN STARS, OF TWO KINDS

• Senior guard Greg Graham was the Hoosier most affected by the offensive rearranging necessary after Alan Henderson's mid-February knee injury. Graham's IU career high up to then was 25 points; he averaged 25 a game the rest of the way. That started with Graham's 32-point contribution to a 93-78 victory over Purdue—on two 3-point field goals and a Big Ten-record 26-for-28 on free throws. Graham was the first to lead the Big Ten in 3-point shooting and overall shooting. His late-season surge boosted him to All-Big Ten and first-round selection in the NBA draft (17th, by Charlotte).

• Actor Nick Nolte and producer William Friedkin spent a March week around Bob Knight and the Hoosiers, at practice and at an Assembly Hall game. Then they filmed *Blue Chips*, with a Knight-like Nolte playing a college coach who gives in to alumni pressures, then rebels. The climactic game—Nolte's "Western" vs. Knight and Indiana—was filmed before 6,000 at Frankfort's Everett Case Fieldhouse. Shaquille O'Neal, Anfernee Hardaway and Hoosier Matt Nover played major movie roles. Seniors Calbert Cheaney, Greg Graham and Chris Reynolds and alumni Joe Hillman, Eric Anderson, Keith Smart and Jamal Meeks wore Indiana uniforms in the film's big game.

HOOSIER LIST

TODD LEARY'S FREE THROW STREAK

Todd Leary set a Big Ten record of 46 consecutive free throws, over a period of nearly four years.

Date	Opponent	FT
1989-90		
Feb. 22	Iowa	4
1991-92		
Jan. 9	Minnesota	2
Jan. 28	Purdue	4
1992-93		
Jan. 6	Iowa	7
Jan. 9	Penn State	2
Jan. 24	Ohio State	4
Jan. 30	at Northwestern	2
Feb. 21	Purdue	2
Feb. 23	at Ohio State	1
Feb. 27	at Minnesota	1
March 4	Northwestern	2
1993-94		
Jan. 16	Michigan	8
Jan. 22	Northwestern	2
Jan. 26	at Minnesota	5

Previous Big Ten record: 45, Steve Smith, Michigan State, 1990-91
Previous IU record (Big Ten only): 37, Keith Smart, 1987-88

LEGEND *Damon Bailey*

AN EARLY STAR

Damon Bailey was the one IU basketball player of modern times who was a full-fledged Hoosier legend before putting on an Indiana uniform.

Bailey was featured in *Sports Illustrated* before his first high school game. He led age-group teams to three national AAU championships, bringing IU coach Bob Knight to Bailey's junior high to watch him play. Knight's comments about him were part of the *Season on the Brink* book excerpt that *SI* ran in the same issue where, separately, Bailey was spotlighted as the Player of the Year in the upcoming freshman class.

The kid from Heltonville led Bedford North Lawrence to the state's Final Four three of the next four years. His senior year a national record crowd of 41,046 in the Hoosier Dome watched Bailey—who two weeks before had broken the state scoring record—score his team's last 12 points to beat undefeated Concord, 63-60, for the state championship.

Then he went to Indiana. In four years, he played in 108 victories, in an IU-record 11 NCAA tournament victories.

His senior year began with a stunning 75-71 loss at Butler. One Saturday later, the nation saw Bailey at his best—29 points in a 96-84 victory over Kentucky. He scored a career-peak 36 points at Kansas, but the Jayhawks won at the overtime buzzer, 86-83.

Alan Henderson come back well from knee surgery, a late-season 41-point game proving that. Shooters Pat Graham, Todd Leary and Brian Evans combined with Bailey as IU led the nation in 3-point percentage. Ironically, a 3-point barrage by Boston College ended the Hoosiers' season in the third round of NCAA tournament play.

Bailey averaged 19.6 for the season and closed his career No. 5 at IU with 1,741 points. As a senior, he was All-Big Ten and third-team All-America.

BIG TEN MEDAL - Vito Maurici & Anne Eastman **GIMBEL AWARD -** Jody Roudebush

ATHLETES OF THE YEAR - Mark Buse & Kristen Kane

ALINE ROBINSON AWARDS
Basketball, Shirley Bryant; Volleyball, Jill Kerkhoff; Track, Regina Frye; Cross Country, Regina Frye; Tennis, Danielle Paradine; Golf, Nicole Hollingsworth; Swimming-Diving, Garland O'Keefe; Softball, Candace Nishina.

BALFOUR AWARDS
Football, Ross Hales; Basketball, Damon Bailey; Baseball, Bob Scafa; Track, Mark Buse; Wrestling, Chris Russo; Swimming, Jason Baumann; Cross Country, Darrell Hughes; Golf, Jody Roudebush; Tennis, None given; Soccer, Wane Lobring.

IUiTEM

LEWIS BREAKOUT AT PENN STATE

Thomas Lewis set a Big Ten record with 285 receiving yards against Penn State.

John Paci

Penn State's Beaver Stadium is not the place to go looking to set offensive records, but on Indiana's first visit there, some happened.

Quarterback John Paci shredded the Lions' defense for 379 yards, 285 of them on 12 connections with junior wideout Thomas Lewis, whose yardage set IU and Big Ten records. Included was the first 99-yard touchdown pass in league history. But the Lions hung on and won, 38-31.

Lewis went on to the second 1,000-yard receiving year in IU history, capping it with a 177-yard game in the Independence Bowl at Shreveport, Louisiana. The Hoosiers went there after a 24-17 victory over Purdue lifted them to 8-3 and qualified them for their sixth bowl game in eight years.

Indiana, trailing Virginia Tech 14-13, was looking for a go-ahead field goal in the last 30 seconds of the first half when an intercepted pass and a fumble runback gave the Hokies 14 stunning points and 28-13 command of a game they won, 45-20.

It was the Hoosiers' last bowl appearance of the Bill Mallory years, and Thomas Lewis' last game. He entered the NFL draft early and was the first-round pick of the New York Giants.

Snapshot In Time

VENTURELLA REWRITES RECORDS

THE CLOSEST THING in IU softball history to the 1992 Triple Crown baseball season by a Smith named Michael was a year put together in 1994 by a Venturella named Michelle.

A junior catcher, Venturella hit .418 and set IU records with 16 home runs and 65 runs batted in. She stepped that up to .486 in league play—her batting average, her 69 total bases and her 33 RBI all Big Ten records.

She was Player of the Year in the conference and a second-team All-American as Indiana won the league championship by three games. Pitcher Gina Ugo (19-2, a Big Ten record for victories) and outfielder Candace Nishina joined her on the All-Conference team under league Coach of the Year Diane Stephenson.

Venturella came back as a senior to hit .377 with 9 home runs and 51 RBI, repeating on the All-Big Ten team and making third-team All-America.

She trained after that with the U.S. National team that won a gold medal at the Atlanta Olympics. She continued to travel and train with the team, aiming toward possible Olympic play in Sydney in 2000.

Michelle Venturella set Big Ten records in batting average, total bases and runs batted in.

IN THOSE DAYS . . .

LEARY'S STREAK LONGEST OF ALL

Todd Leary's Big Ten-record string of free-throw conversions almost certainly will always be the Big Ten's longest.

Someone else may go higher than Leary's 46, but surely not longer.

On February 17, 1990, freshman Leary was 19 when he hit all four free throws he tried in IU's Assembly Hall-record 118-71 victory over Iowa.

He didn't shoot any more that year, and he was red-shirted in the 1990-91 season. Picking up a streak that counted only shots taken in Big Ten games, he hit all six he tried in 1992 and all 21 he shot in the Hoosiers' 17-1 championship season, 1993.

That put his streak at 31, the league record 45 by All-American Steve Smith of Michigan State, who started and finished his in 1991—*after* Leary's streak was under way.

Eight against Michigan and two against Northwestern put Leary at 41. And January 26, 1994, at Assembly Hall—22 days short of four years after his streak began—23-year-old Todd Leary hit five against Minnesota to pass Smith by one.

Then he missed on his next try, ending the streak.

He strung eleven more before his next miss, just one misfire away from a streak of 58. By then, Steve Smith was a third-year pro.

1994 1995

ASSEMBLY HALL'S 50-GAME WINNING STREAK FACTS

Streak Start:
Feb. 24, 1991—Indiana 112, Michigan 79

Wins Over:
Austin Peay (1993)
Boston University (1992)
Butler (1992, 1995)
Central Michigan (1992)
Cincinnati (1993)
Eastern Kentucky (1994)
Illinois (1992, 1993, 1994)
Iowa (1992, 1993, 1994)
Kansas (1995)
Miami (1995)
Michigan (1991, 1992, 1993, 1994)
Michigan State (1992, 1993, 1995)
Minnesota (1991, 1992, 1993, 1994)
Morehead State (1995)
Murray State (1993)
Northwestern (1992, 1993, 1994)
Notre Dame (1992, 1994)
Ohio State (1992, 1993, 1994)
Penn State (1993, 1994)
Purdue (1992, 1993, 1994)
St. John's (1993)
Tennessee Tech (1994)
Tulane (1993)
Vanderbilt (1992)
Washington State (1994)
Western Michigan (1993)
Wisconsin (1992, 1994, 1995)

Biggest Win:
Jan. 9, 1993—Indiana 105, Penn State 57

Overtime Game:
Feb. 2, 1994—Indiana 87, Ohio State 83

Streak End:
Jan. 24, 1995—Michigan 65, Indiana 52

INDIANA

LEGEND *Alan Henderson*

ALL THE WAY BACK, AND THEN SOME

Alan Henderson's knee fits into the same place in IU basketball conjecture as Scott May's arm, Mike Woodson's back, and Randy Wittman's foot—if it hadn't been hurt, would there be more NCAA championship banners at Assembly Hall?

Henderson came back as strongly as the other three did, suggesting the answer is:

You bet there would.

Henderson played well as a junior, building toward his 41-point game at Michigan State the last week of the season and his 34-point NCAA tournament game against Ohio.

His senior year, as the leader of a freshman-filled 19-12 team, ranks with IU's all-time best. His 23.52 scoring average *is* the best in Bob Knight's 28 IU seasons—barely ahead of senior Scott May's 23.50, but ahead of that 1976 Player of the Year, and all other Knight Hoosiers.

In that senior year, Henderson scored 20 or more points 24 times, an IU record. In four years, he had 50 "double-doubles"—double figures in both points and rebounds in the same game. Against Minnesota his senior year he had 26 points and 20 rebounds.

One more game might have made Henderson IU's fifth 2,000-point scorer. He finished at 1,979.

He set IU's career rebounding record, his 1,091 topping by three the IU record Walt Bellamy had held for 34 years.

Henderson, Atlanta's first-round draft pick, had to surmount some more physical problems but became an outstanding player for the Hawks. In 1997-98, he won the NBA's award as Sixth Man of the Year. Then he signed a big contract and became a Hawks starter.

BIG TEN MEDAL - Erik Barrett & Michelle Venturella   **GIMBEL AWARD -** Brian Maisonneuve

ATHLETES OF THE YEAR - Brian Maisonneuve/Todd Yeagley & Michelle Venturella

BALFOUR AWARDS

Football, Troy Drake; Basketball, Alan Henderson; Baseball, Scott Mudd; Track, Mark Buse; Wrestling, Roger Chandler; Swimming, Brian Barnes; Cross Country, Darrell Hughes; Golf, Don Padgett III; Tennis, Erik Barrett; Soccer, Brian Maisonneuve.

ALINE ROBINSON AWARDS

Basketball, Emma Urzua; Volleyball, Michelle McElroy; Track, Phynice Kelley; Cross Country, Nikki Suever; Tennis, Holly Taylor; Golf, Nicole Hollingsworth; Swimming-Diving, Erica Quam; Softball, Michelle Venturella.

IUitem

PAIR OF ACES FOR YEAGLEY

Todd Yeagley and Brian Maisonneuve arrived in Indiana soccer at a fortunate time for them and IU. Yeagley's dad, Jerry, started five freshmen in the season opener. Yeagley had his first goal and Maisonneuve his first assist in that game, Maisonneuve his first goal in the second game. Both were victories.

A pattern had begun. The two stepped right in as leaders of teams that won and won and won—73 times over the next four years. One more would have been all they could have asked.

Brian Maisonneuve

The '94 Hoosiers lost to North Carolina 2-1 in their second game, then won 15 in a row to be No. 1. They lost at Cal State Fullerton, then swept to the Big Ten tournament title and included Fullerton among the four tournament victories that put them in the NCAA finals.

There, Virginia won, 1-0.

Yeagley, a second-team All-American his first three seasons, moved up to first team, as did Maisonneuve, a second-team pick in '93 and two-time Big Ten MVP. Yeagley was the Missouri Athletic Club's Player of the Year. Maisonneuve won IU's fifth Hermann Trophy. They, co-captains Brandon Ward and Mike Clark, and Jeff Bannister and Scott Coufal were All-Big Ten, the fourth time for Yeagley and Maisonneuve.

Soccer News named Yeagley Player of the Year. Maisonneuve was named to the U.S. Under-23 team, which led to his playing in the 1996 Olympics. Maisonneuve received a $5,000 NCAA post-graduate grant. Both Maisonneuve and Yeagley began careers with the Columbus team in the new American professional soccer league, Major League Soccer.

For Coach of the Year Jerry Yeagley, final-game disappointment was personal and profound, but he made a promise: "We'll be back, and I'll be back."

Todd Yeagley

Snapshot In Time

SMITH WITH ROOKIE ROYALTY

WHEN HIGH-SCORING Alex Smith of little Franklin County was named Indiana's first high school "Mr. Football," there were skeptics. Big stats, little school, the doubts ran. Indiana coach Bill Mallory trusted his own looks and liked the idea that Smith had gone to the State as both a wrestler and a sprinter.

Smith had an even bigger freshman year than Mallory hoped for.

The first freshman tailback/halfback to start an IU opener since George Taliaferro 49 years before, Smith popped Cincinnati for 152 yards in a nationally televised 28-3 victory.

He jumped that to 191 yards in a 35-14 victory over Miami of Ohio, then 221—fifth-best in IU history—as Kentucky fell, 59-29. He set a Big Ten freshman record with 232 yards in a 27-20 victory at Iowa, but the Hoosiers went to Purdue with four straight losses, their 5-1 start down to 5-5.

Smith broke for a 66-yard touchdown run in the first quarter and went on to reset his Big Ten record with 245 yards in a 33-29 Indiana victory.

That gave Smith 1,475 yards. Only two freshmen in college football history had topped that: Tony Dorsett and Herschel Walker. Right under Smith on that freshman yardage list are Marshall Faulk and Emmitt Smith. UPI named the state's first "Mr. Football" national Freshman of the Year.

IN THOSE DAYS . . .

'HAMMER' MAKES HIS MARK

At 6-2, 256, John Hammerstein was small only by family standards. Older brothers Mike and Mark were much bigger, which is why they got scholarships to Michigan and John didn't. Both older Hammersteins were Michigan stars, Mike a consensus All-American at defensive tackle in 1985.

Bill Mallory's sons Mike and Doug played with the older Hammersteins, and Mallory was happy to bring young John to Indiana. He got himself a solid defensive starter, and at the end of his junior year, the player Mallory called "Hammer" got something for himself that neither of those older brothers had received.

Hammerstein, carrying a 3.58 grade average in biology, was named first-team Academic All-American.

He was IU's first in 14 years and fifth in history, joining Brad Bomba (1956), Harry Gonso (1967), Glenn Scolnik (1972) and Kevin Speer (1980).

"John gets it done in the classroom and on the field," Mallory said. "You couldn't ask anyone to work harder. This is just terrific."

211

1995 1996

HOOSIER LIST

IU'S BIG TEN GOLF CHAMPIONS

Men

1964 Byron Comstock, 290

1969 Don Padgett, 290

1975 Bob Ackerman, 294

Gary Biddinger, 294

1984 Mike Ingram, 286

1991 Shaun Micheel, 276

Women

1986 Sarah DeKraay, 313

1987 Michele Redman, 297

1990 Shannon Hardesty, 298

1994 Erika Wicoff, 305

1995 Erika Wicoff, 292

1996 Erika Wicoff, 226

1998 Erin Carney, 299

1999 Erin Carney, 301

INDIANA LEGEND — *Erika Wicoff*

ALL-AMERICAN, TWICE

Even in the perennially outstanding IU women's golf program, Erika Wicoff made a strong case for ranking as the Hoosiers' best ever.

Wicoff, from Hartford City, was Big Ten Freshman of the Year in 1993 and then the league's Player of the Year—and conference meet medalist—each of the next three years, a Big Ten first.

In 1995, when her fourth-place 288 at the NCAA championships was the best 72-hole score ever for a Hoosier, Wicoff was the first IU player to be named first-team All-America. She repeated in 1996.

Along the way she won three Indiana Amateur championships and medalist honors at the U.S. Women's Amateur. She led the Hoosiers to two Big Ten championships and to a fifth-place NCAA finish in 1995, IU's highest ever. Her 73.9 stroke average in 1995 and 76.1 career average are IU records.

Wicoff's father introduced her to golf when she was 4. On the IU course that was to become home to her, she won her first of two State Junior championships before entering high school. Blackford County High School didn't have a girls' golf team so she played No. 2 on the boys' team. The next year, she and her younger sister, a freshman, found enough players to form a girls' team. Her senior year the team finished second in the State, and her last three seasons she placed third, second and second at the State.

After college, she qualified for and joined the women's pro tour— "my dream, ever since I was a little girl."

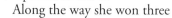
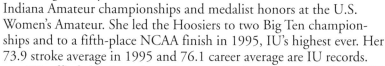

BIG TEN MEDAL - John Hammerstein & Gina Ugo **GIMBEL AWARD -** Sam Gasowski

ANITA ALDRICH AWARD - Kimiko Hirai

ATHLETES OF THE YEAR - Brian Evans & Erika Wicoff/Kimiko Hirai

ALINE ROBINSON AWARDS
Basketball, Lisa Furlin; Volleyball, Stacie Murr; Track, Stephanie Barnum; Cross Country, Stephanie Barnum; Tennis, Lizl Coetsee; Golf, Erika Wicoff; Swimming, Tracy Cook; Diving, Carrie Keckley; Softball, Kelli Brandt; Soccer, Merit Elzey

BALFOUR AWARDS
Football, Eric Smedley; Basketball, Brian Evans; Baseball, Matt Braughler; Track, Nathan Davis; Wrestling, Roger Chandler; Swimming, Sam Gasowski; Cross Country, Keith Ikard; Golf, Randy Leen; Tennis, Hayden Gibson; Soccer, George Crawford.

NCAA CHAMPIONS - Kimiko Hirai, 1-meter diving.

OLYMPIC MEDALISTS - Diving, Mark Lenzi, springboard, bronze.

212

IUitem

TARA MADE IU, U.S. PROUD

Tara VanDerveer played at IU (1973-75) and coached the 1996 U.S. Women's Basketball team to Olympic gold.

As an upstate New York middle-schooler, Tara VanDerveer was her high school boys' basketball team's Bear mascot, so her parents would have to take her to games. She almost got fired because she'd shed the Bear head and watch the game rather than perform.

At Indiana, she was a good player on a strong team, but that wasn't enough. She attended men's practices, too, and took notes on what coach Bob Knight taught with his great 1975 team.

Basketball and coaching, a blended priority in young Tara's life, took her to the top. Her Stanford teams won national championships in 1990 and '92.

The U.S. Olympic Basketball Committee asked her to coach the 1996 American team, with a new twist: She had to give up a Stanford season to coach a team-in-training, for the fall and winter season leading up to Atlanta.

VanDerveer's team went 52-0 against the best U.S. college teams and some international teams. Then at Atlanta, the team generally considered women's basketball's best ever blew through the field and clinched the gold with a 111-87 victory over Brazil.

VanDerveer, inducted into IU's Athletics Hall of Fame in 1995, always credited those hours at Knight's practices with influencing her coaching ideas. She kept Knight and Pete Newell as coaching confidantes. And after an early-round victory at Atlanta when her team took its opponent out of the game right away, VanDerveer said:

"We really put some good defensive pressure on them.

" . . . some good *Indiana* defense."

ATLANTA NOTICED HOOSIERS

BECAUSE COACHES (e.g., Tara VanDerveer) aren't given medals at the Olympic Games, diver Mark Lenzi's bronze was the only medal IU athletes took away from Atlanta.

But Hoosiers were prominent.

On opening night, Hobie Billingsley—unexcelled as a college diving coach, a two-time U.S. Olympic diving coach and, in his retirement, an Olympic diving official—was picked to take the Judges' Oath during the globally televised Opening Ceremonies.

Bob Kennedy and Jim Spivey, Hoosier middle distance stars in the Olympics together for the second time, ran for the U.S. in the 5,000 meters.

Kennedy, a second-time finalist and American recordholder in an event the U.S. has won just once, led early in the last lap but finished sixth in a crowded field. Kennedy called it "a positive thing for me (and) for American distance running—to be competitive and part of an Olympic 5,000 final again, not just out there."

Spivey, America's best at 1,500 meters through his peak years, made it through one round of 5,000-meter trials but had a grand career end with elimination in the semifinals.

Starting the last lap, Spivey said he told himself: "This is the last lap you'll probably ever run." Competively, it was.

After a year as an assistant at North Central College, he became the men's and women's track and cross country coach at the University of Chicago. His women's team placed sixth in the NCAA Division 3 cross country championships.

IN THOSE DAYS . . .

TRIO OF FIRSTS

• After filling in valuably as a freshman for the strong 1993 Hoosiers, Brian Evans was a leader on the next three IU basketball teams. As a senior, carrying a young team to a Big Ten-runnerup finish, he averaged 21.2 points a game—the league's MVP, a first-round NBA draft pick, and, with a 22.2 conference average, Bob Knight's first Big Ten scoring champion.

• Kimiko Hirai's 1996 NCAA one-meter diving championship was IU's first in swimming and diving. Jenny Dixon, a Hirai teammate in Jeff Huber's diving program, was the league's 1995 one-meter champion and 1997 Diver of the Year for winning one- and three-meter titles.

• Bob Morgan's IU baseball team won its last 13 games but lost the regular-season Big Ten championship to Penn State by a half-game. At State College, the Hoosiers—with All-Big Ten pitcher Dan Ferrell earning MVP with his first save in the championship game and league batting champion Matt Braughler helping out— won their first Big Ten Tournament title. IU won one game at Wichita, Kansas, in the NCAA tournament, before being eliminated.

1996 1997

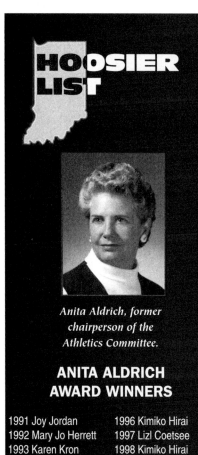

HOOSIER LIST

Anita Aldrich, former chairperson of the Athletics Committee.

ANITA ALDRICH AWARD WINNERS

1991 Joy Jordan
1992 Mary Jo Herrett
1993 Karen Kron
1994 Kris McGrade
1995 Stacy Quilling

1996 Kimiko Hirai
1997 Lizl Coetsee
1998 Kimiko Hirai
    Kelly Fitzgerald
1999 Zahra Ahamed
    Jessica Anderson

FIRST FEMALE RECIPIENTS OF OTHER ANNUAL AWARDS

Big Ten Medal
Karen Marinsek (1982)

Athlete of the Year
Denise Jackson (1983)

Aline Robinson Awards

1990
Zandrea Jefferies, basketball
Joy Jordan, volleyball
Jennifer Goldy, track
Michelle Dekkers, cross country
Gretchen Doninger, tennis
Debbie Lee, golf
Caroline Teskey, swimming
Marjorie Ledgerwood, softball

1996
Merit Elzey, soccer

INDIANA

LEGEND
Randy Leen

TAMED EVEN TIGER

Freshman Randy Leen finished eighth in the 1995 Big Ten golf championships and coach Sam Carmichael was impressed. "He has the capabilities to be exceptional—wonderful putter, just a great touch," Carmichael said.

The next three years, Leen was the Big Ten Player of the Year, the only three-time selection in the 12-year history of the award.

IU's team rose with Leen. Tenth in his freshman year, the Hoosiers finished third in 1996, with a fifth-place tournament finish from senior Don Padgett III, scion of one of Indiana's premier golfing families. In '97, Leen finished second in the Big Ten tournament, two strokes back, and Indiana placed fourth.

That year Leen shot 70-70-74-71 at the NCAA championships to finish 10th. His 72.0 average for the season set IU's record, and he was the sixth Hoosier to be named All-America.

His senior year, teammates Josh Brewer and Corey Sullivan edged him by two strokes at the Big Ten, sharing second with Leen fifth as the Hoosiers won their second league championship since 1975 and their seventh overall.

In the summer of 1996, Leen played with the best in golf at the U.S. Open. After an opening 77, he finished 71-70-73 for 291, the lowest amateur score. That helped put him on the U.S. Walker Cup team, and he contributed two points to America's 18-6 victory.

Caddying for him at the Open was Carmichael, a one-time tour player. And among the amateurs Leen beat was Tiger Woods—by three strokes, just before Woods turned pro.

BIG TEN MEDAL - Tom Lukawski & Mary Vajgrt   **GIMBEL AWARD -** Micah Nori

ATHLETES OF THE YEAR - Roger Chandler & Hilary Bruening
ALINE ROBINSON AWARDS
Basketball, Bridget Porter; Volleyball, Melissa Rooney; Track, Nathalie Belfort; Cross Country, Cassidy Wall; Tennis, Lizl Coetsee; Golf, Erin Carney; Swimming, Charnele Kennedy; Diving, Jennifer Dixon; Softball, Katrina Valencia; Soccer, Jennifer Cantwell.

BALFOUR AWARDS
Football, Jamie Baisley; Basketball, Haris Mujezinovic; Baseball, Ryan Dillon; Track, Nathan Davis; Wrestling, Roger Chandler; Swimming-Diving, Greg Ruminski; Cross Country, Matt Sparks; Golf, Randy Leen; Tennis, Kevin Gabel; Soccer, Scott Coufal.

214

IU item

CAMERON REPLACES MALLORY

Cam Cameron is IU's 24th football coach.

B ill Mallory, whose 13 seasons and six bowl trips represented the longest and most successful IU football coaching tenure since Bo McMillin's, was notified in mid-year that 1996 was his last season.

It was a painful 3-8 year, but the Hoosiers—with 164 yards and two touchdowns from Alex Smith in his last college game—closed it out with an emotional 33-16 victory at Purdue.

Three days later, Washington Redskins quarterback coach Cam Cameron signed a seven-year contract—IU's 24th football coach and first alumnus coach in the 20th century.

At Terre Haute South High, Cameron was an All-State quarterback and a starter on three straight Final Four basketball teams—the Trester Award winner in 1979. He signed a football scholarship at Indiana, but when the football season ended each fall he joined the basketball team and lettered in both sports in 1981-82, '82-83 and '83-84.

Basketball coach Bob Knight's friendship with Michigan football coach Bo Schembechler led to a graduate assistant's spot for Cameron, who a season later was on Schembechler's full-time staff. His nine seasons as a Michigan assistant included six Big Ten championships or co-championships and five Rose Bowl trips. Cameron had been on Norv Turner's Redskins staff for three years when the Indiana offer came.

Cameron's exposure to coaches and coaching styles included—in addition to Knight, Schembechler and Turner—his two IU coaches, Lee Corso (1979-82) and Sam Wyche (1983). It went deeper. His stepfather, Tom Harp, was head coach at Cornell and Duke in Cameron's boyhood days.

BELL BRINGS NCAA TO IU

SAM BELL, a year before his retirement as IU's track coach, began his own grand finale by bringing the NCAA men's and women's outdoor track and field championships to IU.

Bell sold Bloomington to the NCAA sites committee, then had to get a multi-million-dollar spruce-up to IU's Billy Hayes Track financed and completed in time. It was close, but by the June 4-7 event, Hayes Track and the full Robert C. Haugh Complex around it were gleaming—Bell's last enormous contribution to IU track (and a considerable one, too, from Haugh, whose $1.5-million gift enabled the renovation).

Arkansas and LSU extended long reigns in winning the men's and women's titles.

Indiana's women scored two points, on eighth-place finishes by high jumper Nathalie Belfort and javelin thrower Mateja Bezjak. Intermediate hurdler Tom Chorny (ninth) placed highest for the men, who did have an "almost" champion.

High hurdles winner Reggie Torian of Wisconsin was coached in high school by IU's first seven-foot high jumper, Gary Haupert of Northfield. Haupert pointed the hurdler-long jumper (and football wideout) toward Indiana, but IU's math requirements caused a problem.

"I wanted to follow (Haupert's) footsteps," Torian said after his championship, "but it didn't work out."

HOOSIER LIST

IU RADIO: ENBERG TO FISCHER

Dick Yoakam remembers when Indiana University decided to set up a football and basketball radio broadcasting network with student announcers in the early 1960s.

Don Fischer

"Elmer Sulzer was the director of broadcasting and I was an assistant professor in journalism and radio and TV," Yoakam said. "About ten students responded to a *Daily Student* ad. We had tryouts at a football scrimmage."

The first to try was Dick Enberg. "After hearing him for about five minutes, most of the rest of them left," Yoakam said. Enberg, a graduate student in physical education, went from that start to become one of sports broadcasting's brightest stars.

Other students working for the network included Phil Jones (who advanced to White House correspondent for CBS), John Gutowsky (a major league play-by-play man, as John Gordon), and Pat Williams (better known as an NBA general manager with Philadelphia and Orlando).

Among others:

Sam Taylor   Bill Cameron
Ernie Nims   Bill Orwig Jr.

Beginning with the Rose Bowl football season, 1967-68, Max Skirvin was IU's network "voice," with student assistants. In 1973-74, Don Fischer was brought in as the network's chief announcer, teamed with Skirvin for 24 years.

Fischer's acclaim goes beyond IU's fandom. He has been honored more than twenty times as Indiana's Sportscaster of the Year.

LEGEND *Sam Carmichael*

DOUBLE VICTORY IN LAST CHANCE

In 1990, Sam Carmichael became men's golf coach at IU in addition to the women's coaching role he'd had since 1981. He announced early that 1998 would be his last year of double-duty.

His teams sent him out with something they hadn't managed before: a double championship.

The Hoosier women got the double started by setting a league record with 1,196 for a 13-stroke margin over runnerup Ohio State at Penn State. Co-medalist Erin Carney, third-place finisher Jenny Gray and fourth-place finisher Jennifer Seger came in at 299, 300 and 301, and the fourth counting Hoosier, Michelle Hatfield, shared 12th at 305. All four made All-Big Ten.

The next weekend at Michigan State, the Hoosier men took the lead during the second round and packed three players into the top five at the finish for a three-stroke victory over Ohio State. Randy Leen—fifth in the tournament but the league's Player of the Year for a third time—and Josh Brewer made All-Big Ten. Brewer and teammate Corey Sullivan shared second place in the tournament.

Carmichael was Coach of the Year in both—for the second time in men's golf and a seventh time in women's.

Carmichael grew up in Martinsville. He played high school basketball for the Artesians, but he was better known around the state as a golfer. He played golf in college at Louisiana State, on an SEC championship team in 1960. He won all three major men's tournaments in Indiana—Junior, Amateur and Open. He played on the professional tour seven years. In 1973, he was inducted into the Indiana Golf Hall of Fame.

BIG TEN MEDAL - Rob Iglinski & Jennifer Gray   **GIMBEL AWARD -** Andrew Held

ATHLETES OF THE YEAR - Randy Leen & Erin Carney

ALINE ROBINSON AWARDS
Basketball, Quacy Barnes; Volleyball, Julie Flatley; Track, Mateja Bezjak; Cross Country, Amber Macy; Tennis, Correne Stout; Golf, Erin Carney; Swimming, Laurie Kerns; Diving, Kimiko Hirai; Softball, Monica Armendarez; Soccer, Wendy Dillinger; Water Polo, Meredith Cravens.

BALFOUR AWARDS
Football, Joey Eloms; Basketball, Charlie Miller; Baseball, Kyle Boyd; Track, Tom Chorny; Wrestling, Jason DeVries; Swimming-Diving, Michael Collier; Cross Country, Marius Bakken; Golf, Randy Leen; Tennis, Andrew Held; Soccer, Caleb Porter.

IU item

Wally Ogunleye—All-Big Ten in 1997, second-team in 1998.

A PASSING FANCY

Cam Cameron's first coaching victory made a splash in the IU record book. After the Hoosiers lost 23-6 at North Carolina in their opener, they dropped four second-half scoring bombs on Ball State and won 33-6 under the lights at Memorial Stadium.

Quarterback Jay Rodgers hit 27 of 39 passes for an IU-record 408 yards and five touchdowns.

The Hoosiers completed just one touchdown pass the rest of the season. Five straight losses to ranked teams sent them plunging to a 2-9 season that included Cameron's first Big Ten victory: 23-6 over Illinois at IU.

The record was not atypical of first-year IU coaches. Cameron's immediate predecessors had gone: Bill Mallory, 1984, 0-11; Sam Wyche, 1983, 3-8; Lee Corso, 1973, 2-9; John Pont, 1964, 2-8; Phil Dickens, 1958, 5-3-1 (although in the first year of the Dickens' regime, 1957, when Dickens was under Big Ten suspension and assistant Bob Hicks was interim coach, the record was 1-8); Bernie Crimmins, 1952, 2-8, and Clyde Smith, 1948, 2-7.

Sophomore defensive end Adewale Ogunleye was the team's standout. Ogunleye, 6-5 and 260 from Staten Island, N.Y., was credited with 10 sacks and 21 tackles for loss. Big Ten coaches named him first-team All-Conference.

Snapshot In Time

QUACY HOOSIERS' FIRST PRO

QUACY BARNES represented something new in Indiana women's basketball.

A 6-foot-5 center from Benton Harbor, Mich., Barnes on April 30, 1998, became the first Hoosier drafted by a women's professional league. The 22nd player taken in the WNBA draft, she signed and played with the Sacramento Monarchs.

Barnes had an outstanding senior season. She was named to the coaches' All-Big Ten team after leading the 21-12 Hoosiers in points (583, a 17.7 average), rebounds (212, 6.4 a game) and blocked shots (60—down from her school-record 95 her junior year when she led the Big Ten and ranked sixth in the nation). She has IU's career record with 269 blocks.

When she scored 29 points in an 83-75 victory at Michigan State February 22, 1998, she hit 12 of 13 shots, setting IU's one-game shooting-percentage record. Barnes' 165 free throws and 242 free-throw attempts her senior season also are IU records.

Barnes graduated with 1,428 points for her four seasons. That ranks her seventh on an IU career list headed by Denise Jackson, who in 1983 was the first recipient of IU's women's Athlete of the Year Award. Jackson, from 1981 through '84, scored 1,917 points.

Quacy Barnes is IU's first women's professional basketball player.

HOOSIER LIST

LIN LORING'S
ALL-BIG TEN SELECTIONS

Heather Crowe, 1981, 82, 83

Tina McCall, 1981

Bev Ramser, 1981, 82

Jenny Snyder, 1981, 82, 83

Tracy Hoffman, 1982, 83, 84, 85

Anne Hutchens, 1982, 83, 85

Diane McCormick, 1982, 83

Wendy Allen, 1984, 85, 86

Janey Strause, 1984

Reka Monoki, 1985, 86, 87

Janet McCutcheon, 1986, 87

Kelly Mulvihill, 1986, 87, 88, 89

Jane Paulson, 1986

Angela Farley, 1987

Candy Kopetzki, 1987, 88, 89, 90

Gretchen Doninger, 1988, 90

Shawn Foltz, 1988, 89

Stephanie Reece, 1989, 90, 91, 92

Deborah Edelman, 1990, 91, 92, 93

Jody Yin, 1991, 92, 93, 94

Susie Starrett, 1992

Rachel Epstein, 1993, 94, 95

Holly Taylor, 1995

Natasha Joshi, 1996

Lizl Coetsee, 1997

Megan McCarney, 1997

Correne Stout, 1998

Jessica Anderson, 1999

INDIANA LEGEND

1998 Soccer Champions

PERFECT ANSWER TO '97 PAIN

In 1997 they did what no other Indiana soccer team had ever done: they took a perfect record into the NCAA Final Four. There, in the semifinals, in three overtimes, they lost to eventual champion UCLA, 1-0. "So painful," Indiana coach Jerry Yeagley called that loss.

Back from that team came Lazo Alavanja, a "Hoosier Hoosier" from Lake Central who as a senior was to make first-team All-America, win his second Big Ten Player of the Year award and be named IU's male Athlete of the Year.

Back also were Aleksey Korol, Dema Kovalenko and Yuri Lavrinenko—Americans since age 14, Ukrainians when they were born within an 18-week period in mid-1977. They were teammates for the Dynamo Kiev youth club when it came to the U.S. to play and, by pre-arrangement, 10 of the team's players stayed on in Rochester, N.Y. The three future Hoosiers excelled for different Rochester high schools. Kovalenko signed to go to Indiana. Korol and Lavrinenko followed.

The four were the heart of the great '97 team—and of the team that went a step farther and won the 1998 national championship. Others also were keys: among them back Nick Garcia, the Defensive MVP of the finals; backs Andrew Parrish and Gino DiGuardi, who made the All-Final Four team, and goalkeeper T.J. Hannig.

This 22-2 team dominated the Final Four as no recent team has. IU throttled Santa Clara, 4-0—Hannig didn't have to make even one save. Korol, who had both goals in a 2-0 quarterfinal victory over Clemson, had two more, Kovalenko and Garcia the others.

The Hoosiers were almost as dominant in their 3-1 finals victory over Stanford. In the game's seventh minute, Kovalenko scored on an assist from Lavrinenko. By halftime, Lavrinenko and Korol also had scored, around Stanford's lone goal. The last half was a scoreless, 45-minute countdown to the championship-at-last for what St. Louis coach Bob Warming called "probably the greatest team ever assembled in the history of college soccer."

"We may have been the best," Yeagley said. "Maybe some days this year we weren't. Today we're champions."

Lazo Alavanja   *Aleksey Korol*   *Dema Kovalenko*   *Yuri Lavrinenko*

Front Row (left to right): Aleksey Korol, Yuri Lavrinenko, Tommy Keenan, Simon Deery, Colin Rogers, T.J. Hannig, Tony Cerroni, Gino DiGuardi, Lazo Alavanja, Andrew Parrish, Dema Kovalenko. Second Row: Coach Jerry Yeagley, Assistant Coach Mike Freitag, John Swann, Ryan Mack, B.J. Snow, Nick Garcia, Jason Jorgensen, Tyler Hawley, Ryan Hammer, Matt Fundenberger, Dennis Fadeski, Justin Tauber, Eric Ripley, Assistant Coach Ernie Yarborough, Assistant Coach John Trask.

Bloomington *Herald-Times* photo

Hoosiers whoop it up after winning IU's fourth NCAA soccer championship.

Coach Jerry Yeagley and son, Todd, after the championship win. Father and son were denied the title in 1994.

BIG TEN MEDAL

Bryan Holcomb & Melissa Rooney

GIMBEL AWARD

Mike Collier

ATHLETES OF THE YEAR

Lazo Alavanja/Mike Collier & Erin Carney

ALINE ROBINSON AWARDS

Basketball, Cindy Kerns; Volleyball, Jennifer Magelssen; Track, Cori McLeod; Cross Country, None; Tennis, Jessica Anderson; Golf, Michelle Hatfield; Diving, Erin Quinn; Softball, Khara Good; Soccer, Jennifer Cantwell; Water Polo, Kara Fellerhoff

BALFOUR AWARDS

Football, Chris Gall; Basketball, A.J. Guyton; Baseball, Jason Torres; Track, Tom Chorny; Wrestling, Victor Sveda; Swimming-Diving, Tom Davis; Cross Country, Aaron Gillen; Golf, John Barry; Tennis, George McGill; Soccer, Dema Kovalenko.

NCAA CHAMPION

TEAM, Soccer (Jerry Yeagley)

IUitem

ANTWAAN'S DEBUT DAZZLING

Antwaan Randle El set a new IU total offense record with 467 yards in his first collegiate game.

Opening night of the 1998 football season, freshman quarterback Antwaan Randle El introduced himself to IU history.

Before halftime.

Against Western Michigan, Randle El opened as director of an option attack that swept downfield immediately to a touchdown, scoring from the 10 himself on a keeper. Next possession, coach Cam Cameron shelved the option and Randle El imitated John Elway. He completed his first college passing attempt. And his second—his first 13, actually, two for touchdowns. And he popped loose for another 18-yard TD run as IU led at halftime, 31-14.

By then, halfway through his first college game, Randle El had 52 rushing yards and 220 passing—the 272 yards of total offense already 17th-best in IU history. For a full game.

He finished with 385 yards and three touchdowns passing (22-for-29, no interceptions), 82 rushing yards and three touchdowns, and IU's one-game total-offense record.

And his team was successful, too, winning 45-30.

Randle El was Big Ten Freshman of the Year. Then he played basketball, and would have played lots more than he did except the body that took poundings by the dozen in each football game gave in twice to basketball plays that cracked hand bones.

He was fine again by spring football. So was Cameron.

Snapshot In Time

CARNEY KEEPS IT GOING

THE IU CAREERS of Erin Carney and Erika Wicoff overlapped with the Hoosiers' 1996 Big Ten championship season.

Freshman Carney contributed to that title, but she was a much bigger part of Hoosier accomplishments to come.

Carney, from LaCrosse, Wisconsin, was the Big Ten medalist in 1998 and '99, leading the '98 team to another league championship. She finished 20th in the NCAA tournament, helping the team to 13th place, and she joined Wicoff as IU's only first-team All-Americans. Her 74.7 stroke average ranked behind only Wicoff's best year—1995, when as a junior she averaged 73.9 in her first of two All-America years.

Carney's 75.2 average as a senior gave her second and third on IU's all-time list. She won the Big Ten medal by three strokes, but the team finished second.

Wicoff was the first golfer named IU's women's Athlete of the Year, sharing the honor with NCAA diving champion Kimiko Hirai in 1996. Carney was the first golfer to win the award outright, and when she repeated in '99, she became just the third two-time winner—with NCAA cross country champion Michelle Dekkers (the 1989 and '90 winner) and All-America diver Kristen Kane (1994 and '96).

Erin Carney, Big Ten Player-of-the-Year in 1998 and 1999.

IN THOSE DAYS . . .

COLLIER, CUPPERS AND A.J.

• Lazo Alavanja (soccer) and Mike Collier (diving) shared IU's male Athlete of the Year Award—Collier the first diver to win it. Also IU's Gimbel Award winner, Collier was named to the U.S. World University Games team. Placing in the top eight on all three boards made him All-America.

• Ex-Hoosiers Brian Maisonneuve and Chad Deering started side-by-side in midfield for the U.S. in its 1998 World Cup opener against Germany. Maisonneuve had led U.S. scoring in the Atlanta Olympics. Another Hoosier, Juergen Sommer, was a goalkeeper on the 1994 and '98 U.S. World Cup teams.

• A.J. Guyton—officially Arthur James Guyton III—as a sophomore in 1997-98 hit a 3-point shot in every game, an IU basketball first. Guyton's streak, bridging three seasons, reached 39 games before he went 0-for-4 against Syracuse. Ten days later Guyton missed his first eight 3s against Temple, then in the last minute hit two—one to tie, the second to win in the last five seconds, 63-62. His long, high 3 sent a game at Penn State into overtime and he won it with another in the second overtime, 98-95—the highest losing score for an opponent in Bob Knight's 28 seasons.

Year-by-Year Summaries

Baseball

Year	Overall Record	Big Ten Record	Big Ten Finish
1896	6-5	--	--
1897	5-3	--	--
1898	3-1	--	--
1899	7-6	--	--
1900	3-2	--	--
1901	3-3	--	--
1902	6-10	--	--
1903	7-5	--	--
1904	11-5	--	--
1905	11-11	--	--
1906	6-11-1	1-5	6th-T
1907	9-5	2-1	3rd
1908	7-9	2-5	6th
1909	10-5	1-5	6th
1910	5-3	4-3	3rd
1911	7-7	3-3	5th
1912	5-9	0-8	7th
1913	11-4	6-3	3rd
1914	6-6	4-5	5th
1915	1-7	1-7	9th
1916	8-4	4-3	3rd
1917	5-9-1	5-4	3rd
1918	9-7	0-5	8th
1919	10-9-1	2-5	6th
1920	7-7	3-6	5th
1921	10-15	5-7	5th-T
1922	1-2	1-2	8th
1923	3-11	2-6	9th
1924	8-12-1	4-5	7th
1925	**11-6**	**9-2**	**1st**
1926	6-9	3-6	8th
1927	7-13-3	4-8	9th
1928	11-4	5-4	5th
1929	11-6-1	4-6	7th-T
1930	10-10	6-4	3rd
1931	12-6-1	4-4	7th
1932	**13-2**	**6-2**	**1st**
1933	16-3	3-2	4th-T
1934	20-5-1	6-3	2nd
1935	10-9-1	4-6	7th
1936	15-7	6-3	4th
1937	20-6	8-2	2nd

Year	Overall Record	Big Ten Record	Big Ten Finish
1938	**14-7-1**	**7-3**	**1st-T**
1939	15-4	7-3	2nd
1940	11-8	3-5	7th
1941	15-8	7-5	4th-T
1942	12-10	5-7	5th-T
1943	4-1	0-0	--
1944	8-13	2-8	9th
1945	14-7-1	5-4-1	3rd
1946	13-5	5-3	5th
1947	12-8	4-6	7th
1948	14-10	3-9	8th
1949	**18-5**	**8-4**	**1st-T**
1950	11-12	4-4	7th
1951	16-10-1	6-4-1	3rd
1952	7-19	1-13	10th
1953	4-16	0-11	10th
1954	12-14	4-9	8th
1955	16-11	3-10	9th-T
1956	14-15	5-6	6th
1957	13-15	3-10	10th
1958	17-15	7-8	6th-T
1959	18-13	8-7	4th-T
1960	17-13	5-9	9th
1961	21-5-1	11-3	3rd
1962	16-13	6-8	5th
1963	15-14	4-10	10th
1964	23-12	7-8	7th-T
1965	20-15	6-7	6th
1966	17-15-1	6-5	5th
1967	14-23	6-12	8th
1968	19-12	5-8	7th
1969	18-14	8-4	4th
1970	18-23	7-11	8th
1971	13-24	5-11	8th-T
1972	11-24	2-13	10th
1973	20-16	8-10	7th-T
1974	19-21	8-7	5th
1975	22-24	7-11	7th
1976	23-17	10-7	3rd
1977	21-26	4-14	9th
1978	20-23	5-8	7th
1979	11-28	3-13	9th
1980	17-25	6-10	6th-T
1981	23-25-1	5-9	5th*

Year	Overall Record	Big Ten Record	Big Ten Finish
1982	24-29	2-14	5th*
1983	26-21	6-7	3rd*
1984	44-20	6-9	4th*
1985	57-19	8-8	2nd-T*
1986	43-17	7-9	3rd-T*
1987	43-17	7-9	3rd*
1988	39-19	11-17	8th
1989	34-26	5-23	10th
1990	30-27-1	14-14	5th-T
1991	38-23-1	15-12	3rd
1992	35-20	14-14	5th
1993	38-21	15-12	4th
1994	33-23	12-16	7th-T
1995	33-23	12-16	8th-T
1996	**43-18**	**18-8**	**2nd****
1997	33-22	8-16	8th
1998	29-27	14-14	5th
1999	37-17	14-14	5th

*Eastern Division **Won Big Ten Tournament

Field Hockey

Year	Overall Record	Big Ten Record	Big Ten Finish
1978	13-10-4		2nd
1979	9-15-1		3rd
1980	12-10-3		6th
1981	14-13		4th

Football

Year	Overall Record	Big Ten Record	Big Ten Finish	Bowl
1887	0-1-0	0-0-0	--	
1888	0-0-1	0-0-0	--	
1889	0-1-0	0-0-0	--	
1890	0-0-0	0-0-0	--	
1891	1-5-0	0-0-0	--	
1892	2-2-0	0-0-0	--	
1893	1-4-1	0-0-0	--	
1894	0-4-0	0-0-0	--	
1895	4-3-1	0-0-0	--	
1896	6-2-0	0-0-0	--	

Football

Year	Overall Record	Big Ten Record	Big Ten Finish	Bowl
1901	6-3-0	1-2-0	6th	
1902	3-5-1	0-4-0	7th-T	
1903	4-4-0	1-2-0	6th	
1904	6-4-0	0-3-0	7th-T	
1905	8-1-1	0-1-1	6th-T	
1906	4-2-0	0-2-0	6th-T	
1907	2-3-1	0-3-0	5th-T	
1908	3-4-0	1-3-0	4th-T	
1909	4-3-0	1-3-0	5th-T	
1910	6-1-0	3-1-0	3rd	
1911	3-3-1	0-3-1	8th	
1912	2-5-0	0-5-0	8th	
1913	3-4-0	2-4-0	6th-T	
1914	3-4-0	1-4-0	8th	
1915	3-3-1	1-3-0	8th	
1916	2-4-1	0-3-1	8th-T	
1917	5-2-0	1-2-0	7th	
1918	2-2-0	0-0-0	8th-T	
1919	3-4-0	0-2-0	9th-T	
1920	5-2-0	3-1-0	3rd	
1921	3-4-0	1-2-0	6th-T	
1922	1-4-2	0-2-1	9th-T	
1923	3-4-0	2-2-0	5th-T	
1924	4-4-0	1-3-0	7th-T	
1925	3-4-1	0-3-1	9th-T	
1926	3-5-0	0-4-0	8th-T	
1927	3-4-1	1-2-1	8th	
1928	4-4-0	2-4-0	9th	
1929	2-6-1	1-3-1	8th-T	
1930	2-5-1	1-3-0	6th-T	
1931	4-5-1	3-4-1	7th-T	
1932	3-4-1	1-4-1	9th	
1933	1-5-2	0-3-2	8th-T	
1934	3-3-2	1-3-1	8th-T	
1935	4-3-1	2-2-1	3rd-T	
1936	5-2-1	3-1-1	4th-T	
1937	5-3-0	3-2-0	3rd	
1938	1-6-1	1-4-1	9th	
1939	2-4-2	2-3-0	7th-T	
1940	3-5-0	2-3-0	6th-T	
1941	2-6-0	1-3-1	7th-T	
1942	7-3-0	2-2-0	5th-T	
1943	4-4-2	2-3-1	4th-T	
1944	7-3-0	4-3-0	5th	
1945	**9-0-1**	**5-0-1**	**1st**	
1946	6-3-0	4-2-0	3rd	
1947	5-3-1	2-3-1	6th-T	
1948	2-7-0	2-4-0	5th-T	
1949	1-8-1	0-6-0	9th	
1950	3-5-1	1-4-0	8th-T	
1951	2-7-0	1-5-0	8th	
1952	2-7-0	1-5-0	9th	
1953	2-7-0	1-5-0	9th	
1954	3-6-0	2-4-0	7th	
1955	3-6-0	1-5-0	9th	
1956	3-6-0	1-5-0	10th	
1957	1-8-0	0-6-0	9th-T	
1958	5-3-1	3-2-1	5th	
1959	4-4-1	2-4-1	8th-T	
1960	1-8-0	0-0-0*		
1961	2-7-0	0-6-0	9th-T	
1962	3-6-0	1-5-0	9th	
1963	3-6-0	1-5-0	10th	
1964	2-7-0	1-5-0	9th-T	
1965	2-8-0	1-6-0	9th	
1966	1-8-1	1-5-1	9th	
1967	**9-2-0**	**6-1-0**	**1st-T**	**Rose**
1968	6-4-0	4-3-0	5th-T	
1969	4-6-0	3-4-0	5th-T	
1970	1-9-0	1-6-0	9th-T	
1971	3-8-0	2-6-0	9th	
1972	5-6-0	3-5-0	6th-T	
1973	2-9-0	0-8-0	9th-T	
1974	1-10-0	1-7-0	10th	
1975	2-8-1	1-6-1	10th	
1976	5-6-0	4-4-0	3rd-T	
1977	5-5-1	4-3-1	4th	
1978	4-7-0	3-5-0	7th	
1979	8-4-0	5-3-0	4th	Holiday
1980	6-5-0	3-5-0	6th	
1981	3-8-0	3-6-0	8th	
1982	5-6-0	4-5-0	6th	
1983	3-8-0	2-7-0	8th-T	
1984	0-11-0	0-9-0	10th	
1985	4-7-0	1-7-0	9th-T	
1986	6-6-0	3-5-0	6th-T	All-American
1987	8-4-0	6-2-0	2nd-T	Peach
1988	8-3-1	5-3-0	5th	Liberty
1989	5-6-0	3-5-0	6th	
1990	6-5-1	3-4-1	7th	Peach
1991	7-4-1	5-3-0	3rd-T	Copper
1992	5-6-0	3-5-0	6th	
1993	8-4-0	5-3-0	4th-T	Independence
1994	7-4-0	4-4-0	6th-T	
1995	2-9-0	0-8-0	11th	
1996	3-8-0	1-7-0	9th-T	
1997	2-9-0	1-7-0	9th-T	
1998	4-7-0	2-6-0	7th-T	

*Games not counted in Big Ten standings

Men's Basketball

Year	Overall Record	Big Ten Record	Big Ten Finish	NCAA Tourney
1901	1-4	0-2		
1902	4-4	0-2		
1903	8-4	0-2		
1904	5-4	0-2		
1905	5-12	1-1		
1906	7-9	2-2	3rd	
1907	9-5	0-0	--	
1908	9-6	2-4	6th	
1909	5-9	2-6	6th	
1910	5-8	3-7	7th	
1911	11-5	5-5	7th	
1912	6-11	1-9	6th	
1913	5-11	0-10	9th	
1914	2-12	1-11	9th	
1915	4-9	1-9	9th	
1916	6-7	3-5	5th	
1917	13-6	3-5	5th	
1918	10-4	3-3	6th	
1919	10-7	4-6	6th	
1920	13-8	6-4	4th	
1921	15-6	6-5	6th-T	
1922	10-10	3-7	9th	
1923	8-7	5-7	7th	
1924	11-6	7-5	6th-T	
1925	12-5	8-4	2nd-T	
1926	**12-5**	**8-4**	**1st-T**	
1927	13-4	9-3	2nd	
1928	**15-2**	**10-2**	**1st-T**	
1929	7-10	4-8	8th	
1930	8-9	7-5	4th	
1931	9-8	5-7	6th	
1932	8-10	4-8	7th	
1933	10-8	6-6	6th	
1934	13-7	6-6	5th-T	
1935	14-6	8-4	4th-T	
1936	**18-2**	**11-1**	**1st-T**	
1937	13-7	6-6	6th-T	
1938	10-10	4-8	8th	
1939	17-3	9-3	2nd	
1940	**20-3**	**9-3**	**2nd**	**Champion**
1941	17-3	10-2	2nd-T	
1942	15-6	10-5	2nd	
1943	18-2	11-2	2nd	
1944	7-15	2-10	8th-T	
1945	10-11	3-9	9th	
1946	18-3	9-3	2nd	
1947	12-8	8-4	2nd	
1948	8-12	3-9	8th-T	
1949	14-8	6-6	4th-T	
1950	17-5	7-5	3rd-T	
1951	19-3	12-2	2nd	
1952	16-6	9-5	4th	
1953	**23-2**	**17-1**	**1st**	**Champion**
1954	**20-4**	**12-2**	**1st**	**Final 16**
1955	8-14	5-9	6th-T	
1956	13-9	6-8	6th-T	
1957	**14-8**	**10-4**	**1st-T**	**Final 16**
1958	**13-11**	**10-4**	**1st**	**Final 16**
1959	11-11	7-7	5th-T	
1960	20-4	11-3	2nd	
1961	15-9	8-6	4th-T	
1962	13-11	7-7	4th	
1963	13-11	9-5	3rd	
1964	9-15	5-9	8th	
1965	19-5	9-5	4th	
1966	8-16	4-10	9th-T	
1967	**18-8**	**10-4**	**1st-T**	**Final 16**
1968	10-14	4-10	9th-T	
1969	9-15	4-10	10th	
1970	7-17	3-11	10th	
1971	17-7	9-5	4th	
1972	17-8	9-5	3rd-T	
1973	**22-6**	**11-3**	**1st**	**Final 4**
1974	**23-5**	**12-2**	**1st-T**	
1975	**31-1**	**18-0**	**1st**	**Final 8**
1976	**32-0**	**18-0**	**1st**	**Champion**
1977	16-11	11-7	5th	
1978	21-8	12-6	2nd	
1979	22-12	10-8	5th	
1980	**21-8**	**13-5**	**1st**	**Final 16**
1981	**26-9**	**14-4**	**1st**	**Champion**
1982	19-10	12-6	2nd	
1983	**24-6**	**13-5**	**1st**	**Final 16**
1984	**22-9**	**13-5**	**3rd**	**Final 8**
1985	19-14	7-11	7th	
1986	21-8	13-5	2nd	
1987	**30-4**	**15-3**	**1st-T**	**Champion**
1988	19-10	11-7	5th	
1989	**27-8**	**15-3**	**1st**	**Final 16**

Year	Overall Record	Big Ten Record	Big Ten Finish	NCAA Tourney
1990	18-11	8-10	7th	
1991	**29-5**	**15-3**	**1st**	**Final 16**
1992	**27-7**	**14-4**	**2nd**	**Final 4**
1993	**31-4**	**17-1**	**1st**	**Final 8**
1994	**21-9**	**12-6**	**3rd**	**Final 16**
1995	19-12	11-7	3rd-T	
1996	19-12	12-6	2nd-T	
1997	22-11	9-9	6th-T	
1998	20-12	9-7	5th-T	
1999	23-11	9-7	3rd-T	

Men's Cross Country

Year	Overall Record	Big Ten Record	Big Ten Finish
1928			**1st**
1929	**5-0**	**3-0**	**1st**
1930	**4-0**	**3-0**	**1st**
1931	**3-0**	**3-0**	**1st**
1932	**2-0**	**1-0**	**1st**
1933	5-1	2-1	--
1934	4-1	2-1	--
1935	2-0	2-0	--
1936	4-0	3-0	--
1937	4-0	3-0	--
1938	**3-1**	**2-1**	**1st***
1939	4-1	3-1	2nd*
1940	**4-0**	**4-0**	**1st***
1941	2-2	2-2	2nd
1942	**2-0**	**2-0**	**1st****
1943	1-1	1-1	2nd
1944	4-0	3-0	2nd
1945	3-1	3-1	5th
1946	**7-0**	**5-0**	**1st-T**
1947	1-1-1	1-1	3rd-T
1948	2-1	1-1	4th
1949	3-0	2-0	3rd
1950	4-0	3-0	3rd
1951	3-0	2-0	4th
1952	5-0	0-0	2nd
1953	3-0	0-0	2nd
1954	2-1	0-0	4th
1955	2-1	0-0	4th
1956	3-1	0-0	3rd
1957	3-1	0-0	4th
1958	2-2	0-0	3rd
1959	2-1-1	0-0	4th
1960	4-1	0-1	3rd
1961	3-1	0-0	3rd
1962	1-4	0-2	6th
1963	2-3	0-1	4th
1964	3-6	1-2	5th
1965	2-6	1-2	8th
1966	1-6	1-4	5th-T
1967	**6-4-1**	**6-0-1**	**1st**
1968	5-2	2-1	5th
1969	5-3	2-3	6th
1970	5-1	2-1	3rd
1971	9-0	2-0	2nd
1972	**6-3**	**1-0**	**1st**
1973	**7-0-1**	**0-0-1**	**1st**
1974	1-6	0-3	7th
1975	5-1	2-0	3rd
1976	3-1	1-0	7th
1977	3-1	1-1	5th

Year	Overall Record	Big Ten Record	Big Ten Finish
1978	3-1	1-1	4th
1979	1-1	0-1	2nd
1980	**0-0**	**0-0**	**1st-T**
1981	0-0	0-0	5th
1982	0-0	0-0	6th
1983	0-0	0-0	5th
1984	0-0	0-0	5th
1985	0-0	0-0	7th
1986	0-0	0-0	3rd
1987	0-0	0-0	3rd
1988	0-0	0-0	6th
1989	1-1	0-0	7th
1990	0-0	0-0	6th
1991	0-0	0-0	8th
1992	0-0	0-0	5th
1993	0-0	0-0	5th
1994	0-0	0-0	5th
1995	0-0	0-0	5th
1996	0-0	0-0	8th
1997	0-0	0-0	8th
1998	0-0	0-0	10th

*NCAA champion **NCAA co-champion

Men's Golf

Year	Overall Record	Big Ten Record	Big Ten Finish
1926	3-2	0-2	--
1930	7-1	3-1	6th
1931	6-2	1-2	--
1932	4-4	0-3	--
1933	3-1	2-1	7th
1934	4-3	1-2	8th
1935	2-4	0-4	8th
1936	2-1-1	2-1-1	7th
1937	3-2	3-2	5th
1938			9th
1939	2-4	0-4	5th
1940	6-4	3-3	8th
1941	3-4	2-3	7th-T
1942	2-5	1-4	6th
1943	0-2	0-2	--
1944	1-4	0-4	--
1945	0-9-1	0-8-1	7th
1946	5-6-1	0-5	6th
1947	5-5	0-5	8th
1948	8-5	2-5	9th
1949	8-2	3-2	7th
1950	6-6	3-5	5th
1951	5-7	3-4	10th
1952	5-5	2-4	6th
1953	3-3	1-2	7th
1954	4-7	2-6	7th
1955	2-10-1	1-8-1	10th
1956	1-11	0-10	10th
1957	3-9	0-8	10th
1958	11-7-1	8-2-1	2nd
1959	14-4-1	9-3-1	3rd-T
1960	8-4-3	3-3-2	5th
1961	2-5	2-5	5th
1962	**13-3-1**	**7-2**	**1st**
1963	5-5	2-5	6th
1964	11-5-1	8-2	2nd
1965	2-3-1	1-2	3rd
1966	6-8-1	5-7	6th

Year	Overall Record	Big Ten Record	Big Ten Finish
1967	8-10	3-6	7th
1968	**13-2-1**	**8-1-1**	**1st**
1969	4-2	0-0	3rd
1970	**7-1**	**2-0**	**1st**
1971	4-3	2-0	4th
1972	0-0	0-0	2nd
1973	**0-0**	**0-0**	**1st**
1974	**0-0**	**0-0**	**1st**
1975	**1-0**	**0-0**	**1st**
1976	0-0	0-0	2nd
1977	0-0	0-0	2nd
1978	0-0	0-0	2nd
1979	0-0	0-0	2nd
1980	0-0	0-0	3rd
1981	0-0	0-0	3rd
1982	0-0	0-0	2nd
1983	0-0	0-0	2nd
1984	0-0	0-0	2nd
1985	0-0	0-0	6th
1986	0-0	0-0	4th
1987	0-0	0-0	8th
1988	0-0	0-0	3rd
1989	0-0	0-0	7th
1990	0-0	0-0	9th
1991	**0-0**	**0-0**	**1st**
1992	0-0	0-0	6th
1993	0-0	0-0	5th
1994	0-0	0-0	10th
1995	0-0	0-0	10th
1996	0-0	0-0	3rd
1997	0-0	0-0	4th
1998	**0-0**	**0-0**	**1st**
1999	0-0	0-0	10th

Men's Gymnastics

Year	Overall Record	Big Ten Record	Big Ten Finish
1949			6th
1950			5th
1951			8th-T
1952			6th
1953			7th
1954			7th
1955	3-4-1	1-4-1	8th
1956	4-7	1-6	6th
1957	6-5	3-5	6th
1958	7-5	4-4	6th
1959	5-7	2-5	6th
1960	4-8	1-6	6th
1961	5-5	2-4	6th
1962	4-8	1-6	7th
1963	6-7	1-6	7th
1964	5-7	0-7	7th
1965	7-4-1	5-2	5th
1966	7-6	1-6	7th
1967	8-5	3-4	5th
1968	5-8	0-7	8th
1969	6-6	2-5	8th
1970	5-7	2-5	6th
1971	7-5	2-3	4th
1972	3-6	2-3	4th
1973	9-4	4-2	4th
1974	9-3	5-1	5th
1975	5-6	3-2	5th
1976	5-4	3-2	7th

Year	Overall Record	Big Ten Record	Big Ten Finish
1977	6-4	2-2	4th
1978	4-6	3-3	6th
1979	1-7	0-4	8th
1980	4-5	1-4	7th
1981	3-8	0-5	8th
1982	1-9	0-6	8th

Men's Indoor Track

Year	Overall Record	Big Ten Record	Big Ten Finish
1904	2-0	1-0	--
1905			
1906			
1907			
1908			
1909	2-0	1-0	--
1910	0-2	0-2	--
1911			
1912			
1913			
1914			
1915	0-0	0-0	6th
1916			
1917	0-0	0-0	7th
1918	0-0	0-0	7th-T
1919			
1920			
1921			
1922			
1923			
1924			
1925	0-2	0-2	--
1926	0-2	0-2	8th
1927			10th
1928			6th-T
1929			7th-T
1930	3-1	2-0	3rd
1931	3-0	3-0	5th
1932	7-0	7-0	1st
1933	2-0	2-0	1st
1934	1-1	1-1	2nd
1935	2-1	2-1	7th
1936	3-1	3-1	3rd
1937	3-1	1-1	2nd
1938	2-1	2-1	5th
1939	3-1	2-1	3rd
1940	3-0	2-0	2nd
1941	3-0	2-0	1st
1942	0-1	0-1	3rd
1943	1-3	1-2	5th
1944	0-4	0-4	6th
1945	4-1	4-1	6th
1946	3-2	3-2	8th
1947	2-0	2-0	8th
1948	2-1	2-1	5th
1949	0-2	0-2	6th
1950	1-1	1-0	7th
1951	3-0	3-0	4th
1952	1-2	1-1	8th
1953	2-1	0-1	4th
1954	4-0	1-0	2nd
1955	2-0	0-0	3rd
1956	3-0	0-0	5th
1957	3-0	0-0	1st
1958	1-1	0-0	3rd
1959	1-2	0-0	3rd
1960	3-2	1-1	5th
1961	4-1	2-0	2nd
1962	2-3	1-1	7th
1963	1-6	0-4	8th
1964	4-5	3-3	8th
1965	2-4	2-2	9th
1966	1-5	1-3	8th
1967	2-4	2-3	6th
1968	2-3	2-2	5th
1969	4-3	2-2	2nd
1970	3-0	2-0	2nd
1971	2-2	2-1	3rd
1972	1-3	1-2	6th
1973	3-1	2-0	1st
1974	3-1	3-0	1st
1975	1-3	0-2	1st
1976	5-1	2-0	4th
1977	0-3	0-2	2nd
1978	5-0	0-0	2nd
1979	5-1	2-0	1st
1980	3-1	1-0	1st
1981	6-1	1-0	5th
1982	4-0	1-0	2nd
1983	6-0	1-0	1st
1984	4-0	1-0	1st
1985	3-0	0-0	1st
1986	0-2	0-1	3rd-T
1987	1-0	1-0	2nd
1988	0-1	0-1	2nd
1989	2-2	0-1	3rd
1990	3-1	2-0	1st
1991	4-1	3-0	1st
1992	8-0	4-0	1st
1993	5-1	2-1	5th
1994	5-1	4-0	5th
1995	3-2	2-1	7th
1996	3-2	3-1	6th-T
1997	2-4	1-2	6th
1998	2-2	2-0	7th
1999	6-1	4-0	4th

Men's Outdoor Track

Year	Overall Record	Big Ten Record	Big Ten Finish	NCAA Finish
1897	0-1	0-0	--	--
1898	2-0	1-0	--	--
1901	0-1	0-1	--	--
1902	1-1	0-1	--	--
1903	1-1	1-1	--	--
1904	1-1	0-1	--	--
1905	2-0	1-0	--	--
1906	2-3	0-3	--	--
1907	1-3	0-1	--	--
1908	1-3	1-2	--	--
1909	--	--	--	--
1910	--	--	--	--
1911	1-1	0-1	--	--
1912	2-1	0-1	--	--
1913	1-1	0-1	--	--
1914	1-1	0-2	--	--
1915	1-1	0-1	6th	--
1916	5-0	1-0	--	--
1917	1-2	0-2	7th	--
1918	0-1	0-1	7th-T	--
1919	3-1	0-1	--	--
1920	2-2	0-2	--	--
1921	0-4	0-2	--	--
1922	0-1	0-1	--	--
1923	0-7	0-5	--	--
1924	1-7	0-5	--	--
1925	2-2	0-1	--	--
1926	3-0	1-0	8th	--
1927	2-4	2-4	10th	--
1928	1-5	1-5	6th-T	--
1929	1-1	1-1	7th	12-T
1930	3-0	2-0	6th	8th-T
1931	0-0 (?)	0-0	4th	5th
1932	3-1	3-1	3rd	1st
1933	3-0	2-0	2nd	3rd
1934	2-1	1-0	2nd	4th-T
1935	2-0	2-0	4th	--
1936	4-0	4-0	1st	3rd
1937	3-1	3-1	2nd	5th
1938	1-4	1-3	4th	14th
1939	3-1	2-1	3rd	9th-T
1940	1-1	0-1	2nd	6th-T
1941	2-1	1-1	1st	2nd
1942	0-1	0-1	2nd-T	14th
1943	0-0	0-0	8th	--
1944	0-0	0-0	7th	18th-T
1945	1-3	1-2	7th	--
1946	1-2	1-2	6th	8th
1947	4-2	2-2	5th	10th-T
1948	3-3	2-3	5th	--
1949	5-1	4-1	5th	20th-T
1950	2-0	2-0	1st	--
1951	5-0	3-0	3rd	17th-T
1952	6-0	2-0	7th	--
1953	3-0	2-0	6th	--
1954	1-1	1-1	4th	--
1955	0-1	0-1	7th	17th-T
1956	1-1	1-1	3rd	16th
1957	2-1	1-0	1st	10th-T
1958	3-1	1-0	2nd	11th-T
1959	1-1	0-1	3rd	12th
1960	0-1	0-1	7th	--
1961	4-0	1-0	2nd	--
1962	1-2	0-1	6th	--
1963	0-1	0-1	9th	--
1964	1-1	1-1	7th	--
1965	1-4	1-3	10th	--
1966	2-2	1-1	8th	--
1967	8-1	5-1	5th	--
1968	7-1	5-0	8th	--
1969	4-2	1-2	2nd	--
1970	4-2	2-0	1st	16th
1971	6-1	2-0	1st	18th
1972	9-2	2-2	3rd	--
1973	8-0	2-0	1st	--
1974	7-1	2-0	1st	11th
1975	2-2	0-1	2nd	14th-T
1976	0-2	0-1	3rd	--
1977	4-2	2-0	2nd	--
1978	2-2	1-0	2nd	--
1979	0-2-1	0-1	1st	--
1980	3-2	2-0	2nd	--
1981	0-1	0-1	2nd	9th

Year	Overall Record	Big Ten Record	Big Ten Finish	NCAA Finish
1982	1-1	1-0	2nd	15th
1983	1-0	0-0	2nd	11th
1984	0-1	0-0	2nd	10th-T
1985	**4-1**	**1-0**	**1st**	**20th-T**
1986	2-1	0-0	4th	--
1987	4-1	0-0	2nd	--
1988	2-0	0-0	2nd	17th-T
1989	2-0	0-0	3rd	--
1990	**6-1**	**0-0**	**1st**	--
1991	**1-0**	**0-0**	**1st**	**19th-T**
1992	4-0	2-0	2nd	16th
1993	2-1	1-1	5th	7th-T
1994	1-1	1-1	6th	17th-T
1995	0-0	0-0	8th	--
1996	1-0	0-0	5th	--
1997	0-0	0-0	7th	--
1998	0-0	0-0	6th	--
1999	8-1	2-0	8th	--

Men's Soccer

Year	Overall Record	Big Ten Tourney	NCAA Tourney
1973	12-2		
1974	14-3		
1975	13-3-1		
1976	**18-1-1**		2nd
1977	12-2-1		
1978	**23-2-0**		2nd
1979	**19-2-2**		Final 8
1980	**22-3-1**		2nd
1981	**20-3**		Final 8
1982	**21-3-1**		Champion
1983	**21-1-4**		Champion
1984	**22-2-2**		2nd
1985	12-9-1		
1986	9-6-4		
1987	18-3		
1988	**19-3-3**		Champion
1989	**18-2-2**		Final 4
1990	**16-4-2**		Final 8
1991	**19-3-2**		1st Final 4
1992	14-6-4		1st Final 8
1993	17-3-1		
1994	**23-3**	1st	2nd
1995	14-5-2	1st-T	
1996	**15-3-3**	1st	Final 8
1997	**23-1**	1st	Final 4
1998	**23-2**	1st	Champion

Men's Swimming

Year	Overall Record	Big Ten Record	Big Ten Finish	NCAA Finish
1923	0-0	0-0	5th	--
1924	5-1-1	2-1-1	4th-T	--
1925	5-4	1-4	--	--
1926	0-7	0-4	--	--
1927	7-5	2-3	7th-T	--
1928	5-6	0-5	--	--
1929	5-5	1-5	8th	--
1930	4-5	1-4	8th-T	--
1931	0-0	0-0	--	--
1932	0-4	0-3	--	--
1933	0-0	0-0	--	--

Year	Overall Record	Big Ten Record	Big Ten Finish	NCAA Finish
1934	5-3	2-3	7th-T	--
1935	6-4	2-3	8th	--
1936	3-5	3-4	9th	--
1937	5-3	1-3	8th	--
1938	3-3	0-3	8th-T	--
1939	6-3	2-3	9th	--
1940	4-2-1	3-2	8th	--
1941	2-6	0-4	9th	--
1942	4-4	0-3	8th-T	--
1943	3-5	0-2	5th-T	--
1944	0-0	0-0	--	--
1945	5-2	4-2	3rd	10th
1946	1-2	1-2	8th-T	--
1947	4-4-1	0-3-1	8th-T	--
1948	4-3	1-3	8th-T	--
1949	4-4	1-3	7th	--
1950	7-5	2-5	6th	--
1951	4-3	2-3	6th-T	10th
1952	5-3	2-3	8th	--
1953	2-5	1-5	10th	--
1954	4-3	3-3	10th	--
1955	3-5	1-5	6th-T	10th
1956	7-2	4-2	3rd	6th
1957	5-4	3-3	4th	4th
1958	5-2	4-2	6th	11th
1959	6-2	4-2	2nd	3rd
1960	5-0	4-0	2nd	3rd
1961	**8-0**	**4-0**	**1st**	--
1962	**9-0**	**5-0**	**1st**	--
1963	**10-0**	**5-0**	**1st**	--
1964	**9-0**	**5-0**	**1st**	**2nd**
1965	**7-1**	**2-1**	**1st**	**2nd**
1966	**8-1**	**4-1**	**1st**	**2nd**
1967	**9-0**	**5-0**	**1st**	**3rd**
1968	**10-0**	**6-0**	**1st**	**1st**
1969	**11-0**	**7-0**	**1st**	**1st**
1970	**12-0**	**6-0**	**1st**	**1st**
1971	**13-0**	**6-0**	**1st**	**1st**
1972	**11-0**	**8-0**	**1st**	**1st**
1973	**13-0**	**8-0**	**1st**	**1st**
1974	**12-0**	**8-0**	**1st**	**2nd**
1975	**10-0**	**6-0**	**1st**	**2nd**
1976	**9-0**	**7-0**	**1st**	**4th**
1977	**8-0**	**5-0**	**1st**	**4th**
1978	**8-0**	**5-0**	**1st**	**9th**
1979	**9-3-1**	**7-1**	**1st**	**7th**
1980	**10-2**	**4-1**	**1st**	**9th**
1981	12-0	7-0	2nd	14th
1982	9-1	6-0	2nd	16th
1983	**8-3**	**6-1**	**1st**	--
1984	**6-3**	**6-1**	**1st**	**18th**
1985	**10-2**	**6-1**	**1st**	--
1986	3-3	2-1	2nd	--
1987	3-4	3-3	3rd	--
1988	6-2	4-2	3rd	16th
1989	3-3	1-0	4th	12th
1990	4-4	3-4	5th	17th
1991	2-6	2-5	3rd	15th
1992	8-2	6-2	3rd	17th
1993	4-5	2-5	5th	--
1994	4-4	2-3	6th	--
1995	9-5	3-3	4th	17th
1996	6-2	2-2	4th	19th
1997	7-3	3-2	3rd	20th
1998	5-3	2-2	5th	--
1999	9-3	3-1	5th	21st

Men's Tennis

Year	Overall Record	Big Ten Record	Big Ten Finish
1930	1-9	0-5	--
1931	1-6	0-3	--
1932	0-3-1	0-2-1	--
1933	1-3	0-1	--
1934	2-5	0-0	--
1935	2-4	1-1	--
1936	5-4	1-0	--
1937	4-8	3-3	--
1938	3-8	1-4	--
1939	2-9	0-4	--
1940	1-8	0-1	--
1941	3-8	0-2	--
1942	2-7	1-2	--
1943	2-3	0-0	--
1944	0-6	0-1	9th
1945	0-2	0-1	9th
1946	0-11	0-7	9th
1947	1-4	0-1	7th-T
1948	5-1	0-1	9th
1949	5-3	1-2	7th
1950	14-2	5-2	5th
1951	14-2	5-2	4th-T
1952	**13-3**	**8-0**	**1st**
1953	**17-2**	**7-1**	**1st**
1954	**19-0**	**8-0**	**1st**
1955	16-2	7-1	2nd
1956	14-5	6-1	2nd
1957	13-2-1	6-2	3rd
1958	11-11	5-4	5th
1959	10-13	3-6	6th
1960	12-9	4-4	10th
1961	13-3	8-1	3rd
1962	14-4	5-2	6th
1963	20-4	6-2	3rd
1964	**21-2**	**10-1**	**1st**
1965	14-4	8-1	2nd
1966	17-6	7-2	3rd
1967	16-8	5-4	3rd
1968	8-11	3-6	5th
1969	13-7	8-1	2nd
1970	19-3	7-1	2nd
1971	19-5-2	8-1	2nd
1972	15-5-1	8-1	2nd
1973	16-7	6-3	3rd
1974	13-6	8-1	2nd
1975	12-9	5-5	6th
1976	15-8	3-6	7th
1977	15-8	5-4	2nd
1978	5-13	4-5	6th-T
1979	17-10	4-4	6th
1980	18-4	7-2	7th
1981	13-13	2-7	6th-T
1982	8-14	1-8	10th
1983	12-10	5-4	9th
1984	12-14	3-6	8th
1985	22-7	7-5	4th
1986	21-13	7-5	3rd
1987	20-9-1	9-4	5th
1988	18-10	7-5	4th
1989	20-10	7-6	6th
1990	19-7	9-3	2nd
1991	18-8	9-3	3rd
1992	16-8	11-2	2nd

Year	Overall Record	Big Ten Record	Big Ten Finish
1993	12-8	8-4	3rd
1994	6-20	4-8	9th
1995	10-10	7-6	5th
1996	11-11	2-8	9th
1997	15-11	6-4	4th
1998	9-15	4-9	8th
1999	14-10	6-5	5th

Softball

Year	Overall Record	Big Ten Record	Big Ten Finish
1974	6-7	--	--
1975	5-9	--	--
1976	6-6	--	--
1977	16-9	--	--
1978	22-15	--	--
1979	32-14	--	--
1980	33-16	--	--
1981	26-12	--	--
1982	27-14	--	--
1983	**45-22-1**	**11-4**	**1st**
1984	38-22	14-10	3rd
1985	47-20-1	14-12	3rd
1986	**45-18**	**15-9**	**1st-T**
1987	37-23	15-9	3rd
1988	36-20-1	13-10	4th
1989	31-21	13-11	4th
1990	45-18	16-8	3rd
1991	23-30	9-15	5th-T
1992	25-30	14-14	5th
1993	28-23-1	11-17	6th
1994	**49-16**	**23-5**	**1st**
1995	27-28	14-14	5th
1996	37-24	16-7	4th
1997	27-21	11-11	5th
1998	13-31-1	7-16	10th
1999	17-40	3-21	10th

Volleyball

Year	Overall Record	Big Ten Record	Big Ten Finish
1975	16-15-1	4-4-1	--
1976	28-15	12-10	--
1977	28-14-2	11-4	--
1978	16-20-3	5-9	--
1979	26-20-3	3-8	--
1980	22-24	1-10	--
1981	12-19	3-7	8th
1982	10-21	6-12	6th-T
1983	12-26	5-8	6th
1984	16-14	9-4	3rd-T
1985	19-16	10-8	5th
1986	18-13	9-9	5th
1987	20-13	10-8	4th
1988	17-13	9-9	5th-T
1989	19-12	9-9	5th-T
1990	17-11	9-9	6th-T
1991	8-22	5-14	9th
1992	6-23	4-16	9th-T
1993	11-18	7-13	7th-T
1994	16-16	7-13	8th
1995	20-14	12-8	4th-T
1996	10-22	4-16	10th

Year	Overall Record	Big Ten Record	Big Ten Finish
1997	18-15	5-15	8th
1998	17-14	9-11	5th-T

Water Polo

Year	Overall Record	Big Ten Record	Big Ten Finish
1998	26-9-1	--	--
1999	21-18	--	--

Women's Basketball

Year	Overall Record	Big Ten Record	Big Ten Finish
1972	17-2	--	
1973	17-3	--	
1974	16-5	--	
1975	19-5	--	
1976	12-13	--	
1977	13-13	--	
1978	7-16	--	
1979	21-14	--	
1980	18-14	--	
1981	21-16	--	
1982	17-13		
1983	**19-11**	**15-3**	**1st-T**
1984	17-11	11-7	3rd-T
1985	16-12	11-7	4th
1986	17-11	10-8	4th
1987	10-17	5-13	7th
1988	12-16	7-11	6th-T
1989	16-12	9-9	4th-T
1990	12-16	6-12	7th
1991	18-13	8-10	5th-T
1992	16-12	8-10	6th-T
1993	14-13	5-13	9th
1994	19-9	10-8	4th-T
1995	19-10	8-8	5th-T
1996	14-13	5-11	9th
1997	16-13	7-9	8th-T
1998	21-12	10-6	3rd-T
1999	13-18	2-14	10th-T

Women's Cross Country

Year	Overall Record	Big Ten Record	Big Ten Finish
1981	0-0	0-0	6th
1982	0-0	0-0	8th
1983	0-0	0-0	7th
1984	0-0	0-0	7th
1985	0-0	0-0	3rd-T
1986	0-0	0-0	5th
1987	0-0	0-0	4th
1988	0-0	0-0	2nd
1989	**0-0**	**0-0**	**1st**
1990	**0-0**	**0-0**	**1st**
1991	0-0	0-0	10th
1992	0-0	0-0	8th
1993	0-0	0-0	7th
1994	0-0	0-0	10th
1995	0-0	0-0	7th
1996	0-0	0-0	7th
1997	0-0	0-0	7th
1998	0-0	0-0	9th

Women's Golf

Year	Overall Record	Big Ten Record	Big Ten Finish
1976	0-0	0-0	4th
1977	0-0	0-0	3rd
1978	0-0	0-0	4th
1979	0-0	0-0	2nd
1980	0-0	0-0	5th
1981	0-0	0-0	6th
1982	0-0	0-0	7th
1983	0-0	0-0	2nd
1984	0-0	0-0	3rd
1985	0-0	0-0	2nd
1986	**0-0**	**0-0**	**1st**
1987	**0-0**	**0-0**	**1st**
1988	0-0	0-0	3rd
1989	0-0	0-0	2nd
1990	**0-0**	**0-0**	**1st**
1991	0-0	0-0	2nd
1992	**0-0**	**0-0**	**1st**
1993	0-0	0-0	2nd
1994	0-0	0-0	2nd
1995	**0-0**	**0-0**	**1st**
1996	**0-0**	**0-0**	**1st**
1997	0-0	0-0	2nd
1998	**0-0**	**0-0**	**1st**
1999	0-0	0-0	2nd

Women's Gymnastics

Year	Overall Record	Big Ten Record	Big Ten Finish
1979	7-7		6th
1980	11-4		6th
1981	7-4		5th
1982	6-4		5th
1983	13-5		6th
1984	10-23		7th
1985	8-8		7th

Women's Indoor Track

Year	Overall Record	Big Ten Record	Big Ten Finish
1980	0-2	0-1	5th
1981	3-1	0-0	4th
1982	7-1	2-0	3rd
1983	3-2	0-1	3rd
1984	3-0	2-0	2nd
1985	3-0	1-0	2nd
1986	2-1	1-0	2nd
1987	3-0	3-0	3rd
1988	**1-0**	**0-0**	**1st**
1989	1-2	0-1	2nd
1990	2-1	2-0	2nd-T
1991	**2-1**	**2-1**	**1st**
1992	4-3-1	1-2-1	7th
1993	3-4	1-2	5th
1994	3-1	2-1	7th
1995	4-2	3-1	5th
1996	0-4	0-3	9th
1997	2-4	1-2	9th-T
1998	1-2	1-1	8th
1999	3-3	2-2	3rd

Women's Outdoor Track

Year	Overall Record	Big Ten Record	Big Ten Finish
1980	2-1	1-0	4th
1981	2-0	1-0	6th
1982	3-0	2-0	6th-T
1983	3-1	2-1	4th-T
1984	2-1	1-0	2nd
1985	4-0	1-0	2nd
1986	4-1	1-0	6th
1987	5-1	1-0	3rd
1988	2-0	0-0	4th
1989	3-1	0-0	3rd
1990	4-1	0-0	3rd
1991	1-3	0-0	3rd
1992	3-1	2-1	5th
1993	1-2	1-1	9th
1994	2-0	2-0	4th-T
1995	3-3	0-3	6th
1996	0-4	0-1	9th
1997	1-5	0-1	5th
1998	2-2	1-1	8th
1999	5-3	0-1	7th

Women's Soccer

Year	Overall Record	Big Ten Record	Big Ten Finish
1993	12-6	--	--
1994	8-10	3-4	--
1995	8-10-1	3-3-1	--
1996	**11-11**	**2-3**	**1st**
1997	11-9	4-5	--
1998	14-8-1	6-3	--

Women's Swimming

Year	Overall Record	Big Ten Record	Big Ten Finish
1969	7-0	0-0	--
1970	0-0	0-0	--
1971	**0-0**	**0-0**	**1st**
1972	**0-0**	**0-0**	**1st**
1973	0-0	0-0	3rd
1974	0-0	0-0	2nd
1975	0-0	0-0	2nd
1976	0-0	0-0	3rd
1977	2-1	1-0	5th
1978	3-0	0-0	3rd
1979	8-3	0-0	2nd
1980	12-3	6-1	2nd
1981	**11-1**	**0-0**	**1st**
1982	3-3	3-2	3rd
1983	5-3	4-1	5th
1984	4-5-1	4-1-1	5th
1985	7-5	6-1	4th
1986	5-3	5-1	6th
1987	2-6	1-6	9th
1988	9-1-1	7-1-1	6th
1989	4-7	3-5	10th
1990	6-2	5-0	8th
1991	4-5-1	2-5-1	10th
1992	2-6	2-5	8th
1993	4-6	3-5	8th
1994	3-7	1-5	8th
1995	4-6	3-5	9th
1996	7-2	4-2	6th
1997	9-5	2-5	8th
1998	6-4	2-4	5th
1999	6-5	1-3	8th

Women's Tennis

Year	Overall Record	Big Ten Record	Big Ten Finish
1975	10-3	2-0	7th
1976	10-3	1-0	7th
1977	12-7	3-2	7th
1978	10-7	5-5	2nd
1979	28-3	13-0	2nd
1980	**24-4**	**9-0**	**1st**
1981	**29-5**	**18-0**	**1st**
1982	**39-3**	**19-0**	**1st***
1983	**33-9**	**16-0**	**1st**
1984	**33-7**	**13-0**	**1st**
1985	33-3	15-1	2nd
1986	27-7	9-2	2nd
1987	**30-5**	**10-1**	**1st**
1988	**22-6**	**12-0**	**1st**
1989	**26-4**	**11-0**	**1st**
1990	**23-7**	**12-0**	**1st**
1991	**25-8**	**11-1**	**1st**
1992	**22-4**	**12-0**	**1st**
1993	**20-5**	**13-0**	**1st**
1994	**20-5**	**11-2**	**1st**
1995	**24-7**	**13-0**	**1st**
1996	13-13	8-5	3rd
1997	19-9	12-2	2nd
1998	**19-9**	**9-1**	**1st**
1999	10-15	5-7	6th

*AIAW champion

Wrestling

Year	Overall Record	Big Ten Record	Big Ten Finish
1914	**--**	**--**	**1st**
1915	**--**	**--**	**1st-T**
1916	--	--	2nd
1917	--	--	2nd
1918	--	--	--
1919	--	--	--
1920	--	--	2nd
1921	**--**	**--**	**1st**
1922	--	--	--
1923	4-3	4-0	--
1924	**6-0**	**5-0**	**1st**
1925	**7-1**	**4-0**	**1st**
1926	4-2	4-1	--
1927	5-1	3-1	4th
1928	6-4	2-3	--
1929	9-1-2	3-0-2	3rd
1930	8-1	4-1	--
1931	**8-1**	**5-0**	**1st**
1932	**6-0**	**4-0**	**1st***
1933	**6-1**	**4-0**	**1st**
1934	**7-0**	**2-0**	**1st**
1935	11-0	6-0	4th
1936	**9-0**	**4-0**	**1st**
1937	5-2	1-1	4th
1938	7-0	2-0	2nd
1939	**3-2**	**2-1**	**1st**
1940	**4-2**	**2-1**	**1st**
1941	6-1	4-0	2nd-T
1942	2-5	0-4	8th
1943	**4-2**	**4-0**	**1st**
1944	2-1-1	0-2	8th
1945	4-2-1	3-0-2	4th-T
1946	6-0	5-0	2nd
1947	4-4	3-4	6th
1948	4-2	4-2	8th
1949	3-4	2-4	6th
1950	2-6	1-6	8th
1951	2-7	2-7	10th
1952	6-2-1	5-2-1	4th
1953	3-5-1	2-5-1	5th-T
1954	4-5-1	3-5-1	9th
1955	9-4-1	4-4-1	8th
1956	8-3	6-3	5th-T
1957	4-5-1	2-5-1	6th-T
1958	6-4	6-3	5th-T
1959	6-4	6-3	8th
1960	4-5	4-5	6th
1961	6-5	6-5	7th
1962	4-7-2	2-4-2	7th
1963	2-7	2-6	6th
1964	3-6	2-6	3rd
1965	8-4-2	8-4-2	7th
1966	3-5-2	2-5-2	6th
1967	9-5	7-5	7th
1968	15-3	8-1	5th
1969	6-9	5-6	7th-T
1970	3-10	0-10	10th
1971	5-11	1-10	8th
1972	10-6	4-5	8th
1973	4-8	1-8	9th
1974	4-22-2	0-10	8th
1975	6-20-1	0-10	8th-T
1976	11-12-2	1-7-1	10th
1977	10-8-1	2-5-1	6th
1978	6-9	1-6	7th
1979	10-10	1-7	7th
1980	15-9	3-5	9th
1981	14-6-1	2-5-1	6th
1982	11-12	3-6	7th
1983	9-12-1	3-6	10th
1984	2-17	0-9	10th
1985	7-13	0-7	10th
1986	7-13	1-6	8th-T
1987	7-9-1	0-6-1	9th
1988	6-10	1-5	9th
1989	13-8	6-4	5th
1990	14-0	6-0	2nd
1991	5-8	3-3	10th
1992	5-12	2-5	10th
1993	7-11	0-8	11th
1994	12-4	4-3	5th
1995	15-5-1	3-3	10th
1996	16-2	6-1	11th
1997	9-8	1-6	9th
1998	6-7	1-6	11th
1999	11-5-2	2-5-1	9th

*NCAA champions

Indiana Letterwinners

All-Time Indiana University Letter-Winner List

Names, sport and letter years were compiled from I-Men's and I-Women's directories prepared by the Indiana University Alumni Association as approved by the University Athletics Committee, and by Associate Athletic Director Isabella Hutchison. Female athletes are listed by their maiden names. Any corrections or additions should be sent to Media Relations in Assembly Hall. We regret any errors or ommissions.

KEY TO ABBREVIATIONS

BB - Baseball
VB - Volleyball
FB - Football
WBK - Women's Basketball
FH - Field Hockey
WCC - Women's Cross Country
MBK - Men's Basketball
WGO - Women's Golf
MCC - Men's Cross Country
WGY - Women's Gymnastics
MGO - Men's Golf
WP - Water Polo
MGY - Men's Gymnastics
WR - Wrestling
MSO - Men's Soccer
WSO - Women's Soccer
MSW - Men's Swimming
WSW - Women's Swimming
MTN - Men's Tennis
WTN - Women's Tennis
MTR - Men's Track
WTR - Women's Track
R - Rifle
SB - Softball

Aaron, David B.	MSW	1977, 78
Abel, Elizabeth J.	WBK	1978
Abele, William R., Jr.	MCC/MTR	1956, 57, 58, 59
Abell, Jasper A.	MBK	1909
Abell, Julian D.	MTR	1926, 27
Abernathy, Ellis D.	BB	1936, 37
Abernethy, Thomas C.	MBK	1973, 74, 75, 76
Ableman, Mark D.	MTN	1992, 93, 94, 95
Abner, Carol	SB/WBK	1971, 72, 73, 74
Abraham, David D.	MSW	1955
Abram, Karna L.	WBK	1984, 85, 86, 87

Abrams, David F.	FB	1975, 76, 77, 78
Abromson, James J.	MCC/MTR	1927, 28, 29
Abruzzo, Nicholas A.	FB	1997
Abunassar, Joseph	MBK (Mgr.)	1993
Achgill, Chris H. III	MTR	1973, 74, 75
Ackerman, Robert W. III	MGO	1973, 74, 75
Ackermann, Kenneth C.	MSW	1997, 98, 99
Ackman, Taner	MSO	1972
Acre, Harry M.	MTR	1914, 15
Acre, Robert R.	MTR	1916, 17
Adair, Jerrie	WSW	1970, 71, 72
Adam, Donald W.	R	1969
Adama, Dennis R.	MTR	1971, 72, 73, 74
Adams, Barbara A.	WTR	1979
Adams, Daniel D.	FB	1982
Adams, James K.	FB (Mgr.)	1938
Adams, James S.	FB (Mgr.)	1920, 21
Adams, Kellie K.	SB	1994
Adams, Martin A.	MTR	1925
Adams, Michael E.	FB	1967, 68
Adams, Rachel A.	WBK/WTR	1987, 88, 89, 90
Adams, Robert B.	MTR	1975, 76
Adamson, Wendell M.	MSW/WR (Mgr.)	1928
Addams, Abe B.	FB	1944
Addison, Samuel J.	FB	1983
Adkins, David W.	FB (Mgr.)	1985
Adler, Eugene E.	MSW	1959
Adler, Robert E.	BB	1935, 36, 37
Adler, Walter H.	MTR	1940
Agee, Michael S.	MBK (Mgr.)	1983
Agee, Tracee K.	SB	1996, 97
Agnello, Gail A.	SB/WBK	1971, 72
Aguilera, Vilma	WSW	1984, 85, 86
Ahamed, Zahra S.	WTN	1997, 98, 99
Ahlbrand, Jane E.	WGY	1975, 76, 77
Ahler, James R.	FB	1990, 91
Ahlfeld, Steven K.	MBK	1973, 74, 75
Ahting, Gerhard	FB	1978, 79, 80
Aikman, Homer B.	BB	1903, 04
Alatorre, Patricia	WSW	1979, 80
Alavanja, Lazo	MSO	1995, 96, 97, 98
Albershardt, Richard K.	MGY	1952, 55, 56
Albright, Elizabeth J.	VB	1976, 77
Alcini, Amy E.	WTN	1988, 89
Alder, Lyn S.	FH	1980
Aldrich, Wendell R.	MGO	1940, 42
Aldridge, Delmas E.	WR	1930, 31, 32
Aldridge, Lee E.	MBK	1957, 58, 59
Aldridge, Relle T.	MBK/MTR	1921, 22, 23
Alexander, Charles V.	FB	1978, 79, 80
Alexander, Christopher B.	BB	1989, 91, 92
Alexander, Darrell E.	MTN	1947
Alexander, John E.	MCC/MTR	1925, 26
Alexander, Ramon L.	FB	1943
Alford, Adrian N.	FB	1943
Alford, Stephen T.	MBK	1984, 85, 86, 87
Allen, Ann M.	WCC/WTR	1981, 82
Allen, David T.	FB (Mgr.)	1979
Allen, Douglas B.	MBK	1973, 74, 75
Allen, Eric K.	FB	1994, 95, 96, 97
Allen, Frank E.	FB	1914, 15
Allen, James H.	MTR	1937, 38, 39
Allen, John T.	FB	1971
Allen, John W., Jr.	MTR	1955
Allen, Keith B.	MCC/MTR	1985, 86, 87, 88

Allen, Kenneth A.	FB	1984, 85, 86, 87
Allen, Kevin E.	FB	1981, 82, 83, 84
Allen, Kristi	WTR	1984, 85
Allen, Linda A.	SB	1981, 82
Allen, Ottis	MTR	1915, 16
Allen, Richard F.	MSW	1964, 65, 66
Allen, Ruth Ann	WBK (Mgr.)	1981
Allen, Wendy J.	WTN	1983, 84, 85, 86
Allenspach, Mark A.	MGO	1978, 80
Allerdice, James K.	FB	1943
Alleva, David G.	MSW	1983, 84, 85, 86
Allison, Ralph C.	BB	1957
Allotey, Victor	FB	1994, 95, 96, 97
Aloisio, Tony L.	FB	1954, 57, 58
Alsfelder, Robert F.	MSW	1972, 73, 74, 75
Alsop, William M.	BB	1898, 99, 1900
Althauser, Thomas L.	R	1957, 58, 59
Altman, Lori J.	WSW	1982, 83
Altman, William E.	MBK	1960, 61, 62
Alvares, Kenneth M.	MSW	1964, 65
Alvarez, Louis	MSW	1950
Alvear, Cindy S.	VB	1979, 80, 81, 82
Alward, Kenneth J.	MBK	1923, 24, 25
Amabile, Pamela S.	SB	1980
Amacher, Richard C.	MTR	1967
Amberg, Susan M.	WGY	1974, 75, 76
Ambler, John A.	MTN	1946
Ambrose, Frank P.	FB	1992
Amstutz, Gerald J.	FB	1954, 55, 56
Amstutz, Joanne K.	VB	1998
Amwake, Kathryn	WBK	1973, 74
Andersen, Kim K.	MTN	1985
Andersen, Peter A.	MSW	1963, 64, 65
Anderson, Clifton, Jr.	FB/MTR	1949, 50, 51
Anderson, Clyde L., Jr.	FB/WR	1958, 59, 60, 61
Anderson, Eric	MBK	1989, 90, 91, 92
Anderson, Farnum S.	BB/MGY	1916, 17
Anderson, Frank W.	FB (Mgr.)	1937
Anderson, Gerald K.	FB	1951
Anderson, Gordon P.	MTN	1951
Anderson, Gregg C.	MTN	1982, 83, 84, 85
Anderson, Isaac R.	MGY	1958
Anderson, James Ra.	MTR	1951, 52
Anderson, James Ro.	BB (Mgr.)	1939
Anderson, Jerry L.	FB	1961
Anderson, Jessica M.	WTN	1997, 98, 99
Anderson, John C.	MSW	1965
Anderson, John R.	BB	1957, 58, 59
Anderson, Judith L.	SB	1970
Anderson, Lars	FB	1991, 92
Anderson, Michael J.	FB	1982, 83, 84, 85
Anderson, Randy G.	BB	1977
Anderson, Richard C.	MBK (Mgr.)	1961
Anderson, Richard L.	MSW	1969, 70, 71
Anderson, Roy O.	BB	1914
Anderson, Ryan C.	MSW	1993
Anderson, Tina L.	WGO	1977
Anderson, Tony M.	MSW	1982, 83, 84, 85
Anderson, Warren L.	MTR	1954
Anderson, William P.	FB	1935, 36, 37
Andert, Joseph C.	MSO	1975, 76, 77, 78
Andis, Brenda S.	VB	1975, 76, 77
Andres, Ernest H.	BB/MBK	1937, 38, 39
Andrews, Brett W.	FB	1980
Andrews, Elizabeth	WSW	1978, 79
Andrews, Francie	WTR	1985
Andrews, John F.	MGO	1986, 87, 88, 89
Andrews, John M.	FB	1968, 69, 70
Andrews, Theresa	WSW	1981
Ane, David E.	FB	1987, 88, 89, 90
Angel, Jeff R.	WR	1972, 73, 74, 75
Angel, Robert R.	MCC/MTR	1975, 76, 77
Angell, Christopher C.	MTN	1992, 93
Angione, Toni A.	WCC/WTR	1985, 86, 87,88,89
Anglemeyer, Charles E.	FB	1931, 32, 33
Angotti, Arthur A.	MCC	1963
Anhaeuser, Michael	MSO	1988, 89, 90, 91
Anleitner, Scott D.	BB	1996, 97, 98
Anspach, Lawrence C.	MSW (Mgr.)	1973
Anstead, Shannon E.	WSW	1988
Anthony, Craig E.	MTR	1979
Anthony, James R.	WR	1954, 55, 56
Anthony, Jan	WBK/WGO	1972, 73, 74
Anthony, Sandy	VB/WGY	1969, 70, 71
Antibus, Phillip D.	MGO	1955, 56
Antonacci, Robert J.	WR	1939, 40, 41
Antonini, Ettore	FB/MTR	1933, 34, 35
Antonini, Fred	FB	1929, 32, 33
Antonoff, Mark W.	MSW	1974, 75, 76, 77
Applegate, Albert E.	MCC/MTR	1936, 37, 38

Bob Ackerman was Big Ten co-medalist and All-American in 1975.

Dennis Adama won Big Ten high jump titles indoors and outdoors in 1972-73-74.

Applegate, James W.	BB	1954, 55, 56
Applegate, Steve D.	FB	1967, 68, 69
Appleton, Darwin B.	BB	1928
Aranda, Norman	MTR (Mgr.)	1985
Arantes, Romulo D.	MSW	1976, 77, 78, 80
Arbuckle, James L.	MTR	1967, 68, 69
Arbuckle, John W.	WR	1970, 71
Arbuckle, M. Aaron	FB	1977, 78, 79
Archer, Christina M.	FH	1973, 74, 75, 76
Archer, John E.	WR	1942, 43
Archer, Joseph M.	MSO	1974, 75
Archer, Patricia A.	FH/SB/WBK	1970, 71, 72, 73, 74
Archer, Terrie J.	WTR	1979, 80, 81
Ardell, Shalandra D.	WTR	1991
Areddy, Joe	MBK (Mgr.)	1992
Armendarez, Monica M.	SB	1995, 96, 97, 98
Armbrustmacher, E. M.	VB	1985, 86, 87, 88
Armington, Jane	WSW	1985
Armstrong, Charles L.	FB	1945, 46
Armstrong, Freeland H.	MBK	1945
Armstrong, Paul "Curly"	MBK	1939, 40
Armstrong, Robert E.	MBK	1947, 48, 49
Armstrong, William F.	FB	1944, 45, 46
Armstrong, William S.	BB	1940
Armstrong, William S., Jr.	BB/FB	1971, 72, 73, 74
Arnett, Scott G.	FB	1976, 77, 78
Arnold, Eric J.	MSW	1991, 92, 93, 94
Arnold, James H.	MCC/MTR	1988, 89, 90
Arnold, Robert W.	FB (Mgr.)	1941
Arons, Ian F.	MTN	1998, 99
Arp, Lorilee R.	WBK	1979
Arquette, Peggy	WBK	1975, 76
Arthur, Harry L.	WR	1950, 51, 52
Artim, Melanie	FH	1978
Artman, Joseph M.	FB/MTR	1902, 04, 05
Artman, Oliver C.	FB	1911
Artz, Kelly A.	WSW	1985, 86, 87, 88
Arzner, Ryan	MSW (Mgr.)	1998
Aschinger, Cathleen A.	WSW	1981, 82
Ashburner, Richard E.	FB	1951, 52
Ashby, Lucian O.	FB/MBK	1929, 30
Ashby, Samuel R.	MSW	1923
Ashley, Lorenzo	FB	1963, 64
Aspengren, Andrea L.	WSW	1976, 77, 79
Atinay, Charles W.	MSO	1989, 90, 91
Atkins, Craig J.	FB	1995
Atkins, Janet	WTR	1979
Atkinson, David W.	MCC/MTR	1967, 68
Atkinson, J. William	FB	1972, 73, 74
Atkinson, Larry L.	BB	1957, 58, 59
Atkinson, Roy S.	MBK	1968, 69, 70
Atterberry, Linda	FH	1969
Atwater, Munson D.	BB/FB	1893, 94
Aucreman, Ted L.	FB	1958, 59
Auger, Kevin W.	MSW	1980, 81, 82, 83
Ausenbachs, Mara	VB/WTR	1975, 76, 79
Austin, Jane L.	FH	1979, 80, 81
Autry, Gary C.	FB	1976, 77
Autry, Gene "Bucky"	BB	1982, 83, 84
Aveni, John P.	FB	1957, 58
Ax, John R.	MCC/MTR (Mgr.)	1934, 35
Axelberg, Jane	WTR	1979
Aydelotte, Frank	FB	1898, 99
Aydelotte, William E.	FB	1903, 04, 05
Ayers, Linda A.	VB	1973, 74, 75
Aylsworth, Mary Kay	SB	1970

Ayres, Harry E.	MBK	1902, 03
Ayres, Loren D.	MTR	1928, 29

Baas, Susan B.	WBK	1980
Babb, Jesse L.	FB/MTR	1931, 32, 33
Babb, Stuart V.	WSW	1977
Babbidge, Steve	MSW	1963, 65
Babcock, John W.	FB	1972, 73, 74
Bachman, Drew H.	WR	1964
Bachtel, D.K.	MTR	1985, 86
Backer, Herbert J.	MSW	1934, 35, 36
Badar, Jason R.	WR	1999
Badar, Richard C.	FB	1962, 63
Badell, Joab, Jr.	WR	1955
Badger, Emily D.	VB	1992, 93, 94, 95
Baechle, George R.	MGY	1959, 60, 61
Baer, Charles S.	BB/FB	1931, 32
Baer, Michael T.	MTN	1965, 66, 67
Baety, Eddie L.	FB	1991, 92, 93, 94
Bahr, Wilfred A.	FB/MBK	1921, 23
Bailey, Cladie A.	BB	1932
Bailey, Damon L.	MBK	1991, 92, 93, 94
Bailey, James E.	R	1963
Bailey, James R.	FB	1961, 62
Bailey, Jennifer M.	SB	1987, 88
Bailey, J. Douglas	FB	1969, 71
Bailey, Marcus A.	FB	1971, 72, 73
Bailey, Max A.	BB	1961, 62
Bailey, R. Gabe	WR	1992, 93, 94, 95
Bailey, Richard A.	MSW	1974
Bailin, Ann R.	WSW	1988, 89, 90, 91
Baillie, Charles D.	MTR	1938, 39, 40
Baird, William C.	MSW	1969, 70, 71, 72
Baise, William C.	BB	1935, 36
Baisley, Jamie M., Jr.	FB	1993, 94, 95, 96
Bak, Christine A.	MSO (Mgr.)	1988
Bakalar, Robbi L.	MBK (Mgr.)	1999
Baker, Clyde A.	MCC	1924
Baker, George C.	BB	1932, 33, 34
Baker, Gretchen	WTR	1981, 82, 83, 84, 85
Baker, Laura J.	SB/WBK/WSW	1977, 78
Baker, Meg	MTR (Mgr.)	1985
Baker, Sharon	FH	1969
Baker, Thomas L.	MBK	1978
Baker, Tyrus D.	WR	1991, 92
Baker, Ward N.	FB	1927, 28
Baker, William R.	FB	1976
Bakhle, Tara F.	WGO	1992, 93, 94, 95
Bakken, Marius	MCC/MTR	1997, 98
Balay, Paul L.	BB/FB	1927, 28, 29, 30
Balbach, Emily	WTR (Mgr.)	1998
Balcells, Pedro P.	MSW	1974
Balch, James F., Jr.	MGO	1952, 54, 55
Balch, William C.	MBK	1957, 58
Baldridge, Kitty	WBK	1970
Baldwin, Charles W.	MTR	1936, 37
Balfour, Lloyd G.	BB/FB	1905, 06, 07
Balgley, Annemarie	WSO	1996
Ball, Deborah A.	WBK	1976, 77
Ball, Kenneth W.	FB	1979, 80, 81
Ball, Ray N.	MBK	1956, 58
Ballard, Gwyneth J.	WBK	1994
Ballester, Jose L.	MSW	1989
Ballou, David M.	FB	1997
Balsiger, Joseph E.	MTN	1999
Balsley, Kevin D.	BB	1972, 73, 74
Balwinski, Christopher T.	WR	1986, 87, 88
Bane, Paul W., Jr.	WR	1957, 58, 59
Banka, John A.	BB/FB	1930, 31, 32
Banks, Charles O.	MTR	1928, 29, 30
Banks, Clarence A.	MCC/MTR	1928, 29, 30
Banks, D. Rene	FB	1966, 68
Banks, Khalfani O.	FB	1995, 96, 97
Banks, Marcia	WTR	1981
Banks, William H.	FB/MTR	1902, 03, 04, 05
Bankson, Virgil E.	MCC	1964, 65
Bannister, Jeffrey J.	MSO	1992, 93, 94, 95
Banton, Melissa R.	WTR	1999
Barada, Paul W.	MTR (Mgr.)	1967
Barber, Jamie A.	FB	1997
Barber, Kathryn A.	WCC/WTR	1996, 97, 98, 99
Barber, Robert W.	BB	1986, 87, 88, 89
Barbiere, Lawrence E.	MSW	1970, 71, 72, 73

Barbour, Herbert V.	FB	1895
Barclay, Joseph K.	MTR	1903, 04, 05
Barco, Torri M.	WSO	1995, 96
Barczak, Michelle F.	SB	1978
Bardwell, Cameron D.	FB	1991
Barger, Ryan E.	BB	1999
Barilich, Thomas A.	WR	1975, 76
Barish, Ann M.	WSW	1994, 95, 96, 97
Barker, James E.	FB	1966
Barker, Michael D.	MTR (Mgr.)	1960
Barker, Robert M.	MTN	1952, 53, 54
Barkett, Gustav K.	MSO	1972, 73
Barkman, Janie	WSW	1970
Barley, James R.	MBK	1955, 56
Barlow, Earl W.	BB	1927
Barnard, Everette B.	WR	1968, 69, 70, 71
Barnefield, John T.	BB	1974, 75, 76, 77
Barnes, Brian E.	MSW	1992, 93, 94, 95
Barnes, Charissa	WTR	1980, 81
Barnes, Dylan M.	MTR	1992, 93, 94, 95
Barnes, Kenneth D.	MTR	1951
Barnes, Nick T.	FB	1974, 78
Barnes, Priscilla A.	WTR	1994, 95, 96, 97
Barnes, Quacy M.	WBK	1995, 96, 97, 98
Barnett, Jeffrey L.	FB	1971, 72
Barnett, Kristin A.	WTR	1993
Barnhart, Dean L.	MBK	1909, 10, 11
Barnhart, Hugh A.	FB/MBK	1912, 13
Barnhart, Richard J.	FB/WR	1952, 53
Barrett, Eric S.	MTN	1992, 93, 94, 95
Barrett, Laura L.	WTN	1996
Barnett, William K.	MTR	1974
Barnhill, Rose Ann	WCC/WTR	1979, 80, 81, 82, 83, 84
Barnthouse, Token D.	MTR	1995
Barnum, Stephanie A.	WCC/WTR	1992, 93, 94, 95, 96
Barr, Christine R.	WCC	1990
Barrow, Robert K.	MCC	1963, 64
Barrows, Barbara	WSW	1970
Barry, Dianne K.	WSW	1979, 80, 81
Barry, John M.	MGO	1997, 98, 99
Barter, Robert F.	MCC/MTR	1938, 39
Bartgis, Jenny W.	FH	1975, 76
Barth, Richard C.	MGO	1958, 59, 60
Barthold, William C.	MSW	1969, 70
Bartholomew, Harold J.	MGO	1951, 52, 53
Bartkiewicz, Byron M.	WR	1974
Bartkiewicz, John J.	FB	1952, 53, 54, 55
Bartkiewicz, Joseph F.	FB	1946, 47, 48, 49
Bartkiewicz, Leonard S.	FB	1960
Bartkiewicz, Walter C.	FB/MGY	1946, 47, 48, 49, 50
Bartley, Johnnie F.	MTR	1989, 90, 91, 92
Barton, William R.	MSW	1959, 60, 61
Bary, Steven D.	MSO	1975
Barzilauskas, Carl J.	FB	1971, 72, 73
Barzilauskas, Robert "Bo"	FB	1994
Baske, James R.	MGO	1966, 67
Bass, Jerold D.	MBK	1960, 61, 62
Bassett, Martin M.	MCC/MTR	1982, 83, 84, 85, 86, 87
Bassham, Clifford H.	WR	1937
Bastian, Frederick E.	MTN	1919, 20, 21
Bastian, Richmond E.	MTN	1932
Bastianelli, Ann I.	VB	1975, 76, 77
Batalis, George C.	FB	1995, 96
Batdorf, Linda	WBK/WG	1970, 71
Batdorf, Teresa	WBK	1973, 74
Bateman, Bryan J.	MSW	1967, 68, 69
Bateman, Carrolle	WSW	1979
Bates, Robert E.	MTR	1930, 31
Bates, Willie D.	FB	1985, 86, 87, 88
Battaglia, Carla	WTR	1982, 83, 84, 85
Battaglia, Robert L.	FB	1958, 59
Battreall, Ronald W.	FB	1956
Batts, Michael L.	FB	1992, 93, 95
Baublis, Janet A.	WSW	1981, 82, 83, 84
Bauer, Daniel E.	FB	1985, 86, 87, 88
Bauer, Jawn J.	MTR	1974
Bauer, Michelle	WSO	1995
Bauer, Robert L.	BB	1949, 50, 51
Baughman, Cara L.	WCC/WTR	1979, 80
Baughman, Christina	WTN	1972, 73, 74
Baughman, Cindy	WTN	1972
Baughman, Michael A.	BB/FB	1967, 68, 69, 70
Baum, Barbara J.	WCC	1983
Baum, Johnnie C.	MCC/MTR	1994, 95
Bauman, James M.	MTR	1993
Baumann, Jason D.	MSW	1991, 92, 93, 94
Baumgartner, Richard E.	MBK/MTR	1951, 55
Bausback, Danny E.	R	1962, 63
Baxter, Brian T.	MCC/MTR	1984, 85, 86, 87, 88
Baxter, Gary Z.	MTN	1961, 62, 63

Baxter, Kathy A.	WSW	1977, 78
Baxter, Neal E.	FB	1928, 29, 30
Bayles, David R.	MSW	1967, 68, 69
Beachler, Micah A.	MTR	1989, 90, 91, 92
Beals, Christy D.	VB	1988
Beals, Travis W.	MTR	1995, 96, 97, 98
Bean, William E.	FB	1921
Bear, Scott	FB (Mgr.)	1988
Beard, Clarence H.	BB	1890
Bearnarth, Kristin A.	WSW	1988
Beasey, Alan W.	MTR	1991
Beasley, Nelson G.	FB	1934, 35, 36
Beattie, Glenwood R.	MTR	1925
Beatty, G. Ronald	BB	1970, 71
Beatty, Kenny D.	MTR	1999
Beauchamp, Charles A.	FB	1990, 91, 92, 93
Beaudry, Robert	MSW	1980, 81
Beaupre, Anne M.	FH	1981
Beaver, Ernest R.	MGO	1936, 37
Beaver, Howard W.	MGO	1936, 37, 38
Beaver, Richard D.	MSW	1959, 60, 61
Beaverson, David G.	MTR	1982, 83, 84
Beck, Lori L.	WSW	1980, 81, 82, 83
Beck, Lynne E.	SB/VB	1980, 81, 82, 83
Beck, Roland W.	MTR	1916
Beck, Sara E.	WTR	1995
Beck, William E.	FB	1971
Becker, Charles A.	BB	1926
Becker, Christina M.	WCC	1981
Becker, David A.	MSO	1989
Becker, Henry W.	BB	1936, 37, 38
Becker, Tracy	WTN	1984, 85
Becker, Tracy L.	WSW	1988
Beckerle, Janet	WTN	1971
Becket, Melvin H.	FB	1950, 51
Beckles, Ian	FB	1988, 89
Beckley, Larry P.	MSW	1957
Beckner, Arthur J.	FB/MBK	1925, 26, 27, 28
Becks, Brett E.	WR	1999
Beecher, William B.	MTR	1929, 31, 32
Beemer, Jeff M.	MSW	1988
Beeson, Harold	FB	1932, 33, 34
Beeson, Harry	FB	1931
Beggs, Douglas B.	MCC/MTR	1987, 88, 89
Beggs, Jill	VB	1986, 87
Beggs, Webb E.	MSW	1940
Beguin, Steve M.	MCC/MTR	1996, 97, 98
Behling, Christopher S.	WR	1997
Behling, Matthew C.	WR	1996, 97
Behling, Steven M.	MTN	1994, 95, 96
Behr, Mark R.	MTN	1978, 79, 81
Behringer, Marc F.	MSO	1986, 87, 88
Beisler, Randall L.	FB	1963, 64, 65
Beitman, Lisa	WCC/WTR	1993, 94, 95
Belden, Bodine J.	FB	1988
Belfort, Nathalie	WTR	1995, 96, 97, 98
Bell, Brian R.	BB	1985, 86
Bell, Edward	FB	1941, 42
Bell, George	FB	1953, 54
Bell, Gregory C.	MTR	1956, 57, 58
Bell, Horace S.	BB	1928, 29
Bell, Julie S.	MCC (Mgr.)	1976
Bell, Leonard C.	FB	1983, 84, 85, 86
Bell, Robert A.	WR	1930
Bell, Ronald E.	FB (Mgr.)	1959
Bell, Vern S.	FB	1918, 19, 20
Bellamy, Walter	MBK	1959, 60, 61

Bellovich, Sharon L.	SB	1971
Belshaw, Edwin P.	WR	1930, 31, 32
Belshaw, George H.	WR	1930, 31, 32
Belt, Gordon E.	MSW	1954
Beltrame, Rachel J.	WSW	1993, 94
Belu, Michael A.	FB	1995, 96
Bencivenni, Carmen P.	FB	1962
Benckart, Robert G.	MCC	1941, 42
Bender, Robert M.	MBK	1976
Benedetti, Bart P.	MSW	1939, 40, 41
Benner, Wayne M.	FB	1948, 49
Bennett, Charles H.	FB	1926, 27, 28
Bennett, Donald C.	WR	1963, 64, 65
Bennett, Karen	WBK	1976
Bennett, Kenneth W.	FB	1928, 29
Bennett, Richard L.	MTN	1952, 53, 54
Bensen, Hayward S.	FB	1982, 83
Benson, M. Kent	MBK	1974, 75, 76, 77
Benson, Roger L.	MSW	1971
Bente, Paul F.	MCC/MTR	1938, 39
Bentley, Jeffrey T.	WR	1981, 83, 84, 85
Benzel, Charles F.	MTR	1925, 26, 27
Benzel, William H.	MTR (Mgr.)	1938
Benzio, Edward A.	WR	1977, 78
Berard, Monique	WGO	1981, 82, 83
Bere, David L.	MSW	1972, 73, 74
Bere, James F.	MSW	1970, 71, 72
Beres, Robert E.	BB	1952
Berg, Kajsa M.	WSW	1971, 72
Berg, Richard E.	MGO	1957
Berger, Caroline A.	SB/WTR	1983, 84, 85, 86, 87
Berger, Deborah	WBK	1972
Berger, Linda	WBK	1970
Bergman, Sheila K.	WGO	1976, 77
Bergman, William J.	FB	1965, 66, 67
Bergman, William E.	MTR	1952, 53, 54
Bergsman, James R.	MGO	1951
Berkebile, Stella	VB	1984
Berkoben, Deanna L.	MGO	1988, 89
Berkowitz, Kevin B.	MCC	1990
Berndt, Arthur "Cotton"	BB/FB/MBK	1908, 09, 10, 11
Bernoske, Daniel G.	FB	1924, 25
Berry, Kathy	FH	1970, 71
Berry, Kevin J.	MSW	1966, 67, 68
Berry, Linda C.	WBK	1977, 78
Berry, Robert C.	MTR	1977, 78, 79, 80, 81
Bertilsdotter, Nina S.	WSW	1999
Bertram, Russell J.	MSW	1987, 88
Betancourt, P. Armando	MSO	1978, 79, 80
Betner, Donna J.	MGO	1976, 77
Betner, Nathan M.	TR	1968
Bettman, Joan	WSW	1984, 85
Betz, Kimberly S.	WCC/WTR	1986, 87, 88, 89, 90, 91
Betz, Victor O.	MCC/MTR	1971, 72, 73, 74
Bevers, Mark M.	MBK (Mgr.)	1968
Beyer, Thomas H.	MSW	1973, 74, 75, 76
Beyst, Jennifer M.	WCC/WTR	1992, 93
Bezjak, Mateja	WTR	1996, 97, 98
Bezold, C. Lee	MSW	1969, 70
Bianco, Beth A.	FH/VB/WBK	1969, 70, 71, 72
Bibbie, Duane A.	MTR	1982
Bibbs, Andrew H.	FB	1946
Bickel, Mark E.	WR	1976
Bicking, Charles W.	MTR	1933, 34, 35
Biddinger, Gary A.	MGO	1972, 73, 74, 75
Biddinger, Noble L.	MTR	1931, 32, 33
Biedinger, Charles L.	MSW	1930, 32, 34
Bieghler, Peter W.	MCC/MTR	1989, 90
Bieker, Mark A.	FB (Mgr.)	1985
Bierman, Craig W.	MSW	1989, 90, 91, 92
Billish, Daniel R.	MCC/MTR	1996, 97, 98, 99
Bilunas, Thomas C.	FB	1966, 67, 68
Binkley, James K.	WR	1966, 67
Binkley, James L.	MTN	1962, 63, 64
Bird, William J.	FB	1949, 50, 51
Bireline, Robert B.	MSW	1987, 88, 90
Birko, Thomas	BB	1947, 48, 49
Birr, James O.	FB/MBK	1937
Bishop, DeGray R.	MBK (Mgr.)	1936
Bishop, George P.	FB	1925, 26
Bishop, Larry A.	BB	1968, 69, 70
Bishop, Lisa A.	WCC	1984
Bishop, Mark A.	MTN	1970, 71, 72
Bishop, Richard E.	BB (Mgr.)	1959
Biven, Donna L.	WTR	1981
Bizzell, John J.	FB (Mgr.)	1969
Bjelich, Steven C.	MTR	1974, 75, 76
Blab, Uwe K.	MBK	1982, 83, 84, 85
Black, James W.	WR	1965
Black, Joseph B.	MBK (Mgr.)	1982

Larry Barbiere was a 1968 Olympian and NCAA champion in the 100-yard backstroke in 1970.

Cindy Bumgarner, All-Big Ten in 1986, holds the IU record with a 17.3 career point average.

Name	Sport	Years		Name	Sport	Years
Black, Joseph H.	FB	1942		Booth, Walter W.	FB	1975, 76
Black, Joseph M.	BB (Mgr.)	1941		Borden, Nathaniel "Nate"	FB	1951, 52, 53, 54
Black, Karen A.	WTN	1976, 77		Borders, Nathan W.	FB	1981, 82, 83, 84
Black, Thomas E.	MGO	1944		Bordner, William A.	FB	1969
Black, Walt N.	MGY	1949, 50		Boroughs, Carl H.	BB	1928, 29, 30
Black, William S. II	MSW	1987, 88, 89, 90		Borowski, Steve S.	MSW	1967, 68, 69
Blackard, Michael G.	BB	1972, 73		Borse, Christina L.	WSW	1995, 96, 97
Blackburn, Marsh H.	FB	1951		Borst, Henry R.	MSW	1939
Blackburn, Thomas E.	MGO	1945		Borthwick, Robert J.	MGO	1965, 66
Blackburn, William C.	MTN	1946		Bosak, Edward S.	FB	1949, 50
Blackketter, George E.	BB	1891, 92		Bosart, Robert G.	MTN	1941, 46
Blackmon, John N.	MSW	1951, 52, 53		Bose, Donald L.	MCC/MTR	1910, 11, 12, 13
Blackwell, Joseph	MTR	1982, 83, 84		Bose, James	WR	1954, 55, 56
Blackwell, Larry R.	BB	1979, 80, 81, 82		Boshears, Troy A.	MBK (Mgr.)	1992
Blackwell, Robert L.	BB	1962		Bossert, Walter F.	BB/MBK	1906, 07
Blackwell, Ruth	WGY	1972		Bostic, Rachelle R.	WBK	1981, 82, 83, 84
Blaeuer, Karl F.	MCC	1984		Bostwick, Susan E.	WCC/WTR	1984, 85
Blagrave, William N.	MBK	1931		Boswell, Charles H.	MGO	1936, 37
Blair, Kathleen R.	WBK	1988, 89		Boswell, Patricia M.	SB	1978, 79, 80, 81
Blake, Sally L.	WSW	1976, 77		Bothwell, John H.	BB	1866, 67
Blake, Tracey D.	WGY	1981, 82, 83, 84		Bothwell, Michelle	WCC/WTR	1985, 86
Blakeley, Eric R.	BB	1999		Botkin, Suzanne D.	WTR	1999
Blanch, Kelly M.	WTN	1998, 99		Botos, Gregory Z.	MSW	1991, 92
Blanco, Beth	SB	1971		Bottenfield, Carl R.	BB	1917
Bland, Janice I.	SB	1970		Bouchard, Remi	MGO	1985, 86, 87
Blankenship, G. Thomas	WR	1966, 67, 68		Bouchie, Steven D.	MBK	1980, 81, 82, 83
Blankertz, Howard H.	MTN	1939, 40		Boughman, Dixon W.	MTR	1971, 72, 73
Blann, Robert L.	MSW	1957, 58, 59		Boughman, Janice O.	VB	1979
Blastick, Michael G.	FB	1993		Bouslog, Eugene H.	MSW	1946, 47, 48
Blazevic, James D.	BB	1987		Bove, Thomas A.	FB	1969, 70, 71
Bleecker, Dina Z.	WTN	1990		Bowen, Greg A.	FB	1990
Blickenstaff, Jim J.	MSW	1963		Bowen, Matt	MBK (Mgr.)	1994
Blitz, Gregory P.	MTR	1969		Bowerman, Cathy L.	B/VB	1976, 77, 78, 79
Bloom, Benton J.	FB	1903, 04, 05, 06		Bowers, Jason R.	WR (Mgr.)	1999
Bloom, William M.	BB	1939		Bowers, Jerry	FB	1978, 79, 80
Bloss, William H.	FB	1886, 87, 88		Bowers, Judith E.	FH/SB/WBK	1970, 71
Blount, Debbie	WTR	1979		Bowker, William D.	BB	1944
Blubaugh, Dale E.	WR	1981, 82		Bowman, Arnold J.	BB/FB	1949, 50, 51
Blumenthal, Harold J.	BB (Mgr.)	1947		Bowman, Brian D.	MTR	1999
Blythe, Stephen E.	FB	1966		Bowman, Brooke J.	WSW	1988, 89
Boak, Robert J.	FB	1958, 59		Bowser, Harold J.	FB	1916, 17, 19, 20
Board, Jenny	WSW	1982		Bowser, Herschel P.	MBK	1918
Board, Julie Ann	WSW	1984		Boyd, Alonzo H.	R	1953
Boarman, Daniel J.	FB	1971, 72, 73		Boyd, Carl M., Jr.	MSW	1953, 54, 55
Boatman, William S.	FB	1989, 90		Boyd, Douglas N.	MSW	1983, 84, 85, 86
Boaz, Robert C.	MSW	1940, 41		Boyd, Gene	FB	1986, 87, 88, 89
Bobay, Brian J.	FB	1995, 96, 97, 98		Boyd, James C.	MTR	1954, 55, 56
Bobb, Christopher R.	MSO	1972, 73		Boyd, Jason M.	FB	1991, 92, 93, 94
Bochnicka, John	FB/WR	1942, 43		Boyd, John A.	FB	1981, 82
Boddicker, Jay B.	BB	1985, 86, 87, 88		Boyd, Kyle W.	BB	1995, 96, 97, 98
Boden, Charles L.	MGO	1941, 42		Boyd, Trisha L.	SB	199/, 98, 99
Bodenhafer, Walter B.	WR	1911		Boyer, Byron O.	MGY	1953, 54, 55
Bodnar, Brenna C.	WTN	1990, 91		Boyer, Christopher W.	BB	1990, 91
Boehm, Dale E.	BB	1941, 42, 43		Boyle, Cecil W.	MBK	1908
Boehm, John H.	WSW (Mgr.)	1962		Boyle, Edward L.	BB/FB	1904, 05, 06
Boerger, Tricia S.	WSO	1993		Boyle, Herman B.	MTR	1938, 39, 40
Boersma, Anthony J.	MSW	1992, 94		Boyle, James P.	BB	1901, 02, 03, 04
Bogenschutz, Judith L.	WCC/WTR	1984, 85, 86, 87, 88		Boyle, Patrick J.	BB	1902
Boggan, Daniel	FB	1986		Bozdech, Barbara N.	FH	1974
Boggs, Brian E.	MSW	1981, 82, 83		Braadt, William K.	MSW	1987, 88
Boggs, Lowell W.	FB	1920, 21		Brabender, Robert C.	WR	1948, 49, 50
Boggs, William J.	FB (Mgr.)	1978		Brabender, David J.	WR	1973, 75
Bohach, Annette M.	WTR	1980, 81, 82, 83		Brabender, William G.	BB/WR	1948, 49, 50
Bohn, Erwin L.	MTR	1921, 22		Bradbury, Harry H.	BB	1903, 04, 05, 06
Bohnert, William W.	BB	1960, 61, 62		Bradford, Richard B.	FB	1958, 59, 60
Boland, Shannon	WTN (Mgr.)	1998		Bradley, James D.	BB	1978, 79, 80, 81
Boland, William J.	BB/FB	1889, 90		Bradley, London B.	BB	1990, 91, 92
Boldebuck, David J.	MSW	1977		Bradley, Richard	MCC	1954, 55
Bolen, Halfred D.	FB (Mgr.)	1951		Bradley, Robert J.	BB	1960, 61, 62
Bollinger, Robert T.	MSW	1979, 80, 81, 82		Bradley, Steve C.	FB	1983, 84, 85
Bolyard, Robert A.	MSW	1927		Bradley, William B.	MTR	1946, 47, 48, 49
Bolyard, Thomas E.	MBK	1961, 62, 63		Bradshaw, John W.	R	1962
Bolyard, Thomas W.	FB	1988		Bradt, Wilbur E.	MSW	1923
Boman, Tracey	WGY	1980		Brady, Terry D.	FB	1981
Bomba, Beth Anne	WTR	1981		Brafford, Jody	WTN	1972, 73
Bomba, Brad J.	FB	1954, 55, 56		Bragalone, Alfred A.	FB	1939, 40, 41
Bomba, Matthew J.	FB	1990, 91, 92		Brahm, Terry P.	MCC/MTR	1981, 82, 83, 84, 85, 86
Bomball, Walter M.	FB	1991		Bramel, Gordon M.	FB	1997
Boncek, David G.	MSO	1980, 81, 82, 83, 84		Brammell, Richard A.	BB (Mgr.)	1965
Bonchek, Jeff A.	BB	1985		Branam, George E.	MCC/MTR	1950, 51, 52, 53
Boneham, Chris R.	MSW	1984, 85, 86, 87		Branaugh, Michael L.	MBK	1969
Boniecki, George E.	WR (Mgr.)	1934		Branch, Bryant L.	MTR	1976
Bonnell, Scott C.	FB	1989, 90, 91, 92		Branch, Emmett F.	BB	1893
Bonsib, Louis W.	FB	1913, 14, 15		Branch, Melvin	FB	1962, 63, 64
Bonsib, Ray M.	FB/MTR	1907, 08, 10		Brandenburg, Ray E.	MBK	1944, 45
Bonsignore, Salvatore A.	MGY	1954, 55		Brandon, Lewis L.	MTR	1988, 90, 91
Boone, Clarence W.	MTR	1978, 79, 80, 81		Brandon, Thomas E.	WR	1972, 73
Boone, Thomas A.	BB	1970		Brandt, Elizabeth	WBK	1988
Bootes, Damon R.	MSO	1987, 88, 89		Brandt, Kelli M.	SB	1994, 95, 96, 97
Booth, Jonathan D.	MCC/MTR	1994, 95, 96, 97				

Brannan, Burl H.	WR	1929	Brown, Samuel E.	MCC	1933
Brant, Bridane W.	MGO	1934	Brown, Stacy D.	MSW	1984
Brant, John H.	MTR (Mgr.)	1960	Brown, Stephen H.	FB	1969, 70
Brase, Brian J.	MTR	1978, 79, 80, 81	Brown, Thurman J.	MTR	1930, 31, 33
Brase, Shondell M.	WTR	1984	Brown, William R.	MTR	1983, 84, 85, 86
Brattain, John M.	MTR	1927, 28	Brown, William S.	BB (Mgr.)	1936
Brattain, William M.	MTR	1927, 28	Browne, Dorothy	WSW	1971
Brauer, Nancy K.	FH/WBK	1969, 70, 71	Browne, Stacy L.	WCC/WTR	1981
Braughler, Matthew L.	BB	1993, 94, 95, 96	Browning, Tyrone W.	FB	1997, 98
Brawner, Melissa E.	VB	1995, 97	Brownstein, Julius R.	MGO	1940
Breckenridge, Thomas W.	MCC	1996, 97, 98	Browns, Jaime L.	WSW	1996
Bredschneider, Claus B.	MSW	1978	Broyles, James F.	FB	1997, 98
Breedlove, William H.	BB (Mgr.)	1952	Brubaker, Charles L.	BB/FB	1928, 29, 30
Breer, Brooke N.	WSO	1993, 94	Brubaker, Joe B.	MGO	1954
Brenda, Robert S.	BB	1980, 81	Bruce, Robert G.	MTR	1954
Breneman, Bruce R.	WR	1953	Brucker, James G.	MGO	1959, 60
Brennan, Frank X.	MTN	1962, 63	Bruening, Hilary C.	WCC/WTR	1993, 94, 95, 96, 97, 98
Brenner, Allen L.	FB	1904	Brugos, John D.	BB (Mgr.)	1974
Breslin, Julia	WSW	1979	Brun, Carmen L.	WSW	1986, 87, 88, 89
Bretscher, Seth P.	MSW	1981, 82, 83	Brunell, Frank O.	MSW	1960, 61, 62
Brewer, Joshua B.	MGO	1995, 96, 97, 98	Bruner, Brian D.	FB	1994
Brewer, Kenneth W.	FB	1891, 92, 93, 94	Bruner, Mark A.	WR	1993, 95
Brickner, Arthur J.	BB	1946, 47	Bruner, Robert L.	WR	1943, 47
Brickner, Ralph H.	BB	1946, 47	Bruner, Tammy	MTR (Mgr.)	1981
Bridenstine, Emily L.	WSO	1995, 96, 97, 98	Brunner, Clarence E.	BB	1940, 41, 42
Bridgeland, Cindy	FH/WTN	1970, 71, 72, 73	Bruno, Donald C.	MTR	1995, 96, 97
Bridges, Larry	CC	1959	Brunoehler, Richard	MSW	1945, 47, 48, 49
Bridges, R. McIntyre	MSW	1975, 76	Brusse, William R.	FB	1975, 76
Briede, David G.	BB	1983, 84	Bryan, E. Burritt	MGO	1950
Briggs, David M.	MCC/MTR	1989, 90, 91, 92, 93	Bryan, Frederick E.	FB/MTR	1900, 01, 02, 03
Briggs, Ray H.	MCC/MTR	1917, 18, 19	Bryan, Katherine A.	WSW	1977, 78, 79, 80
Bright, Russell	MBK (Mgr.)	1977	Bryan, William Lowe	BB	1884
Brigman, Jana	FH	1979, 80	Bryant, Hallie	MBK	1955, 56, 57
Brill, John R.	BB	1889	Bryant, James R.	MGY	1981
Brill, Pat	FH	1978	Bryant, Reggie L.	FB	1994
Briner, Louis A.	FB	1925, 26, 28	Bryant, Sherri	WTR	1986
Bringle, Ray D.	FB	1938	Bryant, Shirley D.	WBK	1992, 93, 94, 95
Brinkman, Craig C.	FB	1974, 75	Bryant, Stephanie L.	WCC/WTR	1993, 94, 95
Brinkoetter, Steve W.	MGY	1977, 78, 79	Bryce, Thomas M.	WR	1936, 37
Briscoe, Robert H.	MSW	1952, 53, 54	Bryson, Leonard A.	MGY	1959, 60, 61
Brittenham, Thomas G.	MCC	1947	Bubalovic, Mirsad E.	MSO	1990, 91
Brock, Raymond E.	FB	1984	Bucaro, Jamie F.	BB	1975, 76, 77, 78
Brocksmith, Henry A.	MCC/MTR	1930, 31, 32	Bucchianeri, Michael R.	FB	1938, 39, 40
Brodie, Donald C.	FB	1957	Bucci, Ronna M.	WGO	1988, 89
Brodt, Duane A.	MTR	1987	Buchan, John J.	FB	1977
Broertjes, Vernon H.	MCC/MTR	1938, 39, 40, 41	Buchanan, James K.	MTR	1974
Bromley, Amy E.	WSO	1994	Bucher, Clum C.	BB	1926, 27, 28
Brooker, Wesley R.	MTR	1968, 69	Buck, Phillip A.	MBK	1949, 50, 51
Brooks, Cleveland C.	FB	1948	Buck, Thedis M.	FB	1922
Brooks, Delray L.	MBK	1985	Buck, Thomas J.	FB	1973, 74, 75
Brooks, Esther M.	WCC/WTR	1989, 90, 91, 92, 93	Buck, Wallace A.	MCC/MTR	1927, 28
Brooks, Gregory R.	FB	1980, 81	Buckel, Joseph L.	BB	1991, 93
Brooks, Harry T.	FB	1939, 40	Buckley, Jaylene M.	WSW	1984
Brooks, Jennifer M.	WSW	1996, 97, 98, 99	Buckley, Jeffery A.	MBK (Mgr.)	1985
Brooks, John W.	MTR	1964, 65, 66	Buckley, Linnie C.	WTR	1989, 90, 91
Brooks, Neil R.	MTR	1962	Buckley, Roy D.	MTR	1905, 06
Brooks, Russell G.	MTR	1997, 98, 99	Buckner, Doster	MTR	1916
Brooks, William C.	MSO	1972	Buckner, Robert G.	MTR	1963, 64
Broome, L. Byron	FB	1960, 61	Buckner, W. Quinn	FB/MBK	1972, 73, 74, 75, 76
Brothers, James F.	FB (Mgr.)	1989	Buda, Arthur J.	WR	1945
Brough, Curtis R.	FB (Mgr.)	1989	Budacki, Robert M.	BB	1977
Brown, Angela	WTR	1980, 82, 83	Buehling, Richard	MCC/MTR	1949, 50, 51
Brown, Anthony E.	FB	1997, 98	Buerk, Harry A.	BB	1886
Brown, April E.	WTR	1979, 80	Bueter, Daniel E.	FB	1967
Brown, Catherine	WTR	1982	Bufe, Bruce S.	FB	1983, 84, 86
Brown, Christy G.	SB	1988, 89, 90, 91	Buford, Tony C.	FB	1985, 86, 87, 88
Brown, Cynthia	WCC/WTR	1979, 80, 81, 82, 83	Bugh, Robert B.	MTN	1949
Brown, David F.	MTN	1967, 68, 69	Buhler, Anna	MSO (Mgr.)	1991
Brown, D.A. "Tony"	MBK	1980, 81, 82, 83	Bui, Melanie A.	WCC	1986
Brown, Donald R.	BB	1962	Buickel, Howard C.	BB	1947, 48
Brown, Edward S.	MTR	1950, 51, 54	Buickel, Sherry D.	SB/WSW	1973, 74, 75, 76
Brown, Edward T.	MTR	1929, 30, 31	Bullard, Debra	WGO	1982
Brown, Gary L.	BB	1968, 69	Bullington, Mark A.	MGO	1985
Brown, Glen H.	WR	1933	Bullock, Max G.	MTR	1919, 20, 21
Brown, Gregory A.	FB	1968, 70, 71	Bullock, Monique R.	SB	1999
Brown, Gregory A.	FB	1980, 81	Bumgarner, Cynthia D.	WBK	1985, 86, 87, 88
Brown, Gregory L.	BB	1983	Bunce, Linda C.	SB/VB	1969, 70, 71, 72, 73
Brown, Heather M.	WTR	1992, 93, 94, 95	Bundy, Alicia J.	WTR	1997, 98
Brown, Howard K.	FB	1942, 45, 46, 47	Bunger, Leon E., Jr.	FB (Mgr.)	1943
Brown, Ilise	WGY	1970	Bunger, Thomas	FB (Mgr.)	1972
Brown, Jack W.	MBK	1948, 51	Bungum, Brian	MSW	1974, 75, 76, 77
Brown, Jacquline A.	WCC/WTR	1981, 82	Bunke, Anna C.	WSW	1975, 76
Brown, Jay A.	MCC	1967	Bunnell, Horace D.	MCC	1943
Brown, Jennifer N.	WTR	1998, 99	Bunting, Bruce M.	MGY	1977
Brown, Kenneth J.	MTN	1943	Buondonna, Brett W.	MSW	1992, 93, 94, 95
Brown, Lance A.	FB	1991, 92, 93, 94	Burch, Tracy R.	WCC/WTR	1981, 82
Brown, Mark A.	MTR	1981, 82	Burgan, Jack A.	MTR	1961
Brown, Michael A.	FB	1991	Burgess, David H.	MSW	1991, 92
Brown, Orlando, Jr.	FB	1982, 83, 84	Burgess, Thomas E.	FB	1958, 59, 60
Brown, Paul E.	MGY	1958, 59, 60	Burke, Daniel B.	FB	1921

Brian Bungum, was an NCAA champion diver in 1976 and 1977.

Jack Campbell led the Big Ten in batting in 1966 with a .381 average.

Burke, Edmund L.	MTR	1944
Burke, James E.	BB	1964, 65, 66
Burke, James W.	BB	1926, 27, 28
Burke, Kevin T.	FB	1980, 81
Burke, Mary E.	WSW	1993, 94, 95, 96
Burke, Thomas	MTR (Mgr.)	1963
Burkel, John R.	MGY	1960, 61, 62
Burkhart, Gerald E.	BB	1963, 64, 65
Burks, Stephen R.	MSO	1972, 73, 74, 75
Burks, Wendy	WSW	1973, 74
Burnett, Barry R.	BB	1972, 73, 74
Burnett, Darrick T.	FB	1975, 76, 77, 78
Burnett, John A., Jr.	FB	1921
Burnett, Robert E.	MTR	1939, 40, 41
Burnett, Ulysses	FB	1978
Burnham, Robert J.	MTN	1950, 51, 52
Burns, Donald F.	WR	1941
Burns, Jane Ellen	WTR	1985, 86
Burns, Maureen	WSW	1982
Burns, Peter R.	MTR	1973, 74
Burns, Richard	MSW	1963
Burns, Robert W.	WR	1954, 55, 56
Burns, Russell E.	FB	1957
Burnside, Diane	WSW	1970, 73
Burnside, Stephen W.	MSW	1982
Burrell, Donald K.	FB	1976
Burrell, James F.	MTR (Mgr.)	1966
Burrell, William III	MSW	1968
Burrelli, Angelo D.	FB	1976, 77
Burris, Carl C.	MCC	1927
Burrough, Kathy	WSW	1972, 73
Burroughs, Lori L.	WBK	1979, 80, 81
Burt, Meredith G.	SB	1989, 90
Burton, Charles S.	FB	1933, 34
Burton, Daniel L.	MTR	1986, 87, 88, 89, 90
Burton, Elmer	FB	1973
Burton, Gregory E.	MBK (Mgr.)	1989
Burton, Roger H.	R	1956
Burtt, Amos H.	BB	1910, 11
Busbee, Westley F.	FB/MTR	1932, 33, 34, 35
Busby, Lawrence M.	MBK	1921, 22
Buschmann, Charles S.	BB/FB/MBK	1915, 16, 17
Buse, Mark W.	MTR	1992, 93, 94, 95
Bush, Darren D.	FB	1985, 87
Bush, Howard T.	WR	1933, 34, 35
Bush, Joseph K.	MCC/MTR	1920, 21
Bushing, Jodi A.	WP	1998, 99
Buskirk, Philip K.	BB	1881
Bustard, Cynthia J.	FH	1975, 76, 77, 78
Butcher, Jade J.	FB	1967, 68, 69
Butler, Errol S.	MTR	1991, 92, 93
Butler, Evelyn L.	FH/SB/WBK	1972, 73, 74, 75
Butler, John R.	MCC/MTR	1982, 83, 84, 85
Butler, Mary Ann	VB	1976, 77, 78, 79
Butler, Thomas S.	FB	1921, 22, 23, 24
Butte, Charles G.	MBK	1960
Butterfield, David J.	MSO (Mgr.)	1987
Buttorff, Gordon S.	BB/MBK	1919, 20
Butts, Carroll R.	FB	1926, 27, 28
Buzminski, Angela R.	WGO	1990, 91, 92, 93
Byers, G. Herman	FB	1925, 26, 27
Byers, George H., Jr.	FB	1950, 51, 52
Byers, Philip A.	MBK	1953, 54, 55
Byers, Steve D.	MSW	1973, 74
Bynum, Kelly L.	WBK	1983
Bynum, William D.	BB	1866, 67
Byrne, Mitchell L.	R	1963

Byrnes, Charles F.	FB	1971, 72
Byrum, Enoch A.	MBK	1917, 19, 20

Cabel, James R.	MSW	1956, 57
Caffey, Harold	MTR	1956, 57, 58
Cain, Garrett	MTR	1998, 99
Cain, Susan	WSW	1981, 82
Cain, Thomas D.	MSW	1982, 83, 84, 85
Caine, Walter A.	MCC/MTR	1924, 25, 26
Calcaterra, Jeffry J.	BB	1989, 90, 91, 92
Caldemeyer, Daniel F.	MTR	1934, 35, 36
Caldwell, Adam M.	WR	1988, 89, 90, 91
Caldwell, Elvin T.	FB	1957, 58, 59
Caldwell, James E.	FB	1983, 84, 85
Caldwell, Ralph W.	FB	1981, 82
Caldwell, Virginia	WSW	1978, 79, 80
Calhoun, Christopher K.	MCC/MTR	1989, 90, 91
Calkins, Scott P.	MSO	1989, 90
Call, James A.	FB	1894
Callahan, Kelly G.	WSW	1984
Callaway, Stephanie S.	WSW	1993
Callaway, Steve V.	MTR	1971, 72, 73, 74
Callis, Robert	MGO	1952, 53, 54
Calloway, Richard M.	MBK	1986, 87, 88
Calvert, Timothy W.	BB	1981
Calvin, Keith D.	FB	1974, 75, 76, 77
Cameron, Deon A.	MTR	1985, 86, 87, 88
Cameron, Malcolm "Cam"	FB/MBK	1982, 83, 84
Cameron, Robert J.	FB	1986
Cammarata, Ben E.	MCC/MTR	1986, 87, 88
Cammarata, Christy A.	SB	1987, 88, 89, 90
Campagnoli, Tony	FB	1935
Campaigne, Barbara	WTN	1972, 73, 74
Campbell, Andrew J.	MSW	1983, 84, 85, 86
Campbell, Cary C.	MGO	1985
Campbell, Charles A., Jr.	FB	1960
Campbell, Clinton A.	MCC/MTR	1961, 62, 63, 64
Campbell, Earl E.	MGY	1949, 50
Campbell, Jack E.	BB/MBK	1964, 66
Campbell, James A.	MBK	1931, 32
Campbell, Janelle K.	SB	1992, 93, 94, 95
Campbell, Johnny L.	MTR	1993
Campbell, Karen M.	WSW	1996
Campbell, Keith	MBK/MGO	1933, 34, 35
Campbell, Milton G.	FB/MTR	1954, 55
Campbell, Randy C.	WR	1980, 81
Campbell, Robert R.	WR	1964, 65, 66
Campbell, Shavonda C.	WBK	1993, 94
Campbell, Tarviant C.	WTR	1997, 98, 99
Campbell, Thomas L.	FB/MTR	1956, 57, 58
Campins, Luis	MSW	1990
Camplese, Daniel	BB	1953
Campuzano, Sergio, Jr.	MSO	1997
Canfield, Stephen H.	FB	1970
Cannady, John H.	FB	1943, 44, 45, 46
Canning, Arthur J.	MGY	1960, 61, 62
Cannon, Kristin	WSW	1975, 76
Cannon, Larry G.	MBK (Mgr.)	1975
Cannon, Robert W.	MTR	1977, 78, 79, 80
Cannon, Robin A.	FH	1979
Cantwell, Guy	MBK	1902, 03
Cantwell, Jennifer H.	WSO	1995, 96, 97, 98
Cappas, Peter J.	BB	1953, 54
Caplis, James P.	BB	1978, 79, 80
Cappos, Scott A.	MTR	1988, 89, 90, 91
Capron, John C.	BB/FB	1889, 90, 91
Carder, Nancy	WTN	1971
Cardinali, Mario A.	MTR	1989, 90, 91, 92
Cardwell, Lisa E.	WCC/WTR	1986, 87, 88
Cardwell, Richard W.	MGO	1953, 54, 55
Carey, Charles D.	MSW	1948, 49, 50
Carey, Roderick C.	FB	1991, 92, 93
Carey, Tracy	WSW	1981, 82, 83
Carie, Helen A.	WSW	1987
Carl, Dorothy R.	WCC	1981
Carlberg, Jason A.	MSW	1998, 99
Carlin, Robert	WR	1950, 52
Carlino, Ralph A.	WR	1960, 61, 62
Carlson, David A.	MSO	1986
Carlson, John R.	FB	1968
Carlson, Jonathan J.	MSW	1996, 97, 98, 99
Carlson, Robert J.	MSO	1989
Carlton, Nicholas J.	MSW	1966, 67, 68

Carlton, Roseann	WBK	1985, 86, 87, 88
Carmine, Samuel A.	MSW	1969
Carney, Brett D.	MSW	1983, 84
Carney, Erin E.	WGO	1996, 97, 98, 99
Carpenter, Kenneth L.	FB	1972, 74
Carpenter, Kristin J.	WP	1998, 99
Carr, Charles E.	FB/MBK	1902, 03, 04, 05
Carr, Francis J.	BB	1954, 55
Carr, Ryan	MBK (Mgr.)	1996
Carroll, Joseph E.	MTR	1958, 59, 60
Carroll, Joseph L.	MSW	1982, 83, 84, 85
Carroll, Kay L.	SB/WBK	1980, 81
Carroll, Paula A.	WCC/WTR	1984, 85, 86
Carson, William H.	MGO	1995, 96, 97, 98
Carter, Barbara J.	WTR	1993, 94, 95, 96
Carter, C. E. "Butch"	MBK	1977, 78, 79, 80
Carter, Cydryce	VB	1996, 97, 98
Carter, Francis L.	FB	1948
Carter, Hugh M.	WR	1922
Carter, Jennings D.	BB (Mgr.)	1931
Carter, Marshall D.	MGY	1970, 71, 72, 73
Cartwright, Clarence E.	BB/FB	1907, 08
Cary, Stephen J.	MSW	1966, 67
Casaburo, Christopher P.	MSO	1990, 91, 93
Casaburo, Thomas A.	MSO	1987, 88, 89, 91
Casebeer, Paul B.	BB	1918
Casey, Spencer J.	MCC/MTR	1991, 93, 94
Cashman, Kirsten P.	WSW	1993, 94
Cashman, Michael D.	R	1961, 62
Cass, William O.	MSW	1961, 62
Cassady, Heather L.	WBK	1999
Cassells, Gary J.	FB	1966, 67
Casselman, Donald L.	FB	1970, 71
Cassidy, Patrick M.	MTR	1982
Cassidy, Patrick R.	WR	1997, 98, 99
Cassidy, Thomas J.	FB	1953, 54, 55
Castanias, Marilyn	WSW	1973
Castle, Thomas R.	WR	1979, 80
Castleman, Justus C.	BB	1900
Castro-Silva, Rod A.	MSO	1982, 83, 84, 85, 86
Catron, Diane R.	VB	1981, 82, 83
Catterton, Antrim S.	FB	1926, 27
Catterton, Wilbert O.	FB/MGO	1927, 28, 29, 30
Caudill, C. Craig	MTR	1972, 73, 74, 75
Caudle, Laura A.	SB	1982
Cauley, Julia A.	VB	1984
Caulkins, Sally E.	FH/SB	1977, 78, 79, 80, 81
Cavanaugh, Robert M.	MCC/MTR (Mgr.)	1933, 34
Cavallo, Joseph A.	MSO	1995, 96
Cave, George E.	MSW	1947, 48, 49, 50
Cazee, Rachel M.	WTR	1999
Cellini, Oliver G.	WR	1933, 34, 35
Centlivre, Charles F.	R	1953
Ceretto, Ana K.	WTN	1998, 99
Cerovski, Charles J.	MTR	1945
Cerroni, Daniel A.	MSO	1996, 97, 98
Cerroni, J.T.	MSO	1994, 95, 96, 97
Cervasio, Christine E.	WTR	1993, 94, 95
Cesario, Rodney M.	BB	1983, 84
Chaffee, Robert G.	MTR	1962, 63, 64
Chalfie, Ivan M.	MSW	1951, 52
Chamberlin, Ben H.	MTN	1949
Chamberlin, Kenneth R.	WR	1980, 81
Chambers, Betty	WSW	1975, 76
Chambers, Michael P.	MGO	1992, 93, 94
Champa, Benjamin A.	MSW	1996
Chandler, Aletha C.	WGY	1976
Chandler, Roger L. III	WR	1994, 95, 96, 97
Chandler, Val M.	MTR	1969, 70, 71
Chaney, Earl H.	MCC/MTR	1921, 23
Chaney, Jermaine T.	FB/MTR	1992, 93, 94
Chanley, David R.	FB (Mgr.)	1971
Chapman, Jill L.	WBK	1999
Chapman, Tracy L.	WGO	1985, 86, 87, 88
Chappell, Kathleen R.	FH	1979, 80
Chase, David G.	BB	1992
Chase, Steven M.	FB (Mgr.)	1984
Chattin, Clyde N.	MBK	1907, 08, 12
Chattin, Herbert O.	MCC/MTR	1933, 34, 35
Cheaney, Calbert N.	MBK	1990, 91, 92, 93
Chelle, Robert S.	MSW	1996, 97, 98, 99
Cheney, James A.	MGO	1966, 67, 68
Cheney, Johanna L.	WSW	1988, 89, 90, 91
Cherry, George R.	BB	1945, 46
Cherry, Harry C.	FB	1935, 36
Cherry, Susan M.	WCC/WTR	1982, 83, 84, 85
Cherubini, Amy S.	WBK	1989, 90, 91, 92
Chesler, Barbara N.	FH	1975, 76, 77
Chew, George E.	WR	1988, 89
Chiarugi, Jeffrey L.	BB	1976, 77

Chiddister, Daniel L.	MTN	1939, 40, 41
Childress, Tina M.	WSW	1983
Childs, Brandt A.	BB	1998, 99
Childs, Floyd	WR	1925
Chiles, Casey M.	WSW	1999
Chirichetti, Lisa M.	WGO	1985, 86
Chitwood, Morris	WR	1946
Choice, Wallace, Jr.	MBK	1954, 55, 56
Chokey, Douglas D.	MTR	1970, 71, 72
Chorny, Thomas W.	MCC/MTR	1995, 96, 97, 98, 99
Chottikhun, Panya	MGY	1956, 57, 58
Christensen, Dianna L.	SB/VB/WBK	1976, 77, 78, 79, 80
Christie, Ryan	WTN (Mgr.)	1999
Christoff, Joseph A.	MTN	1983, 84, 85, 86
Christophersen, Jane	WBK/WTN	1972, 73, 74
Christy, Al C.	BB/FB	1981, 82
Chubb, Nancy A.	FH	1974, 75, 76, 77
Chumbley, Gary E.	MTR	1968
Churchman, Henry C.	MSW	1921, 22, 23
Chylaszek, Melissa A.	MCC (Mgr.)	1988
Cichowski, Eugene W.	FB	1954, 55, 56
Cieslak, Chester C.	BB	1945
Ciolli, Frank	FB	1943, 44, 45, 46
Ciriaco, Yeronimo	FB	1996, 98
Cisar, D. Jeffrey	BB	1983, 84
Cisco, Jennifer L.	WSW	1990, 91, 92
Cisco, Walter S.	MGO	1937, 38, 39
Cisco, Walter S.	MGO	1967, 68, 69
Claahsen, Mark S.	FB	1983, 84
Clapham, William E.	MCC/MTR	1927, 28, 29, 30
Clark, David	WR	1970, 71, 72, 73
Clark, Dennis F.	FB	1974
Clark, Gerald	BB	1954, 55, 56
Clark, Hezlep W.	FB	1904, 05, 06
Clark, James B.	MTR	1937, 39
Clark, James S.	BB	1936, 37, 38
Clark, Jerald W.	MTR	1952, 53, 54, 55
Clark, Michael	FB	1970
Clark, Michael S.	MSO	1991, 92, 93, 94
Clark, Millie S.	SB	1970, 71
Clark, Paul B.	MSW	1921, 22, 23
Clark, Tamsen	WSW	1979
Clarke, Christopher C.	FB	1963
Clarke, Jerry L.	FB	1994
Clarner, Dawn L.	WCC/WTR	1993, 94
Clary, James T.	WR	1970, 71, 72, 73
Clasen, William E.	FB	1937, 38
Clause, Benjamin D.	BB	1997, 98, 99
Clausen, Christopher W.	FB	1979
Clay, Emmons W.	FB	1920, 21, 22
Clay, Tala G.	WBK/WTN	1973, 74
Clayton, James E.	MTR	1982, 83, 84
Cleary, Michael J.	MCC/MTR	1972, 73, 74, 75
Cleary, Patrick A.	MCC/MTR	1973, 76
Cleary, Sean M.	MTR	1997, 98, 99
Clements, Cindy	FH/SB/VB	1972, 73, 74
Clesner, Sonia	VB/WSW	1970, 71, 72, 73
Cleveland, Robert W.	MGO	1947, 48, 49, 50
Cleveland, Stanley A.	MTN	1966
Clevenger, Zora G.	BB/FB	1900, 01, 02, 03, 04
Click, Cecile	WSW	1970
Clifford, Joseph E.	FB	1925
Clifford, Tim R.	BB/FB	1978, 79, 80
Clifton, James R.	BB	1940, 41
Cline, Charles W.	BB	1969, 70
Cline, James R.	BB	1968
Cline, Robert A.	MTR	1951, 52
Clinton, James L.	MTR	1960, 61, 62
Clippard, Amy E.	WTR	1998, 99
Clippert, Geof J.	MSW	1987, 88, 89, 90
Clodfelter, Jo E.	SB/WBK	1974, 75, 76, 77
Close, Glen C.	MTR	1971, 72, 73, 74
Clouse, Cline E.	FB/MBK	1912, 13
Clouse, Derek W.	MGO	1991, 92, 93, 94
Clutter, C. Steven	MTR	1975
Clutter, Seth S.	MTR	1997
Coachys, Richard M.	FB	1962, 1963
Coahran, David A.	BB	1982
Coahran, Thomas E.	BB	1963, 64, 65
Coakley, Albert	MGY	1942, 43
Cobb, Jeffrey E.	MTR	1986
Cobb, Jennifer A.	WSW	1974, 75, 76, 77
Cobb, Steven M.	MTR	1973, 74, 75
Coble, Thomas C.	MGO	1958, 59, 60
Cochran, Roy B.	MTR	1939, 40, 41
Cochrane, John C.	MTR	1913
Coetsee, Lizl	WTN	1994, 95, 96, 97
Coffee, J.C.	FB	1943, 44
Coffey, Donnita K.	WBK	1978, 79
Coffey, George B.	MBK	1921, 22

Coffey, Robert H.	MGY	1974, 75, 76, 77
Cogan, John M.	BB	1943
Cogdell, Charles R.	MCC/MTR	1957, 58
Cohen, Edward	BB	1944, 45, 46, 47
Cohen, Jeffery S.	MTN	1983, 84, 85, 86
Cohen, Stuart M.	MTN	1960, 61, 62
Colby, Terrance L.	BB/FB	1974, 75, 76, 77, 78
Cole, Kelly L.	WSO	1998
Cole, Terry P.	FB	1965, 66, 67
Cole, Thomas W.	MSW	1979, 80, 81, 82
Coleman, Brian A.	FB	1995, 96
Coleman, Chester F.	FB	1910, 11, 12
Coleman, Erick L.	FB	1985, 86, 87, 88
Coleman, George C.	MTR	1943
Coleman, Harold D.	WR (Mgr.)	1942
Coleman, Kenneth	MGY	1974, 75, 76, 77
Coleman, Larry A.	MGY	1963, 64
Coleman, Larry G.	FB	1960, 61, 62
Coleman, Louis H.	BB	1964
Coleman, Roderick A.	FB	1989, 90, 91
Coleman, William J.	MSW	1980, 81
Colglazier, JoAnn	WGO	1972
Colias, James H.	WR	1981, 82, 83, 84
Collier, Jason J.	MBK	1997
Collier, Michael A.	MSW	1996, 97, 98, 99
Collier, Robert M.	MTR	1935, 36, 37
Collier, Thomas M.	MTR	1918
Collignon, Jeff A.	MTR	1987, 88, 89
Collins, Charles H.	BB	1983, 84
Collins, Eoin P.	MTN	1986, 87, 88
Collins, Jerry V.	MGY	1967, 69
Collins, John H., Jr.	MSW	1965, 66, 67
Collins, Linda	WSW	1981
Collins, Pete C.	MSW	1982, 83
Collins, Vernon R.	MTR	1996, 97, 98, 99
Collis, John S.	MSW	1982, 85
Collum, Debra L.	WTN	1975, 76, 77
Colnitis, Donald J.	BB	1949, 51, 52
Colston, Dennis V.	MCC	1963
Colston, Michael V.	MCC/MTR	1995, 96, 97
Colyer, Heather A.	WTR	1999
Combs, Jan M.	FH	1975, 76, 77, 78, 79
Combs, Shannon	WSW	1998
Compani, Tabrizi B.	MSO	1972
Comparet, Aimee J.	WGY	1976, 77, 78, 79
Compton, Russell T.	FB	1974, 75, 76, 77
Comstock, Byron J.	MGO	1962, 63, 64
Comstock, Terrence L.	MGO	1964, 65
Conaway, Richard W.	WR	1963, 64, 65
Condon, Sheila M.	WCC/WTR	1981, 82, 83, 84
Conelly, Gary R.	MSW	1970, 71, 72, 73
Congdon, John F.	FB	1944
Congie, Samuel E.	FB	1956, 57, 58
Conkle, Frederick A.	FB	1915, 16
Conklin, James E.	WR	1947, 48
Conley, Sean	FB (Mgr.)	1981
Conlon, William E.	FB	1965
Conn, Jack K.	BB	1953
Connelly, Lisa M.	WTR	1996
Connelly, Maureen A.	WGY	1985
Connelly, Timothy M.	MGY	1977, 78, 79, 80
Conner, Joseph H.	WR	1928, 29, 30
Conner, O. J.	FB	1997, 98
Connor, Tammy L.	SB	1985, 86, 87, 88
Connors, John M.	FB	1951, 52, 53
Connors, Ryann C.	VB	1996, 97, 98
Connors, Shawn M.	WR	1978, 79
Conrad, Joseph H.	FB	1913
Conroy, Kathleen C.	WSW	1979, 80, 81
Consolo, Nancy E.	WCC/WTR	1983, 84
Constantinou, Savaas	MTN	1994, 95
Cook, Charles E.	MBK	1907, 08
Cook, Christopher H.	FB	1982, 83, 84
Cook, David M.	FB	1974
Cook, Gabriel P.	WR	1998, 99
Cook, George M.	FB	1895
Cook, Harold L.	MGY (Mgr.)	1952
Cook, James W.	MGO	1949
Cook, Jeff D.	MGO	1981, 82, 83, 84
Cook, Laura	WBK/WGO	1970, 71, 72, 73
Cook, Lewis E., Jr.	MSW	1958, 59, 60
Cook, Robert J.	MGO	1946, 48, 49
Cook, Tamara L.	WSW	1993, 94, 95, 96
Cook, Tracy L.	WSW	1994, 95, 97
Cooke, Aaron	MSW	1990
Cooke, Allison M.	SB	1999
Cooke, Joseph	MBK	1968, 69
Cookinham, Martha J.	FH	1980
Cookson, Thomas A.	MBK	1903, 05
Cooley, Frederick A.	BB	1888, 89, 90, 91

Coomer, Richard H.	BB	1959
Coon, James H.	MSW	1934, 35
Coon, Jesse B.	MSW	1930
Coon, Julius M.	MSW	1930, 32
Cooper, Anne E.	WSW	1987
Cooper, Berigan M.	MGO	1961, 62, 63
Cooper, Diane M.	WGY	1985
Cooper, Donald E.	MBK	1928, 29, 30
Cooper, Gilbert F., Jr.	FB (Mgr.)	1940
Cooper, Kathleen	WTR	1983
Cooper, Larry W.	MBK	1964, 65
Cooper, Philip S.	MSW (Mgr.)	1941
Cooper, Ralph T.	BB	1941
Copeland, James E.	MBK	1945
Copeland, Sarah	WGY	1972
Copeland, William A.	MTR	1976, 77, 78, 79
Copper, Jeffrey T.	MSW	1982, 83, 84, 85
Corbin, Gilbert H.	MTR	1922, 23
Cordes, Kathy	WTN	1972
Cordin, J. Scott	MSW	1965, 66, 67
Corell, Barbara J.	WSW	1971, 72
Cornelius, Mary E.	WGY	1976, 77, 78
Cornell, Bonnie	WSW	1972
Cornell, Fred D.	BB/FB	1886, 87, 88
Cornell, Nana	WGY	1975
Corradini, Ronald H.	FB	1990, 91
Correia, Michael J.	MSO	1986, 87, 88
Correll, John E.	BB	1954
Correll, Ralph T.	BB	1954, 55, 56
Correll, Robert G.	BB/MBK	1926, 27, 28, 29
Corretjer, Lizza M.	WSW	1984
Corriden, John M. Jr.	BB	1939, 40
Corrigan, Robert F.	FB	1958, 59
Corsak, Irene	WSW	1980
Corse, Ralph W.	MTR	1947
Corso, Steven L.	FB	1979, 80
Corwin, Kelly A.	WGY	1977, 78
Cossman, Max	MTR (Mgr.)	1941
Costello, Betsy M.	WSO	1993, 94, 95, 96
Cotherman, Mindy L.	WBK/VB	1982
Cotter, Linda L.	SB/WBK	1970
Cotton, Jason A.	BB	1993, 94, 95
Couch, William H.	FB	1965, 66
Coufal, Scott E.	MSO	1993, 94, 95, 96
Coufalik, Francis J.	FB	1960, 61, 62
Coughlin, Josh J.	MTN	1982
Coulter, Todd C.	WR	1986, 88, 89, 90
Coulter, William L.	MBK	1934
Counsilman, James M.	MSW	1969, 70
Courim, John B.	FB	1925
Courter, John L.	BB	1958, 59
Cousineau, Thomas R.	FB	1955, 56, 57
Cousino, David J.	WR	1963
Couter, William T.	MTR (Mgr.)	1937
Coval, Willis N.	FB/MBK/MTR	1901, 02, 03, 04
Cowan, John D.	MBK (Mgr.)	1991
Cowan, Nancy J.	WBK	1987, 88
Cowan, Robert G.	FB/MBK	1942, 43, 46
Cowan, Todd A.	MSO	1994, 95
Cowden, K. Van	MTR	1985, 86, 87, 88, 89
Cowell, William J.	MTR	1991
Cox, Carol E.	BB	1938, 39
Cox, Courtney K.	WBK/WGO	1990, 91, 92, 93
Cox, Dianna	FH	1970
Cox, Francis G.	MGO	1931, 32, 33
Cox, Frank M.	FB/MTR	1920, 21, 22, 23
Cox, James B.	BB	1948
Cox, Monica L.	WSO	1993
Cox, Robert	MTR	1974
Cox, Robin K.	BB	1973, 74, 75
Cox, Todd M.	MSO	1989
Cox, William M.	BB	1933, 34
Coyer, Matthew H.J.	MSO	1989, 90, 91, 92
Coyle, Gene A.	MGO	1970, 71, 72, 73
Coyle, Kenneth F.	MSW/WR (Mgr.)	1929
Crable, Robert A.	FB	1971, 72
Craddock, Keith	MSW	1961, 62
Craft, Norman A.	FB	1956, 57, 58
Craig, Kimberly T.	WTR	1997, 98, 99
Craig, Pamela E.	SB	1985, 86, 87, 88
Craig, Richard M.	MSW	1943
Craig, Robert I., Jr.	R	1954
Craig, Scott T.	MSW	1978, 79, 80
Craig, William H.	MTR	1962, 63, 64
Craker, Ronald A.	MCC/MTR	1976, 77, 78, 79, 80
Crane, Aaron L.	WR	1996
Cranham, Scott R.	MSW	1973, 74, 76
Crapo, Zane H.	MSW	1978
Crask, Donald R.	MCC & MTR	1966, 67, 68, 69
Craton, Hugh L.	FB	1949, 50

Craton, Hugh L. | FB | 1949, 50

Byron Comstock was IU's first Big Ten golf medalist in 1964.

Chris Dal Sasso, a lineman, scored two touchdowns for the 1936 team he captained.

Curdy, Harold M.	MBK	1967
Curran, James R.	MCC	1975, 76, 77, 78
Curran, James V.	MTN	1980, 81
Curry, Curtis C.	MSW	1934, 35, 36
Curry, Ian D.	MTR	1999
Curths, Bruce A.	WR	1964, 65
Curtis, Michael R.	MTR	1958
Cushing, Joseph C.	BB	1958
Cushing, Michael V.	MSW	1989, 90, 91
Cusick, A. Michael, Jr.	MTR	1953, 54, 55
Custer, George T.	BB	1944
Cuthbert, Marvin P.	MCC/MTR	1931, 32
Cutler, Robert F.	MBK (Mgr.)	1943
Cutter, Roland L.	MBK (Mgr.)	1956
Cysewski, Daniel L.	WR	1974, 76, 77, 78
Czap, Jason N.	FB	1996, 97, 98
Czemerys, Sharon L.	FH/SB/WBK	1971, 72
Czerneda, Daniel L.	FB	1966

D'Achille, Louis J.	FB	1950, 51, 52
D'Alosio, Michael J.	MBK	1989
D'Ambrose, Michael P.	WR	1980, 81, 82, 83, 84
D'Orazio, Anthony J.	FB	1976, 77, 78, 79
Dabbiere, Alan J.	WR	1980
Dable, Chris	WBK	1971
Daffara, Felicia A.	WTN	1994
Dagg, Gary L.	FB	1971
Dagwell, David D.	MTR	1960, 61
Dahlberg, Peder L.	MSW	1969, 70, 71
Dahlin, Gene R.	FB	1966
Dahlin, Rodger G.	FB	1963
Dahlmann, Stacey L.	WSW	1988
Daigh, Danielle	VB	1969
Dailey, Charles G.	BB	1895, 96, 97, 98
Dailey, Frank C.	BB/FB	1889, 90, 91, 92
Dailey, John R.	FB	1977
Dailey, Thomas A.	FB	1952, 53, 54
Dakich, Daniel J.	BB/MBK	1982, 83, 84, 85
Dakwa, Albert D.	MTR	1990, 91, 92
Dale, Rex W.	BB	1917
Daley, Cybele K.	WCC	1981
Dallin, Jean	FH/SB/VB	1975, 76, 77, 78
Dal Sasso, Chris C.	FB	1934, 35, 36
Daly, Mark A.	MCC/MTR (Mgr.)	1975, 76, 77, 79
Dalzell, Wilbur J.	WR	1917, 18
Daniel, Cary O.	BB	1995
Daniel, Jerome C.	MBK (Mgr.)	1957
Daniel, John C.	FB/MTR	1912, 13, 14
Daniel, Karen L.	WCC/WTR	1982, 83, 84, 85, 86
Daniels, Charles G.	MCC/MTR	1939, 40
Daniels, Derrick W.	FB	1986, 87
Daniels, Edward	MBK	1971
Danielson, Donald C.	BB	1939, 40, 41
Dannacher, William D.	WR	1939
Danner, Daniel L.	FB (Mgr.)	1974
Danruther, Charles B.	BB	1910, 11, 12
Darby, Phelps F.	BB/FB/MBK	1900, 01, 02
Darring, Al D.	FB/MTR	1978, 79, 80, 81
Darrow, Heather L.	SB	1989, 90, 91, 92
Dart, Kristin M.	WSW	1992, 93
Dartnall, James T.	R	1954, 55, 56
Das, Biman	MSO	1984
Dascoli, Jody C.	VB	1993, 94
Daubel, Kathleen	WSW	1987
Dauer, Harold W.	BB (Mgr.)	1930
Dauer, Raymond F.	FB	1931, 32, 33
Dauer, Victor P.	FB/MBK	1929, 30, 31, 32
Daugherty, William L.	FB	1951
Daulton, Jack A.	MTR	1964, 65, 66
Dauphin, Philip E., Jr.	BB	1989, 90
Davenport, Cindy	VB	1971
David, Cindy	FH	1969
David, Donna	WSW	1975, 76
David, George	MBK (Mgr.)	1996
David, Ronald	MGY	1956, 57, 58
Davidson, Harry R.	FB	1898, 99, 1900, 01
Davidson, Roger K.	FB	1970, 71
Davidson, Thomas N.	MSW	1997, 98
Davidson, Thomas R.	FB	1904, 05, 06
Davies, James D.	BB	1969, 70, 71
Davis, Ashley M.	WSO	1996, 97, 98
Davis, Debbie	WSW	1971
Davis, Edgar Clarence	FB/MTR/WR	1911, 12, 13, 14

Cravens, Bernard K.	FB	1917, 20
Cravens, Dan M.	MGO	1942
Cravens, Eileen E.	SB	1976, 77, 78
Cravens, Meredith A.	WP	1998
Crawford, Carl E., Jr.	FB	1929
Crawford, Daniel J.	MTR	1997
Crawford, George P.	MSO	1992, 93, 94, 95
Crawford, James H.	MTR	1932
Crawley, Lynn M.	VB	1991, 92, 93, 94
Creag, Alicia D.	WTR	1998
Creek, Megan S.	WTR	1999
Creel, David B.	WR	1992
Creigh, Jessica R.	SB	1997
Creighton, Dana L.	WBK	1992
Cremeens, Dennis J.	FB	1972, 73, 74
Cremin, Ann E.	WSW	1981, 82
Crews, James S.	MBK	1973, 74, 75, 76
Crews, Patrick R.	BB	1985
Creydt, Terri L.	SB	1994
Crisman, Barbara	WGY	1972
Crispen, Lawrence W.	MCC/MTR	1945, 46
Crist, John M.	MSW (Mgr.)	1977
Cristofoli, Louis A.	FB	1980, 81, 83, 84
Cristy, Jennifer L.	WSW	1998, 99
Crites, Robert W.	MTR	1975, 76, 77
Crockford, Brian W.	MSO	1991, 92, 93
Crockford, Jim D.	MSO	1987, 88, 89, 90
Croftcheck, Don A.	FB	1962, 63, 64
Cromer, Donald L.	FB	1959, 60, 61
Cromer, Harold N.	BB	1938, 39
Cromer, William F.	MTR	1918
Cronin, William J.	BB	1942, 43
Crosby, Julie A.	WCC/WTR	1987, 88, 89, 90
Crosby, Thomas W.	FB	1915
Crose, Robert G.	TR (Mgr.)	1950
Cross, Ann E.	WTR	1994, 95
Cross, George W.	MGY	1951
Cross, Michael J.	FB/WR	1978, 79
Crotty, R. Michael	BB	1994, 95, 96, 97
Crouch, Clarence C.	MTR	1931, 32, 33
Crouch, John J.	FB	1943
Crow, Garland J.	BB/FB	1929, 30
Crowe, George W.	FB	1953, 54, 55
Crowe, Heather A.	WTN	1980, 81, 82, 83
Crowe, William S.	MBK	1922
Crowley, Theresa A.	FH/WBK	1978, 79
Crozier, Amy Jo	WCC	1981
Crum, Oren K.	FB	1932, 33
Crusan, Douglas G.	FB	1965, 66, 67
Csejtey, Eva M.	FH	1977
Culbertson, Angela S.	WCC/WTR	1991, 92, 93, 94
Culbertson, Jennifer L.	WCC/WTR	1989, 90, 91, 92, 93
Cullen, James H.	FB	1891, 92
Cullen, Kathy	WTR	1981
Cullisen, Samuel W.	MGY	1969
Cullom, Damian L.	MSW	1994
Culp, David M.	WR (Mgr.)	1946
Cummings, Arthur R.	BB	1908
Cummings, Catherine C.	WTR	1993
Cummings, George W.	BB	1874
Cunkle, Charles H.	MCC/MTR	1936, 37, 38
Cunningham, Ashel	BB/FB	1908, 09, 10, 11
Cunningham, Claire D.	SB/WBK	1976, 77, 78
Cunningham, Linda J.	WBK	1983, 84, 85, 86
Cunningham, Nathanial	FB	1966, 67, 68
Cunningham, William G.	MBK	1977

Davis, Gary B.	FB	1959
Davis, George B.	BB	1887, 88
Davis, George H.	MBK (Mgr.)	1931
Davis, James J.	FB	1991, 92, 93
Davis, Jason F.	MBK (Mgr.)	1994
Davis, Jennifer L.	WBK	1990, 91, 92, 93
Davis, Jerome E.	MBK (Mgr.)	1984
Davis, John L.	FB	1949, 50, 51
Davis, Joseph B.	MTN	1938
Davis, Lana C.	WSW	1984
Davis, M. George	BB	1925, 26, 27
Davis, Merrill S.	FB/MBK	1909, 10, 11, 12
Davis, Michael A.	MTR	1971, 72, 73, 74
Davis, Monica E.	WTR	1999
Davis, Nathan C.	BB (Mgr.)	1999
Davis, Nathan M.	FB/MTR	1993, 94, 95, 96, 97
Davis, Patti A.	WTR	1979, 80, 81
Davis, Paul Y.	FB	1909, 11
Davis, Richard C.	FB/MTR	1934, 35, 37
Davis, Thomas A.	MGY	1966
Davis, Thomas N.	MSW	1996, 97, 98, 99
Davis, Trenton L.	MTR	1996, 97, 98, 99
Davis, Victoria J.	WTR	1983, 84, 85, 86
Davis, Wilbert D.	MTR	1964, 65
Davis, William C.	MSW	1934
Davis, William R.	MTR	1943
Davitt, Ronald R.	MSW (Mgr.)	1959
Davy, Virginia E.	WSW	1975, 76, 77
Dawsey, Stacy L.	FB	1983, 85, 86
Dawson, Halford E.	MTR (Mgr.)	1927
Day, Harold K.	MGO	1938
Day, Jacqueline	SB	1973, 74
Day, James A.	MSW	1977, 78, 79
DeCamilla, Jon B.	FB	1974
Deady, Mark E.	MCC/MTR	1985, 86, 87, 88, 90
Deakin, Joshua D.	MTR	1992, 93, 94, 95
DeaKyne, James F.	MBK	1952, 53, 54
Deal, Kara L.	WCC/WTR	1992, 93, 94, 95, 96
Deal, Leroy T.	MCC/MTR	1945, 46, 47, 48
Deal, Mark R.	FB	1978
Deal, Michael H.	FB	1967, 68, 69
Deal, Russell J., Jr.	FB	1941, 42, 45, 46
Dean, Everett S.	BB/MBK	1919, 20, 21
Dean, Jan L.	WTN	1977
Dean, Robert T.	FB	1942
Dean, Saute K.	FB	1995
Deardon, Craig E.	MGO	1976, 77
DeArmond, Don	BB	1945
DeBaisse, Melissa B.	WP	1999
Debbout, John P.	FB	1969, 71
DeBlasis, Dennis R.	FB	1963
DeBlaze, Dawn	WSW	1986
DeBord, Eric J.	FB	1977, 79, 80
Debro, Carolyn D.	WTR	1983, 84, 85, 86, 87
Debro, Cynthia	WTR	1979
Deckard, Roger V.	WR	1983, 84
Deckard, Thomas M.	MCC/MTR	1935, 36, 37, 38
Decker, Christopher J.	MTN	1990, 91, 92
Decker, Hal B.	MTR	1970
Decker, Henry J.	MBK (Mgr.)	1937
Decker, Robert G.	FB	1969
DeCocq, Aimee M.	WSO	1994
Dedic, Joseph A.	FB	1986, 87
Deem, Paul R.	BB	1959, 60, 61
Deering, Brandon C.	MSO	1989, 90
Deery, Simon M.	MSO	1995, 96, 97, 98

Dees, W. Archie	MBK	1956, 57, 58
DeFord, Stephen K.	BB	1969, 70, 71
Defur, Donnon M.	MBK (Mgr.)	1954
DeGiacomo, Kenneth F.	FB	1963
DeGroh, Diane L.	WCC/WTR	1983, 84, 85, 86, 87
DeHart, John W.	WR	1986
DeHeer, William J.	MBK	1967, 68, 69
Dehority, Edward H.	MBK	1921
Dekkers, Michelle	WCC/WTR	1988, 89, 90
DeKraay, Sarah H.	WGO	1984, 85, 86, 87
Dell, Scott W.	MCC/ MTR	1994, 95, 96
Dellinger, Robert L.	MCC/MTR	1948, 49, 50, 51
DeMar, Aaron B.	WR	1997
DeLong, David W.	WR	1982, 83, 84
DelToro, Erica A.	SB	1998, 99
Deluca, Therese G.	SB	1980, 81, 82, 83
DeMaat, Joan M.	WCC/WTR	1981
Demarco, Robert	FB	1957
DeMarcus, Wilson B.	MTN	1921
Dembinski, Timothy S.	BB	1987, 88
Demers, Laura M.	FH	1980, 81
Demetri, John A.	MGO	1955, 56
Deming, Mark S.	FB/MTR	1972, 73, 75
Demmon, Floyd. E.	WR	1915
Demorotski, David D.	BB (Mgr.)	1972
Demos, Leo	MCC	1944, 45
Dempsey, William J.	BB	1972, 73
Dempster, Barbara	FH	1971, 72, 73
DeMuth, David A.	FB	1974
Denard, Theresa	WGY	1979
DeNardo, Janet E.	FH/B/WBK	1970, 71, 72, 73
Denbo, Vicki	WTR	1979
DeNeff, James E.	BB	1966
Denekas, Mark S.	BB	1982
Denham, Louise	WSW	1972, 73
Denham, Robert B.	R	1957
DeNinno, Lynn S.	FH/WCC/WTR	1979, 81, 82, 83
Denisar, S. Eugene	WR	1966, 67, 68
Denker, Larry A.	WR	1971
Dennen, Richard S.	MSW	1985, 86, 87, 88
Dennerline, Ralph R.	R	1955, 56
Denney, Deborah	WSW	1980
Dennis, Andrea K.	WSO	1994
Dennis, Darrell O.	MGO	1979, 81, 82
Dennis, Hobart S.	BB	1920, 21
Dennison, Judith L.	WGO	1983, 84, 85, 86
Denny, E. Rankin	BB	1922
Denny, Robert O.	MTR	1939, 40
Denny, Stanley R.	BB	1954
Denny, Thomas E.	FB (Mgr.)	1964
Denny, Winfield A.	FB	1894
Dentice, Carl	MTN	1954, 55, 56
Denton, Edward D.	MBK	1941, 42, 43
Deranek, Richard H.	FB	1944, 45, 46, 47
Derloshon, Thomas P., Jr.	BB (Mgr.)	1969
Dern, Timothy J.	MGY	1975, 76, 77, 78
Derr, Harold A.	BB/MBK	1926, 27, 28
DeSalle, Donald J.	FB	1967, 68, 69
DeSana, Jennifer L.	WTR (Mgr.)	1994, 95, 97
Desch, Kristian W.	MTR	1990, 91, 92
DeSmet, Lynn K.	WGO	1979, 80, 81, 82
Desmuke, Daniel C.	MSO	1974
DeStefano, Robert D.	FB	1962, 63, 64
Deter, Carol	WSW	1972
Deters, Matthew R.	WR	1997
Deutsch, Whitney T.	WR	1982
DeVault, Brett W.	FB	1979
DeVestern, Frank	MCC/ MTR	1956, 57
Devine, Patrick H.	WR	1932, 33, 34
Devine, Tracy A.	WGY	1985
DeVore, Douglas R.	BB	1997, 98, 99
DeVries, Jason M.	WR	1995, 96, 97, 98
DeVries, John J.	FB	1992
DeVries, Lexie J.	FH	1980, 81
Dew, Robert J.	MGO	1978, 79, 80
Dewar, James A.	FB	1942, 46
Dewey, Dean H.	MSW	1956
Dewhirst, Tom A.	MSW	1985, 86, 87
DeWitt, Cindy K.	VB	1978, 79
DeWitt, Debra A.	VB	1976, 77, 78, 79
DeWitt, Joshua D.	FB	1992, 93, 94
DeWitte, David B.	MTR	1972, 74, 75
DeWitte, David H.	MCC/MTR	1946, 47, 48, 49, 50
Dewitz, Brian K.	FB	1985, 86, 87, 88
Dewitz, Laura E.	VB	1997, 98
Diamond, Adriane D.	WTR	1984, 85, 87
Diamond, Bernard	WR (Mgr.)	1940
Diamond, Gregory M.	FB (Mgr.)	1972
DiBernardo, Angelo	MSO	1975, 76, 77
DiBernardo, J. Paul	MSO	1980, 81, 82, 83, 84

Russell "Mutt" Deal was captain of IU's undefeated 1945 football team.

Tommy Deckard won the steeplechase in the Penn Relays in 1937, setting a record that stood 20 years.

Dibley, Christine A.	SB	1989, 90, 91
Dice, Clifford O.	FB	1912, 13
Dice, William A.	WR/MSW (Mgr.)	1930
Dick, Alan D.	FB	1970, 71
Dick, Allison J.	WSO	1993, 94
Dickerson, Timothy K.	FB	1984
Dickey, William B.	BB/FB/MBK	1930, 31, 32, 33
Dickinson, Michael J.	MTN	1979, 80, 81, 82
Dickson, Bridgett D.	VB	1984
Dickson, Bruce F.	MSW	1973, 74, 75, 76
Dieterich, William L.	MGY	1973, 74
Diethelm, Diane	WGO	1974, 75, 76, 77
Dietrich, Barbara D.	WSW	1984, 85
Dietz, Karla S.	WTN	1975, 76, 77
DiGuardi, Robert G.	MSO	1995, 96, 97, 98
DiGuilio, James G.	FB	1991, 92, 93, 94
Dildine, Ward E.	MTR	1928, 29
Dileo, William E.	FB	1935, 36
Dill, Jerry L.	BB	1964, 65
Dillard, Charles T.	FB	1956
Dilling, Richard A.	MTR	1965, 66, 67
Dillinger, Wendy M.	WSO	1993, 94, 95, 97
Dillman, Cary J.	WR	1979
Dillman, Kenneth L.	MTN	1955, 56, 57
Dillon, Clarence E.	MCC/MTR(Mgr.)	1974, 75
Dillon, Paisley	SB	1997
Dillon, Ryan T.	BB	1994, 95, 96, 97
Dilly, Don W.	BB/FB	1963, 64
Dimitry, Cindy	WSW	1977
Dingman, Darrin D.	MTN	1988
Dinsley, Thomas E.	MSW	1962, 63
DiSalle, Daniel J.	MSW	1981, 82, 83, 84
DiSalle, John D.	MSW	1983, 84, 85
DiSalvo, Mark E.	FB	1973, 74
Dischinger, Donas H.	FB	1934
Disilvestro, Frank A.	MTR	1997, 98, 99
Dittfach, Jennifer L.	WBK	1994, 95, 96
Dittoe, Christopher J.	FB	1993, 94, 95, 96
Divich, Steve M.	MTR	1932, 33, 34
Dixon, Dean A.	MTN	1957, 58, 59
Dixon, Douglas A.	MCC/MTR	1981
Dixon, Jennifer S.	WSW	1993, 94, 95, 96, 97
Dixon, Karen E.	WTR	1983, 84
Dixon, Michael J.	WR	1998, 99
Doan, Marilyn	WGO	1970
Dobbins, William H.	MBK	1920, 21
Dobrin, Stefanie F.	WTR	1995
Dobson, Robert J.	BB/MBK	1951
Dodd, Werter D.	FB	1893
Dodson, Harry C.	FB	1903
Doe, Linda A.	VB	1974, 75, 76
Doehla, George D.	FB	1975, 76, 77, 78
Doerr, Steve C.	MSO	1976, 77, 78, 79
Doggett, Joe C.	FB	1973, 74, 75, 76
Doherty, Christy S.	WSO	1996, 97
Dolan, John P.	FB	1949, 50
Dolan, Tory E.	WSO	1995, 96, 97, 98
Dolaway, Earl L.	FB	1940, 41, 42
Dolph, Brian A.	WR	1986, 88, 89, 90
Dolson, Scott M.	MBK (Mgr.)	1988
Domenic, Donald A.	BB/FB	1952, 53, 54, 55
Donaghy, Mary	WSW	1982
Donahoe, Candice L.	WTN	1996, 97, 98
Donaldson, Braelon, Jr.	MTR	1955, 56, 57
Donatelli, Gary E.	WR	1971, 72
Donati, Marc A.	MTR	1985
Donchetz, Denise	WTN	1973, 74, 75, 76
Doninger, Clarence H.	MBK	1957
Doninger, Gretchen L.	WTN	1988, 89, 90, 91
Donner, Dennis P.	BB (Mgr.)	1981
Donner, Wilbur S.	MSW	1924
Donovan, Harry W.	FB	1919, 20, 21
Dooley, William P.	BB	1955
Dormann, Michael J.	MTR	1979
Dormans, John P.	MTR	1976
Dorn, Brady R.	FB	1994
Dorsey, Ralph C.	MBK	1938, 39, 40
Doss, Angela M.	WSO	1993
Dougherty, Carl L.	FB	1974
Douglas, Dawn T.	WBK	1990, 91, 92, 93
Douglas, Debra J.	MSW (Mgr.)	1981
Douglas, Dezireno D.	MTR	1986, 87
Douglas, Robert E.	FB	1967, 68
Douglass, Ralph W.	MTR	1903
Dove, Douglas J.	FB	1960
Dowdell, Amy E.	WSO	1994
Dowling, James P.	MGY	1982
Downes, Norbert J.	BB	1933
Downey, Brandt C.	BB	1897, 98
Downey, Julie M.	WTN	1984, 85

Jim DeNeff was a 2nd team All-America second baseman in 1966.

Jenny Dixon was a three-time Big Ten diving champion.

Downing, Stephen	MBK	1971, 72, 73
Downs, Corey P.	BB	1990
Doyle, Maureen A.	VB	1977
Doyle, Teresa L.	WCC	1988
Dozier, William E.	FB	1951, 52
Drake, Russell A.	R	1955, 56
Drake, Susan D.	WSW	1981, 82
Drake, Terri L.	SB	1970
Drake, Troy A.	FB	1991, 92, 93, 94
Draper, Cecil L.	MTR	1911, 12
Dreiman, Paul E.	MTR (Mgr.)	1933
Dreisbach, Clyde F.	FB/MBK/MTR	1902, 03
Dressel, Tiana L.	WSW	1992
Driesall, Patricia	WSW	1974, 75
Driscoll, Garrett O.	BB	1911
Driscoll, John F.	BB	1918, 19, 20
Driscoll, Mary E.	WCC/WTR	1987, 88, 89, 90, 91
Driver, Hal E.	BB/FB/MTR	1904, 07, 08, 09
Driver, Hal V.	MBK	1941
Dro, Robert C.	BB/MBK	1939, 40, 41
Drollinger, Benjamin H.	BB/WR	1914, 15
Dross, Marion J.	BB	1930, 31
Drozda, Joseph M., Jr.	MGO	1998, 99
Drozdowski, John E.	MTR	1962
Druckamiller, Emery L.	BB	1924, 25, 26
Drummond, Marcia L.	VB	1990, 91, 92, 93
Druz, Randall J.	MTN	1977, 78, 79, 80
DuBois, Jill E.	VB	1982
Dubrouillet, Frank D.	FB (Mgr.)	1960
Dudding, Joseph E.	FB	1928, 29
Dudeck, John P.	MTR	1978
Dudek, Edward F.	BB	1946, 47
Dudley, Ruth	WSW	1972, 73, 74
Dudley, Tyrell L.	FB	1972
Duechting, Jay C.	FB	1972
Duffy, Karen E.	WGY	1985
Duffy, Kevin T.	FB	1964, 66, 67
Duffy, Terrence J.	MGY	1975, 76, 77, 78
Duffy, Williard C.	WR	1935, 36, 38
Dugan, Joseph M.	BB	1933
Dugan, Kenneth F.	BB	1932, 33, 34
Duhamel, Peter N.	BB	1967, 68, 69
Duhamell, Marilyn	WGY	1972
Dulberger, Murray E.	MTN	1938, 48, 50
Dum, Steven T.	WR	1976, 78, 79
Dumas, Michael D.	FB	1987, 88, 89, 90
Dumke, Dale E.	FB	1959
Dumke, Michael E.	FB (Mgr.)	1967
Dumke, Michael, Jr.	FB	1939, 40
Dumke, Ray M.	FB	1938, 39, 40
Dunbar, Vaughn A.	FB	1990, 91
Duncan, Jody A.	SB/WBK	1976, 77
Duncan, Scott D.	WR	1986, 87
Duncan, Stuart C.	MSW	1948
Dungan, Laura	WSW	1982
Dunham, Karen L.	VB	1984, 85, 86, 87
Dunham, Patricia	VB	1984, 85, 86, 87
Dunker, Donald J.	BB	1940, 41
Dunker, Thomas J.	MTN	1970, 71, 72, 73
Dunlap, James R.	BB	1905, 06
Dunlop, Lorraine A.	WTR	1998, 99
Dunn, Almira S.	WTR	1982, 83
Dunn, Angela E.	WBK	1985, 86
Dunn, Emily S.	WSW	1994, 95
Dunn, Harold L.	FB	1967
Dunn, Jon W.	MGO	1976
Dunne, Karen T.	WSW	1987, 88, 89, 90
Duran, Martha	WTN	1971
Durban, Jason D.	BB	1993, 94

Bob Dro was a member of IU's NCAA championship basketball team in 1940.

Mike Dumas was a two-time All-Big Ten pick and a 1990 All-American.

Durham, Theodore L.	MTR	1993
Durkott, John F.	FB	1964
Durrant, Julie A.	WTN	1977
Durtschi, Becky A.	VB/WTR	1977, 78, 79
Dutter, Homer W.	FB	1908, 09, 10
Dwyer, Ovrill L.	WTR	1980, 81
Dyar, Robert W.	MGO	1954, 55, 56
Dyer, Christopher L.	FB	1990, 91, 92, 93

Eads, Roy S.	FB	1934, 35, 36
Eagleson, Preston E.	FB	1894
Eakins, Walter M.	WR	1927, 29
Earle, Charles C.	MGY	1969, 70, 71
Earles, William H.	WR	1946
Earley, Ellen E.	FH/WBK/WTN	1969, 70, 71, 72
Earley, Jeanne	FH/WBK/WGO	1969, 70, 71, 72
Earley, Rexanne	WSW	1976, 77
Earley, Richard D.	MGY/MSW	1964, 65, 66
Eash, Cornelius E.	MTR	1907, 08, 09, 11
Easley, Moses L.	FB	1963, 65
Eastman, Anne M.	VB	1991, 92, 93, 94
Easton, Greg T.	BB	1985, 86, 88
Easton, Millard E. "Bill"	MCC/MTR	1926, 27
Easton, W. Richard	MBK	1918, 19, 20
Eaton, Edwin R.	MGO	1937, 38
Eaton, Leslie	VB	1972, 73
Eaton, Mark A.	MSW	1984, 85, 86, 87
Eberhart, Elder J.	FB/MTR	1921, 22, 23, 24
Eberhart, Homer D.	WR	1925
Eckert, Gary S.	FB	1976
Eckert, Timothy R.	FB	1983
Economo, Elaine	WSW	1979
Ecton, Virgil	MGY	1961, 62
Eddings, Darryl W.	FB	1987, 88
Edds, David E.	FB	1972
Edelman, Deborah N.	WTN	1990, 91, 92, 93
Edgar, George O.	FB	1974, 75, 76, 77
Edgeworth, Terrence D.	R	1953, 54
Edmonds, Otis D.	FB	1930, 31, 32
Edmundson, Ryan L.	WR	1994, 95, 96
Edwards, Dennis E.	FB	1981, 82, 83
Edwards, Efren E.	FB	1985
Edwards, Kirk	FB	1973, 74, 75, 76
Edwards, Melvin B.	MTR	1952, 53, 54
Edwards, Michael B.	BB	1999
Edwards, Michael L.	FB	1971
Edwards, Jay C.	MBK	1988, 89
Eells, Scott E.	MBK	1976, 77, 78, 79
Efthimiou, Dino N.	MTR	1999
Egan, Patrick M.	FB	1968
Egenolf, Matthew E.	FB	1989, 90, 91
Eggers, Robert D.	MBK	1995, 96, 97, 98
Eggleston, Thomas A.	MTR (Mgr.)	1925
Ehrensberger, James R.	FB	1977
Ehret, Jason C.	MTR	1996, 97
Eichinger, Frank M.	MSO	1973
Eichrodt, Charles W.	MTR	1911
Eickstead, Jon J.	FB	1964, 65
Eikenberry, Michael J.	FB	1974, 75
Eise, David L.	MSO	1984, 85, 86, 87
Eisel, John A.	MSW	1965

Eiting, Patricia	WTR	1980, 81, 82, 83
Ekman, Christopher J.	MTR	1997, 98, 99
Elder, J. Cal	MSW	1988
Elder, Mark A.	BB	1998
Elderkin, Curt L.	WR	1887
Eldridge, Gail E.	MTN	1939
Eldridge, Thomas J.	MSW	1970, 71, 72
Elfers, Edmund B.	FB/MBK/MTR	1899, 1900, 01, 02
Elisara, Pita P.	FB	1998
Ellenwood, James A.	FB	1938, 39
Ellingson, Eric P.	MSW	1982
Elliott, Beth	FH	1969
Elliott, Frederic D.	MTR	1937, 38, 39
Elliott, Howard R.	FB	1940
Elliott, James M.	FB (Mgr.)	1963
Elliott, Larry G.	FB (Mgr.)	1966
Elliott, Mark A.	WR	1980
Elliott, Robert F.	MTN	1929
Elliott, Trevor J.	WR	1994, 95, 96, 97
Elliott, William C.	MTR	1948, 49
Ellis, James M.	WR	1952, 53, 56
Ellis, Joshua	MTR	1999
Ellis, Kenneth A.	FB	1960, 61, 62
Ellis, Lance C.	WR	1990
Ellis, R. Jerrold	FB	1951, 52, 53
Ellis, Willis S.	BB & FB	1885, 86
Ellwanger, Bruce R.	FB	1962, 63
Elm, Frank	MSW	1951, 52, 53
Elmore, Tiffany	WBK (Mgr.)	1999
Eloms, Joey L.	FB	1994, 95, 96, 97
Elreis, Valda	WGY	1970
Elrod, Lanna J.	WSW	1985
Ely, James A.	MCC/MTR	1953, 54, 55, 56
Elyea, Andrea L.	WTR	1986
Elyea, Willard O.	BB	1961, 62
Elzey, Merit E.	WSO	1994, 95, 96, 97
Emberton, William B.	WR	1997
Embich, Edwin C.	MTR	1919
Embry, William	R	1960
Emmert, James A., Jr.	R	1954
Endicott, Carl E.	FB	1893, 94, 95, 96
Engel, Pamela J.	VB	1976, 77
Englehart, Otto T.	BB	1913, 14
English, Steven G.	FB	1983
Englund, Ann E.	FH	1975, 76, 77, 78, 79
Engstrom, Carl J.	MGO	1924
Enis, Ric L.	FB	1974, 75, 76, 77
Ennis, Barbara J.	WCC/WTR	1980, 81, 82, 83
Epstein, Rachel M.	WTN	1992, 93, 94, 95
Erehart, Archie D.	FB/MTR	1914, 15, 16
Erehart, Mark G.	BB/FB/MTR	1912, 13, 14
Erenburg, Stephen R.	MTN	1964, 65, 66
Erickson, Carrie A.	WCC/WTR	1994, 95
Erickson, Kareen K.	WSW	1988, 89
Erickson, Thomas	BB/FB	1963, 64, 65
Ericson, Nina S.	WSW	1996
Ertel, Frances A.	WGO	1982, 83
Esarey, Ralph E.	MBK	1920
Esberg, James A.	MBK (Mgr.)	1951
Esgate, Pat	FH/VB	1969, 70, 71
Esposito, Sam	BB/MBK	1952
Essenpreis, Ronald R.	MGO	1966, 68
Estavillo, Mary Ellen	WGY	1984, 85
Estes, Ann	WGO	1972
Esteva, Santiago E.	MSW	1971, 73, 74

Rachel Epstein, three-time All-Big Ten, 1992 All-American.

Benny Fernandez was a four-time Big Ten gymnastics champion on still rings and IU's last All-American.

Etherton, Scott J.	FB	1977
Ethridge, Trisha	BB (Mgr.)	1997
Ethridge, Wayne H.	FB	1953
Etnire, Robert K.	MBK	1935, 36, 37
Etnyre, Mark A.	MSW	1986, 87
Etter, James F.	MSW	1954, 55
Etzkorn, Emily A.	WSO	1996, 97, 98
Evans, Anne L.	WTN	1977, 78, 79
Evans, Brian K.	MBK	1993, 94, 95, 96
Evans, David C.	FB	1966, 67
Evans, Dennis G.	FB	1991
Evans, Julie L.	WTR	1985
Evans, Marlin W.	FB	1979, 80, 82
Evans, Maurice D.	BB	1982
Evans, M. Daniel	BB	1984
Everett, Franklin L.	MBK	1966
Everroad, James M.	MGY	1963, 64, 65
Eversole, Shannon P.	MTR	1990
Ewald, James M.	MTR	1977, 78, 79, 80
Ewald, Robert C.	MTN	1960, 61, 62
Ewert, Howard W.	FB	1917
Ewert, Ross T.	BB (Mgr.)	1925
Ewing, Claude M.	FB	1914, 15
Ewing, John W.	BB	1881, 84
Eyl, Steven M.	MBK	1985, 86, 87, 88

Fadeski, Dennis C., Jr.	MSO	1996, 97, 98
Fagley, Sheri J.	WP	1998, 99
Fairfield, Jon E.	MTR	1966
Fairfield, Winston L., Jr.	MBK	1961, 62, 63
Faison, W. Earl	FB	1958, 59, 60
Fajkus, Charlie J.	MSO	1974, 75, 76, 77
Falkenberg, Dean J.	FB (Mgr.)	1984
Fall, Ibrahima	MSO	1972
Falsgraf, Deborah	WSW	1983
Falwell, Lawrence J.	MTR	1942, 43
Farabee, Scott A.	MSW	1989
Faraone, Robert L.	FB (Mgr.)	1968
Fargo, Susan	WTR	1981
Faris, Ann	WSW	1979
Faris, Kenneth E.	MBK	1944, 45, 48
Farley, Angela F.	WTN	1984, 85, 86, 87
Farley, Eric M.	BB	1999
Farley, Richard L.	MBK	1952, 53, 54
Farmer, Jill S.	WSO	1996
Farnsley, Steven L.	WR	1987
Farnsworth, T. Brook	MG	1967
Farr, Joseph M.	WR	1995, 96, 97
Farrall, Gregory P.	FB	1988, 89, 90, 91
Farrell, Heather L.	WBK	1991, 92, 93, 94
Farrell, Herbert E.	WR	1942, 46, 47, 48
Farrington, Elaine S.	FH/WTR	1981, 83
Fattore, Charles E.	MBK (Mgr.)	1983
Faulkenberry, Terrell D.	MSW	1974, 76, 77
Faulkman, Edward A.	MSW	1947, 48
Faunce, Frank H.	FB	1927, 28, 29
Fauser, Christian H.	MSO	1982, 83, 84, 85
Faust, Frank F., Jr.	BB/FB	1918, 19, 20
Faust, Lynn	WSW	1975, 76
Favede, Leon F.	MGO	1957
Fawcett, Charles C.	FB	1961
Fawcett, Valerie P.	VB/WSW	1974, 75
Febrey, Theresa M.	WBK	1978, 79
Fechtig, Mary	WGO	1984, 85, 86, 87
Fechtman, Fred D.	MBK	1935, 36, 37
Federoff, Jack A.	BB	1977, 78
Fedor, Sara E.	WTR	1997, 98, 99
Fedorchak, Alexis C.	WSW	1993, 94, 95, 96
Fedorka, Charles M.	BB	1985, 86
Fedosky, Edward J.	MSW	1951
Fee, Mary E.	WGO	1974, 75, 76, 77
Fee, Robert F.	FB	1954, 55, 56
Feeney, Charles L.	MTR	1949, 50, 51
Fegelman, Susan J.	WGY	1983
Fegley, Michelle M.	WSW	1986
Fehr, Michael	MSW	1963
Feigel, Theran E.	MSW	1937, 38, 39
Feighner, John R.	MTN	1940, 41, 42
Feigl, Frank	MGY	1952, 53, 54
Feinberg, Joel D.	MCC	1994, 95
Feld, Cary W.	MSO	1973, 74, 75, 76
Feldhake, Eric A.	WR	1992
Fell, Robert K.	MCC/MTR	1959, 60, 63

Fella, Brad	BB	1985, 86, 87
Feller, James R.	BB	1981
Fellerhoff, Kara M.	WP	1998, 99
Fellerhoff, Kristin A.	WSW	1994
Fellinger, Patrick J.	FB	1953, 54, 55
Fellingham, Ruth	WCC	1987
Fenwick, Mark A.	MCC	1964
Fenner, Geoffrey C.	MSW	1981, 82, 83, 84
Fennerty, Brian S.	MTN	1982
Fenstermaker, Freda	MGY (Mgr.)	1964
Fentress, Patricia	WTR	1981, 82
Ferdinand, M. Brandy	WGO	1993, 94, 95, 96
Ferguson, Frank G.	BB	1893, 94
Ferguson, Fred E.	BB/FB	1893, 95
Ferguson, Kelly J.	WTN	1979, 80
Ferguson, Scott D.	MTR	1987
Ferguson, William W.	FB/MBK	1922, 23
Ferland, Thomas J.	MSO	1981
Fernandez, Benigno	MGY	1971, 72, 73, 74
Fernandez, Orlando S.	MGY	1972, 73, 74, 75
Ferrara, Krista T.	WCC/WTR	1992, 93, 94, 95, 96, 97
Ferrell, Daniel L.	BB	1994, 95, 96
Ferris, David O.	BB	1998, 99
Ferry, Colleen	WGY	1973, 74
Ferry, Marc D.	FB	1985, 87, 88
Feryo, Michael J.	MGY	1950, 51
Fiacable, Steven J.	FB	1990
Fichter, Charles L.	MTN	1963, 64, 65
Fickenscher, Karl W.	MSW	1979
Fidge, Larry L.	WR	1978
Fieber, Howard W.	MSW	1925
Field, Amanda M.	WTN	1999
Field, Manning R.	MSW	1993, 94
Field, Margaret E.	WSW	1993
Field, Michael L.	MTN	1956, 59
Field, Michael R.	FB	1964, 65
Fields, Albert J.	MTR	1902, 03
Fields, Harold N.	MCC/MTR	1926, 27, 28, 29
Fields, Jes B.	BB	1900
Fife, Dane J.	MBK	1999
Fife, John J.	FB	1961
Fifer, Ronald R.	MBK (Mgr.)	1953
Fihma, Scott D.	MCC	1994, 95
Filburn, Mark F.	FB	1981, 82, 83
Filchock, Frank J.	BB/FB	1935, 36, 37, 38
Filipek, Michael W.	MTN	1994, 95, 96, 97
Filipowski, Stephen J., Jr.	FB	1956, 57, 58
Filippelli, Ronald G.	FB	1963
Fillion, Edward P.	MTR	1923, 25
Fincke, Roberta	WSW	1973, 74
Findley, W. Mark	FB	1970, 71, 72
Findling, Willard H.	FB (Mgr.)	1939
Finfer, Milton G.	MSW	1935
Fink, Richard A.	MTN	1973, 74, 75, 76
Finkle, Louis	MTR	1939
Finlayson, Douglas A.	FB	1970, 71
Finley, Benjamin G.	MGO	1990, 91, 92, 93
Finn, Andrew K.	MCC	1991
Finn, Robert E.	MSW	1973, 74, 75
Finney, Brian W.	FB	1985, 86, 87
Fiorini, Robert L.	FB	1961
Fioritto, Bernard H.	FB	1950, 51, 52
Fisch, Paul B.	MSW	1987, 88, 89, 90
Fischer, James W.	FB (Mgr.)	1941
Fischer, Jim L.	MSW	1986, 87, 88, 89
Fischer, Lynn A.	WSW	1979, 80
Fischer, William T.	FB (Mgr.)	1950
Fiscus, Doyne M.	MCC/MTR	1955, 56, 57, 58
Fish, David D.	WR	1991
Fishback, George F.	MTR (Mgr.)	1932
Fishel, Mark E.	FB	1976, 77, 78, 79
Fisher, Charles R.	WR	1947, 48, 49
Fisher, Earl E. "Pete"	FB	1951, 52, 53
Fisher, George	MGY	1957, 58
Fisher, George L.	FB/MTR/WR	1923, 24, 25
Fisher, Harry M.	FB	1922
Fisher, Howard M.	WR	1954, 55, 56
Fisher, Paul R.	MGY	1977, 78, 79, 80
Fisher, Robert H.	FB	1912
Fisher, Robert H.	FB	1891
Fisher, Robert L.	WR	1953
Fisher, Scott E.	FB/MTR	1922, 24, 25
Fisher, Tiffany B.	WGO	1999
Fisher, Vincent R.	FB/WR	1983, 84, 85, 86
Fisher, Walter H.	FB/MTR/WR	1925, 26, 27
Fisher, Warren T.	MBK	1954, 55, 56
Fitch, Jeff M.	WR	1975, 76, 77, 78
Fitzgerald, Jay E.	MBK	1901
Fitzgerald, Joseph M.	FB	1981, 82, 83, 84
Fitzgerald, Kelly S.	WTN	1996, 97, 98

Name	Sport	Years
Galloway, Terrence A.	FB	1980
Galofaro, Lawrence L.	FB	1956
Galvin, William R.	WR	1961, 62, 63
Galyan, Mark L.	WR	1978, 79, 80, 81, 82
Gambino, Lucien A.	FB	1942
Gamble, Rob M.	BB	1982
Gammell, Lindley L.	WR	1945
Gammon, Kathleen L.	VB	1975, 76, 77, 78
Gandolph, David A.	BB	1989, 90, 91
Ganger, Jack E.	MSW	1940
Gannon, Charles J.	FB	1980, 81, 82
Garbett, Lucy A.	FH/WBK	1974, 75, 76
Garcia, Nicholas C.	MSO	1997, 98
Gard, Robin W.	WTR	1985
Gard, Vedder	BB	1915, 16
Gardis, Grant E.	FB	1975
Gardner, Leo K.	MSW	1948
Gardner, Stephen	MTR (Mgr.)	1965
Garish, Matthew P.	WR	1989
Garland, William E.	WR	1952, 53
Garman, Jennifer W.	WSW	1999
Garmen, Shane	MBK (Mgr.)	1996
Garner, Jaime M.	WBK	1995, 96
Garness, Danny R.	BB	1993, 94
Garnette, Harry J.	MTN	1958, 59, 60
Garnier, Eve	FH	1977
Garnier, Susan J.	FH/SB	1978, 79
Garon, Susan T.	WSW	1978, 79, 80
Garrett, Dean H.	MBK	1987, 88
Garrett, Gregory A.	MTR	1980
Garrett, Tina	WSW	1974, 75, 76
Garrett, William L.	MBK/MTR	1949, 50, 51
Garriotte, Brian M.	MTR	1997, 98, 99
Garrison, Jean	WTN	1972
Garrison, Richard W.	FB	1926, 27, 29
Garrison, Robert L.	FB	1983, 84
Garshwiler, William P.	FB	1891
Gartner, Sven C.	FB	1970, 71, 72
Gasowski, Samuel E.	MSW	1993, 94, 95, 96
Gass, Frank L.	FB	1893, 94
Gastineau, Thomas F.	MSW	1947, 48
Gates, Elmer	MGY	1955
Gates, Jerry W.	BB	1957, 60, 61
Gates, Mary	WSW	1979, 80
Gates, Robert A.	MSW	1957
Gates, Robert E.	MSW (Mgr.)	1942
Gatti, Alfred W.	MGY	1968, 69, 70
Gatti, John D.	MSW	1987, 88, 89
Gatti, Ralph J.	BB	1930, 31, 32
Gault, Lon A.	MTR	1947, 48
Gaunt, Russell E.	MGO	1936
Gause, Frank A.	BB/FB	1897, 98, 1904
Gause, Harry L.	BB	1922, 23, 24
Gauvain, David G.	MSO	1985
Gawrys, Joseph H.	MGY	1952
Gaydos, Paul L.	MTR	1968, 69
Gayer, Ashley R.	SB	1995, 96, 97, 98
Gazarek, J. Martin	BB	1992, 93, 94
Gearhiser, Christy L.	WTR	1983
Gebhart, Courtney	WTN	1983, 84
Gebhart, Leland D.	MTR	1929
Gebler, Jean	WGY	1971, 72
Gecina, Brad J.	FB	1997, 98
Geddes, Trevor R.	MSW/WR (Mgr.)	1923
Gedman, Eugene W.	FB	1950, 51, 52
Gedman, Jeffrey R.	FB	1980, 81, 82
Gee, Samuel B.	MBK	1956, 57, 58
Geers, Robert J.	FB	1969
Gehrhardt, Robert E.	MCC/MTR	1991, 92, 93
Gehrig, Timothy M.	BB	1970, 71
Geiger, David M.	WR	1971
Geiger, Steven A.	MGY	1970, 71, 72
Geiger, William A.	FB	1970, 71, 72
Geil, Cheryl	WSW	1984, 85, 86, 87
Geiman, Thomas A.	MSW	1969, 70
Geisler, Donald R.	FB	1980
Gelon, Dawn M.	WTR	1988, 89, 90, 91
Gemmill, Robert A.	MTR (Mgr.)	1932
Gengler, Sara A.	WSW	1982, 83
Gengler, William J.	MSW	1980, 81, 82
Genson, Jon	FB (Mgr.)	1998
Gentil, Daie A.	BB	1938, 39, 40
Gentile, John J.	FB	1954, 56
Georgakis, Steve	FB	1948, 49, 50
George, Elias, Jr.	WR	1946
George, William H.	BB/FB	1962, 63
George, William J.	BB	1880, 81, 82, 83
Geraci, Mike F.	MTR	1985
Gergely, Robert J.	FB	1962
Gerhart, Thomas F.	FB (Mgr.)	1958
Gerken, Kimberly A.	WCC/WTR	1989, 90, 91, 92, 93
Gertsung, Harriet L.	WGY	1974, 75
Gertsung, Louise	FH/WGY	1972, 73, 74
Gertsung, Ruth	FH/WGY	1971, 72
Getman, Michael S.	MSO	1977, 79, 80
Gettelfinger, Ralph A.	MCC	1932
Geyer, R. Thomas	MBK	1999
Gianakopoulos, George J.	FB	1980, 83
Giangiacomo, John J.	FB	1960, 61
Gibbens, Mark H.	MCC/MTR	1966, 67, 68, 69
Gibbs, Edward Bo	MTN	1994, 96
Gibson, Brian D.	MTR	1988, 89
Gibson, Dan A.	MTR (Mgr.)	1933
Gibson, Hayden R.	MTN	1996, 97
Gibson, Kenneth D.	MCC/MTR	1954, 55
Gibson, Nancy	FH	1972
Gibson, Pam	WSW	1973, 74
Gibson, Sarah E.	WCC	1982
Gidley, Scott A.	BB	1973, 74, 75, 76
Giesel, Lisa R.	WTN	1977
Giff, Raymond T.	MCC/MTR	1973, 74, 75
Gifford, Allen W.	BB	1890
Gifford, Hanson S.	MTR (Mgr.)	1930
Gifford, William L.	BB	1968
Gilbert, Bruce M.	MCC/MTR	1980, 81
Gilbert, Constance	WTN	1971
Gilbert, Richard P.	MSW	1965, 66
Gilbert, Richard W.	MSW	1963, 64, 65
Gilbert, Sara L.	WCC/WTR	1979, 80, 81
Gilbert, Ward O.	BB/MBK/MTR	1913, 14, 16, 22
Gilchrist, Carolyn L.	SB/WBK	1975, 76, 77, 78
Gilgrist, Philip M.	MGO	1953
Gill, Cordell M.	FB	1965, 66, 67
Gill, Daniel F.	WR	1939
Gill, James C.	MBK	1928, 29, 30
Gill, Samuel B.	MTR	1935, 36, 37
Gill, T. Andrew	BB/FB/MTR	1909, 10, 11, 12
Gillen, Aaron E.	MTR	1997, 98, 99
Gilles, Ginger G.	SB/VB	1975, 76, 77, 78, 79
Gillespie, Chase D.	FB	1896, 97
Gilliatt, Neal	MSW (Mgr.)	1939
Gillim, Anna M.	WSW	1989, 90, 91, 92
Gillum, Olden C.	WR	1933, 34, 35
Gilman, Mark A.	MTR	1999
Gilmore, Anne	WSW	1974, 75, 76, 77
Gilmore, Harvey S.	MSW	1969, 70
Ginn, Gary L.	BB	1971, 72, 73
Ginsberg, Craig A.	MSO	1991, 92, 93, 94
Ginter, John D.	FB	1964, 65, 66
Giolas, Lynn F.	FH	1981
Giomi, Michael R.	MBK	1983, 84
Gipson, Larry J.	MBK	1969, 70, 71
Gittens, Denise S.	WTR	1987, 88, 89, 90
Glackman, William G.	BB	1915
Glad, Karen A.	WGY	1982, 83, 84, 85
Gladness, William R.	MBK	1998, 99
Gladstein, Harry	MTR (Mgr.)	1931
Gladstein, Sara A.	WSO	1999
Glander, Steven F.	MGY/MTR	1980, 81, 82, 83, 84
Glaser, Kevin R.	FB	1995, 96, 97
Glasgow, John W.	MSW	1987, 88
Glasser, Harold N.	MTR	1943
Glassner, Myron S.	MCC/MTR (Mgr.)	1939, 40
Glazer, Eli	MTN	1951, 52, 53
Glazier, Michael S.	FB	1973, 74
Gleason, Charles T.	MTR	1947
Gleichman, Robert G.	MGY	1970, 71, 73
Gleissner, Joseph P.	MBK (Mgr.)	1984
Glenn, Richard T.	FB (Mgr.)	1954
Glenn, Rudolph J.	MSO	1975, 76, 77, 78
Glick, Jeffrey T.	MSW	1986, 88
Glover, Edward D.	WR (Mgr.)	1939
Glover, Sean E.	FB	1992, 93, 94, 95
Gmuca, Raymond F.	FB (Mgr.)	1952
Gobbett, Kathleen G.	WCC/WTR	1989, 90, 91, 92
Gobert, Stephen W.	FB	1972
Goble, William C.	BB (Mgr.)	1953
Godat, Kenneth L.	MSO	1986, 87, 88, 89, 90
Godbold, Leslie W.	FB/MTR	1933, 34, 35
Godollei, Ruth Ann	WTR	1979
Goedde, Julie A.	VB/WTR	1986, 87, 88, 89, 90, 91
Goehl, Stephanie N.	VB	1994, 95
Goelzer, Don W.	BB (Mgr.)	1950
Goering, Diane	WSW	1980
Goerlitz, Valerie	WTN	1972, 73, 74
Goetz, Kathleen M.	SB	1976
Goings, Dale A.	WR	1931, 32, 33
Goins, James G.	BB (Mgr.)	1966
Goins, William K.	BB	1991, 92, 93
Gold, Donald D. III	MSW	1998, 99

Mike Goodrich won five Big Ten sprint championships from 1969-71.

Duane Gunn was All-Big Ten in 1980 and 1981 as a wide receiver.

Golden, W. Matt	MTR	1976
Goldin, Jeffrey A.	FB	1979, 80
Goldman, Josh	MTR (Mgr.)	1997, 98
Goldman, Nancy L.	WTR	1990, 91, 92, 93
Goldsberry, John G.	FB/MTR	1945, 46, 47, 48
Goldschmidt, Mark A.	MSO	1977, 78, 79, 80
Goldsmith, Marshall J.	MBK (Mgr.)	1962
Goldstein, Benjamin R.	MBK (Mgr.)	1964
Goldstein, Melvin E.	MSW	1958
Goldston, Ralph P.	FB	1948
Goldy, Jennifer D.	WTR	1987, 88, 89, 90
Golliher, Frank E.	WR (Mgr.)	1931
Golonka, Sigmund J.	WR	1943, 46, 47
Gombai, Steven A.	MSW	1990, 91, 92, 93
Gomer, Ernest D.	MTN	1952, 53, 54
Gomez, Tammy P.	SB	1995, 96
Gomory, James A.	FB/MGY	1949, 50, 51, 52
Gonso, Harry L.	FB	1967, 68, 69
Gonzalez, Amador M.	WR	1989
Gonzalcz, Joey R.	MTN	1978
Good, Khara L.	SB	1996, 97, 98, 99
Good, Larry A.	MSW	1954, 55, 56
Goodman, Daniel V.	FB	1913
Goode, Craig C.	FB	1994, 95, 96
Goode, Curt J.	FB	1995, 96
Gooden, Gary S.	FB/MTR	1985, 86, 87, 88, 89
Goodman, Daniel V.	FB	1913
Goodman, James E.	FB	1922
Goodman, Joslin E.	FB	1997, 98
Goodrich, Kyle S.	MSW	1996, 97, 98, 99
Goodrich, Michael L.	MTR	1969, 70, 71
Goodrich, Stephen C.	FB	1989, 90
Goodwin, Clarence L.	BB	1882, 83
Goodwin, Jaynibeth	VB	1977
Goold, Karen	WGY	1984, 85
Gooliak, Daniel G.	MGY	1973, 74
Gordon, Amy S.	WBK/WSO	1977, 78
Gordon, Barbara	WTN	1975, 76
Gordon, Brock R.	MTN	1976
Gordon, Douglas L.	FB	1973, 74, 75
Gordon, Frank W.	FB	1901
Gordon, Fred E.	BB	1942
Gordon, Hilary	FB (Mgr.)	1990
Gordon, Jerome A.	WR	1978
Gordon, Keith L.	MTR	1929, 30, 31
Gordon, Michael L.	MTN	1962
Gordon, Troy W.	MTR	1982, 83, 84
Gordon, William S., Jr.	BB (Mgr.)	1934
Gore, Karen	WSW	1973, 74, 75, 76
Gorgas, Gayle C.	WSW	1985, 86
Gorkis, John E.	BB	1946, 48, 49, 50
Gornak, Steve	FB	1976
Gorrell, Kenneth D.	BB	1935
Gorrity, Manuel L.	MSO	1979, 81, 82, 83, 84
Goss, David K.	BB	1885
Gosse, Kenneth L.	MGY	1971, 72, 73, 74
Gottlieb, David J.	MBK (Mgr.)	1988
Gottman, Braden R.	WR	1995
Gouchnor, Thomas H.	MGY	1942
Goudreau, Colette M.	WCC/WTR	1983, 84, 85, 86, 87, 88
Gouker, Jane	VB	1972, 73
Gould, Alysa	WSW	1978
Gould, Thomas S.	MGY	1980, 81, 82
Goutanis, Cynthia	WTR	1979
Goyer, Richard N.	FB	1972
Graber, Virginia	WTR	1985

Grabham, Bradley A.	MSW	1992
Grace, Dennis J.	MSO	1974
Grady, Carol J.	SB	1970
Graeber, Willy M.	BB	1994, 95
Graessle, George G.	MBK (Mgr.)	1973
Graessle, James A.	FB	1975
Graf, Frederick R.	BB	1998, 99
Graf, Paul J.	MGY	1967, 68, 69
Graf, Timothy H.	MTR	1977, 78, 79, 80
Graff, Cyndee G.	WGY	1978
Graft, Ryan M.	BB	1995, 96, 97
Grafton, Mark E.	MTR	1980, 82
Graham, Alan M.	MTN	1962, 63, 64
Graham, Casey N.	WR	1988, 89, 90, 91
Graham, Dana L.	WTR	1994
Graham, Derin L.	FB	1998
Graham, Edward C.	MTR	1966, 67, 68
Graham, Eugene	MCC/MTR	1961, 62, 63
Graham, Gregory L	MBK	1990, 91, 92, 93
Graham, J. Patrick	MBK	1990, 91, 93, 94
Graham, Kelly S.	WTR	1983, 84, 85, 86
Graham, Paul W.	FB	1936, 37, 38
Gramer, Mark W.	BB	1985, 86
Granderson, Markell	FB	1987, 88, 89
Granger, David W.	BB/MBK	1962, 63
Granger, Teresa L.	WGO	1979, 80, 81
Granneman, Richard	MSW	1989, 90, 91, 92
Grant, Otto E.	MSW (Mgr.)	1936
Grant, Peter M., Jr.	MGO	1938, 39, 40
Grate, Jeffrey L.	BB	1983, 84, 85
Graves-Klaric, R. Jason	MSW	1998, 99
Graves, Paul A.	BB (Mgr.)	1929
Graves, Philip M.	MBK	1910, 11, 12, 13
Graves, Wendy E.	WSO	1997, 98
Gray, Forrest E.	WR	1973, 74
Gray, Gary J.	BB	1969
Gray, Gerald N.	MCC	1914
Gray, Harold	MCC/MTR	1914, 15, 16
Gray, Harry P.	FB	1915, 16
Gray, Hugh W.	WR	1927
Gray, James H.	FB	1904
Gray, Jennifer K.	WGO	1995, 96, 97, 98
Gray, Moses W.	FB	1958, 59, 60
Gray, Robert S.	MTN	1967
Gray, Robert W.	MTN	1956, 57, 58
Gray, Stephanie L.	WBK	1994, 95
Gray, Stoner L.	FB	1979
Gray, Tonia J.	SB	1980, 81, 82, 83
Greathouse, Charles A.	FB	1891, 92, 93
Grecco, Gerald J.	FB	1966, 67, 68
Green, Daniel T.	MSW	1973, 74, 75, 76
Green, Kristi D.	WBK	1995, 96, 97, 98, 99
Green, Lawrence L.	WR	1926
Green, Sharon F.	WTR	1984, 85
Green, Steven M.	MBK	1973, 74, 75
Green, Trent J.	FB	1990, 91, 92
Green, William A.	WR	1971
Green, William A.	FB	1983, 84, 85, 86
Greene, Andrew K.	FB	1991, 92, 93, 94
Greene, David I.	FB	1966
Greene, Dennis L.	FB	1974
Greene, Leslie M.	WBK	1979
Greene, Matt	MBK (Mgr.)	1993
Greene, Robert B.	BB	1993, 94, 95
Greene, Virgil A.	FB	1893
Greenlee, Adam J.	FB	1994, 95
Greenlee, Kelly A.	WCC/WTR	1981, 82, 83, 84, 85
Greenhut, Ivan R.	R	1957
Greenspan, Joshua J.	WR	1998
Greenstein, Michael C.	FB	1981
Greenwell, Pat	FH	1970
Greenwood, Joseph R.	MGO	1929, 31
Grenda, Gregory C.	MSW	1983
Gregory, Damian K.	FB	1996, 97, 98
Gregory, Ethel M.	SB/WBK	1976, 77, 78
Gregory, William R.	MGY	1951, 52
Gres, Darinda Ann	WGY/WSW	1985, 86
Gresk, Paul D.	FB	1972
Gridley, James O.	MBK	1939, 40, 41
Griebel, Dianne J.	WSW	1981, 82, 83, 84
Grieger, Gary A.	MBK	1964, 65, 66
Grieger, Louis A., Jr.	BB	1936, 37, 38
Grieger, Russell M.	BB	1935, 36, 37
Griffin, Peter J.	MTR (Mgr.)	1961
Griffis, Amanda J.	WGO	1997
Griffith, Charles O.	MGO	1962, 63
Griffith, Charles R.	FB	1972, 74
Griffith, Robert B.	BB	1989
Griffiths, Edward M.	MGO	1949, 50
Griggs, Bradley S.	MSO	1997, 98, 99

Name	Sport	Years
Grill, John A.	WR	1960, 61
Grimes, John C.	MTN	1956, 57
Grimm, Karen S.	WGY	1976
Grimm, Richard A.	BB	1985
Grimm, Sharon K.	WSW	1982, 83
Grimsley, J. Kevin	MTR	1968, 69, 70
Grimsley, John M.	MCC/MTR (Mgr.)	1934, 35
Grindlay, Kevin M.	MTR	1950, 51
Gritton, Kristi	WSW	1981
Grizzell, Betsy R.	WTR	1981, 82
Grochowski, Jay A.	BB	1979, 80, 82
Grode, Raymond C.	MSW	1947
Groeger, Susan M.	WTN	1977, 78
Groepper, Peter S.	MSW	1976
Grogg, Stephen E.	MGY	1973, 74, 75, 76
Grogg, Tim A.	BB	1970
Gronendyke, Maurice C.	BB (Mgr.)	1926
Groomes, Melvin H.	FB/MTR	1945, 46, 47
Grose, Tracy L.	WSO	1997, 98
Gross, Joel E.	FB (Mgr.)	1965
Gross, Leslie A.	WSW	1990, 91, 92, 93
Gross, Mary L.	WBK	1977, 78
Gross, William S.	BB	1960, 61, 62
Grossman, David	WR (Mgr.)	1975
Grossman, Dobby	FB	1975
Grossman, R. Daniel	FB	1970, 71, 72
Grossman, Rex D.	FB	1946, 47
Grosz, Anita H.	FH	1973, 74, 75
Grove, Roger L.	FB	1966, 67
Groves, Laurie	WTN	1970
Grubbs, Deion A.	FB/MTR	1997
Grube, Susan A.	WTR	1984, 85
Gruber, Judy	SB	1980
Grubish, Joseph A.	MBK (Mgr.)	1963
Grummell, Edward J.	WR	1953, 54, 55
Grump, Kevin J.	FB	1974, 75, 76, 77
Grundler, Frank D.	BB	1969, 70, 71
Grunfeld, Rudolph	MTN	1941
Grunwald, Glen E.	MBK	1977, 78, 79, 80, 81
Grunza, Bernie L.	FB	1956
Gucciardi, Lea	WSW	1972, 73
Gudelsky, Marsha G.	WSW	1970
Gudgel, Shana D.	SB	1998, 99
Guendling, James J., Jr.	MCC	1958
Guengerich, Franklin D.	MTN	1985
Guerrerro, Jaime	MSO (Mgr.)	1995, 96
Guhl, Barbara	WBK	1970
Guhl, Bonnie	VB	1970
Guild, Evan	MTR	1983, 84
Guiney, Marianne	WTN	1980, 81, 82, 83
Gulley, Brenda S.	FH	1975, 76
Gulliford, Malaika L.	WTR	1991, 92, 93, 94
Gumz, Terry	MSW	1960
Gunn, Duane N.	FB	1981, 82, 83
Gunn, Laurie A.	WTR	1982
Gunning, Kenneth W.	BB/MBK/MTR	1935, 36, 37
Guntzel, Andre	MSO (Mgr.)	1996
Gupta, Anju B.	WTN	1994
Gustafson, John E.	MCC/MTR	1976, 77, 78, 79, 80
Gustafson, Sara K.	WSO	1998
Gustavsen, Ulf G.	MSW	1969, 70, 71
Gutreuter, Brian K.	FB	1989
Guyton, Arthur J.	MBK	1997, 98, 99
Gwin, Jesse B.	FB	1902, 04, 05
Gwin, Thomas T.	BB	1937, 38, 39
Gyuran, Elizabeth	WSW	1990
Haack, Michelle L.	VB	1987, 88
Haack, Peter A.	MSW	1994, 95, 96, 97
Haak, Robert A.	FB/WR	1936, 37, 38
Haas, James R.	FB	1960, 61
Habbe, J. Edwin	MTR	1920
Habegger, Janet	WSW	1971
Hackel, Glenn F.	WR	1963, 64
Hacker, Brenda K.	WTN	1988, 89, 90, 91
Hacker, Deanna C.	SB	1984, 85
Hacker, Debra	WTR	1986, 87
Hacker, Scott A.	MTR	1985, 86
Hacker, Todd M.	MTN	1986, 87, 88
Hacker, William C.	BB	1941, 43
Hackett, Laura A.	WCC	1982
Hackett, Susan	VB	1972, 73
Hackman, Stephen J.	MTR	1979, 80, 81
Hackman, William H.	FB	1908, 09, 10, 11
Haddock, Patty	WGO	1971
Haegele, Daniel R.	BB	1998, 99
Haenisch, Margaret A.	SB	1991, 92, 93, 94
Hagan, James A.	FB	1998
Hagan, John H.	MCC/MTR	1950, 51, 52, 53
Hagen, Mark B.	FB	1987, 89, 90, 91
Hagenbach, Jacqueline	FH	1981, 82
Hager, John F.	MSW	1971, 72
Hagerman, John R., Jr.	MGY	1979, 80, 81, 82
Hagerty, James E.	BB	1888, 89, 91, 92
Hahn, Brian	MBK (Mgr.)	1996
Hahnfeldt, Jon	MSW	1968, 69
Hairston, Kimberly	VB	1985, 86
Hales, Cynthia	FH	1974, 75
Hales, Ross D.	FB/MBK	1992, 93, 94
Haley, Robert M.	WR	1964, 65
Haley, Timothy J.	WR	1962, 63, 64
Halgas, Michael, Jr.	MCC	1943
Hall, Andre	FB/MTR	1985, 86, 87, 88, 89
Hall, Ann	FH	1969
Hall, Bryan D.	FB (Mgr.)	1977
Hall, Charles G.	BB/MBK	1960, 61, 62
Hall, Frank J.	BB	1866, 67
Hall, Gary W.	MSW	1970, 71, 72, 73
Hall, Joseph M.	MTR	1992, 93, 94
Hall, Kenneth R.	MTR	1967, 68, 69
Hall, Michael	MBK (Mgr.)	1990
Hall, Peter R.	FB	1975, 76
Hall, Robert T.	MSW	1940, 41
Hall, Thomas E.	FB	1953, 54, 55
Hall, Walter, M.	BB	1925, 26
Halladay, John R.	MSW	1973, 75, 76
Haller, Herbert A., Jr.	MSO	1985, 86, 87, 88
Haller, Thomas J.	MGY	1970, 71, 72
Halliburton, James E.	MSW	1978, 79, 80, 81
Halloway, Susan	WGO	1973, 74
Halman, Harold R.	BB	1980, 81
Halpin, Andrea E.	WTR	1990, 91, 92
Halsteen, Liz	VB/WGY	1970, 71, 72, 73
Halus, Michael B.	R	1957, 58, 59
Hamby, Earnest L., Jr.	MGO	1987, 88
Hamer, Matthew D.	MSW	1987
Hamilton, Frank I.	FB (Mgr.)	1970
Hamilton, Garnard F.	MGO	1971, 72
Hamilton, Howard E.	FB	1956
Hamilton, Miller	MGR	1911
Hamilton, Ralph A.	MBK	1942, 43, 47
Hamilton, Todd R.	FB (Mgr.)	1989
Hammel, John F., Jr.	BB	1971
Hammer, Glenn L.	MSW	1964, 65, 66
Hammer, Norman L.	MSW	1929, 30
Hammer, Robert D.	MSW	1932, 34
Hammer, Ryan M.	MSO	1998
Hammerstein, John P.	FB/WR	1992, 93, 94, 95
Hammes, Patricia A.	WCC/WTR	1979, 80
Hammond, Harold W.	MBK (Mgr.)	1923
Hammond, Kenneth H.	MTR	1959, 60
Hampton, Charles E.	MTR	1954, 55, 56
Hampton, Colin C.	MSW	1976, 77, 78, 79
Hampton, Roscoe	MTR	1916
Hamry, Carl J.	MSW	1973, 74, 75, 76
Hanak, Mark P.	FB (Mgr.)	1968
Hancock, John P.	MGO	1950, 51
Hancock, Paul W.	MGO	1947, 48, 49
Hand, Brainard M. II	MSW	1966, 67
Handley, Berry A.	FB	1986
Handrich, Stephen J.	MCC/MTR	1991, 92, 93, 94
Haneline, Richard L.	FB	1966
Haniford, Earl L. IV	FB	1997
Hanna, Clay	VB (Mgr.)	1997
Hanna, Raymond	FB	1916
Hanna, Ronald C.	WR	1969, 70
Hannig, Thomas J.	MSO	1997, 98
Hannon, James M.	FB	1990, 91, 92
Hanny, Frank P.	FB/MTR	1920, 21, 22, 23
Hanrahan, John M.	BB	1975, 76, 77, 78
Hanselman, Mark D.	BB	1988
Hansen, Jack	FB	1929, 31
Hansen, Karen	WBK	1971
Hansen, Matthew D.	FB	1990, 91
Hansen, Richard D.	MSW (Mgr.)	1950
Hansley, Todd F.	FB	1983, 84
Hao, Laurence M.	MSW	1959, 61
Harangody, David J.	FB	1977, 79, 80
Harbison, Robert L.	FB	1945, 46, 47
Harbottle, Tate A.	FB	1991, 92, 93, 94, 95
Harcourt, Jack M.	MGY	1970, 71, 72, 73
Harden, Alan W.	MBK	1963, 64, 65
Hardesty, Shannon G.	WGO	1988, 89, 90, 91

Name	Sport	Years
Harding, Margaret	WSW	1970
Hardman, William R.	MTR	1899, 1900
Hardwick, Cary W.	MTR	1981, 82
Hardy, Markus D.	FB	1977
Hardy, Timothy J.	MSO	1992, 93, 94, 95
Hardgrove, Kimberly S.	WSW	1977
Hare, Albert S.	BB	1915
Hare, Frank K.	BB/FB	1903, 04, 05, 06
Harges, Vida	WSW	1975, 76
Hargitt, Macy E.	WGY	1980, 81, 82
Hargrave, Homer P.	MTR	1916
Haring, David P.	MGO	1944, 47, 48, 49
Harker, Albert C.	MTN	1958
Harkrader, Michael T.	FB	1976, 78, 79, 80
Harkrader, Robert P.	FB	1982
Harmening, Debra	WTR	1985
Harmeson, Chester R.	MBK	1903, 04, 05, 06
Harmet, Harold H.	MTR	1950, 51
Harms, Fred A.	MGY	1974, 75
Harp, William P.	MGY (Mgr.)	1964
Harper, Aaron S.	FB	1990, 91
Harper, Darby J.	WCC/WTR	1987, 88
Harper, Gregory W.	MCC/MTR	1987
Harper, James L.	MTR	1951, 52, 53
Harpold, Donald D.	MTR	1932, 33, 34
Harrell, Charles E.	MBK (Mgr.)/MGO	1931, 32, 33
Harrell, Joseph P.	R	1957
Harrell, Paul J.	BB/FB	1926, 27, 28, 29
Harrell, Robert T.	MGO	1934, 35, 36
Harrell, Russell E.	FB	1941
Harrington, Patrick J.	MSW	1980, 81, 82, 83
Harrington, Patrick M.	MSW	1991, 92
Harris, Andre B.	MBK	1986
Harris, Archie H., Jr.	FB/MTR	1938, 39, 40, 41
Harris, Brian N.	BB	1996, 97
Harris, Charles A.	BB	1898
Harris, Charles E.	MCC/MTR	1959, 60, 61, 62
Harris, Charles E.	BB	1894, 95, 96, 97
Harris, Edward W.	FB	1921
Harris, James "Bubbles"	MBK	1970, 71
Harris, Tory J.	MSO	1995
Harris, Walter L.	FB	1986, 87, 88
Harris, Walter R.	FB	1972, 73, 74
Harris, Welton W., II	BB (Mgr.)	1958
Harrison, Brady A.	WR	1993, 94
Harrison, Edgar L., II	MTN	1953
Harrison, Edward L.	FB	1967, 69
Harrison, Nolan	FB	1987, 88, 89
Harrison, Thomas S.	MTN	1901
Harriston, Tamara D.	WSW	1991, 92, 93
Harrod, Bennie E.	BB	1967, 68, 69
Harsh, Eric A.	MCC	1988, 89, 90
Hart, Frank W.	FB	1906, 07, 08
Hart, Gregory S.	MTR	1991, 92, 93, 94
Hart, Harry D.	MSW	1979, 80, 81, 82
Hart, Sean P.	WR	1986, 87, 88, 89
Hart, Steven R.	MBK	1994, 95
Hartfield, Nichole A.	WCC/WTR	1991, 92, 93, 95
Hartman, Craig	MBK (Mgr.)	1990
Hartman, Marilyn	WTN	1970
Hartmetz, Charles E.	MTR (Mgr.)	1939
Hartschuh, Stephen W.	BB	1985, 86, 87
Harvey, Greg L.	FB	1970, 71
Harvey, Linda	VB	1972, 73
Hasapas, Theodore N.	FB/WR	1941, 42, 47
Hashem, Judy A.	VB/WTN	1969, 70
Haskins, Herman H.	BB	1891
Haskins, Sara	WGY	1971
Haslinger, Mary G.	SB	1984, 85, 86, 87
Hastings, Amanda	WSW	1979
Hastings, Deborah A.	WSW	1989, 90, 91, 92
Haston, Kirk A.	MBK	1999
Hatfield, Cloice W.	FB	1908, 09, 10
Hatfield, Elaine A.	WSW	1987, 88, 89, 90
Hatfield, Jack J.	MCC/MTR (Mgr.)	1968, 69
Hatfield, James E.	MTR	1929, 30, 31
Hatfield, Laura L.	WSW	1987, 88, 89, 90
Hatfield, Michelle L.	WGO	1997, 98, 99
Hathaway, Russell G.	FB	1915, 16, 17
Hatton, Tammi	WTR	1979
Hauck, Nancy	WSW	1981, 82
Haugen, Lars J.	MSO	1989, 90
Haupert, Gary L.	MTR	1969, 70, 71
Hauss, Russell D.	MBK	1921, 22
Haussman, Roy F.	BB	1931, 32, 33
Havey, Timothy G.	R	1961
Hawkins, Clarence B.	WR	1931, 32, 33
Hawkins, Thomas C.	MTR	1985
Hawley, Max C.	FB	1898, 99, 1900
Hawley, Ryan M.	FB	1995, 96, 97
Hawley, Tyler R.	MSO	1998
Haworth, Leland J.	BB	1924, 25
Haws, Lisa A.	WCC/WTR	1981, 82, 83, 84
Hay, Thomas W.	MTN	1948, 49, 50
Hay, W. Morrill	MTN	1987
Hayao, George	MGY	1974, 75
Hayden, Jodi S.	WTR	1991, 92, 93
Hayden, Kristi M.	VB	1997
Hayden, Thomas J.	MSW	1962, 63, 64
Hayes, Albin B., Jr.	BB	1955, 56, 57
Hayes, Cathi	WSW	1980
Hayes, Daniel F.	MCC/MTR	1970, 71, 72, 73, 74
Hayes, Glen H.	MTR	1916
Hayes, Holton	MTR	1943, 45
Hayes, Neil B.	FB	1972, 73
Haymann, Gary C.	WR	1995
Haymore, Mark A.	MBK	1975, 76
Haynes, Darbi J.	WTR	1993
Haynes, Sarah A.	SB	1994, 96
Haynie, Gilmore S.	MTN	1938, 39
Hays, Anna C.	MSO (Mgr.)	1991
Hayward, Coleman L.	MSW	1982
Haywood, Albert L.	FB	1995, 96, 97
Hazelip, Rick A.	BB	1982
Heald, Suzy K.	FH	1975, 76
Heath, George R.	BB	1961
Heath, Ralph T.	MSW	1924, 25
Heaton, George C.	FB	1971
Heaton, John T.	FB	1966
Heavenridge, Jack L.	MBK	1933
Heazlitt, Kathy	WSW	1973, 74
Hebb, Herbert C.	MSW	1961, 62
Heck, David M.	MSW	1989, 90
Heck, Kenneth R.	MSW	1987, 88, 89, 90
Heckaman, Samuel D.	BB/FB	1905, 06, 07
Heckler, Scott W.	MGY	1982
Heckman, Vernon J.	MTR	1931
Hedges, David W.	MCC/MTR	1955
Hedges, Edgar L.	MCC/MTR	1938, 39, 40
Hedges, Jerry D.	BB (Mgr.)	1962
Hedges, Stanley D.	MCC/MTR	1958, 59, 60
Hedl, Andrea M.	WSW	1991, 92
Hedrick, Kevin L.	MSW	1984, 85
Heeschen, Richard E.	MGY	1955, 56
Heid, Angela J.	WCC/WTR	1992, 93, 94, 95
Heidel, Mark J.	FB	1976, 77, 78
Heidenreich, Stephen A.	MCC/MTR	1971, 72, 73, 74, 75, 76
Heidler, Elizabeth	WTN	1979, 80, 81
Heidt, Anne E.	WTN	1986, 87
Heilman, John M.	R	1959
Heilman, William H.	FB (Mgr.)	1936
Heim, Lester	FB	1934
Heimann, Erin E.	VB	1996, 97, 98
Heiniger, Steven J.	MBK	1972
Heiss, William N.	MSW	1971, 72, 73, 74
Heistand, Donald J.	FB	1937
Heitger, Joseph D.	MTR	1903, 04
Heizman, Michael W.	FB	1969, 70, 71
Held, Andrew J.	MTN	1995, 96, 97
Held, David T.	MTN	1990, 91, 92, 93
Held, John E.	WR	1924, 25
Held, Karl W.	MTR/WR	1923, 24
Held, Omar C.	WR	1922, 23
Heldt, William D.	BB	1938
Helfrick, John	FB (Mgr.)	1962
Helinski, Florian D.	FB	1951, 52, 53, 54
Hellman, Arthur	FB	1926, 27
Helm, Dwight E.	MGO	1966
Helm, Mark P.	FB	1891, 92, 93
Helmbrecht, Hope K.	WTR	1985
Helmich, Stephen J.	FB	1970, 71
Helminiak, James L.	FB	1961, 62
Helmuth, Ned D.	MTN	1951, 52
Heltzer, Arnold H.	BB	1957, 59
Hempstead, Thomas A.	MSW	1966
Hendee, Craig A.	MSW	1969, 70
Hendershot, Wilfred G.	MTR	1915
Henderson, Alan L.	MBK	1992, 93, 94, 95
Henderson, Bruce B.	FB	1971
Henderson, Kathryn A.	FH/WBK	1970, 71, 72
Henderson, Lisa	WTR	1979
Hendricks, James F.	BB	1936
Hendricks, James F.	MCC	1963
Hendricks, John C., Jr.	BB	1920, 21
Hendricks, Marcia	WSW	1980, 81, 82
Hendrickson, Leonard J.	MGY	1978, 79, 80
Hendrickson, Thomas J.	FB	1981, 82, 83, 84
Hendron, Sally R.	WGO	1976, 77, 78, 79
Hendryx, Jo A.	WTN	1978
Heneghan, Adam D.	MCC/MTR	1989, 90

Heneman, Herbert G.	MSW	1990, 91, 92
Heninger, Wesley R.	BB	1978, 79
Henley, Joseph E.	BB	1874
Hennessey, Marie C.	WSW	1991, 92
Hennies, Amy M.	WSW	1998
Henning, Alisia J.	WCC/WTR	1985, 86
Henning, Kipp E.	WCC/WTR	1982, 83
Henoch, Frederick E.	MGO	1962, 63
Henriott, Heather A.	SB	1995, 96
Henry, Albert S.	MSW	1977, 78, 79, 80
Henry, Charles W.	FB	1930
Henry, Floyd I.	MBK	1933
Henry, Howard J.	MCC/MTR	1941, 42
Henry, Jack E.	MGY	1975
Henry, James E.	MSW	1968, 69, 70
Hensgen, John M.	MCC	1964
Hensley, Louis S., Jr.	MTN	1949
Henthorn, Bonnie	WGY	1972, 73
Herald, Anne K.	WCC/WTR	1992, 93, 94
Herbert, Edward C.	FB	1938, 39, 41
Herdrich, James L.	MSW	1936, 37, 38
Herkless, Ora W.	FB	1893, 94
Herman, Donna	WTN	1970
Hermann, Kathy	WGO	1973, 74
Hermon, Michael M.	MBK	1995
Hernandez, Charlene M.	WSW	1999
Herr, Cindy M.	WBK	1984, 85, 86
Herr, Julie Ann	WTN	1986
Herrett, Mary Jo	VB	1988, 89, 90, 91
Herrick, Georgina	WSW	1972
Herrick, Teresa L.	VB/WSW	1973, 74, 75, 76
Herrick, Walter S., Jr.	MTN	1970, 71, 72
Herring, Arthur E.	BB	1954, 55, 56
Herring, Kathleen M.	WTN	1995
Herrmann, Mark A.	MTR	1981, 82, 83, 84
Herrmann, Nobert E.	MBK	1945, 46, 47, 48
Herron, John R.	MBK	1944, 45, 46
Herron, William P., Jr.	FB	1943
Hersberger, Julie A.	MTR (Mgr.)	1977
Hersey, Jay L.	MSW	1975, 76, 77, 78
Hertz, Craig W.	MSW	1998, 99
Hess, Arthur A.	FB	1917, 18
Hess, Nigel P.	MTN	1969, 70, 71
Hess, Samuel J.	FB	1919
Heston, Melissa M.	WGY	1983
Heubi, Christine H.	WSO	1997, 98
Heuring, Benjamin H.	BB	1919
Heuring, Byron G.	FB/MTR	1917, 19
Heuser, Stephen M.	FB	1982
Hey, Martin A.	WR	1967, 68, 69, 70
Hiatt, Cassius E.	MBK	1905, 06
Hiatt, Phares N.	BB/FB/MTR	1916, 17, 18, 19
Hibler, Stephen J.	MCC/MTR	1960, 61, 62
Hickcox, Charles B.	MSW	1967, 68, 69
Hickcox, W. Thomas	MSW	1972, 73, 74, 75
Hickerson, Eric W.	FB	1986, 87
Hickey, W. Thomas	BB	1928, 29, 31
Hickman, Clint P.	BB	1992, 93, 94, 95
Hickner, Ann	WGY	1978
Hicks, Malcolm C.	MTR	1936, 37, 38
Hicks, Robert B.	BB	1981, 82, 83, 84
Hienton, Jack W.	FB	1970
Higdon, Kevin J.	MCC/MTR	1979, 80, 81
Higginbotham, Russell B.	FB	1938, 39
Higgins, Gregory T.	MSW	1975, 76, 77, 78
Highbaugh, Larry E.	FB/MTR	1968, 69, 70, 71
Highley, Aiden M.	FB	1899, 1901
Highley, Albert E., Jr.	MSW	1934
Highsmith, Hugh P.	MTR (Mgr.)	1936
Highsmith, William H.	MTR (Mgr.)	1939
Hightshue, David C.	FB	1960
Hildebrand, Lawrence D.	WR	1997, 98, 99
Hildebrand, Mark A.	BB	1975, 76
Hildreth, Jack	FB (Mgr.)	1996
Hiles, D. Scott	MCC/MTR	1969, 70
Hilgenberg, Debbie	WGY	1971, 72
Hilker, Stephen M.	MSO (Mgr.)	1978
Hilkert, C. Kay	MCC	1940
Hill, Anita	WSW	1985
Hill, Carolyn K.	WSW	1979
Hill, Earl B.	FB	1926, 27
Hill, Gary L.	BB	1961
Hill, Jack	MSW	1966, 68
Hill, Kristi A.	WCC/WTR	1986, 87, 88, 89, 90
Hill, Luanna F.	WBK	1979
Hill, Martin F.	MTR	1989, 91, 92, 93
Hill, Nat U.	WR (Mgr.)	1945
Hill, Paula L.	VB	1969, 70, 71
Hill, Philip B.	BB/FB	1904, 05, 06
Hill, Phillip C.	FB (Mgr.)	1972

Hill, Robert H.	MGY	1978, 79, 80, 81
Hill, Sherman E.	MBK/MTR	1950, 51, 52
Hill, Tisha B.	WBK	1989, 90, 91, 92
Hillenbrand, William F.	FB	1941, 42
Hiller, Rembrandt C., Jr.	MSW (Mgr.)	1940
Hiller, Robert S.	MSW (Mgr.)	1973
Hilling, Carl M.	FB	1983, 85, 86
Hillman, Joe T.	BB/MBK	1985, 86, 87, 88, 89
Hillman, John A.	FB	1902
Hilton, Benjamin	R	1953, 54, 55
Himebrook, John W.	MBK (Mgr.)	1986, 87
Himelstein, Morris	BB	1933, 34, 35
Hinckley, William R.	MCC/MTR	1993, 94
Hinding, Ronald W.	MSW	1952, 54
Hinds, James E.	MBK	1958
Hiner, Kurt A.	MSW	1963, 65
Hiner, Steven D.	WR	1989, 91
Hines, Dirk R.	FB	1988
Hines, Frederick E.	BB/MTN	1893, 95
Hines, Linnaeus N.	FB	1891, 93
Hines, Neal O.	MTN	1929, 30
Hines, Robert L.	MBK	1943
Hines, Timothy R.	FB	1981
Hinsch, Scott J.	BB	1973
Hinson, Henry I.	FB	1996
Hinz, Holger	MGY	1977, 78, 79
Hipskind, Andrew S.	MTR	1992, 93, 94, 95
Hipskind, William H.	MBK	1909, 10, 11
Hirai, Kimiko	WSW	1995, 96, 97, 98
Hironimus, John E.	MTN	1952, 53, 54, 55
Hirsch, Michael A.	MGY	1982
Hirschmann, John W.	FB (Mgr.)	1937
Hittle, Brian A.	WR	1982, 83, 84
Hixon, C. Edward	BB (Mgr.)	1938
Hixon, Susan L.	WSW	1984
Hoagland, Merton B.	FB	1956
Hoban, Thomas X.	WR	1982, 83, 84
Hobbs, Gregory B.	FB	1991, 92, 93
Hobbs, Johnny L.	WR	1973, 74, 75, 76
Hobbs, Lesley A.	WCC/WTR	1994, 95
Hobbs, Marmaduke A.	MCC/MTR	1934, 35, 36
Hobbs, Roger R.	BB	1991, 92
Hobson, John L.	BB	1936, 37, 38
Hochstetler, David R.	MTR (Mgr.)	1966
Hocker, Clarence M.	MBK	1904
Hockemeyer, Debra A.	SB/VB/WBK	1973, 74, 75, 76, 77
Hocking, Randy	MSO	1977, 78
Hodel, Denise A.	VB	1981
Hodgdon, Thaddeus B.	BB	1967, 68
Hodge, Bruce	MTR	1972, 73, 74, 76
Hodge, John Daniel	BB	1983, 84
Hodge, Stacey L.	SB	1985, 86, 87, 88
Hodges, Dwayne W.	BB	1948
Hodges, Francis T.	MSW	1929, 30
Hodges, Ronald T.	FB	1977
Hodges, Susan G.	WBK	1978, 79, 80, 81
Hodsdon, W. Geoff	MTN	1969, 70, 71
Hodson, Charles L.	MBK	1955, 56, 57
Hodson, Glendon J.	MBK	1932, 33
Hoehn, David M.	FB	1969
Hoehn, Jacquelyn D.	WCC/WTR	1988, 89
Hoehn, Jorja	SB/WBK	1971, 72, 73, 74
Hoehn, Shannon R.	WCC/WTR	1988, 89
Hoereth, Diane	VB	1989, 90
Hoernschemeyer, Robert J.	FB	1943, 44
Hoerr, Blake M.	WR	1997
Hoerr, Brooke R.	WR	1994, 95, 96
Hoerr, Mary	FH	1977
Hoey, Marybeth	FH/WBK	1972, 73, 74
Hoffar, Taylor T.	MBK	1932, 33
Hoffman, Alison	WTN	1987
Hoffman, Bradley C.	BB	1979
Hoffman, Clifford W.	WR	1924, 25
Hoffman, Curtis R.	WR	1921, 22
Hoffman, Everett G.	BB/MBK	1940, 41, 42
Hoffman, John T.	FB	1974, 75
Hoffman, Jon E.	FB	1971, 72
Hoffman, Martin L.	BB	1885
Hoffman, Peter A.	MSO (Mgr.)	1988
Hoffman, Tracy L.	WTN	1982, 83, 84, 85
Hoffman, Walter G.	BB	1912, 13
Hofstetter, Richard R.	MSW	1977, 78
Hogan, De'Wayne A.	FB	1997
Hogan, Tommy L.	MTR	1973, 74
Hogue, John M.	BB (Mgr.)	1949
Hohlt, Eric W.	FB	1983, 84
Hojnacki, Frank J.	FB	1928, 29
Hoke, Charles W.	MGO	1946, 47
Hoke, Robert I.	MTR	1939, 40
Holblick, Harry W.	FB	1922, 23

Holcomb, Bryan K.	MCC/MTR	1997, 98, 99
Holcomb, Derek R.	MBK	1977
Holcomb, Patricia A.	FH/WSW	1970, 71, 72
Holdaway, Ronald S.	WR	1970
Holdeman, John T.	MTN	1930, 31
Holden, Gerald W.	MTR	1946
Holden, Richard J.	MTN	1992
Holder, Christopher J.	FB	1992
Holder, Deborah L.	WSW	1986
Holder, Jack J., Jr.	FB	1960, 61, 62
Holder, William C.	FB	1966
Holick, Christopher H.	BB	1996, 97
Holland, Augusta D.	FB	1956
Holland, Daniel C.	MTR	1982, 83, 84
Holland, H. Davis	MSW	1986, 87, 88, 89
Holland, Kelleen	WSW	1978
Holland, William E.	MTR	1932
Holleran, Johannah L.	WCC/WTR	1988, 89
Holliday, Sarah M.	WSO	1995
Hollingsworth, Julia L.	SB	1974, 75
Hollingsworth, Nicole J.	WGO	1993, 94, 95
Hollingsworth, Rebecca	WTR	1984
Hollis, Jarrod I.	MSW	1999
Hollister, Kenneth W.	FB	1963, 64
Hollmeyer, Anna M.	WSO	1994, 95, 96, 97
Holloway, Jack H.	MSW/MTN (Mgr.)	1934
Holloway, Jack M.	BB	1965, 66, 67
Holloway, Jennifer L.	SB	1994, 95
Holloway, Kevin L.	MTR	1976, 78, 79
Holloway, Thomas C.	FB	1893
Hollowell, Richard L.	R	1963
Holman, Scott A.	WR	1986, 87, 88, 90
Holmes, Kimberly A.	WSW	1984, 85, 86, 87
Holmes, Reginald C.	FB	1974, 75, 76
Holmes, William W.	BB/FB	1884, 85, 86, 87
Holmquest, P. Stewart	BB/FB	1934, 35, 36
Holtzman, Sally	WGO	1971
Holubar, Glenn E.	FB	1964
Holzbach, William A.	BB/FB	1951, 52, 53
Homme, Barbara L.	WBK	1978
Honan, Thomas M.	BB/FB	1887, 88, 89
Honda, Ronald Y.	MSW	1956, 57, 58
Honegger, Rachel E.	WBK	1997, 98
Hoog, Joseph A.	MGY	1949
Hook, Joseph C.	WR	1916, 17, 18
Hook, Mary	WSW	1982
Hooker, Jennifer	WSW	1980, 81, 82, 83
Hooper, Cheryl L.	WSO	1993
Hooper, Kimberly L.	WBK	1991, 92, 93, 94
Hoover, Clayton C.	FB	1908, 09
Hoover, John C.	FB/MTR	1929, 30
Hoover, Samuel H., Jr.	BB	1950
Hoover, Walter	FB	1908, 09, 10
Hoover, William H.	MTR (Mgr.)	1964
Hopkins, Cynthia C.	WTN	1974, 75, 76
Hopkins, Herbert C.	FB	1914
Hopkins, Rodney D.	FB	1977, 78
Hopkins, Thomas G.	MTR (Mgr.)	1953
Hoppe, Frank W., Jr.	FB	1943, 46, 47, 48
Hoppe, Herbert J., Jr.	MTR (Mgr.)	1950
Hord, Luther J., Jr.	BB	1925, 26
Hori, Richard R.	MSW	1958, 59
Hormann, Howard K.	MGY	1964, 65, 66
Horn, L. Allan	FB	1944, 45
Horn, Leah L.	WTR	1998
Horn, Ronnie L.	MBK	1959
Horn, William F.	FB	1993, 94, 95
Hornaday, Charles L.	MTR	1907
Hornbostel, Charles C.	MCC/MTR	1931, 32, 33, 34
Hornbostel, Karen	WBK/WTN	1971
Horne, Virgil L.	FB	1962
Horner, Harold H.	MCC/MTR	1923, 24, 25
Horsley, Jackson S.	MSW	1970, 71, 72, 73
Horton, William E.	MGO	1939, 40, 41
Hoshaw, Kathy	VB	1969
Hoskins, Harley H.	FB	1885
Hoskins, Kyle F.	MSW	1987, 88
Hosler, Willis E.	BB/MBK	1935, 36, 37
Hottell, Walter E.	FB	1893
Houdeshel, Harry F.	BB	1967
Houlihan, James J.	MGO	1979, 80
Houp, Suzy S.	WTN	1971, 72
House, Gerald W.	R	1958
House, Sarah B.	WCC	1987
Housel, Bob	MBK (Mgr.)	1998
Houser, Craig R.	MCC/MTR	1981
Houston, David R.	MGO	1986
Houts, Leroy T.	FB	1985, 86
Hovanec, Thomas J.	BB (Mgr.)	1967
Hovanec, Timothy J.	MBK (Mgr.)	1970

Jennifer Hooker won seven Big Ten titles, and at 15 was a 1976 Olympic finalist.

Mike Ingram was Big Ten golf medalist in 1984.

Hovater, Louanne E.	WP	1999
Howard, Bobby A.	FB	1982, 83, 84, 85
Howard, C.D. "Chuck"	FB	1983, 84
Howard, James P.	FB	1973
Howard, Jeffrey B.	BB	1986, 87, 88
Howard, Jesse M.	BB	1909, 10, 11
Howard, Joseph H.	FB	1886
Howard, Lorn C.	FB	1921
Howard, Lynn W.	BB/FB	1917, 18, 19, 20
Howard, Robert E.	MBK (Mgr.)	1955
Howe, Alfred R.	BB	1866, 67
Howe, James M.	BB	1957, 59
Howe, John D.	MTR	1954
Howell, Don J.	FB	1956, 57
Howell, Trey W.	MCC	1998
Howorth, Charles L.	BB/FB	1932, 33, 34
Hoy, Clifford R.	BB/MBK	1910, 11
Hsia, Jennifer C.	WTN	1998, 99
Hsu, Kimberly	WGO	1996, 97, 98, 99
Hubbard, Benjamin R.	MCC/MTR	1994, 95
Hubbard, Daniel D.	WR	1991
Hubbard, George C.	FB	1901
Hubbard, John C.	FB	1895, 97, 98, 99
Hubbard, Marshall T.	MBK (Mgr.)	1934
Hubbart, Kenneth G.	FB	1957, 58
Huber, Erika M.	WSW	1986
Huber, Melissa A.	WP	1998
Huber, Ryan L.	MTR	1999
Huck, Chad E.	FB	1979, 80, 81
Huddle, Wiley J.	FB	1898, 99, 1900
Huddleston, Elam A.	MTN	1956, 57
Hudson, James A.	FB	1974
Hudson, James H.	MSW	1987, 88, 89, 90
Hudson, Julia A.	SB/VB	1975, 76, 77, 78, 79
Hudson, Reuben	MSW	1988, 89, 90, 91
Hudson, Robert C.	MTR (Mgr.)	1958
Hudson, Robert L.	MSW	1930
Huff, Fred, Jr.	FB	1941, 42
Huff, J.W.	FB	1971
Huff, Ralph	FB/MTR	1938, 39
Huff, William A.	FB/WR	1964, 65, 66, 67
Huff, William J.	FB	1984, 86, 87, 88
Huffman, Gretchen N.	WR (Mgr.)	1999
Huffman, Marvin	MBK	1938, 39, 40
Huffman, Vernon R.	BB/FB/MBK	1933, 34, 35, 36, 37
Huffman, William C.	MTN	1935
Huggett, Ernest E.	FB	1948
Hughes, Cynthia M.	WTN	1977, 78
Hughes, Darrell A.	MCC/MTR	1991, 92, 93, 94, 95, 96
Hughes, Denise	WSW	1974, 75, 76
Hughes, Edward M.	FB	1928, 29, 30
Hughes, John R.	MTR	1951, 52
Hughes, Patrick J.	WR	1983, 84
Hughes, Richard E.	MTR	1975
Hughes, Sheila M.	VB	1982
Hughes, Stacey M.	VB	1989, 90, 91, 92
Hughes, Thomas E.	MTR	1977, 78, 80, 81
Hull, Jewett M.	FB/MTR	1926, 27
Hulpa, Diane	WGY	1972, 73
Hulsen, Jeanne E.	FH	1981
Humbaugh, Peter W.	FB	1983
Hume, John T.	BB	1897
Humphrey, Debra L.	WSW	1993, 94, 95, 96
Humphrey, John E.	MCC/MTR	1964, 65, 66, 67
Humphrey, Michael T.	BB	1982, 83, 84, 85
Humphrey, Robert O.	MTR	1939
Humphreys, George G.	MTR	1909, 10
Hundley, Donald F.	BB	1939, 40, 41
Hungerford, Stephen W.	MCC	1969, 71, 73

Name	Sport	Years
Hunnicut, Brian D.	FB	1988, 89, 90
Hunt, Ernest	BB/FB	1911, 12, 13
Hunt, John W.	MSW	1929
Hunt, Kevin J.	MSW	1982
Hunt, Lee F.	FB	1895, 96, 97, 98
Hunt, Michael E.	R	1961, 62, 63
Hunt, William E.	MGY	1967, 68, 69
Hunter, Angela B.	VB	1986, 87, 88
Hunter, Anthony M.	WR	1987, 88, 89, 90
Hunter, Benton R.	WSW	1997, 98, 99
Hunter, Cyrus R.	BB	1881
Hunter, Diane	WTR	1980
Hunter, Donn R.	MTN	1945, 46
Hunter, Hugh W.	MCC	1929, 31
Hunter, Jimmy L.	FB	1980, 81, 82
Hunter, Joseph H.	BB	1881
Hunter, Michael B.	FB (Mgr.)	1965
Hunter, Morton T.	BB	1904, 05
Hunter, Roger R.	MTR	1985, 86, 87, 88
Hunter, Wiles R.	FB	1895
Hunter, Willie F.	FB	1959, 60
Hurley, Bridget	WSW	1970
Hurley, Charles W.	WR	1949, 50, 51
Hurley, Garland H.	FB	1897, 98, 99
Hursh, Harold J.	BB/FB	1938, 39, 40
Hurst, Bernard	MTN	1932
Hurt, Richard W.	BB	1980
Hurtubise, Francois N.	MGO	1985, 86
Hussey, Sarah	WTR	1981
Hussey, Thomas J.	MSO	1974, 75, 76
Huston, William P.	MTN	1929, 30, 31
Hutchens, Anne	WTN	1982, 83, 84, 85
Hutcherson, Ronald K.	WR	1960, 61, 62
Hutsell, Douglas J.	WR	1977, 78, 79
Hutsell, Kay W.	WR	1952, 53
Hutsell, Martin W.	WR	1972, 73, 74, 75
Huzvar, John F.	FB	1975
Hyatt, Hollyce	WSW	1979
Hyatt, Ronald D.	MTR	1973, 75, 76
Hyde, Raymond S.	WR	1937, 38, 39
Hyden, William H.	FB	1966
Hylant, Daniel J.	MSW	1970, 71
Hylla, Mike J.	MSO	1980, 81, 82, 83, 84
Hylla, Timothy J.	MSO	1982, 83, 84, 85, 86
Hynes, John P.	FB	1982
Hynes, Thomas V.	FB (Mgr.)	1976
Hyre, Teri	WTR	1979

Name	Sport	Years
Iacino, Peter P., Jr.	FB	1941
Iaquinto, Christina J.	WSW	1998
Iatarola, Robert F.	FB	1978, 79
Ieraci, Frank C.	WR	1958
Iglinski, Robert A.	MSW	1994, 96, 97, 98
Ihnat, George	WR	1958, 59, 60
Ijams, Michael E.	FB	1970
Ikard, Keith E.	MCC/MTR	1993, 94, 95, 96
Ikins, Ray G.	MTR	1915, 16
Imburgia, Carl W.	BB	1975, 76, 77
Imbus, Kimberly S.	WSW	1975, 76
Incandela, Salvatore V.	BB	1997, 98, 99
Ingalls, Frank J.	WR	1991, 92, 93
Ingalls, Kathryn J.	SB/WGO	1971, 72, 73
Ingles, James W.	FB	1916, 17, 18
Ingram, Michael A.	MGO	1981, 82, 83, 84, 85
Ingram, Samuel D.	MTR	1989
Inman, Garnett	WR	1938, 40
Inman, Kenneth A.	MCC/MTR	1961, 62, 63, 64
Inman, Marla M.	WBK	1993
Inniger, Ervin L.	BB/MBK	1965, 66, 67
Inserra, Donald R.	FB	1950, 51, 53
Inskeep, Thomas R.	MGO	1975, 76, 77
Irish, Daniel M.	FB	1995, 96
Irvine, Adriane P.	MTR	1994, 95
Irvine, Mary	WTR	1979
Irving, Raymond M., Jr.	FB	1997
Isberg, Charles J.	WR	1944, 45
Isel, John J.	WR	1967, 68
Isel, Richard T.	WR	1963, 64, 65
Isenbarger, John P.	FB	1967, 68, 69
Isenbarger, Phil L.	MBK	1978, 79, 80, 81
Isenhower, Courtland M.	BB	1915, 16, 17
Isger, Matthew W.	MSO	1987, 88, 89, 90
Ishida, Richard D.	FB	1963, 65
Isom, Jerry R.	MTR	1963

Name	Sport	Years
Isom, Stephen E.	FB	1996
Iung, Orestes D.	MSO	1981
Ivanyo, Edward J., Jr.	FB	1993
Izsak, Sidney A.	MTN	1942

Name	Sport	Years
Jack, Keith A.	MSW	1981
Jackman, Charles F.	FB	1892
Jackowiak, Lisa S.	VB	1988
Jacks, Ronald B.	MSW	1968, 69, 70
Jackson, Benjamin D.	MTR	1997, 98
Jackson, Charles E.	MTR	1972, 73, 74, 75
Jackson, Dave M.	WR	1965
Jackson, Denise M.	WBK	1981, 82, 83, 84
Jackson, Derrick B.	FB	1986
Jackson, James D.	BB	1980
Jackson, John C.	MTR	1988, 89, 90
Jackson, John H.	FB	1959
Jackson, Laurel L.	WGY	1976
Jackson, Owen C.	MTR	1932
Jackson, Reba	WTR	1979, 80, 81, 82
Jackson, Repaunzel	WTR	1989
Jackson, Robert D.	MTR	1952, 53
Jackson, Robert D.	MGO	1974, 75, 76, 77
Jackson, Theodore A.	MTR	1961, 62, 63
Jacobberger, Richard K.	MSW	1964
Jacobs, Leonard M.	BB	1974
Jacobs, Sarah	WSW	1997, 98, 99
Jacobson, Carl A.	MSW	1937, 38, 40
Jacobson, Paul A.	MTN	1999
Jacoby, Charles P.	FB	1941, 42
Jacoby, Diane	WSW	1970
Jacquin, Jerome R.	MGY	1958, 59, 60
Jadlow, Todd M.	MBK	1986, 87, 88, 89
Jagade, Harry	FB	1944, 46, 47, 48
Jagielski, Harry A.	FB/WR	1951, 52, 53, 54
Jahnke, Susan M.	FH/WBK	1969, 70, 71, 72
Jakubowski, Janice L.	SB	1978, 79, 80
Jambois, Steven K.	MSO	1975
Jamerino, Christine M.	WSW	1996, 97, 98, 99
James, Floyd L.	MCC	1929, 30
James, Gary L.	MSW	1970, 71, 72, 74
James, George H.	MTR	1909
James, Rachel L.	WTR	1992
James, Richard F.	BB	1955, 56, 57
Jameson, G. Larry	FB	1972, 73, 74
Jameson, Kathryn Jo	WBK	1977
Janes, Mickey C.	WR	1969
Janiak, Clifford J.	FB	1974, 75
Janney, Jack D.	FB	1960, 62
Jansen, John F.	BB	1980, 81, 83, 84
Janssen, Lori A.	VB	1988
Janzaruk, John D.	FB	1937, 38, 39
Jaques, Eric T.	BB	1986, 87, 88, 89
Jarech, Eugene R.	BB	1946
Jaros, Walter	BB	1929, 30
Jarosz, Patricia A.	FH/SB	1975, 76, 77
Jasper, Paul G.	FB/MBK	1928, 29, 30, 31
Jastremski, Chester A.	MSW	1961, 62, 63
Jastrzebski, Richard F.	MTR	1993
Jaworski, Cynthia A.	FH	1976, 77, 78, 79
Jecmen, Charles J.	MGY	1954
Jefferies, Zandrea E.	WBK	1988, 89, 90, 91
Jeffries, Urban B.	BB/MBK	1918, 19, 20
Jehl, William C.	BB	1982
Jenkins, Dawn E.	WGY	1980
Jenkins, Gregory D.	FB	1995, 96, 97
Jenkins, Marcelleous	MTR	1939, 40, 41
Jenkins, W.E.	FB/MTR	1887, 88, 89, 90, 91
Jenness, Charles W.	MTN	1961, 62
Jennings, Charles A.	MSW	1991, 92, 93
Jensen, Jill J.	SB	1987, 88, 89, 90
Jensen, Louis S.	MBK	1948
Jermak, John G.	MSO	1997
Jessup, Paul S.	WR	1929, 30, 31
Jessup, Robert G.	MSW	1947, 48, 49
Jewell, James W.	MGO	1964, 65, 66
Jimenez, Luke D.	MBK	1997, 98, 99
Joers, Ronald A.	MGO	1946
John, Lisa M.	VB	1986, 87, 88, 89
John, Terry L.	BB	1971
Johns, Gregory A.	BB	1971
Johnson, Albert E.	MBK	1945
Johnson, Azure D.	WSO	1994, 95, 96, 97

Johnson, Barry W.	FB	1955
Johnson, Byran S.	MTR	1993, 94, 95, 96
Johnson, Claudia	WGY	1975, 76
Johnson, Cynthia	WGY	1978
Johnson, Derek R.	BB	1992
Johnson, Donald E.	MTR	1972, 73
Johnson, Douglas W.	WR	1976, 78, 79
Johnson, Fred A.	FB	1934
Johnson, Fred T.	MTR	1948
Johnson, George L.	MTR	1942, 43
Johnson, Glen A.	MBK	1921
Johnson, Gregory W.	MCC/MTR	1971, 72, 73, 74
Johnson, Glynn, Jr.	FB	1997
Johnson, Harrison H.	MTR	1908, 09, 10
Johnson, Homer R.	FB	1930, 32
Johnson, Jack N.	MBK	1965, 66, 67
Johnson, James L.	MTR	1977
Johnson, James N.	MBK (Mgr.)	1928
Johnson, Jeremy S.	FB	1996, 98
Johnson, Jerry L.	FB	1970, 71, 72
Johnson, John B.	MSO	1985, 86
Johnson, John H.	FB	1899
Johnson, John H.	FB	1960, 61, 62
Johnson, John W.	MTR	1988
Johnson, Julie L.	WBK/WTR	1981, 82
Johnson, Kathy M.	WSW	1977, 78, 79, 80
Johnson, Ken	WR	1985
Johnson, Leroy R.	MBK/MTR	1959, 60
Johnson, Lisa M.	WGY	1976
Johnson, Lonnie, Jr.	FB	1978, 79, 80
Johnson, Mark S.	FB	1978, 79
Johnson, Michael E.	FB	1985
Johnson, Morris "Johnny"	BB/FB	1907, 08, 09
Johnson, Ossie S.	BB	1914, 15, 17
Johnson, Philip F.	MTN	1958
Johnson, R. Kenneth	MBK	1968, 69, 70
Johnson, Robert F.	BB	1978, 79
Johnson, Robert J.	FB	1995, 96
Johnson, Robert S.	WR	1946, 47, 49
Johnson, Ronald E.	MGY	1952, 53, 54
Johnson, Scott F.	MTR	1996, 97, 98
Johnson, Sherell, Jr.	MGO	1958, 59
Johnson, Theodore L.	MTR	1907
Johnson, Thomas J.	MGO	1956, 57
Johnson, William J.	BB	1931
Johnson, William S.	MBK	1937, 38, 39
Johnston, John M.	MTR	1959, 64, 65
Johnston, Judith A.	SB	1976, 77
Johnston, Peter M.	MSW	1993
Jolgren, Verner H.	MCC	1968, 69
Jones, Anthony T.	MSW	1979, 80, 81, 82
Jones, Aquilla G.	BB	1867
Jones, Barry L.	BB	1982, 83, 84
Jones, Benyard D.	FB	1995, 96, 97
Jones, Christopher A.	FB	1984
Jones, Dee R.	FB	1893, 94
Jones, Donald C.	MSW	1958
Jones, Eli S.	FB	1911
Jones, Emily	VB (Mgr.)	1998
Jones, Ernest C.	MTR	1942
Jones, Ernest L.	FB	1984, 85, 86, 87
Jones, Forrest T.	MGO	1960, 61, 62
Jones, Frank B.	MTR	1943
Jones, Harry L.	MTR	1916
Jones, Howard	BB	1962
Jones, Jackie E.	R	1953
Jones, John A.	FB	1964
Jones, Lyndon M.	MBK	1988, 89, 90, 91
Jones, Nathan E.	MCC	1997, 98
Jones, Nelson M.	BB (Mgr.)	1928
Jones, Jackie E.	R	1953
Jones, Ralph T.	BB	1976
Jones, Richard O.	BB	1954, 55, 56
Jones, Richard S.	FB (Mgr.)	1929
Jones, Robert E.	FB	1968, 69, 70
Jones, Robert I.	FB/WR	1931, 32, 33
Jones, Robert L., Jr.	MTR	1950
Jones, Ronald P.	MTR	1981, 82, 83, 84
Jones, Shelby F.	MBK (Mgr.)	1946
Jones, Shirley	WSW	1972, 73
Jones, Tara M.	WBK	1998
Jones, Teresa M.	WTR	1979, 80
Jones, Terry A.	BB/FB	1974, 75, 76, 77
Jones, Thomas D.	BB/FB	1906, 07
Jones, Tom G.	MGO	1956
Jones, Trent J.	FB	1996
Jones, Victor W.	FB	1958, 59
Jones, Walter A.	FB	1893, 94
Jones, Walter B.	BB	1912
Jones, William L.	FB	1905

Jones, Willie, Jr.	FB	1973, 74, 75, 76
Jones, Willie D.	FB	1956, 58
Jontz, Jon P., Jr.	MCC/MTR	1988, 89, 90, 91
Jordan, Amy P.	WTN	1981
Jordan, Colleen M.	VB	1988, 89, 90, 91
Jordan, Jane	WSW	1978
Jordan, Jeffrey K.	MTR	1976
Jordan, John J.	FB	1972, 73
Jordan, Joy L.	VB	1987, 88, 89, 90
Jordan, Paul R.	MTR	1902, 03
Jordan, Ricardo J.	MTN	1997, 98, 99
Jordan, Richard C.	MTR	1985, 86, 87
Jordan, William D.	BB	1986, 87, 88, 89
Jorden, Timothy R.	FB	1985, 86, 87, 88
Jorge, Jeff E.	WR	1992, 93, 95
Jorgensen, Michael A.	WR	1977, 79
Joseph, Russell L.	MTR	1905
Joshi, Natasha A.	WTN	1993, 94, 95, 96
Joss, Laura	WTR	1981
Joyce, William J.	MTN	1946
Joyner, Charles E.	MTR	1931, 32
Joyner, Harry C. "Butch"	MBK	1966, 67, 68
Juda, Christine M.	WSW	1982, 83, 84, 85
Judge, Edward A.	FB	1965
Judge, Tom W.	MCC/MTR	1942, 43
Julius, Russell S.	BB/FB	1916, 17, 18, 19
Jurkiewicz, Walter S.	FB	1939, 41

Kabanas, Steven	MSO	1979
Kaczmarek, Kenneth W.	FB	1965, 66, 67
Kaifesh, Larry J.	WR	1987, 88, 89, 90
Kaiser, Christopher E.	MBK (Mgr.)	1985
Kaiser, Mark J.	FB	1981
Kalcevich, Kenneth J.	WR	1974
Kalcheim, Jordan L.	MSW	1994
Kallay, Robert D.	MSO	1990
Kaltenrieder, Amy C.	FH	1980
Kalupa, Edward J.	FB	1963, 64
Kambadellis, Panayiotis J.	MTN	1986, 87, 88
Kamberg, Becky D.	WSW	1996, 97, 98, 99
Kaminski, Jack J.	FB	1971
Kaminski, Leon R.	MBK (Mgr.)/MTN	1943, 44, 45
Kamradt, Allan K.	FB	1966, 67, 68
Kamstra, John R.	MBK	1973, 74, 75
Kamtz, Jennifer E.	WTR	1995, 96, 97, 98
Kan, Alan	WR	1999
Kane, Campbell G.	MCC/MTR	1939, 40, 41, 42
Kane, Chad D.	MSW	1990, 91, 92
Kane, Charles J.	MTN	1963, 64, 65
Kane, Kristen M.	WSW	1991, 92, 93, 94
Kane, Michael J.	MTN	1972
Kanter, Steven B.	MGY	1981
Kapitan, Julius	WR	1950
Kapsalis, Daniel A.	MSO	1982, 83, 84
Kapsalis, Dean A.	MSO	1989, 90, 92, 93
Kapsalis, Paul A.	MSO	1983, 84, 86, 87
Karasawa, Bryce G.	WR	1999
Karchefsky, Jason M.	BB	1997, 98
Karls, Mathew E.	FB	1963
Karns, William K.	FB (Mgr.)	1976
Karras, Ted G.	FB	1953, 54, 55
Karstens, George J.	FB	1946, 47, 48
Kasonovich, Lou	FB	1948
Katalinich, John D.	BB	1991
Katner, Simon N.	MSO	1985, 86, 87, 88
Katsinis, John	MSO	1973, 74
Katterjohn, Cecil C.	BB	1918
Katz, Michael	FB (Mgr.)	1962
Kau, Donald L.	MSW	1957
Kauchak, Elizabeth R.	SB	1991, 92, 93
Kaufman, Alexandra H.	SB	1998, 99
Kaufman, Barton L.	BB	1961, 62
Kaufman, Bernard	WR (Mgr.)	1941
Kaufmanis, Eric	MGO	1978, 79, 80, 81
Kaull, Kevin M.	MSO	1980
Kay, Bret M.	MTR	1985
Kaylor, Jason E.	FB	1992, 93, 94, 95
Kayworth, Alfred E.	MSW	1943
Kealing, Robert J.	MTR	1975, 76, 77
Kean, Raymond L.	MSO	1973, 74, 75, 76
Kearney, Kathleen A.	WCC/WTR	1979, 80
Kearney, Richard C. III	FB	1994, 95
Keating, Charles H.	MSW	1974, 75, 76, 77

Lonnie Johnson in 1980 was the first IU runner with back-to-back 200-yard games.

Kristen Kane was a four-time All-American and won the one-meter title at the U.S. Outdoor Championships in 1992.

Keaton, Walter B.	WR (Mgr.)	1935
Keck, Robert C.	FB	1933, 34, 35
Keck, William H.	BB (Mgr.)	1941
Keckich, John A.	FB	1931, 32
Keckley, Carrie L.	WSW	1993, 94, 95, 96
Keefer, Thomas H.	MCC/MTR	1971, 72, 73
Keegan, Donna	WSW	1979
Keehn, Roy D.	FB	1897
Keeler, Jack L.	MTR	1970, 71, 72
Keeler, John R.	WR	1937, 38
Keeling, Forrest E.	MTR	1917, 19, 20
Keenan, Christopher L.	MCC	1994
Keenan, Christopher T.	MSO	1984, 85, 86
Keenan, Thomas	MTR	1967, 68
Keenan, Thomas R.	MSO	1995, 96, 97, 99
Keever, Charles H.	FB	1916, 17, 18
Kegley, Carol A.	FH/WBK	1972, 73, 74, 75, 76
Kegley, James H.	MSW	1977, 78, 79, 80
Kehrt, Willard M.	BB/MBK	1933, 34, 35
Keiler, David A.	MGY	1966, 67, 68
Keim, Janis A.	VB/WBK	1974, 75, 76, 77
Keim, Kenneth G.	MSW	1976, 77, 78, 79
Keir, Krista M.	WTR	1999
Keisker, William E.	MBK (Mgr.)	1924
Keith, Dean V.	WR	1920
Keithley, Crecia J.	VB	1998
Kelleher, Derek J.	MCC/MTR	1991, 92
Keller, James R.	WR	1950, 51
Keller, Paul L.	MGY	1961
Keller, Raymond J.	MSO	1979, 80
Keller, Ronald L.	BB	1963, 64, 65
Keller, Steven R.	MSO	1991, 92, 93, 94
Kelley, J. Steven	MCC/MTR	1969, 70, 71, 72
Kelley, Joseph P.	MSO	1974, 76
Kelley, Phynice K.	WTR	1992, 93, 94, 95
Kelley, Thomas W.	MGO	1974
Kelliher, Patty A.	WGY	1978
Kellogg, Kevin C.	FB	1977, 78, 79, 80
Kelly, Donna L.	WTR	1986, 87, 88, 89
Kelly, Eboni J.	WTR	1989
Kelly, Francis J.	FB	1901
Kelly, James D.	MBK (Mgr.)	1986
Kelly, James E.	MGO	1999
Kelly, Kevin M.	FB	1986, 87
Kelly, Michael	MBK (Mgr.)	1990
Kelly, Scott A.	WR	1979, 80, 81, 82
Kelsey, Charles V.	MTR	1943
Kelso, Reed H.	FB	1933, 34, 35
Kelso, Robert	FB	1920
Kelso, Russell M.	FB	1925
Kemmer, Charles B.	MSW	1935
Kemp, Charles	BB	1905
Kemp, Robert K.	MCC/MTR	1929, 30, 31, 32
Kemper, Michael K.	MGO	1993, 94, 95, 96
Kempf, Edward J.	BB/FB	1905, 06
Kempf, Joseph L.	FB	1943, 44
Kempf, Susan L.	VB	1974, 75
Kendall, Joseph G.	MTN	1972, 73, 74
Kendall, Paul	MCC/MTR	1941, 42
Kenderdine, Robert L., Jr.	FB	1935, 36, 37
Kendrick, Ralph L.	MSW	1964, 65, 66
Kendrick, Thomas B.	FB	1956, 57, 58
Kenebrew, Leonard D.	FB	1982, 83, 84
Keneipp, Dale M.	FB	1976, 77, 78
Kenley, Kevin C.	FB	1979, 80, 81

Kennady, Richard M.	MSW	1957, 58, 59
Kennedy, Charnele M.	WSW	1994, 95, 96, 97
Kennedy, Gregory W.	MSO	1979, 80, 81, 82, 83
Kennedy, Kevin M.	FB	1983
Kennedy, Robert L.	MTR	1986, 87, 88
Kennedy, Robert O.	MCC/MTR	1966, 67, 68, 69
Kennedy, Robert O.	MCC/MTR	1988, 89, 90, 91, 92
Kennedy, Russell E.	MTR	1945
Kenney, Henry C.	MGO	1933, 35
Kenney, James E.	BB	1960
Kenny, William F.	MSW	1983, 84
Kent, Miller C.	FB	1902, 03
Kenyon, Thomas A.	MSW	1974, 75, 76, 77
Keough, Cheryl L.	WGY	1978
Keppler, Donald R.	MTR (Mgr.)	1953, 54
Kerby, Michael G.	MGO	1969
Kercheval, William R.	MBK/MTR	1905
Kerekes, James I.	FB	1961, 62
Kerkhoff, Jill S.	VB	1990, 91, 92, 93
Kern, Darren J.	MTR	1982, 83, 84, 85
Kernohan, John F.	MGO	1983, 84, 85, 86
Kerns, Cindy M.	WBK	1996, 97, 98, 99
Kerns, Laura B.	WSW	1995, 96, 97, 98
Kerns, Tobi A.	FB	1991, 92
Kerr, John W.	MGO/MSW	1954, 55, 57
Kerr, William T.	FB	1958
Kerry, Mark A.	MSW	1978, 79
Keucher, Thomas R.	FB (Mgr.)	1965
Kidd, Robert L.	BB	1922
Kiddoo, Anne J.	WSW	1988, 89, 90, 91
Kienlen, David A.	FB/MSW (Mgr.)	1966, 67
Kieran, William J.	FB (Mgr.)	1963
Kight, William D.	BB	1922, 24, 25
Kilby, Roy, Jr.	BB/MBK	1942, 46, 47
Killian, Robert A.	WR	1956, 57
Killough, Bruce A.	MSO	1984, 85, 86, 87
Kimball, Brian L.	MTR	1979, 80, 81
Kimble, Frank E.	FB	1907, 08, 09, 10
Kimbo, Conney M.	FB	1952, 53, 56
Kimmell, Ray B.	MCC	1948, 49
Kincade, Leigh A.	WCC/WTR	1979, 80, 81, 82, 83
King, Clarence K.	FB/MTR	1980, 81, 82, 83, 84
King, Daniel M.	MSO	1981, 82, 83, 84
King, Emmett O.	FB	1895, 96, 97
King, Harold A.	FB/MTR	1910, 11
King, J. Raymond	MTR	1938, 40
King, John M.	MSW	1981, 82, 83, 85
King, Joseph	FB	1994, 95, 96, 97
King, Kathryn D.	WBK	1976, 77
King, Sean	MSO	1994
King, William E., Jr.	MTN	1945, 47, 48, 49
Kingdon, Victor R.	MTN	1937, 38, 39
Kinman, Guy M.	FB	1910
Kinniry, David T.	FB	1983, 84, 85, 86
Kinsella, John P.	MSW	1971, 72, 73, 74
Kinsey, Elza D.	BB	1933
Kiplinger, Henry W.	FB	1886, 87
Kirby, Joel A.	FB	1973, 74
Kirchenstien, Terrye J.	MTR	1988, 89, 90, 91, 92
Kirchner, Eric W.	MBK	1978, 79, 80, 81
Kirchner, Robert J.	MSO	1972, 73, 74
Kirchner, Steven A.	MSO	1974, 75
Kirn, Jeffrey A.	FB	1997
Kirn, Tina E.	VB	1990
Kirschner, Eric L.	MTR	1967, 68
Kirk, Robert	FB	1967, 68
Kirkham, Laura M.	WTR	1986, 87, 88, 89
Kirkpatrick, Carl J.	BB	1955, 56, 57
Kirkpatrick, John Q.	MTR	1931
Kirkpatrick, Russell B.	MBK	1914, 15
Kirkwood, Walter B., Jr.	MTR (Mgr.)	1951
Kitchel, Ted D.	MBK	1979, 80, 81, 82, 83
Kitchell, Richard W.	MSW	1960, 61, 62
Kitchen, Rodney P.	MCC/MTR (Mgr.)	1989, 90
Kivett-Ripmaster, Austin	MSO	1998
Kivett, Silas C., Jr.	MSW (Mgr.)	1938
Kivland, Patrick P.	MGY	1967, 68, 69
Kizer, Robert L.	FB	1993, 94
Klaers, Nicholas	MCC	1994
Klafs, Frank A.	MSW	1939, 40, 41
Klapkowski, Joyce	FH	1974, 75
Klaric, Anton J.	MTN	1997
Klassen, Rachel S.	WGY	1979, 80
Kleiman, Janis L.	WGO	1980, 81, 82, 83
Klein, Christopher R.	MSO	1994, 95, 96, 97
Klein, Kathleen A.	WGO	1986, 87, 88, 89
Klein, Paul T.	R	1955, 56
Klein, Sheri L.	WGY	1980, 81, 82
Klenoski, Ronald J.	FB	1974
Kleschen, Mary Z.	FH	1975, 76, 77, 78

Name	Sport	Years
Klezmer, Samuel	MSW	1935, 36
Klim, Richard J.	FB	1955, 56
Klink, Orrin E.	FB	1919
Klitzky, Shelley	WGO	1970
Kloeffler, Lloyd C.	MCC/MGO	1935, 37, 38
Kluska, Jennifer L.	WSO	1997, 98
Klusmeyer, Benjamin L.	FB	1994, 95, 96, 97
Kluszewski, Theodore B.	BB/FB	1944, 45
Klutinoty, George II	FB	1958
Knapp, B. Kathryn	WSW	1986, 87, 88
Knapp, Donald O.	MBK (Mgr.)	1969
Knapp, Willard E.	MCC/MTR (Mgr.)	1928, 29
Knecht, Marvin	R	1957, 58, 59
Knepper, Edwin W.	BB	1897
Kniffin, Sue Ellen	WSW	1970
Knight, Foy W.	FB	1901, 02, 03
Knight, Kerry D.	MTR	1985, 86
Knight, Marion R.	MSW	1952, 53, 54
Knight, Patrick	MBK	1991, 93, 94, 95
Knight, Ralph D.	MSW	1945
Knipple, John H.	MTR	1957, 59
Kniptash, Jennifer L.	SB	1998
Knoll, Karen E.	VB	1985, 86, 87, 88
Knopf, Frank A.	BB	1972, 73, 74, 75
Knowles, David L.	FB	1974, 75, 76
Knox, Kenneth R.	MSW	1975, 76
Knoy, Earl E.	MBK	1923
Knuckles, Franklin B.	MGY	1963, 64, 65
Knudsen, Sanne S.	WSO	1997
Knudson, Traci A.	WCC/WTR	1995, 96, 97, 98
Knue, Beth Ann	WTR	1995
Kobel, Bret W.	MSW	1986, 87, 88, 89
Kobi, Daniel C.	FB	1997
Kobman, Randy L.	FB	1982
Kobulnicky, Paul	FB	1951, 52, 53
Koch, Katrin R.	WTR	1989, 90, 91, 92
Koch, William S.	MTN	1982, 83, 84
Kochell, Howard E.	BB	1977, 78, 79
Koehler, Christopher E.	BB	1991, 92, 93
Koenemann, Edward P.	MSW	1953, 54
Koenig, Brian E.	FB	1966
Koenig, Craig W.	MTR	1963
Koenig, Debbie	WSW	1971
Koenig, Howard A.	BB	1931, 32, 33
Koenig, Walter C.	FB/MTR	1929, 30, 31
Koesters, Scott	FB (Mgr.)	1996
Kohlmeier, Jania L.	WGO	1979
Kohlmeier, Kim C.	MBK (Mgr.)	1977
Kohne, Jacquelyn A.	VB	1969
Kokos, John T.	FB	1945, 46
Koller, Kathleen V.	VB	1973, 74, 75
Kollias, Louis	FB	1953, 56
Komar, Samuel B.	WR	1975, 76, 77, 78
Komasinski, Ralph M.	BB	1966, 67
Kominiarek, Richard J.	FB	1970
Komorowski, Norman T.	WR	1956, 57, 58
Konrad, Michael G.	MCC/MTR (Mgr.)	1988, 90
Konrad, Walter P.	MTR	1920, 22
Kontol, David J.	MTR	1975, 76
Koontz, Theodore V.	WR	1923, 24
Kopatich, Debora A.	VB	1975, 76
Kopetzki, Candice	WTN	1987, 88, 89, 90
Kops, Willard J.	BB	1945, 47, 48
Korallus, Sonja	WSW	1990, 91, 92
Korbelak, Megan L.	WCC/WTR	1994, 95
Koressel, Tim A.	MGO	1980, 81, 82, 83, 84
Korhel, Douglas G.	MTR	1970
Kornhaber, Steven F.	MSO	1972, 73
Kornowa, David R.	FB	1965, 66, 67
Korol, Aleksey Y.	MSO	1996, 97, 98
Kosanic, Ryan T.	MSW	1997, 98, 99
Kosanovich, Louis	FB	1948
Koselke, Norman E.	BB	1957
Kosman, Michael T.	BB	1939, 40, 41
Kost, Karol Ann	WBK	1977
Kostka, Joseph N.	FB	1985
Kotarba, Steven S.	BB	1990
Kouba, Elizabeth J.	WCC/WTR	1994, 95, 96
Kovach, Albert F.	MSW	1984, 85, 86
Kovalenko, Dema A.	MSO	1996, 97, 98
Kovalenko, Jefferson T.	WR	1980
Kovatch, Ernest S.	FB	1948, 49, 50
Kovatch, John R.	FB	1975
Kozar, Kathryn E.	WSO	1993, 94, 95, 96
Kozma, Michael C.	MTR	1980, 81, 82, 83, 84
Kraak, Charles F.	MBK	1952, 53, 54
Kraft, Patrick M.	FB	1998
Krahulik, Frank	WR	1934, 35, 36
Kralovansky, Albert	BB/MBK	1944, 45, 46, 47
Kram, Kelly M.	WSO	1998
Krambeck, Henry F.	MGY	1950
Kramer, Gerald C.	MTR	1933
Kramer, Kathy	FH	1970, 71
Kramer, Kyle K.	BB	1993, 94, 96, 97
Kramer, Paul W.	MTN	1954
Kramer, Robert J.	FB	1973, 74, 76
Kramer, Terry E.	FB	1998
Kramme, David M.	FB	1985, 86, 87
Kraus, Lori F.	WTN	1977
Krause, Arthur C.	FB	1912, 13, 14
Krause, Larry J.	FB (Mgr.)	1970
Krehbrink, Bradley J.	MTR	1989, 90
Kreil, Nicole	WSW	1985, 86, 87, 88
Kreisher, Karl W.	MSW	1996
Kremer, Carl T.	FB (Mgr.)	1962
Kremm, Tim L.	MTN	1976, 77
Krevitz, Nathan M.	BB	1929
Krick, Denny	WR	1954, 55, 56
Krick, Kurt A.	MTR	1997, 98, 99
Krick, Tracy L.	WBK	1984, 85, 86, 87
Krider, David G.	BB (Mgr.)	1961
Krider, Ross K.	BB	1960
Krieger, Barbara J.	SB/WBK	1977, 78, 79, 80
Krieger, Nancy S.	SB	1970, 71, 72
Kriete, Darl	MGO	1957, 58, 59
Krise, Thomas H.	BB (Mgr.)	1942
Krisko, Gregory D.	MSW	1992, 93, 94, 95
Kristan, Terry	MCC (Mgr.)	1988
Krivoshia, Michael	FB	1965, 66, 67
Krockover, Mark A.	BB (Mgr.)	1993
Kron, Karen C.	SB	1991, 92, 93, 94
Kronenberger, Julie C.	WBK	1982, 83
Kropf, Paul L.	FB	1968
Kropschot, Jeffrey S.	MGO	1985
Kropschot, Krissa S.	WGO	1989, 90
Krouse, Laura A.	WCC/WTR	1987, 88, 89
Kruchten, Frank G.	MTR	1932, 33, 34
Krueger, Dennis W.	BB	1963, 64, 65
Krueger, John E.	MTR (Mgr.)	1942
Krueger, Julius E.	MBK	1925, 26, 27
Krueger, Nate D.	MSW	1994
Krug, Ann M.	WSW	1973, 74, 75, 76
Kruger, Carrie	WCC/WTR (Mgr.)	1997, 98, 99
Krulewitch, Edward	FB	1959
Krupa, Raymond F.	BB	1947, 48
Krutzsch, Armin	FB	1907
Kruyer, Thomas E.	FB/WR	1969, 70, 71
Kuberski, Natasha D.	WSW	1995, 96
Kubic, Steve	BB	1935, 37
Kubo, Hazime	MSW	1989
Kuchuris, Paul G., Jr.	FB	1962, 63
Kuechenberg, Rudolph B.	FB	1962, 63, 64
Kuehne, Clem K., Jr.	MSW	1939
Kuhlmeier, Debra R.	FH/SB	1974, 75, 76
Kumerow, Craig J.	FB	1979, 80, 81
Kumfer, Brian K.	MSW	1993, 94
Kun, Lester	FB	1952, 53, 54, 55
Kunkel, Kenneth	BB	1917, 19, 20
Kunkel, William A.	BB	1916
Kunkel, William A. III	BB	1944
Kurfman, Virginia	WGY	1972
Kurtz, William A.	MTR (Mgr.)	1938
Kus, Martin W.	FB	1972
Kushner, Shirah	WCC	1983
Kuss, Melissa A.	WTR	1986
Kuss, Otto R.	FB/MTR/WR	1931, 32, 33, 34
Kutchback, Knoll F.	MTR	1930
Kutchins, Alexander S.	FB	1930, 31
Kuvin, Michele	WSW	1982
Kvietkus, Robert	FB	1973, 74
Kyff, Robert J.	BB	1959, 60, 61
Kyle, John M.	BB	1949, 50, 51
Kyle, John W.	FB/MTR	1919, 20, 21
Laberdie, Terry A.	MSW	1961
LaBerteaux, A.O.	MSW	1946
Labotka, Charles A.	MCC/MTR	1942, 43
LaBrash, James C.	MTR (Mgr.)	1956
LaBrash, John H.	MCC/MTR	1951, 52, 53, 54
Lach, Michael	MGO	1965
Laconi, Reginald L.	MTR	1958, 60, 61
Ladewig, Brock L.	MSW	1972, 73, 74, 75
LaDuke, Edward R.	BB	1960, 61, 62

Laesch, Mark A.	BB	1974, 75, 76		Leach, Frank D.	MSW	1972
LaFave, Michael J.	MBK	1981, 82		Leach, Gilbert E.	MSW (Mgr.)	1973, 74
LaFleur, Michael J.	MGY	1976, 77, 78, 80		Leach, John H.	FB	1933
LaForce, David S.	BB	1888, 89		Leach, William O.	FB (Mgr.)	1957
Lageman, Angela S.	WSW	1994, 95, 96, 97		Leahy, Megan R.	WCC/WTR	1995, 96, 97, 98, 99
LaGrange, Candres A.	WGO	1976, 77, 80		Leake, Alphonso	FB	1976, 77, 78
LaGrange, Constance	WGO	1971, 72, 73		Leakey, Donald J.	BB	1944, 45
Lahoda, Henry L.	BB	1924		Leakey, Marion T.	WR	1931
Lakoff, Victoria A.	WGO	1974, 75, 76, 77		Leary, Todd C.	MBK	1990, 91, 92, 93, 94
Lalaeff, Mike	MGO	1951		Leas, Rodney M.	MCC/MTR	1928, 29, 30, 31
Laland, Dalphia A.	WTR	1980, 83		Lebowitz, Martin S.	MTR	1963, 64, 65
Lallathin, Stephanie	FH/SB/VB	1971, 72, 73, 74		Lebron, Martha T.	SB	1991, 92
Lallman, Ellie R.	WSW	1998, 99		Lechner, Pamela K.	WSW	1985
Lamar, James D.	FB	1996, 97, 98		Leckeitner, Michele	WSW	1985
Lamb, Fred J.	WR	1959, 60		Leckie, Melissa S.	WBK	1980, 81, 82, 83
Lamb, Marlo M.	WCC	1988		Ledgerwood, Marjorie C.	SB	1987, 88, 89, 90
Lambert, James R.	MCC/MTR	1951, 52, 53, 54, 55		Lee, Cara Beth	WTN	1988, 89, 91
Lambert, Mark C.	MSW	1976, 77, 78, 79		Lee, Christopher J.	FB	1995, 96, 97
Lambert, Mark R.	MSW	1972, 73, 74, 75		Lee, Deborah S.	WGO	1987, 88, 89, 90
Lambert, Michele	WTN	1986		Lee, Herbie	MBK	1959
Lambert, William C.	MTR (Mgr.)	1963		Lee, James W.	BB	1966, 67, 68
Lammert, Larry G.	MSW	1969		Lee, Jerry L.	FB	1981, 82
Lampkin, Ann Y.	WCC/WTR	1986, 87, 88, 89, 90		Lee, Pamela J.	SB	1983, 84, 85, 86
Lancaster, Thomas S.	MGY	1959, 60, 61		Lee, Ray A.	MTR	1923, 24
Land, Kim S.	WBK	1981, 82, 83, 84		Lee, Rickey O.	MGO	1968
Landis, Gerald W.	FB	1922		Lee, Stephen R.	FB	1993, 94, 95, 96
Landon, William L.	MCC/MTR	1959, 60, 61, 62		Lee, Wendy	WSW	1979, 80
Landry, Brent L.	MGO	1996, 97, 98, 99		Lee, William Sylvester	MGY	1951, 52
Landshof, Nancy E.	WGY	1981, 82, 83, 84		Leen, Randall T.	MGO	1995, 96, 97, 98
Lane, Clarence R.	MTR	1955, 56, 57		Leene, Eilish	WSW	1980
Lane, Gordon L.	MGO	1961, 62		Leer, Jack R.	MGO	1950, 52, 53
Lang, John J.	MCC/MTR	1989, 90, 91		Leer, Kevin W.	WSW	1997
Lang, Walter B.	BB	1921		Leer, Mary Ann	FH	1969, 70
Lange, Jonathan W.	MTR	1999		Leet, Clarence E.	MTR	1928
Langemak, Kay	WSW	1987		Leftwich, Jerry D.	MTR	1972, 73, 74
Langille, Paul A.	WR	1970		Legacki, Amy Beth	WCC/WTR	1987, 88, 89, 90, 91, 92
Langsdon, Fred R.	FB	1911, 12		Legge, Robert W.	MCC/MTR	1968, 69, 70, 71
Langworthy, David S.	WR	1981, 82		Lehman, Janet C.	WGY	1974, 75, 76
Lanman, Vivian F.	FB/MTR	1924, 25, 26		Lehman, Philip H.	MBK (Mgr.)	1960
Lanscioni, Mark J.	MGO	1989, 90, 91		Lehr, Edgar I.	WR	1926
Lantz, Park G.	BB	1910		Leimbach, Michael P.	MGY	1975, 76, 77
LaPlante, Kathy J.	FH/SB	1974, 75		Leinberger, Gary J.	MBK	1966, 67
LaPlante, Robert W.	MSW	1935, 36		Leissner, Michael D.	MSW	1987, 88
Lappin, Harley G.	WR	1975, 76, 78		Lekas, Maria I.	VB	1997
LaRou, Elizabeth C.	SB	1989, 90		LeMar, Bruce R.	MCC	1966
Larraazabal, Elena A.	WGO	1982, 83		LeMay, Robert G.	MGY	1977, 78, 79, 80
Larrison, Kevin J.	FB	1981		Lemert, Bonnie	WGY	1974, 75
Larrison, Luanne	SB/VB	1972, 73, 74, 75		Lemirande, Jeffrey J.	FB	1983, 84, 85
Larson, James R.	MGO	1960		Lemme, Kevin J.	MBK	1996
Larson, Michael T.	FB	1987, 88		Lenard, Richard A.	BB	1970
LaRusso, Laurie A.	FH	1977		Lenfert, Patricia A.	FH/SB	1973, 74, 75, 76
LaSelle, Thomas J.	MTN	1975, 76		Lenihan, Paul F.	MSW	1981, 82, 83, 84
Lash, Donald R.	MCC/MTR	1934, 35, 36, 37		Lenox, Than H.	MBK (Mgr.)	1972
Lash, Russell E.	MCC/MTR	1959, 60, 61, 62		Lentz, James C.	WR	1967, 68, 69
Laskowski, John J.	MBK	1973, 74, 75		Lentz, Jeffrey J.	BB	1972
Laskowski, Kristin A.	WCC/WTR	1988, 89, 90, 91		Lenzi, Mark E.	MSW	1987, 88, 89, 90
Latshaw, Alan R.	FB	1972		Leo, Charles J.	FB	1954, 55, 59
Latshaw, Susan P.	WCC/WTR	1981, 82		Leon, Christopher G.	WR	1985
Lattaoui, Mohamed	MSW	1982		Leon, Kenneth B.	MSO	1973
Laufenberg, Brandon "Babe"	FB	1981, 82		Leonard, Adam A.	FB	1907, 09, 10, 11
Laughlin, Euel J.	MSW	1970, 71, 72		Leonard, John E.	FB	1919, 20, 21
Lauinger, Craig R.	MSW	1988		Leonard, John H.	MBK/MTR	1927, 28
Lauter, Alfred A.	MSW	1927, 28, 29		Leonard, Kay	WGO	1971, 72, 73
Lauter, Fred A.	FB	1959, 60		Leonard, Raymond B.	MTN	1980, 81
Lauterbach, Lawrence W.	R	1958		Leonard, W. Robert	MBK	1952, 53, 54
LaVenda, John	MBK (Mgr.)	1980		Leonardi, Daniel T.	BB	1987
Lavrinenko, Yuri V.	MSO	1996, 97, 98		Leonhardt, William P.	MTR	1947, 48
Law, Brett A.	FB	1991, 92, 93, 94		Leopold, Charles M	BB (Mgr.)	1964
Lawall, Sara	WSW	1972, 73, 74		Leopold, Judge M.	FB	1897, 98
Lawecki, Joseph S.	BB	1947, 48, 49		Leopold, Richard	BB (Mgr.)	1997
Lawrence, Donald J.	MSO	1988		Leques, Alzira B.	WSO	1997
Lawrence, Philip A.	MTR (Mgr.)	1936		Lescak, John	BB/MCC	1943, 44, 45
Lawrence, Robert E.	BB	1958		Lesniak, Mary E.	WP	1999
Lawrie, Mary K.	WSW	1973, 74		Levenda, John P.	MBK (Mgr.)	1980
Laws, Bert H.	MTR	1930		Levin, Barbara	WGY	1971, 72
Laws, Richard V.	MTR	1964		Levin, Daniel B.	MTN	1974
Lawson, Christopher	MBK	1990, 91		Levin, Michelle L.	SB	1991
Lawson, Harry A., Jr.	MGO	1930		Levin, Sarah R.	WR (Mgr.)	1997
Lawson, Martin R.	R	1960, 61		Levine, Jerry B.	WR	1979, 80, 81
Lawson, Nancy A.	WSW	1978, 79, 80		Levitre, Patrick I.	MSW	1999
Lawson, Randall L.	FB	1979		Levy, Jacob N.	FB (Mgr.)	1959
Lawson, Richard W.	BB	1951		Levy, Morris	FB (Mgr.)	1967
Lawson, Robert E.	MCC/MTR	1955, 56		Levy, Newman	FB (Mgr.)	1957
Lawson, Rodney H.	FB	1972, 73, 74		Lewandowski, Walter F., Jr.	MTR (Mgr.)	1943
Lawson, Thomas R.	R	1961, 63		Lewis, Adolph A.	FB	1938, 40
Laxgang, Mark	MSO	1979, 81, 82, 83, 84		Lewis, Brett M.	BB	1995, 96, 97
Layman, Jeffrey L.	MSO	1981, 84, 85		Lewis, D. Michael	MBK	1997, 98, 99
Layman, Richard C.	MSO	1980, 81		Lewis, James E.	MGY	1968
Layman, Richard E.	FB	1975		Lewis, James K. II	MSW	1958
Lazzara, Angelo	WR	1939, 41		Lewis, Karen L.	WSW/WTR	1985, 86, 87, 88

Jim Lentz was Big Ten wrestling champion in 1969.

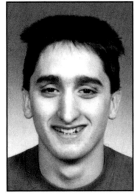

Sergio Lopez, swimming for Spain in 1988, was IU's last Olympic swimming medalist.

Lewis, Laura M.	WCC/WTR	1985, 86, 87, 88, 89
Lewis, Laurie R.	MTR	1975, 76
Lewis, Nathan C.	BB	1991, 92, 93
Lewis, Thomas A.	FB	1992, 93, 94
Lewis, Thomas S.	BB	1972
Lewis, Walter O.	BB/FB	1909, 10, 11
Lewis, Warren W.	MBK	1942, 43
Lewis, William H.	BB	1925
Lewis, Ylonda D.	WBK	1987, 88, 89, 90
Ley, Leo J.	MSO	1972
Leytze, D. Robert	MSO	1982, 83
Liber, Shannon H.	WBK	1989
Lidy, John V.	FB	1996, 97, 98
Lienert, Walter J.	MGY	1950
Ligon, Damita C.	WTR	1984
Lilja, David S.	FB	1984, 85, 86
Lilley, Susan D.	SB/VB/WTR	1976, 77, 78, 79, 80
Lilliston, Andrew W.	BB (Mgr.)	1968
Lilly, Robert F.	MGY	1962, 63, 64
Lind, Patrick G.	BB	1954, 55
Lindeman, Todd J.	MBK	1992, 93, 94, 95, 96
Linder, George E.	WR	1935
Linderbeck, Amy L.	WTR	1997
Lindgren, John A.	FB	1989
Lindgren, Kristina E.	WGY	1977, 78, 79
Lindley, Frank I.	FB	1910
Lindner, Carol L.	WSW	1976
Lindsay, Lawrence W.	MTN	1971, 72, 73, 74
Lindsay, Michael K.	MSW	1978
Lindsey, Ermel E.	MTR	1916
Lindsey, Jason F.	MCC	1970, 71
Link, Charles L.	BB	1925
Linke, Curtis G.	MTR (Mgr.)	1964
Linker, Robert S.	MSW	1943
Linko, Michael	BB	1945, 48
Linnemeier, Thomas J.	MCC/MTR	1955, 56
Linonis, Frank E.	FB	1942
Linsemeyer, Dorothy A.	WSW	1987, 88
Linski, Charles J.	MGO	1998, 99
Lintner, Daniel T.	FB/MTR	1970, 71, 72
Lippitt, Scott K.	MTN	1997
Lipski, Debbie M.	WSW	1995, 96, 97, 98, 99
Lisle, Janice	WGO	1979, 80
Liston, John L.	MBK (Mgr.)	1974
Littell, Clarence G.	FB	1902
Little, J. David	FB	1989
Little, Palmer L.	MCC/MTR	1925, 26, 28, 29
Littlejohn, Ann S.	WSW	1973, 74
Litz, Willard G.	BB	1947, 48, 49, 50
Livingston, Theodore A.	FB	1935, 36
Livovich, Andrew F.	WR	1939, 40
Liwienski, Christopher J.	FB	1994, 95, 96, 97
Lobring, Wayne M.	MSO	1990, 91, 92, 93
Lobus, John A.	BB	1968, 69
Lock, Jenna L.	WTR	1999
Lockett, Harold J.	MTR	1943, 48
Lockhart, Thomas L.	MTN	1978, 79, 80, 81
Lockridge, R. Bruce	FB/MTR	1902, 03
Lockridge, Ross F., Jr.	MCC/MTR	1932, 33, 34
Loftus, Shirley	WSW	1970, 71, 72
Logan, Harlan D.	MBK/MTN/MTR	1924, 25
Logan, James Z.	FB	1937, 38, 39
Logan, John A.	BB/MBK	1941, 42, 43, 46
Logan, Theodore E.	BB	1967
Logsdon, Sue Ellen	WBK	1970, 71, 73, 74
Logue, Lester L.	MTR	1937, 38

Loh, Robert	MSW	1966, 67
Lohman, James M.	MCC	1997
Lohman, Libbie K.	WSW	1997, 98, 99
Lohrei, Jesse D.	FB	1919, 20, 22
Lollar, Robert W.	MBK	1948
Londergan, Benjamin R.	MSO	1995, 96, 97
Long, Clarence W.	FB (Mgr.)	1938
Long, Everett K.	MTR	1942, 43
Long, Gary V.	MBK	1959, 60, 61
Long, Harry	FB	1901
Long, Kenneth W.	FB	1968
Long, Philander L.	FB	1903, 04
Long, Ronald E.	MCC/MTR	1956, 57, 58, 59
Long, Thomas D.	BB	1885, 86, 87
Long, William J.	MGY	1966, 67, 68
Longsdon, Malcolm J.	MTR	1921
Longshore, Marc M.	FB	1979, 81, 82
Lonigro, Aimee E.	SB	1994, 95, 96, 97
Loomis, Robert M.	MTR	1920
Loop, Omer L.	FB	1911
Loos, Lee S.	MTR	1953
Looschen, Clifford H.	MSW	1985, 86
Lopa, Michael J.	FB	1960, 61, 62
Loper, Laura E.	WTR	1994, 95
Lopez, Sergio	MSW	1988, 89
Lorber, Max J.	FB/MBK	1923, 24
Lord, Thomas	MSW	1956, 57, 58
Lortz, Gilbert D., Jr.	MTN	1959, 60, 61
Losh, Brian D.	MSO	1994
Lottner, Jere W.	BB	1953
Loughery, Richard M.	MTR	1972, 74
Lounsbury, Laura M.	WBK	1984, 85, 86, 87
Lovan, Tish R.	WSW	1985, 86, 87, 88
Love, Glenn R.	MTR	1972, 73, 74
Lovejoy, David J.	MSW	1983
Lovell, Suzanne M.	WGY	1977, 78
Lovett, Larry W.	FB	1978, 79
Lovstedt, Roy J., Jr.	MSW	1961, 62, 63
Low, Robert M.	FB	1974
Lowe, Alvin B.	MCC	1926
Lowe, Brenda K.	WBK	1977
Loyal, Michael C.	MSO	1973, 74
Lucas, Elmer L.	WR	1922
Lucas, William F.	MSW	1936, 37
Lucci, Michelle J.	WSW	1986, 87, 88
Lucey, Ellen N.	WSW	1990, 91, 92, 93
Luciano, Andre C.	MSO	1992, 93
Luciano, Michael A.	BB	1975, 77
Luda, Stephen M.	BB	1996
Ludlow, Bonnie J.	VB	1994, 95, 96
Luebbehusen, Mary Lou	SB	1970
Luecke, Michelle E.	WTR	1987, 88
Luft, Don R.	BB/FB/MBK	1949, 50, 51, 52
Lugar, William R.	MTN	1940
Luger, Julie L.	WSW	1992, 93
Lukawski, Thomas J.	FB	1993, 94, 95, 96
Lukemeyer, Robert S.	MBK	1949
Lumm, Robert W.	MTR (Mgr.)	1937
Lundgren, Kenneth B.	MTR	1968, 69, 70
Lundy, Nathanial	FB/MTR	1978, 79, 80, 81
Lundy, Troy A.	BB	1986, 89
Lussow, Frederick H.	FB	1963
Luther, Godfrey M.	MTR	1918, 19
Luther, Lawrence C., Jr.	FB	1984, 85, 86, 87
Luther, Susan	WSW	1979
Luther, William	MSW	1927
Luthman, Amy M.	WSO	1993, 94, 95
Luttinger, William G.	MGY	1949, 50
Lux, Kathryn L.	WCC/WTR	1983, 84, 85
Lybrook, John C.	BB	1911, 12
Lykens, James	FB (Mgr.)	1973
Lynch, Harold D.	BB	1922
Lynch, Ralph D.	WR	1926
Lynch, Thomas C.	MTN	1952
Lyon, Richard E.	WR	1950
Lyons, Fitzhugh R.	FB	1931, 32, 33
Lyons, Jeffrey A.	WR	1989, 90, 91, 92
Lyons, Kathleen A.	WSO	1993
Lysohir, Nick	FB	1945, 48
Lyster, Barbara S.	VB	1974, 75, 76, 77
Lyster, Deborah J.	FH	1974
Lytle, Todd C.	MCC/MTR	1988, 89, 90, 91

MacArthur, Robert J.	MTR	1982
MacAskill, Douglas J.	MSW	1976, 78, 79, 80
MacDonald, Elizabeth K.	WSW	1985, 86, 87, 88
Mace, William M.	MTR	1956, 57
MacEachern, Chris	BB	1990
Macer, Leland E.	BB	1922, 24
Mack, Daniel H.	BB (Mgr.)	1954
Mack, Gary R.	MSO	1998
Mack, Jason D.	FB	1989, 90, 91
Mack, Pamela G.	WBK	1982, 83, 84, 85
Mackey, Alicia R.	WTR	1996
Mackin, Norman L.	BB/FB	1956, 57, 58, 59
Mackle, Robert J.	MSW	1983, 84, 85, 86
Macomb, Doug	MTR (Mgr.)	1992
Macon, David C., Jr.	MTR	1944, 45
MacPherson, Dennis H.	MGY	1962, 64
MacQuivey, Joseph A.	MTR (Mgr.)	1949
Macy, Amber D.	WCC/WTR	1997, 98, 99
Maddick, Russell A.	BB	1961
Maddocks, Todd D.	MTR	1979
Maddox, Clee S.	FB	1938, 39
Maddox, Rosalyn D.	WCC/WTR	1995, 96, 97
Madruga, Djan G.	MSW	1977, 78, 79, 81
Madruga, Rojer G.	MSW	1982, 83, 84, 85, 86
Madry, John T.	MTR	1977, 78
Magaw, James W.	FB	1902
Magee, Raymond J.	BB	1912
Magelssen, Heather J.	VB	1994, 95, 96
Magelssen, Jennifer A.	VB	1995, 96, 97, 98
Mager, Misten	SB	1993, 94, 95, 96
Magley, Richard A.	MCC/MTR	1973, 74, 75, 76
Magley, Stephanie K.	WCC/WTR	1998. 99
Maglish, Joseph M.	FB	1954, 56
Magnabosco, John V.	BB/FB	1927, 28, 29, 30
Magrane, Jean	SB/VB/WSW	1972, 73, 74, 75
Magro, Donna	FH	1978
Maguire, Edward J.	FB	1969, 70
Mahan, James C.	MGO	1971, 72, 73, 74
Maher, Mary	FH	1971, 72, 73
Maholm, Timothy R.	FB (Mgr.)	1977
Maidenberg, Milton	FB (Mgr.)	1932
Main, James D.	WR	1971, 72, 73, 74
Maines, Summar R.	WBK	1996, 97, 98, 99
Maisonneuve, Brian L.	MSO	1991, 92, 93, 94
Majors, Robert B.	MTN	1963
Males, Barbara J.	FH	1970, 71, 72
Maley, Douglas W.	MSW	1981, 82, 83, 84
Malik, Amar	WBK (Mgr.)	1998, 99
Malinchak, William J.	FB	1964, 65, 66
Malinovsky, Victor E.	FB	1969, 70
Mallory, Charles E.	FB	1984
Malmedahl, Jack C.	MGY	1972, 73, 74, 75
Malone, Kenisha L.	WBK	1996, 97, 98, 99
Malott, Claude G.	BB	1893, 94, 95, 99
Malott, Lance E.	FB	1987
Maloy, John	FB	1926
Mamala, Horace	MTR	1946, 48
Mandera, Patrick R.	MCC/MTR	1970, 71, 72, 73, 74
Mandeville, Richard T.	MBK	1994, 95, 96, 97, 98
Mandina, Paul R.	FB	1997, 98
Manford, Stefan	FB (Mgr.)	1993
Mangel, Emil H.	MBK	1910
Mangold, Donald R.	FB	1943
Maniatis, Melina S.	WCC/WTR	1987, 88, 89, 90, 91, 92
Manis, William A.	MTN	1943, 44, 46
Mankowski, Ben M.	FB	1928, 29, 30
Manley, Kara P.	SB	1991, 92, 93, 94
Mann, Craig W.	WR	1974, 77
Mann, Dawn R.	MTR (Mgr.)/WTR	1981, 82, 83, 84
Mann, Deborah S.	WBK	1987
Mann, Frederick C.	MGY	1969
Mann, Hansford C.	MCC	1967
Mann, Lawrence V.	WR	1963, 65
Mann, Robert J.	MGO	1971, 72, 73
Mann, Todd N.	BB	1993, 94
Manna, Anthony L.	MSW	1996, 97, 98, 99
Manning, Susan E.	MSW (Mgr.)	1991
Manolopoulos, Bill A.	FB	1993, 94, 95, 96
Mansberger, Sheryl L.	WSO	1993, 94
Mantel, Richard M.	R	1959, 60, 61
Mantion, Daniel	MGY	1975, 76, 77
Manuszak, Robert G.	BB	1969, 70
Marchewka, Michael R.	MTR	1982, 83, 84
Marchino, Chris	MTR	1992
Marchiol, Tanya M.	VB	1992, 93, 94
Marcus, Demetra A.	VB	1992, 93, 94, 95
Marcus, Merritt E.	MGO	1956
Marencik, Karen	WGO	1979, 80, 81, 82
Margolin, Barry T.	MSO	1986, 87, 88
Marino, Angelo M.	WR	1976, 77, 79, 80
Markel, Ivan J.	FB	1907, 08, 09
Markel, Orrin H.	FB	1901, 02
Marker, David R.	MSW	1970
Marker, Loyal T.	MTR	1935, 37
Marker, Rudolph E.	FB	1923, 24, 25
Markey, Patricia J.	WGY	1975
Markey, Stephen A.	MCC/MTR	1982, 83
Markey, Susan I.	WGY	1974, 75
Markle, Gene L.	BB	1950
Marks, Brown	FB	1966, 67
Marks, Deryck A.	MSW	1983, 84, 85, 87
Marks, Lawrence E.	FB	1923, 24, 25
Marks, R. Craig	FB	1975, 76, 77
Marks, William A.	MSW	1961
Marmion, Abigail A.	WSW	1982, 83
Maroni, John J.	WR	1961, 62
Maroon, Joseph C.	FB	1960
Marotto, Angela M.	WGY	1983
Marple, Paula L.	WGY	1980
Marquart, Michel R.	MGY	1968
Marques, Fabio I.	MSW	1996, 97
Marr, Daniel C.	FB	1973, 74, 75, 76
Marr, Robert G.	BB	1961
Marra, Michael P., Jr.	MBK (Mgr.)	1974
Marrazzo, Julia A.	WTR	1983, 84, 85, 86, 87
Marrs, Jane	WTR	1983
Marsala, Charles L.	MCC/MTR	1984, 85, 86, 87
Marsala, Christopher	MTR	1985, 86, 87
Marsh, Robert E.	MSW	1937, 38, 40
Marshall, Allan F.	MCC/MTR	1963, 64, 65
Marshall, Anne R.	WCC/WTR	1995, 96, 97, 98, 99
Marshall, Arthur H.	BB	1944
Marshall, Claudus H.	MTR	1899, 1900
Marshall, Jana	WGY	1975
Marshall, Jean	VB	1977
Marshall, Lyn	WGY	1973, 74
Marshall, Marsha	WGY	1973, 74
Marshall, Robert J.	MSW	1932
Marshall, Roberta A.	WCC/WTR	1995, 96
Marshall, Todd	FB (Mgr.)	1982
Marte, Carlos J.	FB	1985, 86, 87, 88
Martich, Peter G.	FB/MTR	1931, 32, 33
Martin, Charles V.	MGO	1990, 92, 93, 94
Martin, Craig E.	MTR	1978, 81
Martin, David C.	MTR	1951, 52, 53
Martin, Dennis O.	FB	1960
Martin, Graham E.	FB	1940
Martin, Gregory T.	FB (Mgr.)	1976
Martin, Hugh E.	MBK/MTR	1903, 04, 06
Martin, Hugh E.	WR	1922
Martin, James O.	MTR	1946
Martin, Jonathan C.	FB	1989, 90, 91
Martin, J. Robert, Jr.	MTN	1952, 53, 54, 55
Martin, Kevin L.	MTR	1983, 84, 85, 86
Martin, Nancy R.	WBK	1976, 77
Martin, Peggy E.	FH/SB/WBK	1970, 71, 72
Martin, Randy L.	FB	1974
Martin, Richard A.	MTN	1960, 61
Martin, Roger R.	FB	1972
Martin, W.M.	MSO	1979
Martin, W. David	FB	1959, 60, 61
Martindale, Frank E.	BB	1911, 12, 13
Martinez, Teresa J.	SB	1997, 98, 99
Marvin, Thomas P.	WR	1962, 64
Marx, Jeffrey D.	FB	1988, 89
Marxson, Robert C.	BB/MBK	1920, 21, 23
Marzulo, David C.	MGY	1976
Mash, Thomas P.	WR	1971, 72
Maslovsky, Ronald K.	MSW	1980
Mason, Nancy	VB	1988, 89, 90, 91
Mason, Steven G.	FB	1973
Mason, Troy E.	FB	1988, 89, 90, 91
Massa, Charles P.	R	1953
Masters, Robert W.	MBK/MTN	1950, 51, 52
Mastin, Steve H.	FB	1971, 72, 73
Matejko, Donald M.	FB	1987, 89, 90
Matesic, Joseph T.	FB	1950
Math, Steven A.	MSW	1982, 83
Mather, Debbie	WGO	1971, 72, 73
Mathers, Thomas N.	MSW	1936
Mathews, Anne	WSW	1986, 87
Mathews, William W., Jr.	MSW	1985, 86, 87, 89
Mathias, Harold W.	BB	1923

Miller, Charles	FB	1976
Miller, Charles B.	BB	1968, 69, 70
Miller, Charles J.	MBK	1995, 96, 97, 98
Miller, Charles, Jr.	FB	1973
Miller, Christopher R.	BB	1995, 96
Miller, Cornelius T.	MTR	1962, 63, 64
Miller, David I.	WR	1949, 50, 51
Miller, Dick	FB	1892, 93
Miller, George A.	FB	1935, 36, 37
Miller, Glenn L.	MBK (Mgr.)	1925
Miller, Harper B.	MGO	1928, 29
Miller, Henry H.	MBK	1916, 17
Miller, Henry L.	MTR	1905, 06, 08
Miller, James E.	FB	1959, 60
Miller, Jason H.	MSW	1990
Miller, Jerry R.	MSW	1968
Miller, John D.	MTR	1917
Miller, John D.	BB	1922
Miller, John D.	FB	1989, 90, 91, 92
Miller, John E.	MCC/MTR	1955, 56, 57
Miller, Judith N.	WGY	1976
Miller, Kristin K.	WBK	1996, 97, 98, 99
Miller, L. Andy	MTR	1983, 84
Miller, Laurie A.	FH	1975, 76, 77, 78
Miller, Lionel W., Jr.	MTR	1948, 49
Miller, Mark A.	MSW	1977
Miller, Michael A.	MTR	1970, 71
Miller, Milton J.	WR	1936
Miller, Nancy L.	WP	1998
Miller, Natalie J.	WCC	1979
Miller, Paul G.	WR	1972
Miller, Randolph R.	BB	1972, 73, 74
Miller, Robert G.	FB	1891
Miller, Robert W.	BB/FB	1944, 45, 46
Miller, Ronald J.	FB	1957, 58, 59
Miller, Rutherford B.	MTN	1951
Miller, Samuel H.	MTR	1936, 37, 38
Miller, Tereasa A.	SB/VB	1969, 70
Miller, Thomas L.	R	1957, 58
Miller, William C.	MSW	1927, 28
Miller, William J., Jr.	MGO	1990, 91, 92, 93
Miller, William O.	BB	1923
Miller, Zachary G.	MGO	1996
Millett, Roscoe E.	BB	1901, 02, 03
Milligan, George F.	FB	1981
Mills, Angela D.	WGO	1989, 90, 91, 92
Mills, Dennis M.	FB	1980, 81, 82
Mills, F. Lamar	FB	1991, 92, 93
Mills, Joseph B., Jr.	BB	1956, 57
Mills, Lexie H.	MTR	1942
Mills, Suzanne A.	SB	1982, 83, 84
Mills, Timothy J.	FB	1972, 73, 74
Milne, William B.	MTR (Mgr.)	1948
Miloszewski, Frank	BB	1977, 78
Miltenberger, Larry J.	MGY	1959, 60, 61
Mineau, Kenneth R.	MTR	1965, 66, 67
Mineo, John A.	FB	1980, 81, 82
Miner, Robert L.	BB	1964, 65, 66
Minnick, Lloyd E.	R	1955
Minor, David G.	MBK	1987
Minor, Mark S.	BB	1999
Mintch, Lantz M.	MGY	1974, 75, 76
Minto, Jenner M.	WSW	1993, 94, 95, 96, 97
Minton, John R.	MTN	1948
Minton, Roscoe	BB/FB	1917, 18, 19, 21
Minton, Sherman	BB/FB	1912, 13, 14
Mintzer, Sterling M.	FB	1998
Minzey, Ronald D.	MTR	1954
Miranda, Samuel C.	MBK	1950, 51, 52
Miroballi, Dana L.	WCC/WTR	1988, 89, 90, 91, 92
Misner, William D.	MGY	1962
Misrach, Craig	WTN (Mgr.)	1998, 99
Mitchell, Brad D.	FB	1985, 86, 87
Mitchell, Charles E.	MTR	1963
Mitchell, Earl	MCC/MTR	1942, 46
Mitchell, Eugene E.	MGY	1950, 51
Mitchell, Jenny R.	SB	1992, 93, 94, 95
Mitchell, John J.	FB	1892, 93, 94
Mitchell, Mary Ann	WTR	1979
Mitchell, Pamela A.	FH/WBK	1974, 75, 76, 77
Mitchell, Paul C.	WR	1930, 31
Mitchell, Samuel L.	MBK (Mgr.)	1938
Mitchell, Stephen D.	FB	1979, 80, 81
Mitchell, Thomas J.	MTR	1946, 47, 48, 49
Mitchell, William F.	FB/MTR	1946, 47
Mitchem, John C.	MCC/MTR	1944, 45
Mitrovich, Nick S.	MSO	1984
Mitten, James R.	BB	1912
Mladick, Carolyn J.	WSW	1983, 84, 85
Modak, Mike	BB/FB	1944, 45
Moe, Barbara	WGO	1970
Moeller, Kenneth W.	FB	1941
Moffatt, Kyle P.	FB	1998
Mogge, Arthur R.	MCC/MTR	1916, 17, 18, 19
Molen, Jane L.	FH	1972, 73, 74
Molen, Ronald L.	MCC	1949
Mollaun, Peggy	WSW	1972, 73
Molodet, John A.	BB	1952
Mondini, Elena J.	WTR	1983, 84, 85
Money, Brian K.	BB	1989, 90, 91
Money, D. Brad	FB	1985, 86, 87, 88
Monoki, Reka B.	WTN	1985, 86, 87, 88
Monroe, Brooke N.	SB	1999
Montecino, Ingrid R.	WTN	1972, 73, 74, 75
Montgomery, Heath A.	MSW	1999
Montgomery, James P.	MSW	1974, 75, 76, 77
Montgomery, Meg E.	SB	1994, 95, 96, 97
Montgomery, Orbra F.	BB	1881
Montgomery, Samantha G.	WGO	1997, 98, 99
Montgomery, Sheila	WCC/WTR	1980, 81, 82, 83, 84
Montilla, Gabriel J.	MTN	1997, 98, 99
Montoya, Scott J.	FB	1989, 90, 91
Mooar, Ronald G.	MGY	1963, 64
Mood, Dwight L.	MTR	1980
Moomaw, Earl E.	BB/FB	1922, 23, 24, 25
Moon, Alpheus W.	FB	1895
Mooney, Ann T.	WBK	1986, 87, 88, 89
Moore, Cathy	WSW	1970
Moore, Christine	WSW	1982
Moore, Eric P.	FB	1985, 86, 87
Moore, Frank D.	BB	1893
Moore, George W.	BB	1895, 96, 97, 98
Moore, Harry A.	BB	1949, 50, 51
Moore, Henry T.	WR	1947
Moore, J. Barton	FB	1963
Moore, James L.	WR	1947
Moore, John I.	WR	1920
Moore, John M.	MSW	1923, 24, 25
Moore, John R.	MTR	1948, 50
Moore, Joseph, Jr.	FB	1958, 59
Moore, Julie A.	VB	1993
Moore, Karleen K.	SB	1984, 85, 86, 87
Moore, Linda K.	WBK	1974, 75, 76, 77
Moore, Michele L.	SB	1991
Moore, Prentiss D.	WR	1921
Moore, Richard C.	WR	1946
Moore, Robert J.	MCC	1947, 48, 49
Moore, Robert L.	MTR	1959
Moore, Robert R.	BB	1948, 49
Moore, Sandra	WGY	1978
Moore, Sharon A.	VB	1981
Moore, William L.	FB (Mgr.)	1924
Moore, Woody W.	FB	1960, 61, 62
Moorhead, Thomas M.	FB	1942, 46, 47
Moorin, John H.	MTN	1983, 84
Moorman, Stephen J.	FB	1981, 82
Moran, James M.	MSW	1954
Moran, William J.	MSW	1953, 54
Morandini, Michael R.	BB	1985, 86, 87, 88
More, Walter S.	BB	1906
Moreno, Nester	MCC/MTR	1978, 79, 80
Morgan, Adrienne E.	WSW	1991, 92
Morgan, Alison P.	WTR	1994, 95, 96, 97
Morgan, John, Jr.	FB	1951
Morgan, Kameelah	WBK	1996, 97, 98, 99
Morgan, Keith A.	FB	1984
Morgan, Kenneth C.	MBK	1969, 70, 71
Morgan, Kevin D.	MTR	1978, 79
Morgan, Marjorie A.	FH	1978, 79
Morgan, Megan E.	WP	1998
Morgan, Michael E.	MSW	1981, 82, 83, 84
Morgan, Robert W.	MBK	1982, 83, 84, 85, 86
Moriarty, Brendan R.	FB	1963
Morr, Vicki J.	SB	1986, 87, 88, 89
Morran, D. Keith	FB	1970, 71
Morrical, Gerald G.	FB	1946, 47, 48
Morris, Chris S.	FB	1968, 69, 70
Morris, Craig A.	MBK	1973, 74
Morris, Douglas J.	MTR	1979, 80, 81
Morris, Edward L.	FB	1958, 60
Morris, Emily L.	WSW	1995
Morris, James J.	FB	1932
Morris, Jennifer T.	WSW	1991
Morris, Joseph F.	FB	1930
Morris, Matthew	FB (Mgr.)	1994
Morris, Richard O.	MBK (Mgr.)	1942
Morris, Robert A.	WR	1974
Morrisey, Michael	FB (Mgr.)	1990
Morrison, Bruce A.	BB	1985
Morrison, Clyde W.	MCC/MTR	1911, 12

Name	Sport	Years
Morrison, Donald B.	WR	1957, 58, 59
Morrison, Gilbert H.	MSW (Mgr.)	1932
Morrison, Mingo III	WR	1998, 99
Morrison, Sue	WTR	1979
Morrow, Douglas C.	FB (Mgr.)	1973
Morrow, Melyssa J.	WTR	1982, 83
Morse, Richard G.	MSW	1964, 65, 66
Morton, Howard R.	BB	1947
Morton, Kathy	VB	1970, 71, 72, 73
Morton, Pamela L.	WTR	1985, 86, 87, 88
Morton, Walter P.	MTR	1915
Morwick, Lawrence B.	FB	1969, 70, 71
Moscovic, Derek J.	WR	1994, 95, 96, 97
Moser, Mary Jane	FH/SB/WBK	1969, 70, 71, 72
Moser, Matthew S.	BB	1996, 97, 98, 99
Moss, Peggy	WSW	1972, 73, 74
Moss, William G.	FB/WR	1926, 27, 28, 29
Motil, John M.	FB	1969, 70, 71
Motter, Thomas A.	MBK	1939, 40
Moulton, James K.	MGO	1946
Mount, Carrie R.	WBK	1992, 93
Mounts, David G.	BB/FB	1959, 60
Mourer, Kim E.	SB	1984, 85
Moynihan, Robert A.	FB	1966, 67, 68
Mrofka, Richard M.	BB	1957
Mucci, Kris J.	FB	1993, 94, 95
Muckler, Todd D.	MSW	1975
Mudd, Daniel G.	WR	1966, 67, 68
Mudd, David K.	WR	1965, 66, 67
Mudd, L. Scott	BB	1992, 93, 94, 95
Mudge, Jill D.	VB	1997
Mueller, Edwin C.	MTR	1945
Mueller, Jack L.	MGO	1937, 38, 39
Mueller, Staci M.	WBK	1998, 99
Mueller, William J.	BB	1982, 83, 84, 85
Muffie, Peter F.	MTR	1960
Muhleck, Martina S.	WTR	1998
Muir, Donald W.	MSW	1969, 70, 71, 72, 73
Muirhead, John D.	MBK	1967, 69
Mujezinovic, Haris	MBK	1996, 97
Mukete, Abel	MSO	1972
Mulhern, Thomas V.	MSW	1982, 83
Mullett, D.T., Jr.	MTR	1945
Mullett, DeWitt T.	FB/MBK	1915, 16, 17
Mullins, Dennis J.	MSW	1993, 94, 95, 96
Mulvey, James	MCC/MTR	1994, 95
Mulvihill, Kelly C.	WTN	1986, 87, 88, 89
Mumby, Edward W.	FB/WR	1918, 19, 20, 21
Mumby, Harold F.	WR	1923, 24
Muncy, Harold W.	MSW	1949, 50
Mundy, Deborah S.	FH/SB	1969, 70, 71, 72
Munich, Thomas E.	MTR	1983, 84, 86
Munkelt, Glen H.	MBK	1911, 12, 13
Munn, Duncan M.	WR	1999
Munson, Lindsay K.	WGO	1990
Murao, Peter D.	MGY	1975, 76, 77, 78
Murchie, Lewis K.	FB/MTR	1915, 16
Murchison, Julia A.	WGY	1975
Murdock, Judith W.	FH	1977
Murdock, Samuel H.	FB	1888, 89, 90, 91, 94
Murff, Eric B.	MSW	1984, 85
Murin, Melissa A.	WGY	1980, 81, 82, 83
Murphy, Charles A.	FB	1968
Murphy, Anne C.	WSW	1990
Murphy, Harry L.	MGO	1942
Murphy, James L.	MCC/MTR	1981, 82, 83, 84, 85, 86
Murphy, John J.	MSW	1972, 73, 74, 75
Murphy, John P.	MTR	1973, 75
Murphy, Joseph W.	FB	1888, 89, 90, 91
Murphy, Kathleen M.	WSW	1985, 86
Murphy, Laura C.	WTR	1995
Murphy, Patrick J.	BB	1990, 91
Murphy, Shannon M.	WGO	1980, 81
Murphy, William F.	BB	1892
Murr, Stacie E.	VB	1992, 93, 94, 95
Murray, Abigail E.	WSW	1988
Murray, April	WSW	1973
Murray, Charles W.	BB (Mgr.)	1945
Murray, Edward P.	BB	1945
Murray, Roger F.	FB	1994, 95
Murray, William E.	BB	1945
Mushkin, Michael R.	MTN	1973, 74, 75, 76
Musika, Terry L.	MTR	1968, 69, 70
Mustard, Fred P.	MSW/WR (Mgr.)	1927
Muta, Janet	WSW	1978, 79
Muth, Parke P.	MTR	1976
Muth, Robert D.	MCC/MTR	1972, 73, 74, 75
Mutz, Howard H.	BB	1907
Muyumba, Muuka	MBK (Mgr.)	1997
Muyumba, Walton	MBK (Mgr.)	1994
Myers, Angela K.	WSW	1995
Myers, Clifford R.	WR	1936, 37, 38
Myers, Herman H.	BB (Mgr.)	1924
Myers, Jennifer L.	WGO	1987, 88, 89, 90
Myers, Joseph P.	BB	1895, 96, 97
Myers, Kimberly A.	WTR	1989, 90
Myers, Martin T.	MGY	1972
Myers, Paul V.	WR	1915, 16
Myers, Timothy L.	WR	1997, 98, 99
Myers, William A.	FB	1893
Mygrants, Robert W.	BB	1946, 51
Mynard, Karen	WSW	1984
Myslewski, Alan N.	FB	1964
Nace, Jill J.	WCC/WTR	1993, 94, 95, 96
Nachtrieb, Benjamin D.	WR	1994, 95, 96, 97
Naddeo, Michael R.	FB	1938, 39, 40
Nading, Martin M.	MTR	1928, 29
Nafe, Cleon A.	MTR	1916
Naganobori, Hiroki	MSW	1999
Nagle, Pamela	WTN	1970, 71, 72
Nagle, Zachary A.	WR	1992
Nagy, Steve W., Jr.	FB	1938
Nakamura, Leslie H.	MSW	1958, 59, 60
Nakasone, Kenneth H.	MSW	1961, 62, 63
Napoli, Michael A.	FB	1983
Narewski, Melissa F.	SB	1998, 99
Nash, Audrey E.	WTR	1991, 92, 93
Nash, John F.	FB	1940, 41, 42
Nash, Melvin W.	MSW	1973, 74, 75, 76
Nash, Richard C.	BB	1963, 64, 65
Nash, William P.	MBK	1915, 16, 17
Naso, Mark P.	MCC	1991, 92
Nathan, L. Dedee	WTR	1987, 88, 89, 90
Nave, Joseph S.	BB	1866, 67
Nawrocki, Aloysius D.	MGY	1959, 60
Nay, John M.	MCC/MTR	1922, 23, 24
Neal, H. Richard	MBK	1955, 56, 57
Neal, Julie K.	VB	1983, 84
Neal, Margaret	WTN	1971, 72
Neal, Raymond M.	WR	1933, 34, 35
Nebelsiek, Jacqueline A.	SB	1996, 97
Nebraska, Dave M.	BB	1987, 88
Neel, Charles H.	MSW	1964, 65, 66
Neely, John I.	MTR	1936, 37
Neese, Donald E.	MCC/MTR	1930, 31, 32, 33
Neff, David S.	FB	1970
Neher, Edwin M.	MTR	1899, 1900, 01
Neitzel, Carin L.	WCC	1981
Nelson, Benjamin J.	WR	1994, 95, 96
Nelson, Eric B.	MTR	1976
Nelson, Erika K.	WSW	1988, 89, 90
Nelson, Kent J.	BB	1916, 17
Nelson, Patricia A.	WCC/WTR	1987, 88, 89, 90
Nelson, Robert A.	BB	1980, 81, 82, 83, 84
Nelson, Robert K.	MSO	1973
Nelson, Susan E.	SB	1984
Nesbitt, William W.	MSW	1950
Ness, Roger J.	BB	1980, 81
Nessel, Ferdie D.	FB	1925, 26
Nestel, Diann L.	SB/WBK	1975, 76, 77, 78
Nestor, Carl	FB/WR	1944, 45
Netherton, Ross D.	FB	1907, 08
Netzley, Rebecca	WSW	1975, 76
Neuburger, Eric	MSW (Mgr.)	1999
Neuman, Carl F.	MSW	1963, 64, 65
Neville, Kori E.	WCC/WTR (Mgr.)	1997, 98
New, Bonnie	FH/WTN	1970, 71
New, Willard	BB	1881
Newby, Alonzo C.	MTR	1897
Newcomb, Christopher N.	BB	1990, 91, 92
Newcomer, Zach S.	MSW	1994, 95
Newell, Mark E.	FB	1989, 90
Newman, John H.	MSW	1965, 66, 67
Newman, Karl M.	BB	1896, 97
Newquist, Jay D.	MTR	1990, 91, 92
Newsom, John F.	BB	1889, 90, 91
Newton, Troy D.	FB	1990, 91
Nicholas, Rebecca S.	WBK	1973, 74, 75, 76
Nichols, Gary	FB	1966, 67
Nichols, Orville W.	MBK (Mgr.)	1941
Nichols, Rachel	WTR	1991, 92, 93, 94
Nichols, Robert E.	FB	1967, 68, 69

DeDee Nathan won six Big Ten titles before becoming America's No. 1 heptathlete.

Bob Nelson was an All-American in soccer in 1973.

Nichols, Robert J.	MTR	1943
Nicholson, Joe C.	FB	1938
Nickols, Jeffrey J.	BB	1980
Nido, Carlos J.	MTN	1983, 84
Niehaus, Nan	WSW	1979
Nielsen, Jeffery B.	BB	1980
Nieradka, David J.	WR	1991
Nieves, Daniel	BB	1993
Niezer, Charles M.	FB	1898, 99
Nigh, Tammy J.	WGO	1983, 84
Nigon, Jeannette M.	WSW	1999
Niles, Benjamin M.	MBK	1969, 70
Niles, Michael B.	MBK	1968, 69, 70
Nill, John H.	BB	1938
Niness, Samuel F.	BB/FB	1922, 23, 24, 25
Nino De Rivera, Luis A.	MSW	1966, 67, 68
Nischwitz, Matthew P.	WR	1999
Nishi, Lynden K.	MSW	1962
Nishina, Candace K.	SB	1991, 92, 93, 94
Nitardy, Nancy J.	WSW	1977
Nix, Sunder L.	MTR	1981, 82, 83, 84
Noblet, Amanda L.	WSW	1998, 99
Nocks, Matt A.	SB (Mgr.)	1998, 99
Noel, Ralph W.	MBK	1903, 04, 05
Nolan, James M.	MTN	1965, 66, 67
Nolan, John W.	MSW	1968, 69
Noland, Michael J.	MBK	1968, 69
Noone, Donald G.	FB	1957, 58, 59
Noone, William P.	BB/FB	1956, 57, 58
Noort, Donald J.	MBK	1973, 74, 75
Nordsiek, Cynthia	WGY	1974, 75, 76
Nori, Fred J.	BB	1963, 64, 65
Nori, Micah F.	BB	1994, 95, 96, 97
Norman, Benjamin F.	FB	1967, 68
Norman, Erik I.	MSW	1985, 86, 87, 88
Norman, Joseph D.	FB	1975, 76, 77, 78
Normington, Joseph H.	BB	1946, 47, 48
Norris, Karen L.	FH	1980, 81
Northcutt, Sheila A.	SB/WBK	1974, 75
Norton, Claude W., Jr.	FB	1935, 36
Norton, David M.	MTR	1949, 50
Norton, Martin W.	MCC	1944
Norton, Thomas R.	MSW	1965
Novak, Andrew J.	FB	1990
Novak, Brad J.	MTR	1994
Novak, Gregory R.	MTR	1990, 91, 92, 93, 94
Nover, Jeannene M.	VB	1991
Nover, Matthew J.	MBK	1989, 90, 91, 92, 93
Nowatzke, Thomas M.	FB	1962, 63, 64
Nranian, Andrea N.	WTR	1980, 81, 82, 83
Nunnick, Johannes C.	BB	1975
Nusbaum, Payson L.	BB	1902
Nussel, Charles H.	BB	1911
Nuthak, Stephen C.	MTR	1987, 88
Nyikos, Michael J.	MBK	1923
Nylec, William A.	FB	1931
Nyquist, Robert E.	MGY	1982

O'Banion, Sandy	WGY	1971

O'Brien, J. Grant III	MCC	1994
O'Brien, Kim M.	FH	1980
O'Brien, Lynne E.	MTR (Mgr.)	1985
O'Callaghan, Susan M.	SB	1981, 82, 83
O'Connell, Frank W.	BB	1998, 99
O'Connell, Kathryn M.	WSW	1987, 88
O'Connell, Timothy N.	FB	1993
O'Conner, Donald	MTR (Mgr.)	1992
O'Connor, Kelli J.	WCC/WTR	1997, 98, 99
O'Connor, Patrick J.	MSW	1971, 72, 73, 74
O'Dell, Carol	FH	1978
O'Dell, Stewart H.	FB/MTR	1971, 72, 73, 74
O'Donnell, John P.	BB	1903, 04, 05
O'Hagan, Christopher J.	MBK (Mgr.)	1992
O'Hair, Willard S.	WR (Mgr.)	1937
O'Hara, James P.	FB	1969
O'Hare, Bonnie	SB	1971
O'Haver, Thomas F.	MGO	1933, 35
O'Keefe, Garland M.	WSW	1992, 93, 94
O'Keefe, Robert R.	FB	1977, 78
O'Neal, Karen	WGO	1981
O'Neal, Kathleen	WSW	1979, 80
O'Neal, Perry E.	BB	1914
O'Neill, Dennis M.	MSW	1963, 64, 65
O'Rourke, Hugh J.	FB	1974
O'Rourke, Kelly A.	FH	1981
O'Shea, Christopher J.	MTR (Mgr.)	1972
O'Toole, Kelly S.	WCC/WTR	1978, 79, 80, 81, 82
Oakley, Darrell W.	FB	1978
Obenchain, Roland, Jr.	FB	1934, 35, 36
Oberdorf, Todd A.	FB	1988, 89
Oberholzer, Timothy J.	BB	1974, 75, 76, 77
Oberting, Margaret R.	SB/WBK	1973, 74, 75, 76
Obremskey, Jennifer	WTR	1984
Obremskey, Peter L.	MBK	1956, 57, 58
Odell, James L.	MCC/MTR	1943, 45
Odle, Jarrad K.	MBK	1999
Odusch, John M.	MSW	1960, 61
Ogden, John H.	MSW	1965, 66
Ogg, Margaret	WCC	1979
Ogilby, Trahern C.	MSW	1964, 65
Ogle, Cynthia	WSW	1978
Oglesby, Regina	FH	1970
Ogunleye, Adewale	FB	1996, 97, 98
Oing, Debra M.	WBK	1972, 73, 74, 75
Ojala, Pirjo L.	WTN	1981
Okon, Diana M.	FH	1976
Olas, Joseph	MCC (Mgr.)	1996
Olds, William F.	BB	1976, 77
Olin, Nelson C.	BB	1892
Oliphant, Jeff D.	MBK	1986, 87, 88, 89, 90
Oliver, Jonathan R.	MGO	1999
Oliver, Larry J.	BB	1967, 68, 69
Oliver, Mark A.	MGY	1982
Oliver, Robert C.	MTN	1935, 36
Oliver, Rodolfo A.	MSO	1980
Oliver, Vincent J.	FB	1937, 38
Oliverio, Gabriel P.	MBK	1967, 69
Olkowski, Lori Ann	WTR	1986
Olmstead, Diane M.	VB	1982, 83, 84, 85
Olmstead, John H.	FB	1935, 36, 37
Olsavsky, William J.	FB	1960, 61
Olsen, Daniel W.	MGO	1986, 87, 88, 89
Olsen, Larry E.	FB	1966
Olson, Cynthia E.	VB	1977
Olson, Diana	FH	1975
Olson, Kirk A.	MSW	1987, 88, 89, 90
Olson, Lynn D.	MSW	1968, 69
Olson, Matthew R.	MSO	1986, 88
Olson, Paul D.	MCC/MTR	1969, 70, 71, 72, 73
Olson, Richard E.	FB	1950
Olson, Robert H.	MSW	1964, 65
Olson, Stephanie A.	WTR	1995, 96
Omizo, Debra K.	WBK	1988
Ooley, Clarence E.	MBK	1938
Opasik, Eugene	FB	1930, 31, 32
Oppliger, Peg	FH	1969
Oppliger, Robert A.	MSW (Mgr.)	1967
Oren, Homer G.	FB/MTR	1931
Orfanos, George T.	FB	1944
Orie, Kevin L.	BB	1991, 92, 93
Oristaglio, Jeffrey T.	MSW	1986, 87, 88, 89
Orr, Michael F.	MSW	1990, 91, 92, 93
Orso, Brent C.	FB	1983
Ortega, Lulu	SB	1973, 74
Orth, Gregg R.	FB	1961
Orton, Jason D.	FB	1990, 91, 92, 93
Osborn, Janice	VB	1979
Osborn, Thomas E.	R	1958, 59, 60
Osborne, Kathy A.	FH	1981

Osborne, Maureen	WGY	1970
Osbourne, Maurice	FB	1972
Osburn, William E.	MGO	1935
Osika, Daniel C.	FB	1998
Osler, Peter L.	MTN	1975, 76
Osmon, Cynthia	WCC/WTR	1978, 79
Osmon, Paul R.	FB	1962
Osterburg, Walter S.	MGO	1968
Osterhues, Christine M.	WSW	1990, 91, 92, 93
Ostermann, Jeffrey P.	MSW	1997, 98, 99
Oswald, Christopher S.	MSO	1979, 80, 81, 82, 83
Otte, Nicholas J.	BB	1998, 99
Otte, Zachary M.	BB	1998, 99
Ottenheimer, Lester A., Jr.	MTR	1943
Otto, Michael D.	FB	1980
Oury, John T.	WR	1978, 81
Ousley, James A.	MGO	1991, 92, 93, 94
Ousley, Jeffrey G.	MGO	1990, 91, 92
Overly, Tonner M., Jr.	MSW	1949, 50
Overman, Margaret L.	WSW	1999
Owen, Arnett H.	FB	1915
Owen, Kimberly A.	WCC	1982
Owens, Dave	MBK (Mgr.)	1997
Owens, Frank L.	MCC/MTR	1946, 47, 48, 49, 50
Owens, Pamela L.	WBK	1990, 91
Owens, Phil	FB (Mgr.)	1982
Owens, Ruth M.	WSW	1995
Owens, Taquesha M.	WTR	1995
Owsiany, John F.	MSW	1980
Owsley, Pam	WSW	1971
Oxley, Lane J.	FB	1994, 95
Oyler, Daniel S.	MTR	1960, 61, 62

Paar, Doris M.	FH/SB/VB	1970, 71
Paar, Robert J.	FB	1975, 76
Paci, John P. III	FB	1992, 93, 94
Pack, Paul R.	MBK (Mgr.)	1959
Pack, Ralph W.	BB	1960, 61, 62
Packwood, George H.	MTR	1944
Paddock, Christopher G.	MSO	1984, 85
Paddock, Howard	BB/FB	1907, 08, 09
Paddock, Levi S.	FB	1906, 07, 08
Paddock, Robert F.	MTN	1943, 47, 48
Padgett, David F.	MSW	1967, 68
Padgett, Donald E. II	MGO	1969, 70, 71
Padgett, Donald E. III	MGO	1994, 95, 96, 97
Padgett, Thomas P.	FB	1989
Padgett, William R.	MSW	1981
Page, Mary E.	WSW	1991, 92, 93, 94
Paige, Jerry L., Jr.	FB	1984
Pakucko, Michael M.	MSW	1940, 41, 42
Palacios, Antonio C.	MTR	1987, 88
Palazzo, Michael V.	WR	1991, 92, 93
Palivec, Donna K.	FH/SB/WBK/WSW	1971, 72, 73, 74
Palko, Eddie T.	BB	1964
Pallister, David S.	MSW	1965
Pallotta, Andrew W.	MSW	1980, 81, 82, 83
Palmer, Eddie S.	WR	1995
Pankoke, Amy E.	WP	1998
Pankow, Charles J.	WR	1952, 53, 54
Pankratz, Karl L.	FB	1967, 68, 69
Paradine, Danielle H.	WTN	1991, 92, 93, 94
Paras, Eduardo	FB	1983
Parcao, Nick	MCC (Mgr.)	1981
Parchute, Gerald E.	MTN	1957, 58
Parker, Cynthia C.	VB	1976
Parker, David F.	MCC (Mgr.)	1975
Parker, George A.	FB	1944, 48
Parker, Horace R.	FB	1965
Parker, Patrick T.	FB (Mgr.)	1986
Parker, Paul B.	BB/MBK	1923, 24, 25
Parker, Thomas L.	FB	1971
Parker, Wayne E.	MTN	1946
Parker, William R.	MGO	1976, 77, 78
Parks, Emory	MTR	1929, 31, 32
Parks, Hal	FB	1994
Parks, John E.	MSW	1958, 59, 60
Parmalee, Michael A.	FB	1965, 66
Parmenter, Katherine J.	VB	1998
Parola, Todd A.	BB	1987, 88, 89
Parr, Charles E.	WR	1922, 23
Parr, Nevin F.	MTR	1922

Parr, Robert L.	MBK (Mgr.)	1974
Parrish, Andrew M.	MSO	1995, 96, 97, 98
Parrish, Robert A.	FB	1996, 97, 98
Parrott, Mary C.	WCC/WTR	1983, 84, 85, 86
Parry, Samantha E.	WSW	1998
Parson, William A.	WR	1953
Parsons, Charles D.	MTN	1968, 69, 70
Partenheimer, Brian J.	BB	1994, 95, 96, 97
Pass, Sindi A.	WGY	1978
Pasternack, Joe	MBK (Mgr.)	1999
Pasternak, Rona E.	WCC/WTR	1978, 79, 80, 81
Pate, Susan E.	WCC/WTR	1978, 79, 80, 81
Pate, Wayne H.	MTR	1977, 78, 79, 80
Paternoster, Edvardo J.	MBK (Mgr.)	1974
Patrick, James E.	MTR	1928, 29, 30
Patten, Cheryl	FH	1981
Patten, James C.	FB	1896
Patterson, Andrae M.	MBK	1995, 96, 97, 98
Pattis, Howard E.	BB	1981
Pattis, Lawrence E.	MGY	1976
Patton, Melvin	FB	1977, 78, 79
Patty, Robert H.	WR	1942
Paugh, Russell H.	BB	1927, 28, 29
Paul, Angeline A.	FH	1977, 78, 79, 80
Paul, Jean	FB/MBK	1995, 96, 97
Paul, John D.	MSO	1987, 88, 89, 90
Paulson, Jane S.	WTN	1986, 87
Paulus, Charles W.	FB	1969
Pauly, Catherine D.	VB	1974
Pavis, Robert	BB	1941, 42
Pavlin, Sandra L.	WBK	1978, 79
Pavy, Raymond E.	MBK	1961
Pawlitsch, Joseph A.	FB	1971, 72
Paxton, Norman J.	MSW	1969
Paxton, William E.	WR	1982, 83, 84, 85, 86
Payne, Andrew J.	FB	1997, 98
Payne, Clifton	FB	1975, 76
Payne, Floyd E.	FB	1904, 05
Payne, Kenneth A.	BB	1934, 35
Payne, Vernon	MBK	1966, 67, 68
Paynter, William T.	MCC	1943
Peabody, Danny T.	WR	1979
Peacock, Douglas L.	FB	1976, 77, 78
Peacock, Lewis	BB	1958
Peal, Charles E.	FB	1975, 76, 77
Pearce, Robert R.	MTR	1963, 64, 65
Pearson, Deborah L.	WGY	1974, 75
Pearson, Jimmy	WR	1987, 88, 89, 90
Pease, Melissa M.	WSW	1997
Pease, Ronald L.	MBK/MTR	1963, 64, 65
Peck, Erle P.	BB	1926
Peck, William L.	WR	1922, 23
Peckinpaugh, Earl M.	FB/WR	1914, 15, 16
Pedlow, Donald E.	MTR	1944
Peed, Richard, Jr.	MBK	1944
Peer, Terrie	VB	1977
Peet, Barbara	WGY	1975
Pegram, Michael R.	MSW	1981, 82, 83, 84
Pegram, Raymond S.	BB	1950, 51, 52
Pegram, Steven W.	MSW	1989, 90, 91
Peiffer, Pamela J.	VB/WGY	1973, 74
Peirce, Michael J.	BB	1993
Pelkowski, Magnus M.	MBK	1985, 86, 87, 88, 89
Pell, Robert A.	WR	1974
Peltonen, Craig A.	MSO	1977, 78
Pelz, David T.	MGO	1959, 60, 61
Pemberton, Kim E.	MBK	1971, 72
Pendery, Kim E.	WTN	1974, 75, 76, 77

Debbie Oing was IU's first female All-America basketball player in 1975.

Don Padgett was Big Ten golf medalist in 1969.

Pendleton, Michael R.	FB	1980, 81, 84
Penn, Albert	BB/MBK	1904
Penn, John G., Jr.	BB	1969, 70
Penning, Frank G., Jr.	MGO	1939, 40, 41
Pennington, Melissa D.	WTR	1992
Pentino, Anthony L.	MCC/MTR	1955, 56, 57
Peo, Elizabeth	WGO	1992
Pepper, Robert C.	MTR	1926, 27
Perdue, Cory R.	FB	1891
Perez, Andrea L.	WSW	1996, 97
Perez, Celestino J.	MSW	1968
Perk, Richard L.	MGO	1945
Perkins, Marvin L.	MTR	1931
Perkins, Steven L.	FB	1990, 91, 92, 93
Perkins, Tamara L.	VB	1980, 81, 82, 83
Perkowski, David J.	MSW	1967, 68, 69
Pernell, Robert	FB	1968
Pernus, Russell S.	MTR	1993, 94, 95, 96
Perozzi, Christina M.	WTR	1991, 92, 93, 94
Perry, Andrienne	WSW	1999
Perry, George	MSO	1974, 75, 76
Perry, J. Michael	FB	1967, 68
Perry, Natalie V.	WSW	1970
Perry, Oscar B.	FB	1895
Perry, William M.	FB	1966
Persinger, Delmar M.	MCC	1939, 40
Persinger, Richard L.	BB	1959, 60, 61
Petche, Scott M.	WR	1992, 93, 94, 95
Peters, Arthur	WR	1934, 35, 36
Peters, Charles F.	MTR	1947, 48, 49, 50
Peters, Christopher M.	BB	1992, 93
Peters, Dallas M., Jr.	MGO	1963, 64, 65
Peters, David S.	MCC/MTR	1974, 75
Peters, Doug R.	BB	1987, 88, 89, 90
Peters, Jerome H.	BB (Mgr.)	1942
Peters, Kenneth C.	MSW	1959
Peters, Paige M.	WSO	1994
Peters, Rotimi	MTR	1977, 78, 79, 80
Petersen, Paul C.	MSW	1981, 82, 83
Peterson, Christopher R.	MSO	1979, 80, 81, 82, 83
Peterson, Kevin D.	MSO	1976
Peterson, Leah	WTR	1979
Peterson, Lindley	WSW	1979, 80, 81
Peterson, Stacey L.	WSO	1998
Petrauskas, Raymond R.	FB	1950, 51, 52
Petri, Vernon J.	R	1958
Petrick, Francis J.	FB	1937, 38
Petrick, William A.	MTN	1956, 57, 58
Petronka, Eppie N.	WR	1956, 57, 58
Pettingell, Candy	WSW	1970
Peyser, Ronald G.	MBK	1963, 64, 65
Pfaff, Vernon R.	MBK	1964, 66, 67
Pfaltzgraf, Mark	MSW (Mgr.)	1984
Pfander, Stanley W.	FB	1971, 72, 73
Pfeffer, Amy-Louise	WCC	1981
Pfeifer, Norbert L.	MCC/MTR	1921, 22
Phelan, Mary Beth	WSW	1970, 72, 73
Phelps, David H.	MSW	1978, 79, 80, 81
Phelps, Michael A.	MSW	1976, 77
Phenicie, Greg V.	MGO	1989
Phillips, Albert	FB	1996, 97
Phillips, Alfred B.	MTR	1958, 60
Phillips, Allan L.	MTR	1986, 87, 88, 89
Phillips, Ardith L.	MBK/MTR	1918, 19, 20
Phillips, Callie A.	WSO	1993
Phillips, Clay A.	MTR	1913
Phillips, Elliott V.	MGO	1952, 53, 54
Phillips, Elroy V.	MTR	1979, 81, 82
Phillips, Jesse	FB	1984
Phillips, John H.	BB	1949, 50, 51
Phillips, Nevin E.	MSW	1952, 53
Phillips, Raymond	FB	1956
Philpott, Donald C.	MCC/MTR	1955
Phipps, James J.	MBK	1955, 56
Phipps, Jeffery L.	FB	1976, 77, 78, 79
Phoenix, Janet	FH	1978, 79
Piatek, Joseph P.	MTN	1950
Piccirillo, Peter G.	FB	1956, 57, 58
Pickford, James C.	MSW	1981
Piela, David M.	BB	1986
Pierce, James H.	FB/MTR	1918, 19, 20
Pierce, Lorna	WSW	1985
Pierce, Robert R.	MCC/MTR	1980, 81, 82
Pierce, William E.	MTR	1924
Piercy, Daniel B.	FB	1985, 86, 87, 88
Pieroni, Mark A.	MTR	1977
Pierre, Giles J.	MTR	1929, 30
Pigog, John	FB (Mgr.)	1973
Pihakis, Manuel M.	WR	1954, 55, 56
Pihos, Pete L.	FB	1942, 43, 45, 46

Pike, Phil R.	MTN	1928
Pike, Roy O.	BB/FB	1897, 98, 99, 1900
Pilch, Jonathon M.	FB	1992, 93, 94, 95
Pinnick, Brooks C.	MGO	1946, 47, 48, 49
Pinnick, Charles T.	WR	1973
Pinnock, Louis S.	FB	1992, 93, 94, 95
Piontkowski, Melvin L.	FB	1958
Piper, Laura L.	WTR	1986, 87
Pipp, William J.	FB	1971, 72
Pisano, Laura M.	FH	1980
Pister, William B.	MTR	1997, 98, 99
Pitcher, George C.	BB	1896, 97, 98, 99
Pittenger, Oscar M.	FB	1893
Pittman, Walter R.	MCC	1946
Pitts, Eric W.	WR	1996, 97, 98
Piwarski, Frank J.	FB	1971
Place, Nicholas D.	MTR	1979, 80
Plank, Richard S.	MCC	1963, 64
Platis, Chris S.	BB	1949, 51
Platis, James G.	BB	1949, 51
Platt, Joe M.	MBK	1936, 37, 38
Ploeger, Susan	WTR	1985
Plogsterth, Willard T.	MTN	1919, 20
Plonchek, Jenna	WTR	1981
Plumb, Christopher W.	MSW	1994, 95, 96, 97
Poe, William	BB	1963, 64, 65
Poehls, Ralph D.	FB	1961, 62
Poff, Paul J.	MBK	1953, 54, 55
Pogue, Henry E.	FB	1968, 69, 70
Poindexter, Kim	WTR	1979
Pokorny, Joseph R.	FB (Mgr.)	1981
Pokryzwinski, Bernard C.	FB	1963
Polance, Jack T.	BB	1971
Poland, Donald F.	MTR	1963, 64
Polce, Joseph F.	FB	1946, 47, 48
Polce, Thomas F.	FB	1984, 85, 86, 87
Polizotto, Brett H.	MCC	1987, 88, 89
Polk, Lee	FB	1896
Pollio, Martin A.	MBK (Mgr.)	1993
Pollock, Theodore R.	MGY	1951
Polonchek, Jeanna S.	WBK/WTR	1980, 82, 83
Polowy, Jamie S.	WP	1999
Pomeroy, Traci L.	WSW	1990, 91, 92
Pond, Richard S.	MTR	1958
Pontow, Brad G.	MTN	1982, 83, 84, 85
Poorman, Roger W.	MCC/MTR	1937, 38, 39, 40
Poosuthasee, Ann T.	WTN	1999
Pope, Derek L.	MTN	1995, 96, 97
Pope, Holly A.	WTN	1973, 74, 75, 76
Pope, Rex C.	MCC/MTR	1925, 26, 27
Pope, Spencer G.	FB/MTR	1915, 16, 17, 19
Pope, Thomas M.	MCC/MTR	1962, 63, 64, 65
Popp, Marcia J.	VB	1982, 83, 84, 85
Porter, Bridget D.	WBK/WTR	1994, 95, 96, 97
Porter, Caleb R.	MSO	1994, 95, 96, 97
Porter, Daniel B.	MTR	1990, 91
Porter, David D.	MBK	1961, 62, 63
Porter, David H.	MBK (Mgr.)	1967
Porter, Donald R.	BB	1953, 54
Porter, John R.	MBK	1915, 16
Porter, Kenneth T.	MGY (Mgr.)	1963
Porter, Nichole L.	WSO	1995, 96, 97, 98
Porter, Stephanie S.	WSW	1981, 82, 83, 84
Porter, Stephen W.	FB	1969, 71
Porter, Steven L.	BB	1975, 76
Porter, W. Robert	MBK	1933, 34, 35
Post, John F.	BB	1889
Pot, Catharina C.	FH	1979, 80
Potter, Cynthia A.	WSW	1970, 71, 72
Potts, Philip C.	BB	1952, 53
Poulsen, Charles M.	WR	1985, 88, 89
Powell, Connie	WSW	1973, 74
Powell, Gary B.	FB/MTR	1971, 72, 73, 74
Powell, Gary V.	MGY	1970, 71, 72, 73
Powell, James E.	FB	1956
Powell, Marshall A.	FB	1986, 87
Powell, Michael P.	WR	1996, 97, 98, 99
Powell, Nicole I.	WCC/WTR	1992, 93, 94, 95
Powell, Thomas C.	WR	1975, 77, 78
Power, William D.	MTN	1964, 65, 66
Powers, Gretchen E.	WCC/WTR	1987, 88, 89
Powers, Jan A.	WGY	1978, 79
Powers, Kim R.	SB	1988, 89
Powers, Lea	WSW	1979
Powers, Paul D.	FB	1977, 78
Poyle, Geoff A.	FB	1986
Prather, Clinton C.	FB/MBK	1913, 14, 15, 16
Prather, Geneal	MTR	1925, 26
Prather, Paul D.	FB	1995, 96
Pratt, Dickson J.	MTR	1951, 52, 53

Dave Power was a tennis All-American in 1966.

Michele Redman was Big Ten medalist and a 2nd team All-American in 1987.

Pratt, Nelson B.	MGY	1979, 80, 82
Pratt, Roy N.	FB	1958, 59, 60
Pratzmann, Wendy C.	WSW	1977, 78
Preda, Joseph, Jr.	WR	1950
Preger, Daniel A.	FB	1942
Prentkowski, Sandra L.	WTR	1984
Press, James N.	MCC/MTR	1968, 69, 70, 71
Press, Jeffrey W.	MCC/MTR	1973, 74, 75, 76
Pressler, Paul R.	BB (Mgr.)	1946
Preston, Shelley	WSW	1978
Prewitt, Todd D.	BB	1989
Price, Clarence R.	FB	1967, 68
Price, Gregory A.	MTR	1975, 76, 77
Price, Harry C.	MCC/MTR	1941, 42, 43
Price, Robert B.	MCC/MTR	1993
Price, Vella J.	SB/WBK	1973, 74, 75, 76
Prickett, Dan E.	BB	1961, 62, 63
Priest, David W.	MSO	1987, 88
Prifogle, Elmer W.	MCC/MTR	1945, 46, 47, 48
Primmer, John W.	MSW (Mgr.)	1963
Prince, Harry R.	FB (Mgr.)	1960
Principe, Mimmo	MGY	1979
Prinz, Michelle E.	WCC/WTR	1992, 93
Pritchett, George S.	BB	1884
Pritzke, Ronald R.	BB	1967, 68, 69
Prizant, Simon H.	WR	1947, 48, 49, 50
Proctor, Roger K.	MGO	1970, 71, 72, 73
Proffitt, Patricia	WTR	1979
Props, James K.	WR	1926, 28
Prothro, Marcee J.	VB	1994, 95
Prough, Dan A.	BB	1966, 67
Province, Clarence	BB/FB	1891, 92
Prucha, William J.	FB	1923
Prugh, David S.	FB	1975
Pruitt, Cathryn L.	WTN	1975, 76, 77
Pruitt, Lesli	FH	1978
Prusiecki, Matthew J.	FB	1991
Puchany, Andy J.	BB/WR	1946, 47, 48, 49
Puchyr, Marnie M.	WCC	1990
Pugsley, Andrea L.	WSO	1993, 94
Pukall, Janis L.	WSW	1977
Pullen, Francie	WCC/WTR	1986, 87
Pullon, Jennifer R.	SB	1998
Pulver, Raymond L.	BB	1983, 84, 85, 86
Purcell, George W., Jr.	MTN	1935
Purcell, William W.	MTR	1918, 19, 20
Purdy, Catherine A.	WSO	1993, 94
Purichia, Jeffrey S.	FB (Mgr.)	1988
Purnell, Eric A.	MTR	1994, 95, 96, 97
Purnell, Fred S.	MTR	1903, 04
Putman, Mark E.	MCC/MTR	1981, 82
Putna, John W.	MSO	1975, 76, 77, 78
Putorti, William, Jr.	WR	1958, 61
Putteet, Adrienne D.	WTR	1996
Pyle, Ernest T.	FB (Mgr.)	1922
Pyles, Charles D.	WR	1979

Qualls, Ronald	FB (Mgr.)	1979
Quam, Erica M.	WSW	1993, 94, 95, 96

Queisser, Herbert C.	BB	1935, 36, 37
Queller, Donald E.	MTR	1943
Quenzer, Shirley K.	SB/WBK	1971, 72
Quick, John D.	BB (Mgr.)	1957
Quillin, Emerson S.	BB	1898
Quilling, Stacy K.	WGO	1993, 94, 95, 96
Quimby, Robert J.	WR	1946
Quinkert, Kelly L.	VB	1987
Quinn, Claudius E.	BB	1909
Quinn, Erin L.	WSW	1998, 99
Quinn, Thomas M., Jr.	MTN	1928, 29
Quinter, William H.	FB	1960, 61

Rabb, Albert	BB	1884, 85, 86, 87
Rabideau, Nathan R.	FB	1994, 95, 96
Rabold, John P.	FB (Mgr.)	1967
Rabold, Michael J.	FB	1956, 57, 58
Racey, Megan E.	WTN	1995, 96, 97
Radcliffe, Charles D.	MBK	1945
Rader, C. Andrew	MSW	1984, 85, 86
Radford, Wayne	MBK	1975, 76, 77, 78
Radovich, Frank R.	MBK	1958, 59, 60
Radow, Judy	WTN	1970
Radtke, Timothy S.	FB	1985, 86, 87, 88
Raembke, Jan	WTN	1971
Raese, William T.	MSW	1991, 92, 93, 94, 95
Raffel, Dorothy E.	WBK	1980, 81
Rafik, Roxana P.	SB	1986, 87, 88, 89
Raftery, Scott E.	MGY	1982
Railsback, Walter S.	FB	1901, 02, 03
Raimondi, Benjamin L.	FB	1944, 45, 46
Raine, Teresa G.	SB	1987, 88, 89, 90
Rakita, Nancy	WSW	1970
Rakvica, Milan	MTN	1999
Ramey, Arthur J.	BB	1990, 91, 92
Ramey, Laura	WTN	1987
Ramsay, Floyd N.	BB	1912, 13
Ramser, Beverly M.	WTN	1979, 80, 81, 82
Ramsey, Edgar L. "Dart"	FB	1978, 79, 80, 81
Ramsey, Mark	FB	1978
Ramsey, Michael T.	BB	1987
Ramsey, Nathan L.	FB	1960, 61, 62
Ramsey, Rolla R.	FB	1893, 94
Ramsey, Steven L.	FB (Mgr.)	1974
Ramsey, Susan J.	WBK	1975, 76, 77
Randall, James R.	FB	1966
Randle El, Antwaan L.	FB/MBK	1998, 99
Randle El, Curtis	FB	1996, 97, 98
Randolph, Clare L.	FB	1926, 27, 28
Rapp, Angela L.	SB	1993, 94, 95
Rapp, Daniel J.	MSO	1984
Rapp, George R.	FB (Mgr.)	1934
Rapp, James M.	FB	1963
Rascher, Ambrose H.	BB/FB/WR	1929, 30, 31, 32
Rasheed, Eli H.	FB	1993, 94, 95
Ratchford, Frank T.	MTN	1940
Ratcliff, Orville M.	WR	1921, 22, 23
Rather, Thomas A.	FB (Mgr.)	1971
Ratliff, Roger G.	MBK	1938
Ratterman, Bernard W., Jr.	BB	1956, 57
Rau, John H.	BB	1905, 06, 08
Rauchmiller, Ronald A.	FB	1954, 55
Rausch, Douglas A.	MSW	1948, 49
Rauschenbach, Willard G.	BB	1918, 19, 20
Ravensberg, Robert A.	FB	1943, 44, 45, 4
Rawl, Wilfred E.	FB	1947, 48
Rawlings, Michael J.	MTR	1979
Rawson, Donald R.	MSO	1972, 73
Ray, Charles W.	MTR (Mgr.)	1957
Ray, Frank W.	FB	1895, 96, 97, 98, 99
Ray, Richard E.	BB	1926, 27, 28
Ray, Stephanie Jo	WSW	1991
Rayl, Gerald P.	BB	1943, 46
Rayl, James L.	MBK	1961, 62, 63
Rayl, Roy	BB	1917
Raymond, Robert R.	FB	1921, 22
Razmic, Charles F.	FB	1951, 52, 53
Razmic, Charles J.	FB	1981, 82, 83, 84
Razmic, John P.	FB	1957, 58
Razumich, Jerry Z.	MSO	1973
Rea, Ernest A.	BB	1930, 31, 32
Reason, Raymond, Jr.	WR	1951
Reasoner, Frank	BB	1905

Recker, Lucas A.	MBK	1998, 99
Record, Marnie E.	WSW	1994, 95, 96, 97
Records, Thomas W.	FB/MBK	1900, 01
Rector, Paul W.	BB	1927
Reda, David R.	FB	1961, 62
Redden, Normand W.	MCC/MTR (Mgr.)	1939, 40
Redding, Gerald R.	MGO	1926
Redding, Harlow W.	BB	1935
Redeker, Fred W.	WR	1957, 58, 59
Redenbaugh, Karen D.	WBK	1991, 92, 93, 94, 95
Redenbaugh, Stephen H.	MBK	1963, 64, 65
Redington, Scott K.	WR	1993
Redman, Michele R.	WGO	1984, 85, 86, 87
Redmon, John T.	FB	1915
Redmond, Thomas G.	MSO	1973, 74
Reeb, Paul H.	MTN	1943
Reece, James O.	MSW	1946, 48, 50
Reece, Stephanie	WTN	1989, 90, 91, 92
Reed, Burgess N.	MBK	1995, 96, 97
Reed, Carol	FH/SB/VB	1969, 70
Reed, Charles F.	MTR/WR	1921, 24, 25
Reed, George	MBK	1917
Reed, John D.	MTN	1942
Reed, Philip B.	MCC	1926
Reed, Samuel L.	BB	1954, 55, 56
Reed, Scott W.	MTR	1985, 87
Reed, Stacy L.	WGY/WTR	1982, 83, 84, 85
Reed, Tammy L.	WTR	1985, 86, 87, 88
Reedy, Ricky G.	R	1969
Reel, Leonard R.	WR	1967, 68, 69
Rees, Elizabeth	WSW	1973, 74, 75, 76
Reeves, Earle C.	MCC	1910
Reeves, Emily J.	VB	1980, 81, 82, 83
Regans, Aaron J.	MTR	1988, 89, 90, 91
Rehm, Richard T.	FB	1940
Rehm, William H.	FB	1930, 31, 32
Rehmer, James B.	MCC/MTR	1968, 69, 70
Rehrer, Shanna	WTR (Mgr.)	1999
Reider, David A.	FB	1970
Reidy, Theresa	WGO	1972
Reihman, Sheryl E.	WSW	1975, 76
Reiling, Sara L.	WSW	1999
Reiman, James L.	R	1959
Reineck, Kenneth L.	MCC	1943
Reinhardt, George W.	FB	1927
Reinhart, Bob L.	BB/MBK	1959, 60, 61
Reinke, Dean A.	MCC/MTR	1974, 75, 76
Reisert, William A.	FB	1987, 89
Reish, Steven A.	BB/MBK	1979, 80
Reisig, Edwin C.	MGY/MSW	1949, 50, 51
Reising, Carl J.	MGY	1949
Remak, Heidi	WTN	1972
Remak, Ronald F.	MTN	1977, 78, 79
Renegar, Ralph	FB	1932, 33
Reneke, Johanna E.	WCC/WTR	1981, 82
Renfro, Adam F.	MCC/MTR	1981, 82, 83, 84, 85
Rennie, William D.	MTN	1977, 78
Rentsch, Bonnie L.	WSW	1977
Repetti, Jon P.	MSW	1997, 98, 99
Ress, Alexander B.	MSW (Mgr.)	1991, 92, 94
Ress, L. Colin	MSW	1975, 76, 78, 79
Resseguie, Richard A.	MCC/MTR	1979, 80
Retherford, Claude W., Jr.	MBK	1944
Rexford, Bernadette R.	FH	1979, 80
Reynolds, Dennis D.	WR	1982, 83, 84
Reynolds, Elizabeth	WTN	1972
Reynolds, Holly F.	SB/WBK	1977, 78, 79, 80
Reynolds, Jill K.	WBK	1998
Reynolds, Kassandra L.	SB	1993, 94, 95, 96
Reynolds, Laurel	WGO/VB	1971, 72, 73, 74
Reynolds, R. Christopher	MBK	1990, 91, 92, 93
Rhoade, Susan E.	WSW	1975, 76, 78
Rhodes, Fred D.	MGY	1951
Rhodes, Peter S.	MSW	1966, 67
Rhodus, Daniel D.	FB	1967
Rian, George S.	MSW (Mgr.)	1955
Ribble, Robert H.	MTR	1946
Rice, Erin A.	WSW	1999
Rice, Joseph L.	MTR	1998
Rice, Kathryn	WGY	1979, 80, 81, 82
Rice, Megan M.	WSW	1998, 99
Rich, Claude T.	FB (Mgr.)	1928
Rich, Harold E.	MTR	1936
Rich, John B.	BB	1866, 67, 74
Rich, Norman S.	MSW (Mgr.)	1979
Richards, Charles L.	MSW	1965, 66, 67
Richards, Daniel R.	MTN	1972, 73, 74, 75
Richards, Robert L.	MTR	1951, 52, 53
Richards, Robert L.	BB	1953
Richardson, Clair L.	MTR	1937, 38
Richardson, Earl H.	BB	1903, 04, 05, 06
Richardson, Larry L.	MBK	1996, 97, 98
Richardson, Mose J.	FB	1990, 91, 92, 93
Richardson, Paul B.	FB	1929, 30
Richardson, Walter N.	MTR	1915
Richley, Mike D.	MSW	1997, 98, 99
Ricker, Timothy C.	FB	1989
Ricks, James A.	MTR	1969
Ridenour, Lisa J.	WTR	1987, 88, 89, 90
Ridlen, Daniel L.	MTR	1973, 75, 76, 77
Ridley, Edward S.	BB	1916, 17, 18
Ridley, John E.	MCC/MTR	1982, 83, 84
Riedford, Mary C.	VB	1976, 77
Riehm, Rachel K.	WCC	1988
Rifkin, Samuel	MGY	1943
Rigg, Alan W.	MTR	1978, 79, 80, 81
Riggin, Ronald D.	WR	1987, 88
Riggle, David J.	WR	1975
Riggs-Miller, John H.	MSO	1981
Riley, Charles E.	MCC	1948, 49
Riley, Chris	WGY	1970
Riley, Paul H.	MTR	1940, 41, 42
Riley, Robert H.	FB/WR	1983, 84, 85, 86
Rinehart, Wilmer T.	MTR	1927, 28, 29
Ring, Eugene E.	BB/MBK	1949, 50, 51
Ringwalt, Carroll W.	FB	1927, 28, 29
Rink, Shea	MBK (Mgr.)	1996
Ripley, Eric M.	MSO	1996, 97, 98
Risch, Paul A.	MCC/MTR	1979, 80, 81, 82
Rishe, Frank J.	FB	1966
Risher, John R.	FB	1936
Risk, Sara M.	WCC	1983
Risley, Elliott C.	FB	1919, 20
Risley, Jay A.	MSW	1979, 80
Risley, Stephen A.	MBK	1978, 79, 80, 81
Ritchie, Morris, Jr.	FB (Mgr.)	1939
Ritchie, William D.	MGO	1943
Ritter, David C.	MSW	1976, 77, 78
Ritter, Donald E.	BB/MBK	1947, 48, 49
Ritter, Harry, Jr.	BB	1950
Ritter, John P.	MBK	1971, 72, 73
Ritter, Robert C.	MTR (Mgr.)	1993
Ritterskamp, Godfred H.	MBK	1905, 06
Ritterskamp, Paul H.	MCC	1923
Ritz, Timothy R.	MTR	1963
Ritz, Zachary R.	MTR	1998
Roach, Dorrell C.	MTR (Mgr.)	1947
Robb, Patricia A.	WCC	1984
Robbiano, Lisa	WSW	1981, 82, 83
Robbins, Chester C.	WR	1943, 47, 48
Robbins, Gordon T.	BB	1971
Robbins, Tyrie A.	MBK	1949, 50, 51
Robeen, Craig W.	FB	1997, 98
Roberson, James O.	FB/MTR	1947, 48, 49, 50
Roberson, James O.	MBK	1976, 77, 78
Roberson, John L.	FB/MTR	1950, 51, 54
Roberson, Timothy W., Jr.	FB	1971
Roberts, George M.	FB/MTN	1908, 09, 10, 11
Roberts, Linda	WTR	1985
Roberts, Marc D.	BB	1992, 94
Roberts, Norman K.	MGO	1972, 73, 74, 75
Roberts, Troy C.	FB	1989
Roberts, Victor J.	BB	1933, 34, 35
Robertson, Elaine	WTN	1973, 74, 75, 76
Robertson, Michelle L.	WSO	1993
Robertson, Robert E.	BB/FB	1949, 50, 51, 53, 54
Robertson, Roosevelt	FB	1962
Robin, Daniel K.	MGY	1970, 71, 72
Robinette, Robert D.	FB (Mgr.)	1960
Robins, Harry F.	MCC	1936, 37, 38
Robins, Neill R.	MTR	1973
Robinson, Albert D.	MTR	1983, 84, 85, 86
Robinson, Bernard M.	BB/MBK	1905, 06, 07
Robinson, Frederick S.	MBK	1983, 84, 85, 86
Robinson, Gayle H.	FB	1968
Robinson, James B.	MCC	1933, 34
Robinson, James J.	MCC	1911, 12, 13
Robinson, Lee E.	FB	1967, 68
Robinson, Leonard C.	MTR	1954, 55, 57
Robinson, Marion L. "Jabar"	FB	1995, 96, 97, 98
Robinson, Mark D.	MBK	1988, 89, 90
Robinson, Richard D.	MTR	1966
Robinson, William A.	MTR	1967, 68
Robling, Keith A.	FB (Mgr.)	1980
Robling, Mim A.	WTR	1992
Rocco, Charles A.	FB	1960, 61
Roche, Kelly	WSW	1980, 81
Rochford, Jeremy B.	MTR	1997, 98, 99
Rodabaugh, Edward B.	MSW (Mgr.)	1951
Rodeheaver, Roger L., II	BB	1996, 97, 98

Don Ritter was 1st team All-America in baseball in 1949; he also captained the basketball team that year.

Jody Roudebush was All-Big Ten in 1993 and 1994.

Rodgers, Blake R.	MSO	1990, 91, 92, 93
Rodgers, Jay R.	FB	1996, 1997, 98
Rodholm, Mark N.	MCC/MTR	1986, 87, 88, 89, 90
Rodrigues, Agostinho L.	MTR	1982
Rodriguez, Mark F.	FB	1979, 80, 81, 82
Roehm, Luther S.	MTR	1932
Roelofs, Gabrielle	WSW	1981, 82, 83
Roembke, Margaret A.	WSW	1976, 77, 79
Roemer, Mary V.	VB	1972, 73, 74
Roemer, Ronald E.	FB	1959, 60
Roesch, Pamela L.	WGY	1977
Roest, Han G.	MSO	1985, 86, 87, 88
Roethke, John R.	MSW	1961
Rogers, Amy E.	SB	1989, 90, 91, 92
Rogers, Arthur	MBK	1908, 09
Rogers, Bruce H.	MSW	1979, 80
Rogers, Colin J.	MSO	1998
Rogers, Cort J.	MCC	1941
Rogers, Cynthia	WGY	1980, 81, 82, 83
Rogers, Daniel C.	MSW	1978, 80, 81
Rogers, David L.	FB	1953
Rogers, Joel K.	FB	1983
Rogers, Mark W.	FB	1983, 84, 85
Rogers, Steven A.	MGO	1975, 76, 77, 78
Rogers, Susan L.	WSW	1978
Rogers, Thomas C.	MTN	1978, 79, 80, 81
Roggeman, John J.	FB	1979, 80, 81, 82
Rogus, Margot A.	WTR	1980, 81, 83, 84
Rohan, Matthew J.	FB	1979
Rohdes, Fred D.	MGY	1951
Rohe, Steven M.	FB	1979, 80, 82
Rohleder, Jeffrey M.	BB	1978, 79
Rohrman, Martin J.	WR	1969
Rolak, Bruno J.	WR	1941
Rolak, Michael J.	WR	1943, 46
Rolfsen, Lynn M.	WGO	1976, 77, 78
Roll, Christina C.	WSW	1983, 84
Roll, Christopher J.	FB	1994
Rollandts, Ruth	FH	1970
Rolleri, Christina T.	WCC/WTR	1992, 93
Rollett, Gregory S.	BB	1981, 82, 83, 84
Roman, Barbara	WSW	1975
Roman, Joseph M.	WR	1938, 39, 40, 45
Romanelli, Dominic	MSO	1984
Romberg, Karin R.	WGO	1982, 83, 84, 85
Rompel, Jacqueline S.	WSO	1998
Ronzone, Paschal N.	FB	1942
Rooney, Melissa A.	VB	1995, 96, 97, 98
Root, John H.	MGO	1935
Roper, John M., Jr.	FB	1947
Rosbrugh, Paul C.	BB	1926
Rose, James J.	MTR	1985
Rose, Richard M.	FB	1981, 82, 83
Rose, Robert H.	MCC/MTR	1924, 25, 26
Rose, Robert S.	FB (Mgr.)	1953
Rose, Stephen G.	MGO	1941
Rose, Suzanne J.	WP	1999
Rosen, Martin A.	MGY	1965, 66
Rosen, Scott J.	MSO (Mgr.)	1973, 75
Rosen, Sheryl, I.	WTR	1999
Rosen, Steven H.	FB (Mgr.)	1960
Rosenau, Gordon	MTR (Mgr.)	1959
Rosenberg, Abraham L.	MSW (Mgr.)	1943
Rosenberg, Allen E.	MCC/MTR	1974, 75, 76, 77

Rosenblum, Lynn A.	VB	1972, 73, 74
Roska, Natalie R.	SB	1997
Rosin, Larry J.	BB	1975, 76, 77, 78
Ross, Alan L.	MSW	1970
Ross, Annette	WSW	1981
Ross, Ben R.	FB	1919, 20, 21
Ross, George O.	FB/WR	1928, 29, 30, 31
Ross, Jasper A.	BB/FB	1902, 03, 04
Ross, Kelly L.	WP	1998, 99
Ross, Melvin R.	FB	1959
Ross, Michael L.	MGY	1964, 65, 66
Ross, Susan M.	VB	1975, 76, 77, 78
Ross, Theodore W.	FB	1956
Ross, William B.	MCC/MTR	1949, 50
Rosselet, Cynthia E.	WBK	1980
Rosselli, Kristen A.	VB	1982, 83
Rossero, John S.	WR	1962
Rossi, Joanna	WTN	1990
Rossiter, Chris	MSO	1984
Rostovsky, Lee-Ann	WTN	1994, 95
Roth, David W.	BB	1975, 76
Roth, Edward A.	FB/MTR	1950, 51, 52
Roth, Louis L.	MTN	1959
Roth, Michael G.	FB	1967, 68
Rothberg, Sol	MBK (Mgr.)	1932
Rothmuller, Ilan J.	MTN	1959, 60
Rothrock, David A., Jr.	BB (Mgr.)	1932
Rothschild, Arvin K.	MSW (Mgr.)	1937
Rottinghaus, Ben	VB (Mgr.)	1997, 98
Roudebush, Earl D.	MCC	1911
Roudebush, Jody M.	MGO	1991, 92, 93, 94
Rouhier, Jack A.	MGO	1956, 57
Rounds, Fred O., Jr.	MSW	1960
Rourke, Linda M.	FH	1974
Rourke, Nancy V.	WGO	1985, 86, 87
Rousseau, Richard G.	MGO	1982, 83, 84, 85
Rowe, Bettyann	FH	1978
Rowe, John R.	MCC/MTR	1967
Rowland, Nancy D.	VB	1982, 83, 84, 85
Rowland, Robert A.	MBK	1944
Rowles, P. Christopher	MBK	1996
Rowlette, Marshall J.	MCC/MTR	1945, 46
Rowray, Richard D.	MBK	1982
Roxey, Walter A.	FB/WR	1929, 30, 31
Roy, Shashi B.	MSO	1978, 79
Royer, Amy S.	WTR	1993
Royer, Robert A.	MSW	1927
Royer, Ronald L.	MGO	1958, 59, 60
Rubin, Suzanne T.	WBK	1979
Rubinelli, Peter A.	FB	1943
Ruble, Vern W.	FB (Mgr.)	1923
Rucinski, Edward A.	FB	1938, 39, 40
Ruckelshaus, Leonard C.	BB	1921, 22
Rucker, Alvah J.	FB/MBK/MTN	1900, 01, 02
Rudin, Wesley T.	MSW	1996, 97
Ruff, Loren K.	MSW (Mgr.)	1957
Ruggles, John K.	MGY	1964, 65
Ruhlman, Ann L.	WGY	1977, 78
Ruminski, Gregory A.	MSW	1994, 95, 96, 97
Ruppert, Barry C.	BB	1978, 79, 80, 81
Rusche, Kyle A.	MSW	1997, 98
Russell, Charles M.	MCC/MTR	1965, 66, 67
Russell, David C.	MTN	1990, 91
Russell, Delmar L.	BB/FB/MBK	1944, 45, 47, 48, 49
Russell, Donna	WGO	1972, 73, 74
Russell, Edward W.	MTR	1964
Russell, Jill C.	WSW	1977, 78, 79
Russell, Joel R.	MSO	1990, 91
Russell, Nigel	MTN	1990, 91, 92, 93
Russell, Pat	WGO	1970
Russell, Robert C.	FB	1965, 66, 67
Russell, William P.	MBK	1965, 66, 67
Russo, Christopher T.	WR	1991, 92, 93, 94
Russo, Peter J.	FB	1950, 51, 52
Russo, Ronald T.	MTR	1983
Rust, Gurley S.	BB	1924
Rust, Lloyd A.	BB	1920, 21
Rutledge, Shannon D.	FB	1992, 93
Ryan, Abigail C.	WSO	1995, 96, 98
Ryan, Christie	WTN (Mgr.)	1998
Ryan, Gregory A.	MBK (Mgr.)	1985
Ryan, Maureen	WCC/WTR	1991, 92, 93, 94, 95
Ryann, Joann U.	WBK	1979, 80, 81
Rydzewski, Robert C.	FB	1985, 87, 88
Ryker, Angela J.	WTR	1988, 89, 90, 91
Ryser, Terry A.	BB	1962, 63

Name	Sport	Years
Saban, Louis H.	FB/MTR	1941, 42, 43
Sabik, Adolph J.	FB	1933
Sablosky, Marvin E.	MTR (Mgr.)	1942
Sabo, Michael A.	BB	1985, 86, 87, 88
Sabol, Albert R.	FB	1938, 39, 40
Sachs, Heather E.	VB	1992, 93
Sagstetter, David C.	MSO	1975
St. Clair, Blake E.	BB	1998, 99
St. John, Martha E.	VB/SB	1973, 74
St. Martin, Ronald F.	R	1957
St. Pierre, Kenneth V.	BB/FB	1970, 71, 72, 73, 74
Sakanich, James M.	FB	1980, 81, 82, 83
Saks, Laurence D.	FB (Mgr.)	1981
Salas-Schoofield P.	MTN	1982, 83, 84
Salazar, Douglas R.	MSW	1991
Salmi, Victor J.	FB	1924, 25, 27
Salmon, Rebecca H.	WCC/WTR	1987, 88, 89, 90, 91
Salpeter, Terry	SB	1971
Salters, Johnnie L.	FB	1981, 82, 83
Salters, Marty E.	WR	1989
Salumaa, Gunnar E.	MTN	1988, 90, 91
Salumaa, Sven W.	MTN	1985, 86, 87, 88
Saluski, Stanley	BB/FB	1930, 31, 32, 33
Salzer, Caren J.	WCC/WTR	1985, 86
Sammons, Edward M.	MTR	1989, 90, 91
Sampias, William J.	BB	1952
Sams, James D.	FB	1987, 88
Samse, Leroy P.	MTR	1903, 04, 05, 06
Samuel, Arnold F.	MSW	1953, 54, 55
Sanchez, Stephen M.	MSW	1992, 93
Sanders, Alphonso L.	MTR	1974
Sanders, Chester E.	FB	1943
Sanders, Corby J.	MSW (Mgr.)	1970
Sanders, James E.	BB/MBK	1905, 06, 07
Sanders, James L.	FB	1901
Sanders, James S.	BB	1954, 55, 56
Sanders, Steven A.	FB	1973, 74, 75, 76
Sanderson, Allan J.	MTR	1973, 75
Sanderson, Kristina M.	VB	1996, 97, 98
Sanford, Harold E.	BB/MTR	1922, 23
Sangalis, Gregory T.	MGY	1976, 77
Sangalis, Nicholas T.	MTR (Mgr.)	1956
Sangalis, Theodore D.	WR	1978, 80, 81
Sanquinette, Sally J.	WSW	1977, 78, 79
Saperstein, Morris	MTR	1944
Saracino, Sue	VB	1971
Sargent, Gary T.	BB	1966, 67, 68
Sargent, Tony W.	MCC/MTR (Mgr.)	1979, 80
Sarjent, Christopher W.	MGY	1981, 82
Sartain, Maria B.	WCC	1982
Sattelberg, Christel	WSW	1980, 81, 82
Satter, Karl R.	MBK	1951
Sauer, Edward F.	MSW/WR	1921, 22
Sauer, Mary L.	WSW	1975, 76, 77, 78
Sauers, Debra L.	WCC/WTR	1988, 89, 90, 91, 92
Saul, Ralph O.	WR	1925, 26
Saunders, Keith A.	WR	1979, 80, 81, 82
Saunders, Kevin W.	BB	1980, 81
Saunders, Terrence D.	FB	1986, 87, 88, 89
Saunders, Thomas C.	WR	1999
Savage, Nancy K.	SB	1982, 83, 84, 85
Savage, Schuyler L., Jr.	MSW	1942
Savko, Sheri M.	SB	1999
Sawicki, Halary	FB	1931, 32, 33
Sawicki, Joe R.	FB	1933
Sawyer, Jeffrey W.	MGY	1970, 71, 72
Scafa, Robert D.	BB	1991, 93, 94
Scarff, Kees N.	BB/FB	1964, 65, 66, 67
Scavo, Margaret A.	WSO	1993, 94, 95, 96
Schaab, Charles E.	MBK (Mgr.)	1935
Schabel, Gregory M.	BB	1995, 96, 97, 98
Schade, Ryan L.	BB	1998, 99
Schaefer, Barbara	WSW	1970
Schaefer, Gregory W.	WR	1999
Schaefer, Harry F.	MSW	1953, 55
Schaefer, Herman H.	MBK	1939, 40, 41
Schaefer, Hollie L.	WSO	1994
Schaefer, Steven G.	BB	1990, 91, 92, 93
Schafer, Daniel E.	MGY	1966
Schaffer, Devin K.	FB	1998
Schaftlein, Shari M.	FH/SB	1980, 81, 82, 83, 84
Schaible, Richard A.	MSW	1964, 65
Schank, David M.	BB	1988
Schannen, Richard H.	MBK (Mgr.)	1939
Schanz, Donald C.	FB	1974, 75
Scharnowske, Robert S.	FB	1970
Schaumann, Richard P.	BB	1967
Scheele, Suzanne B.	VB	1982, 83, 84, 85
Scheid, Carl D.	MBK	1928, 29
Scheidel, Pamela	WGO	1983
Scheidemann, Jill A.	WTN	1978, 79, 80
Scheider, Richard A.	MCC	1957
Schelske, Clara M.	WGY	1972
Schenck, Andrew E.	MSW	1987
Scherer, Nancy	WGY	1971, 72
Schermer, Kenneth L.	FB	1952
Scheumann, Edward G.	MTN	1924
Schevers, Terry A.	WBK	1978
Schieck, Jennifer L.	WSO	1993
Schienbein, Edward L.	FB	1943
Schieve, Donald R.	MGO	1954, 55
Schilawski, Ralph H.	FB	1933, 34
Schilling, Susan E.	WGO	1975, 76, 77, 78
Schimmele, Grant S.	MGO	1994, 95, 96, 97
Schlachter, Patsy	SB/WSW	1972, 73, 74
Schlatter, Marc G.	MSW	1977, 78, 79, 80
Schlegel, Lori L.	WBK	1978, 79
Schlegelmilch, Allen D.	MBK	1958, 59, 60
Schlemmer, Norman C.	BB	1914, 15
Schlereth, Douglas E.	FB	1985, 86, 87, 88
Schlicting, Fred W., Jr.	MSW	1962
Schlundt, Donald D.	MBK	1952, 53, 54, 55
Schlundt, Mark A.	MTR	1976
Schmalz, Richard H.	BB (Mgr.)	1940
Schmid, Jennifer J.	WSW	1996, 97, 99
Schmid, Joseph J.	MSO	1979, 80, 82, 83
Schmidt, Aaron D.	WR	1991
Schmidt, Alvin W.	FB	1967, 68
Schmidt, Debbie B.	VB	1969, 70
Schmidt, Douglas E.	MGY	1982
Schmidt, Fred W.	MSW	1963, 64, 65
Schmidt, Harold J., Jr.	MGO	1941
Schmidt, Herman A.	FB	1902, 03
Schmidt, Joy	SB	1974
Schmidt, Karl D.	WR	1970
Schmidt, Lester T.	WR	1945
Schmidt, Nancy M.	WCC/WTR	1978, 79
Schmidt, Tina A.	WSW	1992
Schmidt, Wayne W.	BB	1917
Schmit, Emily M.	WP	1998, 99
Schmit, Robert J.	FB	1983, 84, 85
Schneider, Earl W.	MBK	1967, 68, 69
Schneider, Randy L.	FB	1988, 89, 90, 91
Schneider, Richard J.	MBK	1945
Schneider, Richard P.	MGY	1965, 66
Schneiderman, Julius	MSW/MTR	1935, 36
Schnell, David E.	FB	1986, 87, 88, 89
Schnepf, Paul G.	MBK (Mgr.)	1959, 60
Schnierle, Nancy E.	WTR	1994
Schnute, Justin C.	MSW	1995, 96, 97, 98
Schoeff, Jill	WGY	1979
Scholl, Jack E.	MTR (Mgr.)	1944
Scholl, Janet L.	SB	1978, 79, 80
Scholler, Harry M.	BB/FB	1892, 93, 94, 95, 96
Schooler, Lucinda	WGO	1970
Schooley, James F.	MBK	1951, 52, 53
Schoolfield, William E.	WR	1927, 28
Schrader, Edward A.	MCC/MTR (Mgr.)	1933, 34
Schrage, Michael	MBK (Mgr.)	1998
Schreckengast, Steven R.	FB	1975
Schrems, Bonnie J.	WSW	1991, 92, 93, 94
Schreyer, Susan D.	WGY	1979, 80
Schroeder, Heather E.	WCC/WTR	1990, 91, 92, 93, 94
Schroeder, Peter G.	MBK (Mgr.)	1979, 80
Schroeder, Richard T.	MSW	1962
Schrumpf, Richard D.	MBK	1966, 67
Schuette, Thomas P.	FB	1964, 65, 66
Schuholz, Shauna	WSW	1979, 80
Schulenburg, John E.	MSO	1974, 75
Schuler, Herman E.	BB/MBK	1917, 19, 20, 21
Schulhof, Lary A.	MSW	1962, 63, 64
Schulte, John F.	MSW	1980, 81, 82, 83
Schulte, Mary	SB	1971
Schulte, Norman G.	MGY	1949, 50
Schulte, William J.	MSW	1974, 75, 76, 77
Schultz, Archie F.	BB	1912
Schultz, Carl H.	BB	1912, 13, 14
Schultz, Charles L., Jr.	MGO	1950, 51
Schultz, Donald E.	WR	1961, 62, 63
Schulze, Max H.	R	1959, 60
Schumacher, David R.	MTN	1967, 68, 69
Schuman, Minot K.	MSW	1957, 58
Schumann, Kathy	WSW	1983

Schuppan, Anne L.	WSO	1998
Schurr, Linda	WTR	1979
Schuster, Fred L.	MSW	1983, 84, 85, 86
Schutter, David E.	WR	1982
Schutz, Perri	MGY (Mgr.)	1950
Schwab, Ad.....	FB (Mgr.)	1998
Schwartz, Andy D.	FB (Mgr.)	1988
Schwartz, Eric R.	MCC/MTR	1989, 90, 91, 92
Schwartz, Thomas W.	FB/MBK	1945, 46, 48, 49
Sciortino, Chris J.	MSO	1987, 88
Scolnik, Glenn	FB	1970, 71, 72
Scott, Auree B.	WR	1929, 30
Scott, Burke H.	MBK	1953, 54, 55
Scott, Chad A.	FB	1994
Scott, Charles F.	MBK	1934, 35, 36
Scott, Clair H.	FB	1914, 15
Scott, Karen A.	WTR	1995, 97, 98
Scott, Leroy M.	FB	1896
Scott, Louis A.	MBK	1952, 53, 54
Scott, Marvin R.	WR	1934
Scott, Myron D.	MSW	1971, 72, 73, 75
Scott, Richard K.	BB	1963, 64, 65
Scott, Robert M.	MTN	1964, 65, 66
Scott, Theodore	MTN	1938
Scott, Wilbert J.	FB	1958, 59, 60
Scott, William O.	BB (Mgr.)	1937
Scott, William T.	BB	1982
Scully, Joseph H.	FB	1929
Scully, Roger J.	MGY	1970, 71, 72, 73
Scutt, Cheryl L.	SB/WBK	1970, 71
Seach, William J.	FB	1962
Seaman, Kenneth E.	MSW	1979, 80
Searcy, Sandra K.	WSW	1983
Sears, Brian K.	MTR	1978
Sears, Nicholas R.	MTR	1997, 98, 99
Sebek, Nicholas	FB	1945, 47, 48, 49
Seelinger, Jacqueline A.	WSW	1984
Seelinger, Omer D.	BB	1891
Sefton, James L.	WR	1937, 40
Segan, Tiffany M.	WSW	1993
Seger, Jennifer L.	WGO	1996, 97, 98, 99
Seger, Sherri L.	WGY	1985
Seib, Jay W.	FB	1993, 94, 95, 96
Seidholz, Donn E.	BB	1972, 73, 74
Seifert, Eugene P.	BB	1944
Seifert, Thomas L.	MTR	1961, 62
Seitz, Laura	WSW	1982
Self, David	FB (Mgr.)	1998
Seki, Samuel T.	MSW	1951, 52
Selby, Victor A., Jr.	MTR (Mgr.)	1931
Sellers, Edwin A.	MCC	1917
Sellers, Milan	FB	1948
Sellers, Scott A.	BB	1993, 94
Selthoffer, Steven V.	MSW	1978
Sembower, Charles J.	BB	1891, 92, 93, 94
Semones, Rebecca	WSW	1986
Sendobry, Jeff G.	MSO	1977, 78
Senft, Thomas W.	BB (Mgr.)	1980
Seng, Margaret M.	SB/VB	1977, 78, 79, 80, 81
Sera, Maria D.	WGO	1980, 81
Servies, Richard L.	WR	1959
Sessler, Stanley S.	R	1956
Settina, Alfred J.	WR	1958
Seward, Fred A.	MTR	1905, 06
Seward, James B.	MGO	1936, 38
Sexson, Ward E.	BB (Mgr.)	1955
Sexton, Ronald R.	FB	1966
Shabazz, Ayesha S.	WTR	1996, 97
Shackleton, Laura J.	WTR	1984
Shackleton, Roy	FB/MBK	1902, 03
Shadburne, William L.	MSW	1950, 51, 52
Shafer, John A.	FB/MTN	1891, 92, 93, 94, 95
Shafer, Paul O.	MCC	1928, 29
Shaffer, Leslie M.	SB (Mgr.)	1999
Shaffer, Steve P.	MSW	1978
Shanahan, Hugh N.	FB	1929, 30
Shanel, William C.	MSW	1981, 82, 83, 84
Shanken, Jeff A.	MGY	1976, 77, 78, 79, 80
Shanker, Joel H.	MSO	1992, 93, 94
Shanklin, Josh	MBK (Mgr.)	1998
Shanks, John A.	FB (Mgr.)	1936
Shannon, James R.	MTN	1949, 50, 51
Shapert, Sean E.	MSO	1987, 88, 89, 90
Sharp, Christina L.	WTN	1995, 96, 97, 98
Sharp, Donald G.	MGO	1951
Sharp, Robert I.	MGO	1932
Sharp, Sophia S.	WTR	1983
Sharpe, Charles S.	MSW	1978, 79, 80, 81
Sharpless, Keith A.	MTR	1982, 83, 84
Shaw, George E.	BB	1900, 01, 02, 03
Shaw, Patrick	FB	1996, 97, 98
Shaw, Ronald L.	MTR	1976, 77
Shaw, Steven J.	R	1971
Shea, Joseph H.	BB	1888, 89
Shea, Karen	SB	1971
Sheehan, Michael J.	WR	1975, 76, 77
Sheek, Daniel W.	FB	1894, 95, 96, 97
Sheets, Kenneth P.	WR	1980, 81
Sheetz, Eldridge M.	WR	1938
Sheire, Denise M.	WTR	1979, 80
Shelby, Robert I.	MBK (Mgr.)	1971
Shelley, Robert L.	MSW	1924
Shelton, David S.	MSO	1973, 74, 75, 76
Shelton, Gary D.	MCC/MTR	1978, 79, 80, 81
Shelton, Patrick F.	MGO	1998, 99
Shepherd, David P.	MBK	1972
Shepherd, Krista L.	WGY	1979
Shepherd, Stacie L.	WBK	1991
Shepler, Richard G.	FB	1986
Sherfick, Larry G.	MBK (Mgr.)	1975
Sheridan, Gary D.	MCC/MTR (Mgr.)	1977
Sheridan, John K.	BB	1895, 96
Sherman, Joseph W.	MCC	1974
Sherman, Ruth E.	WBK	1978, 79
Sherman, Warren C.	BB	1874
Shickell, Tighlman H.	FB	1984
Shideler, Thad R.	MTR	1904
Shields, Bradley D.	FB	1986, 87
Shields, Brady A.	FB	1995, 96, 97, 98
Shields, John C.	MGY	1974, 75
Shields, Marianne	WGY	1970
Shields, Mitchell M.	BB	1886
Shields, Oscar R.	MTR	1902
Shields, Paul C.	MBK	1944
Shields, William G.	FB	1927, 28, 29
Shima, Kevin T.	MSW	1993
Shin, Duke K.	MSW	1995, 96, 97, 98
Shine, Tiffany	WSO	1993, 94
Shinn, William M.	R	1957
Shircliff, Wayne J.	MGO	1969, 70, 71
Shire, Nicole E.	WSW	1991, 92
Shirk, Jeremiah J.	MBK (Mgr.)	1999
Shirley, Hardy L.	MCC/MTR	1921
Shively, George J.	BB	1914, 15, 16
Shivers, Jay S.	MSW	1949, 50, 51
Shivner, Julia C.	SB/WBK	1976, 77
Shockley, Ernest V.	MTR	1899, 1900, 01, 02
Shoemaker, David M.	MTR	1960, 61, 62
Shoemaker, Merle A.	MTR	1936, 37, 38
Shoemaker, Morrell M.	MCC/MTR	1910, 12, 13
Sholty, Lloyd O.	FB	1909, 10, 11
Sholty, William M.	FB	1935, 36
Shonkwiler, Fred A.	FB	1914, 15
Shonkwiler, George W.	MCC	1930
Shonkwiler, John W.	MGY	1966
Shook, Joseph A.	WR	1956, 57
Short, Kerrwin J.	BB	1977, 78, 79, 80
Shorter, Marti	WBK	1972
Shoup, James A.	BB	1971, 72
Shoup, Susanne	WTN	1972
Showley, Douglas D.	MCC/MTR	1994, 95, 96
Shrader, Carl E., Sr.	WR	1929
Shrader, Donald A.	FB	1985, 86, 87, 88
Shriver, Harry J.	MCC/MTR	1964, 65, 66
Shroyer, Mark D.	MTR	1976, 77, 78, 79
Shroyer, Todd F.	FB	1981
Shu, Joyce	WSW	1989
Shuck, James A.	MSW	1983, 84, 85, 86
Shuck, James L.	FB	1972, 73, 74, 75
Shumaker, Charles J.	BB	1940, 41, 42
Shumaker, John D.	FB	1971, 72, 73
Shumaker, Leo W.	MTR (Mgr.)	1926
Shuppert, Karen J.	WSW	1982, 83, 84, 85
Shy, Terry L.	MCC/MTR	1962, 63, 64, 65
Sibley, Frank H.	FB/MBK	1924, 25, 26, 27
Sickafus, Schlaura N.	WSW	1996, 97
Siddall, Deanna L.	WSW	1985
Sidereas, Lori Ann	WGY	1975
Siderewicz, Joseph W.	FB (Mgr.)	1985
Sidwell, John E.	FB	1943
Siebenthal, Tait E.	BB	1906, 08
Sieber, Eric W.	BB	1987, 88, 89, 90
Siefert, Robert R.	WR	1973
Siegal, Mark A.	MBK (Mgr.)	1974
Siesky, Charles L.	MCC/MTR	1958, 59, 60, 61
Siesky, Larry L.	MCC/MTR	1962, 63, 64, 65
Sigfusson, Paul B.	MSW	1976, 77, 78, 79
Sigler, Christopher L.	BB/FB	1981, 82, 83, 84, 85
Sigler, Diane	WTN	1975
Signs, Charles O.	FB	1895

Sikland, Hardeep S.	FB (Mgr.)	1985	
Sikora, Michael W.	FB	1946, 47	
Sikora, Robert A.	FB	1983	
Silas, Donald E.	FB	1968	
Silberstein, William	MBK	1936	
Sill, Robert W.	MGO	1939, 40	
Silva, Edward O.	MSW	1990	
Silver, Robert L.	MSW	1970, 71	
Silverman, Louis E.	WR	1989, 90, 91	
Simanton, Mark D.	MSO	1975, 76, 77, 78	
Simchick, Julius A.	FB	1943	
Simic, Curtis R.	MBK (Mgr.)	1993	
Simios, John S.	BB	1985, 86, 87, 88	
Simmons, Joseph C.	FB	1987	
Simmons, Martin R.	MBK	1984, 85	
Simon, Eric B.	BB	1993	
Simon, Michael E.	BB	1901	
Simon, William H.	FB	1969	
Simone, Debra J.	WP	1998, 99	
Simons, Christopher J.	FB	1985, 86, 87, 88	
Simos, Mikko J.	MCC/MTR	1997, 98, 99	
Simpson, Harry D.	FB	1891	
Simpson, James G. III	FB	1994	
Simpson, John R.	BB	1985	
Simpson, Paul D.	BB	1981, 82	
Simpson, Terry D.	MTR	1989, 90, 92, 93	
Simpson, Tracy A.	FH	1980	
Simpson, William T.	MSW	1945, 46	
Sims, Charles E.	BB/FB	1883, 84, 85, 86	
Sims, Gary D.	MBK (Mgr.)	1982	
Sims, Mark A.	MBK (Mgr.)	1986	
Sims, Melvin L.	MCC	1980	
Sindelar, Jody	WTN	1970	
Singer, Diane E.	FH	1973, 74, 75	
Singleton, Palmer C.	WR (Mgr.)	1943	
Singleton, Robert E.	BB	1962, 63, 64	
Sinn, Melinda	WSW	1974, 75, 76	
Sintz, Peter V.	MSW	1960, 61, 62	
Sisk, Caroline E.	WTN	1994	
Sisk, Thomas W., Jr.	MSW	1990, 91, 92	
Sisson, Adam D.	MTR	1982	
Sisti, Lori A.	SB	1981, 82, 83	
Sitterding, Cathy	WBK	1972	
Sitzberger, Kenneth R.	MSW	1965, 66, 67	
Sivoy, Barbara	SB	1973, 74	
Sizemore, Beth	VB	1993	
Sizemore, Duane E.	FB	1982	
Sjoholm, Gustav E.	BB	1957	
Skarshaug, Kirsten R.	WSW	1990, 91, 92, 93	
Skarzynski, Jean E.	SB	1989, 90, 91, 92	
Skeeters, Roy N.	BB	1954, 55, 56	
Skibinski, David J.	MBK (Mgr.)	1979, 80	
Skiff, Bradford C.	BB	1988, 89, 90	
Skiles, Julie A.	WGO	1977, 78	
Skinner, Kathryn G.	WTR	1992	
Skoronski, Robert F.	FB	1953, 54, 55	
Skoronski, Stephen M.	MBK (Mgr.)	1981	
Skvara, Michael J.	FB (Mgr.)	1969	
Slabaugh, Jeffrey L.	FB	1960, 61, 62	
Slack, Marilynn	WGO	1971	
Slevin, Michael P.	BB	1977, 78	
Sloan, Brian K.	MBK	1985, 86, 87, 88, 89	
Sloane, Michael A.	MSO	1984, 85	
Sloate, Joseph F.	BB/FB/MBK	1922, 23, 24	
Sloniker, Elizabeth A.	MGY (Mgr.)	1977	
Slont, Alvin C.	BB	1979	
Slosky, Edward R.	FB	1953	
Sloss, Russell M.	FB	1936, 37, 38	
Small, Diana J.	WBK	1985, 86, 87, 88	
Smalley, Donald A.	MTR	1927, 28, 29	
Smart, J. Keith	MBK	1987, 88	
Smedley, Eric A.	FB	1993, 94, 95	
Smella, Steven D.	BB	1993, 94, 95, 96	
Smialek, Linda	WSW	1981	
Smiley, Brian M.	WR	1998, 99	
Smiley, Rahman E.	MTN	1999	
Smiley, Thomas C.	MTR	1915	
Smillie, Ronald P.	MSW	1946	
Smith, Alex G.	BB	1982, 83, 85, 86	
Smith, Alexander G.	FB	1994, 95, 96	
Smith, Allison K.	SB	1993, 94	
Smith, Amanda	WSO (Mgr.)	1998	
Smith, Angela D.	WBK	1976, 77	
Smith, Anitra	WTR	1981	
Smith, Arthur H.	MSW	1964, 65, 66	
Smith, Benjamin W.	FB	1993	
Smith, Byard H.	MBK	1919	
Smith, Cara M.	WSW	1991	
Smith, Cari	WTR	1980	
Smith, Carl	FB	1974, 75, 76, 78	
Smith, Carol	FH/SB	1974, 75, 76, 77	
Smith, Chad L.	BB	1996, 97, 98, 99	
Smith, Charles W.	BB	1956, 57, 58	
Smith, Christopher S.	FB	1992, 93, 94	
Smith, Clare F.	WTR	1979, 80	
Smith, Claudia E.	WTR	1982, 83	
Smith, David C.	MSW	1961	
Smith, Denver	FB	1979, 80, 82	
Smith, Douglas R.	FB	1981, 82, 83, 84	
Smith, Edgar R.	FB	1922	
Smith, Elisa R.	VB	1987, 88, 89, 90, 91	
Smith, Everett J.	FB	1901, 02, 03	
Smith, Franklin H.	FB	1938, 39, 40	
Smith, Franklin H.	MSW	1970, 71	
Smith, George H.	WR	1919, 20, 21	
Smith, George T., Jr.	FB	1957, 58, 59	
Smith, George W.	MSW	1969, 70, 71	
Smith, James A.	FB	1965, 66	
Smith, James, Jr.	MBK	1943	
Smith, James T.	MCC/MTR	1935, 36, 37, 38	
Smith, Jennifer J.	SB	1998, 99	
Smith, John E.	FB	1943	
Smith, John G.	WR	1940	
Smith, Joseph A.	MBK (Mgr.)	1930	
Smith, Julie A.	SB	1984, 85, 86, 87	
Smith, Justin C.	FB	1998	
Smith, Kathleen A.	WP	1999	
Smith, Kenneth L.	FB	1939, 41	
Smith, Kenneth R.	BB	1957, 59, 60	
Smith, Kimberly L.	WSW	1975, 76, 77	
Smith, Kim W.	WSW	1976, 77, 78, 79	
Smith, Kreigh	MBK	1985, 86, 87, 88, 89	
Smith, Lester	MTR	1983, 84	
Smith, Linda Jo	WSW	1980	
Smith, Max J.	FB	1989, 90	
Smith, Megan R.	WSW	1996, 97, 98	
Smith, Merritt W.	FB	1951, 52	
Smith, Michael A.	BB	1989, 90, 91, 92	
Smith, Michael J.	MTR	1958	
Smith, Nelson T.	BB	1881	
Smith, Peter J.	MSW	1972	
Smith, Ralph E.	BB	1971, 72, 73	
Smith, Raymond V.	MTR	1968	
Smith, Richey E.	MSW	1948	
Smith, Robert T.	BB	1943	
Smith, Robin M.	VB/WTN	1970, 71, 72	
Smith, Roscoe W.	FB	1900, 01	
Smith, Russell E.	WR	1960	
Smith, Samuel E.	BB	1878, 79, 80, 81	
Smith, Samuel S.	MTR	1900, 01, 02	
Smith, Stephen T.	MTR (Mgr.)	1979	
Smith, Temple	FB/MTR	1922, 26, 27	
Smith, Terrence J.	FB	1981, 82, 83, 84	
Smith, Todd M.	FB	1990, 91, 92, 93	
Smith, William S.	FB	1938, 39, 40	
Smith, William S.	FB	1948, 49, 50	
Smith, William T.	BB	1938	
Smits, Linda J.	WSW	1977, 79	
Smock, John R.	MTR	1928, 29, 30	
Smock, Trent R.	FB/MBK	1972, 73, 74, 75	
Smrt, Charles E.	FB	1972, 73, 74	
Smullen, Willard C.	MCC/MTR	1933, 34, 35	
Smythe, James M.	FB	1979, 80, 82, 83	
Snedden, David R.	BB	1991, 92, 93	
Sniadecki, James B.	FB	1966, 67, 68	
Snively, Darrell D.	MTN	1968, 69, 70	
Snow, Brian J.	MSO	1996, 97, 98	
Snow, Kenneth T. III	MSO	1987, 88, 89, 90	
Snow, Richard E.	MTR (Mgr.)	1969	
Snow, Steven L.	MSO	1989	
Snowden, Calvin R.	FB	1966, 67, 68	
Snowden, Charles D.	MSW	1947	
Snyder, Courtney	FB	1973, 74, 75, 76	
Snyder, Donal M.	MTR	1947	
Snyder, Hugh P.	MTR	1950	
Snyder, Inga V.	WGO	1998, 99	
Snyder, James L.	BB	1963, 64, 65	
Snyder, Jenny H.	WTN	1980, 81, 82, 83	
Snyder, Kimberly M.	WSW	1995	
Snyder, Mark C.	FB	1984	
Snyder, Matthew T.	FB	1997, 98	
Snyder, Thomas M.	MTN	1970, 71, 72	
Snyder, Willam H.	MGO	1932, 33	
Soare, James B.	MSW	1992, 93, 94, 95	
Sobczak, Robert R.	FB	1954, 55, 56	
Soderberg, Susan L.	WGO	1989, 90, 91	
Sojka, Gene W.	FB	1971	
Sojka, Lisa K.	WTR	1982	
Solano, Nicholas F.	MGY	1979, 80, 81, 82	
Soldati, Adam P.	MSW	1995, 96, 97	

Mike Stamm, NCAA champion and Olympic gold medalist.

Diane Stephenson, softball All-American in 1981.

Somers, Alan B.	MSW	1961, 62, 63
Somesan, Robert A.	MCC/MTR	1969, 70, 71, 72, 73
Sommer, Joergen P.	MSO	1987, 88, 89, 90
Sommer, Jon W.	MGO	1958, 59, 60
Songer, Cynthia M.	FH	1981
Sorensen, Holly M.	WSW	1992
Sorgius, Steve W.	BB	1972, 73, 74
Sorrells, Molly J.	WCC/WTR	1986, 87, 88, 89, 90
Soulti, Lydia G.	WTN	1990, 92
South, Walter N.	MTR (Mgr.)	1957
Southard, Harold O.	R	1958
Southard, Teresa L.	VB	1982
Southerland, Jo E.	WBK	1974, 75, 76, 77
Southward, C. Fred	MSW	1968, 69, 70
Southwick, Dwight G.	MSW/WR (Mgr.)	1924
Sowinski, Joseph J.	FB/WR	1943, 44, 45, 46
Spagnolo, Linda	SB	1979, 80, 81
Spangler, Jeffery S.	MCC	1975, 76
Spannuth, William G.	FB	1930, 31, 32
Sparhawk, William F.	FB	1972, 73, 74
Sparkman, Melinda J.	WBK	1980, 81, 82, 83
Sparks, Joseph C.	WR	1941
Sparks, Katherine	VB	1973, 74
Sparks, Matthew W.	MCC/MTR	1993, 94, 95, 96, 97
Sparks, Michael S.	WR	1969, 70
Sparks, Richard L.	BB/MBK	1962
Sparks, Will C.	FB	1898, 1900
Spear, Jason H.	FB	1996, 97, 98
Speer, Kevin P.	FB	1979, 80
Spellman, Brian W.	MSW	1979
Spence, Donald	BB	1942
Spence, Wesley L.	MTN	1968, 69, 70
Spencer, Gordon J.	MSW	1974, 75
Spencer, Jesse E., Jr.	MGY	1955, 56
Spencer, O.J.	FB	1997, 98
Spencer, Sara	WSW	1973, 74
Spicer, Douglas H.	FB	1963, 64
Spicer, Robert E.	FB	1974
Spicer, Robin E.	FB	1970, 71, 72
Spickard, Richard W.	FB	1965, 67, 68
Spickelmier, Carl F.	MBK (Mgr.)	1948
Spillman, Barton	MGO	1957
Spinks, Glen C.	FB	1981, 83
Spisak, Michael L.	BB	1996, 97, 98
Spitz, Mark A.	MSW	1969, 70, 71, 72
Spivey, James C.	MCC/MTR	1978, 79, 80, 81, 82, 83
Spivey, Raymond D.	MTR	1959, 61
Sponsler, Palmer A.	MBK	1924, 25, 26
Sprauer, John E.	FB	1932, 33, 34
Spray, Adam M.	MSW	1997
Spray, Richard J.	MSO	1974, 75
Sprenger, Karen	WSW	1972, 73, 74, 75
Springer, Charles H.	BB	1885, 86, 87, 88, 89
Springer, Charles I.	FB	1922, 23, 24
Sprouse, Norbert L.	MTR (Mgr.)	1949, 50
Sprowls, Jennifer T.	WCC/WTR	1995, 96, 97, 98, 99
Squires, Fred H.	FB (Mgr.)	1931
Spungen, David A.	FB	1971, 72
Sramek, Richard J.	FB	1970
Staats, Robert E.	MGO	1947, 48, 53
Stabile, Christine	WCC	1985
Stack, James J.	MTR	1987, 88, 90, 91
Stackhouse, Lisa	VB	1977
Stacy, Ann C.	WGO	1982
Stadler, Darlene	WSW	1981
Stadler, Ernest F.	MSW	1942
Stadler, Matthew L.	MSW	1982, 83, 84, 85
Stajkovic, Niki	MSW	1978, 79, 80, 81

Stalker, Charles H.	BB	1898
Stalter, Todd M.	MSO	1989, 90
Stamats, Donald E.	FB	1925
Stamm, Michael E.	MSW	1971, 72, 73, 74
Stanbro, Richard D.	MSW	1932
Stanfield, Erin L.	WSW	1997
Stangle, William J.	FB (Mgr.)	1957
Stanley, Albert F.	WR	1921
Stanley, John D.	MGY	1981, 82
Stanley, Kevin J.	WR	1998, 99
Stanley, Vickie J.	VB	1976
Stapp, Charles P.	MTR	1974, 75, 76, 77
Starbuck, Edwin D.	BB	1888, 89
Starbuck, Walter H.	FB (Mgr.)	1933
Starck, Colleen A.	VB	1970, 71
Starek, Collen	VB	1969
Starling, Kenneth W.	FB	1971, 72, 73
Starr, Maurice A.	MBK	1927, 28
Starrett, Susan S.	WTN	1992, 93
Stastny, Robert C.	BB	1998, 99
Stavroff, Frank	FB	1963, 65, 66
Stavroff, Frank	FB	1973, 74, 75
Stavroff, Jeffrey D.	MGO	1990, 91, 92, 93
Stavros, John M.	MSW	1979, 80, 81, 82
Stayton, Chester A.	MBK	1911, 12
Stealy, Jason P.	FB	1997, 98
Stearman, William L.	BB	1947, 48, 49
Stebbins, Robert J.	FB	1948, 49, 50
Stebbins, Robert J.	FB	1987
Stebbins, Sheryl	VB	1969
Stebing, Walter E.	MTR	1938, 40
Steckel, Charles R.	FB	1911
Steckel, Lou Ann	SB	1973, 74
Stedman, Susan	WSW	1971, 72
Steele, Ann	WCC	1981
Steele, Charles A.	FB	1940, 41
Steele, Edwin C.	MCC	1928
Steele, Frank M., Jr.	MTR	1943, 45
Steele, George H.	FB	1904, 05, 06
Steele, Richard M.	MTR	1943
Steele, Robert F.	BB (Mgr.)	1935
Steers, Edwin K.	MSW (Mgr.)	1935
Steeves, Arnold J.	FB	1955, 56, 57
Stefanic, John	MGO	1943
Steffey, Kathy L.	VB	1977
Steffey, Raymond C.	MSW	1941
Stein, Bernard A.	MTN	1961
Stein, John D.	MTR	1994
Stein, Lisa R.	VB	1976, 77
Stein, Raymond I.	MTR	1935, 37
Stein, Yitah H.	FH	1977
Steinback, Michael A.	BB	1974, 75, 76
Steinhagen, William H.	FB (Mgr.)	1935
Stekert, David M.	MSW	1985, 86, 87, 88
Stemen, Mary Ann	WBK	1984, 85
Stenback, Charles R.	MGY	1966
Stenberg, William D.	MBK	1967, 68, 69
Stephens, Herbert C.	BB	1924
Stephens, Jennifer L.	WTN	1990
Stephens, Jerry L.	MSW	1993, 94
Stephens, Joan A.	FH	1969, 70
Stephens, Sol D.	MTR	1995, 96
Stephenson, Diane M.	SB/WTR	1978, 79, 80, 81
Stephenson, Lou A.	VB/WBK	1973, 74, 75, 76
Stephenson, Nancy	WTN	1978, 79, 80, 81
Stephenson, Robert E.	FB	1978, 79, 80, 81
Stephenson, William R.	FB/MTR	1926, 27, 28
Stepler, James E.	MBK	1946
Stepp, Thomas M.	FB (Mgr.)	1977
Steptoe, Robert J.	MTR	1962
Stettner, Meredith L.	WSW	1999
Steube, Michelle M.	WBK	1978
Stevens, Kenneth R.	FB	1924
Stevens, Mark R.	FB	1970
Stevens, Maryanne	WSW	1973, 74
Stevens, Pamela	FH	1972, 73
Stevens, W. Scott	WR	1982, 83, 84
Stevens, William F.	FB	1937, 38
Stevenson, George T.	FB/MTR	1931, 32, 33, 34
Stevenson, Jack K.	MBK	1939
Stevenson, James R.	MTR	1982
Stevenson, Lou Ann	VB/WBK	1973, 74, 75
Stevenson, Robert L.	FB	1937, 38
Stevenson, Robin	WBK	1975, 76
Stevenson, Roderick M.	MGO	1946, 47
Stevenson, Stanley R.	MTR	1934, 36
Steward, Karann	WSW	1970, 72, 73, 74
Stewart, David C.	BB	1881, 82, 83
Stewart, David W.	FB	1977, 78, 79
Stewart, Edward	MTN	1983, 84

Ted Stickles was a world record holder in swimming.

Ken St. Pierre was All-American catcher in 1974.

Stewart, Elmer B.	BB/FB	1884, 85, 86, 87
Stewart, Henry G.	BB	1884
Stewart, J. Derek	MSO	1984
Stewart, Jerome L.	WR	1973, 74
Stewart, William L.	MBK (Mgr.)	1958
Stickann, Frank C.	FB	1932
Stickl, Gary J.	MGO	1978, 79, 80, 81
Stickles, Edward A. "Ted"	MSW	1962, 63, 64
Stiers, John E.	MBK (Mgr.)	1940
Stillabower, Mark W.	MCC/MTR	1978, 79, 80, 81
Stinchfield, Guy F.	FB	1897
Stinnett, William A.	MGO	1967, 68, 69
Stinson, Laurel L.	WGO	1989, 90, 91, 92
Stock, Cameron T.	MSW	1962, 63, 64
Stock, Robert J.	MBK (Mgr.)	1950
Stock, Wade R.	MSW	1980, 81, 82, 83
Stocker, Daniel E.	WR	1944
Stocksdale, Jeffrey D.	MBK	1969, 70, 71
Stoddard, John W.	FB	1902
Stohler, L. Robert	MBK (Mgr.)	1963
Stohr, Stanley E.	WR	1927
Stokes, James E.	BB	1966, 67
Stolberg, Eric C.	FB	1967, 68, 69
Stoll, James P.	BB	1986, 87
Stollmeyer, John M.	MSO	1981, 82, 83, 84, 85
Stoma, Anne M.	FH	1969, 70, 71
Stone, Chris J.	MBK (Mgr.)	1980
Stone, James E.	FB/MTR	1954, 55
Stone, Janice	VB	1969
Stone, William H.	MBK	1902, 03
Stoneman, Randall M.	MCC/MTR	1976, 77, 78, 79, 80
Stoner, Ajamu H.	FB	1994, 95, 96
Stoner, Rebecca	WGY	1973, 74
Stonikas, Robert M.	MGO	1985
Storemont, David L.	WR	1917, 18, 19
Stoshitch, Bozidar	BB	1938, 39, 40
Stotter, Roscoe O.	BB/MBK	1909, 10, 11
Stouffer, Craig A.	MSW	1982, 83, 84
Stout, Correne	WTN	1997, 98
Stout, Cynthia	SB/WBK	1974, 75, 76
Stout, Jeff M.	BB	1985, 86, 87, 88
Stout, Lester L.	MBK	1934, 35, 36
Stout, Michael B.	MCC/MTR	1966, 67, 68
Stout, Sherri L.	VB	1989
Stowell, Cynthia L.	FH/SB/WBK	1969, 70, 71, 72
Stoyanovich, Pete M.	FB/MSO	1985, 86, 87, 88
Strachan, William A.	MCC/MTR	1963, 64
Strack, Joseph P.	MSW	1934, 35, 36
Strakowski, Jeffrey A.	MCC/MTR	1982, 83, 84, 85, 86
Strange, Ernest E.	MBK	1901
Straub, Clarence E., Jr.	MGY	1955, 56
Straub, Steven P.	FB	1978, 79
Straus, Stephen	R	1955
Strause, Sara Jane	WTN	1984
Strayhorn, Jerry L.	MTR	1978, 79, 80
Streaker, Lee H.	BB	1894, 95, 96, 97
Streaker, Lee H.	MBK	1927
Streeter, Larry	FB/MTR	1982, 83, 84, 85
Streib, Erik W.	MSW	1988, 89, 90, 91
Streicher, Abraham B.	MTR	1930, 31, 32
Strickland, James D.	MBK	1928, 29, 30
Strickland, Joseph C.	BB	1885
Strickland, Pamela J.	WGY	1978, 79, 80, 81
Stringer, Jaynee M.	WCC/WTR	1978, 79
Strobel, Donald D.	WR	1982
Stroble, Chris P.	BB	1998
Strome, Robert C.	MTN	1949, 50
Strong, Allen V.	MTR (Mgr.)	1953, 54

Strong, Cynthia S.	WGY	1976
Stroup, Todd A.	BB	1982, 83, 84
Stryker, Brian R.	MSW	1999
Stryzinski, Daniel T.	FB	1985, 86, 87
Stucker, Ricke P.	MCC	1966
Stuckey, Jeffrey D.	MBK (Mgr.)	1986
Stuckey, Jonathan C.	MBK (Mgr.)	1992
Stuckey, Larry D.	MCC/MTR	1959, 60, 61, 62
Stucky, Victoria L.	WGY	1976
Studer, Walter J.	MTN	1935
Stuebe, Michelle M.	WBK	1978
Stultz, Robert D.	MGO	1952
Stumpf, Michael J.	FB	1992, 93, 94
Stumpner, Robert L.	MSW	1945
Sturgeon, Anndi L.	VB	1987
Sturgeon, Sandy	WBK/WTN	1971
Sturges, Duke A.	FB	1990
Sturges, Laura E.	WSO	1998
Sturgis, Jack D.	FB (Mgr.)	1942
Sturtz, Joseph W.	BB	1991, 92, 93
Stutesman, Frank M., Jr.	FB	1915, 16
Stuteville, Jerry A.	MBK	1948, 49, 50
Sudbury, Bedford V.	BB	1886, 87, 88, 89
Suddith, Arnold	MBK	1932
Suever, Nicole M.	WCC/WTR	1992, 93, 94, 95
Sugar, Manuel J.	WR (Mgr.)	1932
Sukurs, Charles P. II	FB	1971, 72, 73
Sulewski, Richard M.	MTR	1988, 89, 90, 91
Sullivan, Corey L.	MGO	1997, 98, 99
Sullivan, Donna	VB	1969
Sullivan, Douglas W.	MTN	1972, 73, 74, 75
Sullivan, Jack K.	MTR	1989, 90, 91, 92
Sullivan, Kamau K.	MTR	1990, 91, 92
Sullivan, Kevin P.	MCC/MTR	1993, 94, 95, 96
Sullivan, Michael B.	MTR	1993, 94, 95, 96
Sullivan, Paul R.	FB (Mgr.)	1956
Sullivan, Robert L.	FB	1994
Sullivan, Trudy L.	WBK	1977
Sullivan, William C.	FB	1966
Summerall, James	FB	1989, 90, 91
Summers, Frank M.	MTR	1915
Summers, Harold H.	BB	1955
Sumpter, Vincent B.	MSW (Mgr.)	1982
Sundheim, George M.	FB	1944
Sungail, John P.	FB	1958
Supernaw, Kywin D.	FB	1996, 97
Surface, Matthew J.	FB	1994, 95, 96
Susic, Phillip A.	BB	1958
Suskiewich, James V.	BB	1968
Susmilch, Mark A.	WR	1975
Sutheimer, Alvin F.	BB	1919
Sutherland, Louis L.	FB	1933
Sutkowski, Alan J.	FB	1995, 96, 97
Sutor, Mark A.	FB	1979, 80, 81, 82
Sutor, Joseph P.	FB	1963, 64, 65
Sutphin, John O.	BB/FB	1907, 08, 09
Sutphin, Winfield A.	BB	1900, 01
Sutlin, Joel M.	MGY	1965, 66, 67
Sutter, Karl V., Jr.	MSW	1962
Sutters, John D.	MTR	1988
Sutton, Harley H.	BB	1874
Sutton, James W.	MBK	1963, 64
Sutton, Jennifer L.	VB	1992, 93, 94, 95
Svyantek, William S.	FB	1951, 52
Sveda, Viktor J.	WR	1999
Swafford, Doug L.	FB	1980, 81, 82
Swain, Charles O.	WR	1924, 25, 28
Swain, James O.	WR	1921
Swain, John M.	MCC	1920
Swain, Sally A.	WGY	1982, 83, 84, 85
Swan, Kenneth	MTR	1992, 93
Swanson, Connie	SB/WBK	1974, 75, 76
Swanson, Irwin E.	MBK	1941, 42, 43
Swartz, Christopher	FB	1989
Swayne, Charles B.	BB	1916, 17
Sweazy, Damon J.	FB	1985, 86
Sweden, Paula H.	WCC	1984
Sweeney, Colleen M.	WSO	1997
Sweeney, James T.	MSW	1988, 89, 90, 91
Sweeney, Joseph M.	FB	1973
Sweet, Mark S.	MSO	1986
Swenson, Charles J.	MBK (Mgr.)	1974, 76
Swift, Richard D.	MTR	1966, 67, 68
Swihart, Edgar D.	FB	1940, 41
Swihart, Fred C.	FB	1928
Swinehart, John F.	FB	1977, 78
Swingley, Roland K.	MBK (Mgr.)	1949
Swiss, Thomas M., Jr.	MSW	1986, 87, 88
Switzer, J. Gannon	MCC/MTR	1991, 92, 93
Swope, Joseph A.	BB/FB	1914, 15, 16

Swygart, Daniel L.	MGY	1975
Sybert, Douglas L.	FB	1976, 77, 78
Sydnor, John R.	FB	1983
Synowiec, Paul A.	MTR	1993
Sypniecski, Edward L.	MCC	1947
Sypniewski, Jeffrey S.	MCC/MTR	1982, 83, 84
Szabo, Joseph	FB	1936, 37
Szymakowski, Stanley M.	FB	1972, 74
Szymczak, Matthew R.	BB	1979, 81, 82

Tabaka, Peter F.	FB	1970
Taber, Earl R.	MBK	1904, 05
Tabereaux, Ryan H.	MSW	1998, 99
Tackett, Richard D.	FB	1942
Tackitt, Sylvan W.	FB (Mgr.)	1930
Taffe, Michael L.	MGY	1970, 71, 72
Takacs, William E.	FB	1956, 57
Talarico, Sam J.	FB	1949, 50, 52
Talbot, Frank M.	BB	1934
Talbot, George W.	MBK (Mgr.)	1926
Talbot, Phillip S.	MGO	1930, 31
Talbot, Robert M.	FB (Mgr.)	1927
Talbott, John E.	FB	1906, 07, 08
Talbott, Tammy L.	VB	1987
Taliaferro, George	FB	1945, 47, 48
Tallen, Terrence P.	FB	1978, 79, 80
Tallon, Harry A.	FB	1956
Tanabe, Richard T.	MSW	1955, 56, 57
Tankersley, Kevin C.	WR	1993
Tankersley, Michael J.	MCC/MTR	1994, 95, 96, 97
Tanner, Dale H.	FB	1937
Tanner, David A.	MSW	1970, 71, 72
Tanner, Leonard E., Jr.	MTR (Mgr.)	1955
Tardy, M. Eugene, Jr.	MTN	1955
Taroli, Kenneth S.	WR	1982, 83, 84
Tate, Joseph P.	FB	1963, 64, 65
Tatum, John R.	WR	1936
Tauber, Justin C.	MSO	1997, 98
Tavener, John H.	FB	1941, 42, 43, 44
Tavenner, Fred W.	MTR	1916
Taylor, Charles F.	MTR	1968, 69, 70
Taylor, Corey A.	FB	1990, 91
Taylor, Geoffrey S.	MTR	1989, 90, 91, 92
Taylor, JaMille C.	VB	1990, 91
Taylor, John H.	FB	1979, 80
Taylor, Karla	FH	1970
Taylor, Michael C.	MSW	1982, 83, 84, 85
Taylor, Rex M.	MBK (Mgr.)	1978
Taylor, Roosevelt, Jr.	BB	1958
Taylor, William B.	MTR	1981, 82, 83, 84
Taylor, William M.	MTR	1950, 51, 52
Taylor, Winslow R.	MTR	1972, 73, 74, 75
Teeters, Donald F.	BB	1919, 20
Tegarden, Scott K.	FB	1969, 70
Teipen, Jonathan D.	MCC/MTR	1996, 97, 98
Telfer, Daphane	WGO	1988
Templeton, Frederick S.	MCC/MTR	1950, 51, 52, 53
Templeton, Philip H.	MTR	1922
Tepley, Thomas J.	MCC/MTR	1975, 76, 77, 78, 79
Terrell, Derrick R.	FB	1992, 93, 94
Terrell, Ronald R.	MGO	1956, 57, 58
Terry, Glenn C.	MTR	1990, 91, 92, 93
Terry, Raymond L.	FB	1964, 65
Teskey, Caroline J.	WSW	1988, 89, 90, 91
Teskey, Luke "Mac"	MSW	1977, 78, 81
Teskey, Mary J.	WGY/WSW	1983, 84, 85, 86
Teter, George E.	FB/MBK/MTR	1899, 1901, 05
Teter, James L.	FB/MTR	1969, 70
Teter, John W.	FB	1899, 1900
Teter, Sanford F.	FB	1892
Tetrick, Jeffrey S.	MCC	1992, 93, 94
Thake, Dale R.	BB	1971, 73, 74, 75
Thaler, Brenda L.	SB	1981, 82, 83, 84
Thaler, Linda A.	SB	1981, 82, 83, 84
Thaxton, Gregory	FB	1967
Thedford, Jaime R.	SB	1996, 98, 99
Theil, John D.	BB	1986, 87, 88, 89
Thies, Susan G.	WCC/WTR	1978, 79, 80
Thistlewaite, John M.	FB	1897
Thomas, Andrea L.	WSW	1985
Thomas, Bill E.	MTR	1992, 93, 94, 95, 96
Thomas, Charles A.	BB/FB	1929, 30, 31
Thomas, Daniel J.	FB	1949, 50, 51

Linda Thaler, 1984 softball All-American.

Donnie Thomas was a two time MVP and third-team 1975 All-American at linebacker.

Thomas, Daryl	MBK	1984, 85, 86, 87
Thomas, David G.	MGO	1980, 81, 82, 83, 84
Thomas, De Lawrence E.	MTR	1996, 97
Thomas, Donnie M.	FB	1973, 74, 75
Thomas, Dorothy	FH	1974, 75
Thomas, Eddie L.	FB	1988, 89, 90, 91
Thomas, Eugene S.	BB/FB/MBK/MTR	1920, 21, 22, 23
Thomas, Isiah L.	MBK	1980, 81
Thomas, James E.	MBK	1980, 81, 82, 83
Thomas, Jeffrey D.	MTR	1978, 79, 80
Thomas, Jonathon R.	MTR	1982, 83, 84, 85
Thomas, Krista	WGY	1973, 74
Thomas, Kristi L.	WTN	1992
Thomas, Mifflin K.	MSW	1938, 39, 40
Thomas, Pat	FH	1971
Thomas, Richard A.	MSW	1975, 76, 77, 78
Thomas, Richard C.	WR	1972, 73
Thomas, Richard J.	MGO	1999
Thomas, Robert S.	R	1954, 55, 56
Thomas, Sara T.	WSW	1997
Thomas, Shane L.	FB	1993
Thomas, Shawn	VB (Mgr.)	1998
Thomas, Susan A.	WCC/WTR	1996, 97, 98
Thomas, Thomas J.	MGO	1962, 64
Thomas, Thomas N.	MGO	1970, 71, 72
Thomas, Tracey	WSO	1993
Thomason, John	FB (Mgr.)	1989
Thompson, A.	BB/FB	1896, 97
Thompson, Andrew R.	WR	1966, 67, 68
Thompson, Angela L.	WBK	1989, 90, 91
Thompson, Anthony Q.	FB	1986, 87, 88, 89
Thompson, Brent A.	MBK (Mgr.)	1992
Thompson, Carol A.	WSW	1978, 79, 80, 81
Thompson, Caroline	WSW	1984
Thompson, Charles B.	WR	1951, 52
Thompson, Daniel P.	FB	1990, 91, 92, 93
Thompson, Donald F.	FB (Mgr.)	1935
Thompson, Earl L.	MTR (Mgr.)	1946, 47
Thompson, Ernie	FB	1989, 90
Thompson, Francis M.	BB/FB	1908, 09
Thompson, Frank	BB/MBK	1908, 09
Thompson, George D.	MCC	1911, 12
Thompson, George I.	MTN	1907
Thompson, George W.	MTR	1905, 06
Thompson, Gregg E.	MSO	1977, 79, 80, 81
Thompson, Jerry L.	MBK	1956, 57, 58
Thompson, Kimberly A.	WBK	1978
Thompson, Paul E.	MSW	1922
Thompson, Ralph F., Jr.	FB	1944
Thompson, Ralph L.	BB	1936, 37
Thompson, Raymond D.	BB/FB	1895, 96
Thompson, Rick L.	FB	1968, 70
Thompson, Robert P.	MTR	1960, 61
Thompson, Shalandra D.	MTR (Mgr.)	1994
Thompson, Suellen	VB	1982, 83
Thompson, Terry L.	WR	1962
Thompson, Theodore H.	MCC/MTR	1933
Thompson, Thomas W.	MGO	1943, 44, 45, 46
Thompson, W. Claude Jr.	MSW	1962, 63
Thomson, Claus B.	MSW	1980
Thomson, Malcolm E.	MSW	1924, 25
Thomson, William C.	FB	1969, 70
Thorn, Peter D.	FB	1968
Thornberry, Darlyn	SB	1973, 74
Thorne, Donald S.	MTN	1960, 61
Thorne, Kimberly B.	FH	1980, 81
Thornton, Jeffrey D.	FB	1988
Thornton, Kristen M.	WSO	1993

Gina Ugo was third team All-America pitcher in 1996 and a two-time All-Big Ten pick.

Amy Unterbrink, a 1986 All-American, pitched seven no-hit games.

Thornton, Ross O.	BB	1901, 02, 03, 04
Thrapp, Gary	MTR	1970
Thrasher, Phillip H.	WR	1951
Thrush, Danielle M.	WBK	1996, 97, 98, 99
Thurman, Alphonso II	FB	1991, 92, 93, 94
Thurman, Jill M.	WSO	1993
Tidwell, Donald W.	MTR	1994, 96, 97
Tieman, Edward H.	MTN	1935, 36, 37
Tieman, Jamie	WSW	1975, 76
Tiernan, Richard J.	FB	1932
Tiernan, William J.	BB	1953
Tighe, Charles P.	FB	1905, 06, 07
Tillery, Robert J.	FB	1979
Tillery, Steve A.	FB	1980
Tillman, Roger L.	R	1957, 59
Tilton, William F.	WR	1969
Timbrook, Henry, Jr.	MGO	1940, 42
Timmons, Dale L.	WR	1964, 65
Tipmore, Floyd L. "Bill"	FB	1938, 39, 40
Tippman, Kurt	FB (Mgr.)	1993
Tipton, Dawna C.	VB	1974
Tipton, George W.	MBK/MTR	1943, 44
Tirey, Ralph N.	BB	1903
Tisdale, Brent A.	FB	1977, 78, 79, 80
Tobias, George E.	MTR	1934
Tobin, Paul E.	BB/FB	1925, 26, 27
Todd, Robert L.	FB/MTR	1927, 28, 29, 30
Toensing, Craig E.	MTR	1957, 58, 59
Toensing, Trent D.	MSW	1959, 60
Tofil, Gary J.	FB	1963, 64, 65
Tofil, Joseph J.	FB	1938, 39, 40
Tolbert, Lester C.	MCC	1942
Tolbert, Ray L.	MBK	1978, 79, 80, 81
Tolliver, Wayne E.	MCC/MTR	1939, 40, 41
Tolton, Becky	SB	1973, 74
Tomaselli, Joe W., Jr.	MGO	1991, 92, 93, 94
Tomczak, Edmund A.	MTN	1948, 49
Toole, Katherine D.	WP	1998
Topolgus, James N.	MGO	1964
Toran, Derrick L.	FB	1983
Torok, Frank J.	FB	1943
Torphy, William L.	MBK	1940, 41, 42
Torres, James Jr.	WR	1997, 98
Torres, Jason M.	BB	1996, 97, 98, 99
Torrijas, Brian R.	BB	1980
Tosheff, William	BB/MBK	1949, 50, 51
Tosswill, Susan	FH	1972, 73
Toth, Mark E.	MGO	1967
Toth, Melody E.	FH/SB	1970, 71, 72, 73
Toth, Nancy	VB	1972, 73
Townsend, Oliver K.	MSW	1963, 64, 65
Toy, James I., Jr.	BB (Mgr.)	1948
Toyama, Wendy J.	WGY	1980, 81, 82, 83
Tracy, Elizabeth A.	WGO	1972, 73, 74, 75
Trager, Brad	MSW	1987, 88
Traicoff, Christopher	WR	1937, 38, 39
Trainer, Tomas F.	FB	1960, 61
Trant, Brian	BB	1985
Trask, John T.	MSO	1984, 85, 86, 87
Traster, Fern L.	WR	1949
Traster, Harry B.	WR	1941, 42, 43
Treadway, Robert L.	FB	1896
Tremblay, Yves C.	MGO	1977, 79, 80, 81
Tremewan, Cary P.	MSW	1962, 63, 64
Tremor, Victor F.	WR	1917, 20
Trent, Joseph K.	MSW	1998, 99

Trent, Tia T.	WTR	1999
Trent, Thomas B.	MSW	1995, 96, 97, 98
Trethewey, Thomas G.	MSW	1964, 65, 66
Trevino, Andy D.	WR	1993, 94, 95, 96
Trigg, Robert M.	MSO	1987
Trimble, George	FB/MBK	1908, 09
Trimble, James W.	FB/WR	1939, 40, 41
Trimborn, Marcia	WSW	1975, 76
Trimpe, Barbara	SB	1972
Trinter, Philip D.	FB	1988, 89, 90, 91
Tripp, Delbert H.	FB	1923
Tripp, Ernest H.	BB	1874
Trobaugh, Raymond J.	FB	1927, 28
Troesch, Amy L.	WSW	1994, 95, 96, 97
Trombetta, Alexander D.	FB	1961
Troop, Laura M.	SB	1990
Trout, Anthony J.	BB	1980, 81
Trout, Arthur L.	FB	1911, 12, 13
Trowbridge, Kenneth L.	MGO	1970, 71
Troy, Dennis A.	MGO	1966
Troy, Douglas P.	MTN	1986
Troy, Michael F.	MSW	1960, 61, 62
Truax, William J.	MTR	1966
Trudell, Lindsay J.	VB	1995
True, Jeff F.	MTN	1977, 79, 80, 81
Truex, Kenneth P.	MTR	1930
Truex, Wayne O.	MGY	1952, 53, 54
Trummer, Arnold J.	MGY	1942, 43
Trust, Stephen C.	MBK (Mgr.)	1989
Trutt, Melverne I.	MCC/MTR	1936, 37, 38, 39
Trzaskowski, Larry M.	BB	1970
Tsandes, Ted R.	MSO	1988
Tsoukatos, Pantelis G.	MSW	1999
Tucker, Maurice D.	FB	1998
Tucker, Michael W.	BB	1966
Turak, Jeffrey A.	BB	1984
Turchyn, Leo R.	MCC/MTR	1977, 78, 79
Turley, Ann	WTN	1970
Turley, Ira S.	FB	1911
Turner, Alan M.	MTR	1989, 90, 91, 92
Turner, Ann V.	WSW	1970
Turner, Constance	WSW	1975, 76
Turner, Deborah L.	WSW	1970
Turner, Howard K.	FB	1916
Turner, Joey J.	FB	1984
Turner, John D.	MGY	1974, 75, 76, 77
Turner, Landon M.	MBK	1979, 80, 81
Turner, LaToya M.	WTR	1997, 98, 99
Turner, Rob	MBK	1998, 99
Turner, Robert D.	FB	1987, 88, 90
Turner, Shawna Y.	WTR	1988, 89
Turner, Steven B.	MTR	1981, 82, 83, 84
Turpen, Larry W.	MBK	1965, 66, 67
Tuthill, John B.	MTN	1937, 38
Tutsie, Albert P.	FB	1949, 50
Tuttle, Annette M.	SB	1989, 90, 91, 92, 93
Tuttle, Carl R.	R	1958, 60
Tuttle, Jay L.	FB	1989
Tuttle, Steven C.	FB	1972
Twineham, Arthur P.	BB	1866, 67
Tye, Judy	FH	1970
Tyler, Frederick D.	MSW	1973, 74, 75, 76

Udvardi, William F.	MGY	1951, 52
Uebele, Susan	WGO	1987
Uecker, William F.	FB	1944
Ugo, Gina J.	SB	1993, 94, 95, 96
Uhl, Melanie J.	WTR	1987, 88, 89, 90
Uhrin, Joan	WBK	1978
Ulen, Earl C., Jr.	FB (Mgr.)	1940
Umbarger, Charles E.	MCC/MTR	1961, 62
Umphrey, Lawrence L.	MTN	1932
Underwood, John R.	MGY	1978, 79, 80
Underwood, Paul E.	BB	1953
Unger, Fred W.	FB	1958
Unger, Jacob W.	FB/WR	1928, 29, 30
Unnewehr, Charles A.	MBK	1901, 02
Unsworth, Valerie M.	WSW	1984, 85
Unterbrink, Amy	SB	1983, 84, 85, 86
Unthank, Katherine W.	WBK	1972, 73, 74, 75
Upshaw, Curtis W.	MTR	1986, 87
Urdal, Robert M.	R	1956, 57, 58

Uremovich, Emil	FB/MTR	1938, 39, 40
Urzua, Emma A.	WBK	1993, 94, 95
Usrey, David F.	MSW	1967, 68
Utley, William A.	MSW	1966, 67, 68
Utroske, Theresa J.	WCC/WTR	1982, 83, 84
Utter, Clifton C.	BB/FB	1891, 92, 93, 94

Vajgrt, Mary E.	WGO	1993, 94, 95, 96, 97
Valavicius, Richard J.	MBK	1976, 77
Valderrama, Paige	WTR	1986, 87, 88, 89
Valencia, Katrina M.	SB	1995, 96, 97, 98
Valentine, Nicole A.	VB	1991
Valerio, Victoria A.	FH	1974, 75
Valiska, Tami L.	WGY	1977, 78
Valle, Miguel A.	MTR	1973, 74
Vallejo, Juan Carlos	MSW	1985, 86, 87, 88
VanArsdale, Richard A.	MBK	1963, 64, 65
VanArsdale, Thomas A.	MBK	1963, 64, 65
VanBoven, Andrea D.	FH	1976
VanBuskirk, John M.	MSO	1990, 91, 92, 93, 94
Vandenbark, James A.	MTR	1963
Vanderoef, Craig D.	MCC	1993
Vandersluis, David K.	MSW	1984
VanDerveer, Tara A.	WBK	1973, 74, 75
VanDorn, Paul R.	MSW	1963
VanDuren, Allen	MSW	1941, 42
VanDyck, Thomas A.	FB	1981, 82, 83, 84
Vaneck, Leonard F.	MCC/MTR	1952, 53, 54, 55
VanHook, James K.	MTR (Mgr.)	1928
VanHorn, Wilber H., Jr.	MGO	1940, 41
Vann, Ina	WTR	1981
VanOoyen, Jerry L.	FB	1949, 50, 51
VanPelt, Robert C.	FB	1964, 65, 66
VanSchoyck, Amy K.	VB	1990, 91
VanSlyke, James J.	FB	1986
VanTrees, Harry W.	WR	1984, 85
VanVleet, Robert L.	WR	1978, 79
VanVliet, Robert D.	FB	1985, 86
VanVooren, Jason L.	MCC	1991
VanWinkle, Gregory B.	MCC/MTR	1979, 80, 81, 82
Vargo, Ronald V.	FB	1986, 87, 88, 89
Veale, Marcia A.	FH	1974, 75, 77
Vecchio, Robert F.	FB	1960, 61
Veit, Dorothy	WCC/WTR	1978, 79, 81
Veldman, Thomas F.	MSO	1972
Veller, Claron W. "Lefty"	BB/MBK	1929, 30, 31
Veller, Don A.	FB	1932, 33, 34
Venturella, Michelle	SB	1992, 93, 94, 95
Verbarg, Holly C.	WTR	1996, 97
Vercuski, Bruno V.	FB	1932, 33, 34
Verhoeven, Gary A.	MSW	1963, 64, 65
Verlihay, F. Ted	FB	1967
Verost, Adam W.	MCC	1994
Verth, Thomas W.	MSW	1960, 61, 62
Vesel, James A.	FB	1952, 53
Vesel, Tatjana	WBK	1994, 95, 96, 97
Vich, Edgardo	MGY	1982
Vieau, Dale J.	MBK	1951, 52
Viehofer, Kerstin	WTR	1997
Vieira, Kim T.	MSO	1972, 73
Vine, Douglas P.	MTR	1971, 72, 73, 75
Visher, John E.	MSW	1939
Visnich, Michael R.	FB	1971, 72, 73
Visscher, Daniel W.	MCC/MTR	1974, 75, 76, 77, 78
Vitou, James E.	MGO	1959, 61
Vittoz, Robert L.	BB	1941, 42
Vlassis, George P.	MBK (Mgr.)	1952
Voelker, Rebecca L.	WSO (Mgr.)	1994, 95, 96
Vogel, Ernest H.	MSW	1943
Vogel, Herbert L.	MGY	1951, 52, 53
Vogel, Jaime L.	SB	1990
Vohs, Margaret F.	WBK	1978
Voigt, Erick C.	BB	1979
Voisard, Andrew P.	MTN	1950
Vojtech, George A.	BB	1926
Voliva, Richard L.	FB/WR	1932, 33, 34
Volk, Myron	MSW	1945
Volz, David A.	MTR	1981, 82, 83, 84
Vonderheide, Dean M.	FB	1972, 74
VonTress, Edward C.	FB/MBK	1921
Voorhis, William A.	FB	1964
Vordermark, Don F.	MSW	1928, 29
Voss, C.F. Walter	FB/MTR	1914, 15

Vozel, Richard G.	BB	1989, 90, 91, 92
Vranek, Greg C.	MGY	1973, 74
Vrydaghs, Joseph M.	MTR	1990
Vuskalns, Victor V.	MCC/MTR	1985, 86, 87, 88

Wachowiak, Barbara D.	FH/WTR	1981, 82
Waddell, Ermel W.	WR	1953
Waddell, Mary Jo	VB	1985, 86
Waddell, Michael J.	FB	1991
Wade, Allison M.	WSO	1994, 95
Wade, Franklin C.	FB	1903, 05, 06
Wade, Jack L.	WR	1999
Wade, Jeffrey F.	FB	1983, 84, 85, 86
Wade, John B.	FB	1943
Wade, Mark R.	MTR	1970, 71
Wade, Richard T.	BB	1942
Waggoner, Darrell E.	MGY	1951
Wagner, Christina E.	WCC/WTR	1978, 79, 80, 81
Wagner, John A.	MSW	1963, 64, 65
Wagner, Ralph J.	FB	1946, 47
Wagner, Steven R.	MGY	1979, 80
Wagner, Susan	WGO	1970, 71
Wagner, Susan U.	FH	1976, 78, 79
Wagnon, Lloyd L.	FB/WR	1948, 49
Wahl, Christine R.	WTR	1993, 94
Wahl, Erwin H.	MSW	1946
Wahl, Henry E., Jr.	BB	1934, 35, 36
Wahl, Kermit E.	BB	1942, 44
Wainman, Jonathan N.	MSW	1999
Waite, Alphonse A.	MTR	1932
Waite, Nancy	WSW	1982
Waite, Robert A.	BB	1981, 82
Waiters, Van A.	FB	1983, 85, 86, 87
Wakefield, Markham C.	BB/MBK	1919, 20
Wakefield, Patricia A.	SB/WBK	1972, 73, 74
Walden, Rodney F.	FB	1979, 80, 81
Walden, Ronald L.	MGY	1957, 58, 59
Waldman, John B.	MSW	1983, 84, 85
Waldo, Ralph E.	MSW (Mgr.)	1964
Waldschmidt, James M.	MSO	1973, 74
Walker, Andra B.	VB	1986
Walker, David C.	MBK	1946, 47
Walker, Harrison A.	FB	1912, 13
Walker, James B.	BB	1920, 21, 22
Walker, James M.	MTR	1962, 63, 64
Walker, James R.	MGO	1950
Walker, James S.	MSW	1962, 63
Walker, John S.	MSW	1961, 62, 63
Walker, Joseph A.	WSW (Mgr.)	1998, 99
Walker, Lewis W.	FB/MBK	1933, 34, 35, 36
Walker, Max W.	MBK	1964, 65, 66
Walker, Melinda K.	WTR	1989
Walker, Paul K.	FB	1942
Walker, Paul R.	MTR	1975
Walker, Steve G.	MTN	1982, 83, 84
Walker, Todd A.	FB	1987, 89, 90, 91
Walker, Tracy	VB/WSW	1972, 73
Walker, W. Timothy	MBK (Mgr.)	1976
Wall, Cassidy R.	WCC/WTR	1996, 97, 98
Wall, Merl M.	WR	1915
Wallace, Byron F.	MCC/MTR	1924, 25
Wallace, J. Lucky	FB	1978, 79, 80
Wallace, John A.	BB/MBK	1946, 47
Wallace, Leon H.	WR (Mgr.)	1926
Wallace, Mark B.	MSW (Mgr.)	1969
Wallace, Marvin V.	MTR	1903, 04, 06
Wallace, Megan D.	WSO	1997, 98
Wallace, Robert C.	MGO	1946
Wallace, Russell S.	FB/MCC/MTR	1913, 14, 15, 16
Wallace, Sharrod J.	FB	1998
Wallace, William P.	MTR	1915
Wallace, William R.	MTR	1972, 73, 74, 75
Wallenstein, Karin A.	VB	1980, 81
Wallihan, Rebecca G.	WTN	1997, 98, 99
Walling, Kenneth V.	MSW	1922, 23
Walls, Craig S.	FB	1979, 80, 81
Walsh, John B.	FB	1981, 82, 83, 84
Walsh, Patrick W.	BB	1985, 86
Walsh, Thomas W.	MTR	1933
Walsh, Tim K.	MSO	1977, 78, 79, 80
Walsh, William J.	MCC/MTR	1943, 44, 46
Walsworth, Timothy V.	WR	1983, 84, 85, 86, 87
Walters, Timothy P.	MSO	1975, 76, 77, 78

Name	Sport	Years		Name	Sport	Years
Walters, Trent	FB	1963, 64, 65		Weir, Woodrow R.	MBK	1932, 33, 34
Walther, Joseph E.	MTR	1933		Weishar, Marcia A.	WSW	1977, 78, 79, 80
Walther, Stacey M.	WTR	1994, 95, 96, 97		Weiss, Brad A.	MSO	1992
Walton, Ardith	WBK	1972		Weiss, Brian D.	MSW	1986, 87, 88, 89
Walton, Constance S.	FH	1979, 80, 81		Weiss, Catherine E.	WGY /WSW	1979, 80
Walton, David T.	MCC/MTR	1982, 83, 84		Weiss, Harry M.	MSO	1992, 93, 94, 95
Walton, Jeffrey A.	MGO	1986		Weiss, Seymour	WR	1938, 40
Walton, Lee	WSW	1971		Weiss, Sidney	FB	1937
Waltz, Richard B.	FB	1968		Weiss, Steven J.	MCC/MTR	1971, 73
Wampler, Orbin M.	WR	1927		Weisser, Steven J.	MSW	1976, 77
Wanezek, Thomas P.	MSW	1996, 97, 98, 99		Weissert, Stephen J.	FB	1976, 78, 79
Warburton, Thomas K.	MSW	1969, 70		Weitzel, B.	FH	1969
Ward, Brandon R.	MSO	1991, 92, 93, 94		Welch, David R.	WR	1975, 76, 77, 78
Ward, Darin A.	FB	1993, 95, 96		Weldon, Carol J.	WGY	1976, 77, 78
Ward, Donald M.	MTR	1955, 56		Weldy, John D.	MTR	1969
Ward, Douglas A.	MGY/MSW	1970, 72		Welklin, David J.	MSW	1985
Ward, Michael J.	BB	1968, 69, 70		Wellman, Guy L.	BB	1941, 42, 43
Ward, Thomas B.	FB (Mgr.)	1989		Wellman, Jack	MCC/MTR	1951, 52, 53, 54
Wardlow, Harry J.	FB	1990, 91		Wellman, Karen	WSW	1981
Ware, B. Jermaine	FB	1994, 95, 96		Wellman, Michael S.	MCC/MTR	1978, 79, 80, 81
Ware, Steven B.	MSW	1968, 69, 70		Wellman, Willard F.	BB	1948
Warm, Edward M.	FB (Mgr.)	1986		Wells, Clark P.	MGY	1965, 66, 67
Warman, Chester M.	MTR	1937		Wells, Elmo D.	BB/MBK	1927, 28, 29
Warnecke, Aaron D.	FB	1994, 95, 96, 97		Wells, Garrett A.	MTR	1957, 58
Warner, Donald A.	FB	1967, 68, 69		Wells, George W.	MCC	1967, 68
Warner, Sarah J.	WBK	1995, 96, 97, 98		Wells, Paulette	FH/SB	1972, 73, 74
Warren, Christopher A.	MGY	1979		Wells, Timothy C.	FB (Mgr.)	1976
Warren, Rustey	WSW	1971		Welte, James R.	MCC/MTR	1979, 80, 81, 82
Warren, Truman G.	MBK (Mgr.)	1929		Welter, Amanda M.	VB	1997, 98
Warrick, Homer L.	MCC/MTR	1923, 24		Welton, Kevin D.	MSW	1979, 80, 81, 82
Warrick, Jeffrey A.	MSW	1991, 92, 93, 94		Wells, Melanie D.	WTR	1996
Warrick, John L.	MCC/MTR	1920, 21, 22, 23		Wendel, Mark A.	BB	1996
Warriner, Thomas E.	FB	1969		Weninger, Michael P.	FB	1976
Warthan, Jennifer F.	WCC/WTR	1992, 93, 94		Wenstrom, Fred G.	TN	1961
Wasdovich, Michael A.	FB	1960, 61, 62		Wenzel, Jim L.	FB	1973, 74
Washburn, Regina M.	WCC/WTR	1979, 80, 81		Werd, Norman F.	BB	1972, 73
Washington, Gary N.	MCC/MTR	1974, 75, 76		Wermuth, Mary Ellen	WCC/WTR	1984, 85, 86
Washington, Isaac I.	FB	1985, 86, 87		Wernet, John J.	MSW (Mgr.)	1972
Washington, Lynn A.	MBK	1999		Werskey, James R.	FB	1974, 76
Wason, Robert P.	MGY	1961, 62		Wertschnig, Charles J.	WR	1967, 68, 69
Watanabe, Shelley T.	WCC	1979		Wervey, Richard D.	FB	1962
Waterbury, James L.	MSW	1982, 83, 84, 85		Wessel, Jennifer M.	WSO	1993, 94
Watercutter, David A.	FB	1986		Wesselhoff, Matthew B.	MTR	1985
Waterhouse, Harold A.	FB	1974, 75, 76		Wesselman, Robyn A.	SB/VB	1976, 77, 78
Waterhouse, Kenneth G.	MCC/MTR	1982, 83, 84		Westbrook, Steven P.	MSO	1976, 77, 78, 79
Watkins, Marvin J.	BB	1942		Westenfelder, Louis L.	MGY	1981
Watson, Fred	MTR	1952, 53, 54		Westfall, Phillip K.	FB	1962, 63
Watson, J. Clifford	MCC/MTR	1930, 31, 32, 33		Westover, Kevin T.	FB	1974, 76
Watson, Louis C.	BB/MBK	1947, 48, 49, 50		Wetzel, Walter J.	BB (Mgr.)	1923
Watson, Mary Ann	WTR	1980, 81, 82, 83		Weybright, Teague T.	BB	1991
Watson, Sunday L.	WBK	1997		Wham, Robert B.	MTN	1963, 64, 65
Watson, Theresa A.	SB	1971, 72		Wham, William F.	MTN	1963, 64, 65
Watterson, Brad S.	MSW	1993, 94, 95, 96		Whatmore, Douglas E.	BB	1988, 89, 90, 91
Watts, Carrie L.	WSO	1996, 97, 98		Wheatcroft, Steven J.	MGO	1998, 99
Watts, Damon S.	FB	1990, 91, 92, 93		Wheeler, Jeffrey B.	MCC/MTR	1985, 86, 87, 90
Watts, Jennifer L.	WSW	1998, 99		Wheeler, Rena S.	SB	1991
Watts, J. Michael	FB	1974		Whipple, Lloyd G.	BB	1940
Watts, Susan A.	WBK	1981, 82, 83, 84		Whitaker, Berry M.	FB/MTR	1911, 12, 13
Watts, William P.	MGY	1973, 74, 75, 76		Whitaker, Frank B.	BB/FB/MBK	1913, 14, 15, 16
Waugh, Lloyd A.	FB	1904, 05, 06		Whitaker, Kimberly	WSW	1975, 76, 78
Way, Barry B.	FB	1986, 88		Whitaker, Lynne E.	WCC/WTR	1981, 82, 83
Waymire, Elbert S.	FB	1907		Whitcomb, Kyle	WSW	1979
Wear, George H.	MTR	1916		White, Albert S.	MCC/MTR	1925, 26
Weaver, Carol	WBK	1973, 74		White, Arthur P.	MGO	1961, 62, 63
Weaver, Karen B.	WGY	1977, 78, 79		White, Bradley	BB	1985, 86, 87
Weaver, Ralph W.	FB/WR	1926, 27, 28, 29		White, Cornelius "Bootsie"	MBK	1971, 72
Weaver, Thomas R.	BB (Mgr.)	1960		White, David L.	MTR	1950, 51, 52
Webb, Kenneth M.	MSW	1966, 67		White, Eugene "Gene"	FB	1939, 40, 41
Webb, Ronald J.	MTR (Mgr.)	1959		White, E.G.	FB	1967, 69, 70
Weber, Albert J.	BB	1950, 51, 52		White, James M.	MCC/MTR	1985, 86, 87, 88, 89, 90
Weber, Daniel S.	WR	1998		White, John H.	MBK	1989
Weber, Jennifer M.	WTR	1990, 91		White, Nicholas	MSW	1952, 53
Weber, JoAnn	WSW	1974, 75		White, Richard E.	MBK/MGO	1952, 53, 54, 55
Weber, Joel J.	WR (Mgr.)	1936		White, Robert B.	MSW	1945, 47, 48, 49
Weber, Kevin F.	WR	1980, 81, 82, 83, 84		White, Robert H.	MTR	1966, 67, 68
Weber, Robert R.	MTN	1941, 42		White, Robert J.	BB/FB	1940, 41, 42, 43
Webster, Kimberly E.	WTN	1993, 94		White, Robert L.	FB	1968, 69
Wechsler, Karen M.	WTR	1979, 80, 81		White, Sean T.	FB	1990
Weddle, Randall J.	MTR	1964, 65, 66		White, Whitney E.	WSO	1993, 94
Weeks, W. William	FB	1973, 74		Whitehead, Edward E.	BB	1956, 58
Wehner, John P.	BB	1987, 88		Whitely, John H.	BB	1897, 98, 99
Weidenbenner, Thomas A.	FB	1983, 84, 85, 86		Whiteman, Roy S.	MCC/MTR	1950, 51, 52
Weiland, Paul H.	FB	1914, 15, 16		Whitis, Anita	VB	1974
Weiler, Mark P.	FB	1981, 82, 83, 84		Whitman, Cindy J.	WGY	1978
Weinberg, James J.	FB	1982		Whitman, Garrett	MGO	1954
Weiner, Becky	WSW	1970		Whitman, Susan B.	WTN	1974, 75, 76
Weiner, Scott D.	BB	1976, 77, 78		Whitmore, David C.	MSW	1980, 81, 82, 83
Weinhoeft, Peggy D.	WCC/WTR	1983, 84, 85		Whitney, Claude B.	MBK	1910, 11
Weir, Allan G.	MCC	1933, 34, 35		Whitney, Jason R.	MTR	1993, 94
Weir, David M.	FB	1979, 80, 81		Whitsell, David A.	FB	1956, 57

Whitson, David B.	MGO	1995		Williamson, Robert E.	MSW	1964, 65, 66
Whittington, Bernard	FB	1990, 91, 92, 93		Williamson, Robert L.	MTR	1952, 53, 54
Wible, Everest E.	MTR	1941		Willis, Kemya R.	WBK	1983, 84, 85, 86
Wible, Ralph W.	FB (Mgr.)	1957		Willis, Kendal J.	WSO/WTR	1997, 98, 99
Wicht, Rosalie-Anne	WSW	1984, 85, 86		Willis, Randle C.	MSW	1924
Wichterman, Walter V.	BB	1923, 24		Wills, Gretchen M.	WSW	1992, 93
Wicker, Roger A.	MSO	1977, 78, 79, 80		Willson, John P.	WR	1970, 71, 72
Wicks, John S.	MTR	1913, 14		Willson, Romney L.	BB	1896, 97, 98, 99
Wickstrand, Katherine J.	WSW	1977, 79, 80		Wilmot, Trevor R.	FB	1993, 94
Wicoff, Erika C.	WGO	1993, 94, 95, 96		Wilsey, Robert E.	BB/FB	1886, 87, 88
Widaman, John D.	FB	1937, 38		Wilshere, Seward E.	BB	1939
Widney, Otto L.	BB	1896		Wilshere, Vernon "Whitey"	BB	1933, 34
Wiebell, Jeffrey A.	FB	1979, 80, 81, 82		Wilson, Albert J.	MTR	1953, 54
Wiechers, Sarah J.	WP	1998		Wilson, Ayanna T.	WBK	1994
Wiedman, Timothy D.	MCC	1965		Wilson, Ben, Jr.	WR	1940, 41
Wiegand, Dana S.	WSW	1984, 85		Wilson, Brittany D.	WSW	1995, 97
Wiegand, Mary	SB	1973, 74		Wilson, Cal J.	FB	1965, 66, 67
Wieneke, Kyle C.	MGO	1991, 92, 93, 94		Wilson, Christopher S.	BB	1997, 98, 99
Wiersman, Debbie	VB	1971		Wilson, David D.	BB/MCC	1958, 59
Wiese, George T.	MTN	1990, 91, 92, 93		Wilson, David L.	BB	1972, 73, 74, 75
Wiese, Julie L.	FH	1980		Wilson, Donald B.	MTR	1928
Wietecha, Edwin J.	FB	1954, 55, 56		Wilson, Edwin A.	MSW	1966
Wilbur, Gary	BB	1963		Wilson, Franklin D.	MBK	1971, 72, 73
Wilbur, Timothy L.	FB	1978, 79, 80, 82		Wilson, Heidi	WSW	1988, 89
Wilcott, Elizabeth M.	WBK	1979		Wilson, Hugh E., III	WR	1945
Wilcox, Michael L.	FB	1989		Wilson, John W.	WR	1944, 45
Wilcox, Toby L.	MSO	1990		Wilson, Kelly A.	WSO	1994, 95, 96, 97
Wilcoxson, Scott A.	MTR	1988, 90, 91, 92		Wilson, L. Webster	WR	1986
Wilder, Clem	FB/WR	1913, 14		Wilson, Murlyn E.	MCC	1940
Wilder, Richard R.	WR	1951, 52		Wilson, Ralph	WR	1924, 26, 27
Wildermuth, Michael F.	WR	1976		Wilson, Robert E.	MGO	1943
Wiley, Anthony D.	FB	1994		Wilson, Robert E.	WR	1915
Wiley, Chester E.	FB/WR	1916, 17, 19, 20		Wilson, Robert W.	BB	1887
Wiley, Daniel L.	WR	1974, 75		Wilson, Ronald R.	MGY	1979, 80, 81, 82
Wiley, Everett	MTR	1902		Wilson, Roy S.	MTR	1924, 26
Wilfong, Jennifer K.	WBK	1983, 84, 85, 86		Wilson, Sarah C.	WCC/WTR	1995, 96
Wilhelm, Gregory R.	MGO	1987		Wilson, Sylvester E.	MTR	1974, 75, 76
Wilhelm, Helena E.	WSW	1999		Wilson, Theron C.	BB	1934, 36
Wilhoit, Ernie L.	BB/MBK	1960, 61, 62		Wilson, Thomas W.	BB	1882, 83, 84
Wilke, Ruth A.	WGY	1978		Wilson, William B.	FB	1974, 75, 76, 77
Wilke, Steve M.	MSO	1975, 76		Wilt, Frederick L.	MCC/MTR	1941
Wilkens, Elmer S.	FB	1921, 22, 23		Wimmer, Greta	FH	1980, 81
Wilkerson, Dorian V.	FB	1994, 95, 96		Winchell, Robert C.	MTR	1969, 70, 71
Wilkerson, Robert L.	MBK	1974, 75, 76		Winchester, Teresa J.	SB/WBK	1973, 74, 75, 76
Wilkerson, Sherron E.	MBK	1994		Windle, Robert G.	MSW	1966, 67, 68
Wilkins, Stanley F.	MTR	1949, 51		Windsor, John R.	MSW	1938
Wilkinson, James J.	WR	1943, 47		Winekoff, Carl K.	WR	1980, 81
Wilkinson, Mary	VB	1971		Wines, Ronald L.	MGY	1961, 62
Wilkinson, Robert E.	MBK/MGO	1958, 60		Wininger, Henry T.	MCC	1953, 54
Wille, Naverne	MCC/MTR	1957, 58		Winstandley, John B.	BB	1889
Willerer, Thomas J.	BB	1997, 98, 99		Winslow, Michael T.	FB	1973, 74
Willetts, William B.	WR	1970, 71, 72, 73		Winston, John M.	FB/MBK	1925, 26, 27
Willhite, James R.	FB/MTR	1977, 78, 79, 80		Winston, Kenneth A.	BB	1968, 69
Williams, Aaron C.	FB	1996, 97, 98		Winston, Kevin C.	FB	1987
Williams, Allan D.	BB	1945		Winston, Robert A.	MSW	1927, 28, 29
Williams, Berry	MTR	1957, 58, 59		Winston, Sam L.	FB	1948, 49, 50
Williams, Carolyn	WSW	1971		Winter, Olice	BB/FB	1908, 09, 10, 11
Williams, Clay A.	FB	1992, 93, 94, 95		Winters, Brad M.	MBK (Mgr.)	1974, 75
Williams, Clyde H.	FB	1931		Winters, Daniel B.	BB	1982, 83, 84
Williams, Craig A.	BB	1987, 88, 89, 90		Winters, Matthew	BB/FB	1912, 14, 15
Williams, Dale M.	WR (Mgr.)	1933		Wise, Byron E.	MTR	1937
Williams, G.H.	MTR	1917		Wise, Clayton R.	MTR	1903, 04
Williams, Heber D.	MBK/MTR	1917, 19, 20		Wise, Harry E.	BB/FB	1885, 86
Williams, James D.	R	1960, 61		Wise, Harry O.	BB/FB	1886, 91
Williams, Jason M.	BB	1998, 99		Wise, Hillary E.	VB	1997
Williams, Jerry J.	MGO	1961		Wise, Walter A.	WR	1922
Williams, Joyce A.	WGY	1976, 77		Wise, William	FB	1913
Williams, Kenyetta D.	FB	1993		Wise, William H.	BB	1978
Williams, Levron L.	FB	1998		Wiseman, Gerald W.	FB	1970
Williams, Marla	SB	1971, 72		Wiser, Melvin D.	MGY	1967, 68, 69
Williams, Mary L.	WSW	1977, 78		Wishart, Wendy R.	WSW	1985
Williams, Paul B.	FB	1989, 90, 91		Wisman, James A.	MBK	1975, 76, 77, 78
Williams, Paul J.	MGO	1963, 64, 65		Wisuri, William P.	BB	1979, 81
Williams, Ralph J.	WR	1914, 15		Witmer, Robert L.	MGY	1967, 68, 69
Williams, Randolph, Jr.	FB	1958, 60		Witmer, Wayne L.	BB	1964, 65, 66
Williams, Raquel S.	WSW	1986, 87		Witte, James C.	MBK	1984, 85, 86
Williams, Richard K.	MGO	1955		Witte, Norbert W.	MBK	1959, 60
Williams, Ronald L.	WR	1994		Witteman, Carole L.	WTN	1992, 93
Williams, Russell S.	FB	1919, 21		Wittenbraker, Richard W.	MBK	1942, 43, 46
Williams, Scott T.	MCC/MTR	1985, 86, 87, 88, 89, 90		Wittman, Randy S.	MBK	1979, 80, 81, 82, 83
Williams, Sharmesa K.	WTR	1989, 90		Witucki, Casimir L. "Slug"	FB	1946, 47, 48, 49
Williams, Sydney J.	MCC	1944		Woehr, Robert A.	BB	1938
Williams, Tamara A.	FH	1972, 73, 74, 75		Woessner, Susan S.	WSW	1999
Williams, Travis B.	FB	1913, 14, 15		Wolf, Diane K.	WSW	1977, 78
Williams, Ward M.	BB/MBK	1943, 47, 48		Wolf, Fred R.	MTN	1941, 42
Williamson, Charles F.	BB	1906, 07		Wolf, Martha A.	FH	1972, 73, 74
Williamson, Clifford "Corky"	MBK	1955, 56		Wolfe, Martin L.	BB	1989, 90, 91, 92
Williamson, Cristopher J.	MGO	1988		Wolfe, William H.	FB	1967, 68, 69
Williamson, C. William	MTN	1946		Wolkowitz, Quincy R.	WSO	1993, 94, 95, 96
Williamson, John A.	R	1958		Wolter, Robert E.	MCC/MTR	1943, 44

Karen Wechsler set IU's indoor hurdles record in 1981 and still holds it.

Jody Yin, four-time All-Big Ten and 1994 Big Ten Player-of-the-Year in tennis.

Xiang, Zheng	VB (Mgr.)	1998

Yaeger, Sara A.	WSW	1996, 97, 99
Yakey, Joseph W.	FB	1889
Yakovac, Jean M.	FH	1980, 81
Yale, Richard A.	WR	1979
Yang, Michael	BB (Mgr.)	1999
Yap, H. Barry	MSW	1956, 57, 58
Yarborough, Ernest L.	MSO	1992, 93, 94, 95
Yarian, Paul A.	FB	1977
Yassin, Azmil M.	MSO	1972, 73
Yeager, Ty L.	MTR	1994, 97, 98
Yeagley, Todd J.	MSO	1991, 92, 93, 94
Yelch, Harry L.	MTR	1907
Yeldell, Greg M.	FB/MTR	1998, 99
Yengo, Christopher M.	WR	1991
Yin, Jody	WTN	1991, 92, 93, 94
Yinger, Ronald A.	MTR	1975
Yocum, Paul S., Jr.	MSW	1945
Yoder, Albert C., Jr.	MTN	1934
Yoder, Don L.	FB	1933, 34
Yoder, Harry L.	MTR	1907
Yore, James E.	FB	1956, 57
York, Stephen S.	MTR	1970, 71, 72, 73
Youmans, Todd	FB (Mgr.)	1996
Young, Edwin F.	MSW	1967, 68, 69
Young, Janet S.	WSW	1977, 78
Young, Jerry N.	WR	1954
Young, Kimberly D.	WTR	1982, 84, 85
Young, Kristine N.	WBK	1985, 86
Young, Marty D.	FB	1979, 81
Young, Norman D.	BB	1954, 57, 58
Young, Robert H.	FB	1946, 47
Young, Samuel S.	MBK	1944
Youngblood, Robert M.	FB (Mgr.)	1976
Youngflesh, Jay F.	R	1962, 63
Youngquist, Kristin R.	WCC	1988
Youngquist, Martha	WGO	1970
Youtsler, William D.	FB	1897, 98
Yovanovich, Timothy M.	MTR	1992, 93
Yuska, Melissa L.	WBK	1998

Wong, Peter T.	MSO	1972
Wood, Carl E.	BB/FB	1890, 91, 92, 93
Wood, James B.	MTN	1940, 41, 42
Wood, John E.	MBK	1952, 55
Wood, Mary Jo	WGO	1976, 77, 78, 79
Wood, Michelle C.	WGO	1991, 92, 93
Wood, Richard G.	MTN	1943
Wood, Robert N.	MTN	1947
Wood, Sally A.	SB	1981, 82, 83
Wood, Terence M.	MGY	1981
Wood, William L.	FB	1968, 69
Woodard, Debbie	WGY	1971, 73, 74
Woodburn, James A.	BB/MTN	1874, 75, 84, 85, 86, 87, 88
Woodburn, Terry V.	FB	1971, 73
Woodman, Kelly E.	WCC/WTR	1987, 88, 89, 90, 91
Woodruff, Todd E.	MBK (Mgr.)	1975
Woods, Brenda	WCC/WTR	1978, 79
Woods, Howard M.	WR	1935
Woods, Reginald W.	BB/FB	1964, 65, 66
Woods, Robert A.	BB	1879, 80, 81
Woodson, Marvin L.	FB	1961, 62
Woodson, Michael D.	MBK	1977, 78, 79, 80
Woodward, Bobby J.	BB	1966
Woodward, James E.	MGY	1961, 62, 63
Woodward, Richard L.	BB/FB	1922, 23, 24, 25
Woody, Clark	MBK	1910
Woody, Clifford	MBK	1908
Woolard, Jason	FB (Mgr.)	1994
Wooldridge, Byron	MTR	1918
Woolsey, Mary	FH	1969, 70
Woolsey, William T.	MSW	1955, 56, 57
Woosnam, Elizabeth C.	SB	1991
Wooton, Melvin E.	BB	1920
Worcester, Edward "Ted"	FB	1963
Worsey, Arlington S.	FB/MTR	1912, 13, 14, 15
Worstell, James M.	FB	1973
Worthington, David R.	MSW	1982, 83
Wortley, George E.	FB	1968
Woschitz, Joseph F.	BB	1978, 79
Wright, Charles M.	MTN	1986, 87, 88
Wright, Charles N.	MSW	1929
Wright, Clifton A.	BB	1931, 32
Wright, David A.	MSO	1991, 94, 95
Wright, Heather	VB	1988
Wright, Howard R.	MSW	1946
Wright, James I.	MTR	1959
Wright, Jeryl L.	MGY	1956, 57, 58
Wright, Joby A.	MBK	1970, 71, 72
Wright, Joseph E.	MGO	1978, 79, 80
Wright, Karin A.	SB	1970
Wright, Larry A.	FB	1971
Wright, L. J.	MBK (Mgr.)	1990
Wright, Nicole M.	WTR	1996, 97
Wright, Verle	R	1953
Wright, Vernon L.	FB	1963
Wube, Lisa G.	WBK	1997, 98
Wunker, Swift E.	MBK	1942
Wurst, Bryan C.	MTR	1997
Wyatt, Dewey M.	MSW	1983
Wyatt, Patrick G.	MTR	1961
Wyse, Ingrid J.	WSW	1983
Wysong, Phillip R.	MCC/MTR	1972, 73, 74, 76

Zabek, Edward L.	BB	1945, 46
Zagar, Frank L.	FB (Mgr.)	1976
Zahasky, Monica M.	SB	1997, 98, 99
Zahller, Joshua J.	BB	1995, 96
Zahner, Keri B.	WCC/WTR	1996, 97
Zaiser, Robert M.	MSW	1925, 27
Zaiser, William H., Jr.	FB	1923, 25
Zaitzeff, Zoe A.	WSW	1999
Zaleski, Kevin P.	BB	1994, 95, 96
Zana, Peter L.	MSW	1990, 91, 92
Zanolla, Daniel A.	BB	1990
Zapich, Brian	MBK (Mgr.)	1995
Zarco, Cruz A.	WCC/WTR	1990, 91, 92, 93
Zaring, Ivan A.	FB	1912, 14
Zarlingo, Daniel A.	FB	1974, 75, 76, 77
Zarr, Joseph J.	MSO	1997
Zboray, Richard T.	WR	1959, 60, 61
Zeigler, Debra M.	WGO	1981
Zeigler, Joseph R.	FB	1986, 87, 88, 89
Zeller, Joseph T.	FB/MBK	1929, 30, 31, 32
Zeller, William M.	MBK	1918, 19
Zellers, Elizabeth A.	WBK	1988, 89, 90
Zellers, Frances L.	MCC/MTR	1951, 52, 53, 54
Zellmer, Mark W.	FB	1971, 72, 73
Zemla, Jaime N.	WSO	1994
Zendejas, Teresa	WTR	1979
Zender, Denise	WSW	1975, 76

Zeoli, David A.	FB	1981
Zieles, Robert S.	MGY	1981, 82
Zifchak, Peter G.	MTR	1975, 76, 77
Zike, John E.	MTN	1959
Zilkowski, Ronald R.	FB	1978
Zimmer, Andrew M.	MBK	1940, 41, 42
Zimmer, Harold L.	FB	1939, 40
Zimmerman, John M.	MSW	1969
Zimmerman, Kerry V.	MTR	1980, 81, 82, 83, 84
Zimmerman, Patricia A.	SB/WBK	1970
Zimmerman, Scott E.	BB	1987
Zimny, Robert J.	FB	1941, 42
Zingrang, Karen L.	WTN	1979
Zink, Michael C.	MTR	1975
Zinselmeier, Steven E.	MTR	1976, 77
Zirzow, William A.	MSW	1959
Ziska, Michelle A.	VB	1977, 78, 79, 80
Zivich, John M.	FB	1923
Zody, Charles F.	MGY	1957, 59
Zody, Kenneth R.	MGY	1956, 57
Zoellin, John F.	MTR	1946
Zoll, Richard D.	FB	1965, 66
Zoll, Richard M.	FB	1933, 35, 36
Zoll, Robert W.	FB	1966
Zubizarreta, Iker J.	MSO	1981, 82, 83, 84
Zuerner, David A.	BB	1977, 78, 79, 80
Zuger, John T.	FB	1951, 52, 53
Zuhl, Walter H.	MGO	1943, 44, 45
Zumerchik, Patricia E.	VB	1983, 84, 85, 86
Zweig, Daniel J.	MBK (Mgr.)	1974
Zych, Theodore	BB	1946
Zyzda, David L.	FB	1981, 82, 83, 84

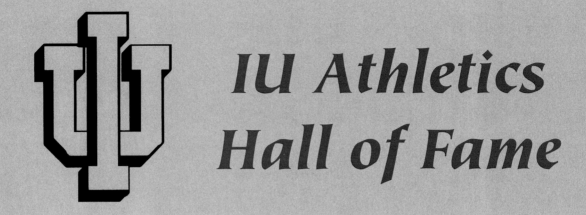

IU Athletics Hall of Fame

1982

Greg Bell
Walt Bellamy
Howard Brown
Milt Campbell
Z.G. Clevenger
Everett Dean
Harry Gonso
Gary Hall
E.C. (Billy) Hayes
Charlie Hickcox
Vern Huffman
Ted Kluszewski
Don Lash
Bobby Leonard
Branch McCracken
Charley McDaniel
Frank McKinney
Bo McMillin
Pete Pihos
Lou Saban
Don Schlundt
Bob Skoronski
Mark Spitz
Billy Thom
Mike Troy

1983

Ernie Andres
Archie Dees
Paul (Pooch) Harrell
Billy Hillenbrand
Chet Jastremski

1984

Bill Garrett
Jim Henry
Bob Hoernschemeyer
Charles Hornbostel
Dr. Herman B Wells

1985

Bob Dro
Campbell Kane
Sid Robinson
Dick VanArsdale
Tom VanArsdale

1986

Quinn Buckner
Gordon Fisher
Scott May
Don Veller
Fred Wilt

1987

Lesley Bush
Roy Cochran
Doug Crusan
Bill Orwig
Dick Voliva

1988

Jade Butcher
Chris Dal Sasso
Ivan Fuqua
John Kinsella
Claude Rich

1989

Frank Allen
Kent Benson
Marv Huffman
Cynthia Potter
Bob Ravensberg

1990

Earl Faison
Jim Montgomery
John Tavener
Lou Watson

1991

James "Doc" Counsilman
Corby Davis
Angelo DiBernardo
John Isenbarger
Jimmy Rayl

1992

Armando Betancourt
Tom Deckard
John Pont
George Taliaferro
Mike Woodson

1993

Russ Deal
Tom Miller
Jim Spivey
Mike Stamm
Isiah Thomas

1994

Dick Albershardt
Bill Armstrong
Hobie Billingsley
Brad Bomba
Heather Crowe

1995

Steve Heidenreich
Tom Nowatzke
Chuck Peters
Tara VanDerveer
Randy Wittman

1996

Anita Aldrich
Ted Kitchel
Sunder Nix
Ken Sitzberger
Whitey Wilshere

1997

Steve Alford
A.H. (Cotton) Berndt
Ralph Floyd
Rick Gilbert
Debbie Oing

1998

Tom Bolyard
Hallie Bryant
Kathleen Ellis
Ted Stickles
Ed Williams

IU Personnel

This personnel section was compiled through research of Indiana University sports information records and the Big Ten Conference record book. We regret any errors or omissions. Please contact the IU media relations office if you discover errors.

Faculty Representatives

1900-06	M.W. Sampson
1906-07	U.G. Weatherly
1907-08	E.O. Holland
1908-12	H.W. Johnston
1912-19	Charles W. Sembower
1919-41	William J. Moenkhaus
1941-42	Bernard C. Gavit
1942-43	Lee Norvelle
1943-51	William R. Breneman
1951-62	John F. Mee
1962-73	Edwin H. Cady
1973-78	Dan W. Miller
1978-85	Jack R. Wentworth
1985-93	Haydn H. Murray
1986-93	Marianne H. Mitchell
1994-	William C. Perkins

Directors of Athletics

1894-96	Edgar Syrett
1897-98	Madison G. Gonterman
1899-05	James H. Horne
1906	Zora G. Clevenger
1907-10	James M. Sheldon
1911-13	Dr. C.P. Hutchins
1914-15	Clarence C. Childs
1916-22	Ewald O. Stiehm
1923-46	Zora G. Clevenger
1946-47	A.N. (Bo) McMillin
1948-54	Paul J. Harrell
1954-55	W.W. Patty (acting)
1955-61	Frank Allen
1961-75	J.W. (Bill) Orwig
1975-78	Paul F. Dietzel
1978-90	Ralph N. Floyd
1990-91	Edgar G. Williams (interim)
1991-	Clarence H. Doninger

Women's Athletic Administrators

1973-79	Leanne Grotke
1979-80	Ann Lawver (interim)
1980-94	Isabella Hutchison
1995-	Mary Ann Rohleder

Sports Information Directors

1935-39	George Gardner
1939-44	Bob Cook
1944-46	Jack Overmyer (acting)
1946-53	Bob Cook
1953-82	Tom Miller
1983-	Kit Klingelhoffer

Athletic Trainers

1949-	Carey Colpitts & Dwayne Dixon
1954-60	Dwayne (Spike) Dixon
1961-67	Warren Ariail
1968-71	Tom Healion
1972-81	Bob Young
1981-	Tim Garl (Basketball)
1982-87	John Schrader
1987-	Walter "Kip" Smith

Equipment Managers

1946-82	Floyd (Red) Grow
1983-88	Warren McGuire
1989	Tony Anderson
1990-	Marty Clark

Ticket Managers

1938-60	L.L. Fisher
1960-76	George Keough
1976-99	Bill King
1999	Mike Roberts

Baseball Coaches

1899-00	James Horne

1901	Robert Wicker
1902	George Moore
1903-04	Philip O'Neil
1905-06	Zora Clevenger
1907	Jake Stahl
1908	Robert Wicker
1909-11	Ralph Roach
1912	John Corbett
1913-15	Arthur (Cotton) Berndt
1916	Frederick Beebe
1917	Roy Whisman
1918	Guy Rathbun
1919-20	Harry Scholler
1921-22	George Levis
1923-24	Roscoe Minton
1925-38	Everett Dean
1939-47	Paul Harrell
1948	Danny Danielson
1949-73	Ernie Andres
1974-80	Bob Lawrence
1981-83	Larry Smith
1984-	Bob Morgan

Basketball Coaches (Men's)

1901	James Horne
1902	Phelps Darby
1903-04	Willis Coval
1905-06	Zora Clevenger
1907	James Sheldon
1908	Edward Cook
1909	Robert Harris
1910	John Georgen
1911	Oscar Rackle
1912	James Kase
1913	Arthur Powell
1914-15	Arthur (Cotton) Berndt
1916	Allan Willisford
1917	Guy Lowman
1918-19	Dana Evans
1920	Ewald (Jumbo) Stiehm
1921-22	George Levis
1923-24	Leslie Mann
1925-38	Everett Dean
1939-43	Branch McCracken
1944-46	Harry Good (interim)
1947-65	Branch McCracken
1965-69	Lou Watson
1970	Jerry Oliver (acting)
1971	Lou Watson
1972-	Bob Knight

Basketball Coaches (Women's)

1972-76	Bea Gorton
1977-80	Joy Malchodi
1981-85	Maryalyce Jeremiah
1986-88	Jorja Hoehn
1989-	Jim Izard

Cross Country Coaches (Men's)

1912-14	C.V. Hutchins
1915-16	W.A. Cogshall
1917	Harvey Cohn
1918-19	Dana Evans

1920-21	W.A. Cogshall
1922	Lester Null
1923-24	Jesse Ferguson
1925-43	E.C. (Billy) Hayes
1944	J.C. Watson
1945-61	Gordon Fisher
1962-68	Jim Lavery
1969-97	Sam Bell
1998-	Robert Chapman

Cross Country Coaches (Women's)

1978-80	Mark Witten
1981-89	Carol Stevenson
1990-97	Roseann Wilson
1998-	Judy Bogenschutz

Diving Coaches (Men's & Women's)

| 1959-89 | Hobie Billingsley |
| 1990- | Jeff Huber |

Field Hockey Coaches

1975-76	Kay Burris
1977-81	Pat Fabozzi
1982	Patty Foster

Football Coaches

1887	A.B. Woodford
1891	Billy Herod
1894	Ferbert & Huddleson
1895	Osgood & Wren
1896-97	Madison Gonterman
1898-04	James Horne
1905-13	James Sheldon
1914-15	Clarence Childs
1916-21	Ewald (Jumbo) Stiehm
1922	James Herron
1923-25	Bill Ingram
1926-30	E.C. (Billy) Hayes
1934-47	A.N. (Bo) McMillin
1948-51	Clyde Smith
1952-56	Bernie Crimmins
1957	Bob Hicks (acting)
1958-64	Phil Dickens
1965-72	John Pont
1973-82	Lee Corso
1983	Sam Wyche
1984-96	Bill Mallory
1997-	Cam Cameron

Golf Coaches (Men's)

1929	Harper Miller
1930	Gerald Redding
1931	Joe Greenwood
1932	Phil Talbot
1934-41	Hugh Willis
1942-47	James Souter
1948-57	Owen (Chili) Cochrane
1958-89	Bob Fitch
1990-98	Sam Carmichael
1998-	Mike Mayer

Golf Coaches (Women's)

1975-79	Margaret Cummins
1979-81	Bruce Cohen
1982-	Sam Carmichael

Gymnastics Coaches (Men)

1948-70	Otto Ryser
1971-82	Jim Brown

Gymnastics Coaches (Women)

1975-85	Diane Schulz

Rifle Coaches

1952-54	Louie Donoho
1955-57	Jack Darden
1958-59	Joseph Spitler

Soccer Coaches (Men's)

1973-	Jerry Yeagley

Soccer Coaches (Women's)

1993-	Joe Kelley

Softball Coaches

1973-74	Jenny Johnson
1975-76	Louetta Bloecher
1977-79	Ann Lawver
1980-87	Gayle Blevins
1988-	Diane Stephenson

Swimming Coaches (Men's)

1919-20	Guy Rathbun
1921	Robert Shafer
1922	Lester Null
1923-25	William Merriam
1926	Oscar Tharp
1927-30	Paul Thompson
1932-44	Robert Royer
1945-46	Robert Stumpner (interim)
1947-57	Robert Royer
1958-90	James "Doc" Counsilman
1991-	Kris Kirchner

Swimming Coaches (Women's)

1975-79	Don Glass
1980-81	Pat Barry
1982	Terry Townsend (acting)
1983-86	Bob Bruce
1987-91	Chet Jastremski
1992	Jill Sterkel
1993-98	Nancy Nitardy
1999	Dorsey Tierney

Tennis Coaches (Men's)

1930	Harlan Logan
1931-33	Ralph Esarey
1934-40	Ralph Graham
1941-43	Ralph Collins
1944	Emory Clark (interim)
1945-46	Ralph Collins
1947	William Johnson
1948	Don Veller
1949-57	Dale Lewis
1958-72	Bill Landin
1973-81	Scott Greer
1982-85	Steve Greco
1986-	Ken Hydinger

Tennis Coaches (Women's)

1975-76	Dean Summers
1977-	Lin Loring

Track & Field Coaches (Men's)

1915-16	Clarence Childs
1917	Harvey Cohn
1918-19	Dana Evans
1920	Guy Rathbun
1921	John Millen
1922	Lester Null
1923-24	Jesse Ferguson
1925-43	E.C. (Billy) Hayes
1944	Clifford Watson
1945-62	Gordon Fisher
1963-69	Jim Lavery
1970-98	Sam Bell
1999	Marshall Goss

Track & Field Coaches (Women's)

1978-80	Mark Witten
1980-89	Carol Stephenson
1990-98	Roseann Wilson
1999-	Randy Heisler

Volleyball Coaches

1975-83	Ann Lawver
1984-87	Doug West
1988-92	Tom Shoji
1993-	Katie Weismiller

Water Polo

1998-	Barry King

Wrestling Coaches

1910-14	Elmer Jones
1915-16	Edgar Davis
1917-21	James Kase
1922	Guy Rathbun
1923-27	Jack Reynolds
1928-45	W.H. (Billy) Thom
1946-72	Charley McDaniel
1973-84	Doug Blubaugh
1985-89	Jim Humphrey
1990-91	Joe McFarland
1992-	Duane Goldman

Index

Castro, Rod	185
Catterton, Wilbert	34,62
Caudill, Craig	76,162,163
Cerroni, Tony	219
Chambers, Goethe	116
Chandler, Roger	32,180,210,212,214,215
Chapman, Tracy	193
Cheaney, Calbert	6,126,140,154,180,202,203,206,207
Cheney, Jim	144,146
Cherubini, Amy	202
Childs, Clarence	33,34,36,58
Choice, Wally	6,107,122
Chorny, Tom	215,216,219
Christoff, Joey	184
Cichowski, Gene "Chick"	123
Ciolli, Frank	98,103
Cisco, Walt	150
Clapham, Ed	61,62,64,104
Clark, Hezlep	13,17
Clark, Mike	34,203,206,211
Clark, Thomas D.	9,19,21,41
Cleveland, Bob	16,110
Clevenger, Z.G.	5,8,10,13,16,22,32,36,42,43,50,51,52,58,64, 65,75,77,79,81,85,95,97,107,205
Clifford, Tim	60,94,174,175,179
Clinton, Jim	134
Clippert, Geof	199
Clouse, Derek	202
Cobb, Steve	162
Cochran, Roy	52,70,78,79,82,91,106,122
Coetsee, Lizl	16,212,214,216,218
Cohn, Harvey	37
Cole, Terry	146,147,150
Cole, Tom	180
Collier, Jeanne	145
Collier, Mike	34,180,216,219,220
Collier, Robert	52,78
Collins, Eoin	194,196
Colnitis, Don	72
Compton, Russ	169
Comstock, Byron	138,212
Conelly, Gary	144,158
Connelly, Tim	172,174
Conway, Dick	140
Cook, Charles	40
Cook, Ed	4,50
Cook, George	31
Cook, Tracy	212
Cooke, Joe	149
Cordin, Scott	144
Correll, Robert	4,59
Corriden, John Jr.	96
Corso, Lee	161,169,175,183,215,217
Cotton, Chris	182
Coufal, Scott	211,214
Coulter, John	82
Counsilman, Jim "Doc"	66,74,128,129,131,133,134,137,139, 144,146,149,150,151,152,154,155,156, 158,159,160,167, 169,175,179,195,199
Counsilman, Jim Jr.	151
Counsilman, Marge	175
Coval, Willis	48,50
Cox, Bill	73
Cox, Courtney	188,200,206
Coyer, Matt	203,206
Craddock, Keith	133
Craig, George	71
Cravens, Meredith	216
Crawford, George	212
Creigmile, Kathryn	63
Crews, Jim	164,165,167,177
Crimmins, Bernie	117,121,123,217
Croftcheck, Don	20,137,150
Cross, George	112
Crotty, Mike	202

Crowe, Heather	171,180,181,186,218
Crusan, Doug	80,146,150,153
Cunningham, Arthur "Heze"	21,25
Cunningham, Linda	194
Cunningham, Nate	146,147
Curtis, Judy	133
Cusick, Mike	104,120
D'Achille, Lou	113
Dahlberg, Peder	151
Dailey, Frank	61
Dailey, Tom	34,120
Daily, William	82
Dakich, Dan	6,184,185,192
DalSasso, Chris	12,78
Dalzell, Wilbur	34,38,104
Danielson, Danny	10
Darby, Phelps	4,6,7,48,50
Darrow, Heather	200
Dauer, Ray	12,65,72,104
Dauphin, Phil	118,196,198
David, Ron	124
Davis, Corby	60,79,80,81,83,150
Davis, Edgar	10,22,25,32,48
Davis, Jene	177
Davis, Joseph	12
Davis, Merrill	4,10,27
Davis, Nathan	20,212,214,215
Davis, Paul	24
Davis, Tom	219
Davis, Vicky	76,186
Deady, Mark	195
Deakyne, Jim	116
Deal, LeRoy	104,106
Deal, Russ	12,20,93,98,102,103,105,115,150
Dean, Everett	4,10,30,40,43,44,50,51,53,58,59, 62,64,67, 73,77, 78, 81,89,91,104,107
Deckard, Tommy	10,77,78,79,83,90,91,151
Deem, Paul	132
Deering, Chad	196,220
Deery, Simon	218
Dees, Archie	125,126,127,130,140,154,206
DeFord, Kent	152
DeHeer, Bill	6,145
Dekkers, Michelle	64,184,186,196,197,198,201,214,220
DeKraay, Sarah	193,212
Delo, Elmer	68
DeLong, Dave	182
DeMarcus, Bruce	45
Demmon, Floyd	32
Denisar, Gene	106,146
Dennis, Denny	180
Dennison, Lynn	188
Dentice, Carl	44,119,120
Denton, Ed	93
Deranek, Dick	98,103
DeSalle, Don	20
Devine, Pat	32,70,71
DeVore, Doug	118
DeVries, Jason	216
Dew, Robbie	174
Diamond, Adriane	76,186
DiBernardo, Angelo	169,170,187,196
DiBernardo, Paul	180,182,186,187
Dickens, Phil	127,129,133,139,142,217
Dickey, William	48
Dickinson, Mike	172,180
Dickson, Bruce	106,165
Dietzel, Paul	36,163,171

"Bob Hammel knows about all the big sports stories in the history of Indiana University, and was on press row for a high percentage of them. What a gift that he has put all that knowledge into one book."

Bob Zaltsberg
Editor, Herald-Times

Recognizing Bob Hammel for 45 years of great sportswriting.

The Herald-Times congratulates Hammel on the completion of "Glory of Old IU."

The Herald-Times

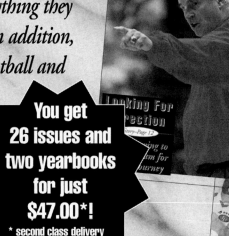

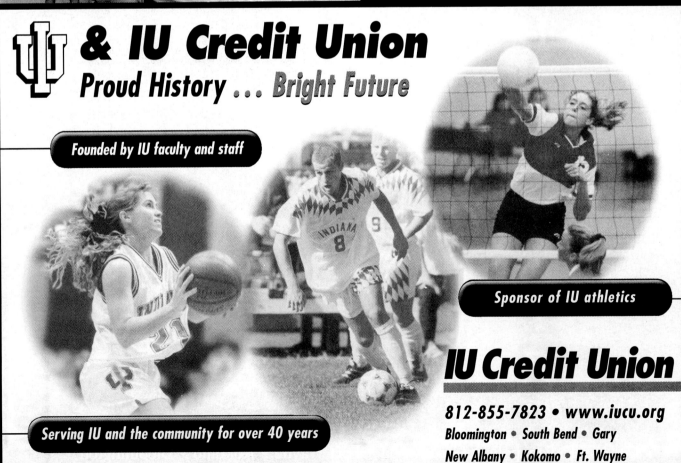

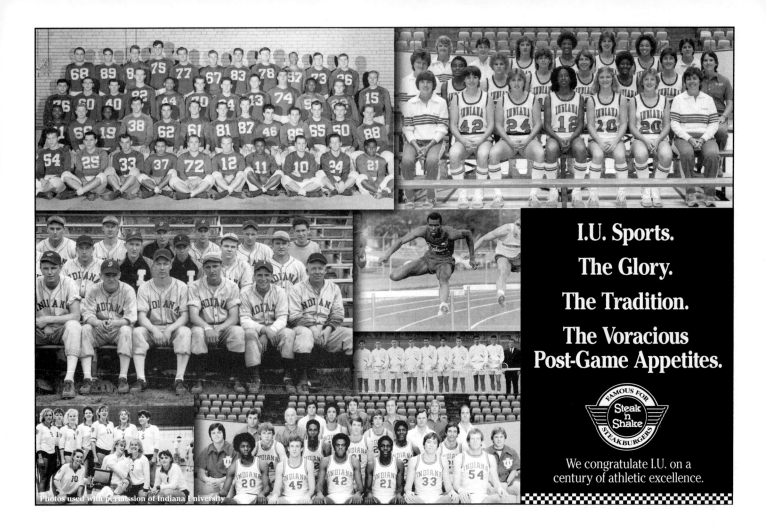

Your Home For I.U. Sports
In Bloomington!

96.7 FM —— **An Artistic Media Partners Station**